BTEC NATIONAL

Early Years

Penny Tassoni
Sarah Horne
Maureen Smith
Andrew Boak
Joan Butcher
Harriet Eldridge
Carol Runciman

Endorsed by Edexcel

Heinemann Educational Publishers,
Halley Court, Jordan Hill, Oxford OX2 8EJ
Part of Harcourt Education

Heinemann is the registered trademark of Harcourt Education Limited

© Yvonne Nolan, Andy Boak, Joan Butcher, Harriet Eldridge, Sarah Horne,
Maureen Smith, Penny Tassoni 2002
Complete work © Harcourt Education Limited

First published 2002
2006 2005
10 9 8 7 6 5

A catalogue record for this book is available from the British Library on
request.

ISBN 0 435 45518 4

Pages designed by Artistix, Thame, Oxon
Typeset and illustrated by Techtype, Abingdon, Oxon
Printed and bound in Great Britain by Scotprint, East Lothian

Websites

Please note that the examples of websites suggested in this book were up to
date at the time of writing. It is essential for tutors to preview each site before
using it to ensure that the URL is still accurate and the content is appropriate.
We suggest that tutors bookmark useful sites and consider enabling students to
access them through the school or college intranet.

Tel: 01865 888058 www.heinemann.co.uk

Contents

Core Units

Optional Units

Introduction

A career in Early Years is one of the most rewarding opportunities available. The chance to influence young lives and to promote effective learning experiences that will help to form children's attitudes to learning and leisure throughout their lives, is a joy and privilege worth working for. The BTEC National is one of the well-respected and valued routes into working in Early Years, and is a qualification that will provide you with a firm foundation for your future work and training. It will require commitment and hard work, but it is exciting and rewarding work that will repay you well for the efforts you make.

About this book

This book contains everything you need to succeed in your BTEC National Early Years qualification. The content of the units matches the BTEC specification and covers all of the core units as well as some of the optional units. Each unit provides you with just the right amount of theory and makes links to real-life childcare practice.

The eight core units are:

- Equality, diversity and rights
- Research and Project
- Protecting children
- Learning in the early years
- Communication and supportive skills
- Safe environments
- Professional practice
- Childcare practice.

The externally assessed optional units included in this book are:

- Human growth and development
- Child health.

The internally assessed optional units included in this book are:

- Play and learning activities
- Special needs.
- Developmental psychology

Course structure

The structure of the BTEC National is based on the study of compulsory core units as well as specialist units that enable you to study particular areas in depth.

The BTEC National Certificate in Early Years is made up of 12 units – seven core units and four specialist units. The BTEC National Diploma in Early Years is made up of 18 units – eight core units and nine specialist units.

The core unit in Professional Practice counts as one unit for both the Certificate and Diploma and includes work placements with a range of age groups.

Assessment

All units are assessed and graded, and an overall grade for the qualification is awarded.

Features of the book

Throughout the text there are a number of features that are designed to encourage reflection and discussion and to help relate theory to practice in an early years context. The features are:

What you will need to learn	a list of the knowledge points that you will have learnt by the end of the unit
Think it over	thought-provoking questions and dilemmas that can be used for individual reflection or group discussion
Theory into practice	practical activities that require you to apply your theoretical knowledge to the workplace
Key issues	contemporary issues in childcare that you should be aware of
Assessment activities	activities that address the assessment requirements of the course
Case studies	examples of 'real' situations to help you link theory to practice

A wide range of experienced professionals have contributed their expertise to this book; their purpose in doing so is to support you in your chosen studies and to provide you with a firm knowledge foundation from which you can extend and develop your particular interests.

We do hope that you enjoy your BTEC National in Early Years course and wish you good luck and every success in achieving your qualification and in your future work.

Yvonne Nolan
General Editor

Picture Acknowledgements

The authors and publisher would like to thank the following for permission to reproduce photographs and other material:

Associated Photos/Jacqueline Arzt p.4
Circa Photo Library/John Smith p.3
Gareth Boden p.54, 133, 243, 288, 451
Gerald Sunderland p.29, 241, 249, 347, 467, 493
Haddon Davies p.9, 29
Michael Dunning p.32
Science Photo Library/Chris Priest p.400
Science Photo Library/Matt Clarke p.374
Science Photo Library/Sheila Terry p.370

The photos on pages 118 and 140 were provided by Sarah Horne.

Equality, diversity and rights

Introduction

This unit introduces the concepts of equality, diversity and rights. These concepts form the foundation of your work with young children and their families. As you grow in your understanding of equality, diversity and rights you will see that these important concepts are integral to the ways in which early years settings and early years practitioners provide their service. Concepts of equality, diversity and rights are also very important to the social care and the health care sectors, so much of this unit is applicable in those settings as well.

What you need to learn

- The importance of equality, diversity and rights to health, care and early years services
- How care services recognise and promote equality, diversity and rights
- How individual workers recognise and promote equality, diversity and rights in their own practice
- Values and underlying principles for the early years care and education sector

The importance of equality, diversity and rights to health, care and early years services

Terminology

There are many terms used when talking about equality, diversity and rights, some of which are explained below. Other terms are included in the glossary. Each time you see a new word, check it out so that you understand precisely what it means.

Equality: in our society, 'equality' is about fairness and ensuring people have the same rights regardless of their background or who they are. Any society that ensures its people have equal chances and equal treatment is building for its future by encouraging equality of opportunity for all.

Diversity: diversity means 'difference', e.g. difference in gender, disability, race, age, culture, religion, social class, child rearing practices, appearance, employment status or sexuality. These differences enrich our society and make it an exciting and challenging place to be.

Rights and responsibilities: our society recognises that all its members have responsibilities as well as rights. Rights are what we are entitled to as members of society, e.g. we have a right to live in peace but with a responsibility to be peaceful ourselves. These rights are sometimes called 'moral rights' based on ideas about what is right or wrong, fair or unfair, just or unjust.

Values: values are held by all of us – they are the beliefs and moral principles by which we live. We are likely to share many of the values of our society, e.g. respect for human life and opposition to murder, but there is less agreement on issues such as capital punishment for people who commit murder.

Ethics: these are closely linked to values covering what is good and bad, and with moral beliefs, duty and obligation. Ethics are difficult balancing acts as often there are no clear-cut answers. For example, an individual health worker may not agree with abortion. When asked to assist in an abortion clinic they have an ethical dilemma – should they break their own ethical and moral code and undertake this work?

British society

The UK is said to be a democratic society in which people can elect someone through the voting system to represent their views in Parliament or assembly. In a democracy, people are allowed to hold different political views and different values. British society is a competitive society where people compete for the best education or the best jobs but it is not an equal society as there are major differences between, for example, the top elite and the poor or homeless. Also society is divided in many different ways. The government itself divides society into a social scale as follows:

1. Higher managerial and professional occupations.
    1.1 Employers and managers in larger organisations (e.g. company directors, senior company managers, senior civil servants, senior officers in police and armed forces).
    1.2 Higher professionals (e.g. doctors, lawyers, clergy, teachers and social workers).
2. Lower managerial and professional occupations (e.g. nurses and midwives, journalists, actors, musicians, prison officers, lower ranks of police and armed forces).
3. Intermediate occupations (e.g. clerks, secretaries, driving instructors, telephone fitters).
4. Small employers and own account workers (e.g. publicans, farmers, taxi drivers, window cleaners, painters and decorators).
5. Lower supervisory, craft and related occupations (e.g. printers, plumbers, television engineers, train drivers, butchers).
6. Semi-routine occupations (e.g. shop assistants, hairdressers, bus drivers, cooks).
7. Routine occupations (e.g. couriers, labourers, waiters and refuse collectors).
8. The eighth category covers those who have never had paid work and the long-term unemployed.

The values and principles of British society have developed over centuries based on philosophical and religious concepts, e.g. the Christian faith, which (along with other world faiths) has always emphasised the value of caring for the poor although this aspect of belief has changed over the centuries.

The Victorians believed that there were the deserving and undeserving poor. If you were elderly or disabled you might be considered deserving whereas others who could not work for other reasons (for example, the unemployed or mentally ill) were labelled undeserving. The 'undeserving poor' would often find themselves on the streets and many died from cold and hunger.

Despite different interpretations influenced by religion and society, the principle of caring for the poor has persisted throughout the centuries. Today the principles are being taken forward by the UK government through its policies for social welfare and social inclusion.

Although government policy is to support social need, there is still a requirement for voluntary groups such as charities for the homeless or care offered by groups such as the Salvation Army. Voluntary groups are often closer to the communities they serve and see the needs and gaps in government services.

Voluntary groups provide services for the community which are not covered by government

The principle of equity

Equity is about fairness, natural justice, being impartial and reasonable. Many people will use the term equity in the same way as they would talk about equality. The principle of equity is very important and should be the hallmark of a civilised mature society. British society, through its laws and practices, supports the view that fairness, tolerance and equity are important moral principles. A society that is not based on principles of equity will be an unequal divided society, but even where society, at least in its laws and constitution, supports equity, there are still many gaps between rich and poor. Equity is not just about poverty, but if you are poor, you suffer most from a range of different problems and deprivations.

A national survey carried out by the Office for National Statistics (ONS, 2000) has revealed important information on the extent of social deprivation in the UK. Interviews with a sample of individuals were used to draw up a list of items and activities that a majority considered 'necessities'. These were defined as those things that everyone should be 'able to afford and which they should not have to go without'. A follow-up survey was then conducted, weighted towards those with lower incomes, to find out how many actually lacked these necessities and to accumulate additional information on poverty.

Over 90 per cent of the people questioned defined necessities as a bed, heating, a damp-free home, the ability to visit family and friends in hospital, two meals a day and medical prescriptions. Less than 10 per cent considered dishwashers, mobile phones, and Internet access or satellite television to be necessities. The method used by the researchers enabled them to compare their findings with results from two earlier 'Breadline Britain' surveys.

Here are some of their findings:

- More than one in six children are growing up in poverty in the UK.
- 24 per cent of people were living in poverty in 1999.
- Two million children go without basic food and clothing.
- One in 50 children go without new shoes, warm waterproof coats or fresh fruit and vegetables daily.

- Unemployed lone parents and those from some ethnic groups are the poorest.
- 9.5 million Britons live in badly heated homes.
- 8.5 million cannot afford a fridge, telephone or carpets.

Another report funded by the Joseph Rowntree Foundation, 'Monitoring Poverty and Social Exclusion' (New Policy Institute, 1999), found that:

One in six children grow up in poverty in the UK

- the highest number of low earners are located in Scotland, the North West, Wales and the North East
- health inequalities have worsened with premature deaths located in low-income areas
- there are higher rates of suicide in young men without a known occupation
- one million pensioners rely solely on their state retirement pension and state benefits
- better-off pensioners spend 25 per cent more on food than those relying on the state.

Poverty and women

Much of the work on how to reduce poverty has been targeted at tackling unemployment. Overwhelmingly women want to work but need affordable childcare, and employment structures that do not penalise women for having a family. Also a more equal sharing of care responsibilities is essential to reducing poverty. Women's poverty can be linked to a working life interrupted by caring and family responsibilities leading to:

- taking lower paid jobs
- having less chance of building an occupational pension
- having an interrupted National Insurance record which restricts the benefits they are entitled to.

It is clear that despite efforts to bring about a more equitable society there is still a long way to go. It remains to be seen whether the government's agenda for social inclusion, and a more equal society with better public services for all, will be achieved.

I am never going to make the meeting – is this called 'Having it all'?!

Tackling social exclusion

Generally groups who experience discrimination do not have power or influence in our society and are often marginalised to a greater or lesser extent. These people are sometimes called the socially excluded. Currently government policy is to promote social inclusion with such initiatives as Surestart and to empower communities and give people the skills for employment. Surestart's aim is:

'To work with parents, parents-to-be and children to promote the physical, intellectual and social development of babies and young children – particularly those that are disadvantaged – so that they can flourish at home and when they get to school, and thereby break the cycle of disadvantage for the current generation of young children' (DFES, 2001).

The cycle of disadvantage is where generations of the same families are trapped into a vicious circle and face multiple problems such as poverty, unemployment, poor environments and low aspirations. Often these are fragile families located in troubled communities. Surestart and other initiatives are usually family and community focused. These families often have many strengths and successful programmes will build on these.

There are other new ideas and initiatives growing in the UK around the concept of social entrepreneurship. These new initiatives have the potential to break into the cycle of disadvantage. Social entrepreneurs are individuals or groups with a vision to change society by pioneering new solutions to social problems and by empowering the societies they serve. Examples include setting up programmes for housing estates with high rates of teenage pregnancy or working in prisons to educate young male inmates in how to care for children. Social entrepreneurs are much needed in disadvantaged communities and there is an increased feeling of optimism that solutions may be found to what have been really difficult on-going problems.

Think It Over

Get some information on Surestart on both a local and national level. In a group, think about the following questions:

- Is the UK an equitable society?
- How can the cycle of disadvantage be broken?
- How can the Surestart programme help with this?

UN Convention on the Rights of the Child

The UN Convention on the Rights of the Child has influenced law and public policy with respect to children in the UK. The UN Convention is a formal statement designed to protect children's rights agreed by many nations. Its main points cover children from 0–18 years, whether rich or poor, and cover a whole range of rights including the following:

- All rights apply to all children whatever their background and the State has an obligation to protect children against discrimination. (Article 2)
- Children's best interests must come first. (Article 3)
- Children have a right to be heard. (Article 12)
- Children must be protected from violence, abuse and neglect. (Article 19)
- Children with disabilities and learning difficulties must have their rights protected. (Article 23)

Think It Over

Young girls in some parts of the world are subjected to what is known as female genital mutilation (female circumcision) when parts of their external genital organs are altered or removed in order to minimise sexual pleasure and encourage chastity. This is illegal in the UK but sometimes young girls who live here are taken to other countries to be circumcised as it is considered to be a part of their culture.

- Discuss in a group how the UK views this practice and how prevalent it is in the rest of the world. Can any culture justify female genital mutilation?
- How does the practice accord with the UN Convention on the Rights of the Child?

Values and principles

Most occupations have some kind of value base or professional code of ethics that underpins how they work. These value statements generally recognise the importance of good standards of provision and public safety according to the type of occupation and many recognise principles of equality and rights.

The code of ethics or value base covers an occupation's approach to its service users and to the work it actually undertakes. These values will be evident in the work of the setting and demonstrated through the kind of service offered and the attitudes and behaviour of the staff. This unit focuses on work with young children and their families but many of the concepts of equality, diversity and rights are common across health, social care and early years.

Health and social care services have a set of values and principles stated clearly within the national occupational standards for that sector and although there are many similarities these are slightly different from the early years values. Occupational standards are based on the functions people undertake when working and are published by standard setting bodies for different types of employment, e.g. health and social care, catering, engineering. They are grouped into units that lay out the standard of service expected by employers and government and include the values of the occupation. It is important for you to become familiar with the values of the early years sector as you will need to make sure you can work to these values when you are in placement and in employment.

These values and principles are stated in full at the end of this unit. They are so important that they are integrated into every unit within the occupational standards for early years care and education. Each unit indicates the particular values and principles contained within the unit. You can find out more about occupational standards by contacting the relevant standard setting body.

Diversity and difference

Learning about differences between people is very important. The UK today is a diverse society with many different languages, ethnic groups and cultures. There are many dimensions of diversity or difference but those most commonly recognised are described in the following table.

Difference	Comment
Gender	In the past men had more rights than women and were seen as more important. Women still earn less than men for similar work and find difficulty in breaking through the 'glass ceiling' to the most senior positions at work. There are far more derogatory terms such as 'slag' used to describe women than men
Ethnic origin and race	People categorise themselves and others based on race and ethnicity, e.g. being black or white, European or Asian. Ethnic origin is different from race and usually covers a shared history, social customs and common ancestry. Our society still places a value on white skin and Western European background. Derogatory terms for black people are still used
Culture	All of us have a cultural background, i.e. activities, beliefs, values, knowledge and ideas shared by a group of people from the same tradition or background. White, middle class culture still dominates the media and is seen as most valuable. People feel more comfortable with others of a similar cultural background and groups who hold power and influence in society tend to value others like themselves
Religion	People are brought up with varying religious backgrounds. Religion is closely linked with culture and is often used as a cover up for prejudice
Age	Youth is generally valued above old age, although the very young are often not valued. There are problems for older people in employment and in relation to issues such as health care
Disability	This refers to differences in physical or mental ability or sensory impairment. People make assumptions about disability and make negative judgements about those who are seen as disabled
Class	This refers to differences in social background, education, income, lifestyle. Assumptions are made about people who are poor or with limited lifestyle
Employment status	People who are employed are often valued above those who are unemployed regardless of the reasons. One of the first questions people ask each other is 'What do you do?'
Health	People with illnesses are often made to feel different and outside mainstream society, especially if they are seen as somehow being responsible for their own disease, e.g. AIDS or lung cancer. This is especially true for mental health problems
Relationships	This refers to differences in family or social relationships, e.g. lone parents, same sex relationships. These are often not valued as much as heterosexual relationships and two-parent families
Language	English is seen as the UK's mainstream language. Other languages are often seen as less important
Marital status	Divorced, separated or single people are often made to feel different
Sexuality	Being a gay man or lesbian woman. Homosexual relationships are often not valued as much as heterosexual relationships, and can suffer prejudice

The UK is multicultural and early years practitioners are responsible for helping all children to recognise and appreciate diversity

The table can only include broad categories and one of the important lessons is that we are all different. For example, the category 'gender' can only cover broad terms but we all know there are huge differences between men and other men, and women and other women. The main lesson is that the similarities between us are usually greater than the differences and we should always see people as individuals rather than as part of a particular group. Also, it is important not to judge by appearances as people with hidden disabilities, e.g. autism, deafness or mental health problems, may look just like anyone else. This can lead to reverse discrimination where people with real needs are overlooked because they look like everyone else.

Think It Over

Jo is a seven-year-old girl with cerebral palsy. Her family are black and live on a South London housing estate with their three other children. Discuss in pairs:

- What is your feeling about Jo and her family? What sort of life do you think she has? What assumptions have you made?

In fact both Jo's parents are lawyers and she lives in a private estate of large detached houses. Jo's cerebral palsy is very mild. Jo is a gifted musician and academically already performing at the highest level. She has twin elder sisters and an elder brother all of whom are devoted to her.

It is important that we do not judge people who are 'different' from us as either inferior or lacking in some way. Our society, in common with most others, values particular characteristics. These messages are often not deliberate but are picked up by young children from their families and the world around them and reinforced throughout life by our experiences, influential people and the media.

For many of us, learning about diversity and relating to those who are different can be stressful as we may feel our own culture and values are under threat. We need to be aware of this and be willing to see the benefits of diversity in our society and in the workplace.

Positive benefits of diversity

The UK has a rich cultural and ethnic mix that has many positive effects. Today we live in a globalised society. Countries have links with other countries across the world, communication is instant and understanding other cultures has positive benefits to business and commerce. Immigration over the years has brought skills and knowledge into the UK and has enriched our national life. People who accept difference in cultures can be more flexible and creative, and understand the needs of others.

Cultural enrichment takes many forms. On a day-to-day basis there are new foods to try, different clothes to wear and new forms of relating, e.g. Asian communities are well known for their hospitality and for their respect for and care of the elderly. Cultural enrichment is also present in music and the arts. It is almost impossible to imagine UK society without reggae or rap music, both of which have their origins in immigrant groups. Different cultures are represented in the media and sports and help the UK to succeed in all these areas.

Early years and diversity

There are particular advantages in recognising diversity within early years settings. In schools and nurseries there are children from many different races and cultures speaking many different languages. If we are positive about diversity it can enrich our lives and that of the children in our care. It is important to make sure that different people and groups are equally respected.

Early years settings can develop and use the differences in culture, ethnic group, gender language and religion to make the nursery a learning experience for all children and their families. Looking positively at other cultures and different ways of life helps children to understand the wider world, to grow up to be tolerant and to accept, without fear and as equals, people who are different.

Children who, as part of their overall social development, learn to respect the views and needs of others and to value difference, are more likely to become tolerant adults who are able to contribute to a fairer society.

Appreciation of diversity promotes tolerance and acceptance without fear

Assessment activity 1.1

Re-read the sections above on difference.

- Draw up a table of advantages and disadvantages of living in a diverse society. For each advantage or disadvantage write a short analysis giving your reasons. You may wish to talk to a variety of other people to assist in the task.
- After completing the table evaluate your findings. State why you reach particular conclusions.

Attitudes and values

To be able to work using the values of any sector it is important to understand your own attitudes and values. Attitudes are about the way you view something and usually include how you judge or evaluate. For example, your attitude to war is likely to include views about whether you agree or disagree with the idea. Together, your attitudes and values are of major importance for how you view the world and the people in it.

You will need to be sure that you are aware if you hold any prejudiced and stereotyped attitudes as these may lead you to behave unfairly towards people. Prejudice usually means an unfavourable view of someone or something based on inadequate facts. The dictionary defines a stereotype as 'a standardised image or conception of a type of person'. Most stereotypes are based on prejudices and involve labelling, and all are untrue as they do not look at the individual. There are people, for example, who are long-term unemployed because they are disabled, ill or not able to move to another part of the country because of family commitments. People in this position are sometimes labelled lazy or scroungers when there are very good reasons why they cannot get a job. Most of us hold stereotypes without necessarily realising it and apply those stereotypes to people we meet. It is our behaviour based on our stereotypes that can be unfair and discriminatory.

Key issues

You are aware that there are several families using the nursery who are asylum seekers and that part of a local estate seems to have many houses and flats where families claiming asylum live. The press reports that local children cannot get school places near to home due to the influx of children from abroad.

- Do we think of asylum seekers as one group or many groups each with different reasons for being here?
- Are we prejudiced – if so – why?
- Do we mind if someone accuses us of prejudice?
- Do we think we are superior?
- Do we think asylum seekers are getting something they don't deserve?

How we learn our attitudes and values

Attitudes, values and prejudices are usually learned in our early years. Children as young as two years are able to make judgements based on race or gender as they learn to put a higher value on certain types of physical appearance.

Young children develop their attitudes and values as a result of early learning from their families, friends, nursery, school and from television and other media. The family is a very powerful influence on children's values and attitudes and it is often in the home that they first learn to stereotype other people or groups. Children pick up the attitudes of their parents or carers through observing their behaviour and then copying it. Boys who are always given 'boy's toys' such as construction equipment for making cars and girls who are always given 'girl's toys' such as dolls and who are also encouraged to behave in stereotyped ways are likely to hold back from trying new ideas and ways of relating that cross those stereotypes.

Often individual prejudices have come about through history and experience as well as misinformation. Prejudices are often shared with a larger social group and have become part of what we all believe and what we express to our children regardless of whether there is any factual basis for them. For example, a common prejudice is against obese people who are often judged as lazy or out of control.

Remember: children have a right *not* to learn negative attitudes and prejudices from people around them.

Think It Over

Working on your own or with a partner ask yourself the following questions:

- Can I remember an example(s) of times when I felt I was receiving unfair treatment and why?
- How did that experience make me feel?
- Do I hold stereotyped views about race, gender, disability or other people who are different from me?

Discrimination

This chapter uses the term 'discrimination' to refer to situations when individuals or institutions behave unfairly or in negative, hostile or damaging ways to other individuals or groups. Discrimination usually arises from stereotyped or prejudiced attitudes that may or may not be deliberate. Sometimes people experience discrimination for no apparent reason, e.g. being bullied just because the bully wants to feel superior.

Discriminatory practices are sometimes present because no one in an organisation realises they are discriminating and there is lack of thought or understanding, or, on rare occasions where staff simply can't be bothered. Examples are:

- where a setting uses books and learning materials that only reflect white children
- where a setting only allows the English language to be used when it has many bi-lingual children and children with English as an additional language
- asking boys to play outside and girls to stay in and help staff clear away
- when disabled children are steered away from certain activities that with appropriate support they could undertake very successfully.

Individual discrimination

Discrimination by individuals can be open and obvious such as name calling, bullying or racial abuse. Or, it can be subtle such as individual practitioners having lower expectations of children because they are from an ethnic minority. Again it can be because practitioners are unaware that they are discriminating.

Institutional discrimination

Institutional discrimination is not usually a result of deliberate acts but occurs as the result of an organisation's long-standing policies, practices and assumptions which have never been challenged and which are discriminatory.

In the workplace, an example of institutional discrimination would be a company who always advertises for staff who are 'fit and active', even in jobs that do not require any physical activity. Requiring all staff to be fit and active when the job is, for example, office based, discriminates against people with certain physical difficulties who may be quite able to do the job.

Structural discrimination

This type of discrimination relates to traditional long-standing structures in our society and the ways in which these can discriminate. For example, parents from some ethnic groups are more likely to have to work full time and are more likely to have to use expensive full-day care. These parents are less likely to be able to use free nursery education that is only available three hours per day. Therefore the structures of local nursery education discriminate against this type of parent.

The Race Relations (Amendment) Act 2000

This Act identifies four types of discrimination which can also be institutional, individual or structural:

- Direct discrimination – treating a person less favourably on racial grounds such as refusing a child a place at nursery because they were black, Asian or white.
- Indirect discrimination – applying a requirement to everyone that certain racial groups either cannot fulfil or only a small proportion can fulfil, e.g. insistence that girls wear skirts can be unlawful as it indirectly discriminates against certain religions.
- Victimisation – being treated less favourably because someone is using race relations legislation or alleging discrimination.
- Segregation – segregating on racial grounds may constitute discriminatory treatment, e.g. grouping children by colour at mealtimes or when in line.

These types of discrimination are equally applicable to other groups who suffer discrimination, e.g. the disabled, being a girl or a member of a particular religion.

Harassment

This is illegal under both the Race Relations Act and the Sex Discrimination Acts. Harassment in these contexts can mean subjecting people to unwanted sexual attention or racial abuse. This covers a whole range of behaviours such as verbal or physical bullying, jokes and taunts or excluding people because or their race or gender. No one has to put up with this sort of behaviour and can expect the law to be on their side if harassment is proven.

Case Study

Megan is an office worker. She is teased constantly by her boss who uses sexual innuendo and who also puts pressure on her to meet him outside work hours. Megan feels she wants to leave her job as the situation is so bad. Megan talks to another senior manager who is not sympathetic and suggests she is being over sensitive. Megan talks to a colleague who takes her seriously and advises her to go to her union. The union is taking up the case but Megan is not sure whether it's worth all the stress.

Anti-discrimination

Anti-discrimination actively opposes discrimination by implementing policies and practices designed to rid society of barriers and discrimination, e.g. when women are paid less for the same work as men and legal action is taken against the employer under the Equal Pay Act.

Anti-discrimination puts equal opportunities into action and means that positive steps are taken to combat the various types of discrimination, such as racism.

Within early years settings anti-discriminatory practice is considered to be best practice and this is dealt with in more detail later in the unit.

Groups vulnerable to discrimination

Most of us experience discrimination sometime in our lives but some people and groups experience it more than others. As we have already, discussed being different in some way often brings discrimination.

Access to early years services

Tied up with social exclusion is the issue of access to services. To gain access to services people need to know they exist and that they can use them. This means information must be open and in all community languages. The services also need to be accessible and affordable. Finally services must welcome children and families and involve them at all levels, including management and service development.

Case Study

A rural initiative has been set up to work with children under five and their families in several small villages. There are real difficulties for these families as many have been affected by the foot and mouth disease epidemic and have lost their jobs or their farms. The initiative has been very successful due to its motivated and talented organiser and has attracted funding for several projects to help children and families. The success has been in taking the services to the communities and meeting the real needs of young families in isolated settings.

- Research the needs of rural communities for early years services. Identify ways in which the needs have been met or could be met.

Effects of discrimination

Think It Over

Imagine you are a young Asian woman in a bus queue and everyone kept ignoring you and pushing past to get on the bus. When you eventually got to the front of the queue the bus driver would not let you on and was hostile and unhelpful. You might feel angry and argue the point or decide to go by train next time. If this was your experience every day, in all sorts of different situations discuss how would you feel.

Discrimination affects everyone. People, including children, who experience discrimination, are damaged in many ways. As well as personal feelings which hold people back from realising their true potential, the effects of discrimination spread out to the wider community. This can lead to increased marginalisation and social exclusion of whole groups, e.g. young males. Some communities find increased levels of violence and aggression and social problems like crime and drug taking. Discrimination is both a moral issue and a social issue having wide consequences.

Key issues

People who hold discriminatory attitudes often have:

- feelings that some groups are 'less human'
- little empathy and consideration for others
- less respect for others.
- a false sense of superiority
- unreal perceptions of life

Discrimination affects children almost from birth. During their early years, children are developing their sense of identity, self worth and self-esteem. They are learning how others see them and react to them, especially outside their home. For example, black children may be bullied or called names such as 'paki' and alongside this they may see advertising where blonde, blue-eyed children are portrayed positively as successful and beautiful.

If children grow up with a view of themselves as inferior (or superior), this will affect their whole future. Children with poor self-esteem may achieve less at school and they may have serious emotional and behavioural problems.

Key issues

The effects of discrimination on self-esteem include:

- lack of confidence
- unwilling to take risks
- feeling unsafe and vulnerable
- feeling excluded
- self-fulfilling prophecy
- depression and hopelessness.
- low self-esteem
- fear of rejection
- withdrawal
- loss of motivation to achieve
- stress and illness

How care services recognise and promote equality, diversity and rights

Early years and care services are operated within a framework of laws and regulations designed, amongst other things, to support equality, diversity and rights. They have policies, procedures and codes of practice in place as a matter of best practice and to make sure that the law is upheld. The main thrust of these policies is to ensure that people are allowed equal treatment and that individual's rights are protected. Work practices, administration and organisation should all reflect this.

Treating everyone fairly is not the same as treating everyone in the same way. Fair treatment in any organisation or in an early years setting means meeting the needs of individuals. Individual needs are always different and need to be met in different ways as long as these are fair in terms of the law and the policies of the setting. This is not favouritism – giving all children the same activity and materials does not allow for the fact that some children, because of disability, will not be able to do the activity without additional assistance. The disabled child will be treated differently but only to ensure he or she has an equal chance with everyone else.

Formal policies

Policies are overall statements, aims and intentions and include the general goals and values of the organisation. Policies are powerful tools to make sure that the organisation's values and beliefs are implemented in everyday practice.

Policies that cover equality, diversity and rights have a role in ensuring high quality services relating closely to the values of the sector. Quality services are difficult to achieve if systems are not in place to protect staff and service users.

Each policy will have a code of practice and/or statements of procedures that set out in general terms how the policy will operate and what actions are to be taken in particular situations, e.g. what staff do if a parent makes a racist comment.

Many policies are primarily designed to promote individual's rights and freedoms when in employment whereas other policies are designed to protect service users. For example, a harassment policy protects employees from different forms of harassment or bullying, whereas a policy on behaviour is designed both to give staff clear guidance and to protect children.

Policies covering equality are required in early years settings' legislation and policy should include an appeals and complaints procedure that should be implemented fairly and without prejudice.

Every organisation and setting should have an equal opportunities policy that includes race even where they do not see themselves as needing one. For example, a nursery in a rural area where all its children are white should still ensure that equipment, activities books and so on, clearly reflect positive images of black and Asian children. This is also true of disability. Children need to understand that they live in a diverse society and learn to value and respect other people.

Common policies in early years settings covering equality and rights	Examples of policy goals
Recruitment and selection of staff	Open and transparent recruitment and selection that does not put up barriers to any section of the community. Designed to encourage a multi-racial workforce that reflects the proportion of different races in the community, including male staff and those with disabilities
Equal opportunities	Both for staff as well as children and families. Equal opportunities should form a part of all other policies to bring about equal treatment and equal chances. A 'no blame' culture to cope with change and service development
Anti-discrimination	Actively opposing and challenging discrimination in every area of work including discriminatory language, bullying, hidden or unintentional discrimination
Harassment	To give clear guidance on all forms of harassment experienced by staff, children and families, e.g. racial or sexual harassment
Admissions	Open, fair and transparent admissions systems ensuring access to service by all parts of the community. Ensuring materials translated into community language and extending knowledge of the services into 'hard to reach' groups such as travellers
Curriculum	The curriculum, resources, equipment, activities should be fully accessible to all children including disabled children, those with special needs or with English as an additional language. Positive images of groups who experience discrimination should be used throughout. Links with the community should be strong and diversity celebrated
Relations with parents	This policy will state the setting's attitudes and values regarding parents as partners
Staff development and training	On-going training to raise awareness of discrimination and to ensure staff both understand the issues and support the solutions
Quality assurance	This may incorporate elements of other policies but is designed to ensure that levels of service meet high quality standards across all the work of the setting. Settings may have written quality standards that they aim to achieve and a quality assurance policy will include these together with mechanisms for obtaining and using feedback from service users and other agencies involved. Inspections, regulations, codes of practice and the underlying principles will all contribute to the quality standards

Work practices

It is very easy to have a policy but it is more difficult to make sure that the policy is put into practice and that everybody knows about it and sticks to it. Organisations and settings should regularly evaluate the success of their policy in achieving its objectives. This also means that organisations will have to use management strategies such as appraisal and performance management to make sure policies and procedures are followed by individuals and monitored regularly. Many organisations now have whistle-blowing procedures whereby staff can report problems of all types including bullying, harassment and poor work practice. A whistle-blowing policy should protect, not penalise, the whistle-blower.

Adequate staff training and development follows on from appraisal. Regular in-house and off-the-job training sessions on equality of opportunity, anti-discriminatory practice and so forth will help the organisation to meet its goals. Staff should work together on developing policies for their work with children and policies that affect them as an employee. They should be clear on what policies protect them and how they do so.

Legislation

Many areas of discrimination have been addressed through laws which have been passed to make it illegal to discriminate on various grounds. These are outlined in the diagram on page 18.

Success of legislation in opposing discrimination

It would be wrong to assume that all legislation designed to oppose discrimination was entirely successful. Despite laws being in place, certain groups still experience discrimination, e.g. black people are still under-represented in professions such as law or medicine and women are under-represented in Parliament.

Under the Race Relations Act, it is still difficult to prove discrimination and obtain evidence that makes comparisons with other racial groups. Cases take a long time and are often stressful. There are possibilities under the Act for positive action in certain cases, e.g. where an employer wishes to advertise for a black member of staff and can justify why they are allowed to do so, perhaps to work with people from a specific ethnic group.

The Sex Discrimination Act has still not succeeded in bringing equality for women, who earn on average 82 per cent of men's hourly earnings for broadly the same work. The pay gap isn't just bad news for women. It means that women's abilities and skills are not being fully utilised in businesses and in the economy.

Women are still kept from rising to top positions at work because of the 'glass ceiling'. This is a term used to describe the barriers in place to prevent women getting beyond middle management.

There are other structural barriers to women succeeding, e.g. poor childcare facilities, lack of family friendly policies at work, inflexible working hours and low status given to part-time work. Many UK employers expect staff to work the longest hours in Europe if they are to rise in the company and women still take the major burden of caring for the home and family making the pressures on them enormous.

The 'glass ceiling' at work

Race
Race Relations Act 1976
Protects individuals against discrimination when:

- applying for a job
- at work
- joining a club
- renting a home
- house sale and purchase
- in education and training.

The Commission for Racial Equality (CRE) was set up to enforce the Act and to give advice on improving equality of opportunity in the area of race and ethnicity.

Human Rights
Human Rights Act 1998
Ensures that the European Convention for Human Rights is enforceable in UK courts. The convention covers fundamental freedoms and rights such as right to life, right to respect for family life, right to education. There is a Human Rights Unit in the Home Office.

Disability
Disability Discrimination Act 1995
Protects individuals against discrimination on grounds of disability. Covers those who have or who have had a disability.

Main points are:

- new rights for disabled employees and job applicants
- access to goods and services
- rights when buying or renting.

No commission set up to enforce the Act.

Equality of opportunity legislation

Children
Children Act 1989
Far reaching legislation affecting children and their rights.

Main points of the Act:

- the well-being of the child is paramount
- parental responsibility stressed
- introduced statutory services for children 'in need'
- partnership with parents
- individual child's own race, culture, language and religion to be respected
- services to be co-ordinated
- services designed to meet the needs of individual families
- child protection
- children are best cared for in their own families
- children's own feelings and wishes to be taken into account
- parents and extended families continue to play a role in child's life even when child lives away from home
- registration and inspection of early years providers.

Education
The Education Act 1981
brought about:

- introduction of concept of 'special educational needs'
- assessment could result in a 'statement of special educational needs'
- local authorities were required by the law to make special educational provision for children with special needs.

Gender
Sex Discrimination Act 1975 and 1986
Protects individuals from sex discrimination when:

- applying for a job
- at work
- renting a home
- house sale and purchase
- in education
- using goods and services.

Men and women entitled to fair and equal treatment.

Equal Pay Act 1972
Stated that wages should be same for a particular job regardless of whether it is a man or a woman worker. The Equal Opportunities Commission was set up to support the laws affecting sexual discrimination.

As well as laws, social attitudes are also required to change and this takes much longer. Many organisations still discriminate against certain groups whether deliberately or not.

The Children Act 1989 and National Standards for Under Eights Day Care and Childminding

This is a very important piece of legislation that affects many aspects of the way in which children are cared for. The Act covers children who are disabled and is described in more detail in the diagram above. It states that health, education and social services for children should be co-ordinated so that a seamless service may be offered.

In England the regulations under the Children Act (DFES, 2001) require early years providers to meet a set of fourteen standards and supporting criteria. OFSTED inspect early years settings taking account of these standards. The standards most closely linked to equality, diversity and rights are as follows:

- Standard 9 Equal opportunities: This standard will ensure that settings actively promote equality of opportunity and anti-discriminatory practice for all children.
- Standard 10 Special needs (including special educational needs and disabilities): This standard will ensure that settings are aware that some children will have special needs and that they are proactive in taking action when such children are identified or admitted to the provision. This means settings will have to take steps to promote the welfare and development of the child in partnership with parents/carers.

Key issues

If you live in Wales, Scotland or Northern Ireland the systems for registration and inspection are different. Find out what these are in your area and how they relate to equality, diversity and rights.

Human Rights Act 1998

This Act incorporates the European Convention on Human Rights into UK law across England, Wales, Scotland and Northern Ireland. The Act allows residents to seek justice through the courts if they feel a public authority has infringed their human rights. The term 'public authority' covers:

- local authorities (including social services)
- government departments
- police
- NHS (including GPs, dentists, etc., when doing NHS work)
- other public bodies (covers a wide range of organisations that have a public function).

The Act is designed to modernise relationships between people and the state based on the values of fairness, respect for human dignity, and inclusiveness in public services. The law is divided into sections, all of which affect broad human rights. The main exceptions to the goal of promoting individual human rights are to do with ensuring the safety of the individual or the wider common good.

The main areas that have been incorporated into UK law are listed in the table below with a brief commentary of those sections most relevant to early years work.

Rights and freedoms (Part 1)	Commentary
Article 2 Right to life	Public authorities must not cause death. There are some exceptions, e.g. when necessary force has been used to protect someone from unlawful violence and this has resulted in death. This article could affect decisions on abortion, life saving operations, and end-of-life decisions. It will also affect decisions about access to treatment, withdrawal of treatment, and investigations of suspicious deaths whilst in health or care settings
Article 3 Prohibition of torture	No one should be subjected to inhuman and degrading treatment. This article could affect decisions about taking children into care where they are experiencing inhuman or degrading conditions

Rights and freedoms (Part 1)	Commentary
Article 4 Prohibition of slavery and forced labour	People must not be 'owned' by anyone like slaves or forced to work and unable to leave. There are some exceptions, e.g. during emergencies affecting the community or in prison
Article 5 Right to liberty and security	Everyone has rights to liberty except when detained by law, e.g. convicted criminals, those with mental illness or when entering the country illegally. This article could affect people detained under Mental Health Acts when there is a delay in dealing with their case
Article 6 Right to a fair trial	People have a right to a fair trial within a reasonable time and are innocent until proved guilty. This part of the Act gives everyone the right to a public trial/hearing by an independent tribunal. Covers criminal and many civil cases, tribunals and hearings
Article 7 No punishment without law	No one can be held guilty of a criminal offence for something they did in the past, when under the law at the time, what they did was not criminal
Article 8 Right to respect for private and family life	Public authorities are not allowed to interfere in people's private affairs unless they have legal authority to do so, e.g. in cases of national security, public safety, protecting others. Health and social care services can affect family life, e.g. taking children into care
Article 9 Freedom of thought, conscience and religion	Freedom to change religions, and to practise religion. Covers issues such as taking time off for religious festivals, refusing life saving treatment such as blood transfusions on religious grounds, children practising religion when in care, and adoption practices based on religion
Article 10 Freedom of expression	Freedom to hold opinions, and to receive and impart information. This covers the media, the Internet, books – any type of communication
Article 11 Freedom of assembly and association	Right to demonstrate and to join (or not to join) trade unions

Rights and freedoms (Part 1)	Commentary
Article 12 Right to marry	Right to marry and found a family. The article will affect adoption and fostering. Local authorities' policies on who can adopt may need reviewing to ensure they do not discriminate on grounds of race or age or other criteria such as obesity
Article 13 Prohibition of discrimination	The rights and freedoms under the Act do not discriminate between people, e.g. on grounds of race, colour, sex, language, religion, political opinion, national or social origin, being part of a minority, property, birth or other status
Article 14 Freedom from discrimination in respect of protected rights (not a separate article)	Prohibits discrimination. It could cover a whole range of different scenarios such as organ donation or denying treatment because of age. This article recognises not all differences in treatment are discriminatory, only those with no reasonable justification
Rights and freedoms (Part 2 The First Protocol of the Act)	
Article 1 Protection of property	Gives people entitlement to peaceful enjoyment of their property and possessions so long as the public interest is not affected or removing property is allowed under law
Article 2 Right to education	No one is to be denied education and the state will respect the right of parents to ensure education for their children conforms with their principles, e.g. religion. The rights have to be measured against the available resources. This article could affect the rights of children with special educational needs or children who are excluded from schools
Article 3 Right to free elections	Covers rights to a free election with secret ballot
Rights and freedoms (Part 2 The Sixth Protocol of the Act)	
Article 1 The death penalty shall be abolished	No one shall be executed. Exceptions in Article 2 cover times of war

Overriding individuals' rights

Practitioners working in early years settings have to be very careful not to override individual rights and freedoms. This is particularly the case when dealing with vulnerable children and families. The principle of parents as the most important people in the child's life is very important. What parents want for their children or children want for themselves should be respected. Practitioners do not always agree with parents or children's choices and this can cause some difficulties. However, in most cases practitioners should not force the child or family to undertake a certain course of action even when its perceived as being for their 'own good' but should allow them to make an informed decision.

Case Study

Adam is a new child in the nursery. His parents are very traditional in their views of gender roles. Adam loves playing in the home corner and one day his father visits and finds him 'ironing' and playing with dolls. His father comments loudly, 'Come out of there Adam, boys don't do ironing, leave that to the girls!' The practitioner takes Adam's father to one side and tries to explain the benefits of allowing Adam to explore different roles. Adam's father asks that his son be prevented from playing in the home corner in future.

- In a group, discuss how the setting could deal with this. Role play a meeting between Adam's father and the practitioner.

There have been occasions when children who are finicky with food have been 'force fed' in early years settings sometimes with the best of motives. This kind of behaviour is totally unacceptable. No matter how young the child their views and opinions should be sought and should generally direct what happens to them. Children should be allowed choice and autonomy within the bounds of safe practice. This is not the same as a free for all where children are not given boundaries and frameworks for positive behaviour. Practitioners do need to prevent children hurting one another or to prevent and manage self-destructive behaviour.

In many situations dealing with young children practitioners have 'power' over the child or its family and must use this ethically. For example, where a child discloses abuse or where you suspect that a child is being abused a particularly difficult situation arises. The child may well say that 'This is a secret'. In this case you will have to say immediately to the child that it cannot remain a secret and make clear that you are obliged to tell other people. Equally if a parent states they suspect a third party of abuse you cannot collude with secrecy and have to override their rights for confidentiality.

There are times when individual human rights have to be put aside for the good of the person and for society; for example:

- the Mental Health Act 1983 – permits the detention of someone in hospital, e.g. if they are suicidal or a threat to others
- the Children Act 1989 – children must grow up in a safe and protected environment and their interests are paramount. Children's rights change and increase as they grow older and are considered more able to take their own decisions. However, age is not always the deciding factor. For example, the Gillick case where a mother tried to get

a court judgement preventing her underage daughter getting contraceptive advice from her GP. Victoria Gillick failed in her attempt and a precedent was established whereby children can consent to a range of medical procedures when they are deemed to have sufficient understanding.

Practice implications of confidentiality

Confidentiality is an important principle in work with children and families. If confidences are broken and sensitive information leaks out through accident or careless practice, this has major implications for all concerned and leads to loss of confidence in the setting. Parents or other service users are at liberty to take legal action against the setting in some cases.

How confidential information comes into the setting, how it is recorded and stored and how it is retrieved from storage are all points where the wrong people can find out things that are confidential. If information is received by fax or email, it can sometimes be seen by those for whom it is not intended. Therefore the setting will need to have systems for receiving, recording and storing confidential information. Clearly children's records should be stored securely as well as medical or court reports, case conference material and so forth. Staff must be clear about who has access to what and in what circumstances. Use of IT can be controlled and made secure by the use of passwords and other means of limiting access.

Where face-to-face interviews and discussions take place, participants should be clear at the start that what is said must be confidential including any notes or minutes taken and where recording devices or video have been used.

In most circumstances the relationship between children, their parents and the early years practitioner is one of trust based on a professional relationship where confidentiality is the rule. Parents must feel able to share with staff issues that affect children and many of these will be deeply personal, e.g. changes to the household when a parent moves out or another adult moves in. Students in placement must never discuss or write about the children and families in their care outside the setting except with prior written permission.

The relationship between the early years practitioner and parent should be based on trust

Day-to-day work with children and families will necessitate some recording of information; this should be done sensitively and accurately. You should record what you see and hear objectively and without bias. You should not express opinion unless it is firmly based on evidence.

There are, however, some circumstances where confidentiality cannot be guaranteed and these are mainly to do with child protection. If a child discloses abuse of any type and where the practitioner suspects abuse they must report this immediately to a responsible, senior member of staff. In turn senior staff will act according to the setting's policies and procedures for child protection. If a child or anyone close to the child reports abuse they must be told that this information cannot remain confidential (see Unit 5 for more information).

Assessment activity 1.2

Identify scenarios when you may wish to discuss children and/or families outside the setting.

- How might families feel if you break their confidence?
- Identify legislation that both protects the rights of the individual and sometimes may override the rights of individuals and think of examples affecting children and families.
- Write a report evaluating your examples and how legislation works to provide for the rights of individuals.

There are other issues that may interfere with the confidential relationship between families and the setting, e.g. drug dealing on the setting's premises, or where theft is a problem. These issues always have to be dealt with on their own merits but are likely to involve the police and may result in the necessary sharing of confidential information.

All individuals in the UK have some protection through the Data Protection Act 1998. This Act gives legal rights to individuals in respect of personal data held about them by others. However there is no other requirement or absolute right to confidentiality. In practice it would be difficult to keep confidentiality in settings where information has to be exchanged between staff and between agencies. If information is sensitive, permission should be sought before passing to others.

Empowerment and advocacy

Disability legislation and practice stresses the need to encourage children to make their own decisions and gain some control over their lives. This is known as empowerment and is a right for every child. Sometimes children with special needs find it difficult to communicate their needs and desires and require an independent adult (an advocate) to speak for them. Sometimes parents can be their child's advocate or a child's health visitor or social worker. Some local authorities employ children's rights officers.

Case Study

A nursery in an inner city had an established equal opportunities policy which ensured that discrimination, when identified, was dealt with immediately. The officer in charge insisted that all staff had training in anti-discriminatory practice as soon as they started at the nursery.

A new family had a place for their two-year-old at the nursery and were assigned a black key worker. They met with the officer in charge and stated that they did not wish their child's key worker to be black or Asian. The officer in charge was able to show the family the equal opportunities policy and to talk to them about the benefits to their child of meeting people from other backgrounds. The family understood that the policy meant that their request could not be granted although they were free to take their child elsewhere.

- What positive actions had the officer in charge taken? Why were the actions appropriate?
- How might the family be feeling? How could their attitudes affect their own child?

Assessment activity 1.3

- Find examples of equal opportunities policies from your placement or college tutor. Compare them and see if they cover the same areas. Ask yourself if there are missing areas.
- Discuss how such a policy helps early years services to promote rights and monitor good practice.

How individual workers recognise and promote equality, diversity and rights in their own practice

Early years practitioners have to ensure that they promote equality, diversity and rights in their own practice and work to the underlying values and principles of the sector. This section looks at how individuals can apply these principles in their work.

Discrimination and behaviour

How we behave to each other and to those around is the outward face of our inner attitudes and values. None of us is likely to be completely free of prejudice but we must make sure that the way we behave at work is always true to the values and principles of the sector. In other words we must never behave in ways that discriminate either intentionally or unintentionally. This means constantly checking the ways we relate to service users and the kind of service we provide. Settings do this in many different ways including feedback from parents and children and through inspections and self-assessment. All the work of the setting will be covered and the feedback will inform future planning. Individual staff can use this feedback to inform their own practice.

Theory into practice

Identify how your setting gets feedback from service users, inspections and other sources to help them to be more effective in implementing the values of the early years sector. Use that information towards your own action plan. Identify what support or information you may need.

Stereotyping

Stereotyping affects the ways we treat individual children. For example, we may feel that girls, in general, enjoy quiet activities and are less competitive than boys. We may feel that boys are usually noisier and enjoy competitive games and vigorous outdoor play. Equally we may think that black children are stronger and more athletic than others and that Asian girls are quiet and submissive. Our expectations of children are known to be a key factor in their achievement. If we hold stereotypes we may expect less of some children in some areas of their learning and development and they may not reach their true potential.

Early years best practice looks at individual children with their individual needs, personalities, likes and dislikes rather than whether they are boys or girls, or black or white. Holding stereotypical views about children based on their gender, race, ability or any other feature is not acceptable within early years settings and should never be tolerated.

Anti-discrimination in the early years setting

All forms of discrimination should be removed immediately they are evident in the setting. This means tackling discrimination and discriminatory remarks as soon as possible – preferably immediately. Staff need to be clear about the policies they are working to and be sure of the support of management.

As well as dealing with discrimination from people and organisations, early years practitioners have a duty to provide a curriculum that promotes children's development and learning but is also in itself anti-discriminatory. Louise Derman Sparks (1989) uses the term 'anti-bias' to describe a curriculum that should permeate every aspect of the early years provision and goes beyond celebrating the occasional festival. All nursery activities and equipment should reflect anti-bias and ensure that all children feel valued and at home in the setting regardless of their background.

Think It Over

A mixed race candidate is on placement in a large nursery in a rural area. There are a few black or ethnic minority children in the setting. The supervisor in the room where the candidate is working is very welcoming and helpful but says firmly that all the children are treated the same and that none of the children, who are two and three years old are aware of colour of skin. When the candidate hears a child make a racist remark to one of the black children she tells the supervisor immediately who comments that she is over sensitive and won't last long if she accuses young children of racism every five minutes. There are no witnesses to the conversation.

- How should the candidate proceed?

Children and parents discriminate too

Occasionally you will have to deal with children who behave inappropriately or make discriminatory remarks. Children may not know the views they are expressing are inappropriate and need to be told clearly and calmly with appropriate explanation. For example, in a home corner a group of girls say to a boy wishing to join them 'We don't want boys in here – they're dirty' or comments are made in the school playground to an Asian child, 'Go home, we don't like pakis'. In these circumstances you should explain clearly to the child that you do not like what they have said and explain why their remarks were hurtful. According to Iram Siraj-Blatchford (1994) you should support and physically comfort the abused child making sure they know you support their identity.

If parents are openly racist and ask that their child does not sit with a child from a different ethnic group or if children use abusive and discriminatory language or behaviour, there is usually an established procedure for these situations. This behaviour needs to be addressed – doing nothing is not an option.

Check your language

Some languages are considered more important than others. Bullying or teasing children because of their home language or their name seriously affects how they feel about themselves.

Many people find it difficult to know what language is acceptable when talking about discrimination. They are afraid of offending someone by being unintentionally insulting. For example, many older people describe black people as coloured as they feel using the term 'black' could be offensive, whereas most black people find the word 'coloured' reminds them of the days of slavery and apartheid. Similarly, words to describe disability are not always clear.

Most people know what constitutes discriminatory language. There are many derogatory terms used against women, black people or disabled people – there are far fewer against white men. Language gives a powerful message about our values.

It is also important to learn the names of the children and their families and be able to know which is their first name and which is their family name. Correct pronunciation is also important as this shows concern for the individual.

Disability discrimination

The effects of discrimination are discussed earlier in this chapter and apply equally to disabled people. Each child is different and has areas where they are especially talented or skilled, and areas where they may lag behind others of their age. Yet when we think about children who have a disability, it is easy to think about the disability first, putting the child into a category with other 'disabled children', and rarely stopping to think further about the individual behind the label.

Children who are disabled or who have other special needs have the same rights and should receive the same opportunities as other children. They should be treated as unique individuals and should not be labelled or stereotyped as this is discrimination.

Role modelling

Early years practitioners model good practice to children by the way they behave and what they say. 'Actions speak louder than words' is never truer than for young children who are watching you very carefully and soon see if you say one thing and do another. The key issue is to demonstrate respectful attitudes and fairness and to positively welcome and build on the diversity in our society.

Think It Over

Do you demonstrate respectful attitudes to children and their families, visiting adults and other staff? How can you be sure your approach is effective?

Empowering children

Children need to be encouraged from a very early age to deal with bullying and discriminatory attitudes, although adults must always support and protect them. Children can be taught techniques which empower them, i.e. give them strategies to use to defend themselves. Children's self-esteem and confidence grows if they feel they have some control over their lives and if they feel that they and their families are valued.

Derman Sparks (1989) suggests that for children to feel good and confident about themselves they need to be able to say 'That's not fair' or 'I don't like that' if they are the targets of discrimination. If they see a child abusing another child they should have the confidence to say 'I don't like what you are doing'. We should help children as much as we can to have the confidence to stand up for themselves and others in these situations.

Children with English as an additional language are vulnerable to discrimination if they cannot communicate, as are other children with communication difficulties. Communication support is very important and may involve using interpreters and bringing in those who speak the child's language. Children who cannot understand or communicate in English will need to be clear that their home language is valuable and examples of bi-lingual books, story tapes and posters need to be available. Multi-lingual children often cope very well if they have more than one language and can derive real benefits but may also need support. Children with other communication difficulties must have appropriate specialist support. Practitioners will find that drawing attention to dialect, accents, sign language and so forth is a good way of complementing discussions on community languages.

Think It Over

What strategies can you develop in your own practice that empower children? Identify what support or information you may need.

Promoting equality, diversity and rights in the early years setting

Promoting equality, diversity and rights through play

Everyday interactions

- Treat every child as an individual.
- Encourage boys to talk and express their feelings appropriately.
- Encourage girls to use construction equipment and outdoor equipment such as bikes or climbing frames.
- Encourage boys to use the home corner.
- Don't expect the girls to tidy up after the boys.
- Ask for strong children to help, not just strong boys.
- Don't expect girls to be quiet and boys to be noisy.
- Don't allow gangs of boys playing superheroes to terrorise the rest of the children.
- Encourage all parents to participate in the life of the nursery.

Circle time

- Use this time for discussion about feelings – what have you enjoyed? What has been difficult?
- Use this time for questions and discussion appropriate to the age of the children in ways that stress similarities between people and races rather than emphasising differences. This is a much more effective way of ensuring co-operation and respect. It is also important to encourage children to look at other points of view, e.g. if someone said that unkind thing to you how would you feel?
- Use the time to suggest ways of sharing, resolving conflicts.
- Discuss differences, e.g. in colour or shape of face or features, personality or ability, always in a positive and sensitive way without labelling.
- Set rules for circle time such as no interruptions and accepting that others have comments and feelings to share.

Activities, equipment, books and pictures

- Learn to use these thoughtfully and with understanding.
- Use equipment with which children can identify and that reflects diversity, e.g. black dolls, dressing up clothes from different cultures, multi-ethnic kitchen utensils.
- Ensure that there are positive images of girls, disability and ethnic minority groups in the nursery.
- Value languages that are not English and support bi-lingual children.

- Encourage children to use their home language during role play.
- Use dual language books, labels and posters.
- Ensure that all nursery activities are adapted for use by children with special needs.
- Persona dolls – these are special dolls that represent different people and are not usually kept with the toys and equipment. These dolls can be very helpful in explaining diversity and exploring concepts of discrimination with children, e.g. the doll could represent a child from an ethnic minority and can be used to discuss feelings and difficult issues one step removed from the children.

Theory into practice

Undertake an audit of two or three types of resources in the setting, e.g. books, domestic play equipment, posters and pictures, dolls, puzzles and games.

- Check the resources for an anti-bias approach and whether they promote equality, diversity and rights.

- Select the resource that best encourages equality of opportunity. Say why you have chosen this resource instead of one of the others.

Events and opportunities

- Settings should explore with their communities whether celebrating religious and cultural events is appropriate.
- Use festivals to celebrate diversity not just to pay lip service to different cultures or religions, e.g. be authentic and don't just dwell on the exotic aspects.
- Invite parents and members of the community in to talk to children and work with them.

Assessment activity 1.4

- Devise a leaflet for an early years setting explaining to parents the policy on equality, diversity and rights and how early years practitioners will promote these.
- Talk to other candidates and think of frequently asked questions (FAQs) about these topics to include in your leaflet with a model answer for each.

Values and underlying principles for the early years care and education sector

The welfare of the child

The welfare of the child is paramount. All early years practitioners must give precedence to the rights and well-being of the children they work with. Children should be listened to, and their opinions and concerns treated seriously. Management of children's behaviour should emphasise positive expectations for that behaviour, and responses to unwanted behaviour should be suited to the child's stage of development. A child must never be slapped, smacked, shaken or humiliated.

Keeping children safe

Work practice should help prevent accidents to children and adults, and should protect their health. Emergency procedures of the work setting, including record keeping, must be adhered to. Every early years practitioner has a responsibility to contribute to the protection of children from abuse, according to their work role.

Working in partnership with parents/families

Parents and families occupy a central position in their children's lives, and early years practitioners must never try to take over that role inappropriately. Parents and families should be listened to as experts on their own child. Information about children's development and progress should be shared openly with parents. Respect must be shown for families' traditions and child care practices, and every effort made to comply with parents' wishes for their children.

Children's learning and development

Children learn more and faster in their earliest years than at any other times in life. Development and learning in these early years lay the foundations for abilities, characteristics and skills later in life. Learning begins at birth. The care and education of children are interwoven.

Children should be offered a range of experiences and activities which support all aspects of their development: social, physical, intellectual, communication and emotional. The choice of experiences and activities ('the curriculum') should depend on accurate assessment of the stage of development reached by the child, following observation and discussion with families. Early years practitioners have varying responsibilities concerning the planning and implementation of the curriculum, according to their work role, but all contributions to such planning and implementation should set high expectations for children and build on their achievements and interests. Child-initiated play and activities should be valued and recognised, as well as the adult planned curriculum. Written records should be kept of children's progress, and these records should be shared with parents.

Equality of opportunity

Each child should be offered equality of access to opportunities to learn and develop, and so work towards their potential. Each child is a unique individual; early years practitioners must respect this individuality; children should not be treated 'all the same'. In order to meet a child's needs, it is necessary to treat each child 'with equal concern': some children need more and/or different support in order to have equality of opportunity. It is essential to avoid stereotyping children on the basis of gender, racial origins, cultural or social background (including religion, language, class and family pattern), or disability: such stereotypes may act as barriers to equality of access to opportunity. Early years practitioners should demonstrate their valuing of children's racial and other personal characteristics in order to help them develop self-esteem.

These principles of equality of access to opportunity and avoidance of stereotyping must also be applied to interactions with adult family members, colleagues and other professionals.

Anti-discrimination

Early years practitioners must not discriminate against any child, family or group in society on the grounds of gender, racial origins, cultural or social background (including religion, language, class and family pattern), disability or sexuality. They must acknowledge and address any personal beliefs or opinions which prevent them from respecting the value systems of other people, and comply with legislation and the policies of their work setting relating to discrimination. Children learn prejudice from their earliest years, and must be provided with accurate information to help them avoid prejudice. Expressions of prejudice by children or adults should be challenged, and support offered to those children or adults who are the objects of prejudice and discrimination. Early years practitioners have a powerful role to play in nurturing greater harmony amongst various groups in our society for future generations.

Celebrating diversity

The UK is a multi-racial, multi-cultural society. The contributions made to this society by a variety of cultural groups should be viewed in a positive light, and information about varying traditions, customs and festivals should be presented as a source of pleasure and enjoyment to all children, including those in areas where there are few members of minority ethnic groups. Children should be helped to develop a sense of their identity within their racial, cultural and social groups, as well as having the opportunity to learn about cultures different to their own. No one culture should be represented as superior to any other: pride in one's own cultural and social background does not require condemnation of that of other people.

Working with other professionals

Advice and support should be sought from other professionals in the best interests of children and families, and information shared with them, subject to the principle of confidentiality. Respect should be shown for the roles of other professionals.

The reflective practitioner

Early years practitioners should use any opportunity they are offered or which arises to reflect on their practice and principles, and make use of the conclusions from such reflection in developing and extending their practice. Seeking advice and support to help resolve queries and problems should be seen as a form of strength and professionalism. Opportunities for in-service training and continuous professional development should be used to the maximum.

Assessment activity 1.5

Look at the underlying principles for early years on pages 31–33.

- Do they support the view that equality, diversity and rights are important in early years work?
- Take each heading and try to explain its meaning using your own words. Include the terms equality, diversity and rights in your explanations as appropriate.

End-of-unit test

1 Explain briefly the meaning of the terms 'equal opportunity'?
2 What are values or codes of ethics?
3 Outline two key points from the UN Convention on the Rights of the Child.
4 Differences in our society make us a 'diverse' society, e.g. we may belong to different social classes. List five other areas that make our society diverse.
5 Briefly explain three reasons why an understanding of equality, diversity and rights is important to early years services.
6 Describe three ways in which diversity in our society can be celebrated within the early years setting.
7 How can holding prejudiced views affect our work with children and families. Give two examples.
8 Briefly explain how children learn attitudes and values.
9 Briefly explain the meaning of the term 'discrimination' as applied to race and gender.
10 Give an example of when a family's right to confidentiality may be overridden.
11 In the nursery you overhear a member of staff telling an parent, 'We treat all the children exactly the same in this nursery'. Briefly discuss whether this attitude encourages equality of opportunity.
12 How can 'Persona' dolls assist children's understanding of equality and diversity?
13 Explain briefly what is meant by 'empowering children to cope with bullying and discrimination'.
14 Identify three ways in which circle time can be used to promote anti-discrimination in the nursery.

References and further reading

Bandura, A. (1989), 'Perceived self-efficacy in the exercise of personal agency', *The Psychologist* 2(10), 411–24

Commission for Racial Equality, (1989), *From Cradle to School*, London: CRE

Council for the Disabled, (1995), *Help Starts Here*, London: NCB

Dare, A. and O' Donovan, M. (1997), *Good Practice in caring for Young Children with Special Needs*, Cheltenham: Stanley Thornes

Department of Health, (1989), *Children Act*, London: HMSO

Derman-Sparks, L. (1989), *Anti-Bias Curriculum*, Washington, DC: National Association for the Education of Young Children

DfEE, (1994), *Code of Practice on the identification and assessment of special educational needs*, London: HMSO

Early Childhood Education Forum, (1998), *Quality and Diversity in Early Learning*, London: National Children's Bureau,

Equal Opportunities Commission, *An Equal Start*, Manchester: EOC

Equal Opportunities Commission (Scotland), *An Equal Opportunities Guide for Parents*, Glasgow: EOC

Lane, J. (1999), *Action for Racial Equality in the Early Years*, London: NEYN

Maxime, J. (1991), *Towards a Transcultural Approach to Working with Under Sevens*, Conference report for the Early Years Trainers Anti-racist network and the National Children's Bureau, Wallasey: EYTARN

Milner, D. (1983), *Children and Race: 10 years on*, Ward Lock Educational

Siraj-Blatchford, I. and Clarke, P. (2000), *Supporting Identity, Diversity and Language in the Early Years*, Oxford: OUP

Siraj-Blatchford, I. (1994), *The Early Years – Laying the Foundation for Racial Equality*, Staffordshire: Trentham Books

Surestart – a Guide for Fourth Wave Programmes, (2001), Nottingham, DFEE

The Children Act Guidance and Regulations, Vol. 6, Children with Disabilities, (1991), London: HMSO

Woolfson, R. (1991), *Children with Special Needs*, London: Faber and Faber

Working Group against Racism in Children's Resources, (1990), *Guidelines for the Evaluation and selection of toys and other resources for children*, London: WGARCR

Useful websites

Commission for Racial Equality – www.cre.org.uk

Equal Opportunities Commission – www.eoc.org.uk

Home Office (for information on Human Rights Unit) – www.homeoffice.gov.uk

National Disability Council – www.disability-council.gov.uk

Communication and supportive skills

Introduction

In order to work in the care and education sector, adults must have high levels of communication and interpersonal skills. This unit describes the skills that are required in order to develop strong relationships, not only with children and their families, but also with other professionals. Practitioners working with babies and very young children will also need to be good communicators in order to stimulate their language development.

What you need to learn

- Interpersonal interaction and communication
- Supportive skills
- Communication
- Supportive skills with distressed individuals, children and their families

Interpersonal interaction and communication

Why is communication so important?

Communication is an essential part of most people's everyday lives. Without good communication, we would not gain information, form relationships and maintain friendships. Babies and children rely on adults around them to be good interpreters of their body language and first words, and so early years practitioners have to be skilled communicators.

Interpersonal interaction

The term **interpersonal interaction** refers to a wide range of ways in which we might make contact and develop a relationship with someone else. The need to be with others and to form relationships is a very powerful instinct in most humans. We all make relationships on different levels and this affects the type and intensity of the interpersonal skills that are used. Some relationships will be fleeting, e.g. when you sit next to someone on a train, whilst others may be lifelong, e.g. relationships with friends and family members.

What is communication?

The process of communication is often shown as a model called the **communication cycle**. There are seven stages in this model (see diagram on page 36).

Stage 1 – Information: the sender has to decide what they want to convey.

Stage 2 – Encoding: the sender chooses a medium in which to send their message – this can be using spoken language, written, non-verbal or visual. She thinks of what to say.

Stage 3 – Transfer of information: at this point the information is sent out. She says 'Well done'.

Stage 4 – Reception of information: the receiver now hears or takes in the information. The child hears 'Well done'.

Stage 5 – Decoding of information: the information is now interpreted. The child realises that they have been praised.

Stage 6 – Feedback: the receiver of the information may show some reaction. Sometimes the sender of the information may not see the feedback, e.g. if a letter is sent. The child may blink and then smile.

Stage 7 – Response: they may then wish to send information themselves in which case the cycle continues.

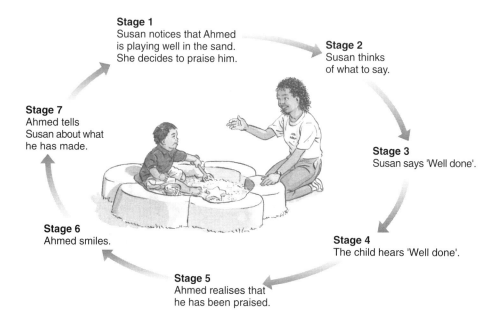

Stage 1
Susan notices that Ahmed is playing well in the sand. She decides to praise him.

Stage 2
Susan thinks of what to say.

Stage 3
Susan says 'Well done'.

Stage 4
The child hears 'Well done'.

Stage 5
Ahmed realises that he has been praised.

Stage 6
Ahmed smiles.

Stage 7
Ahmed tells Susan about what he has made.

Difficulties during the communication cycle

There are many factors that can interrupt and disrupt the communication cycle.

Noise

Factors that are not caused by the sender or receiver are sometimes referred to as 'noise'. Sometimes these factors can be technical, e.g. an email failing to send a message or noise on the telephone line. Other examples of 'noise' include:

- background noise – noisy environment, loud music
- poor handwriting
- poor telephone line
- lack of lighting – this can affect non-verbal and written communication.

Distortion

The communication cycle can also be disrupted if the way the message is sent is unclear or if the sender does not pick up the message properly. This means that the message becomes distorted. This is a common cause of misunderstandings, e.g. a cartoon may have been drawn in order to make someone laugh, but the receiver may not have the same sense of humour. This will mean that the message will have been distorted.

Types of communication

Although language often springs to mind when considering communication, it is important to remember that there are several ways in which communications can be sent. There are four key types of communication: **verbal communication, non-verbal communication, written communication** and **visual communication.**

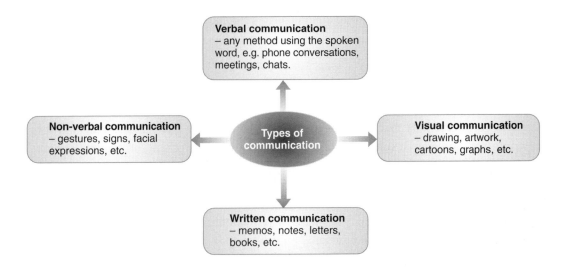

Assessment activity 2.1

In pairs, think about the communications that you have 'sent' and 'received' today.

Fill in the following table.

Type of communication	Sent or received	Message
Written		
Oral		
Visual		
Non-verbal		

Within each of the four key types of communication, there are further sub-classifications. Developments in technology and people's work and social patterns have had an effect on everyday communication. There has also been a greater understanding of the need to find ways to communicate with groups of people who previously may have found communication difficult. This has resulted in the development of systems such as **Makaton, BLISS** boards and the use of interpreters and advocates.

Types of communication	Examples
Language – spoken	Face to face, by telephone, through video and web-cams, story telling, radio, story tapes, taped information
Signing	British Sign Language, Makaton, social signs such as thumbs up, pointing

Types of communication	Examples
Music and drama	Rap, country and western, opera, classical music, pop music, ballads, plays, dialogues
Arts and crafts	Painting, drawing, collage, ceramics, embroidery, tapestry
Body language	Frowns, smiles, shrug of shoulders, hand gestures
Written language including Braille	Letters, text messages, notice boards, emails, websites, newspapers, memos

Personal space

The type of interactions that take place are often governed by physical distance and the environment. Some environments and layouts are better than others for communication. Noisy, bustling environments will make it harder for people to share sensitive information whilst calmer and more relaxed environments can assist in communication. The importance of the environment in assisting communication is increasingly being recognised and many early years settings now pay attention to creating welcoming reception areas. The seating arrangements and the way in which people are placed can also affect communication. In early years settings, communication is encouraged between children and so chairs may be grouped around tables to stimulate discussion. In other educational situations, tables and chairs may be in straight lines to encourage children to focus on the teacher, e.g. science lessons.

Barriers to interpersonal interaction

Good communicators also have to be aware of potential difficulties that some people may have in communicating.

Language

Spoken language relies on both speakers finding a common language in which to communicate. An inequality in levels of language can create frustration as one person may not feel that they are adequately able to express what they wish to say or may misinterpret what is being said. Young children who have a different home language from the one used in their setting will need particular support in order to convey their needs. To overcome this potential barrier to interaction, interpreters may be used in early years settings (see page 57).

Language disorders

Some interaction may be hindered by specific language and speech disorders such as aphasia and dysphasia as well as communication impairments caused by conditions such as autism.

Disability

It is a mistake to imagine that anyone with a disability will necessarily have difficulties in making their wishes and needs understood. Difficulties in interpersonal interaction are sometimes the result of others feeling uncomfortable with a person with a disability. Overcompensation, withdrawal and embarrassment sometimes create situations where interaction becomes tense.

Personality

People have different personalities and behaviour types. Some personality types find it easier than others to communicate with others. A person who is very shy may find it hard to engage in conversation or respond if they are approached.

In some cases, people's differences in personality can create difficulties. This is sometimes called a 'personality clash' although the root cause is often the inability of one party to respect and value the other or to listen carefully. Practitioners working with children cannot use 'personality differences' as an excuse for not forming an effective relationship with a child as children tend only to reflect back.

Time

Time can be a strong barrier to communication. Most relationships take some time to develop, for people to become familiar with others and for confidence in a relationship to grow. In situations where time is not easily available, it is harder to communicate and the level of relationship is therefore limited, e.g. in the morning, a child may be dropped off at nursery or school and there may be little time for parents and early years practitioners to communicate. In situations where time is limited, misunderstanding can take place.

Cultural and ethnic differences

Cultural differences and ethnic differences can affect interaction. Many gestures and the use of eye contact do not have universal meanings so they can be open to misinterpretation. In these situations, interpreters can be invaluable because as well as interpreting the oral communications, they can also explain what the non-verbal communication means (see page 56).

Differences in interpretation of language

Even between speakers of the same language, there can be distortion. This can occur if a phrase or tone of voice is misinterpreted or if vocabulary being used is not universally understood. Regional dialects often have particular expressions, e.g. the word 'coochie' is often used for 'cuddle' in Wales, whilst 'mardy' means bad tempered in parts of the north of England.

Think It Over

Have you ever realised that you have not completely understood someone because they have used a term or expression that you are not familiar with? Discuss your experiences in a group and list them.

Interacting with parents

A major part of interpersonal interaction and communication will take place with parents. Parents and families tend to play a large role in children's lives and early years practitioners need to work in partnership with them if they are going to meet children's needs.

Understanding family structures and lifestyles

A good starting point is to be aware of some of the different family structures that exist in our society. Below is an outline of some of the classic family structures, although it is always important to understand that any form of classification can lead to stereotyping, and the key to avoiding possible distortion in the communication cycle is to understand and find out about them.

Nuclear families

The nuclear family consists of two parents and their children.

Extended families

The extended family consists of several family members living in the same household or very near by and having a strong role in bringing up the children. Extended families were commonplace in the last century, today many ethnic minority communities live as extended families. There are many advantages to this family structure as children grow up alongside the older generation and form strong bonds with other family members.

Step families/reconstructed families

The high divorce and separation rate means that many practitioners will be working with reconstructed families. A reconstructed family is where a child lives with one birth parent and a step parent. The step parent may have their own children and the couple might also have further children creating half siblings.

Relationships in reconstructed families can seem complicated as children might have contact with step grandparents, step aunts and uncles as well as with their original family members. Many children also have their time divided between natural parents depending on the custody arrangements in place. Some children will be part of two separate reconstructed families in situations where both of their natural parents have formed new relationships.

Gay and lesbian parents

Some children might also be living in gay or lesbian households with some or no contact with the other natural parent. As there are still some prejudices against same-sex relationships, children living with gay or lesbian parents can find themselves being teased or being made to feel different. In some cases, couples may not present themselves as being in same-sex relationships.

Lone parent families

Many children are brought up by one parent. There are many misconceptions about lone parents with the media often giving the impression that the majority of lone parent families are created by teenage mothers. This is not the case as the majority of lone parent families consist of parents who have separated from their partners or where one partner has died.

Foster families

There are some children who are the sole or joint responsibility of the local authority. These children are often referred to as 'looked after' children. Some of these children may live in foster families and may or may not have continuing contact with their natural parents. Foster care can be temporary or in some cases an interim step before permanent adoption takes place.

Nomadic families

Nomadic families travel from area to area. The traditional travellers are gypsies who have their own language, culture and traditions. As well as gypsies, there are a new group of nomadic families often referred to as 'new age' travellers.

Backgrounds and lifestyles

Practitioners might also find themselves working with children from a wide range of backgrounds. Some families might be reliant on state benefits, whilst other families might be affluent. Being sensitive to the socio-economic background of families is important as some families might not be able to afford 'extras' such as school photographs and outings, and practitioners may need to consider this when planning extra activities and fund raising. It is also important to remember that in many households the main breadwinner may not be the man and that the majority of mothers are now engaged in some type of work. The wide variety of backgrounds and lifestyles of parents means that practitioners should be careful not to make assumptions if they are to establish effective relationships.

Cultural and ethnic influences

The UK is a multi-cultural society and although Christianity is the traditional religion and English is the predominant language, there are many children who are being brought up in other religions and speaking more than one language. This again means that practitioners should not make assumptions when working with children and their families. Some families do not celebrate birthdays, while many children do not celebrate Christmas and Easter. Practitioners need to be careful to find out about and respect the customs of other cultures and be aware that children will be gaining a variety of experiences outside of care and education settings.

Geographical location

Where families live can also make a difference to children's experiences and so we need to be aware of them. A child living in a rural location will have different needs and experiences to a child who is living in temporary bed and breakfast accommodation or a three-bedroomed semi-detached house in the suburbs.

Assessment activity 2.2

Simone is a lone parent who is generally in a hurry first thing in the morning. She has a high income job and is used to working in a 'service' culture. The nursery opens at 8.00am and she needs to drop off her son and get to the office for 8.30am which is a 15–20 minute drive depending on the traffic. Today she is running slightly late because her car would not start. Her concern about running late tends to make her aggressive and brusque in manner. Today one of the members of staff asks her if she has remembered to bring in some nappies. She is very sharp saying 'Look, can't I just give you the money some time? I really can't be bothered with all of this messing about!' The member of staff interprets this remark as that she does not care about her son.

- Examine the underlying barriers to interpersonal interaction in this scenario.
- Consider the possible effects that they may have on the care of the child.

Supportive skills

Practitioners have to be able to work and form relationships with people whose backgrounds and lifestyles may be very different to their own. The ability to form working relationships with a wide range of people relies on having good interpersonal skills. This section considers a range of skills that early years practitioners will require.

Warmth, gentleness and empathy

Carl Rogers, whose work has greatly influenced counselling methods, suggests that there are three important elements that are needed to create situations where people could talk openly: acceptance, gentleness and empathy.

Acceptance is about trying not to judge others as we listen to them. To do this we have to understand our own values and attitudes (see page 60).

Gentleness, sometimes referred to as sincerity, is about responding in an open and positive way – not just saying things because they are the 'right' things to say.

Empathy is about trying to understand how the other person is feeling and seeing things from their perspective.

Positive body language

Body language is a powerful tool in interpersonal interaction and communication. Good communicators use positive body language to help others feel at ease. The three elements of warmth, gentleness and empathy can be conveyed through positive body language. Children are very quick to pick up on adults' body language and respond well to caring, open gestures. It is also important for early years practitioners to notice babies and children's body language especially where children have limited language.

Stance

The way people sit and stand sends out silent messages.

Crossed arms and legs – these can indicate that people are not comfortable in a situation. It is as if they are trying to hold themselves back or defend themselves.

Learning forward or back – in some situations, a listener who sits back away from a speaker can send out a message of not being interested whilst a listener who leans slightly forward can give the impression of attention.

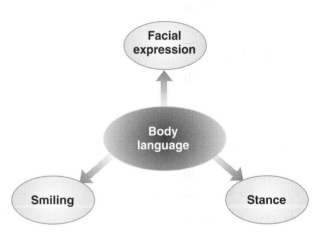

Facial expression

Facial expression is a strong element in non-verbal communication, although in some Eastern cultures facial expressions are more restricted. People can show a lot of their feelings through their faces as facial muscles tense when people are anxious or under stress. As a practitioner, it is helpful to note people's expressions because if they are particularly stressed or tense, this might mean that we will need to alter our approach. As a communicator, you should try to show warmth and interest in your face. Smiling and inclining the head are ways of conveying interest and warmth non-verbally. It is also interesting to note whether or not hands are being used to cover up the mouth or face. This can mean that someone is not comfortable or trying to conceal their feelings.

Listening skills

Being able to communicate using verbal communication and signing is partly linked to being able to listen/respond to others effectively. The term 'listening' in this section will be used to cover situations where people may also be signing. By listening carefully to others, we can gain trust and find out more about others' points of view. Active listening can be used as a way of understanding another person's perspective as well as checking that we have understood what someone really means.

Good communicators including counsellors use a range of strategies that help them to listen actively. Whilst learning and using these techniques will help you to communicate more effectively, remember that they do not confer 'counsellor' status!

Reflecting and paraphrasing

This strategy makes people feel that they are being listened to and understood. Essentially, the strategy is quite simple as the listener takes what the speaker has said and either directly repeats the words (direct reflection) or summarises what has been said (paraphrasing) using an interested tone of voice. This strategy allows the focus of the conversation to stay with the speaker whilst acknowledging what they are saying. Empathy should also be shown with the speaker.

It is important that reflection is not taken to extremes, otherwise the conversation will be stilted, and generally paraphrasing is considered to be the better method of reflection providing that the summary is accurate. Reflective listening is a technique that is used to help counsel people because in some ways it acts like a mirror on people's thoughts and so can help them to clarify them.

Think It Over

Look at the conversation below:

Parent: 'Sometimes he doesn't want to play with other children when they come around and he just goes up to his room.'

Early years practitioner: 'So he just goes up into his room.'

Parent: 'Yes, he just goes into his room and then I get really cross with him because I'm the one who has to sort out his friends and that really makes me angry.'

Early years practitioner: 'So there you are left with his friends and feeling angry.'

Parent: 'And I don't really know what I should do – does he act like this when he's here?'

- Find the examples of direct reflection and paraphrasing in this conversation.
- Examine the importance of correctly paraphrasing what a speaker has said.

Written skills

As well as interacting with people using spoken language, early years practitioners need to be able to use written language effectively. Writing is a useful form of communication, but can have disadvantages as the reader does not usually see the body language of the sender and so misunderstandings can sometimes arise if the tone of the writing is not appropriate. This means that being able to write using an appropriate style is an important skill.

Type	Purpose	Audience	Comments
Letter	To give information To make a request	Parents Other professionals Organisations	Letters are formal ways of recording information and a request. They might be used in settings to inform parents of trips, to confirm a place or to invite parents to open days and evenings
Memo	To give information To make a request	Colleagues	Memos are informal ways of passing information or making requests
Noticeboards	To give information To advertise To make requests	Parents Visitors	Noticeboards are public ways of passing on information. It is essential that writing on display is accurate and appropriate
Emails	To give information	Colleagues Other professionals	Emails are popular ways of passing information quickly. They tend to be informal in tone
Records	To store information for future reference	Parents Colleagues Other professionals Oneself	Records may include observations of children, assessment records. They must be accurate, legible and conform with data protection
Reports	To record summarised information	Parents Colleagues Other professionals	Reports might be given to parents to summarise their child's progress. Reports might also be sent to other professionals when a child starts at another setting

Effective writing skills

Many people find writing difficult and even daunting. Common fears include spelling, punctuation and not being sure about the layout and style. There are many points to consider before starting any writing project – see the diagram below.

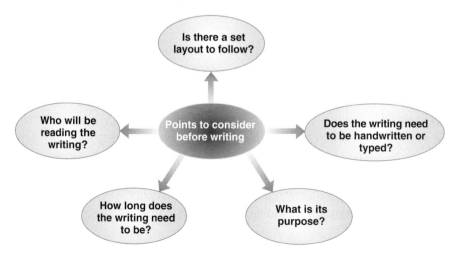

Spelling

Spelling is an area that many people identify as one of their weaknesses. There are, however, some strategies that can be used to overcome this difficulty.

Using a spell checker

This is a useful tool if you are working on a computer, but check carefully that the computer has not altered the meaning, e.g. 'quite' and 'quiet' are two words that have different meanings but are spelt very similarly. Also note that some computers show American spellings.

Ask others to read through the document

This is one of the best ways of getting help. Choose someone who is a good speller, but is also sympathetic. Asking for help shows a mature attitude rather than being seen as a weakness.

Use a dictionary

This is helpful when the first few letters of a word are already known. Check carefully that the word found has the same meaning as the one intended.

Report writing

Most early years practitioners will need to be able to write reports. Reports are ways of passing on summarised information, e.g. an accident report form or a report on a child's progress. The easiest types of reports to write are those which need completing on a form. Organisations use report forms to ensure that all the information that needs to be noted is recorded. Headings or boxes provide guidance as to the content.

Where reports are not to be recorded on forms, it is important to find out if there is a set organisational 'style' in terms of order, headings and whether it needs to be typed or hand written. It is essential to consider who will be reading the report and to ensure that it is as accurate and factual as possible.

Most reports require the following:

- clear headings and structure
- formal style of writing
- accurate and concise language.

References

The word 'plagiarism' is used when someone copies or uses written material without the author's permission or without acknowledging them as the source. In report or essay writing this is considered to be unacceptable as it is seen as taking credit for someone else's work. To avoid plagiarism, references should be used to source the material that is being used.

Record keeping

A range of records is kept in most early years settings. These include registers, records about children's progress as well as records which ensure the smooth running of a setting, e.g. stock ordering.

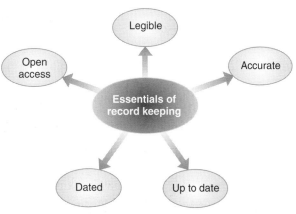

Children's records

Keeping children's records up to date is an essential task in early years settings. Most settings have a folder for each child. This may contain emergency contact details, health information as well as notes and observations to help staff and parents evaluate children's progress (see Observations, page 00).

Curriculum vitae

A curriculum vitae or CV gives an employer a summary of your working life including your qualifications, experience and education. The best CVs are concise and are usually no longer than two pages of A4. They need to be typed and several computer word processing packages are available to help people lay out their information. It is usual for CVs to end with the names and addresses of two referees who will be able to provide more information about you. It is courteous to inform people that you would like to use them as referees before using them.

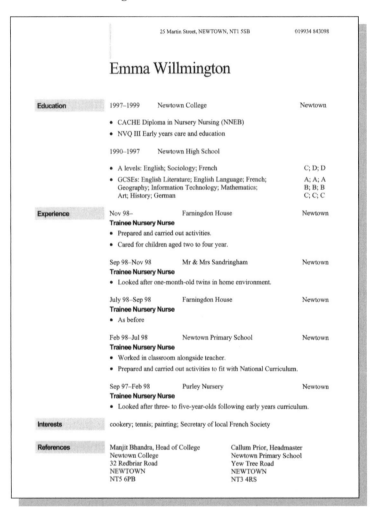

25 Martin Street, NEWTOWN, NT1 5SB   019934 843098

Emma Willmington

Education			
	1997–1999	Newtown College	Newtown

- CACHE Diploma in Nursery Nursing (NNEB)
- NVQ III Early years care and education

| | 1990–1997 | Newtown High School | |

A levels: English; Sociology; French			C; D; D
GCSEs: English Literature; English Language; French; Geography; Information Technology; Mathematics; Art; History; German			A; A; A B; B; B C; C; C

Experience

Nov 98–   Farningdon House   Newtown
Trainee Nursery Nurse
- Prepared and carried out activities.
- Cared for children aged two to four year.

Sep 98–Nov 98   Mr & Mrs Sandringham   Newtown
Trainee Nursery Nurse
- Looked after one-month-old twins in home environment.

July 98–Sep 98   Farningdon House   Newtown
Trainee Nursery Nurse
- As before

Feb 98–Jul 98   Newtown Primary School   Newtown
Trainee Nursery Nurse
- Worked in classroom alongside teacher.
- Prepared and carried out activities to fit with National Curriculum.

Sep 97–Feb 98   Purley Nursery   Newtown
Trainee Nursery Nurse
- Looked after three- to five-year-olds following early years curriculum.

Interests   cookery; tennis; painting; Secretary of local French Society

References   Manjit Bhandra, Head of College   Callum Prior, Headmaster
Newtown College   Newtown Primary School
32 Redbriar Road   Yew Tree Road
NEWTOWN   NEWTOWN
NT5 6PB   NT3 4RS

Letter of application

Letters of application are sometimes asked for by employers instead of a curriculum vitae. A letter of application should provide the employer with information about your skills, qualifications and experience as well as details about why you feel that you would be suitable for the post. It is now usual to present employers with a typed letter of application, although some employers state that they require a handwritten letter.

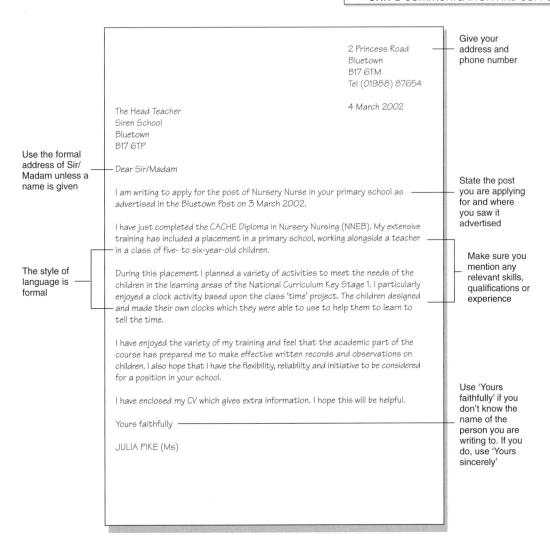

Give your address and phone number

2 Princess Road
Bluetown
B17 6TM
Tel (01988) 87654

4 March 2002

The Head Teacher
Siren School
Bluetown
B17 6TP

Use the formal address of Sir/ Madam unless a name is given

Dear Sir/Madam

I am writing to apply for the post of Nursery Nurse in your primary school as advertised in the Bluetown Post on 3 March 2002.

State the post you are applying for and where you saw it advertised

I have just completed the CACHE Diploma in Nursery Nursing (NNEB). My extensive training has included a placement in a primary school, working alongside a teacher in a class of five- to six-year-old children.

The style of language is formal

During this placement I planned a variety of activities to meet the needs of the children in the learning areas of the National Curriculum Key Stage 1. I particularly enjoyed a clock activity based upon the class 'time' project. The children designed and made their own clocks which they were able to use to help them to learn to tell the time.

Make sure you mention any relevant skills, qualifications or experience

I have enjoyed the variety of my training and feel that the academic part of the course has prepared me to make effective written records and observations on children. I also hope that I have the flexibility, reliablilty and initiative to be considered for a position in your school.

I have enclosed my CV which gives extra information. I hope this will be helpful.

Yours faithfully

JULIA PIKE (Ms)

Use 'Yours faithfully' if you don't know the name of the person you are writing to. If you do, use 'Yours sincerely'

Visual forms of presenting information

There is a range of visual forms of presenting information. These include photographs, posters, videos and cartoons. Information that is visual is often more easily remembered as the brain can store images more easily than words. Visual forms of presenting information can be particularly helpful for communicating when people have difficulties with either the spoken language or with handling written information (see page 58).

Case Study

A refugee family has been settled into accommodation in the local town. The youngest child is attending the nursery class attached to the primary school and the teacher is keen to communicate with the parents. She decides to take a series of pictures of the child during the day doing a variety of different activities. She hopes that this will help communication between her and the parents when they next meet.

In pairs consider the following questions:

- Why might the photographs help the parents to feel welcomed?
- Think of two other situations where photographs might act as a tool for communication.

Non-visual information

The majority of methods of communicating have some visual element – but for groups of people who have a visual impairment these can be handicapping. Non-visual forms of presenting information can be useful such as tape recordings, telephone and touch.

Tape recordings

Tape recordings are often used as a way of presenting information to people who have a visual impairment. Newsletters, reports and messages can be put onto tape as a way of helping to stay in contact. Remember:

- Keep background noises to a minimum.
- If possible use a microphone, rather than the built-in microphone.
- Speak naturally, but as clearly as possible.
- Try to visualise the listener as you speak to inject warmth into your voice.
- Prepare a script or list of points to avoid lengthy hesitations.

Telephone

The telephone is one of the most used forms of communication when people are not face to face. It is immediate and allows people to respond to each other. The tone of voice used on a telephone is critical and so it is essential to visualise the other speaker and also to avoid distractions during a call. Remember:

- Use your normal voice – do not put on a 'phone' voice.
- Speak clearly and slightly slower than usual if necessary.
- Show the speaker that you are listening and understanding by using phrases such as 'Yes, I see' – a telephone version of nodding and smiling.
- Always repeat or spell out unusual names.
- Repeat and take care over numbers – 14 and 40 sound similar.

Key issues – making a call

- Consider whether using the phone is the best form of communication – the telephone is not usually a suitable form of communication to discuss sensitive issues such as a child's behaviour.
- Mentally run through the purpose of the call beforehand.
- Consider the timing of the call – is this an appropriate time?
- Establish identity at the start of a call.
- Be courteous – do not attempt to do any other tasks during the call.
- Have a pen and paper to hand to keep notes of a conversation or to record information.

Key issues – answering a call

- Establish your identity and if necessary your position in the setting.
- Listen carefully to the needs of the caller, e.g. who they wish to speak to.
- If a message is to be left, note down the name of the person calling, the message and repeat it back to the caller to ensure that the details are correct.
- If a call needs to be returned, ask for the contact number.
- Immediately following the call, write up the message along with the time and the date of call.
- Make sure that the message is passed on swiftly.

Assessment activity 2.3

A three-year-old child in a nursery has been sick and is complaining of a headache. A telephone call needs to be made to the parent to ask them to collect the child. In pairs, role play this phone call. (This can be videotaped or taped to provide evidence of your telephone skills.)

Produce a fact sheet about non-visual forms of communication. Your fact sheet should:

- consider situations when non-visual forms of communication might be useful
- explain ways in which non-visual forms of communication can be made effective.

Self-esteem

Whatever way we choose to communicate with children, parents, colleagues or other professionals, it is essential that respect and courtesy is shown. Flippant remarks, lack of interest or even tone of voice can make people feel insecure and can create a barrier to future communication. A poorly presented letter or hastily scribbled note can equally give the recipient the impression that they are not valued. Remember:

- Always acknowledge another speaker by making eye contact, nodding or smiling.
- Find out how parents and children wish to be addressed.
- Make sure that remarks and speech are respectful and appropriate.

Making communication more equal

For good communication, people should be as equal as possible in the process. A person who has limited vocabulary will find it hard to express their viewpoint and so may be disadvantaged even though they understand what is being said. Advocates, interpreters and translators may be used to assist people who otherwise would be disadvantaged in their communication.

Advocacy

Vulnerable groups such as 'looked after' children or adults with severe learning difficulties may find it hard to be listened to or to express their needs and feelings powerfully. To empower such groups so that they can be active rather than passive in decisions being taken about them, an advocate might be appointed for them. An advocate speaks and argues for someone else so that their viewpoints can be put forward and should be completely independent, although family members and friends can be advocates provided they do not have a conflict of interest.

The importance of empowering people who may have communication differences is being increasingly recognised and many support groups are able to give information about paid or volunteer advocates. Legal advocates are appointed by the court when children are taken into the care of the local authority.

Case Study

Katie is in a residential children's home. She is four years old and under the 1989 Children Act has been appointed an advocate. The advocate represents her when her case is being discussed by social services and lawyers for her parents. Her advocate is independent and although she is a trained solicitor, she does not have any involvement with social services or the solicitors representing her parents. She visits Katie before her case is reviewed to find out clearly what Katie is feeling.

- How would the advocate communicate with Katie to make her feel comfortable?
- Why is it so important that Katie is able to communicate clearly with her advocate?

Interpreters and translators

For communication to be effective, both parties need to understand each other, but also need to be able to put forward their ideas, feelings and reactions. Interpreters and translators are used when the level of someone's language may be a barrier to effective communication. An interpreter is used to translate spoken or signed language whilst a translator translates written text (see page 58).

Interpersonal skills
Relationships in early years settings

There are many people with whom early years practitioners will need to form sound relationships. These include parents, children, colleagues and other professionals. It is easy for early years practitioners to consider that their relationships with children are the most important, but that is not the case as all of these relationships are essential as they are usually interlinked and a poor relationship can affect others.

Key workers

To help babies and very young children settle into child-care settings, a key worker is usually designated to each child. A key worker's role is to form a special relationship with the child and the parent. Key workers should be able to form an attachment that will enable the child to feel reassured, safe and secure when their parent is absent. Key workers need particular skills. They need to be patient, warm and thoughtful so that the child can feel comfortable with them. Key workers also form a vital link between the setting and the parents. In settings with an established key worker system, they are responsible for record keeping and passing on routine information about the child's day.

Understanding the needs of parents

Inexperienced and young early years practitioners can find it hard to approach parents, mainly because of the age difference and also because they do not feel confident. The parents' role in a child's life is one of the most critical relationships in their lives. Parents give children a sense of belonging, love and security and also a child's cultural and ethnic identity. As a starting point for forming a relationship with a parent, it is useful to understand parents' needs.

Most parents need to:

- be confident that their child is safe
- be sure that their child is receiving the best care and education possible
- know that their child is loved and liked
- be involved in decisions about their child
- be sure that the values that they are promoting at home are not being undermined in the setting
- gain reassurance that their knowledge and skills about the child are respected.

Ways in which settings may interact with parents

The day-to-day ability of parents to interact with staff in a setting will vary enormously. Some parents are able to drop and collect their child each day, whilst others may have complicated arrangements. This means that a flexible approach needs to be taken by child-care settings. Many settings have a home-setting book which allows parents and staff to communicate in writing. The majority of settings have also adopted an 'open door' approach which allows parents to talk to staff at the beginning or end of the days or in some cases whilst a session is running. Settings also encourage parents to become involved in settings in a variety of ways including fund raising, helping during sessions and on outings.

Theory into practice – working with parents

- Be courteous.
- Provide regular feedback about their child's progress and development.
- Take time to tell parents about their child's day and 'achievements'.
- Ask parents about how their child is when at home.
- Find out about any preferences that they may have regarding diet, skin care or behaviour management.
- Listen carefully to parents' concerns and acknowledge them.

Breaching confidentiality

Breaching confidentiality means breaching an individual's or organisation's trust in you. This is a serious matter and can result in disciplinary action. Most organisations have a policy on confidentiality to help guide individuals and usually confidentiality is only breached as a last resort in cases where there is bad practice that cannot be resolved from within an organisation. Practitioners during the course of their work will have access to a range of information about children and their families. This may include personal, medical and professional information that is required in order to meet a child's needs. Practitioners also gain information about their colleagues and work settings which may also be confidential. It is usual to consider any personal information that is gained in the course of work and is not generally available to others, as confidential.

In situations where a child's health or security is at risk, it is good practice to explain to a child or a family member that this type of information cannot be regarded as totally confidential (see Unit 5, Child protection).

Theory into practice – confidentiality

- Assume that information that is not common knowledge and has been gained in the course of your work is confidential, e.g. the financial difficulties of a family.
- Always seek advice if you are unsure as to whether or not information is confidential.

Think It Over

In pairs look at the following scenarios.

- Paul, a nursery nurse, has been asked by Tom's mother if he could give her the phone number of another parent because she wishes to invite the child over for tea.
- Jasmine, an early years teacher, has been asked by another school if she could send over her school's policy on behaviour.
- Emily is working in a pre-school which her daughter's friend attends. Over a cup of tea, the friend asks whether Emily's daughter is being picked on by another child.
- Mary, a childminder, is telephoned by another childminder who asks for information about a child she used to look after. The childminder wants to know how the child settled in when he was being looked after by her.
- A child tells an early years practitioner that her step father has beaten her with a belt. She asks the early years practitioner not to tell anyone else.

For each scenario, analyse the consequences of passing on information and under what conditions information could be exchanged.

Reviewing

Organisations and individuals need to be aware of how well they are communicating and building relationships with others. Evaluations are formal ways of reviewing performance, but most good communicators review their personal performance by looking at people's responses, comments and body language whilst communication is taking place. This type of reviewing process is sometimes referred to as monitoring and evaluating.

Communication

At the beginning of this unit, we considered the communication cycle. Seeing communication as a cycle is important as many people tend to concentrate on their 'speech' or 'message' role rather than their listening and responding role. For early years practitioners, it is essential that they see communication in terms of a cycle in order to help build children's language. Good practitioners are careful to provide opportunities for young children to talk and try hard to listen to them rather than to 'talk' at them. By being a good communicator, the early years practitioner is also teaching children how to communicate effectively as children will model the behaviour they have been seeing.

Verbal and non-verbal behaviour

In order to maintain the communication cycle, good communicators need a variety of skills and have to be able to interpret correctly others' verbal and non-verbal behaviour.

Monitoring and evaluating

During the communication cycle, it is important to monitor how well it is going and consider what is, as well as what is not, being said. It also means monitoring one's own communication skills and considering if the approach taken is working. Evidence that we are communicating well will often be communicated through the other person's body language (non-verbal communication) as well as their contributions. In some situations it is very easy to take over a conversation rather than listen to what is being said – monitoring whether this is happening is therefore an important skill.

Tone of voice

The tone of voice that is used during spoken language either in face-to-face situations or when using the telephone is extremely important. Tone of voice can actually be stronger than the words that are said and can also reflect what the speaker is truly thinking. Good communicators use warm voice tones and this means that conversations are comfortable with them. Warmth in the voice has to be 'thought' and so warm thoughts are also needed. Trainers teaching people to use the telephone effectively encourage them to smile as they speak so that their voices develop warm tones.

Questioning skills

In some situations, questions might be used to help the person we are communicating with express themselves to gain more information. For example, if a child comes in crying, we may need to help them tell us what has happened. If we ask some questions whilst we are listening to someone, it can help them feel that we are listening to them. Questions can be used as a positive tool, although if not used carefully and with the wrong tone of voice can make others fell defensive and threatened.

There are two types of questions – open and closed. Closed questions allow the other person to reply using very few words, e.g. 'Did you tell Mrs Smith about this?' will probably elicit either a yes or a no response. Closed questions do not therefore yield much information, but can make the other person feel safe as they do not have to reveal much. Open questions encourage the other person to reveal more information and can be used to help people explain their thoughts or their reactions, e.g. 'Why did you not tell Mrs Smith that you had fallen over?'.

Combining open and closed questions

Many skilled communicators use a combination of open and closed questions to help others express themselves. This can be a useful technique especially with children who may need some guidance and encouragement to talk. For example:

Early years practitioner: 'Did you have a nice birthday tea yesterday?'

Child: 'Yes.'

Early years practitioner: 'Tell me about your cake. What was it like?'

Child: 'It was really big and had lot and lots of candles that I blew out by myself.'

Silence

There are times when communicators need to be quiet! Generally people who do not know each other tend to fill in natural silences within conversations as these can at times feel uncomfortable. Silence can however be necessary when people need time to collect their thoughts or consider questions especially if they have had to absorb information as in the example below:

Early years practitioner: 'I am afraid that Matt fell over and bumped his head today. He seems much better now. I have filled in an accident report, but you may need to keep an eye on him.'

(Short silence)

Parent: 'Yes, I will – is he all right now?'

Eye contact

Eyes are powerful tools when interacting with someone face to face. In traditional European culture, eye contact is considered to be an important part of interacting with someone else and withholding eye contact can signal a range of feelings including displeasure, anger and embarrassment. Speakers usually notice whether or not the listener's eyes are focused on them – looking behind the speaker or down sends signals of not being interested.

Eye contact is a powerful communication tool

Gazing

Eye contact which is comfortable for both parties usually consists of gazing and glancing at someone's whole face rather than just on their eyes. Looking at someone when they are speaking provides reassurance that they are being listened to.

Intense eye contact/staring

Intense eye contact can be threatening and unnerving. It sends out a range of messages including intimidation, aggressiveness as well as intimacy and confusion.

Body direction

Non-verbal communication refers to the signals that our bodies send out. The way we stand, move or even touch someone can send out signals. Good communicators notice and react to the signals that other people are sending out. They also monitor their own body language with the aim of making it as positive and non-threatening as possible.

Body movement and gesture

Body movements and gestures can reflect our moods. A child who sucks their thumb may be indicating that they are tired, bored or distressed, whilst an adult who points and jabs their finger towards another person is likely to be showing anger. Accurately reading someone's body language requires experience but some signs are easy to read such as a child fiddling nervously with their sleeve. Good communicators monitor their own movements and gestures to ensure that they are not distracting a speaker by, for example, rubbing their eyes or tapping their feet!

Head movements

Nodding and shaking are the most common head movements. Nodding suggests agreement and understanding whilst shaking usually conveys disagreement. The more vigorous the movements, the stronger the signals given out. Good communicators usually tend to moderate their head movements to avoid distracting the speaker. Early years practitioners need to look at babies' and toddlers' head movements and acknowledge them, e.g. a practitioner may say to a baby 'You don't want any more?' when he turns its head away from a spoon. Remember:

- Avoid gestures that might distract.
- Be aware that some gestures may be misinterpreted.
- Acknowledge babies' and children's gestures and head movements by paraphrasing what you think they mean.

Posture

The way someone stands, leans forward or sits back in a chair sends out signals about their state of confidence and their interest in the conversation. Sitting forward slightly is a good position to adopt when listening and speaking to another person, especially to a child because it makes them feel listened to.

It is important to monitor your body posture as leaning forward too close may feel intimidating. It is also interesting to note changes in body postures. A person who is feeling increasingly relaxed may gradually 'unfold' by uncrossing their legs or arms. This is a positive signal as it shows that they are feeling more confident in your company.

Muscle tension

Good communicators tend to notice the 'whole' person when they are communicating with them. As part of this process, it is useful to look for tension in the body. Stress causes muscular tension in people's bodies and common signs include raised shoulders, tight hands or nervous twitches and ticks. Once signs of stress have been noted, it will be important to look for ways to help the other person feel more at ease.

Touch

Physical contact with another person is extremely powerful. In the right circumstances it can show understanding, give comfort and show warmth and friendship. It can also be seen as invasive and threatening if misunderstood. Touch is often an important element in communicating with babies and young children whose receptive language is limited and who need physical reassurance. Touch is not usually an immediate response to adults or even children, as most people need to have established some type of interaction first. It is also important to recognise that some adults and children dislike being touched and that trying to touch them may make them withdraw as they feel uncomfortable.

The way in which the touch is delivered affects its interpretation. A pat on the arm is less threatening than being held by the hand which is usually perceived as being a more intimate gesture. Wherever possible, a touch should be offered rather than forced upon the other person – an early years practitioner may offer an outstretched hand for a child to take rather than automatically take the child's hand. Avoid touching or patting children on the head – this suggests that you are in control.

Proximity

Proximity refers to the distance between the speakers. Being very close can suggest intimacy whilst a large distance can make people feel that they are being treated impersonally. Early years practitioners often find that they need to be quite near to a child so that the child feels that they are being listened to. Young children also get a feeling of comfort and reassurance by a familiar adult's close presence. Being very close to an adult, however, may not be appropriate as most people need 'personal space' and getting too close will make them feel uncomfortable.

Orientation

The term orientation is used to refer to the way in which the body is facing. Turning away whilst another person is talking will give the impression of being uninterested whilst facing another person signifies more involvement. People who are finding it hard to communicate particular details may look away whilst they are speaking, e.g. a child who is embarrassed may talk to the floor rather than directly to you.

As a communicator, it is a good idea to sit slightly to the side of people as this is not an intense position, but allows people to make or break eye contact with you easily.

- Make sure that you are facing babies and young children when you are talking to them – children rely on facial expression.
- Face adults or children with a hearing impairment so that they can see you more clearly especially if they are lip reading.

Cultural differences in verbal and non-verbal communication

Verbal and non-verbal communication is not universal. Every culture has different ways of using non-verbal and verbal communication with, for instance, a large variance between the way touch and proximity is used. It is not uncommon for some cultures to use handshaking at the start and end of routine interactions, e.g. shaking hands with the hairdresser before having a haircut. People may also sit closer to each other in some cultures whilst in others this would feel intimidating. The differences in verbal and non-verbal communication can therefore lead to misunderstandings when a person from one culture interacts with someone from a different culture. Early years practitioners need to be aware of the cultural background of the people they are working with, including children, to avoid potential misunderstandings. If you are unsure about whether eye contact or physical contact is appropriate, it is worth finding out from an interpreter or from the person themselves.

Listening skills

To complete the communication cycle, it is important to listen to the other person's response. Active listening is a skill that takes time to learn as it means thinking carefully about what the other person is saying and formulating thoughts after rather than before they have finished talking! Listening to others is also about making sure that they have enough time and opportunity to fully explain, make their points and feel valued. This means that most communicators use techniques such as paraphrasing and reflective listening (see page 43).

It is also important to remember things that people have said, especially when you meet them again as this shows that you have really thought and listened to what they have said. An early years practitioner may say to a child 'Did you have a nice time yesterday at Jo's house?'. This would show the child that the practitioner had listened to them as well as giving them an opportunity to use their language.

Communication differences

Distortion

This is the term used when the communication cycle is broken because the receiver does not get the message that was intended. The table below shows some of the reasons why this may happen.

Interpretation of expression	Tone of voice or expressions used can be misunderstood. A puzzled tone of voice may appear to the receiver as being 'difficult' or 'bored'
Language differences	Regional expressions as well as changes in tone resulting from translating a language may cause distortion of the message. People using signed language also find that there can be differences in the way that signs are produced. British Sign Language is different to American Sign Language. There are also variations with some of the visual signs that Makaton users produce
Emotional distress	Misunderstandings can easily occur when people are in distressed states. This is usually because they are not able to take in information as efficiently because they are distracted. People in distress may easily misread or mishear what is being said to them and may also not be in control of their own body language
Environment: noise, room layout, lighting	Communication can be hindered by the environment. Noises can distract the listener, interrupt the speaker or even prevent the listener hearing the message Room layout can be a distraction and can cause difficulties, e.g. if people are walking by or if a sensitive conversation needs privacy Lighting can cause difficulties as visually impaired people using lip reading need to be able to see the speakers face clearly
Assumptions, belief systems and attitudes	People can interpret situations and language differently depending on their lifestyles and cultural background. This is why communicators need to be aware of their own values and attitudes (see page 60) as well as those of others. A common cause of misunderstanding is making assumptions about what is being said rather than listening actively

Overcoming barriers

Early years practitioners have to be proactive in finding solutions to communication differences as it is essential that they are able to communicate effectively with parents, children and others in the setting.

Using interpreters and translators

Interpreters and translators can be invaluable in enabling early years practitioners to bridge the language gap. There are however many potential difficulties when using interpreters and translators.

Impartiality and objectivity of interpreters and translators

Professional translators and interpreters are often used because they have been trained to deliver, but not alter the message. This is essential in translation because otherwise there is a danger of interpreters putting forward their own viewpoints or advice to the other speaker.

Inherent difficulties in accurate translation
Every language has its own expressions and levels of vocabulary. This means that it can be hard to directly translate concepts or expressions from one language into another without losing some of the underlying values or feelings.

Think It Over

A good example of an English expression that is difficult to translate into other languages is 'looking forward'. It is used in everyday situations such as 'I am looking forward to meeting you'.

*   In pairs, work out exactly what this expression means. What is the underlying concept and feeling that it is expressing?
*   Can you find another way of saying the same thing without losing any of the sense of this expression?

Using non-professional interpreters and translators

There may be occasions when settings ask for a family member or even an older child to translate documents or act as an interpreter. Whilst this may be a good arrangement for everyday issues, there is always a danger that the quality of interpretation may not be sufficient when tackling sensitive issues. Using older children to interpret should therefore be avoided and also to avoid emotionally burdening them with information. Non-professional interpreters may not be aware of potential pitfalls in translating or may not have sufficient skill in each of the languages to accurately translate. There is also the danger that they may find it hard to stay in the role of 'translator' and begin acting as an adviser. It can also be hard for non-professional interpreters to remember to keep sensitive information confidential.

Communication aids

There is a range of communication aids that facilitate interaction between people when one or more person has difficulties in communicating. Whilst aids are extremely valuable in allowing people with difficulties to break through the potential communication barrier, many still rely on the other person to actively try and understand the other person's needs through questioning and observing reactions.

Talking aids: these allow the user to press a picture or a symbol which then produces a word or phrase.

Picture cards/communication boards: a bank of pictures or words give the user the opportunity to communicate by selecting the picture or word that they need. Communication boards allow the user to see at a glance the visual sign that they wish to select.

Using picture cards can aid communication

Non-verbal aids: these allow someone with limited physical movement and who are severely impaired to use their eyes or limited limb movements to show the other person what they want.

Adaptive aids: some equipment that is used for communication is adapted to allow people to use them. Telephones can be made with large keypads and have boosted sound to help the user, whilst keypads attached to the computer can produce voice messages.

The importance of clear speech and accuracy

To avoid potential misunderstandings, it is essential for communicators to speak clearly and at a suitable pace to meet the listener's needs. A person with English as an additional language may need to be spoken to more slowly and time will need to be spent checking that they have understood. Babies and young children need a more repetitive style of speech with emphasis being placed on key words. Most early years practitioners do this naturally and linguists call this style of speech 'motherese'.

Language also needs to be accurate to avoid misunderstandings. Vague statements such as 'I still need some things' may create confusion if the listener is not sure what is meant by 'things'.

Communication skills for calming a situation

When people are distressed, it is harder for them to give and receive information. This means that communicators need to find ways of calming situations to allow communication to take place. Children, for instance, may need to be physically soothed if they have fallen down or are upset whilst adults may need to sit down and be allowed a moment to collect their thoughts (see Unit 4, page 122). Remember:

- Encourage adults to sit down.
- Get down to children's level.
- Make sure that your tone of voice is gentle and lower it if necessary.
- Avoid bombarding children or adults with information.

Interpreting non-verbal behaviour

Looking at another person's non-verbal behaviour will provide important clues as to how they are feeling. A good communicator uses this to consider their approach to the situation. For example, if you see that a child has clenched fists and is physically restless, it will be important to begin any interaction by calming the child down and making them feel more relaxed.

Advocacy

In situations where decisions are being made, an advocate may be required in order to put forward the adult's or the child's point of view. For advocacy to work well, it is important that they have established a trusting relationship with the person. This means that arrangements have to made in plenty of time so that the child can feel comfortable with their advocate (see page 49).

Adapting the environment

Creating a good environment can prevent communication differences. In some situations it will be important to find an area that will give some privacy, especially if a conversation is personal or sensitive. This may mean taking someone into an office or creating an environment by adjusting the layout of furniture. Comfort is also important

– standing outside or against a wall might make a conversation feel rushed whilst taking time to sit somewhere will give the communication more importance.

Checking understanding

One of the key ways in which communication differences can be overcome or avoided is by carefully checking that each person understands what is being said and has the same perceptions about how it is meant. The skills of active listening are important here as well as using questions to check and clarify. Many good communicators rephrase important points that they are making to ensure that the other person can take in the information. Good communicators also make sure that the other person has time to think and reflect. Allowing enough time is particularly important with young children.

Using other skilled communicators

In some situations, early years practitioners will need to recognise that they are not the best people to communicate with somebody. A child who is having behavioural difficulties because of a bereavement may need to be helped by a counsellor or play therapist. Recognising that people may need the assistance and support of others is therefore an important part of interacting.

Values and attitudes

A good starting point is to understand that people have a right to be as they are. This requires practitioners to adopt an accepting attitude towards others if communication is to be open and honest. This is not always easy to do because sometimes our value bases can prevent us from being tolerant and accepting. Value bases are the set of values and attitudes that are developed during people's lives, especially during the formative years of childhood. They envelope us like a hidden cloak that remains invisible to us but can be perceived by others. People's sets of values determine who they are likely to feel at ease with as most people subconsciously relate better to others who have similar values.

Having different value bases can affect the way we communicate with people. Most people simply feel ill at ease without necessarily understanding why – their body language in turn often reflects their unease causing potential alienation from the person with whom they wish to communicate. Different attitudes stemming from value bases can also be the cause of prejudice and discrimination against others. A practitioner who feels ill at ease with a parent may not spend as much time with them as with another parent whom they feel comfortable with. This is discrimination and is therefore unprofessional.

Key issues – values and attitudes
- Recognise that you have values and attitudes.
- Understand how they may affect your communication.
- Remember that others have a right to their 'lifestyle'.

Self-esteem

The way we think of ourselves can influence the quality of our interactions. People with high self-esteem are likely to be more confident and able to put forward their views whilst people who are unsure about themselves may find it harder. The level of self-esteem can affect people's behaviour types (see pages 62–3).

The development of self-esteem

People are not born with high or low self-esteem. It develops as babies and then children learn about themselves mainly from looking at the reactions of others to them. Children or adults who have repeated bad experiences in their interactions with others are therefore likely to develop low self-esteem. This has several implications for early years practitioners as they will be in part responsible for building the self-esteem of the children they work with. Children will need to feel listened to and have their comments respected. They will also need to see positive facial expressions from adults and feel that they are being supported and encouraged as they speak.

How self-esteem may be developed and maintained as a result of positive interactions

It is not unusual for early years practitioners to work with children, adults and others who may have low self-esteem. Whilst there is no magic cure for low self-esteem, it is possible to raise people's self esteem by making them feel that they are valued and that the relationship with them is important.

- Positively acknowledge them, e.g. by greeting them in a friendly manner.
- Use active listening skills (see page 43).
- Avoid rushed 'interactions' – if you cannot talk to someone, explain why and if possible arrange a better time to talk to them.
- Look for ways of acknowledging their achievements and contributions, e.g. 'I saw that Sam had a new haircut. He said that you did it. It looks really good'.

The importance of conveying respect and value

All of our interactions should be positive and convey respect to others. Failure to show respect creates tension and prevents people from sharing information. This in turn can cause misunderstandings which sometimes develop into feelings of alienation and mistrust.

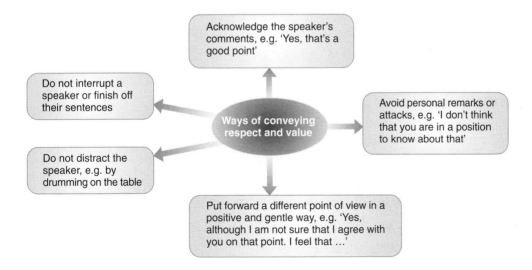

Think It Over
- Make a list of the people that you have seen today. In what ways did a 'connection' take place – e.g. did you make eye contact with anyone unfamiliar to you?
- On a scale of 1–10, with 10 being the most intense, decide how intense the connection was.

Confidentiality – written information

The amount of personal information that organisations hold about individuals has been a matter of concern and recent legislation has enabled individuals to have access to information that is stored about them.

1998 Data Protection Act

The 1998 Data Protection Act (DPA) came into force in March 2000 replacing the 1984 Data Protection Act which covered only information that was stored on computer systems. It also replaced the 1987 Access to Personal Files Act and the 1990 Access to Health Records Act.

The current Act requires anyone who is processing personal information to register with the Data Protection Commission. This includes paper-based information as well as anything held on computers.

There are eight enforceable principles of good practice as listed below. Information must be:

- fairly and lawfully processed
- processed for limited purposes
- secure
- accurate
- not kept for longer than necessary
- processed in accordance with data subjects' rights
- adequate, relevant and not excessive
- not transferable to other countries without adequate protection.

Types of behaviour

It is useful as a communicator to be able to recognise different types of behaviour that people may show, as this allows us to consider ways of best working with them. It is also important for communicators to consider if their behaviour is affecting the communication cycle.

Assertive behaviour

People showing assertive behaviour have accepted themselves and have self-confidence. They do not need to be competitive with others, they accept and can cope with responsibility and are accepting of others. They are likely to be able to accept change, constructive criticism and feel in control of their work and lives.

Key characteristics include the following:

- Self confidence and high self-esteem.
- Interested in others' thoughts and feelings.
- Listens to others and not afraid of conflicting viewpoints.
- Takes on responsibility.
- Asks others for feedback.

Submissive behaviour

This type of behaviour is sometimes referred to as 'passive' behaviour. People showing submissive behaviour may have reached the conclusion that others around them are 'better' than them and so merely go along with others' demands and views. In situations such as team meetings they may never volunteer an alternative viewpoint and are likely to listen rather than be active.

Key characteristics include the following:

- Lack of confidence and self-esteem.
- Puts down self in front of others and inwardly.
- Feelings of insecurity.
- Assumes others' viewpoints are superior.
- Prefers others to take responsibility and to be in control.
- Feels guilty.

Aggressive behaviour

People showing aggressive behaviour are often lacking in self-confidence and have adopted a defensive and aggressive attitude as a coping mechanism. They tend to appear as though they are confident.

Key characteristics may include the following:

- Lack of self-confidence and low self-esteem.
- Lack of respect towards others.
- Feelings of superiority.
- Like to be in control of situations.
- Not interested in others' points of view.
- See others' viewpoints as a personal challenge or slight to them; may make fun at others' expense.

Manipulative behaviour

A person showing manipulative behaviour may well blame others around them rather than take on any responsibility for what has happened. People showing this type of behaviour are ill at ease with themselves and therefore find fault with everything and everyone. They feel 'hard done by' and are usually lacking in self-esteem and confidence.

Key characteristics may include the following:

- Lack of confidence and self-esteem.
- Mistrustful of others' intentions.
- May spread rumours or dissatisfaction.
- Depressed and demotivated.

Supportive skills with distressed individuals, children and families

There are times when children or adults may show distressed behaviour. Early years practitioners may find that a child will become upset when their parent leaves or a parent may come into a setting feeling angry about the care of their child. Finding ways to communicate and be supportive in these situations is therefore important.

Distressed behaviour

The reactions of people to being stressed can vary enormously and depends on the coping skills and mechanisms that they have acquired. Children's reactions are often more straightforward as they are less able to control their feelings and therefore show strong reactions.

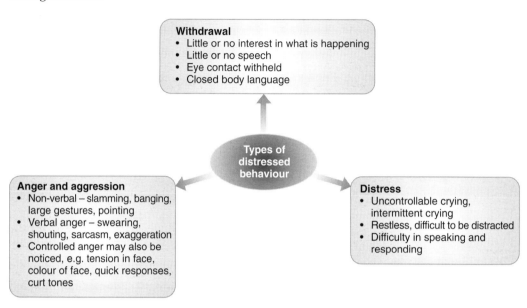

Withdrawal
- Little or no interest in what is happening
- Little or no speech
- Eye contact withheld
- Closed body language

Types of distressed behaviour

Anger and aggression
- Non-verbal – slamming, banging, large gestures, pointing
- Verbal anger – swearing, shouting, sarcasm, exaggeration
- Controlled anger may also be noticed, e.g. tension in face, colour of face, quick responses, curt tones

Distress
- Uncontrollable crying, intermittent crying
- Restless, difficult to be distracted
- Difficulty in speaking and responding

Reasons for distressed behaviour

There are many reasons why people may show distressed behaviour. These include family bereavements, misunderstandings, pressure at work or at home. Early years practitioners find that one of the most common causes of babies' and young children's distressed behaviour is separation anxiety. From around 8 months, babies begin to become distressed if their primary carer leaves them. The table below outlines the causes and signs of distressed behaviour in children.

Cause	Signs	Examples in children
Pain	Children in pain often cry or show their distress by using comfort behaviour such as rocking or sucking their thumb. Adults reaction to pain can vary according to their coping skills but includes irritation, withdrawal and tearfulness	Falling down Feeling poorly Minor/major accidents
Grief	The loss of someone or something creates powerful emotions. Children who feel upset when they leave their parents are actually grieving. As grief is a process, the behaviour shown by people may change, e.g. shock and disbelief may change into anger	Absence of parent Death of pet Lost toys or comfort objects

Cause	Signs	Examples in children
Communication differences	Misunderstandings can cause distressed behaviour. Feelings of hurt and betrayal can create aggressive or withdrawn behaviour	Stammering Children misunderstanding what has been said to them
Frustration	Frustration occurs when people feel that they are not in control of what is happening. A toddler may become frustrated because they cannot convey to an adult what they need, whilst an adult may become frustrated because they are late for work. Feelings of frustration are often translated into aggressive behaviour as a way of protesting; if someone is constantly frustrated they may use withdrawal as a way of coping	Tantrums
Perceived loss of rights or unfairness	Protecting family members and property creates powerful feelings. Early years practitioners often find that angry parents are often 'protecting' their offspring in some way, e.g. a parent may complain if they feel that their child has not received proper care or has been disadvantaged in some way. Squabbles and aggression in young children are often caused by problems over toys or objects as children find it difficult to share but quickly learn to defend possessions	Squabbles over turns, toys and possessions
Threats to self-esteem	Negative actions or words from others that are taken personally create distressed behaviour. An aggressive stance taken by an adult can be the result of a defence mechanism to avoid being 'hurt'. Children often show withdrawal or aggression if their confidence is being undermined	Distress because of bullying (school-aged children)

Skills for working with individuals

Ability to remain calm

When working with an adult or child who is distressed, it is important to remain calm. Strong reactions can often fuel the distressed behaviour rather than diffuse it. Shouting back at someone who is shouting tends to increase the anger and likelihood of more aggressive behaviour. It is also important to judge the seriousness of a situation quickly and seek help if necessary.

Communication techniques that encourage calm responses

Most early years practitioners will find that they quite often have to work with children who are distressed, e.g. a child has fallen down or is upset because of a lost toy.

The following techniques are often helpful in calming down children, but can be adapted in some situations with adults:

- Use gentle, soft tones.
- Get down to the child's level.
- Tell the child that you are listening.
- Use paraphrasing and reflection to help the child feel listened to.
- Use questioning skills to help the child express themselves logically.
- Physically soothe the child (if appropriate).
- Look for practical ways of addressing the source of the child's distress, e.g. ask the child if they would like to help you to look for their lost teddy bear.
- Do not dismiss the child's feeling as being petty.

Assessment activity 2.4

Write a reflective account of how you calmed a distressed child. Your account should evaluate the effectiveness of the communication skills that you used.

1 Discuss strategies that could have been used in a situation where the child had limited understanding of language, e.g. not understanding English, communication difficulty, etc.
2 Explain the importance of using other people including advocates and translators to overcome communication difficulties.
3 Consider ways in which effective communication can support vulnerable children and adults.

Responding to submissive, aggressive and manipulative behaviour

Submissive, aggressive and manipulative behaviours are ways that people have developed to cope with their feelings of low self-confidence. At times of distress, people may show clearly these types of behaviour (see page 63). Responding can be difficult, but good communicators need to develop their own assertiveness and aim to nurture others' self-confidence.

The difference between aggressiveness and assertiveness

Many people confuse assertiveness with aggressiveness. The two are very different as assertiveness is about having enough confidence in yourself to be able to put forward your viewpoint in a positive way whilst aggressiveness is about trying to take control away from others.

Strategies for assertiveness

There is a range of strategies that can help us to be assertive, whilst also responding to others' behaviour.

Positive recognition

Positive recognition means thinking positively about ourselves and others. It shows in our interactions with others and is therefore likely to attract positive responses from others. Positive recognition can be non-verbal as well as verbal. Examples of non-verbal positive recognition can include making eye contact with others, nodding in agreement with them and smiling. These non-verbal behaviours can diffuse tensions and aggressiveness whilst encouraging a person showing submissive behaviour to interact.

As well as showing non-verbal recognition, it is also important to verbalise positive recognition and acknowledge others' contributions. Making comments such as 'Thank you for taking the time to come in and talk to me' is an example of positive recognition and may be helpful at the start of a potentially hostile exchange.

Being able to receive positive comments is also an important part of positive recognition. Refusing to take a compliment or praise can make the other person feel less positive about themselves and you.

Think It Over

Mary is a nursery nurse and has brought in some fabric from home to give to a colleague who is preparing an interest table. Look at the two variations of the conversation below.

Conversation A

Emily: 'Thank you for bringing this in – it's fantastic. You have managed to get just the right colour. It will really make this display.'

Mary: 'Well (head down) I was going to throw it out anyhow.'

Conversation B

Emily: 'Thank you for bringing this in – it's fantastic. You have managed to get just the right colour. It will really make this display.'

Mary: 'It was no problem and I am pleased that I remembered that I had it. By the time you have finished, the display will look really good.'

- How might Emily feel after conversation A?
- What makes conversation B a more positive one?
- How easy do you find it to receive positive recognition?

Positive visualisation

Positive visualisation is a technique designed to help people imagine their way through a potentially difficult encounter. The idea behind this technique is that if you are able to visualise yourself behaving positively, you will be able to go on into the situation and create a positive outcome. This is particularly useful for situations where previously poor communication had taken place.

Case Study

Sam is working in a family centre and is uncomfortable working with one of the parents. The parent had been in to see him to say that his son had come home with paint on his clothes and was angry. Sam in response had shown manipulative behaviour saying that it was not his fault and that the parents would be better off making sure that their child was wearing more sensible clothes in the future. The interaction ended with both parties feeling irritated with each other and since then Sam has avoided meeting this particular parent.

Sam is now learning some techniques of assertiveness and is considering how at the next parents' meeting he will interact with this parent. Using positive visualisation he imagines that he will:

- acknowledge the parent warmly
- make eye contact and smile
- make a positive comment about the child
- make a positive comment about the parents' involvement with the child
- use active listening skills to show the parent that he wants to understand any concerns.

In his mind he can imagine that the meeting will be positive and so on the day of the meeting feels more positive. The parent is at first defensive, but gradually responds to the more positive attitude and the meeting is mutually beneficial.

Using language for assertiveness

In order to be assertive, it is important that the language we use is positive and reflects our thoughts and needs. People who are not confident often find difficulty in expressing clearly what they need to say.

'I statements'

One of the ways in which to make communication simple is to use 'I statements', e.g. instead of saying 'We need to tidy up the cloakroom', the statement may be 'I think that we need to sort out the cloakroom'. 'I statements' show that we are taking responsibility for our thoughts, words and actions. They help others understand what we are trying to do or say.

Using language accurately

Using language accurately is important as it prevents misunderstandings and also allows others to put forward their own points of view. As part of using language accurately, good communicators distinguish between fact, feelings and ideas in their speech, whilst it is common for most people to mix these up. Phrases such as 'I know' should be used for facts rather than for thoughts and feelings especially in cases where we might be trying to empathise with others, e.g. 'I know how you are feeling' is a classic example of using unhelpful language and potentially alienating the other speaker.

Assessment activity 2.5

It is first thing in the morning and the setting is bustling with parents dropping off their children and hanging up coats. A parent has come into the setting to complain that her baby had been sent home with a nappy that obviously needed changing. She is on her way to work and is very angry. She is standing in the doorway of the setting demanding to speak to her baby's key worker. You are the key worker!

In pairs, role play how you would deal with this situation. (This role play could be videotaped or recorded as evidence.)

Write a report about how this type of situation could be managed successfully. Your report should:

- analyse the reasons behind the parent's distress
- consider potential barriers to effective communication and ways of managing these
- evaluate strategies for successful interaction in relation to the communication cycle.

Sources of support for carers

People working in emotionally charged situations should seek support from others. This provides a 'safety mechanism' for all concerned.

Supervision

Supervision is usually used by counsellors as a way of preventing them from becoming too emotionally involved with the people they are working with. It helps them spread the emotional load and assists them in evaluating and reflecting upon their work. Early years practitioners who are not counsellors may seek support from senior members of the setting. This can help as they may be experienced and able to give advice about how best to manage future situations.

Counselling

There are times when early years practitioners may feel that they need counselling in order to 'off load' and cope with their strong feelings, e.g. an early years practitioner may find it hard to cope if a child they work with dies suddenly or a child has made a disclosure about abuse. Receiving counselling is no longer seen as being 'weak' as it is recognised that denying feelings can lead to psychological damage.

Training

Working with children and adults is a skill and learning to communicate effectively in difficult circumstances does not come naturally to everyone. Communication and assertiveness training is therefore very popular amongst people who care for others.

Peer support

Support from colleagues can be invaluable when coping with stressful situations. Colleagues are likely to be sympathetic, although may lack the necessary objectivity to guide you if you have mishandled a situation.

Support within own social network

Many early years practitioners find support from within their family and friends. Whilst they can provide a sympathetic ear, it is essential that talk about work should be kept in the broadest terms to avoid possible breaches of confidentiality. Most people use their social network as a way of 'switching off' from work which allows them to relax.

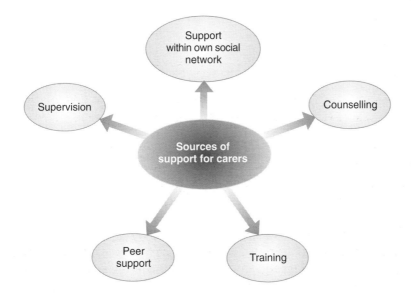

End-of-unit test

1 Explain how the communication cycle works.

2 List three factors that might disrupt the communication cycle.

3 What is meant by the term 'stance'?

4 Give one example of a non-verbal method of communication.

5 Why can it be helpful to understand a child's family structure?

6 Give one advantage and one disadvantage of using a translator.

7 What is meant by the term 'active listening'?

8 Explain three ways in which a person can show active listening.

9 What is the difference between an open and a closed question?

10 Explain what is meant by 'advocacy' and give an example of when it might be used.

11 How can the layout of the environment affect interaction?

12 How might early years practitioners convey 'respect' in their interactions with parents and children?

13 What is the Data Protection Act?

14 List three strategies that you might use to communicate effectively with young children.

15 What is the difference between assertive and aggressive behaviour?

3 Research and Project

Introduction

This unit provides an understanding of research, the research process and its application in the early years setting. Through increasing your understanding of research and by providing the opportunity to develop your research skills, you will be better placed to complete many of the activities required of you for other units, in particular the core units of Human growth and development and Learning in the early years.

What you need to learn

- What is research?
- Undertaking secondary research
- The primary research process
- The use and misuse of statistics
- Validity and reliability
- Ethics and confidentiality

What is research?

Have you ever been shopping in your local high street and been pounced upon by someone holding a clipboard who just wants a few minutes of your time only to ask a seemingly endless stream of questions? If so, then you will probably have been involved in market research to determine, for example, different people's shopping preferences.

You will almost certainly have completed a registration card after purchasing a new stereo or TV that will have involved ticking a number of boxes to a variety of questions. This is another type of market research.

You may have taken part in the National Census or even been interviewed about your views on some topic in the news. These are examples of social research.

Scientific research is used by many people, not just scientists. In science classes at school you will have carried out experimental investigations that are the basis of scientific research. Another example might be where you have been asked by your doctor to be involved in the trial of a new type of drug.

Purpose of research

As indicated above, research is used in all sorts of different ways and can be regarded broadly as a tool to develop a better understanding of the world we live in. Organisations and professionals concerned with young children are continually undertaking research for many different reasons. These can be for:

- studying childhood education
- investigating health issues
- examining social care issues
- evaluating services.

The range of research is vast though at any one time it often reflects issues of political importance simply because a large amount of research is government funded. For instance, in the UK there has been an enormous amount of research on literacy and numeracy in the early years relating to the introduction of the Literacy and Numeracy Hours in primary schools.

Look at the following examples of recent research studies to get an idea of the breadth of research carried out in different countries and by different organisations.

Central USA University study finds gender-based disparity in spatial reasoning of children

By the age of four and a half, boys have an advantage over girls in spatial reasoning, according to a study conducted by Central USA University. While a gap in the spatial reasoning abilities of the sexes had been documented in older age groups, the study shows that this difference arises much earlier than previously thought. These spatial skills are used by people to figure out maps, to interpret technical drawings and to affect performance in school and on the job.

SMALLER FAMILIES PLAY MINOR ROLE IN ASTHMA RATES

Some experts have suggested that declining family size might be one reason that increasing numbers of people are developing asthma. However, results of a study from New Zealand suggest that this is not the case. Past research has shown that the larger a family, the less likely a child is to have asthma. For example, a British study in 1997 found that single children were twice as likely to be asthmatic or wheezy as children with two or more siblings.

NEW RESEARCH ON INDIVIDUAL STYLES IN LEARNING TO SPELL

A Swedish government research project has shown that, by focusing on an individual's learning style it is possible to improve spelling age. It suggests that by recognising and teaching to a child's strengths and weaknesses, learning can be made more effective. For example, children with dyslexia often show an ability to support their phonological weaknesses through the use of visual and semantic strengths.

Babies of vaccinated mothers susceptible to measles

Babies whose mothers were vaccinated against measles as children may be more susceptible to measles than those born to mothers who were not vaccinated, US government researchers report.

Figure 3.1: Examples of recent research in the early years field

Types of research

There are many different ways of undertaking research and all involve the use of what is termed **primary** and **secondary** research. Primary research is the gathering of information by the person or persons carrying out the research. Primary research provides up-to-date and hopefully relevant information about the topic being studied. You will use primary research to carry out your own studies such as observing children in a nursery or classroom or carrying out a survey of parents.

Secondary research is the use of information that others have collected. You will undertake secondary research to gather information for the completion of much of your course work. The information you obtain may come from a variety of sources and will be based upon the published work of the original researcher or an interpretation of their work by someone else.

Secondary research is an essential part of primary research as the researcher needs to be fully aware of what other people have studied in relation to their own work. It may be that one piece of research is based upon the work of someone else or that the same research is being carried out in a different context, i.e. in a different place or with different people.

The type of information obtained by primary or secondary research can be identified as either **quantitative** or **qualitative**. Quantitative information describes information or data that is in the form of numbers, e.g. the number of children attending different forms of day care provision, whereas qualitative information is descriptive and in the form of the written or spoken word, e.g. mothers' experiences of childbirth.

Further distinctions can occur as a consequence of research in the early years field involving the study of people. These include **cross-sectional** and **longitudinal** studies. A cross-sectional study is based upon the investigation of people at a particular moment in time. Such research may form part of investigations into the differences or relationships that can occur between individuals or groups, e.g. finding out about the difference in ability to conserve (see *Experimental method*, case study, page 87). Alternatively, longitudinal research studies individuals or groups over a period of time, in some cases many years, e.g. studying the development of a baby for the first six months of life.

The problem with longitudinal studies is the time required to complete them. Whilst the example given might be feasible for you to carry out, others may not, e.g. a lifetime study of the social and emotional development of twins. After all, your course has been designed to be completed within two years!

Undertaking secondary research

As already stated, secondary research involves finding out facts and figures on topics you may be studying that have been produced by others. Some thought needs to be given to potential sources of such information.

Secondary sources

Books, newspapers, magazines, specialist publications

Books obtained from your school or college will probably be your main source of information initially, particularly if you have not had experience of using other sources of information. Whilst your tutors may direct you to some books and give you lists, you will have to search out others for yourself. This can be quite a task if a library is well stocked. However, most libraries now possess computerised search facilities and these can be a great source of help in finding resources that cover the area of work you are studying. As well as the school/college library, your local library may have useful material and depending upon where you live it may be possible for you to access more specialist libraries, e.g. universities or local authority education centres which usually have libraries for teachers (access to such facilities may be restricted or involve paying a subscription).

Libraries often subscribe to, and keep back copies of, one or more daily newspapers, magazines and more specialist publications produced for people working in specific industries/organisations. The types of publications you might find helpful include:

- *Nursery World* – weekly publication for early years curriculum professionals
- *The Nursing Times* – a weekly publication produced for nurses and other professionals in the health and caring services. Often contains specialist articles relating to children
- *The Times Educational Supplement* – published weekly covering newsworthy topics and developments in education
- *Social Trends* – published annually this is an invaluable source of official statistics covering amongst others information on families, housing, health, education and work
- *Regional Trends* – similar to *Social Trends* but contains information on a regional basis. Useful if you want data relevant to the area you live in.

People

By talking to people who work in early years settings, your tutors, family and friends, you can get different views and ideas on subjects. Such views may reflect changing attitudes towards parenting and education and as such support or refute information obtained from books.

Organisations

There are voluntary and statutory organisations that you will have found out about by reading other parts of this book and through input from your tutors. They can be an invaluable source of help and information on specific topics.

Whilst the statutory services are available throughout the country, voluntary organisations may be concentrated in larger towns or cities. However, a good starting point to look for such organisations is your local newspaper or the library. Whilst many organisations offer support to sufferers and carers they are usually more than happy to talk to, or provide students with, information that helps to further their cause.

Computers

Computers can be used to obtain information from CD-ROMs, the Internet or intranets.

CD-ROMs (Compact-Disc Read Only Memory) are digitally recorded stores of information. Some are like electronic encyclopaedias containing textual and visual information on a wide range of topics. Others are digital copies of the publications mentioned above that are updated annually. CD-ROMs are now the usual source of computer programs, many of which have an educational content.

The Internet is a worldwide information base which anyone can contribute to or access. Accessing the Internet requires a computer to be fitted with a modem that links it to worldwide communication systems. A computer program then allows the computer to gain access to the Internet via an Internet Service Provider (ISP). You can then use 'search engines' to find the information you require. However, you can waste an awful lot of time searching the 'web' and getting nowhere. You need to be quite specific in your search, but not so specific that the search engine comes up with nothing. Most search engines have help facilities to assist you in your quest.

Intranet sites are local versions of the Internet used by organisations for exchange of information within that establishment. The organisation may choose to allow access to others via an Internet website, but may limit use to specific parts of the site.

Other media

TV, national and local radio as sources of up-to-date information are often used to reflect current attitudes and opinions about different issues. However, like newspapers, they may reflect the biased views of the publishers and in order to attract a maximum audience will latch onto subjects that are topical, e.g. the Louise Woodward case in America.

Museums

These are often disregarded but are potentially useful in terms of local history and the subsequent social changes in local communities. Such changes may reflect on a wide range of issues relating to parenting and the development, education and experience of children in a community. Many museums operate interactive displays or operate as living museums to reflect social history, e.g. Beamish Museum.

Using secondary research

Remember that information obtained from secondary sources is second-hand. As such it may be biased towards the views of the person or organisation that has produced it. In addition the information may be out of date as the book or article may have been written some time after the original research was undertaken and you may be reading the material some years after publication. You should always treat such information with caution and have evidence from different sources to support your work and provide a balanced picture.

Avoiding plagiarism and summarising information

Plagiarism is the direct copying of someone else's work, which is against copyright law. However, copyright does allow for other work to be used for research purposes as long as the original author is acknowledged. The use of secondary information means that you must produce a summary of the original. You can make a direct quote where the information contains specific facts or data relating to your study, but the information should be enclosed within inverted commas ('...'). Whether you have summarised or used a direct quote, you must also include a reference or acknowledgement to the author or producer of the information and its source (see *Producing a bibliography* on page 106).

With the advent of computers and the Internet, plagiarism has become a widespread problem with students cutting and pasting large chunks of material for inclusion in their work. It has been known for students to copy information from such publications as Encarta and not even take the trouble to remove the copyright symbol! Teachers and lecturers are becoming more adept at spotting such transgressions and students may be asked to do the whole assignment again.

Key issues – the Literacy Hour and the Numeracy Hour

Literacy and numeracy are important features of the UK government thinking on education. The introduction of the Literacy Hour and the Numeracy Hour and other government education initiatives are a consequence of research that suggests this country lags behind other Western democracies in terms of the standards set in English and maths. Preparation for, and the evaluation of, the initiative's success has resulted in a wide range of projects being undertaken to study the impact of this and other initiatives to improve the standards of literacy and numeracy both here and abroad.

Through vocational practice in schools you will become involved in supporting children during the Literacy Hour and the Numeracy Hour.

Theory into practice

To develop your research skills you should know how to conduct an information search. By undertaking this activity you will gain a deeper understanding of the Literacy and Numeracy Hours initiative.

Go to your local or college library and look for texts on the subject or chapters or articles in books or publications. Note down the titles, the authors, date and place of publication (see *Producing a bibliography* on page 106).

Now carry out a search on the Internet. Try using different search engines to identify online information on the Literacy and Numeracy Hours. Check out some of the website addresses and if they seem to contain relevant information, note down or copy the titles of the research together with their author and website address. If you have not used the Internet before, ask your tutor, school, college or local library to help.

The primary research process

Whilst secondary research can provide the background and basis for many of your studies you will also need to be familiar with the process of primary research and the different primary research methods used. Whatever the nature of the research being undertaken, researchers make use of different methods to help them answer the questions they have posed. These include:

- surveys
- interviews
- experiments.
- observations
- case studies

You might find by reading specialist books on research that these methods are presented in different ways and that there are others. Each method has its own advantages and disadvantages and will consequently be used by researchers in different circumstances.

Before considering each method in turn, together with an explanation of the method and examples of their application, you need to be aware of the processes you must go through to plan your research effectively.

Research is regarded as a cyclical process that involves the following general approach:

1 Identifying a topic to research
2 Producing a research question or hypothesis
3 Selecting research and sampling methods (designing)
4 Collecting the information
5 Presenting the information
6 Analysing the information
7 Evaluating and discussing the research.

Discussion and evaluation of the research can lead to further or continuing investigations to complete the cycle.

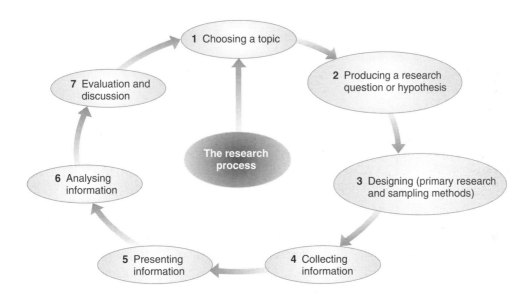

The first three statements in the cycle are all about planning and the more effort put into planning and organising your activities, particularly where the research is a project for which you have been allocated a term or longer to complete, the better the end result. Once you have planned the research you are then ready to collect the data, after which you need to sort it out ready for presentation and analysis.

At the end of this unit a checklist is provided to help you with the organisation and planning of any research or project you undertake (see page 107).

Identifying a topic to research

This can be based upon the following:

• Reading or hearing about something which you think would be interesting and enjoyable to find out more about.
• Your own ideas.
• The ideas of others.

Your tutor may be able to get you started on suggesting topics that previous students have investigated, but you and your fellow students could try a 'brainstorming' session as described below.

Key issues – brainstorming

A popular technique used by businesses and organisations to generate ideas is brainstorming. You need a flipchart and marker pens. Your tutor may have given you a broad idea to think about or left things very open. As a class, or in smaller groups of four to seven, agree who will write down the ideas (they need to be written large so everyone can see). The group should then start to think about what they could research and any idea that is suggested should be written down no matter how silly it may seem. Sometimes it can be difficult to get started but ideas will soon flow easily.

From the list, choose two or three topics that sound interesting. Either as a whole class or in groups, discuss the ideas to see if they are realistic (in the time allocated, with the resources available, considering relevant ethical or confidentiality issues, etc.) and what research methods could be used. Your tutor will help you with this process. This process should result in a research idea that you can begin to consider in more detail.

Case Study

A group of students was asked to undertake some research into childhood infectious diseases. In order for each student to select a disease to investigate, the tutor asked the group to brainstorm different childhood diseases they knew or had heard about. They came up with the following list:

Meningitis	Chickenpox	Measles
Headaches	Gastroenteritis	Impetigo
Eczema	Mumps	Threadworm
Whooping cough	Flu	Scabies
Nits	Asthma	AIDS
Scarlet fever	Tonsillitis	Polio
Diarrhoea	Thrush	Cystic fibrosis
Coughs	Diphtheria	Colds

Then the tutor went through the list to identify actual infectious diseases rather than non-infectious diseases. Students individually selected a disease to study.

Course syllabus

Another starting point is the course syllabus, which should be available through your tutor. The syllabus identifies the outcomes and assessment evidence requirements for the units you will be studying. By reading through these it should be possible to identify a topic that could be based upon a research project. Indeed, your tutor may give some direction or set specific assignments to ensure you meet such outcomes and assessment criteria. A number of units, both core and optional refer to research projects as possible means of assessment.

Talking to others

Talking to other people can be invaluable for helping to generate ideas and may include any of the following:

Family – by virtue of being your parents/guardians, your mother and father will have a wealth of knowledge about bringing up children and, apart from seeing how difficult a job it is, you may be able to gain information from them that will enable you to focus in on your study. Other relations may also be of assistance, not only as potential parents themselves, but possibly as someone who works with or on behalf of children.

Friends – talking to each other about your work will help spark off different ideas and make you think more deeply about your work that can help you become more focused.

Tutors – your tutor will probably want you to study something that is related to the course, but their experience and understanding of the subject and of past students' work make them an invaluable resource to be exploited at every opportunity, even though they may be busy!

Employers and workplace supervisors – if you work in a 'caring' organisation either voluntarily, through an organised placement or as an employee you could ask for advice and may find that they would like you to carry out some research for them.

The research question or hypothesis

Having selected the topic or list of topics that you would like to, or are thinking about studying, you must now begin to refine your ideas focusing on what you would specifically like to find out. This will lead to producing a **research question** or **hypothesis**.

A research question simply states the question or questions you want your research to answer.

A hypothesis is a special type of research question that tends to be used in surveys or experiments. It proposes the existence of a relationship between variables or factors and tends to suggest how the relationship will be tested (see Experimental method, page 86).

Students often find identifying a research question one of the more difficult parts of the whole process and consequently try to opt out of making a decision about this until later. This is an error that results in students being unclear about the focus of their study. Time needs to be given to what you hope to find out. This part of the research process will involve you in doing some secondary research, reading around the topic, looking at recent research and talking to others. In this way you will begin to find out more about the area you are going to study that can then lead to the selection of a specific topic.

One way to focus on a subject for the purpose of identifying a suitable research question or hypothesis is to produce a spider diagram to explore the different issues relating to a chosen subject as exemplified in the following case study.

Case Study

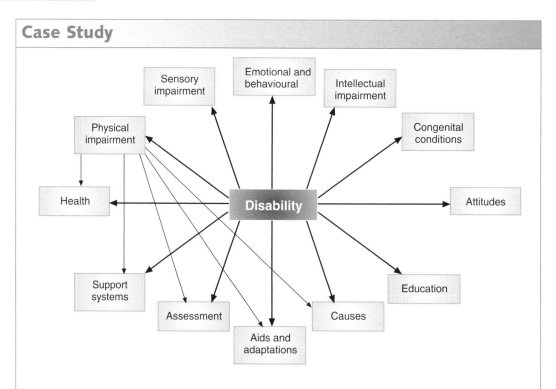

This is the start of a spider diagram designed to focus on a research topic related to disability. There are many different issues and there may be others worthy of inclusion. In addition, it is possible to make connections between different subtopics that begin to show how complex a subject can become if it lacks a specific focus. However, by identifying the possible strands, it allows you to focus on one or a small number of aspects that makes a research programme feasible. For example, this researcher chose to investigate the availability and cost of aids and adaptations for children with cerebral palsy as a result of talking to people she got to know through voluntary work in a day care centre.

- Are there any more links to be made between physical conditions and any of the other subtopics?

Think It Over

On the basis of a subject you are interested in, produce your own spider diagram. From this spider diagram identify a topic to research and produce a research question or hypothesis that will form the basis of a research project.

In writing your research question or hypothesis simply start by noting what questions you would like your study to answer. If you have several questions, try to narrow them down to one or two. This will make your project more manageable.

Research methods

This section concentrates on giving you information about the different methods you were introduced to earlier and how to use them. To remind you, the different methods to be considered are:

- surveys
- interviews
- experiments.
- observations
- case studies

Surveys

Survey research is based upon asking questions. This can be in the form of a question-naire or an intensive one-to-one, in-depth interview.

Questionnaires

Questionnaires are usually a pen-and-paper exercise that people complete. The completion of a questionnaire can be carried out through a mail drop or group activity or as a one-to-one structured interview. The advantages of using a questionnaire are as follows:

- They are relatively inexpensive to administer, apart from the cost of photocopying and postage stamps.
- It can be sent to a large number of people.
- Respondents may fill it out at their own convenience.

However, there are some disadvantages, which include the following:

- Response rates from mail surveys are often very low.
- Postal surveys are not the best way of asking for detailed information.

The disadvantage of response rate can be overcome by carrying out the survey face to face, e.g. in your local high street. This also allows for questioning the respondent to clarify any questions or to gain a more insightful response. If you decide to use this method it is important for personal safety that you conduct the activity in a small group and that you have some form of identification.

Alternatively, a group administered questionnaire is an effective way of getting people to respond to a questionnaire. It guarantees a high response rate and can draw on people who are readily available, such as in college, a school or workplace, though it may limit the total number of people surveyed and can create a biased sample (see *Sampling methodology*, page 92). Respondents are handed the questionnaire and can be asked to complete it immediately or you can offer to collect it the following week or whenever convenient.

How you administer the questionnaire is relatively easy compared to producing it. You might think it is easy to run off a few questions about, for example, the views of parents on raising children and keeping pets. You will find that it takes time, thought and practice to ensure that the questions give you the answers you are seeking. You will also find that you need to undertake a trial to find out if it works.

The types of question you can ask vary and include the following:

Closed and open questions – closed questions lead to a yes/no answer whereas open questions prompt the respondent to say something more, e.g. closed question 'Are you married?', open question 'What are your views on marriage?'. Closed questions give information that can be easily quantified whilst open-ended questions allow the respondent to express their own views. The difficulty with open-ended questions is that respondents may have slightly different views making the presentation of such information more difficult.

Information gathering questions which usually ask for some numerical data, e.g.:

- How many children do you have?
- What is your age?
- In what year were you born?

(The last is regarded as a more sensitive way of asking someone their age than the second.)

Category questions offer a number of possibilities only one of which the respondent can fit into, e.g.:

- Are you:
  Male
  Female

- Are you:
  Married
  Single

- Tick which age group you fit into:
  15-25
  26-35
  36-45
  46-55
  56+

The use of categories such as age groups is another way of obtaining information that may be regarded as sensitive. It can also be useful to allocate people to age ranges if you want to see if there is any difference in response to your questionnaire between age groups, e.g. attitudes or changes to parenting between younger and older age groups.

Ranking questions are used to place answers in order and are useful for obtaining information on views or attitudes, e.g.:

- Number the following emotional and social needs of children in order of importance:
  Security
  Discipline
  Love
  Encouragement
  Responsible behaviour

- In order of importance number your preferred method of pain relief during childbirth:
  Gas
  Pethidine
  Epidural
  Breathing and relaxation techniques

Scale questions can also be used to obtain information about attitudes and beliefs, but must be used with care, e.g.:

- Tick the box that best describes how you feel about the following statements:

A child should be smacked if they:	Strongly Agree	Agree	Disagree	Strongly Disagree
hit or bite another child				
wet themselves when being toilet trained				
have a temper tantrum				
play with their genitals				

The above scale question is quite controversial and may not be appropriate within a college-based project. However, it helps to illustrate how controversial topics may be investigated without having to ask someone directly about the subject, i.e. do they smack their children.

A less controversial subject for using a scale question might be:

- Tick the box that best describes your views on:

	Strongly Agree	Agree	Neither agree nor disagree	Disagree Disagree	Strongly Disagree
Breast feeding					
Fluoridation of water					
Homework for infant school children					

In this example note how an extra column has been added to include the neutral response of neither agree nor disagree. Whilst this allows people to express a neutral view, it can result in people avoiding the subject.

In addition to the style of questions used you also need to consider the construction and presentation of your questionnaire. The following pointers should be taken into account:

- Keep your questions as simple as possible. Two or three simple questions may be easier to answer than one difficult one.
- Do not ask too many questions. If there are too many, people will get fed up.
- Make sure your questions are unambiguous, e.g. 'Should a child be disciplined for being naughty?'. This question begs the response, 'What form of discipline are you referring to and how do you define naughty?'.
- Do not ask leading questions that imply a particular response, e.g. 'Do you think that it is better to breast feed rather than bottle feed a new baby?'. The response is likely to be: 'Yes, but I'd rather bottle feed.'
- Avoid grouping together questions that have a negative or sensitive context or, if you are seeking a more personal view, place them towards the end of the questionnaire, e.g. asking people's views on abortion, child abuse or drugs.
- Do not ask too many open-ended questions as they can take time to answer and are difficult to analyse. Again these are best placed towards the end of the questionnaire and can be a useful way of getting a response to more contentious subjects.
- Type or print your questionnaire in a format that is clear and legible.

- Set the questionnaire out so that simple closed questions that only require yes/no or one-word answers come first followed by ranking and scale-type questions and finish with open-ended questions to allow subjects to express their opinions more fully.
- Ensure that you include an explanation of who you are, where you are from and the purpose of the questionnaire. Also provide clear instructions and a statement to assure respondents that the questionnaire is confidential (see *Ethics and confidentiality*, page 104).

Pilot study

You may be quite happy with your first draft of the questionnaire but when it comes to people answering the questions, problems can arise over the meaning of words or misinterpreting of questions. Consequently, it is advisable to practise using your questionnaire on a small number of people to see whether questions need modifying to make them clearer. This is called a **pilot** or **trial study**, the results of which may still be used if you have not had to make any changes.

Be prepared to answer questions about your survey and remember to thank the respondent at the end.

Interviews

As you read through this section you will see that interviews, particularly at their simplest level, are no more than extended survey questionnaires. However, interviews are a far more personal form of research and can provide more detailed information particularly on sensitive subjects. They are usually carried out on a one-to-one basis.

Whilst interviews are generally easier for the respondent, especially if what is sought is opinions or impressions, they are not necessarily easier for you. Interviews can be very time consuming and they require good communication skills to complete effectively.

Interviews can be structured, semi-structured or open-ended. Structured interviews are based upon a set of questions requiring specific answers and are not very different from a questionnaire. Open-ended interviews may have little, if any, format and may take the form of a discussion whilst semi-structured interviews are a bit of both. If you use this form of research, semi-structured interviews are probably the most appropriate procedure to follow.

You are most likely to use interviews to find out about people's feelings, attitudes and experiences of, for example, childbirth, raising children, caring for a sick child, managing children's behaviour or the education of children. As a result you will tend to choose one or more people to interview from those you know, have had contact with or have been put in touch with by your tutor or workplace supervisor.

As a consequence of knowing or having been introduced to the person to be interviewed you should give a brief explanation of the purpose of your interview and make arrangements as to the date, time and place of the interview. This will help prepare both the interviewee and yourself for the event. In addition you should make preparations for recording the interview. You can choose to use a tape recorder or take notes, both of which have their advantages and disadvantages as shown in the table below:

Tape recording	Note taking
Able to concentrate on interviewee and what they have to say and the questions to be asked	Need to give attention to both interviewee and note taking
Can make respondents anxious and not able to talk about sensitive issues	Can be distracting
Provides a complete account of what has been said but can take a long time to transcribe and analyse	Allows a summary of what has been said to be noted and the main features identified so analysis is easier. Important facts or remarks may be missed

Whichever method is used, ensure you have the agreement of the interviewee and, if note taking, have a spare pen or pencil and devise a system for abbreviating certain responses such as 'Q:' for your question, 'A:' for the respondent's answer, 'DK' for don't know, etc.

In conducting the interview you need to take into account the beginning, middle and end. The beginning includes making appropriate opening remarks that put the interviewee at ease and doesn't ask too much of them. This can be achieved by explaining who you are, where you are from and re-emphasising what the research is for. The main thing here is not to be long winded. Also provide reassurance that the interview will remain confidential. This can also include asking simple questions that only require one-word or short answers such as how many children do you have, what age and gender are they. These simple questions can be memorised enabling you to give attention to the interviewee so helping to establish a trusting, honest, and non-threatening relationship that can lead into a more open-ended discussion about the main issues.

If you are interviewing more than one person for your research, you must ensure that the questions asked are exactly the same, as altering them in any way can change their whole meaning and, as a result, the response you get. Ask all the questions in the order arranged prior to the interview so that nothing is missed out either by you or the interviewee. Do not finish people's sentences for them because it might not have been what they were going to say. If the beginning has gone well, it should lead naturally into the middle part of the interview where you hope to elicit a more open or detailed response.

Techniques for encouraging a detailed response

- Silence – one of the most effective ways to encourage someone to say more is to do nothing at all – just pause and wait. It works because people are generally uncomfortable with pauses or silence and it suggests that you are waiting, listening for what they will say next.
- Encouraging remarks – something as simple as 'Uh-huh' or 'OK' after the respondent completes a thought can encourage the respondent directly.
- Elaboration – by asking a question such as 'Is there anything else you would like to add?' can result in the respondent providing more information.

- Ask for clarification – by asking the interviewee to talk in more detail about something said earlier can allow the discussion to explore new areas. This type of question also shows that you have been listening, which can encourage the interviewee.
- Reflecting – by repeating back part of what the respondent has said, you say something without really saying anything new. For instance, the respondent just described a traumatic experience they had in childhood. You might say 'What I'm hearing you say is that you found that experience very traumatic.' Then, you should pause. The respondent is likely to say something like 'Well, yes, and it affected the rest of my family as well. In fact, my younger sister...' and so on.

When the interview ends conclude by thanking the respondent and offering them the opportunity to read your completed work or at least a summary of it. Do give the respondent time to ask any further questions about you, your course or your research before you leave.

You may have observations about the interview that you weren't able to write down while you were with the respondent. As such you should immediately go over your notes and include any other comments and observations making sure you distinguish these from the notes made during the interview.

Think It Over

Interviews require good communication skills and take practice. If you are unsure about conducting an interview, try this activity to practise.

In groups of three, take turns in being an observer, interviewer or interviewee. Choose a topic which each of you feels able to talk about. Jot down some questions that will require closed and open answers. Start by the interviewer asking a simple question with the observer making notes on the responses. Move on to more open questions and note the responses, to see if the interviewee says more.

If you found this easy, try repeating the exercise with a controversial or sensitive topic such as abortion, embryo research or cancer.

The experimental method

The experimental method is a standard scientific procedure whereby the researcher, possibly after some preliminary work, devises a research question in the form of a hypothesis by which they hope to explain the initial findings.

The hypothesis forms the basis of an experiment or series of experiments that enable the researcher to find the answers to the problem being investigated, i.e. the experiment tests the hypothesis. As such the hypothesis tends to be a very precise question, statement or prediction which the experiment can answer as probably yes or probably no. The word probably is used since you can never be 100 per cent certain that your study can be repeated over and over again to give the same answer.

A hypothesis suggests that there is a **relationship** or **difference** between two or more factors or variables where a **variable** is something that changes or can be changed. A relationship, often referred to as a **correlation** or **association** between variables, results from changes in one variable being *related* to changes in another, e.g. the number of children suffering from asthma may be correlated to the increase in house dust mite infestations through increased use of central heating. A difference between variables can be regarded as changes in one variable causing an *effect* in another variable, e.g. girls learn quicker than boys, often referred to as a cause and effect relationship.

The hypothesis can also be written in one of two formats, the **experimental** and the **null** hypothesis:

- The experimental hypothesis – predicts the outcome of an experiment, e.g. the number of children suffering from asthma increases with increased numbers of house dust mites.
- The null hypothesis – does not predict an outcome, i.e. states that there is no effect or relationship between variables, e.g. there is no relationship or correlation between the number of children suffering from asthma and the increased numbers of house dust mites.

The next step is to design a suitable experiment that will prove or disprove the hypothesis. The idea is to look at how one variable alters in response to changes in the other. With the cause-effect type of experiment the researcher deliberately alters the variable known as the **Independent Variable** (IV) that is thought to be causing the effect and measures changes in the other **Dependent Variable** (DV). The problem with this approach, particularly when applied to research on humans, is that there may be many other factors that could influence the results. These are called **confounding** or **extraneous variables**. Consequently, the effect of such variables has to be eradicated or minimalised. This can be achieved by attempting to control as many of the factors as possible by ensuring the subjects are of the same or similar age, the same gender, etc. Alternatively the experiment can be designed using one of two approaches:

- Repeated measures design – this type of study is carried out by working with one group of subjects so that each subject experiences both experimental conditions, e.g. in an experiment looking at the effect of providing water during classes on children's attention span – each child experiences both conditions, i.e. having no water or water at different times.
- Independent subjects design – in this case each experimental condition is experienced by two different groups of subjects, e.g. in the effects of water on attention span, two groups of children would be chosen, one of which has water available and the other doesn't.

Think It Over

Discuss the problems that might be associated with the repeated measures and independent subjects design approach. Use the case study below to help you decide which approach would work best.

Case Study

This experiment will provide you with an example of how you could use the experimental method to investigate an aspect of your choice. It shows how the experimental and null hypotheses are presented and the need to design a suitable test.

Suppose you want to find out more about Piaget's theories of cognitive development and conservation. You probably already know that up to the age of about six or seven years, children do not understand that the amount or quantity of something can be presented in different ways, i.e. they are unable to conserve. Your experimental hypothesis would state that children under six years cannot conserve mass compared to older children. The null hypothesis would state that there will be no difference in the ability of children under the age of six compared to children over seven to conserve mass.

You now need to design an experiment to test your hypothesis. This involves selecting the children to take part in your study and designing a way of testing the hypothesis. Selecting the children involves taking a sample (see *Sampling methodology*, page 92) of under sixes and another group of over sevens. In selecting the children you also hope to manage or control some of the extraneous variables that could affect the outcome. The test is quite easy since you could use playdough moulded into two balls of the same size with each child asked if there is the same amount of playdough in each ball. Those children who answer correctly can proceed to the next part of the test which involves rolling one of the balls into a different shape so that the child can see, and the child again asked if each ball contains the same amount of dough. This would be repeated for every child and the results noted.

Assessment activity 3.1

Produce an experiment and null hypothesis for a similar experiment on either the conservation of capacity (volume), length or number. Design the method with a suitable sampling regime. This can be extended to undertaking the experiment on groups of children in your placement having gained the appropriate permission (see *Ethics and confidentiality*, page 104).

This type of experiment could be extended to investigate the work of Vygotsky and Bruner who saw that the intervention of others could affect the child's learning ability.

* In this experiment what extraneous variables could there be that might affect the results and how could these be managed or controlled?

Observations

You will be aware of many different types of observation as a result of undertaking the Early Years course and activities completed during vocational practice. Observation can be defined as the recording of facts or data through close examination of situations or events.

There are two principal types of observation, **participant** and **non-participant**. In the former, you, as the observer, become involved in the activities you intend to observe. In non-participant or passive observation you observe as an outsider and do not become involved. In all likelihood you will probably find yourself undertaking observations through placement activities that incorporate aspects of both types of observation. A good example would be during play activities where you might be assisting younger children whilst observing the interaction between individuals.

Observations can also be regarded as either structured or unstructured. Structured observations are based upon pre-determined criteria that will measure the duration, frequency, type or consequences of events. A form can be devised that enables a record of such observations to be carried out with relative ease (see below).

	A structured observation sheet for observing time on/off task for a child undertaking different classroom activities			
	Times on task	**Number of minutes**	**Times off task**	**Number of minutes**
Literacy	0900—0910	10	0910—0915	5
	0915—0930	15		
Numeracy				
Art				

Figure 3.2: Example of a recording form for carrying out an observation (part complete) – the same form was used for observing each child

How you structure the form depends upon what it is you are looking at, i.e. what is your research question? In the above example, a student wanted to find out if there was any difference between the amount of 'hands-on' time children spend in different subjects. The student sat in on lessons for the subjects identified and noted the length of time a child was actively involved in a planned activity. In order to obtain information from a number of children the observations took place over several days, as it was only feasible to carry out observations on one child at a time. You would have to be very alert to observe several children at once!

Think It Over
- Why do you think the student observed several children rather than just one?
- What problems might result from making observations on different children over a number of days?
- What is meant by being on task and off task? For instance, when a child was not 'on task' did it mean that they weren't doing anything, or appeared to be thinking or discussing the problem with other children or the teacher, or were they talking to others about something entirely different?
- How else could you use this type of observation?

The opposite of a structured observation is the open-ended, unstructured approach. At the extreme, this method involves the researcher having some vague notion of what they wish to study, but through the observation process gathers information that provides a focus for developing a research question or hypothesis (the opposite of what has been suggested so far). The advantage of this approach is there are no pre-conceived notions or expectations about what the outcome of the research will be. As such a large amount of information is gathered which over time can begin to show patterns that can lead to broad generalisations. Herein lies the problem with this type of research – you need time both to carry out the research and to analyse the information.

The advantages of the observation method is that it is adaptable to many situations, can reveal unexpected relationships, draws on data not available using other methods, and can be used in conjunction with the experimental method. For example, the observation of behaviour before and after the introduction of a behaviour modification programme to assess its success or otherwise.

Case studies

The case study is not a method in itself, but an approach to research that is based upon the observation of an individual, organisation or culture. Case studies take into account historical evidence and are used to study the consequences of past and present events on the subject being studied. They can provide a unique insight into an individual or organisation but; can be intrusive therefore care must be exercised in carrying them out to ensure you have informed consent and to maintain confidentiality (see *Ethics and confidentiality*, page 104).

Think It Over

In the late 1960s researchers randomly selected children within schools, before telling their teachers the degree of talent they should expect of such children, in order to study the effect of such information on their education. It was found that the selected children ended up doing better than their peers even though they were not necessarily more able initially.

From 1946 to 1956, nineteen mentally retarded boys at the State Residential School, Fernald, Massachusetts (USA) were fed radioactive iron and calcium in their breakfast cereal. The goal of the study was to gather information about nutrition and metabolism, and the parents, who consented to the study, were not told about the radioactive substances.

How might people involved in experiments today protect themselves using the legal requirements for informed consent?

The gathering of information for a case study should initially be focused upon the gathering of historical information to prepare what is called a case history. This will usually be based upon interviews with the parents, teachers or other people associated with the child being studied followed by observations of the child in different settings depending upon their age, i.e. home, playgroup or school, outdoors, in social groups.

Case studies also form part of a social worker's kit in relation to child abuse and whilst it would be inappropriate for you to be taking such an approach, you will find case studies very useful for finding out about the effects of disabling conditions such as

Down's syndrome, cystic fibrosis or autism for example, on a child's physical, emotional and social development. More in-depth studies may also consider the effects on the family or carers and the implications for health, education and social services.

Case studies are particularly useful for early years research being undertaken by students as they allow the opportunity to study something in depth over a relatively short space of time. They are also valuable for studying individual children as they enable a picture of the child to be revealed from which conclusions about their patterns of behaviour, their learning, their socialisation skills, etc., can be drawn and used to assist their development.

Action research

This technique involves observing the effects of making a change or changes within an organisation with a view to improving the way things are done. It usually involves a number of people either as implementers, observers or participants. The implementer will introduce the change and the observer will record the effects on the participants. A simple example of action research is a teacher introducing a new teaching method to a group of pupils. The teacher acts as researcher, implementer and observer whilst the pupils are the participants. The teacher hopes that the new method enables the pupils to learn more effectively, a result that may be measured by improved SATS test results or improved behaviour.

Action research is a very powerful tool aimed at improving work practice and focusing on specific problems whilst involving all concerned, allowing the processes of the research cycle as shown on page 77 to be linked together.

To complete this section on different methods, try the portfolio activity that follows to help you in selecting the most appropriate method or methods for your study.

Assessment activity 3.2

Review the different methods of research and identify the advantages and disadvantages of each. Read the following research problems and evaluate which method would be most appropriate. Justify your reasons.

- *Competent children at 5: families and early education (Cathy Wylie, Jean Thompson and Anne Kerslake Hendricks).* The aim of this project is to discover what impact children's family resources and early childhood educational experiences have on the development of their cognitive, social, communicative and problem-solving skills. This report describes the skills of 307 children in the Wellington region of New Zealand and highlights the variables which affect the levels of such skills.
- *Computers in classrooms (Sally Boyd).* Using computers in the primary school classroom and integrating their use into the curriculum can work. Boyd's study on a small number of primary schools identifies a number of themes such as the importance of plans and policies about computer use; how the use of software is integrated into the curriculum; technical support; staff development; and factors which encourage computer use in the schools.

Sampling methodology

As well as choosing the primary research methods, some thought has to be given to the subjects who will be involved with the research. It is necessary to consider some form of subject selection process since it won't be possible to include everyone. This selection process is known as sampling.

A sample is regarded as being representative of the group or population of people from which it is taken. Researchers hope to be able to draw conclusions about the population as a result of their work on the sample.

Taking the example of Piaget's experiment on conservation discussed in the experimental method (page 87), the purpose of the experiment is to see if there is any difference in the ability to conserve between children under six and children over seven years old. Obviously, it would be impossible to carry out the study on all children, so the way forward is to observe a small number of children that can be regarded as representative of children under six and children over seven years old. This group (or groups) of children will become your sample and the group from which they are selected is the population. For your work to be truly representative of the whole population, the sample selected must be random. This means that everyone in the population has an equal chance of being chosen to take part in your study.

Not all forms of sampling are random and the method chosen to select your sample will for the most part be dependent on the nature of the study, how easy it is to gain access to the people you hope to do research on and how much time you have.

Random sampling
Subjects are selected at random from a list created by yourself or someone else, e.g. class register, telephone directory or electoral register. It involves everyone in the list being allocated a number and then using a random number generator to select a sample of appropriate size. A random number generator is like the machine that spews out the Lotto numbers every week. Most calculators have a random number generator button that will perform this task for you.

Systematic sampling
From a list, every nth case is selected, i.e. every fifth or tenth person. So if you wanted to choose five children from a class of 25 you would allocate everyone a number from 1 to 25, then select the fifth, tenth, fifteenth, twentieth and twenty-fifth child.

Stratified sampling
Stratified sampling involves taking a random or systematic sample from groups within a population. For example, you may wish to find out if there is any difference in educational attainment or learning ability between girls and boys, in which case you would take a random sample from within the two groups.

Quota sampling
Quota sampling is more or less the same as stratified sampling, but relies on the groups coming from a conveniently available population. In the stratified sampling example, the school in which you are on placement would be a convenient population from which to take your sample of boys and girls.

Opportunity sampling
This is the most common form of sampling employed by students as it simply relies upon the sample being drawn from the population with which the student is associated.

Voluntary and snowball sampling

Involves people volunteering to be part of the research sample and may lead to others becoming involved through word of mouth.

Purposive sampling

The selection of typical or interesting cases. Particularly suited to case study research or the investigation of a specific problem, such as a congenital disease.

Whilst quota and opportunity sampling are the most likely methods you will use, whichever method you employ there may be people chosen who either don't start/join in or don't finish/give up. Never pressurise people into taking part.

Data collection and presentation

Having determined what method or methods you will use and the sampling strategy you will employ, you need to start collecting your data/information.

It is important here to plan your activities. It would not be wise to organise a survey questionnaire in your local high street when the weather forecast is for gales or heavy showers or to find you had forgotten your recording materials when carrying out an observation or interview.

Whichever method you use it will be necessary to carry out the following to ensure the research is undertaken in an effective and efficient manner:

- Check your tutor is happy with what you are going to research and how you are going to do it. Make sure they have vetted your questions for a questionnaire, interview or case study or the way you intend to conduct an experiment or observation.
- Obtain written permission from anyone who may have some responsibility for your research. Verbal permission is adequate for a simple survey.
- Organise when and where the research will be undertaken:
  - Is it at college, in a school, nursery or playgroup, your local high street or shopping centre, at your own house or that of a relation or friend?
  - Timing can be important. For instance, Mondays tend to be quieter in town centres, young children may be more tired in an afternoon if you are conducting an observation or experiment, parents may be in too much of a rush to get involved when they are dropping off or picking up children from playgroup, school or nursery.

- Organise and prepare any materials or resources required:
  - Photocopy adequate numbers of questionnaires having a few for spares if any get spoilt.
  - Have you got/do you need paper, pens or flip charts for you or the participants to write on?

- If you are conducting the research in a group make sure:
  - everyone knows what they are doing
  - everyone follows the same procedures
  - everyone uses the same style of questioning. The way a question is asked can alter its whole meaning.

Having got yourself organised you can now begin to collect the information/data. Once completed, the information collected will need to be prepared for presentation. This will be dependent upon whether it is qualitative or quantitative.

As explained above, qualitative data is descriptive information and can therefore be regarded as information collected in the format of words, whilst quantitative data is based upon numerical information. You may find that your study produces both types of information.

Dealing with qualitative information

Qualitative information may be in the form of directly written words, such as may be transcribed from an interview or written notes that summarise what occurred. Both forms may reflect some selectivity on the part of the person who provided the information or by the researcher in summarising the information. In effect this shows that some analysis has already taken place and further analysis involves additional selection and refinement of the data.

Initially you should take time to organise or manage the data so that the analysis and refining process becomes easier. Whilst you can do this in many different ways, here are some suggestions to assist you with the process:

- Use different coloured highlighter pens to highlight words or passages that say the same thing, that support or refute your research question and support or refute theoretical arguments.
- Add notes or comments alongside highlighted words or phrases that can help you relate the information to the research question or theory. This can include adding references to articles or books on the subject.
- Use a coding system to process information that repeats itself or could be grouped, e.g. males and females, different ages.
- Use tables to categorise words or phrases in particular groups. Open questions from an interview or questionnaire may elicit a wide range of responses. However, it may be possible to identify words or phrases that mean the same thing allowing them to be grouped together. You need to be clear about how you have done this in presenting the data to show that you have avoided being biased.
- Cross out information that is irrelevant.

Once you have processed the information in the above fashion you can begin to select and summarise those bits of data that support or refute your research. Whilst this might seem like doing the whole thing again it allows you to present a coherent argument in favour of or against your research question. It also enables you to tie your research into the information you will have gained by means of secondary research.

Where the information can be categorised into groups as with words or phrases that occur frequently, then the information may be summarised as numerical values, e.g. five respondents to an open-ended question on experiences of childbirth referred to the desire for giving birth naturally rather than with medical intervention, whilst four preferred to have medical assistance. In such cases the information can then be regarded as quantitative.

Dealing with quantitative data

Quantitative data will be based upon direct measurements; categories that have been assigned a value (e.g. the number of males, females, the number in specified age groups), percentages or averages. Percentages and averages can form part of the next step to summarise and refine your data in order to make it clearer. You may also have obtained data as a result of secondary research that you need to prepare for presentation.

Numerical information can be termed **discrete** or **continuous**. Discrete data is usually based on whole numbers that fit into categories, e.g. the number of boys and girls in a class. Continuous data is any numerical value within a range and can be a fraction of a whole number, e.g. heights and weights.

The purpose of data presentation, be it discrete or continuous, is to make it easier to digest. This is achieved by taking the following steps:

1 Organising the data into tables. Tables allow information to be set out in a structured way and can show simple trends and differences between numbers where there is not too much information.
2 Using graphs to summarise more complex information that is difficult to digest from a table.
3 Preparing statistics to analyse data in order to establish the proof or otherwise of the research question or hypothesis.

Modern computer programs enable you to complete all the above by entering the data into a spreadsheet program. Such programs include Microsoft Excel, Lotus 1-2-3 and more specialised statistical packages such as MINITAB, SPSS (Statistical Package for Social Science) and STATVIEW.

Figure 3.3 on page 96 shows some data entered into a spreadsheet that is easily formatted into a table. Graphs can then be produced and formatted to show off your results to best effect. The difficulty is in deciding which graph is the most appropriate. The whole purpose of a graph is to make large amounts of data or more complex data more easily interpreted than might be possible from a table. This does not mean all data should be displayed graphically. The following information on the different types of graph is designed to help you choose which type to use given the data you have collected.

Pie charts
Pie charts are used when you have a single value for each category or set of data collected. They show each set as a percentage of the whole. The table below shows the number of three and four year-olds in education in England, Scotland, Wales and Northern Ireland in 2000 together with the total.

Region of UK	England	Wales	Scotland	Northern Ireland	Total
Number of 3- and 4-year-olds in early years education (thousands)	1137.7	55.4	89.2	27.8	1310.1

It can be seen that each bit of data is a proportion of the total. To produce the pie chart each value in the table has to be converted into a percentage of the total. Each percentage has then to be converted to the number of degrees as part of the 360° that make up a circle prior to constructing the chart. Figure 3.4 shows the pie chart for this data produced using a spreadsheet program that does away with the need for changing to percentages and degrees required for producing the chart by hand.

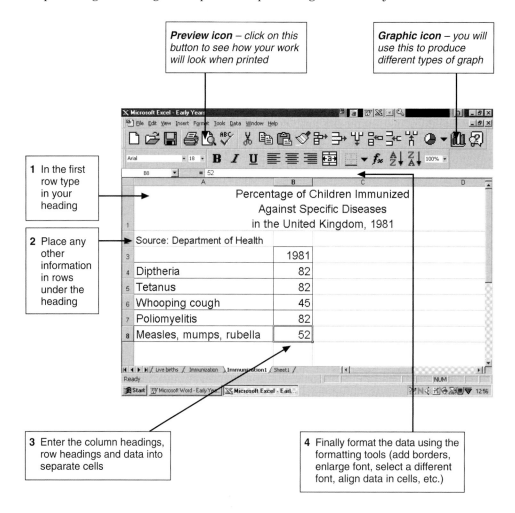

Preview icon – *click on this button to see how your work will look when printed*

Graphic icon – *you will use this to produce different types of graph*

1 In the first row type in your heading

2 Place any other information in rows under the heading

3 Enter the column headings, row headings and data into separate cells

4 Finally format the data using the formatting tools (add borders, enlarge font, select a different font, align data in cells, etc.)

Figure 3.3: Entering data into a spreadsheet (created in Microsoft Excel)

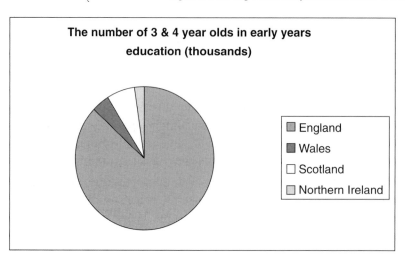

The number of 3 & 4 year olds in early years education (thousands)

- England
- Wales
- Scotland
- Northern Ireland

Figure 3.4: Pie chart

It is important to note that if we didn't know the total number of children we couldn't work out the proportion of each and a pie chart could not be produced. For example, it wouldn't be possible to produce a pie chart of different types of behavioural difficulty existing in a school because we are unlikely to know the total amount of behavioural problems exhibited. You should avoid a pie chart where there are more than six sets of data as the information begins to look confused.

Bar charts
These can be used as an alternative to pie charts for displaying data as either percentages or whole numbers and can be used where there are too many categories to display in a pie chart. The table below gives the numbers of children in different types of day care in England and Wales in 1997.

	Thousands
Day nurseries	202
Childminders	383
Playgroups	413

The types of day care are distinct from one another so the resulting bar chart displays each group as a separate bar or line (Figure 3.5). It doesn't matter how wide the bars or gaps between the bars are.

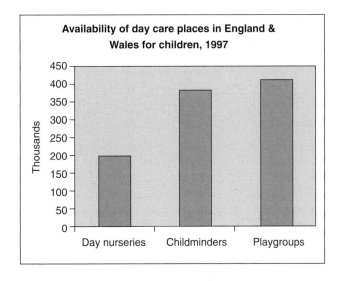

Figure 3.5: Bar chart

Line graphs
When you have a considerable amount of data, especially when it is based on measurements taken over a period of time, the line graph is the best choice. Figure 3.6 shows the increase in the number of children under five participating in education since 1979. This type of chart allows several lines displaying changes to several groups of data over a period of time to be displayed. This should only be done if it is necessary to compare different groups of data. As with the pie charts, avoid having too much data, i.e. too many lines.

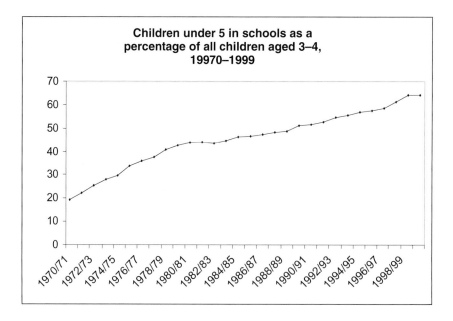

Figure 3.6: Line graph

Sometimes students aren't sure whether to join the data points with a line or a curve. A simple rule of thumb is that if the points for the graph when joined together look like a curve, then draw a curve. If the points form a line, connect the points to form a line. If points are scattered you can draw a best fit line (see Scattergrams, page 99).

Frequency distributions (frequency histograms and frequency polygons)
These are rather more sophisticated graphs that are often confused with bar charts. They are used exclusively with continuous data. The data is grouped into what are termed class intervals where the number or frequency of values falling into each class is found. In order to produce a frequency distribution the raw data requires some manipulation prior to entering into a spreadsheet. This involves producing a tally chart (see Figure 3.7) and then entering the class intervals and frequency into a spreadsheet.

Weights (g)	Tally	Frequency
\multicolumn{3}{c}{Live birth weights of babies born to a random sample of 128 women}		
1000–1499		0
1500–1999		0
2000–2499	‖	2
2500–2999	₩₩ ₩₩ ‖‖‖‖	14
3000–3499	₩₩ ₩₩ ₩₩ ₩₩ ₩₩ ₩₩ ₩₩ ₩₩ ₩₩ ‖	47
3500–3999	₩₩ ₩₩ ₩₩ ₩₩ ₩₩ ₩₩ ₩₩ ₩₩ ₩₩	45
4000+	₩₩ ₩₩ ₩₩ ₩₩	20

Figure 3.7: Tally chart

Creating the chart (see Figure 3.8) is easier on some programs than others but an IT tutor should be able to help you through any difficulties.

If you wish to compare frequency distributions of two or more sets of data it is preferable to present the frequency distribution as a frequency polygon rather than a

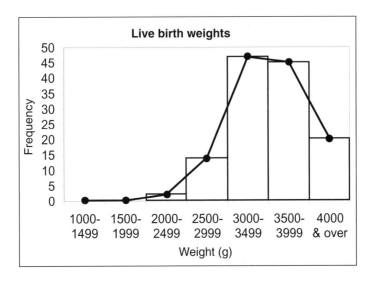

Figure 3.8: Frequency distribution

frequency histogram. A frequency polygon is simply a line joining the tops of each bar at their mid-points, though it is not necessary to do this when using a spreadsheet as you can simply follow the same instructions as for a line graph.

Scattergrams

Scattergrams are used specifically for displaying the results of correlational studies, i.e. data collected to compare one variable with another. It simply involves plotting the results of one variable against the other as a series of markers. The pattern created by the marks once the scattergram has been completed can indicate whether or not there is a relationship between the two variables. If it appears possible to draw a straight line through the markers then a relationship exists. In a spreadsheet the computer can draw in the line. This trend line describes either a positive or negative correlation. If positive it shows that as one variable increases so does the other, e.g. increase in weight correlates with an increase in height (see Figure 3.9). If negative, as one variable increases the other decreases, e.g. the increase in media attention given to problems

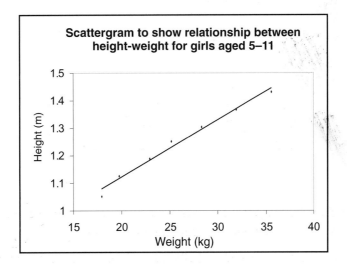

Figure 3.9: Scattergram

associated with vaccination correlates with a decrease in the number of children being vaccinated.

However, beware! Just because a correlation exists does not mean that a change in one variable results in a change in the other, e.g. did you know that the amount of bananas imported into the UK after World War II correlated with an increase in the number of pregnant women? It is possible that the change in both variables is due to some other unrelated factor. Another example is the rise in asthma amongst children during the 1980s and 1990s. It has been found that this increase correlates well with the increasing use of diesel engine motor vehicles. Researchers proposed that this was due to the size of soot particles in vehicle exhausts polluting the air and irritating the lungs. However, there is also a correlation between the increase in rates of asthma and the use of double glazing in homes, central heating and fitted carpets, which encourage the increase in numbers of dust mites that also irritate the lungs. Consequently, don't be tempted to draw a conclusion about a correlation unless it is backed up by the research of others, i.e. your secondary sources.

Think It Over
A line of best fit has been added to Figure 3.9 to show that there is a positive correlation between height and weight. How would the scattergram appear if:

* the correlation was negative
* there was no correlation?

Mean, median, mode and standard deviation
Apart from graphs, numerical data can also be simplified and made more meaningful by determining the **mode**, **median** or **mean**. These terms describe different forms of averages known as measures of **central tendency**. The mode is the most frequently occurring number in a set. The median is simply the middle value in a set of results that have been arranged in ascending or descending order. The mean, as you are probably already aware, is calculated from adding up all the values and dividing by the number of values to give the 'average'.

The median is used where the data is discrete and is often used in conjunction with the **range** (the difference between the lowest and highest values in a set of data) to summarise the data. The range gives a measure of the spread of the data. Whilst this is satisfactory for many circumstances the range will include extreme values and as a consequence may not be representative of the majority of the data, e.g. SATS results may include one or two very high or very low scores with the majority clustered around the median. As a result it may be more appropriate to use the **interquartile range** covering the middle 50 per cent of the data.

The median and range, or interquartile range, are useful when working with discrete data but where the data is continuous the mean and another statistic, the **standard deviation**, tend to be of more value. This is because the standard deviation, whilst giving an idea of how much the data is spread either side of the mean also excludes extreme values and as a result is more representative of the majority of subjects in the sample. Whilst it is difficult to generalise, the larger the standard deviation, the greater the spread of the data about the mean.

The standard deviation is rather more difficult to calculate than the mean. However, scientific calculators that have statistical functions can determine the standard deviation at the same time as the mean. Alternatively, the standard deviation can be obtained from data entered into a spreadsheet.

The standard deviation and mean can be used to determine whether two sets of data, e.g. reading test results before and after an intensive reading programme, are **significantly different** from one another. Fortunately for you, the Early Years syllabus does not expect you to take your data analysis this far! However, if you have a morbid curiosity for fiddling around with numbers, the statistics books in the References and further reading section will show you how this can be done, though it would be preferable to seek the help of the tutor who can do this sort of thing with their eyes shut!

Discussing and evaluating your results

This is perhaps the most skilled part of the research process that is used by tutors to confirm decisions regarding the award of higher grades.

It is best to start the discussion with a review of the problem you chose to investigate together with the research question or hypothesis. This sets the scene and also helps to focus your mind on what all the data collection and presentation was about, as if you had forgotten!

You should then look at your results and summarise what they show. The idea is to highlight those features of your results that are important to your research question or hypothesis, i.e. whether the information supports or refutes the research question or hypothesis. Preparing your report for a presentation is a good way of summarising and picking out the most important features.

In the same way, you need to compare your findings with the information obtained through secondary research. Does this information support your study or contradict it? Differences between your work and those of others may reflect real differences due to the local nature of your research or it may highlight weaknesses in your study. Alternatively, the results may reflect something you hadn't thought of that could lead to the need for further research. In this case, you should attempt to suggest what that research could be.

If your results fail to support your research question or hypothesis, do not be tempted to manipulate them; instead draw on the information provided in the next two sections (*use and misuse of statistics* and *validity and reliability*) to evaluate the presentation of your data and the research and sampling methods used.

A further way of preparing your discussion is to talk to people who have had some involvement with your research and see if they agree with your conclusions, including your tutor. You could also sit down with someone else on the course and tell them what you have found out. If it makes sense to them then it should make sense on paper. You can do the same for them.

If your research was part of a group project – even better. Whilst you will probably be expected to submit individual reports you can discuss your findings and help each other to draw relevant conclusions, evaluate and justify your approach to the topic.

If your research was based on interviews with just a few people or a case study, then it can be appropriate to discuss your findings with them. Not only can they make suggestions or identify things you have missed, but it also keeps them fully informed in line with the ethical requirements for informed consent.

Use and misuse of statistics

Statistics provide a valuable tool for presenting and interpreting information so that the results of research are more readily understood. The use and misuse of statistics can arise as a result of problems with different aspects of the research process and not just the presentation and interpretation of the results. Such difficulties include the following:

- **Lack of clarity in the research question or hypothesis,** i.e. being unsure about what you want to find out. If you are unclear about the focus of your study it can lead to selecting the wrong methods and consequently the production of data or information that is difficult to explain. It may also lead to a misreading of the results in trying to make them fit the hypothesis or research question. For example, you may have chosen to observe the behaviour of young children in a playgroup, but not clarified what sort of behaviour it is you are interested in. In all likelihood you will observe a wide range of behaviours and frequency of such behaviours that may produce too much information to organise and simplify with ease.
- **Use of inappropriate methods.** The method must allow you to gather information that will support your research question or hypothesis. This means choosing a method that enables you to find out what you want to and that it is reproducible. These features of the method are known as validity and reliability and will be discussed in more detail in the next section.
- **Unrepresentative sampling.** Remember that the purpose of sampling is to use people in your research who are representative of the whole population which relies on obtaining a random sample of subjects. As discussed earlier, this is no easy task and there is often bias within a sample whatever the sampling method chosen. In particular, the most common sampling method used by students is the opportunity sample. As the people chosen are probably following some further education course like you then the sample is biased towards students and misses out on all other people.
- **Inaccurate recording of information (sloppy techniques).** Failure to construct a questionnaire with care or to undertake a trial can result in questions being misunderstood and answers being ambiguous. If you are administering a questionnaire as a group, failure for everyone to follow the same procedure can give misleading results. The results of an interview that you haven't prepared for in terms of questioning or recording may bear little resemblance to the actual interview itself and is more open to being biased towards your own views. A poorly prepared observation sheet or failure to conduct an experiment with care and precision will give inaccurate results.
- **Inappropriate presentation or misinterpretation of data.** The following examples serve to show how results can be presented in such a way as to change their meaning or to give misleading information. The figure overleaf compares the attainment of children at Key Stage 1 in two schools A and B.

You can see that school A appears to be far more effective at enabling the children to reach Level 2 of Key Stage 1 than school B. However, what you don't know is that

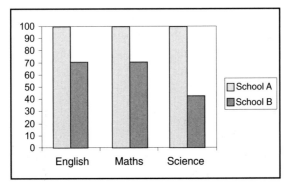

Percentage of children at National Curriculum Level 2 (Key Stage 1) in two schools

school A is an independent school and school B has three times as many pupils as school A, and the children entering the schools come from different social backgrounds.

Key issues – how to avoid misusing information

- Be clear about what you are trying to find out, i.e. ensure your research is focused.
- Be sure to use the most appropriate method or methods for your study.
- Try to ensure your sample is representative of the population in which you are interested.
- Don't try to use statistical methods in presenting your data to make it fit your research question when it doesn't, i.e. be honest. In using graphs make sure they are accurate.
- Don't misinterpret the data, i.e. don't say something is true when it blatantly isn't or say the results don't show anything when they do. Look carefully at and use all the results.
- Don't try to draw conclusions that don't exist. These can become discussion points for further research.

Assessment activity 3.3

Complete a table that shows:

- the methods of presenting statistics
- when you would use the methods
- the advantages and disadvantages of using particular methods.
- which computer packages you could use to present your statistics.

Validity and reliability

These terms have already been mentioned with respect to one or two of the different primary research methods and they need to be taken into account when selecting the most appropriate research method for any research you undertake.

Validity is about whether the results you obtain using a particular method tell you what you want to find out.

Reliability is to do with the method being reproducible, i.e. if someone else repeated your work would they get the same answers?

A method may be reliable but not necessarily valid. Whilst some methods are more reliable and others more valid, it is probably true that the level of reliability and validity is dependent upon how carefully the research has been undertaken. This surprisingly comes down to the conscientiousness of the researcher! One way of improving reliability and validity is to use more than one method in your study.

Assessment activity 3.4

Read the brief evaluation of the reliability and validity of questionnaires below before evaluating the effectiveness of other research methods in terms of reliability and validity. Also consider how different methods could be combined to improve the reliability and validity.

Questionnaires can have high reliability and validity depending on how well they are produced. If the questions have been worded appropriately and the answers are not ambiguous, then the results should tell you what you need to know and are therefore valid. Furthermore, it should also be feasible for someone else to repeat your work and get similar answers, making the research reliable. However, if you tend to get mixed responses to questions that you thought were straightforward, then the validity and reliability will be poor. The best way to ensure good reliability and validity with a questionnaire is to do a trial first in order to iron out any problems.

Ethics and confidentiality

Before undertaking any primary research that involves questioning, experimenting or observing people you must consider the ethics of conducting your research and any issues of confidentiality that may be raised.

Ethics has been an issue in research ever since World War II when the Nazis were found to have submitted individuals to horrific experiments that resulted in death, disfigurement or psychological trauma. The Nuremberg trials that followed the war made researchers aware of the dangers of carrying out experiments on non-consenting subjects and it led to the development of a code of ethics for working with human subjects. Even so, there have been many cases of research carried out since the war that have subjected people to physical and/or psychological pain. One famous experiment on obedience carried out during the 1960s by Stanley Millgram involved allowing participants to administer electric shocks to other people they could see. Unknown to the participants the subjects being electrocuted were actors faking increasing discomfort as shocks were applied. Participants were told that they had to continue applying shocks of increasing voltage even though the person being 'electrocuted' appeared to be in obvious pain. Whilst the experiment proved that people would follow 'orders' irrespective of the suffering they may cause, the justification for such deception of participants was regarded as immoral. Not only had Millgram deceived the participants, but had attempted to alter their behaviour and used secret recordings to observe them.

Whilst deception may be unethical, many drug trials rely on this to determine the effects of new drugs. Such trials, known as blind trials, involve two groups of volunteers, one of which receives the drug and the other a placebo (sugar pill). This experimental type of research works on the basis that any effect of the drug will only be seen in the group taking the drug as neither group knows whether they are taking the placebo or the drug under test. It has been found that some drugs have had as much effect on the placebo group as the test group!

Anyone participating in research is now covered by the United Nations Declaration of Human Rights, which is supported by European legislation enshrined in the EU Directive on Data Protection (1995) and nationally by the Data Protection Act (1998). Organisations conducting research implement a code of ethics to ensure these rights are protected. Such codes include the need for participants to give their informed consent. This means that they are fully informed as to the nature and purpose of the research, what will happen, how and where it will take place. It also gives participants the right to refuse or to withdraw at any time and that the anonymity of participants is preserved. Many researchers also include the requirement to debrief the participants about the nature of the research and why any deception may have been necessary.

As far as your research is concerned you would be unwise to set about collecting data it were to cause distress to the people involved either as a result of the methods chosen, or the sampling process or the reporting of your work. Aspects of these issues have been alluded to at different points and include the need to:

- gain permission from appropriate authorities (employers, teachers, tutors) to conduct the research. This is important, as you may need the support of such people if any problems occur. It is generally recognised that research undertaken at this level will be underwritten by your tutors and/or workplace supervisors due to your inexperience
- ask the subjects, or where children are concerned their parents or guardians, if they wish to take part
- as a consequence of the first two points be in a position to explain your research
- be able to reassure participants or again their guardians about the measures taken to maintain confidentiality.

Confidentiality

With regard to confidentiality, you must ensure the anonymity of all participants. This involves the following:

- Changing names of subjects particularly when using interview, observation, experimental and case study methods where the sample size might be small. False names, letters or numbers can be used instead, e.g., Fred, Miss X, subject 9.
- Avoiding descriptive language that could give away a person's identity as can occur in case studies, e.g. Mrs Y, the leader of the local Labour party, does give the game away a bit! You need to think whether such information is important to your study and if so, how else it can be worded, e.g. subject 8, a local politician.
- In conducting taped interviews care must be taken when transposing the taped interview into a written format so as to avoid identifying the interviewee. It is important to recognise that the interviewee has the right to request that all or part of the tape is erased or destroyed at any time, and in any case the tapes should be erased once you have completed your work.

Another issue concerns what you may find out as part of your research. When gaining permission to conduct the research you need to be clear about what you must do in the event of being told or finding out something of a confidential nature. If you find out or suspect that abuse has taken place, you need to know what your responsibilities are and to whom you should refer. These responsibilities should also form part of the information given to potential participants before the research is carried out.

Assessment activity 3.5

1 Undertake a literature search to find out about embryonic stem cell research and use this information to present arguments for and against such research. Evaluate the evidence on the basis of your own stated position on such research in relation to children, i.e. belief in the rights of the unborn child or the rights of the child with bone marrow disease to treatment that could cure them.

2 Investigate another contemporary issue of your choice that is currently being researched in the health care or early years fields.
  * What is the purpose of the research?
  * What are the ethical issues that are raised by doing the research?
  * Analyse and evaluate the evidence of each piece of research and write two reports comparing the issues, purpose and need for each piece of research.

Your research as a presentation

You may have been asked to present the findings of your research to your peer group or others as part of the assessment process. You will not be alone in dreading this part of the project and be unsure about what you should put into the presentation and what to leave out. A good way of tackling this is to produce an abstract or summary of your work. This is a paragraph or two of 100–200 words that states:

* the purpose of your research, the research question or hypothesis
* the methods chosen
* the most significant results that either support or refute your research
* the conclusions drawn together with any suggestions for further work.

The abstract can then be the basis for your presentation, which can be expanded on with references to:

* aspects of secondary research
* interesting parts of the data collection process (the interview that went wrong!)
* tables, diagrams and charts that display quantitative findings to good effect
* acknowledgements of the people who took part.

Producing a bibliography

In producing your work you will hopefully have used a range of books, articles and other sources. Since you have summarised or extracted sections from such material for inclusion in your work, it is essential that you acknowledge the producers or providers of this information. Consequently, you need to produce a reference section, bibliography and/or acknowledgements section. Whilst these words can be used to mean the same thing they are used here as follows:

* A reference section is generally used for acknowledging information taken from the original author(s) work.

- A bibliography or further reading is used for information extracted from more general textbooks where the author(s) has drawn a wide range of material together from different sources.
- An acknowledgements section is to identify and thank those people who have given help or support or have contributed directly to your work by being a subject (remember not to identify anyone for whom confidentiality was promised).

You do not have to use this system and your tutors may prefer everything to be acknowledged within a bibliography only. However, whatever form you use, adopt a style or format for identifying information and material used.

One of the most commonly accepted formats for referencing is known as the Harvard system. Within the body of your report any book/periodical/newspaper report, etc. used must identify the author, the year of publication and the page number(s) referred to, e.g.

'Observation is particularly suited to the study of phenomena such as non-verbal communication and tactile skills (Lynes, 1999, p. 315)'.

If the author's surname is part of the sentence, then the date and page number(s) are sufficient, e.g.

'Lynes (1999, p. 315) suggested that observation is useful for studying non-verbal communication and tactile skills'.

If reference to a table or diagram is made, then the following is appropriate:

'Analysis of the results (White, 1995, p. 13, table 2)...' or 'White (1995, p. 13, table 2) in his results showed that many single mothers... '.

If you have copied or used part of a table or diagram from another source this must also be acknowledged. This is normally done by identifying the author of the work and year of publication after the title of the table or diagram.

At the end of the assignment the information sources referred to are listed alphabetically by surname. The format depends on the type of resource referred to and is best shown by example as follows.

For textbooks:

Gibb, C. and Randall, P. (1989) *Professionals and Parents, Managing Children's Behaviour.* Basingstoke, Macmillan Education.

For articles from newspapers/periodicals/magazines:

Lynes, D. (1999) 'Using observation for data collection'. *Professional Nurse*, Vol. 14, No. 5, pp. 315–17.

Seek advice from tutors with regards to other types of resource you may have referenced.

Some of this may appear rather confusing, but once you have got used to the idea you will find that it helps in organising and presenting your work in a logical manner.

A checklist for carrying out a research project

- Find out how much time you have got. You may have been given a deadline that only allows you a few weeks or even days to complete the work. Alternatively, you may be looking at a whole year. Whichever, you will need to plan your time effectively to ensure the work is completed on time and is of the standard that you feel justifies the grade you are aiming for. Don't leave things to the last minute particularly with a longer term project.

- Select a topic. If you only have a short period of time you need to select a topic that does not involve more complex secondary or primary research. For instance, it would be no good choosing a topic that involves obtaining information from obscure sources or is reliant on postal questionnaires. You may not get the information back in time, if at all.

- Start reading around your chosen topic to help in focusing on your study in order to produce a research question or hypothesis.

- Select the primary research and sampling methods appropriate to your study. With a short-term project choose just one or two research methods that will provide information quickly whereas a longer term study should involve a variety of methods and allow a more in-depth investigation to be carried out.

- Identify what resources you will require to complete your study. Do you need specialist equipment? Where will you get such equipment? Will there be a charge and how long can you have it for?

- Produce an action plan that identifies your research topic, research question or hypothesis, resources required for the primary research and secondary resources, an approximate time allocation for each section. Submit this to your tutor for approval.

- Continue reading around the subject, making notes that provide background information and that support or refute your research question or hypothesis.

- Draft an introduction and have it checked by your tutor.

- Carry out the primary research.

- Collate and present the results.

- Analyse, discuss and evaluate your research.

End-of-unit test

1 Explain what is meant by the terms primary, secondary, qualitative, quantitative, cross-sectional and longitudinal research

2 Identify three forms of secondary information.

3 Identify the main primary research methods.

4 In surveys, how would you differentiate between a questionnaire and an interview?

5 What is the difference between a structured, semi-structured and unstructured interview?

6 In preparing a questionnaire, in what order would you place the following types of questions (i) open ended; (ii) closed; (iii) scale; (iv) category?

7 Produce an experimental and null hypothesis for the observation that girls appear to achieve academically more than boys.

8 Read the following extract of a case study on an autistic child and undertake secondary research to see how the child's symptoms match up with what would be expected:

The child was developing like a 'normal' child until she reached the age of two and a half. Soon after she reached this age she began to isolate herself from others, stopped talking and feeding herself, and started to hit her head and bite her hand. She would also avoid eye contact and have 'crying' episodes for long periods of time then she would stop and laugh for no reason. She began to spend a lot of time sitting looking out of the window at clouds and trees as they moved.

9 Select the most appropriate graph/chart to present the following category of data:

  a The number of children being immunised against measles, mumps and rubella (MMR) between 1985 and 2000.

  b The number of children achieving different attainment Levels for Key Stage 1 in English, Mathematics and Science in a school for the year 2000.

  c The weight of babies at birth.

10 Select the most appropriate measure of central tendency for the following:

  a The number of parent helpers attending a school on each day of the week over a year.

  b The amount of time children spend watching television.

11 Decide whether the mean, median or mode would best summarise the following data:

24 children in a class were asked how many books they had read in the past month. The raw results were:

1	2	3	4	5	6	7	8	9	10	11	12	13	14	15	16	17	18	19	20	21	22	23	24
3	5	2	6	4	4	5	1	1	3	4	7	6	6	4	3	1	2	6	8	5	6	2	4

What do the results suggest?

References and further reading

Bell, J. (1993) *Doing Your Research Project* (2nd edition), Buckingham: Open University Press

Blaxter, L., Hughes, C. and Tight, M. (1996) *How to Research*, Buckingham: Open University, Press

Corston, R. (1992) *Research Methods and Statistics in the Social Sciences*, Durham: Casder

Davenport, G.C. (1988) *An Introduction to Child Development*, London: Unwin Hyman

Marshall, P. (1997) *Research Methods. How to Design and Conduct a Successful Project*, Plymouth: How to Books

Owen, D. and Davis, M. (1991) *Help With Your Project: A Guide for Students of Health Care*, London: Edward Arnold

Peterson, R.A. (2000) *Constructing Effective Questionnaires*, London: Sage

Safe environments

Introduction

Safety is an essential basic element for sustaining life. As such it is difficult to examine issues of safety in isolation, as the provision of a safe and secure environment is central to all aspects of work with young children. Whether exploring the links between safety and childcare and development, or ensuring that appropriate procedures are in place when planning the educational provision, it is important that safety is seen as an integral aspect of the whole service. This unit has very close links to the work covered in the Professional practice and Childcare practice units. It will also be relevant to the units Protecting children and Learning in the early years.

This unit addresses safety and emergency procedures within early years settings and introduces first aid procedures. It explores the legislation and the resulting policies and procedures that ensure safe practice. It addresses issues of safety within the physical environment, both inside and outside, and investigates the safe provision of play resources. The importance of regular safety checks and of identifying and reporting hazards in the environment is addressed. Providing a secure environment with adequate supervision is essential in an early years setting. The unit examines health and hygiene requirements in relation to providing for children's physical needs, limiting cross-infection and administering and recording medications.

What you need to learn

- Safety and emergency procedures
- Safe and secure environments
- Health and safety procedures

Safety and emergency procedures

First aid procedures

'First aid is the immediate assistance or treatment given to someone who has been injured or taken ill before the arrival of an ambulance, doctor or other appropriately qualified person. The aims of first aid are as follows:

- To preserve life
- To limit the worsening of the condition
- To promote recovery.'

(*First Aid Manual*, 1999)

It is essential that any intervention should not harm the casualty. You must ensure that any treatment you give will be of benefit and that you should not take action just for the sake of doing something. For this reason it is important that everyone who works with children should attend a specialist first aid course with a trained instructor where they can practise techniques such as resuscitation. The following information provides an outline of the procedures to be taken in an emergency, but is no substitute for attending an appropriate course. Specific requirements in relation to first aid procedures are sometimes changed in the light of new knowledge and first aiders are re-examined on a regular basis to ensure that they have updated their knowledge and skills.

Checking for signs and symptoms

Most of the incidents you will deal with as a nursery nurse will be minor injuries, but there may sometimes be more serious complications from what may appear to be a minor injury. It is therefore important that you have a good procedure for responding to accidents and recognising the signs and symptoms of injury. In an accident situation, as a student, your first priority is to summon help from your supervisor, the identified first aider, or the professional services.

Below is a useful procedure for the assessment and diagnosis of injury.

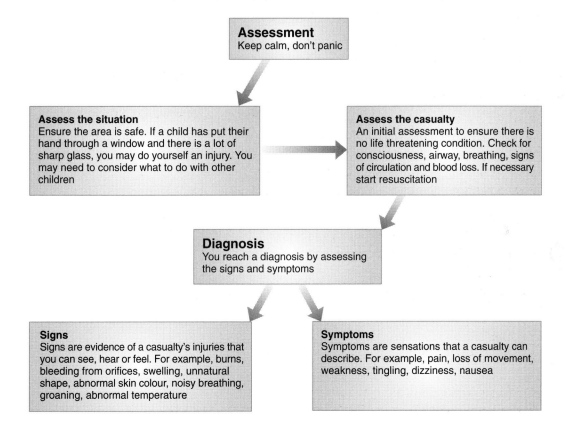

Assessment
Keep calm, don't panic

Assess the situation
Ensure the area is safe. If a child has put their hand through a window and there is a lot of sharp glass, you may do yourself an injury. You may need to consider what to do with other children

Assess the casualty
An initial assessment to ensure there is no life threatening condition. Check for consciousness, airway, breathing, signs of circulation and blood loss. If necessary start resuscitation

Diagnosis
You reach a diagnosis by assessing the signs and symptoms

Signs
Signs are evidence of a casualty's injuries that you can see, hear or feel. For example, burns, bleeding from orifices, swelling, unnatural shape, abnormal skin colour, noisy breathing, groaning, abnormal temperature

Symptoms
Symptoms are sensations that a casualty can describe. For example, pain, loss of movement, weakness, tingling, dizziness, nausea

Prioritising treatment

Having completed this process of assessment you need to be able to prioritise your treatment. Remember, the three main aims for first aid treatment are: to preserve life, to limit the worsening effect of the condition and to promote recovery. The following list taken from the *First Aid Manual* (1999) provides guidance for prioritising treatment.

- Follow the ABC of resuscitation.
- Maintain a clear airway and breathing: if unconscious and breathing, place in the recovery position.
- Control bleeding.

- Treat large wounds and burns.
- Immobilise bone and joint injuries.
- Give appropriate treatment for other injuries and conditions.
- Check airway, breathing and pulse regularly and deal with any problems immediately.

Dealing with an unconscious casualty

An important aspect of first aid provision is the ability to deal with an unconscious person. These skills are best practised on a recognised first aid course. The chart below aims only to provide basic guidelines.

THE ABC OF RESUSCITATION	
CHECK RESPONSE	
Child (1–7)  Talk calmly and shake very gently	Baby (under 1) 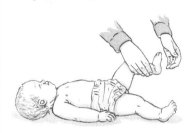 Gently tap or flick sole of foot. DO NOT SHAKE A BABY
CHECK AIRWAY	
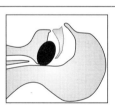 1. When unconscious the muscles relax and the tongue falls back	
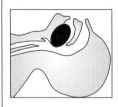 2. When the head is tilted and the chin lifted, the tongue will lift from the back of the throat	
Open airway. Tilt head back slightly, one hand on forehead, two fingers under chin 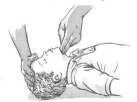	Open airway. Tilt head back very slightly, one hand on baby's head, one finger under chin 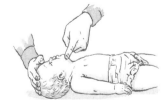

CHECK BREATHING	
Child (1–7)	Baby (under 1)
Place cheek next to child's mouth. Listen for sounds of breathing and watch chest for movement. Listen for up to 10 seconds	
If breathing is not present, carefully remove any obvious obstructions from mouth. DO NOT poke down throat. Pinch child's nose, seal lips round mouth and breathe into the lungs till the chest rises. Give five breaths, one every three seconds. Look for signs of recovery	Carefully remove obvious obstruction. Seal lips round mouth and nose and breath into the baby's lungs. Give five breaths, one every three seconds. Look for signs of recovery
CHECK CIRCULATION	
Feel the carotid artery by placing two fingers lightly on the side of the neck and observe for other signs of circulation	Lightly press two fingers on inside of upper arm and observe for other signs of circulation
If there is no sign of circulation, begin cardio-pulmonary resuscitation	If no sign of circulation, or baby's pulse is less than 60 per minute, begin resuscitation
Place heel of one hand one finger's breadth from the base of the breastbone. Press down one-third the depth of the chest five times at a rate of 100 per minute	Place one finger in the middle of the chest between the nipples. Place two fingers below this and use these two fingers to press down one-third of the depth of the breast of the chest five times at a rate of 100 per minute
Simple check 5 chest compressions with one hand 1 breath through the mouth	**Simple check** 5 chest compressions with two fingers 1 breath through mouth and nose

The recovery position

When you attend a recognised first aid course you will be able to practise this technique.

Step 1: Place two fingers under the child's chin and place other hand on the forehead, gently tilt the head back.

Step 2: Straighten the limbs and place the arm nearest to you so it lies at right angles to the child's body. Check pockets for any bulky objects.

Step 3: Bring the child's other arm across the chest and place the hand against the child's cheek with palm facing outwards. Holding that hand in position use your other hand to pull up the child's far leg. Hold the leg just above the knee.

Step 4: Gently pull the far leg towards you rolling the child forward till they are lying on their side. Use your knees to prevent the child rolling too far forwards. Keep your other hand holding the child's hand to their cheek.

Step 5: Bend the upper leg so that it is at right angles to the body.

Step 6: Throughout the procedure, ensure that the child's head remains well back and is supported on their hand to keep their airway open.

Treatment of major and minor injuries
Major injuries

- Assess for danger
- Make it safe
- Protect yourself
- Wear disposable gloves
- Give emergency first aid
- Check ABC
- Keep calm and support others
- Summon help.

This list provides some basic information for use in an emergency until expert help arrives and highlights the actions you must not take. Remember, it is essential that any action of yours does not harm the individual or make the injury any worse.

Emergency	Action	DO NOT!
Bleeding	• Lay child down to reduce the possibility of shock. Cover wound with pad or dressing • Apply pressure for up to 15 minutes. If there is a large foreign body in the wound, apply pressure on either side of wound • Raise and support the injured part • Bandage the wound	• DO NOT remove glass or objects from a deep wound • DO NOT apply a tourniquet, it can worsen the bleeding
Burns and scalds	• Cool with cold water for at least 10 minutes • Remove constricting clothing from injured area • Cover with a clean cloth	• DO NOT remove anything sticking to the burn • DO NOT apply any lotions or plasters
Choking	• If obstruction visible, hook out with your finger • Lean older child forward, or support baby's face down along forearm and give five brisk slaps between shoulder blades	• DO NOT risk pushing it further down • DO NOT ever hold a baby or young child upside down and slap their back, you could break their neck

Emergency	Action	DO NOT!
Choking	• Stand behind child, place fist on lower breastbone, hold with other hand and press in sharply five times. For baby, use two fingers on lower breastbone	
Convulsions	• Cool the child by sponging with tepid water if they have a high temperature • Clear area and protect from injury by placing pillows or padding around the child • Sponge with tepid water • Put child in recovery position once convulsions have ceased	• DO NOT put anything in the child's mouth
Fractures	• Keep the child still	• DO NOT move the child until the injured part is immobilised
Head injury	• Control any bleeding • Monitor for consciousness, headache, drowsiness, vomiting, or blood loss from nose, mouth or ears • If unconscious, check ABC and respond appropriately	• If there has been a back or neck injury, DO NOT attempt to move • DO NOT leave the child alone
Poisons	• Check ABC • Save sample of poison	• DO NOT make the child vomit
Shock	• Lay the child down, raise legs and keep warm • Loosen tight clothing • Treat any injury • Monitor condition	• DO NOT leave the child alone • DO NOT give the child food or drink

When to call for professional assistance In any major incident it is likely that you will call for professional assistance. There are however some specific situations when it is essential that you call for an ambulance. It may be tempting to put the child in a car to take them to the hospital, but some situations can deteriorate very quickly and you may need professional help and the ability to move through the traffic very quickly. If any of the following situations occur you must call an ambulance:

- unconscious
- difficulty in breathing
- severe bleeding
- serious burns.

Minor conditions and risk assessment
While it is fairly unlikely that you will have to deal with many major accidents, you will regularly be called upon to deal with minor injuries. Many minor injuries will respond

to a cuddle and some adult attention, but however minor the incident you will always be expected to monitor the child's condition to identify any underlying problem. You must be aware that you may need to call for professional assistance even for what may appear to be a minor injury. The chart below provides details of some minor injuries and identifies some specific complications that may occur. Should any of these complications arise you will need to seek medical attention.

Injury	Treatment	Monitor
Bump to head	Cold water compress	For drowsiness, vomiting, headache, bleeding from ears, nose or mouth
Nose bleed	Tip head forward and pinch nose below the bridge for up to 10 minutes	If it continues for more than 30 minutes seek medical attention
Grazed skin	Rinse with clean water, do not rub embedded grit. While in the childcare setting the wound should be covered to prevent infection and inhibit spread of leaking body fluids	For signs of infection, reddening of skin or discharge
Trapped fingers	Cold water compress	Check surface of skin for abnormal shape, or possible fracture

Calling for professional assistance The chart above identifies the situations where you would be expected to seek professional assistance following a minor injury. However, the final advice to any childcare practitioner is always that if at any time you are concerned about the welfare of the child you should refer the situation for medical attention.

First aid box

The Health and Safety (First Aid) Regulations 1981 require that all settings must provide a first aid box. The box should be green and marked with a white cross and should be waterproof and airtight. It must be kept in an accessible place which is clearly marked, so that it can be easily found in the case of an emergency. A designated member of staff should be responsible for checking the contents of the first aid box, and replenishing it as necessary. A first aid box should contain the following:

* 20 individually wrapped sterile adhesive dressings
* 2 sterile eye pads
* 6 individually wrapped triangular bandages
* 6 safety pins
* 6 medium-sized individually wrapped sterile wound dressings
* 2 large individually wrapped sterile wound dressings
* 2 pairs of disposable gloves
* 1 pair blunt ended scissors
* some boxes may include a small first aid manual (*First Aid Manual*, 1999)

Emergencies

While prevention is obviously a priority, emergencies do happen. The Health and Safety at Work Act 1974 requires that all settings provide procedures for use in the event of an emergency to ensure that everyone in the setting can respond quickly and effectively during any emergency incident. The chart below provides examples of some of the emergency situations that most settings will prepare for.

Key issues – emergencies

Emergencies that require evacuation of the building	Other emergencies
Fire	Accident
Gas leak	Sudden illness
Flood	Intruder
Bomb scare	Missing child

The emergency process

It is not enough simply to plan the response to an emergency situation. The process must involve a cycle of specific procedures as shown in the diagram.

How to carry out and modify procedures

Each setting will prepare procedures that meet the individual needs of its environment. In this section we examine some emergency situations following the process identified above.

Fire emergency

Fire procedures checklist
All settings will prepare specific procedures that are relevant to their individual situations. However, a fire procedure will include the following guidelines:

- Prominent display of fire procedure notices which inform people of the action to take in the event of a fire.
- Ensure all adults in the building are aware of notices' location and content.
- Provide fire extinguishers and fire blankets in areas where they may be needed, such as the kitchen.
- Provide training in the use of extinguishers.
- Ensure all fire equipment is serviced once a year.
- Fire exits should be clearly signed, unobstructed and checked for ease of opening.

Prevention
Having an awareness of the causes of emergencies, and taking direct action to minimise these effects

Procedures
Creating procedures that should be followed in the event of an emergency. Ensuring all adults are informed

Rehearse
All procedures need to be practised regularly to ensure that all adults and children in the setting are aware of the actions they should take

Record and review
Each practice will be recorded and reviewed immediately following the event, and an annual review will also be undertaken. This information will feed back into the process of PREVENTION

Prevention
And the cycle is complete!

The cycle of specific procedures required to prepare for an emergency

- Evacuation routes should be planned with consideration for the different situations where a fire may occur.
- Fire practices must be carried out regularly at different times of day and using different evacuation routes.
- Fire practices must be recorded and evaluated.
- Registers must be completed as the children enter the building and must include arrival and departure time.
- Registers should include each child's emergency contact number and be held in an accessible place.
- Access must be maintained for emergency vehicles.

Even if you have fire fighting equipment, the first priority is to evacuate the building. Do not fight a fire unless you know what you are doing.

Rehearsing the evacuation of children
Some settings encourage children to line up at the door and walk out with one member of staff at the front, the centre and the back of the group. Other settings gather in key worker groups. Some nursery settings use a rope that the children all hold as they walk outside. Once outside they stand in a circle inside the rope. Staff will ensure that they make provision for any children with special needs who may need additional help to

leave the building quickly. It is important that even in domestic situations evacuation routes are planned and practised with the children.

If procedures are to be effective, all adults and children in the building need to be familiar with them.

Children with rope during fire practice

Case Study

Kittens pre-school has four regular full-time and three part-time members of staff. Some parents provide rota help on a regular basis and many other parents attend special events. A grandparent attends for one hour on a Wednesday and Friday to run the book club. The pre-school provides placements for students from the local college who attend for three months at a time, and in the summer term children from the local school come for two weeks' work experience. The vicar usually pops in most weeks for a few minutes. A small number of parents have English as an additional language.

- How will you ensure that all these adults are aware of the fire procedure?
- How can you help parents who are not confident in their use of English?
- What would be the result if some adults were not aware of their responsibilities?

Think It Over

Below are two examples of fire procedure notices.

- Read each sign and identify the main differences.
- Decide which notice is the most useful and give reasons for your choice.
- Compare them to the signs in your current workplace.
- Discuss how you found out about the fire procedures in your workplace.

Write your answers down and then share them with a friend and see if you agree with each other.

FIRE PROCEDURE

On discovery of a fire SOUND THE ALARM

The nearest alarm is in the entrance hall

Leave the building by the nearest safe exit

Do not collect belongings

Assemble at the far side of the car park

FIRE PROCEDURE

The person to discover the fire must activate the fire alarm

Manager call the Fire Brigade

Deputy to collect the register

Fire Officer to check the toilets, close all windows and doors and ensure no-one left in the building

All other staff, students and visitors to help escort children out of the building. Keep calm

Assemble under the tree

GET OUT – STAY OUT

Reviewing the fire practice

In order to ensure that fire practices are meaningful experiences, you will need to prepare criteria for evaluating their effectiveness.

Think It Over

Read the evaluation of the fire practice undertaken at the Happy Days Nursery. Using your knowledge of the requirements of a fire procedure make a list of any problems that the staff should address before undertaking their next practice. Consider what would happen if there was a fire at arrival time before the register had been taken.

Happy Days Nursery has just held a fire practice. In the past the staff have sounded the alarm and the children were led out through the main door. On this occasion, Sheila, the manager, placed a large sign saying 'fire' beside a radiator in the main entrance, so that the evacuation could not take place through the main door.

- Adults: 2 staff in baby room, 2 in play room, 2 college students and 1 school work experience student
- Children: 5 in baby/toddler room, 15 in play room
- Date and time 5 December, 1.30 p.m.

(*The Happy Days Nursery referred to throughout this chapter is entirely fictional.*)

Criteria	Response	Action plan
Did everyone respond to the alarm?	Yes, although no one was aware of the location of the fire and time was wasted as staff discovered that they could not leave by the main door and had to decide which exit to leave by	Undertake additional practices with the fire in different locations. Include the effects of smoke, and the need to crawl
Did everyone know what to do?	The children who started this term had to be guided. Rebecca (on work experience from school) did not know what to do. Mandy has left for a new job so no one checked the toilets. Who called the fire brigade?	Discuss fire practices early in the term. Make all adults sign to confirm that they have read the procedures and know what to do
Did all groups of children gather together quickly?	The pre-school children were excited and gathered with the rope very quickly. It took some time to remove the babies from the high chairs. The two adults in the baby/toddler room could not carry all five children	Discuss staffing issues. Discuss what might have happened if Jamie had been at nursery today in his wheelchair
Did the children remain calm?	Staff were very efficient, talking quietly to the children, calming the excited children, and holding the hands of two timid toddlers. Some of the babies were frightened by the noise of the alarm. Staff calmed them quickly	No action
Did all people reach the assembly point?	Yes. But as Sheila had organised the practice no one else thought to take the register outside so it was impossible to check that everyone was there. The staff and children in the baby room took the longest time to evacuate the building	Ensure that all members of staff are aware of their responsibilities
De-briefing discussion with children	Useful discussion with children about Sheila 'finding' the fire, and what they would have done had they found something wrong	Arrange visit from the fire brigade in the Spring term
Comment on the effects of the timing of the fire drill	There are fewer children at lunch time as the part-time children have gone home	Repeat so all children can participate. Have another practice at arrival or departure time to include parents
Evacuation time	Too long!	

Gas leak procedure

This is an example for another emergency that will require evacuation of the building.

- Raise the alarm. (Do not use an electrical alarm system.)
- Turn the gas off at the mains.

- Open all doors and windows.
- Evacuate the building in a calm and orderly manner.
- Phone the Emergency Gas Number (keep the number by the phone).

Theory into practice

- Provide a detailed log account of a fire practice you have participated in.
- Evaluate the effectiveness of your role during the fire practice and identify how you met the requirements of the policy in your setting.
- State which legislation underpins the requirements of the fire procedure in your workplace.

Accident emergency

The Child Accident Prevention Trust states that more than two million children under the age of fifteen, one in five, visit hospital after an accident. The majority of accidents in day care settings are minor, being caused by falls and collisions. They result in bumps, bruises and minor cuts. However, there have been a number of serious injuries and even some accidental deaths at nurseries or pre-school settings. The table below shows the causes of some accidents and how they can be prevented.

Cause	Reason	Action to prevent accidents
Falls	Babies left unattended may roll off furniture	Never leave a baby unattended
	Toddlers may fall out of prams or high chairs	Safety equipment/ harness etc
	Running and climbing	Safe surfaces, clear space/stair gates. Older children separated from crawling and toddling children
	Fall out of windows	Window locks
	Falls at adventure playgrounds	Safe surface under play equipment
Crushing and cutting	Fingers trapped in door	Slow close mechanism/door safety
	Cuts with sharp or broken toys	Safety checks of all resources
	Cut with knives	Age appropriate use of knives
	Sharp objects on the ground	Check ground before children play
Suffocation and choking	Plastic bags, cords on clothing, pillows	No access to plastic bags/check clothing
	Inadequate supervision at meal times	Supervise all feeding
Poisoning	Cleaners, medications, DIY equipment Alcohol	Safe storage of all substances
Scalds and burns	Hot bath water, hot drinks near children	Check bath water. No hot drinks
	Fires and heaters, lighters and matches	Fire guards
Drowning	Drowning in bath, garden ponds and pools	Never leave alone near water Teach older children to swim

Accident procedures checklist

Accident procedures are specific to individual settings but will probably include the following points:

- A trained first aider must be on duty at all times. This will mean that more than one person in each setting should be a qualified first aider.
- All adults should know who the first aider is.
- The person who witnesses the accident should inform a first aider.
- First aider will assess the situation and the injury and summon help if required.
- Another member of staff will comfort any other child involved in the incident.
- Remaining staff will maintain a normal play environment. They may need to move all children into another area if the accident appears serious.
- If necessary, inform the parents or emergency contact if a parent cannot be found.
- In an emergency dial 999 to call an ambulance. A member of staff may accompany the child to hospital if the parent has not arrived (ensure that the adult/child ratio in the setting is still appropriate).
- For other hospital visits, check if staff are insured to take the child in a private vehicle. The child must be accompanied.

Children and accidents

A child who has had an accident will be in pain, and frightened. They will want to see a parent figure. You will keep the child calm, talk quietly and reassuringly and if the injury is serious contact the parent as soon as possible after contacting the emergency services. Other children may also be frightened. You should reassure them, distract their attention, and not apportion blame. They may be feeling guilty already!

Reporting Injuries, Diseases and Dangerous Occurrences Regulations 1984 (RIDDOR) require settings to provide an accident report book. The member of staff attending to the injury is responsible for completing the accident report and ensuring that the parent signs the report.

> **Accident report**
>
> Name _Farinda Patel_
>
> Day/date _Tuesday 15 February, 2002_
>
> Time _11.45 at home time_
>
> Place _in the pre-school room_
>
> Circumstances of accident _Farinda and another child were running to get their coats. They collided, banged heads and Farina fell to the ground_
>
> Nature of incident _slight bump on the head_
>
> Action taken _Cold water compress_
>
> Person who dealt with injury _Zameera_
>
> Witness _Caroline_
>
> Parent's signature ____

Injuries must be recorded in the setting's accident report book

Informing parents

Parents will obviously be very anxious when they hear that their child has been injured, so the news must be given to them in a calm and gentle manner. The staff may also be upset by the incident, but they must be careful not to pass on their own sense of anxiety.

If the accident has been very serious, a parent may experience emotional shock and should be treated appropriately. Parents may demonstrate their distress by being angry and accusing. You should remain calm, and not become defensive or participate in argument. If the injury was caused by another child (biting or hitting), this information should be treated sensitively and public accusations avoided. Following an accident a parent will be asked to sign the accident book to agree that they have been informed about the accident. Care must be taken to ensure that they are not able to read details of other accidents when they sign the accident record book. Following a head injury, parents should be provided with information to help them to recognise symptoms of a more serious injury.

Head injury information

Your child has had a minor bump on his/her head today. If you notice any of the following symptoms contact your doctor:

- Intense headache
- Unusually drowsy
- Vomiting
- Unequal or dilated pupils
- Clear fluid or blood from the nose or ears
- Visual disturbance, blurred vision or seeing 'stars'

Information sheet for parents

Reviewing accident procedures

All accident procedures must be reviewed regularly and should involve an examination of the accident book. This will enable staff to identify any common features, such as the time of day or specific activities that regularly appear to cause accidents. This information can then be used to improve the accident prevention measures.

Theory into practice – accident emergency

- Ask if you can look at the accident report book at your current workplace.
- Identify a variety of different types of accidents that have been reported in the book, e.g. falls or trapped fingers.
- State how they may have been prevented.
- Observe the day, time and place of each accident to determine if there is any pattern.
- List five activities or situations where accidents may occur and describe what you would do to prevent them.

Assessment activity 4.1

Farzana and Kevin have been playing on their bikes racing round the playground. They have had a collision by the side of the climbing frame. Both children are lying on the ground. Three more children who are playing on the climbing frame are jumping up and down and leaning over the side of the frame as they call for help. Farzana is crying loudly and has a lot of blood coming from a nasty cut on her knee. Kevin is unconscious and breathing.

Describe what you will do to in relation to the following:

a) assessing the situation, b) assessing the casualty, c) diagnosing the injuries, d) prioritising treatment, e) providing treatment for both children, f) recording the incident, g) informing the parents.

Remember in most situations you would call your supervisor, or the identified first aider who will make any necessary decisions.

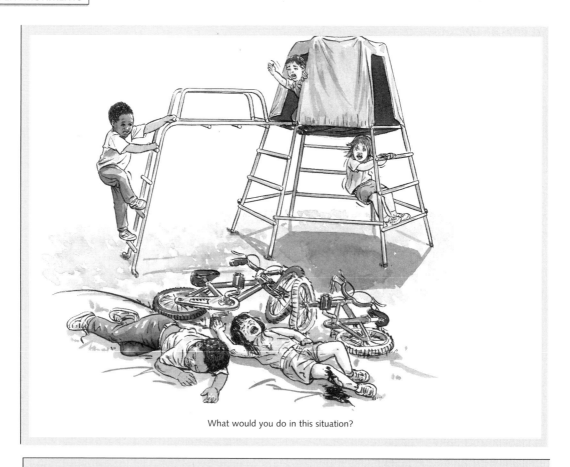

What would you do in this situation?

Assessment activity 4.2

Fire emergency

- Draw a plan of your workplace. Identify the position of the fire procedure, fire extinguishers and emergency exits.
- State why you think they have been placed where they are.
- Identify three areas or situations where a fire may occur.
- Plan an evacuation route for each fire situation.
- List some measures you could take to limit the chances of a fire starting in these positions.

Safe and secure environments

Statutory authorities and legislation

'Your health, safety and welfare are protected by law. Your employer has a duty to protect and keep you informed about health and safety. You have a responsibility to look after others.' (Health & Safety Executive, 1999)

Everyone working with young children must therefore be aware of their legal obligations in relation to maintaining the safety of the children in their care.

The role of the Health & Safety Executive (HSE)

The Health & Safety Executive is the government agency which is responsible for Health and Safety. The HSE has responsibility for:

- 'Inspecting some places where people work
- Investigating accidents and causes of ill health
- Enforcing good standards by advising people how to comply with the law
- Publishing guidance and advice
- Providing an information service
- Carrying out research'. (HSE).

The **Health and Safety at Work Act 1974** is the most important piece of legislation relating to health and safety and includes the following:

- Employers must ensure, as far as is reasonably practicable, the health, safety and welfare of employees and those affected by their work. (*This means ensuring the safety of the staff, children and parents, and any person who may enter the premises, such as a caretaker, student or visitor.*)
- Settings with five or more employees must have a written safety policy which must include specific procedures to cover emergencies such as accidents and events that require evacuation of the building (see Emergencies, page 117).
- Settings with five or more employees must carry out a risk assessment and show how risks are minimised (see Potential hazards, page 130).
- Employers must provide for health and safety in relation to the provision, maintenance and use of premises and equipment (see pages 131–4).

Additional regulations, addressing specific areas of health and safety, have been added since the introduction of the Act. (*Each of the following will be referred to in the relevant part of the text.*)

Reporting Injuries, Diseases and Dangerous Occurrences Regulations 1984 (RIDDOR) require that all settings must provide an accident report book with separate sections for reporting accidents to children and adults (see page 122). All fatal and major injuries and dangerous occurrences not resulting in injury at work must be reported to the appropriate authority. Any injury that requires a member of staff to take more than three days off work must also be reported. The local Environmental Health or Social Services Department will advise on the reporting procedures.

Health and Safety (Information for Employees) Regulations 1989 require employers to display official posters or provide leaflets for workers giving basic information on health and safety law. This is the reason that health and safety notices or leaflets will be on display in your workplace.

Control of Substances Hazardous to Health Regulations 1994 (COSHH) requires that hazardous substances be kept separately in a marked, locked cupboard. It is important that staff are all aware of appropriate methods for using such materials. Instructions about protective clothing and first aid information should be kept (see page 140).

Health and Safety (First Aid) Regulation 1981 state that there should be at least one person appointed to take charge in an emergency and to be responsible for the first aid equipment. It also requires that someone in each workplace must be a trained in first aid (see page 110).

Fire Precautions (Workplace) Regulations 1997 state that it is essential that all settings have plans and procedures for action in the event of a fire and signs showing what to do in the event of a fire should be placed in every room. Regular evacuation practices must be carried out at least every three months and fire extinguisher, smoke detectors and fire alarms should be tested regularly (see page 117).

Electricity at Work Regulations 1989 require that all electrical equipment and systems in non-domestic premises should be safe to use, be properly installed and should be maintained and tested by competent persons. A record of all electrical equipment must be kept, giving details of when each item was tested and the date for re-testing.

Food Handling Regulations 1995 state that settings which prepare or provide food for children must register with the Environmental Health Department in the local authority. They must ensure that people handling food have appropriate training such as the Basic Food Hygiene certificate (see page 144).

Local authority provision

Environmental Health Department
The Environmental Health Department has responsibility among other things for dealing with issues related to food control, health and safety and pollution control. The department provides advice and education and has responsibility for enforcing relevant legislation. The work includes inspecting premises, food poisoning and infectious disease control and registering and licensing food premises.

Local Education Authority
The Health and Safety Unit within the local authority has the responsibility to oversee the implementation of the Health and Safety at Work Act within schools. The authority has responsibility for the provision of the following:

- departmental policies
- procedures, information and guidance
- competent support and advice
- health and safety training
- monitoring and review of health and safety matters.

The governing body of a school has responsibility for policies and procedures development and implementation at a local level. The head teacher has the responsibility of site manager and control of the school premises to ensure that the school is safe for use. All employees have a general duty to themselves and others to ensure safety.

The National Standards Under Eights Day Care and Childminding
The National Standards apply to all childcare providers from September 2001. The responsibility for Registration and Inspection of Early Years settings used to lie with the local authority Social Services Registration and Inspection Unit which inspected settings in relation to the requirements of the Children Act 1989. These responsibilities have now passed to a new Early Years Directorate in OFSTED which will inspect settings against the National Standards and the supporting criteria. The National Standards are a set of 'outcomes' that providers should aim to achieve. Regulations under the Children Act require providers to meet the fourteen standards. Each standard describes a particular quality outcome. The criteria within each standard are matched and are specific to five different types of day care and childminding provision – full day care, sessional day care, creches, out of school care and childminders. Throughout this section we will be referring to the National Standards for full day care. This unit is concerned specifically with Standards 6 and 7.

Standard 6, Safety, includes	Standard 7, Health, includes
• Risk assessment • Security • Safety in the outside area • Fire safety • Outings and transport	• Hygiene • Animals • Sandpits • Food • Medicine • First aid • Sick children • Smoking

Issues of safety are also encompassed within aspects of the following standards

Standard 2, Organisation
• Adult child ratios
• Staff training and qualifications

Standard 4, Physical
• Space requirements
• Maintenance of premises

Standard 5, Equipment environment
• Safety standards

Key issues – National Standards research

As this is the most recent and comprehensive piece of legislation to affect early years settings, it is important that you develop a good understanding of the document. All the issues addressed within this unit are encompassed within the Guidance to the National Standards and this exercise will enable you to develop the work of this unit.

• You are asked to examine a copy of the National Standards for Full Day Care and identify all the aspects which relate to safety. You will prepare a fact file for your reference that details all the specific criteria relating to safety within all 14 standards.
• You will examine the Full Day Care Guidance to the National Standards document and list the Children Act Regulations within the standards. You will then state which policy in your setting provides for the requirements of the Children Act Regulations.

Both documents can be obtained from DfES Publications (tel: 0845 6022260) or at www.ofsted.gov.uk.

Policies and procedures

The implementation of the legislation requires settings to prepare policies and procedures that inform working practices. There will already be policies and procedures within your setting, but it is useful to have an understanding of how these policies are created.

Question. Why do we need policies?

Answer. They are a legal requirement, they provide for quality and they provide an agreed framework for action.

Question. Who is responsible for the policies?

Answer.   The management is responsible for creating the policies and for checking that they are being followed.
The staff are responsible for implementing the policies.

Question.   What is the difference between a policy and a procedure?

Answer.   A policy statement underpins a number of procedures. For example, the health and safety policy will provide procedures for fire, accident, food preparation, etc.

Question.   How does this all link into the legislation?

Answer.   Legislation → Policies → Procedure.

The following list makes links between the policies and procedures that you will find in your workplace and the relevant National Standard under which they have been developed. We examine most of these policies in different sections of this unit. As all staff and parents must be aware of these policies you will often find them on a noticeboard, or in the setting's brochure.

Health and safety policies and procedures
- Health and hygiene (Standard 7)
- Arrival and departures (Standard 6)
- Child protection (Standard 13)
- Behaviour management policy (Standard 11)
- Smoking and drinking policy (Standard 7)
- Fire procedure (Standard 6)
- Medication procedure (Standard 7)
- Illness, accident and emergency procedure (Standard 7)

Some specific issues addressed within the legislation
Adult/child ratios: Standard 2
The staffing ratios within settings are determined to ensure the safety and well-being of the children in the group. The National Standards require that the group size should never exceed 26 children. They also recommend that children should be in key worker groups. This means that each child has a named member of staff who is responsible for their well-being and knows all the details of the child and the family. (It does not mean that they spend all the time with that member of staff.)

The minimum appropriate adult/child ratios in sessional care, full day care and out of school care is as follows:

- 1 : 3 children aged 0–two years
- 1 : 4 children aged two years
- 1 : 8 children aged three–seven years.

Childminder/child ratio
Where a childminder is working alone in her own home the ratios are as follows:

- six children under the age of eight
- of these six, no more than three children may be under five years of age
- and of these three, no more that two may be under two years.

Adult/child ratios in schools

The adult/child ratio in Local Education Authority nursery schools and nursery classes is as follows:

- Two adults for 26 children aged three to five. One adult will be a qualified teacher.
- A private nursery school differs from a day nursery in that it is only open during the period of the school day in term time, it takes children aged three to five who are under the care of a qualified teacher. The ratio is also 2 : 26.

Supervision

These ratios are defined to protect children, as the younger the child, the more observation, guidance and support they require to ensure safety. The level of supervision will vary depending on the age of the child, the environment they are in and the activity they are undertaking. There are three distinct levels of supervision as follows:

- General supervision – ensuring that you can see the children and are aware of what they are doing, e.g. being aware of what the children are doing whilst playing in the garden.
- Close supervision – being on hand while they undertake specific activities to help if required, e.g. sitting at the collage table to help with aprons or writing names on the paper.
- Constant supervision – interacting with the child during a risky activity, e.g. supporting children during a woodwork or baking activity.

Your responsibility is to ensure that children have the appropriate supervision at all times.

Think It Over

This chart describes the activities of some children in a private day nursery. Using the information supplied, identify the correct adult/child ratio and level of supervision for the children and situations.

Age of children	Activity	Adult/child ratio	Level of supervision
3 years 3 months	Playing in the home corner		
18 months	Playing with hammer and peg game		
4 years	Playing on sit and ride toys		
2 years 8 months	On the climbing frame		
5 years 6 months	Playing with a train set		

Access to premises

In order to ensure that the environment is secure, a setting will create procedures for managing access to the premises with arrival and departure procedures for the children. These procedures must ensure that children are safe. This is particularly important where there are situations in individual families where one or other parent may have restricted access to the child. This poses difficulties as there may be issues relating to freedom of access and personal liberty. The Children Act 1989 states that parents have the right to see their children although sometimes this may need to be in a supervised situation if there has been a court order specifying when and where the parent can see the child. A setting will also want to provide some control over the people who are able to enter the building. Many settings maintain a visitors book.

The diagram below identifies some of the security measures taken to ensure the following:

- the safe arrival and departure of children
- that children are not able to leave the premises unsupervised
- that strangers are not able to enter the building.

Locks/buzzers on doors

The locks on doors and gates will be placed so children cannot reach them. Buzzers will alert adults to opening doors

Named personnel

Settings will ask parents to identify any adults who may collect their child. The child will not be allowed to leave the building with any other adult

Vehicles

Many children are brought to the setting by car. Safe car parking arrangements are important

Voice-activated or video access

Some settings may have voice or video identification systems. In large settings staff may have identification badges

SECURITY
Arrival and departure procedures

Care for all children

Settings will have a specific procedure to ensure that all children are cared for whilst other members of staff talk to parents

Signing in

All settings will record the time children arrive and leave, many settings ask parents to sign their children in and out

Transfer of responsibility

The policy will identify the point at which responsibility for the child transfers from the staff to the parent. This may be when the parent enters the building, or when the parent leaves the building

A parent forgets to collect a child

Procedures will be in place to contact the parent or another adult

Potential hazards

The National Standards require that all settings should undertake risk assessment.

Good practice for risk assessment

As with all aspects of quality provision, procedures will be in place for the management of the risk assessment process. The responsibility for risk assessment ultimately lies with the management of the setting. However, the most efficient methods will include all members of staff.

- Identify the hazard. Settings will decide a mechanism for doing this which may include looking at specific areas or events within the setting as identified in the chart below.
- Identify the danger. This may include identifying **who** is at risk (e.g. a member of staff using a cleaning product) or **what** specifically the risk is (e.g. bacteria flourishing in the toilet).
- Identify control measures to ensure the risk is minimised.
- Identify who is responsible for taking action to minimise the risk.

- Record the assessment. Ensure that the assessment is dated and signed.
- Identify a time scale for the review of the risk assessment (e.g. this may be an annual inspection of the whole setting, or may be instigated if there is a change of staff or a new piece of equipment is purchased).
- Monitor and document that the control measures are in fact in place and working effectively.

Having already looked at specific measures for fire prevention, and at the common causes of accidents for young children we will consider each of the following hazards in turn:

- Premises: the indoor environment
- Premises: outside environment
- Equipment and resources
- Specific times of the day
- Animals
- Dangerous substances

Premises: the indoor environment
There are certain dangerous or non-secure areas within the setting where accidents are more likely to occur. Consider the sample risk assessment for Happy Days Nursery below.

In practice, a risk assessment form will also include a column which identifies the person responsible for taking action.

Area	The danger	Action taken to reduce risk
The toilet	<ul><li>Children may lock themselves inside the cubicle</li><li>Children may slip on wet floors</li><li>Children may fall climbing on to high toilets</li><li>Bacteria flourish</li><li>Burns from hot water</li><li>Cleaning materials</li></ul>	<ul><li>High locks on cubicle doors</li><li>Teach children about toilet safety</li><li>Wet floors wiped immediately</li><li>Child steps provided</li><li>Appropriate hygiene procedures</li><li>Ensure thermostat controls temperature</li><li>Store cleaning materials in locked cupboard</li></ul>
The kitchen	<ul><li>Sharp knives and hot equipment</li></ul>	<ul><li>NO access to kitchen area</li></ul>
The floor	<ul><li>Children may slip on wet or polished floor</li><li>Children may trip on the carpet join</li><li>There may be rubbish left on floor by another user of the room</li></ul>	<ul><li>Non-slip floor covering. Special absorbent mat placed under water tray</li><li>All carpets and mats fixed to floor with nails or tape</li><li>Sweep and check floor before use each day</li></ul>
Stairs	<ul><li>Children may fall</li></ul>	<ul><li>Ensure safety gates always closed</li><li>Accompany children on the stairs ensuring they hold the hand rail</li><li>Teach children safe use of the stairs</li></ul>

Area	The danger	Action taken to reduce risk
Windows	• Children may fall out	• Safety glass installed • Provide window locks and keep the key out of reach of children • Do not open window further than the child safety lock allows
Doors	• Children may 'escape' • Children may trap fingers	• Locks on the doors, but keep the key in an accessible place • Check the situation in relation to fire doors • Supervise home time • Provide slow closing mechanism and internal doors which are open during the session must be fixed open
Plug sockets	• Children may poke objects into sockets	• Socket covers provided for all sockets

Premises: outside environment

Outdoor play is an essential aspect of care and education for young children. Below are some of the factors which need to be considered when preparing the outdoor environment.

Plants	Careful checks must be taken to avoid plants with poisonous leaves and berries.
Safe surfaces	Safe surfaces should be installed under climbing equipment Areas where bikes are used must be flat and clear Animal droppings must be cleared and disinfected Surfaces must be checked for vandalism e.g. broken glass
Access and fencing	Gates must be self-closing and at least 1.2m high and locked Fences must not have horizontal bars that children can climb Fences and gates must be kept in good repair
Dustbins and rubbish	Dustbins must be kept out of reach of children If children are encouraged to pick up litter, they must wash their hands immediately afterwards
Equipment	Large equipment to be checked for wear and tear and cleaned regularly Age appropriate equipment provided Supervision at all times Sand pits must be covered and if any sign of animal droppings must have the sand changed No water play and checks must be made in any place that water collects Check position of equipment. Metal slides may become very hot in the sun
Sun	Areas of shade should be provided Sun screen and sun hats should be worn Children should not be outside in the midday sun

Think It Over

This exercise will help you practise the skills of risk assessment. The chart above identifies the hazards and the action taken to reduce the risk. These comprise columns one and three in the sample risk assessment chart below. For each of the sections in the chart above can you identify what the dangers are. Make a chart of your own as described below and complete the central column.

The area or hazard	Danger	Action taken to reduce risk
Sun	Sunburn leading to skin conditions in later life	Shade and sun hats

Equipment and resources

There are many safety factors you need to consider when providing equipment and resources for young children.

- Purchasing
- Storage
- Cleanliness

- Age appropriate
- Maintenance

Supervising children in an outdoor play area

Purchasing

All toys and equipment bought for children should conform to recognised standards. These are some examples of the standard marks you will find on toys and equipment.

You will need to be particularly careful if you are offered second-hand toys and equipment and always check for the safety mark.

Age appropriate

All equipment and resources must be appropriate for the age of the child. You should check the labelling on the packaging of new toys. Young children can choke on the small pieces in some toys, or they may fall off larger toys such as sit and rides or climbing frames. It is also important to provide appropriately sized furniture. A small child may fall off a chair that is too high, or an older child may break a small plastic toddler chair.

Storage

Resources and equipment must be stored safely. Items that children access themselves must be easy to reach. The shelves themselves must be securely fixed to the wall. Resources such as paint, glue and play dough should be checked regularly for freshness and disposed of appropriately. Where large items need to be stored, thought must be given to methods of transportation, as carrying heavy loads may cause injury to a member of staff. Staff should be taught safe handling techniques.

Cleanliness

Special care needs to be taken to ensure that the toys and equipment the children use are regularly cleaned to prevent the spread of infection. Young children put things in their mouths and have not yet learnt the usual habits of hygiene. Plastic toys and rattles that babies and toddlers use should be sterilised in a hyperchlorite solution. Other toys can be washed in soap and water or wiped down with a cloth impregnated with an antibacterial solution. Soft toys and bedding should be washed or disinfected following manufacturers' instructions. The sandpit needs to be cleaned out regularly.

Maintenance

All toys and equipment must be checked regularly. Plastic items may chip or crack, wooden toys may have flaking paint or splinters, metal equipment may rust and moving parts may break. Any defect in equipment must be reported to your supervisor as soon as possible, and the toy removed until it has been mended or replaced. You may be able to undertake minor repairs yourself, but it is important that all other repairs should be carried out by a qualified person. It is often cheaper to replace a small item than to repair it.

Opposite is a sample safety check that a setting may use when undertaking regular assessment of toys and equipment.

Equipment safety check	
Cleaning	**Date cleaned**
Sand tray	-----------
Construction toys	-----------
Dolls and dolls clothes	-----------
Large mobile toys	-----------
Baby toys	-----------
Painting aprons	-----------
Maintenance	**Date checked**
Climbing frame erected securely	-----------
Jigsaws complete	-----------
Car box checked	-----------
Farm complete	-----------
Dolls house	-----------
Train set complete	-----------
All toys in correctly labelled containers	-----------
Containers in correct place on shelves	-----------
Home corner equipment	-----------
Renewable materials	**Date checked**
Paint	-----------
Glue	-----------
Play dough	-----------
Signed _____	

Case Study

You are having a busy day at the nursery. When you are setting up the home corner in the morning, you notice that one of the hinges on the cooker door is loose and the door no longer shuts properly. Whilst setting up the construction table you see that some of the Duplo bricks have got dried play dough stuck on the inside. They were being used yesterday for a printing activity. Later on, whilst reading a story book to a small group of children, you find that there is a tear in one of the pages. After break you are asked to check the outside play area before the children play outside and you notice that the paint on the swing is flaking and that rusty areas are beginning to show. At dinner time you are preparing the high chairs and notice dried food has stuck to the underside of the table. At the end of the day when clearing up, you find that one of the jigsaws has a piece missing.

- Discuss your day with a colleague on your course and prepare a list of the actions you will take during the day in relation to the cleanliness and maintenance of equipment.

Specific times of day

There are specific times in the day when accidents may be more likely to happen. These times may be obvious as, in the table below, or they may be identified by a review of the accident book which may demonstrate a particular pattern in relation to accidental injuries.

Sample risk assessment for Happy Days Nursery

Time	Hazard	Action to minimise danger
Arrival and departure	• Children may escape! (see page 129)	• Suitable deployment of staff
Meal times	• Children may choke • Children may be allergic to specific foods • Children may pick up infections	• Increased supervision • Check children's details for allergies • Ensure children wash hands
Just before lunch and tea	• Children are tired and more likely to have falls and fights	• Provide calm activities whilst waiting for meals
During outdoor play	• More opportunity for collisions and falls as children run about or use physically challenging equipment	• Supervision and teaching the children about the dangers • Provision of safe equipment
Sleep times	• Children may fall from cots or beds • Danger of suffocation • Danger of choking • Danger of overheating	• Age appropriate beds • No pillows for babies or toddlers and place babies on their backs • No long ribbons on garments or toys • Ensure children are not overdressed and the room temperature is suitable • ALWAYS CHECK SLEEPING CHILDREN

Animals

There are aspects within the Early Years Curriculum that encourage children to develop an awareness of animals. Some settings keep pets, visit farms or bring animals in for the children to touch or observe. There are however specific issues in relation to keeping animals in early years settings. The animals may be exposed to over handling and may have long periods alone at weekends. Wild animals such as tadpoles may not actually be in their best environment in a tank in a nursery. There are other ways to consider the needs of animals without actually keeping them on the premises. Children can be encouraged to feed the birds, or undertake topic work about animals, or examine mini-beasts in the environment.

Scrupulous hygiene precautions are necessary in relation to any contact with animals. The following list describes some essential requirements:

- Wash hands before and after handling animals.
- Only introduce animals that are used to children.
- Always supervise children when with animals.
- Dispose of animal waste.
- Keep cages hygienic with a regular cleaning routine.
- Litter boxes should not be accessible to children.
- Keep all animal feeding utensils separately.
- Do not allow animals near children's food.
- Ensure that animals have regular checks with the vet and follow any vaccination requirements.
- Worm animals regularly.
- Check for fleas and treat appropriately.

Department of Health Guidelines recommend precautions for school visits to farms, and this information can be found on the PHLS website.

Dangerous substances

There are many substances in early years settings which may be hazardous. The Control of Substances Hazardous to Health Regulations 1994 (COSHH) require settings to list dangerous materials, and show how the risks are minimised.

Substance	Hazard	Action to minimise risk
Cleaning materials Washing-up liquid Toilet cleaners Bleaching agents	Poisoning Unstable if mixed together Skin irritant	Store in a locked cupboard Ensure bottles are labelled Never transfer to another bottle Never mix different agents, e.g. toilet cleaners Wear protective gloves
Body waste Faeces Urine Vomit Blood	Transfer of infection	Wear disposable gloves and aprons Wash hands before and after dealing with incident Clean area after use Dispose of body waste and soiled nappies in separate container (see page 140)
Medicines	Poisoning	Keep medicines in a locked cupboard Follow 'administering medications policy' (see page 142)

The physical environment

The planning of the layout of the setting will have a direct effect on the children's experiences during the day. The children's concentration, behaviour and sense of security will all be affected by the way in which the room has been prepared. The National Standards address issues related to the physical environment. There should be an area where confidential information can be kept and where staff may talk to parents. Staff should have a room away from the children for their breaks and there should be separate toilet facilities for adults. There should be a kitchen which conforms to environmental health and food safety regulations.

Factors to consider when planning the environment

- There should be a good variety of activities available at all times which can be changed during the session to ensure that children have plenty of challenging experiences throughout the day.
- There must be space to move between activities, to ensure no disruptions. A child concentrating on a jigsaw will be disturbed if their chair is constantly being bumped as people walk by.
- There should be some secure, stable storage at the child's height for self selection of activities.
- Noisy activities should be kept away from areas near doors to ensure safety by the doors and a sense of calm for people entering the premises.
- Quiet areas where children can rest or read should be away from the noisy activities.
- Messy activities should be near a source of water for hand washing.
- Large rooms can be made cosy or small rooms spacious by sensitive positioning of furniture.
- There should be clear space for energetic play, or the furniture may be moved for part of the session to provide for energetic play.
- Ensure that fire exits are unobstructed.
- Ensure good visibility throughout the room to aid supervision.

Adaptations for children with special needs

Children who may have special needs attend many childcare and education settings. The environment and equipment can be adapted to meet their individual needs. It is important to consult the parents or any professional who may be working with the child, as each child will have a different need. Some examples of adaptations may include providing ramps or wide doors for wheelchairs or a particularly quiet environment where background noise is reduced for a child with a hearing difficulty. A child with a visual difficulty may require a safe area where they can move around by touching the furniture, or be introduced to tactile materials and resources. Where a child has a visual difficulty it is important to keep the floor area particularly tidy to limit hazards on the floor. It is often possible to take the activity to the child, perhaps by putting painting on a table rather than an easel, or having activities on the floor.

Think It Over

Examine the plan of Happy Days Nursery. Evaluate the physical layout of the nursery using the information provided on page 137 as guidance.

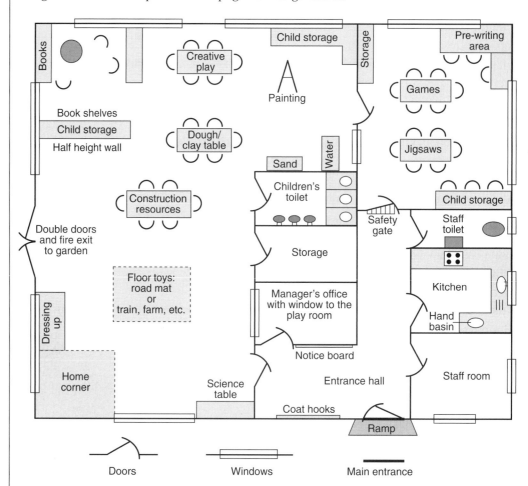

Specific considerations within the physical environment

Having arranged the layout, the furniture and the equipment, it is important to give some consideration to other aspects of the environment which affect the comfort and well being of the children in your care.

Heating	Hot children are often irritable, cold children lethargic
	The temperature should be kept at 18-21°C
	The temperature must be monitored during the day
	Heating systems must be maintained
	Radiators must be protected
	Carbon monoxide monitors should be provided
Lighting	Lighting can affect mood e.g. a sunny day can make people feel happier
	Good lighting will avoid eye strain
	Good use must be made of artificial and natural light
	Flickering fluorescent light should be avoided
	Consider the use of daylight bulbs
Ventilation	Good ventilation can limit the build up of bacteria, viruses and carbon monoxide
	It should be possible to open windows to ensure a supply of fresh air

Assessment activity 4.3

1 Read the following safety report prepared for Happy Days Nursery. Write down two lists: one to identify which pieces of legislation are being adhered to and one to identify which pieces of legislation are being ignored. Give reasons for your choice.

A large notice board by the door displays the following information:
- a Health and Safety at Work poster
- procedure in the event of a fire
- accident procedures
- photos of all members of staff
- health and safety policy
- behaviour policy
- a 'no smoking' sign.

No member of staff is identified as a trained first aider.

An examination of safety records demonstrates that the most recent fire practice was over six months ago. There was no record of any electrical equipment having been tested since purchase although the nursery uses a television, a tape recorder, and has two computers. The accident book was completed appropriately although accidents to staff and children were recorded on the same page.

All cleaning materials are kept in a cupboard under the sink in the kitchen to which the children have no access. A stock list is taped inside the door. An appropriate first aid kit is kept in the staff cupboard. No one person has responsibility for maintaining the supply of first aid equipment. Staff report that whoever uses the equipment is responsible for replacing it. The battery in the smoke detector was dead.

2 While the inspector was on the premises he witnessed the home time procedure. There are 24 children and three members of staff on duty. The children are sitting on the mat having just had a story read to them. The supervisor is at the door ready to unlock it. She gives all the parents a letter about the summer trip as they come into the hall. The children all run to greet their parents who help them on with their coats. All the staff are busy talking to parents telling them about the plans for the trip, and about the work that the children have been doing in preparation for the trip. Four of the children are running round the room. Shaheen and Charlotte are climbing on the table. When all the parents have gone it appears that William has not been collected. A few minutes later George's mum appears to collect him. George has left already with his father. Nobody told the nursery that George's father was not allowed to collect him. Then Rachel's mum appears. Where is Rachel? Has she slipped out with the other children to look for her mum in the car park?

Which aspects of security has the nursery breached? Now rewrite the scene describing how you would like to organise the departure procedure in this setting.

Assessment activity 4.4

1 You are asked to carry out a risk assessment within your current workplace. You will identify potential hazards and describe the actions that have been put in place to reduce the risks. You must address the following issues:

- inside and outside the premises
- equipment and resources
- dangerous substances.

2 Describe the process you undertook whilst carrying out the risk assessment and give reasons for your actions.

Health and safety procedures

Policies and procedures

In addition to the procedures for managing emergency situations and providing a safe environment, a setting will prepare policies and procedures related specifically to issues of health and hygiene. In this section we will investigate some of the procedures you will find in your workplace.

Children cleaning dolls

Procedures for handling body fluids

The legislation which underpins this procedure is to be found in the Control of Substances Hazardous to Health Regulations 1994 (COSHH) (see page 125). The definition of 'substances hazardous to health' is given in Regulation 2 of these regulations and it covers all substances that are capable of causing disease or adverse health effects. It is therefore obvious that body fluids, blood, faeces, urine or vomit that may carry infections must be treated as hazardous substances.

While there is general concern about infections such as HIV (and small amounts of HIV have been found in body fluids like saliva, faeces and urine) there is no evidence to suggest that HIV can spread through these body fluids. However there is a risk that blood-borne viruses such as hepatitis B and hepatitis C and HIV may be spread by blood to blood contact.

A child may be HIV positive or have hepatitis without the carers knowing about it, so it is essential that all accidents or incidents that involve body fluids are managed by following the appropriate procedures.

Procedures for dealing with body fluids will include the following:

- disposable gloves to be worn at all times
- where possible, hands should be washed before carrying out any first aid procedure involving broken skin

- hands to be washed after dealing with any spillages, even if gloves have been worn
- cover any skin abrasion with a waterproof plaster
- blood splashed onto the skin should be washed off with soap and water
- splashes of blood in the eyes or mouth to be washed out immediately with plenty of water
- spillages should be cleaned up as soon as possible using a solution of bleach diluted 1 part in 10 parts of water
- spillages should be wiped up with paper towels which are then disposed of as contaminated waste
- soiled clothing and linen should be rinsed in a cold wash and then washed in a hot wash, preferably at 90°C
- soiled items may be flushed down the toilet, burnt, or double bagged in plastic bags which have been properly secured and the waste collected for incineration
- all gloves or aprons that have been worn must be disposed of with the affected items.

Any carer who is concerned about the transfer of blood should seek medical advice from their doctor.

Children's personal hygiene

Health and safety procedures are particularly important when you are caring for young children who will not have good personal hygiene skills. There are many opportunities for the spread of infection and you must ensure that you follow the policy of the setting. It is important that you consider all the following points:

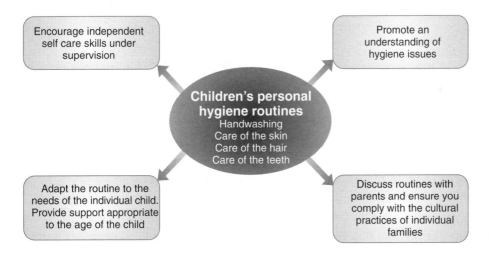

Handwashing

Everyone's hands carry bacteria. Children who regularly put their hands in their mouths are particularly at risk from infection. It is therefore essential that children are taught at an early age how to wash their hands properly. You can act as a good role model for children when they are learning about hygiene.

Care of the skin

Children need to wash regularly to keep the skin clean, to reduce smells and to stop sore areas developing in skin creases. In a day care setting you will not be responsible for bathing routines, but people working in domestic settings, such as nannies or childminders, may have this responsibility.

Some particular conditions affect the skin, and you need to be aware of these when caring for children's personal hygiene. Should you have any concerns about any condition you must consult your supervisor who will take appropriate action. This will include informing the parents who may then seek medical advice.

Children in nappies

Nappies must be changed in a designated area away from the play area. Soiled nappies must be wrapped in a plastic bag before disposal in a bin which should be controlled by a foot pedal. The baby's skin should be cleaned with a disposable wipe and any cream or lotion used should only be that provided by the parent. The changing mat must be cleaned between each use and checked for tears. If the plastic has torn, the mat must be replaced at once. Staff must wash and dry their hands after every nappy change. Where children are using potties, the potties should be washed in soapy water between uses. A specifically designated sink must be used.

Care of the hair

People working in day care settings will not usually be responsible for washing children's hair, although people working in a domestic setting may have this responsibility so it is important that you are aware of the basic procedures. In some day care settings children will have their own brush or comb for daily use.

Care of the teeth

Many day care settings now encourage children to bring a soft toothbrush. These should be clearly marked for individual use.

Case Study

Janice and Caroline are supervising toilet time at Happy Days Nursery. There are three sinks and three cubicles. The children line up at the door. Janice helps them pull down their clothes and lifts them on and off the toilet. Caroline supervises the hand washing. Each basin is filled with water and the children enjoy playing with the bar of soap. There are three towels, one for each sink. Mumtaz drops her towel on the floor as she leaves the room. Lewis has had an accident. 'You silly boy – why did you not tell me you wanted to go to the toilet?' Janice says as she changes his clothes. She puts the dirty clothes in the corner and says 'I will clear these up later while the others are having their snack'. By this time Caroline is dealing with Joseph who appears to have diarrhoea. 'He was like this yesterday, I wonder did anyone tell his mum?', Caroline asks. The staff are so busy that no one noticed that Robert had a rash on his bottom.

- Make a list of all the mistakes that Janice and Caroline have made. Describe what you would have done instead and give reasons for your answers.

Administration and recording of medication

There are two specific types of medication; that which is prescribed by a doctor, and that which can be bought over the counter. In early years settings, only medicines that have been prescribed by a doctor would normally be given.

People tend to think of pills and syrups when talking about medicines, but medications can be administered in many different ways, including:

- pills
- elixirs or syrups
- creams and ointments
- nose, eye, or ear drops
- inhalers
- injections.

The National Standards provide specific guidelines regarding the administration of medications and all settings are expected to create a medications policy.

The following aspects will be addressed within the policy:

- Medication will only be given if written permission has been provided by the parent, and if the medicine has been prescribed by a general practitioner.
- Written permission must include the name of the medicine, the dose, the time and instructions about administering the medicine, e.g. before meals, after meals, etc.
- The medicine must be stored in the original container in a locked cupboard. Some medicines may need to be stored in the fridge, in which case the fridge should ideally be locked.
- When the medicine is administered another member of staff will act as a witness.
- The exact time and dose will be recorded and will be signed by both parties.
- A parent will also sign the record to verify the administration of the medication.
- The carer should be given written information about any medication. This is particularly important as many children may go to different carers during the day, and they must all know what medication has been administered.
- Where medications such as inhalers or injections are to be used, the carer will receive specific training from a health professional on how to administer the medication to that particular child.
- When medications are to be used 'as necessary' the parent will give precise instructions about when it should be administered.

Administering the medication
Both members of staff involved will check the label and ensure that the correct child has been identified. The bottle will be shaken and the correct dose measured using a spoon or cup measure. When pouring out the medicine the bottle will be held with the label facing upwards, to ensure that no medicine runs down the bottle and obscures the label. A younger child may sit on the adult's knee. The member of staff will talk to the child in a calm and reassuring manner, encouraging them to take the medicine. Most medicines have a flavour added to provide a pleasant taste, but it is sometimes useful to have a drink ready to follow the medicine. Remember to praise the child if they swallow the medicine without any fuss!

Happy Days Nursery medication record

Child's name _____
Date of birth _____
Parent/carer's name _____
Emergency contact _____

Name of medication _____
Storage instructions _____
Dose _____
Instructions _____
Time to be given _____

I the parent of _____ give permission for the medication specified above to be administered by the staff at the stated time/s. I confirm that the medication was prescribed by the child's GP.

Signed _____ Date _____

Date _____ Time _____
Medication _____ Dose _____

Administered by _____
Witnessed by _____

Parent's signature _____

An example of a medication record form

Never pour the dose into a drink, as the child may not finish the drink and you will not know how much they have taken. Both members of staff will then complete and sign the medication record.

You will see from the medication record shown above, that the top half contains the instructions about administering the medication and the lower part of the form details the actual record of administration.

Hygiene in the kitchen

All foods may be potentially hazardous if they are not handled correctly, therefore good hygiene in the kitchen is essential. Anyone who is involved in food preparation should undertake the Basic Food Hygiene Certificate. This unit only provides simple basic guidelines as demonstrated in the chart below.

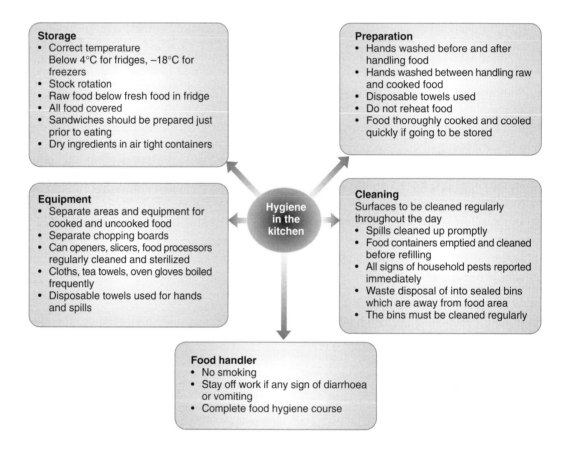

Storage
- Correct temperature
  Below 4°C for fridges, −18°C for freezers
- Stock rotation
- Raw food below fresh food in fridge
- All food covered
- Sandwiches should be prepared just prior to eating
- Dry ingredients in air tight containers

Preparation
- Hands washed before and after handling food
- Hands washed between handling raw and cooked food
- Disposable towels used
- Do not reheat food
- Food thoroughly cooked and cooled quickly if going to be stored

Equipment
- Separate areas and equipment for cooked and uncooked food
- Separate chopping boards
- Can openers, slicers, food processors regularly cleaned and sterilized
- Cloths, tea towels, oven gloves boiled frequently
- Disposable towels used for hands and spills

Cleaning
Surfaces to be cleaned regularly throughout the day
- Spills cleaned up promptly
- Food containers emptied and cleaned before refilling
- All signs of household pests reported immediately
- Waste disposal of into sealed bins which are away from food area
- The bins must be cleaned regularly

Hygiene in the kitchen

Food handler
- No smoking
- Stay off work if any sign of diarrhoea or vomiting
- Complete food hygiene course

Cross-infection

Preventing cross-infection

To appreciate the methods used to prevent cross-infection you need to have an understanding of how infection is spread. The following chart describes the different ways that infection is carried and identifies the precautions that are taken to minimise the spread of infection.

Micro-organisms enter the body via	Methods of prevention
Inhalation Breathed in through the nose and mouth	• Good ventilation (see Physical environment, page 138) • Encourage hygiene practices such as covering mouth when coughing • Hygiene procedures in relation to keeping the environment and resources clean (see Potential hazards, page 134) • Excluding children with communicable diseases
Ingestion Swallowed through the mouth	• Handwashing procedures (see page 141) • Food preparation procedures (see Potential hazards, page 130) • Hygiene procedures in relation to keeping the environment and resources clean (see Potential hazards, page 130) • Hygiene procedures in relation to animals (see page 136) • Exclusion of children with communicable diseases • Safe disposal of waste products (see Dealing with body fluids, page 140)
Inoculation Penetrating the skin through cut or injection	• Covering open wounds (see First aid, page 114) • Safe disposal of waste products (see Dealing with body fluids, page 140) • Separate personal hygiene equipment (see Personal hygiene, page 142) • Use of rubber gloves

Theory into practice

Plan a food preparation activity for a group of children which will enable you to promote issues of health and hygiene. The aim of the activity could be linked to the early learning goal for health and bodily awareness. Ensure you include promoting hygiene during (a) hand washing; and (b) food handling.

Communicable diseases

There are many infectious childhood conditions. They vary in severity and can affect people in different ways at different times of life. Immunisation is available for some of the diseases, but not all families participate in immunisation programmes. Some diseases can be very serious for particular groups of people such as pregnant women and children with certain medical conditions that make them vulnerable to infections. The Department of Health provides guidance on infection control in schools and nurseries and includes exclusion times. You will note however that there is a period of time between the micro-organism which causes the infection entering the body and the symptoms appearing. During this time the child may pass the infection onto other children.

The National Standards require that settings provide a policy for the exclusion of children who are ill to limit the spread of infection.

The chart identifies the incubation and exclusion time for some common childhood infections and lists some of the specific complications. (Exclusion details are taken from the Department of Health Guidance on infection control poster.)

Infections	Incubation	Recommended period to be kept away from school (once the child is well)	Complications
Chicken pox	14–21 days	Five days from the onset of the rash	Scarring or secondary infection from scratching Can affect the pregnancy of a women who is not immune
Diarrhoea and/or vomiting (with or without a specified diagnosis)		For 24 hours after the diarrhoea and vomiting have stopped	Dehydration
Impetigo	1–3 days	Until the lesions are crusted or healed. If the lesions can be kept covered, exclusion may be shortened	Side effects are uncommon
Measles	7–15 days	Five days from the onset of the rash	Ear and eye infections, pneumonia and encephalitis
Meningitis	2–10 days	The Consultant in Communicable Diseases may be informed and will give advice. National Meningitis Trust help line (0845 6000 800) will also advise	Deafness, brain damage and death
Mumps	14–21 days	The child is infectious seven days before the swelling and up to nine days afterwards	Meningitis (very rare) Infection of the testes in young men
Rubella (German Measles)	12–25 days	Five days from the onset of the rash	If contracted by women in first 3 months of pregnancy can cause serious defects in the unborn baby
Scabies		Until treated	
Whooping cough	7–10 days	Five days from commencing antibiotic treatment	Weight loss, dehydration Pneumonia

Children who are not well should not be at school or nursery even if they are not infectious, neither should children and adults with diarrhoea unless the diarrhoea is known to be of a non-infectious cause (e.g. coeliac disease).

Outbreaks

If there appears to be an outbreak of a particular condition the setting must report the matter to staff at the Public Health Department. The Consultant on Communicable Disease Control will assess the situation. If the outbreak is food related this must be reported immediately to the Local Authorities Environmental Health Department.

Informing parents and reporting procedures

Parents are recognised as being the most important influence within a child's life and the concept of 'shared care' is never so important as when supporting the needs of very young children. This cannot happen unless there is a good procedure for sharing information. Communication is an essential aspect of the process. Parents will provide a wealth of information about their own child and will be able to inform the carers about particular family values and practices which must then be incorporated into the care routine for that particular child. Sharing information is a two-way process and the carer also has a responsibility to provide information to parents. The chart below demonstrates some information regularly given to parents in relation to issues of health and safety.

Information about communicable diseases

There are two distinct types of information regularly exchanged between carer and parent. The chart below provides some examples of the information exchanged with parents.

Examples of general information provided for parents	Examples of specific information shared with parents
• Leaflets about childhood illnesses • Leaflets about meningitis • Leaflets about immunisation • Leaflets about head lice • Leaflets about nutrition	• Specific information for an individual parent about their own child • Specific information to all parents about a particular situation, e.g. a case of meningitis in the nursery where a letter which allays parents' fears may well be distributed • An outbreak of head lice in the setting • A child in the setting has developed Rubella

Contacting parents

It is essential that accurate up-to-date records of the parents' home and work contact numbers are maintained to ensure that a parent can be contacted quickly and easily in the event of an emergency. This information will be kept in a central place, and regularly updated.

Developing children's understanding of health and hygiene

The Early Years Curriculum requires that children should develop an understanding of the importance of keeping healthy and develop an awareness of the factors that contribute to health. Staff who work with children of all ages have a responsibility to encourage children to develop good hygiene practices. This is achieved by discussing issues of hygiene during daily routines, and by including planned experiences within the formal curriculum. Some suggestions are given in the following chart.

Formal planned activities	Informal opportunities for discussion
Topic work to cover • My body • The food we eat • Keeping clean Individual planned activities • Cooking activities • Cleaning the home corner • Washing the dolls • Washing the construction toys • Activities involving animals	• During toilet times • When hand washing after paint or glue activities • When preparing for meal times • When using paper hankies • When disposing of paper hankies • When children have a cold and cough and sneeze • After minor accidents involving scratches or cuts

Key issues: community information research

Most settings will provide a variety of leaflets and information covering issues of health and safety. This exercise will enable you to research local information to develop your knowledge of the services provided in your local community. You could work in small groups and prepare a presentation for the rest of your class.

Find the addresses and contact numbers for: the School Nurse, the Environmental Health Department, the Health Promotion Unit, the Fire Safety Officer, the Road Safety Officer and the Council for Voluntary Services.

Collect a wide range of leaflets about health hygiene and safety issues that you could give to a parent.

Reporting procedures

Information can be exchanged verbally, or in written format. It is appropriate that the correct method of communication is used for the correct purpose. The following chart identifies a variety of methods of exchanging information and investigates the advantages and disadvantages of each method.

Verbal	Advantages	Disadvantages
Daily exchange of information as parents collect or deliver children	• Up-to-date information can be shared in an informal relaxed situation. Regular contact enables good relations to develop	• There may not be enough time if parents or staff are in a hurry • Important information may not be passed on to other staff, e.g. a parent tells the staff that the child bumped her head that morning and other staff need to know this information • Parents who are not confident may find it difficult to talk to a member of staff

Verbal	Advantages	Disadvantages
		• There may be barriers to communication if a parent has a hearing difficulty or uses English as an additional language
Verbal information given in group meetings such as new parents evenings	• The same general information can be given to many people	• Parents may not remember all that has been said • Information about individual children cannot be shared

Written	Advantages	Disadvantages
Letters	• Clear precise information can be provided • The information can be retained and referred to at a later date	• Some parents may not be able to access the information. They may use English as an additional language or they may have literacy difficulties themselves • The letter may be lost before the parent receives it • The style the letter has been written in will affect how the parent perceives the information
Posters and leaflets on the notice board	• Detailed information about specific issues can be provided • The information can be kept and referred to in the future	• Parents who do not visit the setting will not see them. Remember many children are brought to nursery and school by childminders, grandparents or neighbours
Accident report slip	• Basic information about a specific minor accident	• A parent may be concerned and want to have greater detail than provided in the report

Case Study

It is the weekly staff meeting at Kittens pre-school. One of the items on the agenda each week is titled 'Working with parents'. At this part of the meeting the staff discuss any issues related to involving parents in the setting. This week some of the questions under discussion are as follows:

- Three children have head lice. Should this information be shared with the parents?
- The topic for next month is about 'my body'. How can we provide information to parents so that they can support the topic work at home?
- Part of the 'my body' topic includes an investigation of healthy eating. We would like to ask Mrs Patel if she will come and do a demonstration of making chapatis. How and when can we do this?
- A new child who is coming into pre-school next term has asthma and needs to use an inhaler. What preparation should we make?

- This term there are three new children from refugee families who have recently moved into the area. The staff are concerned that much of the information they regularly share with families is not accessible as the children and families are not yet confident in their use of English. How can we help these families?

Having read the report of the meeting can you decide:

- what the staff should do in each situation
- who should be responsible for each situation – the manager, the key worker, or all the staff
- what is the best method of communicating with the parents in each situation?

Write down your answers and then share them with a colleague and see if you agree.

When sharing specific information with an individual parent you must be aware of the following:

- Arrange a private place for the conversation.
- Explain the situation clearly and accurately.
- Be calm and understanding.
- If the parent has communication difficulties, e.g. hearing difficulty or uses English as an additional language, ensure that someone who can interpret is available.
- Value the parents' opinion.
- Do not enter into any disagreement.
- In all communications with parents ensure that confidentiality is maintained.

Confidentiality or access to information

The National Standards require that confidentiality must be maintained in relation to all information about families and children. Often breaches of confidentiality happen as the result of thoughtless behaviour rather than direct maliciousness, so you must take particular care to ensure that you do not discuss issues about children and families when you are outside the setting. A confidentiality policy should include some of the following:

- Individual records will be maintained for all children, and will be kept in a secure place.
- Details of individual children and families will not be discussed with anyone.
- Parents will be able to talk to members of staff in a private place where they cannot be overheard.
- If a parent wants to disclose private information, they must first be informed that the member of staff may need to pass the information on (this relates particularly to issues of child protection).
- Information must only be shared on a 'need to know' basis.

When deciding about a 'need to know' situation you can ask yourself the following questions. Will my colleagues be able to look after the child more effectively if they know? Are there dangers for the child or the family if the information is not passed on?

Think It Over

You may often hear things about children and families in your care. Read the following situations and consider what you will say and who you will tell, if anyone. Explain the reason for your decision.

- Amy's mother has told you that Amy is HIV positive.
- When you are changing Charlene's nappy you notice she has a bad rash.
- During lunch time in the staffroom the other students are joking about the dirty underwear worn by two of the children from the same family.
- You are going home on the bus with one of your friends and she tells you that she thinks a child in the class she is working in has just got meningitis.
- You are standing at the school gate and you overhear one of the parents telling her friend that she has left her husband.
- A parent who is very distressed starts to tell you that last night her husband hit her child. She asks you not to tell anyone.

Assessment activity 4.5

What legislation provides guidelines for the administration of medication? Describe in detail what you will do in the following three situations:

- Sarah has had earache during the night. Her father buys a bottle of Calpol on the way to nursery and asks you to give Sarah some medicine if she needs it during the day.
- Robert has had a chest infection. The doctor has prescribed a course of antibiotics. Robert's mother asks you to see that Robert takes this medicine regularly as he does not like taking it and may even have a tantrum.
- Shirin has just started attending your pre-school. You notice on her admission form that she has asthma and needs to use an inhaler quite regularly.

Create a form that could be used in an early years setting to satisfy the reporting requirements for the administration of medication.

Assessment activity 4.6

- Describe the policy in your setting for handling and disposing of body fluids.
- Identify how micro-organisms can enter the body and list some methods of reducing cross-infection.
- Write a log account of dealing with a toileting accident and describe the steps you took to limit cross-infection giving reasons for your actions.

End-of-unit test

1   Decide whether the following statements are true or false. Give reasons to explain your choice.

   • A child has fallen on a broken bottle. There is a large piece of glass in the wound. You should take it out.   T   F
   • You should place a burn in cold water for ten minutes.   T   F
   • If a baby is choking you should hold them upside down and slap their back.   T   F
   • If a child is having a convulsion you should put a pad in their mouth so they do not bite their tongue.   T   F
   • If a child is in shock you should lie them down and keep them warm.   T   F
   • If a child has swallowed some cleaning fluid, you should make them sick.   T   F

2   Respond to the following accident situations:

   • Elizabeth (aged four) has fallen from the climbing frame and is unconscious. Describe the procedure you will follow as you manage the situation:
   • Thomas (aged eighteen months) is choking on a piece of apple. Describe what you will do.
   • Javaria has spilt a cup of hot tea and burnt her hand. Describe what you will do.
   • The next day Elizabeth's mother comes to nursery. She is very angry, is shouting at the manager and blaming her for allowing Elizabeth to be injured. Identify why she is so angry and describe in detail what you will do.

3   Identify any legislation that relates to fire emergency situations. Create a list of all the fire prevention measures that are taken in your workplace.

4   Falls, suffocation, scalds and drowning are common causes of accidents for young children. List two actions you can take to reduce the possibility of each of these accidents. Give reasons for your choices.

5   Which pieces of legislation do the following terms stand for: COSHH and RIDDOR? Name the policies your workplace has developed in response to this legislation. Describe how this legislation affects the practice in your workplace.

6   List five policies and procedures that an early years setting will develop to meet the requirements of the National Standards.

7   Describe a range of measures that can be taken to ensure the safe arrival and departure of children.

8   Describe how your setting ensures that only authorised people can enter the premises. Discuss how issues such as freedom of access and personal liberty may be affected when taking account of the supervision and security of children in early years settings.

9   A child has been sick during snack time. The table, the floor and their clothes are covered with vomit. Describe in detail what you would do. Give reasons for your actions.

10 If a parent came into nursery and asked you to give her son some Calpol, as he has a bit of earache what would you do? Give reasons for your answer.

11 List the requirements of the medication policy in your workplace.

12 Create a list of activities that you could deliver during a pre-school session for children aged three to five which would introduce both formal and informal opportunities to discuss issues of hygiene.

13 You are going to open a new nursery and need to prepare an accident report form. Make a list of the information you need to include on the form.

14 Reporting procedures. Describe how you would share the following information:

- A child has trapped his finger in the door. His nail has turned black.
- One of the children has developed Rubella.
- One of the children has been bitten by another child.
- You are having a visit from the dental hygienist to promote dental care.
- Four children have diarrhoea.

References and further reading

Bruce, T. and Meggitt, C. (1999) *Childcare and Education* (2nd edition), London: Hodder and Stoughton

Coffey, J. (1995) *Care of the Sick Child*, London: Hodder and Stoughton

First Aid Manual: Authorised Manual of the Voluntary Aid Societies (1999), London: Dorling Kindersley

Full Day Care: Guidance to the National Standards

Laidman, P. (1992) *Accident Prevention in Day Care and Play Settings*, Child Accident Prevention Trust

Meggitt, C., Stevens, J. and Bruce, T. (2000) *An Introduction to Child Care and Education*, Hodder and Stoughton

National Standards for Under Eights Day Care and Childminding Full Day Care

Pre-School Learning Alliance, (1991) *Accident Prevention and First Aid for use in Pre-schools*

Tassoni, P., Beith, K., Eldridge, H. and Gough, A. (2000) *Diploma Child Care and Education*, Oxford: Heinemann

Tassoni, P. and Bulman, K. (1999) *Early Years Care and Education NVQ Level 3*, Oxford: Heinemann

Useful websites

Food Safety (General Food Hygiene Regulations) – www.doh.gov.uk/busguide/hygrc.htm

Government health – www.wiredforhealth.gov.uk

Health and Safety Executive – www.hse.gov.uk

Infection control in schools and nurseries – www.phls.co.uk

National Standards and Guidance for National Standards – www.ofsted.gov.uk

Protecting children

Introduction

In the UK, in your town or city, and in your neighbourhood, there are children who are being physically, sexually and emotionally abused, and neglected. There are adults who intentionally harm children or put them at risk from harm through neglect. The majority of families, however, care for their children appropriately and will not need intervention from professional services. This unit looks at how early years practitioners in providing stimulating play and learning experiences for young children are likely to become aware of children who give rise to concern because their behaviour and development are suffering. Early years practitioners are therefore in a prime position to alert others to possible abuse, support the child through any investigation that might take place and provide help for children who are known to have been abused. Because of this, it is important that early years practitioners equip themselves with knowledge about child abuse, why it may occur, how it may be recognised, its effects on young children and their families and what to do if they are concerned.

What you need to learn
- The range of child abuse
- Methods to support parents
- Strategies for supporting children and families
- Good practice in child care settings

The range of child abuse

The work addressed in this unit is of a sensitive nature. Child abuse may be a hidden aspect of some people's lives. It is important that when discussing issues in class you are aware of this.

Variation in family functioning
Family types
The family, in whatever form, is the unit that provides a home and care for dependent children. There are a variety of family types within our society:

Nuclear family	Parents and children live in an independent unit separately from other relatives. This may mean that the family is better off economically, but may also mean that if anything goes wrong between the parents, the family will experience considerable disruption

Reconstituted family	Partners with children from previous relationship live together. This may provide a good level of support, but may also bring tensions for some individuals
Extended family	Parents, children, grandparents, uncles and aunts live together in a supportive unit which has many advantages but may limit the personal independence of some members
Lone parent	A single parent, father or mother, living alone with a child. This may lead to financial hardship, or may induce a feelings of isolation and lack of support

Changing face of the family

While these definitions are fairly specific, it is important to be aware that there are many different combinations. The structure of the family has altered as a result of changes within the wider society. The increased incidence of divorce and remarriage, the development of a multicultural society and increased life expectancy has resulted in changes in family lifestyles and practices. Children may live in two households, moving from one to another at weekends or holidays; they may live with parents in a homosexual relationship, or grow up living with foster carers. Whilst family structures may vary in different cultures, it is very important not to generalise about any family situation.

More specifically, a change within any individual family structure such as moving away from relatives, a grandparent dying or moving to a different country can be quite disruptive for the family and the child. All families are different, have different practices and different values: there is no one particular ideal model. What is important is that the children are fed, clothed and sheltered, are loved and have the opportunity to learn within a protective and caring environment.

Social disadvantage

There are many pressures on families, not least those caused by social or financial hardship. The cycle of poverty is difficult to escape and places added pressures on the family. The table below identifies some of the factors which affect families.

Factor	Effect
Poor housing which may be overcrowded, damp and unheated with limited outside play space	Chest infections from living in damp conditions Lack of privacy or personal space Noise No safe outdoor play which may leave young children playing on the streets
Poor diet, cheap food with limited nutrients, high intake of fast foods, too much sugar and starch and too little fruit and vegetables	Illness and infections May affect growth Sets a pattern of poor eating habits which will last for life
Inadequate clothing	Discomfort in bad weather and may produce illness

Factor	Effect
Lack of stimulation and quality play resources, no holidays and limited travel	May effect intellectual development Makes times like Christmas additionally stressful
Low self-esteem	Feeling of worthlessness May cause depression May develop alcohol or drug dependency Leads to a feeling of being 'trapped'

Different concepts of discipline

All families have different values and standards. These will have developed as a result of the personal experiences of the parents, who will bring their values and family practices from their own childhood and past experiences.

Think It Over

To demonstrate the differences between families, complete the following exercise. Make a list of the rules within your household when you were a child. Ask yourself the following questions:

- Were you allowed to bounce on the settee as a five-year-old?
- Were you allowed to swear in the house as a nine-year-old?
- Were you allowed to hit your siblings at any time?
- Were you allowed to stay out after 10 p.m. when you were twelve?
- Were you smacked by your parents?
- What other punishments were used for minor misdemeanours?
- When you have children will you expect the same standards from them?

Now share your answers with a group of friends and see if you share the same experiences. You will find that there are many differences in relation to the expectations for behaviour and the methods of discipline that were used. There is no one definitive description of acceptable standards and practices will always vary in different family circumstances.

Abuse within families

Contrary to popular belief, most child abuse and neglect takes place within the child's own home and family, by somebody (usually a parent) that the child knows. Child abuse and neglect crosses all boundaries of culture, ethnic origin, religion and social status.

Pre-disposing factors

While no single factor can be seen to be responsible for causing an abusive situation, there are some factors which may make an abusive situation more likely.

Parents

Research into child abuse has shown that certain characteristics and experiences may predispose particular individuals to be more likely to abuse a child in their care than another individual. These include:

- parents who themselves have been abused
- parents who have experienced poor parenting themselves
- very young parents who may be unaware of the child's needs or are in fact still growing up themselves
- people who have unrealistic expectations of their child's behaviour
- parents who experience poverty, poor housing and social isolation
- parents who have a low self-esteem
- a history of alcohol or drug abuse
- parents with mental health issues
- an unwanted pregnancy and/or difficult birth.

None of these categories is applicable to all adults who may abuse or neglect their children, but do need to be considered when addressing individual issues of child protection.

Children

Some children are more vulnerable to abuse than others, for example:

- a child with a disability
- an eldest child
- a child who has been separated from the mother soon after birth
- a loner
- a child who has been previously abused
- a child who cries a lot or is difficult to feed.

These factors are obviously not applicable for all children, but may be pre-disposing factors.

Children with disabilities

All the indicators listed above apply to children with disabilities; however, the question still remains why children with disabilities are more vulnerable. Some reasons are listed below:

- They receive less information on abuse and their rights, and may be less likely to understand it.
- They are more dependent on physical care from different people.
- They may receive less affection from family and friends and so be more accepting of sexual attention.
- They may be less likely to tell what has happened due to communication barriers.
- They are likely to have low self-esteem and feel less in control.
- They may find it difficult to distinguish between good and bad touches.

Theories of child abuse

In spite of the large number of theories put forward as to why child abuse occurs, there is no one theory which can be applied to all cases of abuse and neglect. Each situation is different and occurs for different reasons and therefore needs to be viewed individually. The four main theories as to why child abuse and neglect occur are defined in the the following diagram.

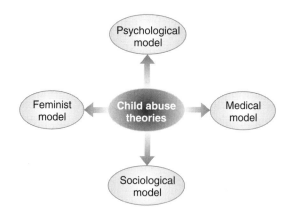

Medical model

This theory addresses issues around the idea that the causes of child abuse were viewed as a disease. This came from the phrase coined by Kempe and Kempe (1962): the 'battered child syndrome'. This was later changed in 1976 to 'child abuse and neglect'. Kempe and Kempe applied Bowlby's thinking around 'attachment theory' directly to child abuse and neglect. They concluded that many mothers (the main caregiver who the bond is made with) who had abused their children had themselves suffered from poor attachment experiences in early childhood. Their response to this was to ensure that children in abusive situations were removed to places of safety and the parents were given 'treatment' to help with the bonding process.

Sociological model

This theory looked at changing patterns within society and believed that unemployment, poverty, poor housing and health deprivation were reasons for people abusing their children. Children need to live in healthy environments if they are to grow up healthy and well adjusted. Research has shown that there are links between rates of reported abuse and characteristics of social deprivation, e.g. a high proportion of low-income families.

Psychological model

Family dysfunction theorists look at the dynamics within a family relationship. If this becomes poor or distorted, the family ceases to function as a unit. Dysfunction usually begins with the adult partners who may then 'scapegoat', which means that all the family's problems become identified in one family member. Theorists argue that the 'scapegoat' has become necessary for the survival of the family unit.

Feminist model

This perspective addresses the imbalance of power between men and women within society and with particular reference to child sexual abuse and the abuse of adult male power.

Case Study

Read the scenarios below and:

- identify the family structure involved
- link the example to the appropriate theoretical model
- give reasons for your choice

Scenario 1: Robert and Leanne and their baby live with Robert's parents in a small terraced house that has been condemned as unfit for habitation. Much of the family money is spent by Robert who has a drug habit. There are concerns about the baby.

Scenario 2: Karen lives with her two children in a high-rise block of flats. Although her mother lives in a neighbouring block, Karen never sees her. She says, 'I never got on with my mother.' There are concerns about the children.

Scenario 3: Sarah and Jeff live with their four children in a detached house on an expensive estate. Both parents work, Jeff is often away from home and even when he is at home there are many arguments. There are concerns about the eldest child.

Definitions of abuse

'Somebody may abuse or neglect a child by inflicting harm, or by failing to act to prevent harm. Children may be abused in a family or in an institutional or community setting; by those known to them or, more rarely, by a stranger.' (*Working Together to Safeguard Children*, 1999)

Physical abuse and injury

'Physical abuse may involve hitting, shaking, throwing, poisoning, burning or scalding, drowning, suffocating, or otherwise causing physical harm to a child. Physical harm may also be caused when a parent or carer feigns the symptoms of, or deliberately causes ill health to a child whom they are looking after. This situation is commonly described as Munchausen syndrome by proxy.' (*Working Together to Safeguard Children*, 1999)

The following characteristics may be observed in a physically abused child.

Physical indicators	Behavioural indicators
Unexplained multiple bruises in unusual places (thighs, behind the knee, upper arm, back, neck, back of legs, etc. – see Figure 5.1)	Unlikely or inconsistent explanations for injuries
	Withdrawn and overly compliant
	Aggressive
Frequent bruises at different stages of healing	Poor social skills
Bruises in the shape of objects, e.g. belts, rope, etc.	Low self-esteem
Fingertip bruises	Unusually fearful
Unexplained/untreated burns and scalds	Hyper-alert to the environment (frozen watchfulness)
Unexplained/untreated fractures	Reluctant to change clothing for swimming or PE
Any bruising on a young baby who is not yet mobile	
Cigarette burns	Plays inappropriately with or without toys
Bite marks	Inappropriately clinging to, or cowering from parent or carer
Internal injuries which can cause pain, fever, vomiting, etc.	

It is important to remember that young children regularly develop bumps and bruises through falls and squabbles with siblings. You should also consider the age and stage of development of the child. For example, regular bumps on the head of a toddler who may fall or bang his head on furniture may be viewed differently from that of a six-year-old who regularly appears with bumps or bruises on the head. When making a decision about a specific injury you should also consider any explanation that has been given to you regarding the injury.

However, the physical signs of abuse are often different from those acquired through normal causes, as shown in the figures below.

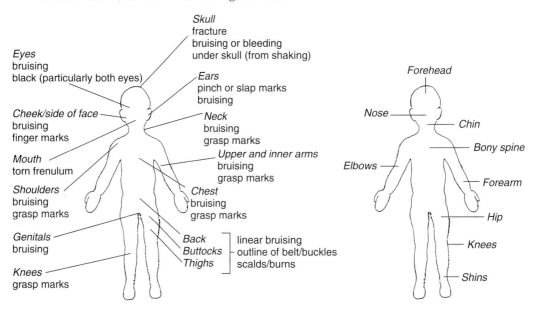

Figure 5.1: Non-accidental injuries

Figure 5.2: Accidental injuries

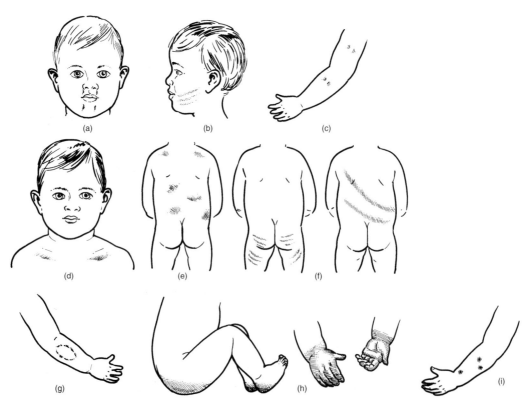

Figure 5.3: Signs of physical abuse: (a) facial squeezing, (b) diffuse facial bruising, (c) pinch marks, (d) grip marks, (e) body bruising, (f) identifiable lesions, (g) bite marks, (h) burns or scalds, (i) cigarette burns

Parental attitude is important in assessing accidental and non-accidental injuries – when a child is suffering a severe and painful injury most parents would seek medical help. It is also important to remember that children of mixed race, of African or Asian heritage, may have dark pigmented areas at the tip of the spine, which at times extends into the buttocks. These spots are known as 'Mongolian Blue Spot'. They are always of the same colour and do not go through changes of colour like bruises do.

Think It Over
Draw or trace a body outline. Shade in four different injuries. Ensure that some are accidental and some non-accidental. Now exchange your picture with a partner and identify the injuries on your partner's picture.

Emotional abuse
'Emotional abuse is the persistent emotional ill-treatment of a child such as to cause severe and adverse effects on the child's emotional development. It may involve conveying to children that they are worthless or unloved, inadequate, or valued only insofar as they meet the needs of another person... Some level of emotional abuse is involved in all types of ill-treatment of a child, though it may occur alone.' (*Working Together to Safeguard Children*, 1999)

The following characteristics may be observed in an emotionally abused child.

Behavioural indicators

Attention seeking	Indiscriminately affectionate
Withdrawn and isolated	Fearful of parents/carers
Stealing or telling lies	Self-mutilation, e.g. head banging, hair
Inability to have fun	pulling, picking at skin
Low self-esteem	Comfort seeking behaviour, thumb sucking
Tantrums at an inappropriate age	or rocking
Speech disorders	Poor concentration
Inability to play	Frequent toileting accidents in older children

Emotional abuse is perhaps the most difficult form of abuse to detect because there are no physical indicators. There are also many other reasons why a child may be displaying these signs. Children may be unsettled by a change in the family function. There may be a new baby, a close relative may have died, parents may be experiencing a stressful time, such as divorce or separation, or the family may be moving home.

Sexual abuse
'Sexual abuse involves forcing or enticing a child or young person to take part in sexual activities, whether or not the child is aware of what is happening. The activities may involve physical contact, including penetrative (e.g. rape or buggery) or non-penetrative acts. They may include non-contact activities, such as involving children in looking at, or in the production of, pornographic material or watching sexual activities, or

encouraging children to behave in sexually inappropriate ways.' (*Working Together to Safeguard Children*, 1999)

The following characteristics may be observed in a sexually abused child.

Physical indicators	Behavioural indicators
Pain, itching or discomfort in the genital area	Nightmares, night terrors and sleep disturbances
Difficulty when having a bowel movement, urinating or swallowing	Dramatic behavioural changes causing disruption of child care activities
Recurring complaints such as frequent stomachaches and headaches	Clinging or compulsively seeking attention from both boys and girls
Eating disorders such as refusing to eat or eating constantly	Overly co-operative or aggressive
Torn, stained or bloody underwear	Destructive or anti-social behaviour
Bruising/bites to breasts, buttocks, lower abdomen, thighs, genital or anal areas	Apparent sadness almost all the time
	Poor relationships with other children and lack of self-confidence
	Frequent lying without apparent reason
Sexually transmitted diseases, promiscuity or pregnancy	Self-destructive behaviour, e.g. biting oneself, pulling out hair, wrist-cutting, head banging
Semen on skin, clothes or in the vagina or anus	Unusual distrust or fear of adults or specific adults
	May fear going home or being left alone
	Unusually secretive, 'special' relationship with an older person
	Unusual sexual knowledge and persistent, inappropriate sexual play for the child's age and stage of development

Neglect

'Neglect is the persistent failure to meet a child's basic physical and/or psychological needs, likely to result in the serious impairment of the child's health or development. It may involve a parent or carer failing to provide adequate food, shelter and clothing.' (*Working Together to Safeguard Children*, 1999)

The following characteristics may be observed in a child who is neglected.

Physical indicators	Behavioural indicators
Poor hygiene	Lack of interest, difficult to stimulate
Inadequate clothing, dirty, torn or inappropriate for weather conditions	Indiscriminately affectionate
Untreated medical problems	Persistently late to school or frequently misses school
Persistent nappy rash	Withdrawn
Poor nourishment	Low self-esteem
Emaciation	
Poor levels of physical development, underweight, short in stature	

Physical indicators	Behavioural indicators
Appears thin and looks generally unhealthy Tired, listless and unkempt Persistent minor illnesses Hungry, overeating when food is available	

Even with the indicators outlined above it is still difficult to determine whether a child has been abused or not. Most of these indicators could quite easily have a valid reason or explanation other than abuse. For example, persistent minor illnesses may in fact be a medical condition or poor hygiene may be the result of limited hot water or bathing facilities or an apparently underweight small child may have very small slight parents. You may consider additional factors such as evidence of visits to the doctor, or the lack of age appropriate supervision or evidence of the parent's interest in the child's experiences and development. It is important as a child care worker not to jump to conclusions and if you are unsure, then discuss your concerns with a colleague or line manager/supervisor.

Consequences and effects of child abuse and neglect

Studies have shown that child abuse has been a consistent factor in the backgrounds of criminals, substance abusers, prostitutes and runaways. Children who have experienced child abuse are likely to continue or create the cycle of violence when they become adults. They assume that pain naturally accompanies intimacy. They turn to physical abuse, as well as substance abuse, in order to forget what have happened or is happening to them. Child abuse and neglect lower self-esteem and has a long-term damaging effect on the person's confidence, faith, relationships and future. Long-term effects of child abuse include fear, anxiety, depression, anger, hostility, inappropriate sexual behaviour, poor self-esteem, tendency towards substance abuse and difficulty with close relationships (Browne and Finkelhor, 1986).

While these effects are not always obvious, they are very important. Knowing this, there can be little doubt that children who are abused, as well as adults who were abused as children, need assistance to resolve the questions that the abuse experience has raised, even if that assistance does not come until years after the abuse.

Legal framework

As stated in the United Nations Declaration of the Rights of the Child (1959), all children should have 'the right to protection against all forms of neglect, cruelty and exploitation'. This was later implemented within the Children Act 1989 and the United Nations Convention on the Rights of the Child which states that all children have a 'right to protection from abuse and neglect'. It therefore gives a responsibility to those working with children to ensure that all are protected.

Historical perspectives

Prior to the implementation of the Children Act, there were many pieces of child care legislation which were thought to be far too complex and incomplete for the needs of children, their families and the professionals working with them. As society's ideas and attitudes were changing towards child abuse, for example more people were becoming aware of its existence and were no longer prepared to 'bury their heads in the sand, it was evident that the existing legislation had to be updated. Another reason for this was the reports into the deaths of Jasmine Beckford (1985), Kimberley Carlile (1985), Tyra Henry (1985) and an inquiry into the handling of alleged child sexual abuse in Cleveland (1987).

The Children Act

The Children Act 1989 came into force on 14 October 1991. It is the most important reform of the law concerning children over the last century. It makes the law simpler and easier to use. It brings together the legislation concerning the care and upbringing of children in both private law, which applies to children affected by a private dispute such as divorce proceedings, and public law, which covers children who are in need of help from a local authority.

Above all the Act is about how we as a society believe children should be cared for. It creates a code of law about the upbringing of children to ensure that we achieve the very best for this and future generations. It aims to help children in need get the best deal possible by providing services to their families.

The five principles underpinning the act are as follows:

- At all times, the *welfare of the child* must be the paramount consideration.
- A new concept of *parental responsibility.*
- The '*no order*' principle, whereby courts are instructed not to make statutory orders unless they are satisfied that the only way to safeguard the first principle (welfare of the child) is to make such an order.
- The '*no delay*' principle, where children are involved in cases before the court, the court must set a timetable and ensure that the case is heard as quickly as possible.
- The principles of '*corporate responsibility*' and '*partnership*'.

Paramountcy principle
The Children Act states that when the courts are involved in making a decision in the child's life, that child's welfare must always be the 'first and paramount consideration' and, with regard to this, a welfare 'check list' is set out within the Act stating that the court must take into account:

- the ascertainable wishes and feelings of the child concerned (considered in the light of his age and understanding)
- his physical, emotional and educational needs
- the likely effect on him of any change in his circumstances
- his age, sex, background and any characteristics of his which the court considers relevant
- any harm which he has suffered or is at risk of suffering
- how capable each of his parents, and any other person in relation to whom the court considers the question to be relevant, is of meeting his needs
- the range of powers available to the court under this Act in the proceedings in question.
  (Children Act 1989, Section 1(3).)

The Act in practice

- Makes children's welfare a priority
- Recognises that children are best brought up within their families wherever possible
- Aims to prevent unwarranted interference in family life
- Requires local authorities to provide services for children and families in need
- Promotes partnership between children, parents and local authorities
- Improves the way courts deal with children and their families
- Gives rights of appeal against court decisions
- Protects the rights of parents with children being looked after by local authorities
- Aims to ensure that children being looked after by local authorities are provided with a good standard of care.

Part V of the Children Act 1989 contains all the relevant orders for protecting children. It is these that local authorities or the NSPCC will apply to the courts for in order to safeguard children who are deemed to be at risk.

Child Assessment Order: a child is removed for an assessment of their physical or mental condition. Lasts for seven days.

Emergency Protection Order: gives the power to remove a child to a place of safety. Lasts for eight days and can be extended for a further seven days.

Care Order: the child is placed in the care of the local authority. Lasts until the child is eighteen. Parental responsibility is shared between the parent and the local authority.

Police Protection Order: gives the police the power to remove children to a place of safety. Lasts for 72 hours.

Supervision Order: the child is placed under the supervision of the local authority, which does not have parental responsibility. It lasts up to one year, and can be extended to three years.

Interim Care Order: lasts for 28 days and is made in the situation where a full hearing cannot yet take place, usually pending a full investigation.

The National Standards for Under Eights Day Care and Childminding

Regulations under the Children Act require providers (technically the registered person in each registered setting) to meet the fourteen Standards and have regard to the supporting criteria.

Standard 13 relating to Child Protection states:

> 'The registered person complies with local child protection procedure approved by the Area Child Protection Committee and ensures that all adults working with and looking after children in the provision are able to put the procedures into practice.' *National Standards for Under Eights Day Care and Childminding – Full Day Care.*

The supporting criteria with the standards also require that the setting has a written statement based on the Area Child Protection Committee procedures. This statement, or policy, should include staff responsibilities with regard to reporting suspected child abuse. There must be a designated person who has attended child protection training who is responsible for liaison with the child protection agencies. All members of staff must be aware of possible signs and symptoms of abuse and all staff must be able to implement any child protection procedures. There is a requirement to keep concerns confidential to as few people as possible.

The Area Child Protection Committee

The Area Child Protection Committee (ACPC) is a committee of senior managers from all agencies working with children and their families within a local authority area. It will include the police, and health and social services. It is responsible for ensuring that all the agencies work together to protect children and ensures that national policies and procedures relating to child protection are in place. Each ACPC will provide guidance relating to child protection procedures.

The United Nations Convention on the Rights of the Child

This was approved by the UK on 12 December 1991. The Convention, which has the status of international law, affects all people under the age of eighteen years. The Convention has been reproduced for all 191 countries of the world. Over 180 have gone through ratification, which means that they have agreed to be bound by the Convention.

Human Rights Act 1998

This Act came into force on 2 October 2000 and details the basic rights of humans in our society. The Human Rights Act outlines rules to order and protect every person.

Rules of the Human Rights Act include the right to life, protection from slavery, the right to education and the right to marriage. These seem as though they go without saying, however, without the Human Rights Act we could live in a very different society. There are places around the world where freedom is restricted, people are made to work as slaves or are not allowed an education. The Human Rights Act is vital in keeping our society as fair and equal as possible and fortunately most of us have no idea what it would be like without such laws. We have the right to have an opinion – even that is not allowed in some societies.

Key issues

Research a child abuse or neglect case that occurred before the Children Act 1989, e.g. the case of Maria Colwell or Tyra Henry.

- What went wrong?
- Who was to blame (if anybody)?
- Could things have been done differently?
- Think about how the case would be handled now, in the light of the Children Act 1989, the Human Rights Act 1998 and the United Nations Convention on the Rights of a Child.
- Have there been any improvements?

Referral

Reporting within the setting

As a student, your first priority in relation to any suspicions of abuse is to talk to your line manager or supervisor. The procedures for reporting abuse will be described in the setting's child protection policy and will usually include the following details:

- Staff should be aware of the signs of abuse.
- All incidents and concerns should be recorded in the incident book.
- If appropriate, additional observations may be carried out to gather supporting evidence.
- Confidential discussions may be held with some other staff.
- Concerns may be discussed with the parents.

Assessment activity 5.1

Read the case studies outlined below.

- Decide whether you think each of these children is being abused. If so ,what type of abuse are they experiencing? Give reasons for your choice.
- List any other signs you might look for.
- Describe the effects for the child and the consequences of any abuse.
- Identify what you as a nursery nurse would do for each situation.

Case study 1: Dominic is four years old and attends a local day nursery. In recent weeks nursery staff have noticed a change in his behaviour. He is using sexualised play with his friends and has begun to swear a lot in everyday conversation. On one particular day a nursery nurse found Dominic lying on top of another child. When he asked him what he was doing, Dominic told him that he was 'rugging'.

Case study 2: Joanne comes to nursery in inadequate clothing; she often has no coat in winter and wears sandals. She usually has a runny nose. At snack time she regularly has an extra slice of toast. She appears to be very quiet and shy and does not mix very well with the other children and seems to have a very low self-esteem. Whenever a new student comes into the nursery she becomes very affectionate.

Case study 3: Kevin often comes to nursery with bumps and bruises on his shins and forehead. On Tuesday he had a very obvious small bite mark on his forearm. His mother said his younger brother has bitten him.

Case study 4: Feroza has always enjoyed nursery. Recently she has been reluctant to come to the setting and she appears very withdrawn and has become very possessive. If anyone tries to remove something she is playing with she reacts by hitting the other child.

Methods to support parents

Good enough parenting
What constitutes a good parent?

This is a difficult question to answer as we all have different views on the subject. We accept that a parent should be able to meet their child's basic needs. These include the ability to love, to nurture and care for the child, to feed, and to protect from harm. A parent should be able to communicate with the child and be able to cope with stress and manage conflict. There are, however, no reliable or valid criteria for determining what constitutes 'good enough' parenting.

The majority of parents, even those who abuse their children, do love them very much and want to do the best for them. It is important that you do not judge any parent and, despite any personal feelings you may have about their management of the child, you must treat them with professional respect. We are taught that to promote self-esteem we respond to a child who is behaving inappropriately by saying 'I do not like what you are doing, but I still love you'. In the same way we can encourage a parent's self-esteem by acknowledging that as people and parents they are valued even though they may not be meeting all their child's needs. If you can initiate good relationships with the parents and work to promote their self-esteem, they will develop confidence in your ability to help and advise them.

Many people learn parenting skills within their own family but some parents, particularly young people and parents who have not experienced parenting themselves, may need help to develop these skills.

Encouraging parents to develop their caring role

There are many ways of helping families to develop parenting skills. Working with parents is important because:

- parenting programmes can work in changing parents' behaviour and increasing their range of skills
- programmes can reduce the proportion of negative parenting
- parenting must be seen in the context of the relationship between the couple and other external stresses.

Effective intervention with parents needs the following elements:
- offering skills and support to parents
- focusing precisely on desired outcomes – this involves creating a specific action plan with specific outcomes
- collaboration between the parents and professional agencies
- highly structured intervention
- community based, and building on existing services
- regular evaluation which is fed back to the parents both verbally and in writing.

So what specifically can we do to help parents who may be struggling with the parenting role? It is often difficult for parents to admit that they are not coping, and many parents may feel intimidated by professionals whether they be nursery nurses, social workers or health visitors. As a nursery nurse in an early years setting you have a role to play in helping parents to develop their skills.

Methods of encouraging parents to develop their caring role and involving parents in the childcare setting

It is easier to be responsive to parents' needs if you understand their difficulties. The following table addresses some of these difficulties and identifies strategies to support parents. Many of these activities will be introduced in all early years settings, but some will be used within settings where parents are required to bring their child under a child protection order.

Skills	Difficulties faced by some parents	Strategies to support parents
Relating to children positively	Parents may not have experienced good parenting themselves and do not know how to relate to children In a stressful family situation, responding to children is a low priority, e.g mental health problems, drug-related situations	Provide positive feedback whenever possible Encourage the parent to work beside you (role modelling) Help parents to develop listening skills Provide opportunities for parents to talk to and share experiences with children Address any additional difficulties the parent may be experiencing such as accessing financial support
Informing parents about child care and development	Parents may not see it as a priority to know about their child's development Parents may feel that the nursery is the expert and will deal with all such matters Parents may have literacy difficulties themselves and be reluctant that this should be 'found out', or have difficulty accessing information	Positively reinforce the value of shared care Exchange information on a daily basis Regular parents meetings to discuss children's learning Visits from the health visitor or dental hygienist Signs and pictures around the setting describing development milestones related to individual activities Written reports about development in jargon-free format which is accessible to parents
Developing practical caring skills	Parents may not have experienced the basic caring skills Parents may be isolated and have no support network and therefore no role models	Do not challenge the parent's method of working with their child. Suggest that there may also be some other ways of managing the situation. For example, rather than say a diet of spaghetti hoops is not nourishing, suggest additional things that the child could eat Staff demonstrate practical skills such as nappy changing, bottle and hygiene routines Involve the parent in cooking activities or meal times Identify or instigate support networks within the family and the community
Participating in play and learning	Parents may not have experienced play themselves Play may not be seen as a priority Learning may be viewed as the role of the nursery or school Financial difficulties may limit the provision of play materials or stimulating experiences	Provide opportunities for parents to share play experiences with children in the early years setting Provide workshop activities where parents can enjoy the play experience and make games or puppets to share with their child at home Toy libraries In-house 'stress free' courses

Skills	Difficulties faced by some parents	Strategies to support parents
Adapting as children develop	For first children, parents may not know what to expect at different ages and stages, e.g. some parents will continue baby food long after the time the child should be on solid food Some parents have a need to be needed and are reluctant to allow their children to develop	Discussion about future developments, e.g. preparing for temper tantrums Verbal exchange on a daily basis preparing the way for additional development Linking the parent into family and community support networks Family workshop activities which enable the parent to meet other parents and observe the development of different children
Facilitating change	Accepting the need to change requires an individual to confront the fact that they may not have been doing well enough. This is very threatening	Parents need all the support they can to accept the need for change and to move forward positively. This relies on them receiving positive feedback and encouragement and the belief that they are valued as parents

Think It Over

It is Wednesday morning at Happy Days Nursery. Below is a list of situations that Rebecca dealt with during the morning.

- A group of mothers is waiting at the door. They are chatting to each other. One toddler is screaming in his pushchair. 'Will you shut up?' the child's mother shouts.
- Anisa is new to the group today. Her health visitor has asked that she attend the nursery as she is worried by her small size, and difficult eating patterns. Anisa's mum does not speak very much English and is very nervous about coming to the group.
- Tom's mum is staying to help in the group today. She is sitting at the dough table busy playing with the dough herself. She is not paying any attention to the other children at the table.
- Katy's mother is attending the nursery at dinner time. She is cutting up Katy's food and feeding her with a spoon even though Katy is three years old.
- At home time Rececca gives Joanne her large painting. Joanne shows it to her mum proudly. Mum responds by saying 'Oh what a mess, can't you do better than that? How on earth are we going to get that home, we are going into town now, just leave it here!'
- Kerry is four years old and at home time her dad is putting her coat on for her.

What would you do to support each of these parents? Identify the following:

- What particular skills do the parents need to develop?
- Why may they be having difficulty meeting the child's needs?
- What exactly are you going to say to the parent in each situation?
- Write your ideas on a piece of paper and then share them with a friend.

Helping parents modify children's behaviour
Rewards and punishments
Many theorists have researched children's positive and negative behaviour such as

Skinner and Bandura (see Unit 12). Skinner was a behavioural psychologist who developed the concept of positive and negative reinforcement. Positive reinforcements and rewards are used to modify behaviour. It is important, however, to remember that while rewards such as stickers, praise and treats are regularly used, for many children the attention they receive when being punished may also act as a positive reinforcer.

The notion of reasonable chastisement

This is a very contentious debate, as England is one of the few remaining countries in Europe that allows parents and carers to smack children. Smacking has recently become illegal in Scotland. There are many organisations throughout the country that would wish to see an end to physical violence/punishment towards children such as EPOCH, the NSPCC and the National Children's Bureau.

Most parents, however, disagree with this and feel that it is an infringement on their civil liberties and rights as parents. Views expressed include 'It never did me any harm' or 'Children need firm discipline if they are to learn right from wrong'. It is interesting to note that parents seldom say 'I hit my child' they are more likely to say, 'I smack my child'. It is as though there is a subtle difference between hitting and smacking, although of course both have the same effect. However, physical discipline may get out of hand if the parent's frustration or increasing temper, when the child refuses to conform, leads them to lose control.

Cultural and social variations

Whilst helping parents with their child's behaviour, it is important to take into account cultural and social factors. What might be viewed as unacceptable in one society may be viewed as the norm in another. We have already seen that standards of acceptable behaviour vary in different families (see page 156) and it may be difficult for children to conform to another expected standard within the early years setting. It is therefore very important to work with parents to achieve a consistent approach to managing behaviour.

Communication barriers may also pose a problem when working with parents for whom English is an additional language – therefore a translator should be called upon. The same is said for parents with a hearing impairment, and a signer should be requested.

Communicating with parents about behaviour

As shown in the diagram below, staff will use a variety and combination of strategies to support parents as they attempt to modify children's behaviour.

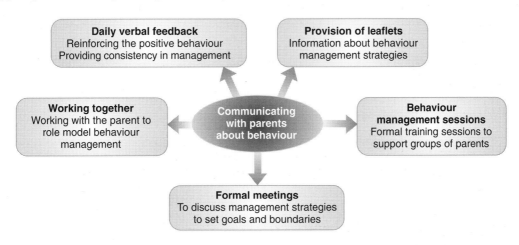

Daily verbal feedback
Reinforcing the positive behaviour
Providing consistency in management

Provision of leaflets
Information about behaviour
management strategies

Working together
Working with the parent to
role model behaviour
management

Communicating with parents about behaviour

Behaviour management sessions
Formal training sessions to
support groups of parents

Formal meetings
To discuss management strategies
to set goals and boundaries

Facilitating change

A family may get stuck in a cycle where the child's inappropriate behaviour causes the parent to behave in an inappropriate manner. To ensure change, both children and parents may need help to modify their behaviour. There are many strategies for promoting positive behaviour. These can be reinforced through a variety of shared experiences, as shown in the table below.

Activity	Strategies to encourage behaviour modification
Women's group	The process is started by promoting the parents' self-esteem by providing the parents with some quality time where they can experience activities such as aromatherapy, make-up sessions, relaxation or stress management. An opportunity to have time for themselves and pamper themselves
Family workshop	An opportunity for staff to work with the whole family, promoting positive behaviour such as encouraging parents to praise good behaviour, to give children lots of attention and encourage the child's self-control. There are opportunities for one-to-one support to help parents reduce the need to smack
Outings such as shopping	This is a situation where children and parents often behave inappropriately. Staff can demonstrate effective behaviour management such as giving the child responsibility, or using distraction techniques and reinforcing appropriate behaviour
Residentials	An opportunity for children and parents to experience new and stimulating activities whilst staff introduce effective management techniques during normal family activities such as meal times and bed time routines. Staff reinforce the importance of a consistent approach, of not nagging the child and of firmly reinforcing appropriate behaviour
Home visits	Staff can visit at meal times to support what may be difficult situations, encouraging the family to sit at the table and to participate in conversation. Parents will be encouraged to set a good example and reward desirable behaviour. They can then encourage play experiences with new and exciting resources from the toy library

Case Study

Read the following passage and identify all the strategies that the family workers took to support Cathy in changing Fred's behaviour.

It is tea time at the family centre. Three families are attending today. Cathy is a single mother who is depressed and has a drug habit. Fred who is aged six has been excluded from lunch times at school, and Charlene, who is three has been referred by her health visitor who was concerned about her physical development. All the parents are encouraged to play with the older children whilst the younger children are read a story. Cathy and Fred are working on the computer. Fred is fooling around because he wants to play a different game. Cathy gives him a clip around the ear and says, 'If you don't behave you won't get to play with any game!'

A family worker asks Cathy to help her prepare the tea, and when she is out of the room and away from Fred she asks her why she felt she needed to hit Fred. She then suggested some different methods for resolving Fred's difficulties. Perhaps he was bored with the game she had chosen and could select his own. She suggests that perhaps Cathy hit Fred because she was frustrated with Fred's behaviour.

At tea time Fred is running round the room refusing to sit at the table. A family worker shows Cathy how to make Fred sit at the table without hurting him. She reminds Cathy that she needs to ensure Fred always sits at the table. The family worker then praises Fred for sitting still.

The other parents are now talking about the problems with their partners. A family worker quickly suggests they leave the conversation till the women's group on Wednesday, and encourages all the parents to give their attention to the children. They all start to talk about the proposed trip to the theme park. Later the families discuss the toys that they will choose from the toy library for when the family worker visits at home.

Providing feedback to parents about their parenting

Factors to consider when providing feedback to parents are outlined in the diagram below.

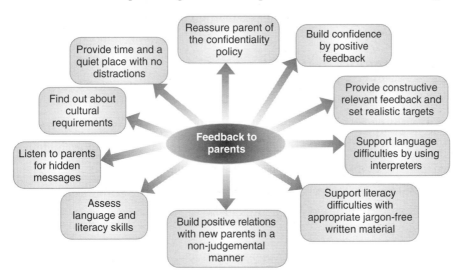

Parental responsibility

Parental responsibility is defined in the Children Act as 'all the rights, duties, powers, responsibilities and authority which by law a parent has in relation to a child and his property'. Parental responsibility covers both rights and duties. It includes the following rights:

- To give consent to medical treatment.
- To determine the child's religion.
- To choose the child's surname.

- To apply discipline.
- To give consent to marriage from the age of 16 to 18.
- To give consent before their child can be adopted.
- To appoint a guardian in the event of the death of the other parent.

It also includes the following duties:

- To look after children in a way which is not cruel or deliberately neglectful, and does not expose children to the risk of significant harm.
- To provide maintenance.
- To ensure that children of five and over receive full-time education.

Who has parental responsibility?

All mothers and married fathers
They automatically have parental responsibility for their children.

Divorced or separated married parents
Both parents, regardless of who the child lives with, retain parental responsibility.

Unmarried fathers
They do not have parental responsibility but may acquire it by formal agreement with the mother or by a court order.

Parental responsibility is very rarely lost except on adoption. Even where a care order is made parental responsibility is retained, although the local authority may limit the extent to which that responsibility is exercised. This changes the position under the old law whereby care orders extinguished parental rights and duties and has led to greater involvement of parent/carers with their children in care.

Community support networks

The challenges faced by families who are involved in abusive situations are considerable and cannot be addressed by one agency. A range of professionals with different skills and expertise will be able to work together to support the family.

Under the Children Act social services has a duty to provide services for children and families in need. The law defines 'in need' in a very broad way. It covers:

- children who are not achieving a reasonable standard of health or development
- children whose health or development is likely to be damaged
- children with disabilities.

The services provided by social services may include:
- advice, guidance and counselling
- occupational, social, cultural and leisure activities
- home help
- holiday provision
- day care provision for under-fives and specified activities after school and in the holidays for under-eights
- accommodation for children where the person caring for them has been prevented for any reason from providing accommodation or care, e.g. hospitalisation.

Voluntary and private organisations also offer services to families who are in need. The NSPCC is a voluntary organisation, which has the statutory power to remove children who are deemed to be at risk of significant harm from their homes. The NSPCC has been providing support to families in many communities for many years. Services vary widely based on the needs of the local community.

Key issues

Visit the NSPCC website and identify the role of the following organisations. Then visit the appropriate websites to identify additional facts about the organisations.

- The Children's Legal Centre
- Deafchild International
- National Association of Child Contact Centres
- Parentline Plus
- Planet One Parent
- The Samaritans
- Women's Aid

Statutory support

The following list demonstrates the roles of some of the professionals who may supervise and support families to enable them to stay together:

- social workers
- health visitors
- educational psychologists
- family workers
- child protection officers
- doctors
- probation officers
- drug and alcohol counsellors
- psychiatrists
- play therapists
- psychologists
- schools.

As part of the National Childcare Strategy, new initiatives are being created which will help to support parents and families.

Sure Start

Sure Start is a vital part of the government's anti-poverty strategy aiming to break the cycle of deprivation and give children under the age of four a 'Sure Start' in life. One of the national targets in relation to improving social and emotional development is a 20 per cent reduction of children re-registered within the space of one year on the Child Protection Register.

Neighbourhood Nurseries

Neighbourhood Nurseries offer quality child care and early education learning places in disadvantaged areas to reduce unemployment. The responsibility for setting up Neighbourhood Nurseries lies with the Early Years Development and Childcare Partnerships. Neighbourhood Nurseries will be expected to work with other services available to families.

Assessment activity 5.2

1   Working in a small group, research a voluntary organisation such as the NSPCC, Barnardos or Kidscape and prepare a presentation for the rest of your group. Address the following points, and present your findings to the rest of the group:

   * the history of the organisation
   * the aims and objectives
   * the main areas of work
   * funding issues
   * local contacts
   * the role of the organisation in offering joint services with local authorities.

2   Re-read the case study about Cathy and her family on page 172 and answer the following questions:

   * Describe a range of methods available to early years practitioners to support Cathy and her family.
   * Identify a variety of community support networks which may support the family and describe the help that they can provide.
   * Describe the benefits of interprofessional working for Cathy and her children.

Strategies for supporting children and their families

Supporting children who disclose

In any early years setting, there may come a time when a child tells you that they are being abused or have been abused. This is known as **disclosure**. Indirect disclosure is when the child identifies abuse through their play. For example, they may demonstrate a knowledge of abuse while playing in the home corner, or make comments during a painting activity. In a direct disclosure situation you must ensure that you give them your full attention. The child obviously feels they can trust you and you must not betray this trust. You may feel shocked by what the child tells you, but you must remain calm and not allow your own feelings to show, as this may affect what information the child then shares. Below is a list of do's and donts' when dealing with disclosure and responding to the child.

Do	Don't
Listen to the child calmly Tell the child they were right to tell you Believe them Tell the child that what has happened is not their fault or responsibility Acknowledge that they have been brave to tell you Reassure the child, telling them that their situation is not unique Be honest about your own position, who you will have to tell and why	Make promises that you cannot keep, such as keeping 'secrets' Ask the child lots of questions – investigation of the alleged abuse will be undertaken by a trained social worker Cast doubt on what the child tells you. It has taken a great deal of courage for them to tell you Say anything which may make the child feel responsible for the abuse, e.g. Why haven't you told anyone before?

Do	Don't
Keep the child fully informed about what you are doing and what is happening at every stage	Communicate feelings of anger
	Ask leading questions, e.g. Was it your mummy that hurt you?
Give the child information about other confidential sources of help, e.g. Childline	Panic. When confronted with the reality of abuse there is often a feeling of needing to 'act immediately'. Action taken too hastily can be counter-productive

Once the child has divulged this information it is your responsibility to record what has been said as soon as you can after the event and report it to your supervisor/line manager. When recording the event it is important to give a factual account stating what the child said as clearly as you can remember. Do not make assumptions about the child's feelings or about the truth of what the child has told you. The good practice guidelines for observations and reporting should be followed. It is also important that you tell the child that they can come back and discuss it further if they wish.

Why children do not disclose

You can understand children's reluctance to talk about their abuse if you consider the following:

- Very young children may not possess the language skills to tell you.
- The abusing adult may threaten the child physically or emotionally to keep the secret.
- Some children may think it is normal if they have never experienced anything else.
- Children may be afraid that adults will not believe them.
- Children may feel that it is their fault.

Dealing with your own emotional reaction

Responding to a child's disclosure can be a very distressing experience and may make you feel angry and upset. It is therefore important that you discuss your feelings with your line manager who will be able to support you. You must not discuss the situation with other members of staff, or friends or family outside the setting. It is also important that you do not let your personal feelings interfere with your relationship with the family.

Potential impact of disclosure on the child and the family

Disclosure may result in the following:

- The provision of services to support the family and enable the child to remain at home.
- The abusing parent may be asked to leave the family home.
- The child may be removed to place of safety.
- Break up of the family structure.

If the abuser comes from outside the direct family circle such as an uncle or baby sitter, additional pressures relating to the wider community will be apparent.

Any of these situations will make the family feel very threatened. Parents may be angry because the setting has raised concerns. The initial shock may be hard to take in and promote a feeling of disbelief. The shock is quickly followed by anger. This anger may be directed at the setting, the child or the partner.

There may often be feelings of guilt, as the non-abusing parent worries about their inability to protect their child and the abusing parent may be guilty about what they have done. The abusing parent, however, may feel that the complaint is unjustified, 'I was only disciplining the child'. There will also be a feeling of shame and embarrassment that the situation may become public. The child will also experience feelings of guilt and feel responsible for the family situation. This is particularly relevant if the abusing parent has issued threats about secrecy during the abuse.

Communication

All human interactions involve communication, and many difficulties or conflicts may arise from failure to communicate effectively. Situations relating to abuse and the challenging of a parent's basic care of their child are very sensitive and as such require particularly sophisticated communication skills. For this reason, direct work with children and families who are in abusive situations will be undertaken by specially trained professionals. However, it is important that you develop an understanding of essential communication skills. Much of this communication may be non-verbal, requiring careful observation to accurately interpret the messages being sent, especially emotions or feelings, e.g. through facial expression, gestures, body posture, lack of eye contact or tone of voice.

Good communication firstly involves establishing and maintaining a good working relationship with the child and parent.

Communicating with parents

Communication involves various elements outlined in the diagram below.

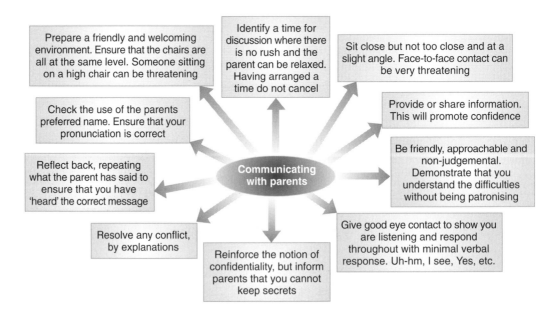

Barriers to communication

There are many barriers to effective communication. The table below identifies some of these and suggests some possible action that can be taken to promote quality communication.

Barriers	Reasons	Actions
The early years worker may not be listening effectively	They may be hearing what they want to hear rather than what is intended	Listen carefully, do not pre-judge, reflect back to the parent or child to confirm what has been said
The parent may be reluctant to speak	They may be apprehensive about the effects of what they will say on the early years worker's opinion of them. They may not trust the professionals	Initiating good relationships by reinforcing the non-judgemental approach. Reflecting back positively Gaining the trust of the parent by valuing their role
Language barrier	The parent may use English as an additional language, and therefore feel under extra pressure	Provide a family member or interpreter. Check with the parent for the preferred choice Confirm your understanding of the difficulties they may have relating to the language barrier Take additional time
Hearing difficulty	A parent with a hearing difficulty	Provide a signer

Think It Over

Read the account of the family workshop session outlined below and answer the following questions.

- Identify areas of good or bad practice in relation to communicating with the families. Give reasons for your choices
- Describe how the factors you have identified will affect the relationships between the parent and the carers.

Family workshop session: Three families who have been in abusive situations are attending. It has been a very stressful day, the staff are running late and have not managed to prepare the room. It is Mrs Patel's first day. Jo greets her at the door with a welcoming smile: 'Hello, it is Mrs Patel isn't it? Come in, it is good to see you'. Jo uses hand gestures to encourage Mrs Patel to sit on a chair in the entrance and then asks one of the students to go and get Feroza who is going to interpret and work with Mrs Patel who has limited use of English.

At the same time Hayley arrives with her son Robert. Shirley, who is Hayley's family worker, comes into the hall and says, 'So you've turned up today. We thought you had left town. You know you are expected to come every Wednesday; this is not good enough. Why have you missed the last two weeks without letting us know?' Hayley begins to reply, 'I have not been well' and Shirley interrupts her to say 'You tell me that every time and it is not good enough!'

By now Robert is throwing the leaflets from the display stand all over the floor so Shirley gathers them up and they all go into the family room where Mandy has just finished setting out the resources and settling Zareena and her son Zuber with the play dough.

A little later Feroza brings Mrs Patel and Anisa to the dough table so Mandy is able to take Zareena into the parents room. She has arranged two low chairs at an angle with a low table with a box of tissues on it. She asks Zareena how she has been getting on and then tells her some positive comments from a conversation she has had with the health visitor following a home visit. They then discuss the difficulties Zareena has been having. Mandy repeats her comments, often adding supporting statements.

Communicating with children

Remember to ensure that your communication with children is age appropriate. Your experience of working with children will be your guide.

- Use age-appropriate language.
- Check vocabulary and ensure that the child understands.
- Use pictures or drawings with younger children.
- Communicate at the child's pace; do not force the subject.
- Play therapists may use anatomically correct dolls to promote conversation.
- Do not lead the child.
- Employ effective listening.
- Work at the child's level; ensure good eye contact.

Children's rights and parents' rights and responsibilities

Parents' *rights* have been changed to *responsibilities* under the Children Act and the new concept of 'parental responsibility' (see page 174 for definition). This means that children are no longer seen as possessions of their parents, therefore parents no longer have 'absolute rights' for their children. The mother and married parents never lose parental responsibility (unless the child is adopted) or when the child is taken into care on a care order, and then parental responsibility is 'shared'.

Parents have the right to appeal against any court decisions; the right to contact with their child whatever the circumstances and providing the child is in agreement (pending age and stage of development); and the right to be involved in their child's upbringing whilst they are subject to a care order.

Children's rights have become increasingly important and grown from the Children Act 1989 and the United Nations Convention on the Rights of the Child. The table below shows some of the European and national rights of children.

Children Act 1989	United Nations Convention on the Rights of the Child
The wishes and feelings of the child must be taken into consideration	Right to non-discrimination
	Right to have best interests as a primary consideration
The right to be brought up within their own families wherever possible	Right to an identity
	Rights when separated from parents
The right to decline medical treatment (Gillick v. West Norfolk Health Authority)	Right to express views and opinions
	Right to freedom of thought, conscience and religion

Children Act 1989	United Nations Convention on the Rights of the Child
The right to adequate/appropriate services	Right to protection from abuse and neglect Rights of disabled children Rights to an adequate standard of living Right to an education Rights of children from minority ethnic communities

Theory into practice

Research the case Gillick v. West Norfolk Health Authority, whereby a parent took a health authority to court because they had prescribed her daughter (who was under 16) with the contraceptive pill.

- What were the outcomes of this case?
- What implication does this have on children and young people in respect of their rights?

The table below outlines children's and parents' rights during an investigation of abuse.

Children's rights	Parents' rights
To have their views and wishes taken into consideration To be kept informed To be listened to To have their own solicitor in court if action is taken	To be informed about any concerns others may have about their child To be told what action is being taken to deal with the concerns To have their views expressed at case conferences, so long as it does not remove the focus from the needs of the child

Empowering children to exercise their rights

The following diagram outlines the skills that a child requires to enable them to exercise their rights.

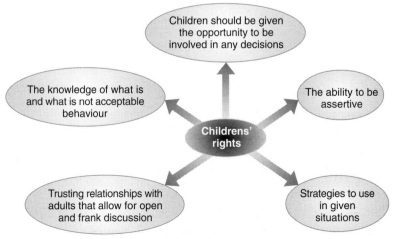

Alleviating the effects of abuse

Once a child has disclosed that they are or have been abused, or you have observed indicators of abuse and referred to social services, your work with that child is just beginning. Below is a list of suggestions which may help with the after-effects of abuse:

- Consult other professionals for advice.
- Always be willing to listen to the child should they wish to talk further about the abuse, but do not question the child.
- Always continue to reassure the child (as at disclosure), stressing that they are not to blame.
- Meet the child's individual needs. Remember many children who have been abused display challenging behaviour.
- Provide appropriate play experiences to allow the child to explore feelings and promote self-image and self-esteem.

Play experiences

The child may be referred to a play therapist whose role is to help children express trauma or emotions through play. You should **not** undertake play therapy experiences yourself unless you are working directly with a play therapist. You will however be able to offer a range of different play experiences, which will support all children's emotional and social development. The table below identifies some of these.

Child's needs	Play activities
Expressing their feelings	Appropriate books dealing with issues such as bullying, or moving into foster care Dough, clay and malleable materials where children can give vent to powerful feelings Sand, water and messy play activities Happy/sad faces drawing activities to allow the children to give words to their feelings Self-portrait activities with sensitive non-questioning discussion Expressing feeling through music and dance Opportunities to explore feelings through role play activities Controlled noise making activities such as banging a drum, shouting out loud, etc. Puppets and doll play where children can describe feelings
Improving self-image	Body image activities such as self-portraits, use of mirrors, etc. Dressing up with mirrors and supportive discussion Books and stories such as 'Little duck and the bad eye glasses' Circle time and discussion about objects from home Create 'A book about me' Invite parents from different cultural groups to the setting to share cooking or clothing experiences
Building self-esteem	Positive feedback during all interactions Dressing up activities to develop independence skills Provide tasks and responsibilities, e.g. handing out biscuits, feeding the animals, looking after younger children

Theory into practice

Plan an activity to enable a group of children to explore feelings or improve self-image. Include the following:

- The aim of the activity.
- The age of child you will work with.
- The adult/child ratio.
- The resources you intend to use.
- Any safety issues.
- Describe your planning identifying some of the conversation or language you may promote.
- Provide a description of the activity.
- Evaluate your activity in relation to meeting your aim.

The role of family centres

Family centres are often jointly funded by social services education and health departments. Their role is to provide a multidisciplinary approach to meeting the needs of children and parents. Family centres facilitate communication between the many agencies who may be working with one family. In addition to the professionals described on page 175, the following people may also work with children and families who are or have been in abusive situations.

Play therapists: children are encouraged to play with puppets and dolls, etc., including anatomically correct dolls (life-like), whereby they demonstrate or 'act out' what has happened to them.

Family therapists: children along with their parents and siblings attend family therapy sessions which look at how to improve relationships and family dynamics.

Counsellors: will provide one-to-one support for either the child or parent.

Guardian *ad litem*: appointed by the court to represent the child's best interests and wishes.

Home visiting

The role of home visiting is as follows:

- To support the family.
- To avoid the need for the child to be taken into public care.
- To provide a realistic environment where the carer can work with the family, for example in the kitchen at mealtimes.
- To enable the professional to address 'real' issues, such as the provision of fireguards and safety factors.
- May seem less threatening for a family than a public visit to a centre. However, it may seem more threatening as some parents are apprehensive about a professional seeing their living conditions, particularly if they are very undesirable.

The following table identifies some of the professionals who visit families at home and describes their area of work.

Childcare professional	Role and function
Health visitor	May visit weekly, particularly in 'failure to thrive' situations Will provide support and advice about diet, health and safety Will provide support and advice to the adult about issues of their health
Family worker	May visit as required May visit to get children out of bed, fed and out to school May support the main carer in case of disability Will work with the parents to promote play activities To support meal times To promote positive behaviour Collect older children from school and take them home, sometimes supporting bed time routines Take families on outings, for shopping or for hospital appointments
Social worker	If the child is on the Child Protection Register the social worker will visit on a regular basis To ensure that the requirements of the case conferences are being adhered to To provide support for the family and help them to access additional help if required
Psychiatric nurses	May visit the home if required
Probation officer	May visit the home if necessary
Homestart volunteers	May provide practical support acting as a friend, e.g. shopping or looking after a child
Environmental health department	The department may be involved in cleaning up seriously dirty households

Co-operation with other professionals

The Children Act 1989 makes it a legal requirement that the different agencies work together for the well being of children. We have already examined the roles and responsibilities of the many professionals who may work with children and families. The diagram on page 185 identifies issues of good practice for multidiscliplinary working.

Confidentiality

Confidentiality is vital whilst working with parents in abusive situations. Issues must only be discussed with colleagues on a 'need to know' basis. It is also important that parents are aware of the boundaries that confidentiality brings; for example, they may wish to confide in you about an issue relating to the abuse. Although you may have built up a good working relationship with the parent, you are never in a position to continue the 'secret' and must always pass information of this nature onto your supervisor/line manger, remembering to record all the details. Your line manager in turn will make the decision about referring the information to other professionals.

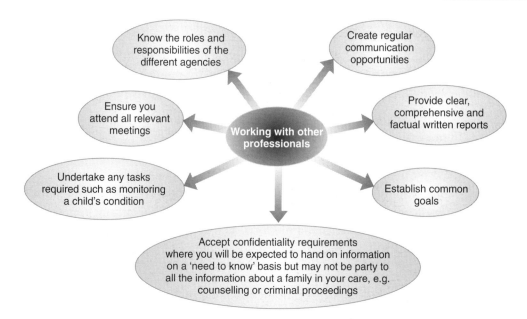

Alternative forms of care

If, due to child abuse and neglect, a child has to be removed from the family home, they will be placed in foster care or in a children's home. Fostering, however, is seen as a good alternative to residential care in that:

- it can provide a family environment
- it can be used for short or long-term placements
- it avoids children becoming institutionalised
- it enables children who have been abused, and as a result possibly experiencing behavioural problems, the opportunity to experience family life.

Residential establishments for children are mainly provided by local authorities. However, voluntary organisations such as Barnardos and the NCH also provide this service. There has also been an increase in privately run children's homes. These establishments consist of small family group homes, community homes and resource and reception centres.

Adoption is seen as another alternative to a child growing up in an abusive situation. This is governed by the Adoption Act 1976 and the Children Act 1989 and is a legal undertaking with all the responsibilities of caring for a natural child. As mentioned previously, with adoption, the birth parents lose parental responsibility, which is automatically given to the adoptive parents once the adoption certificate is processed.

Respite care can also be advantageous for children who have been abused or neglected. Residential care is given to a child for a short period only, giving the parent and child the opportunity for some 'time out'.

Assessment activity 5.3

Read the case studies and answer the relevant questions.

- Identify the type of abuse that has taken place.
- Give reasons for your answer.
- Describe what initial steps you will take to protect the children.

- Describe the effects of this child's disclosure on the family.
- Identify the parents' and the child's rights during any investigation.
- Identify the professionals who may provide additional support for the parent.
- Describe a range of strategies you can use to support the child.

Case study 1: One Tuesday morning Ben came into nursery with a large red bump on his head. 'Oh my goodness, what have you done?' said Julie. 'I fell off my bike' Ben replied. Julie noticed that the tips of Ben's ears were also rather bruised. Ben ran off to play. Later in the morning while Ben was sitting at the dough table bashing and thumping a large lump of dough, Julie went to sit with him and talk about what he was making. Shortly afterwards, quite casually Ben said 'I didn't fall off my bike you know, Mum pulled my ears and banged my head against the fireplace'. 'I will have to ask your Mum about this' Julie replied. 'Please don't tell her, she will be mad' says Ben.

Case study 2: Sam used to live with her mother and had no contact with her father who is a heroin addict. Sam is four years old and has been attending your establishment since she was two years old. Recently her mother died, and Sam was placed into the care of her father. Within weeks of this, Sam began to lose confidence and self-esteem. She would no longer join in any of the activities and mix with the other children. She has recently stated to you that she is left on her own a lot at home and sometimes her daddy does not return at all.

Good practice in early years settings

Good practice within any early years setting involves working as part of a team, both within the setting and in respect of other professionals. This section enables you to explore specific issues of good practice related to protecting children.

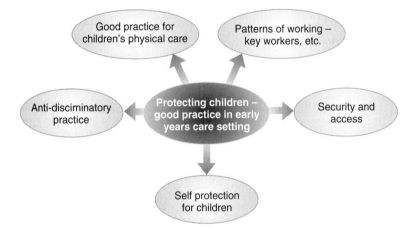

Good practice with children
Physical care
You will have already developed many skills to support you in your work with young children. The following table identifies some specific issues related to children's physical care and child protection.

Promoting good practice	Examples of practical experiences
Appropriate physical care enables children to have respect for their body and to learn about the personal control they should have over their own body and what their personal boundaries are	Providing privacy during toileting Respecting privacy when dressing Encouraging independence in physical care routines such as bathing, feeding, toileting Promoting discrete behaviour such as not pulling your trousers down in public Drawing activities where the children can discuss: • who has the right to touch your body, e.g. doctors • what parts of the body should not be touched by others, i.e. areas covered by swimwear
Appropriate physical care enables a child to learn about their body	Younger children learn body part vocabulary Age appropriate discussion about bodily functions
Appropriate physical care gives young children the opportunity for individual attention and appropriate affectionate touch which will enable them to recognise inappropriate touches	The cuddles a baby receives during nappy changing The physical touch during dressing activities The appropriate bed time routine with bathing, story and cuddle
Appropriate physical care enables a child to develop good self-image and self-esteem	Demonstrating respect during physical care activities, explaining to the child what you are doing; 'We are going to take your socks off now' rather than just pulling the socks off Positive comments during dressing activities can promote self-image
Appropriate physical care demonstrates how adults should behave towards children	Appropriate support for toileting and bathing

Affection

All children need physical demonstrations of affection. They need to experience appropriate touches during respectful contact. If they do not have experience of appropriate affection, they will not be able to judge what is inappropriate. Similarly a child who has limited experience of physical affection may be so desperate for affection that they accept inappropriate advances from adults. For this reason it is important to role model appropriate expressions of affection.

All children are different and all families have different ways of demonstrating affection. It is wrong to demand expressions of affection such as sitting on your knee or being kissed if the child does not offer spontaneously. Some children who crave affection may approach any new adult in the setting with overt physical attention. They may want to hold your hand, sit on your knee and always be physically close. For many new students in placement this message can be misunderstood and it is important that in this situation you do not promote unnecessary physical contact and maintain a professional approach to all children.

Communication

This section enables you to explore good practice in communication, specifically in relation to issues of child protection.

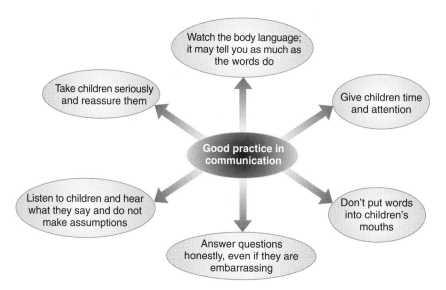

Patterns of working

Following the introduction of the Early Years Curriculum, the concept of key workers is now firmly established within early years care and education settings. However, for many years, settings which provided for children's care have been operating key worker systems. Advantages of a key worker system are as follows:

- The key worker becomes a familiar figure for the child.
- The parent has one specific individual to communicate with.
- The key worker can build up a meaningful relationship with the family.
- The key worker can monitor and record progress and details of the child's care.
- Greater knowledge of the family situation will make the key worker more responsive to individual needs.
- When representing the family at meetings with other professionals the close relationship and knowledge of the individual family is an asset.
- It provides consistency of care which is of particular advantage for a child who is experiencing a traumatic period in their life.

Anti-discriminatory practice

You will have developed a good understanding of anti-discriminatory practice in Unit 1. However, there are some issues which relate specifically to issues of child protection.

It is important that early years practitioners have an awareness of the different cultures and social status within our society and are not judgemental anyway. You must never be critical of another person's way of doing things, just because you don't view it as the 'norm'. For example, a child who is allowed to stay up in the evenings until the parents go to bed may not meet your views about the amount of sleep a child needs, but does not consider the additional adult attention the child may gain during this period. Here are some issues to consider with regard to child protection:

- Don't assume that a family from a particular background is more or less likely to abuse their children.
- Ensure that children and parents for whom English is an additional language use their preferred interpreter and access all the information they may need.
- Promote anti-discriminatory practice with the children. Challenge inappropriate behaviour.

Security of and access to the premises

Children's safety within the early years setting is just as important as their safety at home. It is therefore important to ensure that children do not leave the premises alone or that unknown visitors are not free to come and go as they please. There have been some disturbing incidents in settings where children are cared for and this has raised awareness of the need for increased security in early years settings.

It is important to find a balance between security and a welcoming environment. If simple procedures such as those outlined in the diagram below are explained to parents, they may welcome the concept of safety within your setting. For example, a family where there is a custody issue will be grateful for these procedures.

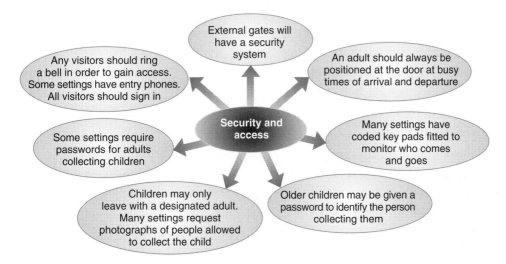

Theory into practice

Write a report detailing the security procedures in your current workplace. You must consider all the aspects identified above. Compare your report with others and identify any differences in how settings manage security. You may find that a primary school, a nursery, a family centre and pre-school may have different procedures.

Dealing with unwanted visitors and raising the alarm

Dealing with unwanted visitors may not be a regular aspect of your work with children. However, some settings that are sited in areas of high deprivation, or where the families attending present with challenging problems, may experience unwanted visitors. Strategies for dealing with unwanted visitors include the following:

- Initially you will not have allowed an unwanted visitor into the premises.
- Ask the person to leave the premises.
- Explain the consequences of not leaving the premises, i.e. we may call the police.
- Stay calm.
- Remove the children to a place of safety if required.
- Do not become involved in confrontation or argument.
- If your safety is threatened call the police.

Many settings that experience these problems may have alarms and panic buttons fitted within the centre, and staff attending home visits will do so in pairs and will carry panic alarms.

Teaching children self-protection

The most important aspect of self-protection is the promotion of children's confidence and self-esteem. However, there are many other ways that early years practitioners can empower children to protect themselves. This can be achieved by giving them information, promoting awareness and encouraging coping skills. You can teach children:

- the difference between good and bad touches
- to say 'No!' to adults that they know as well as to strangers
- the difference between good and bad 'secrets'
- that their body belongs to them
- that they have a right to privacy
- ways of coping with bullying
- how to get help.

The following table identifies specific strategies that can be introduced to enable children to protect themselves. It is important to remember that children should not be made to feel totally responsible for their own protection, as in reality the adults who care for them are ultimately responsible.

Concept	Strategies
Good and bad touches Children should be able to identify good and bad touches. Touches that hurt, are rude or make them feel uncomfortable are not acceptable	Promote through appropriate daily physical care routines Support children who say 'No' to tickling games, hugs or kisses For older children, discussions such as 'I like hugs from... I would not like a hug from...'
To say 'No!' to adults they know as well as to strangers While it is important to promote the concept of 'stranger danger', more children are at risk from adults that they know well	Role play Books and videos, i.e. NSPCC 'Emily and the Stranger' or Rolf Harris 'Say No' video Visits from a police officer Discussion about people you trust
Good and bad secrets You can provide opportunities for children to discuss good and bad secrets	Discussion about good and bad secrets. No one should ever ask children to keep a hug, touch or smack secret, e.g. 'Don't tell Mummy what we have bought for her

Concept	Strategies
	birthday' = good secret 'Don't tell Mummy that I hit you' = bad secret
That their body belongs to them Children should be encouraged to know that their body belongs to them and that they have control over what happens to it	Young children can be helped by learning body vocabulary Songs such as 'Head, shoulders, knees and toes...' Books such as *My first body book* (Early Learning Centre) Appropriate physical care routines Draw a picture of a body and discuss which parts of the body are the 'private' parts Body 'beetle game'
That they have the right to privacy Children have the right to their own privacy	Physical care routines (see page 187)
Getting help There are some situations where children can help themselves by getting help	Children should be taught their address and phone number in case they get lost Learning about which adults they can go to for help, e.g. the police, the person at the shop till, a lollipop lady, a mother with a pram or school teacher Visits from a police officer Shouting 'No!'

Theory into practice

Make a game and plan an activity for children to develop body awareness. Include the following:

- The aim of the activity.
- The age of children you will work with.
- The adult/child ratio.
- The resources you intend to use.
- Any safety issues.
- Describe your planning identifying some of the language or conversation you may promote.
- Provide a description of the activity.
- Evaluate your activity in relation to meeting your aim.

Coping with bullying

While we often assume that adults are responsible for creating abusive situations, for many children bullying is a difficult aspect of their lives. Bullying can happen within family circles but is also common in schools, clubs and on the streets. Bullying can take many forms and what appear to be minor events to adults when extended over a period of time can make children very miserable and frightened.

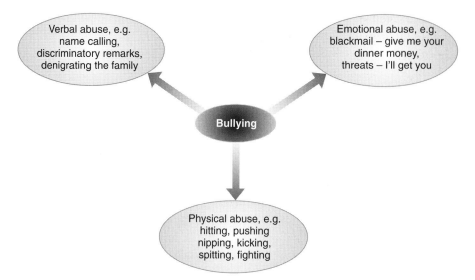

Theory into practice

Design a leaflet or poster that you could give to children aged 5–7 to promote anti-bullying strategies. It should be colourful, include pictures and be easy to understand in age-appropriate language.

Key issues

Research the history, aims and objectives of Kidscape. Investigate the range of resources provided by the organisation and identify how they can be used to help children protect themselves.

Child protection policy

All early years settings must have a number of policies which outline procedures workers must follow in particular situations, e.g. health and safety, anti-bullying. They must also have a child protection policy which contains information about what to do if you suspect that a child in your care is being abused or neglected. These procedures should be written in a format that is easy to read for early years workers, volunteers and parents. It is important that they are reviewed regularly, keeping abreast of any local and national changes in policy and law.

Standard 13 of the National Standards for Under Eights Day Care and Childminding – Full Day Care states:

> 'The registered person has a written statement based on the ACPC procedures clearly stating staff responsibilities with regard to reporting of suspected child abuse or neglect, including contact names and telephone numbers. It also includes procedures to be followed in the event of an allegation being made against a member of staff or volunteer.'

The Standards also state that there must be a designated member of staff who is responsible for liaison with child protection agencies in any child protection situation. The guidance to the National Standards – Full Day Care provides the following advice to help settings prepare their child protection policy:

- Your commitment to the protection of children.
- The responsibilities of all staff in child protection matters.
- The steps to be taken when a concern is raised.
- The name of the designated member of staff for child protection liaison and their role and responsibilities.
- How and under what circumstances parents will be informed about concerns and any actions taken, and how confidentiality will be managed.

The guidance in relation to allegations made against a member of staff could include:

- the action to be taken with regard to the member of staff
- who should be informed
- how any investigation will be conducted and by whom
- how confidentiality will be managed.

Settings will also include statements about training opportunities, and the need to share the policy with all parents. An example of a child protection policy is shown below.

Child Protection Policy

Happy Days Nursery aims to provide an environment where children are safe from abuse and where any suspicion of abuse is promptly and appropriately responded to. In order to achieve this we will:

- Ensure that all staff have police clearance prior to the onset of employment
- Require at least one reference which will always be followed up. Doubts regarding previous employment or gaps in employment should be clearly explained
- Require all appointments to be subject to a probationary period
- Ensure that all staff are trained in the identification of signs and symptoms of possible abuse
- Be vigilant when undertaking everyday routines to allow for observation of the children
- Refer any suspicions to the manager who will then take the decision as to whether further investigation is needed
- Ensure that all matters in relation to any child protection issue will be treated according to the Confidentiality Policy of the setting
- Ensure that all parents will be made aware of the Child Protection Policy when their children first enter the nursery
- Ensure that parents will be informed of any changes noticed in behaviour or appearance of their child
- Contact with social services or the NSPCC will be at the discretion of the manager
- Recognise the expertise of professional statutory and voluntary organisations and will endeavour to work closely with them should the need arise
- Comply with the local ACPC procedures. The file is kept in the manager's office and can be examined at any time
- Allegations of abuse against staff members/volunteers will be investigated immediately and relevant staff members will be suspended from their posts until investigations are complete. The manager will inform the Area Child Protection Team who will undertake the necessary investigations. Persons found to be guilty of abuse of any nature will be referred to the appropriate agency. Support will be given to staff who may be the subject of wrongful allegations

Child Protection Officer – The Manager

Theory into practice

Examine the child protection policy at your current workplace to identify the factors described in the list above.

Record keeping

Early years settings all have their own procedures for recording issues relating to child protection. Any suspicions of abuse or instances of disclosure will be recorded in the accident report book (see page 122).

Staff who are working directly with a family in relation to issues of concern maintain a contact sheet which provides details of all contact with the family.

While record keeping is an important aspect of the care and education of all children, recording issues relating to child protection have particular importance. Any decisions that are made for a family may rely on the evidence gathered within the child's individual record. For this reason it is important that all recording is:

- completed as soon after the incident as possible
- factual
- relevant
- detailed
- clearly written
- free from opinion.

Gathering information

When reporting information relating to individual children it is important to distinguish between directly observed evidence and evidence that someone else has told you. Second-hand stories may not actually be true, or they may have someone else's interpretation which is quite misleading. For example, the statement from a concerned neighbour that 'It's a terrible house, the children are screaming all night', may simply mean that there is a new baby in the house who cries all evening, or it may mean that children are being abused. As an early years practitioner you need to be able to identify relevant information that is directly observed, factual and relevant.

Think It Over

During a staff meeting at Happy Days Nursery the following information about Irfan is discussed. The staff say they are fed up with him, he is getting far too wild and destructive and is setting a bad example to the younger children. Irfan's neighbour has told one of the members of staff who lives in the next street that Irfan's father often hits the children. The incident book records show that Irfan had a bump on his head last week which his mother said was caused by him running into a door. His mother tells the manager that Irfan's elder brother who has been attending hospital for some time has leukaemia.

- Identify the relevant information in this passage. Do you think that Irfan is being abused? Give reasons for your answers.
- Share your decisions with a friend and compare answers.

Confidentiality and security of records

In early years settings children's records are always shared with the parents. However, when a family is receiving specific support in relation to issues of child protection there will be an additional section within a child's file for the storage of confidential records which will be clearly marked as confidential.

Whilst records relating to child protection may be available to the parents, only the manager, or key worker would access these records – they would not automatically be available for all members of staff. The diagram below provides guidelines for the storage of records.

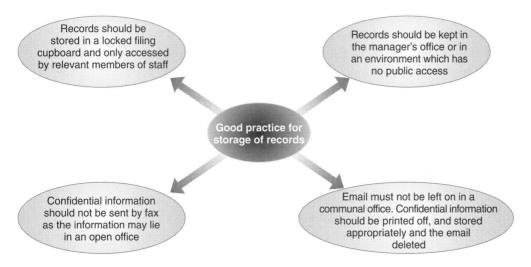

Records should be stored in a locked filing cupboard and only accessed by relevant members of staff

Records should be kept in the manager's office or in an environment which has no public access

Good practice for storage of records

Confidential information should not be sent by fax as the information may lie in an open office

Email must not be left on in a communal office. Confidential information should be printed off, and stored appropriately and the email deleted

---

Assessment activity 5.4

1 You are asked to create a child protection policy for Happy Days Nursery. Ensure you address all the issues required in the National Standards.
2 Discuss the importance of teaching children self-protection. Describe a range of strategies you could use with a group of four-year-olds and a group of seven-year-olds.

End-of-unit test

1 Name the four main types of child abuse. Provide a definition of neglect. List four indicators of emotional abuse.

2 List four types of family structures.

3 When considering pre-disposing factors related to child abuse, list five factors that may make a parent more likely to abuse a child in their care and three factors that may make a child more vulnerable to abuse.

4 Name the four main theories in relation to abuse. Provide a brief description of each.

5 Sandy lives with her four children in a damp, run-down terraced house. She has not worked since she left school. When the family worker first visited the house there was animal excrement in all the rooms, the children slept on uncovered wet mattresses and the pile of rubbish in the garden was higher than the window sills. There was no heating in the house and two of the children had bad asthma.

- Identify the theoretical model of abuse within this case study.
- List the consequences of abuse for the children in this family.

6 State the five main principles of the Children Act and identify how effective these are to child protection.

7 Briefly describe what a care order is.

8 Define parental responsibility.

9 Sajid was seven years old when he came to the attention of social services. He lived with his mother and father and fourteen-year-old brother in a very run-down terraced house. He slept on a mattress in one of the downstairs rooms and rodents have been seen to be nibbling at his toes. Most of his food consisted of 'takeaways' and fast food and as a result he was very underweight and small in size for his age. You have been asked by Sajid's social worker if he can attend your nursery, as he is underdeveloped in all areas. The social worker has told you that the parents are somewhat reluctant to work with social services, as they are worried that they will take Sajid into care.

- How can you support Sadjid's mother as he settles into the nursery?
- What additional professional services may support Sajid's mother?
- What additional community resources can support Sajid's mother?

10 Why are children often afraid to tell that they have been abused?

11 List the techniques you should use when responding to a child's disclosure.

12 Describe the effects on the family following a child's disclosure that the father has been abusing her.

13 Describe three activities you could share with a five-year-old child to promote self-protection.

14 Why does an early years setting need to have a child protection policy? State how the policy affects daily practice.

15 List four factors that provide security in an early years setting.

References and further reading

Brown, A and Finkelhor, D. (1986), 'Impact of child sexual abuse: a review of research', *Psychological Bulletin*, vol 99, pp. 66–77

Bruce, T. and Meggitt, C. (1999), *Childcare and Education* (2nd Edition), London: Hodder and Stoughton

Finkelhor, D. (1984), *Child Sexual Abuse: New Theory and Research*, New Jersey: Prentice Hall

Framework for the Assessment of Children in Need and their Families (1999), London: The Stationery Office

Full Day Care Guidance to the National Standards (2001) DFES

Herbert, M. (1996), *Working with Children and the Children Act*, Leicester: BPS Books

Hobbart and Frankel (1998), *Good Practice in Child Protection*, Cheltenham: Nelson Thornes

Kemp, C. *et al* (1962), 'The Battered Child Syndrome', *Journal of American Medical Association*, vol 181, pp. 17–24

Kempe, R. and Kempe, C. (1978), *Child Abuse*, London: Fontana

Lindon, J. (1998), *Child Protection and Early Years Work*, London: Hodder and Stoughton

National Standards for Under Eights Day Care and Childminding – Full Day Care (2001) DFES

O'Hagan and Smith (1993), *Special Issues in Child Care*, Bailliere Tindall

Reder, P. et al. (1999), *Beyond Blame: Child Abuse Tragedies Revisited*, London: Routledge

Tassoni, P. and Bulman, K. (1999), *Early Years Care and Education NVQ 3*, Oxford: Heinemann

Working Together to Safeguard Children (1999), London: The Stationery Office

Resources for children

Emily and the Stranger, NSPCC

Elliott, M. (1998), *Feeling Happy, Feeling Safe*, London: Hodder and Stoughton (colour picture book for ages 3–7)

Jody and the Biscuit Bully, NSPCC

Videos

Cosmo and Dibs Keep Safe, Kidscape and BBC (for children aged 3–6, teaching notes included)

Useful websites

Barnado's – www.barnardos.org.uk

Bullying Online – www.bullying.co.uk

Childline – www.childline.org.uk

Children's Legal Centre – www.essex.ac.uk/clc

Children's Society – www.the-childrens-society.org.uk

Deafchild International – www.deafchild.org

Gingerbread – www.gingerbread.org.uk

Kidscape – www.kidscape.org.uk

National Association of Child Contact Centres – www.nacc.org.uk

National Children's Bureau – www.ncb.org.uk

NCH – www.nch.org.uk

Parentline Plus – www.parentlineplus.org.uk

Planet One Parent – www.planetoneparent.com

Women's Aid – www.womensaid.org.uk

Professional practice

This unit will help you to look at your own skills in the care of children in the early years and to focus on what you need to work effectively as an early years professional.

Introduction

All child care and early years practitioners have to learn to care for children as individuals, learning how to observe them and respond to their needs. When you are working with young children you will need to behave as a professional carer, promoting equality of opportunity to all the children and adults you work with, whether they are other professionals, parents or adults with whom you come into contact.

What you need to learn
- What is professional practice?
- Policies and procedures
- Expectations of a professional carer
- Professional relationships: supporting children, their families and carers

What is professional practice?

You will learn how to make sure the children are safe, understand the issues around child protection and how to deal with emergency situations. As well as encouraging each child's development through providing a stimulating learning environment, you will learn to look at your own development, evaluating your progress and setting targets for the future. You will also need to understand the requirements of employers and the demands of working with colleagues as a professional.

This unit links with many of the others so that you can use all your knowledge and the skills you have acquired in a professional working environment. Throughout the course of achieving your qualification, you will have the opportunity to work in a range of settings.

This means that you will have the chance to look at both the differences and similarities between working with children of different ages, with different needs and in different settings. All of this experience will help you to become clear about the area of early years practice which is right for you. You will need to use the experiences from your workplace to achieve the assessments for this unit; the assessment is based on you being able to demonstrate your skills and abilities as a professional early years worker. You cannot achieve this unit by writing about caring for children – you must be able to show that you can do the job.

Observing and identifying the individual needs of the child

The first section of this unit considers how you observe and identify the individual needs of the child appropriate to the requirements of the setting. Working with children from birth to eight years of age, you will find out how rapidly children develop and how different they all are. Each child is an individual and this shows from a very young age. Even when babies seem the same, or very similar, for example children who are twins, they can be very different and their parents and carers can tell them apart very quickly, often by their behaviour rather than their appearance.

Observing children is one of the most important skills the early years practitioner develops; observation is a professional skill and an important tool for assessing children. This is different from watching people, particularly young children, which is always fascinating. Watching children and using the information you notice is also an essential part of becoming a professional; being observant is a key skill of good communication.

Think It Over
Think about two children that you know or have seen, that are about the same age.

- Make some notes on what is the same and what is different about them
- If you can, compare notes with someone in your group or class
- Keep your notes so that you can use them later.

Individual needs of children

Understanding how children grow and develop is an essential skill of a professional child care worker, it is the use of observation which is one of the keys to identifying the individual needs of children. To understand what you see, you need to know what you are looking for. There is a chart for you to check the developmental stage of the observation you are recording in Unit 9 (page 327).

Children's development is divided into four different aspects:

- physical
- social and emotional
- cognitive
- language.

Although children develop at different rates, they all go through the same sequence. The patterns of development always follow the same order, for example, a baby will sit before walking and walk before running. It is usual to refer to a child's stage of development rather than a chronological age, although if you are referring to age, it should be in years and months, as a child who is just two years old will be very different from a child who is two years and eleven months. Children differ greatly in their progression through the stages of development and often you will find that one aspect of development is more advanced than another. For example, the child that talks fluently may not be demonstrating very well developed physical skills, and the child who shows well developed cognitive skills may prefer the company of adults, and not relate well to his or her peer group.

Observing and recording children and their development

There are certain conventions to be used when you observe children and record what you see. The child care worker will be observing all the time and may only need to record their observations in particular circumstances, but the student will need to gather together a collection of observations to contribute to the portfolio of work submitted as evidence for this unit.

You should decide what you are going to observe, for example, a particular aspect of the child's development or its play, or a particular part of the day such as welcomes, farewells, lunch or play time, and then plan your observation carefully.

You will need to make sure that supervisors know about your observation, so that you have their permission to carry it out. You must also be certain to reassure them that the information you record will be confidential. The child should be referred to by its first initial and age, not its full name, and the information should only be shared with your supervisor and your tutor at college, and never discussed elsewhere. This issue of confidentiality is most important.

Observations can be recorded in many ways. Firstly, you must give some background information:

- How old is the child?
- Where is it (place and time of day)?
- Who else is around (adults and children)?
- Is the child a boy or a girl?
- A description of the child and any information you have been given about its background is needed. Always say 'I have been told that...' rather than making statements that may seem like personal judgements. For example 'I have been told that the family has many problems at home' is factual but saying, 'This is a problem family' is a judgement that is inappropriate and unprofessional – it labels and stereotypes the family.
- Say what you are trying to observe and how you are going to record it. Be sure to add the date, including the year, so that those reading it later will be quite clear about when it took place.
- Write down only what you see and hear; do not make personal comments or get distracted by other events.
- After you have recorded your observation you can then interpret it. You should use the developmental charts in this or other textbooks.
- You need to recognise variations from what you would expect. These should be recorded and reported to your supervisor.
- When you have written your interpretation or evaluation, you can then note any plans you could make to encourage the child's development in the future, such as more complex jigsaws if the child found the jigsaw it was doing was easy, or a new skill for an older child, such as skipping or knitting.
- Remember to store your observation in an appropriate place and do not leave it lying around – the contents are confidential.

Assessing individual needs

When you have learnt to observe the child and interpret your observations using your knowledge of child development, then you are able to assess the child's individual needs. Each child has their own needs and you can never respond to all children in the same way because every child's needs are different. For example:

- A child who has a hearing difficulty may not be able to sit on your knee and listen to a story told to them very quietly. This child may need to sit where he or she can see your face in a good light with you speaking clearly.
- Joining in a noisy outdoor game may overwhelm a child who has never had the opportunity to mix with other children. A gentle introduction to a quiet game with one or two others may be a much better option.

In order to function as an effective professional you will need to learn the skills and techniques of identifying the individual needs of every child you look after.

Case Study

It is the start of the autumn term and you are welcoming children to the nursery. Two children arrive, both of them are just three years old. Sam comes first and looks around quickly. Spotting the water tray, Sam rushes over and immediately joins in with the other children. There are lots of filling and emptying toys, such as jugs, kettles, bowls and watering cans and Sam has great fun playing with them. You have great difficulty persuading Sam to put on an apron, but the others are encouraging, and you eventually get it on and get Sam's clothes protected.

Meanwhile, Chris is still by the door and is obviously upset because Mummy has gone. Chris has a little rabbit and holds it very tightly. You try to talk to Chris so that you can find out if there is anything that is familiar and easy to play with. It takes a lot of persuading to get Chris to come to the book corner and listen to you quietly reading a simple story with lots of bright, clear pictures.

Why do they behave like this when they are the same age? It could be that:

- Sam is used to going out and playing with other children and Chris is not.
- Chris may have been at home a lot and may not have a large family or group of friends nearby.
- Sam's mother may have may relatives who get together regularly and for Sam, large groups of children are not threatening.
- Chris may live away from the rest of the extended family and the nursery may be a very new and strange experience.

These are just a few of the possible reasons – you cannot possibly know from initial impressions why each child reacts in the way they do. In order to understand why, you will need to understand much more about the child's background and history. What you can do at this stage is to decide how you will respond to each child, and recognise that each child needs a different response from you to meet different needs.

Assessment activity 6.1

1 You are working with a childminder in her home with two children, Connor, aged one year, two months and Leah aged two years and eight months. Connor has been pulling himself up on the furniture for some time, then sitting down suddenly when he lets go. Leah is looking forward to going to school and likes to pretend that she is at school. Suggest two activities, one for each child, which will help them progress. Explain how the activities that you suggest will support the children's development. Consider physical development in particular for Connor and language development for Leah. Refer to the developmental chart in Unit 9 to help you to do this.

2 You are working in a hospital alongside the playworker. You meet three seven-year-olds, James, Naseem and Noah, who have had operations recently and have some limits on their physical activity and tire easily. However, they are bright and lively and getting better and you can see they will be bored if you cannot find something for them to do. Suggest three different activities suitable for children of this age that would encourage their cognitive development. Think carefully about any health and safety issues and mention any particular care that you would take in these circumstances.

3 You are helping a nursery class where there are several children with special needs. You are working with Jade, who is four years and five months. She has great energy and enthusiasm and a severe visual impairment. Suggest ways in which you could adapt the environment so that she can safely enjoy outdoor play with the other children.

All children have a range of needs which have to be met that fall broadly into the following categories:

Physical needs: warmth, shelter, food, exercise, sleep and rest.

Emotional needs: security, unconditional love, affection, close relationships with others.

Social needs: contact with others, belonging to a group, sharing, friendship.

Intellectual needs: intellectual stimulation, interest and challenge, opportunities to learn, access to new information, positive responses to new discoveries.

As a part of your professional role, you will need to make sure that you take the whole range of a child's needs into account and do not only concentrate on one aspect.

Different settings

Whilst you are undertaking your qualification, you will usually work in three or four different early years settings. You may work in a home, as a nanny or with a childminder, in a nursery or pre-school group (private, voluntary or local authority) or a school, hospital, or special needs setting, where you will experience working with older children. People with different backgrounds, training and skills will run each of them in a different way. Each will have different resources, maybe only one or two adults in a home, to many different professionals, all with particular roles, in a hospital.

Assessment activity 6.2

In a school some of the professionals you may meet are listed in the diagram below. Find our about as many as you can and make some notes on each one. It is important that you understand their training and their different roles and responsibilities.

Policies and procedures

Each professional will work to a code of practice which they will have learnt through their training and the expectations of the setting in which they are working. These will vary depending on the professional involved, but your primary concern is to comply with the Code of Practice and underlying values for early years practitioners, teachers, playworkers, physiotherapists, and nurses. It is interesting to find out about the codes of practice of professional colleagues and to explore the differences and similarities.

The values and underlying principles for the early years care and education sector are listed in Unit 1 (pages 31–33). These principles draw on the UN Convention on the Rights of the Child. They are based on the premise that the earliest years of children's lives are a unique stage of human development, and that quality early years provision benefits the wider society and is an investment for the future.

What you need to do about the principles

You should take time to read and understand the values and principles and follow the guidance they give you. These principles are the basis on which all professionals in the sector work, and you must comply with them at all times. The principles underpin all good practice in the sector. If you ever have doubts about the right way to approach a situation, consider how you would apply the underlying principles, and this should inform your actions.

Other policies

Each setting will also have a set of policies giving guidance on areas such as health and safety and equal opportunities.

Health and safety will cover:

- checking of equipment, ranging from toys to fire extinguishers
- the responsibilities of workers to avoid and report hazards and deal with emergencies.

Equal opportunities policies may include:

- equipment and training of staff
- the equal treatment of families and children
- the provision of particular play opportunities and equipment.

Assessment activity 6.3

To gather evidence for the log that you will be presenting at the end of your course, you will need to collect copies of policies and procedures. Find copies of:

- codes of practice
- the health and safety policy
- equal opportunities policies.

You will need to include a commentary on each and, when you have been in more than one setting, compare them and explain why there are differences and similarities.

Clearly a health and safety policy in the home of a childminder has to be different from the health and safety policy in a large primary school, where there are many children, lots of rooms and plenty of staff available to help in emergencies. However, the basic principles will be the same and key safety concerns such as the administration of medicines and the storage of dangerous substances (such as bleach) as well as the safety and security of outdoor areas are very similar, although the ways they are put into place are different. It is very important that you read and understand the health and safety policy of your setting so that you will know what to do in emergencies. If your setting is large enough, they may have a health and safety representative on the staff and you should make the opportunity to talk to them about any special issues in your particular setting.

Think It Over

Look at the equal opportunities policy for your setting. Now consider how equal opportunities are promoted. Use the following checklist to make notes on what you find.

- What toys do you see in the home corner? Are there different types of dolls or different cooking and eating facilities? How do they promote equal opportunities and cultural awareness in the learning environment?
- What festivals are celebrated in your setting? Are they from a variety of religions and different cultural traditions? Make some notes about each one, including when it is celebrated and how.
- Look at the toys and equipment provided. Are both girls and boys encouraged to play with everything? Do the boys and the girls have toys that they prefer to play with in gender groups? If so, think about why and discuss it with your supervisor.

- Look at the pictures, posters and books in your setting. Make a note of those that show children from other cultures or who have special needs. Now look for those that avoid stereotypes, such as a male nurse or a female firefighter. Remember that role models are very important to children.
- Talk to your supervisor about the ways that anti-discriminatory practice is promoted in your setting. You may find that there are ways this can be done that may not have been obvious to you, such as specialist training for staff, or policies on the ways relationships with parents are conducted.
- Find out how you can contribute to the promotion of equality of opportunity in your setting. Your supervisor will be able to help you here and you should make notes about what you find out, checking that you are putting it into practice during the time you are on placement.

Expectations of a professional carer

Becoming a professional is a process that takes place throughout your training. It is often useful to have a checklist that you consider at regular intervals to make sure that you are behaving in a professional manner. People will judge you by what they see and the way that you behave. If you observe the team that you work with, you will see that they maintain certain standards that are important to them in their work.

Assessment activity 6.4

Devise a checklist for yourself that you could use to ensure that you are reaching a professional standard. It should include:

- personal presentation, such as standards of dress and cleanliness
- behaviour, such as reliability, punctuality and attendance
- commitment to the job you are doing, which would include attention to the children's needs
- health and safety and other legal requirements
- respect for parents and other professionals with whom you work.

You will need to think about the requirements for each setting you are in, as these may change. Use it at regular intervals, so that you think about what is expected of you and how you are working towards achieving the expectations of the profession

You could lay it out as a table and note specific examples of things that you did under each heading. You could then make a note of what you felt went well and what did not go so well. Then you could suggest how you could improve your professional performance if you are in similar circumstances at another time.

This type of personal checklist can be used on your own or can be discussed with your tutor.

Think It Over

Think of someone you know who you feel is a professional. Try to note down what it is about them that makes you think about them in this way. Now have a look at the following diagram and compare what you see there with your notes.

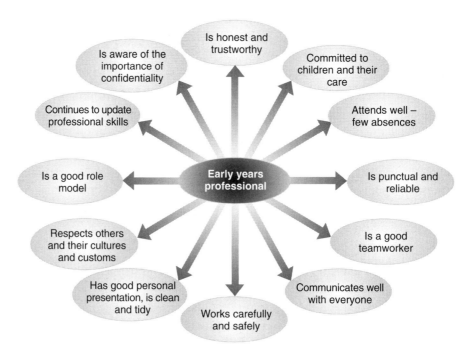

Safe, secure and healthy environment

Creating a safe, secure and healthy environment is one of the fundamentally important jobs of an early years practitioner. It is essential that you have an awareness of safety all the time and that you are observing the children's environment for any potential risks and hazards, ensuring that action is taken promptly. Working with small children is a fast-changing occupation, where situations arise without warning, however careful you have been, demanding quick responses.

Assessing the risks

Children have little awareness of the risks in their surroundings and do not realise what the results of their actions will be, so the early years practitioner must watch out for them. Children will be able to play happily in an environment that is safe and secure, and that will help their emotional well-being, if the early years worker is alert to the sounds and signs of danger.

It is important that the whole play area has been checked before the children start to use it and any potential dangers removed or minimised. For example, in an outside area, any glass or sharp stones can be removed, but you may not repair a broken gate to be repaired quickly and may have to be cordoned off, or outside play stopped until it can be made safe.

Equipment should be checked regularly to make sure that it is not cracked, broken or dirty, and regular, careful cleaning should take place. Unit 4 gives you more details of these procedures, but keep on the alert for any equipment that is not up to standard or could form a potential hazard.

Always being clean and tidy, washing your hands before eating and after using the toilet, covering your nose and mouth when you cough or sneeze, and tidying up regularly are just some of the things a good early years practitioner can do to show the children that good habits are important. Never underestimate how much the children watch you and copy what you do.

When children are ill, their behaviour will change. Watch out for a tired, unhappy child, a child that is flushed and unsettled, or the child who is whining and irritable. Any of these may indicate that the child is not well and you will need to report this to your supervisor. Observe the child carefully. What you see needs to be recorded, as it may be a symptom of a more serious problem. Remember to note the date, time and place of the observation, the name and age of the child, any adults involved and exactly what you saw. Be careful not to include your opinion, or that of others, unless you clearly say that it is an opinion rather than a fact. You will find more details about this in Unit 10.

Assessment activity 6.5

Choose an area of your workplace in which to do a hazard check. If possible, choose an outside play area. Use the following system:

1 Look carefully at your work area.
2 Identify any potential hazards you find and note them on the form.
3 Assess the risk from the potential hazard. Is it potentially critical, serious or minor?
4 Prioritise any actions needed.

You should record your findings. The form below is an example of how you might do it.

Risk assessment summary	Assessment area _____

Form number _____

Name of assessor _____   Review date _____

Ref no.	Activity/task	Hazards	Persons in danger	Probability 1 to 3	Severity 1–3	Risk factor	Person responsible	Comments	Results
1	Water play	Wet floor	Children and staff	2	1	Low	Nursery nurse	Wiped up immediately	A

After you have done the hazard check, it is important that something is done with the results. An important part of the process is making sure the required actions are carried out. All work places must have a healthy and safety policy and many, particularly the larger ones, will have a health and safety officer.

You need to read the policy and talk to the officer or other workers to understand what your responsibilities are. Both you and your employer should work together to ensure that there is a healthy and safe environment for the children in your care, so that they can play happily and comfortably together.

Promoting a stimulating learning environment

You will be able to see the similarities and differences between different settings during your placements. Look at the following table to see the different settings and their structures.

Setting	Structure and purpose
Childminders	Care for children from approximately six months to teenagers in their own homes. Offer all day childcare as well as care before and after school. Fees are paid
Pre-schools/playgroups	Offer sessional care to children from approximately two years six months to school age. Often run by a voluntary management committee with parents helping a qualified leader. May be linked to an out-of-school club. Fees are paid
Private nurseries	Some are small, some are part of a large chain. They offer all-day care to pre-school age children, often with places for babies. Fees are charged at a commercial rate
LEA nurseries	Early education places are provided for three- and four-year-old children often on a sessional basis. Run by a qualified teacher
Infant schools	Part of the primary school, providing free education for five- to seven-year-olds, under the charge of a qualified teacher. Infant schools follow the National Curriculum
Out-of-school clubs	Care for children before and/or after school (sometimes during lunch hours for pre-school children). Usually run by a qualified leader with a voluntary management committee. Fees are paid
Holiday clubs	Care for children during the school holidays. Usually run by a qualified play leader and a voluntary management committee, sometimes with the help of parents

All these settings will be registered with and monitored by OFSTED and will have to comply with certain standards, such as the space and facilities available and the staff and equipment provided. All settings will also have to show that they are delivering the Foundation Stage Curriculum for all three and four year olds in their care. Settings have to ensure that activities are planned and implemented which allow children to make progress towards the Early Learning Goals. OFSTED reports must be made available to the public, so that those who want to use the service can read them before they decide which is best for their child.

The CIS and EYDCP

Information about which setting to chose can be obtained from the Children's Information Service (CIS) for the area. It will have a helpline and a website where information about all registered settings can be accessed. Many CIS websites are lively and interesting and you can gain a lot of useful information from them about all the settings available.

The CIS is part of the local Early Years Development and Childcare Partnership (EYDCP) for your area. Representatives of many groups involved in early years come together on the Partnership to plan and expand provision for the children in their area. They provide a framework within which early years settings work, and can provide funding for places, for training, for expanding provision, to help out when there are emergencies and so on. One of their main tasks is to expand provision for all age groups in every type of setting and they work closely with OFSTED to prepare new settings registration and to support those who are inspected. The EYDCP will also have a website that you can access. It is part of the education department of your local council, so see if you can find it.

Think It Over
Find the address of your local CIS website and explore it to find out about early years settings in your area.

Assessment activity 6.6
Consider your work placement.

- What are its aims?
- How does it plan so that the needs of the children are met?
- Draw a diagram to show how it is organised and your place in the work that it does.
- Now make a list of the resources provided in your setting.

Provision for play and activities
The key principle of early years care and education is that play and learning are inseparable and are both equally vital to a child's development. Regardless of the setting, there will always be a range of activities and most will include those in the following diagram.

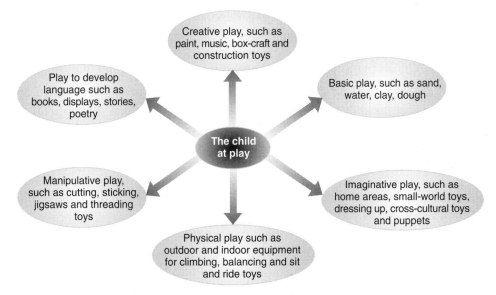

This is usually the basic provision that all settings will offer, although there may be some differences. For example, a childminder may have a garden and outside play may be available all the time, whereas a school may have a playground, which may only be available at set times. On the other hand, a school may have an excellent library with plenty of books for children in the early years, whereas a pre-school may have to get all of its equipment out and put it away each session, so they may not have as many books available.

The needs of the children

If children with special needs use the early years setting, it will have special equipment for them so that the environment is as user friendly as possible. All settings should ensure that all the children are able to communicate with each other and should make sure that any special methods of communication are taught to all children and staff.

Here are some examples of provision of equipment and support for special needs:

Children with visual impairments	Textures to feel and enjoy such as different papers and fabrics Brightly coloured toys Toys which make noises
Children who use wheelchairs	Plenty of space to move about Tables at the right height for the chair
Children with auditory problems	Quiet surroundings for stories with a good view of the adult's face Support to join in with others and communicate in a group
Children with learning difficulties	Individual attention Simple toys and equipment to attract and keep attention. Patience and understanding from everyone.

Very often, the early years practitioners who work with children with special needs will have had specialist training and plenty of experience of dealing with all types of children. Some schools and nurseries will have a particular unit or base room for the children, but in most settings, children with special needs will be integrated and play alongside everyone else. There will be a SENCO (Special Education Needs Co-ordinator) whose task is to ensure that the child's needs are catered for properly and that staff are well informed about the child and how they can support play and education activities.

Planning, implementing and evaluating activities

When you are planning activities, you will usually find that the long-term plans are made by the team you are working with, rather than you done. If you are working in a school, the teacher will usually have topics planned according to the requirements of the National Curriculum. It is important that you find out about these plans to make sure that you are fitting in with the overall strategy of the setting. Planning is usually in three stages and is likely to follow the pattern in the points below.

* Long-term plans – the team meets to discuss how the aims of each area of learning and each early learning goal can be met, alongside the developmental needs of the children, both as a group and individually. Planning often includes special events such as religious festivals, Halloween, Chinese New Year or May Day.

- Medium-term plans – these will often cover particular topics or subjects which may be the focus of a few weeks work, say a month or even half a term. It is very important that you find out about the plan that will be running when you are in placement, as any work that you do will need to contribute to it.
- Short-term plans – you will have a part to play here, which may be focused on both individual children and a topic or subject area. For example, if you and your team are implementing a plan around the Chinese New Year, you could be working with an individual child to develop language skills by working on a display where you and a group of children work together.

A child that needs your special attention could be encouraged to join in the group, name the colours, talk to the other children, share and take turns, as well as being encouraged to talk to you about what they are doing.

The plan for the whole topic might include the food and visits to nearby Chinese shops, or visitors from Chinese communities. The home area could be turned into a Chinese shop, with suitable labels, coins, costumes and things to buy and sell, for example, prawn crackers and bean sprouts.

If you need to do a display or a play activity for an assessment or to undertake an observation of a particular child, you could include these opportunities within the plan.

When you have carried out the activity or the plan, you should review and evaluate it carefully. This is usually undertaken as a team, with everyone who has been involved, and look at what happened. The team will consider what went well and achieved the aims and what did not go so well and why. Suggestions will be made as to how it could be improved in the future. The evaluation of plans for an individual child will need to record what the child knew before, what has been learned through the activity and what the next progress needs to be.

The evaluation of plans for the activity will need to record what happened, what was used, who was involved, how successful it was and how future plans can be made from the work that was done.

Remember that the age of the child or children will affect your planning. Plans to wean a baby from liquid to solid food or to encourage a toddler to talk will be individual and related to that particular child and its circumstances. Plans for a group of older children in an out-of-school club will often be negotiated with the children and may be a specific group activity, such as a visit to the pantomime at the local theatre.

You will find more details on curriculum planning in Unit 7, Learning in the early years.

Activities for supporting learning, displays, visits and first-hand experiences

As you have seen with ideas for activities about the Chinese New Year, there are many ways to support learning. Displays are important, as are first-hand experiences, visits and appropriate types of play. Displays can use children's work in many ways; some of them are illustrated in the following diagram.

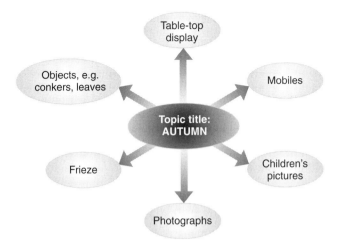

Visits and first-hand experiences

To enhance this activity, which is all based on the topic of Autumn, your plans could include a visit to collect leaves, twigs and conkers or acorns in the local park or wood. Visits like this, although they are quickly and relatively simply arranged, are enjoyable experiences for the children. You will need to make sure you go with a qualified member of staff and that the parents have given permission before you start.

It can be a good opportunity to teach the children basic road safety, so you will need enough adults for the number of children you are taking. For small children one adult to two children is ideal, as then an adult can hold the hands of both children. You will need to check before you go and make sure each child is suitably dressed in warm clothing before you set off.

Bringing back what you have found and putting it on the display table is a job for you and the children together. You may need to choose pictures they have painted or drawn to add to the display, or mobiles that they have made. It is important that it is their work and not yours, so you will need to label it clearly, 'John's conkers', 'Susan's leaves', 'Sam and Anwara's twigs', and so on. Labels should be in lower case letters and everything on the table should be safe for children to handle.

Children will learn by touching, smelling, listening and tasting, as well as looking, so see if you can find something for all five senses. Check your spelling, laminate the labels if necessary, be prepared to maintain the display as it gets used whilst it is up, and plan when you are going to take it down and replace it with something else. There should always be more input from the children than from you. You are just the person that makes it all happen.

Theory into practice

Plan a display that you could put together with the children in your setting. Choose a theme that could be part of the plans for the setting and then make notes on what you will need, what the children will do, how it will be organised and what it will look like when it is completed. If you can carry out your plan, take some photographs of what you did, compare them with your original plan and evaluate how well it went.

Promoting learning with parents

Working with parents is an essential part of your role as an early years practitioner. Parents are the main carers and the most important influence on the children. You must always involve parents in all activities in the early years setting; it is not only about inviting parents in to see displays or to help with visits. Many parents will welcome the chance to be involved in what their children are doing and to see the results of their efforts. It makes a good opportunity for parents to get to know you. A stimulating learning environment includes children and parents alongside the early years practitioners, all co-operating to develop the children's skills and abilities.

Communication is an essential part of the job of the professional early years worker. It is important to be able to communicate well with the team in which you are working, as well as the children in your care and their parents and carers. Other professionals may visit your setting and you should be clear about their roles and how they fit with yours.

Most early years settings will involve you in working as part of a team. Working with colleagues is a skill that you must develop. It is never possible to like everyone you work with, but as a professional you will work hard at overcoming personal likes and dislikes and recognise the value of the contribution which all staff members make.

In order to become an effective team member you should:

- use good communication skills with colleagues just as much as the children
- recognise and value the work others do
- always ask for help if there is something you are unsure of
- never pretend to know more than you do
- do not allow personal feelings to affect your working relationships
- make sure that you are clear about your role in any team projects
- never alter team plans or ways of working without getting the agreement of your supervisor
- don't gossip about colleagues!

The reflective practitioner

All professionals, in any field, need to be able to reflect on their own practice. You will be able to undertake some of this with the support of your supervisor by learning to use appraisal effectively. Appraisal or review of your working performance will give you the chance to hear about your work from your supervisor, this is a useful opportunity to find out about areas of work in which you are performing well and are your areas of strength. You can also find out about areas of your work where you need some more support and a chance to develop your skills.

In discussion with your supervisor, you should set targets for your own professional development. Your targets must be SMART targets, such as those shown in the table below:

Specific	I will improve my activity planning
Measurable	I will plan at least one activity for each day for the next two weeks
Achievable	I will attend a Food Hygiene course in the next three months
Realistic	I will read Nursery World regularly to keep up-to-date
Timed	I will review my own performance with my supervisor weekly

Assessment activity 6.7

Look back at the diagram which has the early years practitioner in its centre (page 206). Now think about yourself very honestly. Which of the qualities can you say you have? Which are you developing? And which need more work?

From this, you can make your own personal action plan. Give yourself realistic target dates for each one you wish to achieve, then make sure you review them on the date you have set yourself.

When you set your own personal targets, try to be quite clear about how you are going to develop the skills needed to reach them. It may be that you need to do some further reading, or you may need to work on your own qualities in a private and personal way, but setting yourself challenges is the mark of a professional and a habit you will continue to develop throughout your professional life.

Another skill of the professional, that of being responsive and adaptable in changing needs and situations, is one which you will need to develop. Consider the following case study situations and make some notes about how you would deal with them. If you can, discuss your ideas with your tutor or supervisor.

Case Study

You have been working as one of the team in an early years setting for some months and have enjoyed working with Susie, a small, quiet, shy girl, who is now three. Susie had problems settling in, but as you started nursery when she started, she took a liking to you and always starts the day by playing with you for a while before going off and playing with other children in the group. One morning Susie arrives with her mother and it is clear that both of them are distressed and upset. You try to settle Susie down, but she clings to her mother and won't let go. Susie's mother says she wants to go as she has to see a solicitor about what has happened at home, but she doesn't want to talk about what this is. The other children in your group cluster round, curious about what is going on. You need to deal with Susie and her mother and you need to ensure that other children are dealt with too.

- What can you do to help to sort out this unexpected situation?
- Make some notes and try to put them in some order of priority.

Case Study

You are working in a school setting, helping a teacher with a group of seven-year-olds. They are going to do a play for their parents at Christmas and are getting very excited about it. The teacher feels it is very important that both of you keep the children on a steady course, so that they do not lose sight of their everyday work in the Christmas rush.

- What can you do to support the teacher in her objective?
- How could you help the children to prepare for the forthcoming event without missing out on their day-to-day work or becoming over-excited and difficult to manage?

Don't forget that the preparation time must be enjoyable to everyone, the children, their parents, the teacher and you and the rest of the staff and pupils of the school.

You will also need to look at the information you have worked on in Unit 2, so that you consider your interpersonal skills. A good professional is a skilled communicator and is always aware that good communication involves far more than language and verbal communication.

Professional relationships: supporting children, their families and carers

One of the most important ways to support children in their learning is to communicate with them. In Unit 2 you will have learnt a lot about communication skills and how to look at your own skills and improve them. You will need to make sure you put what you have learnt into practice in your day to day work, especially with when dealing with children of different ages, or with children or families who have particular communication needs such as a need for signing, or for any printed material to be in Braille or in large print.

Look at the following case studies and consider how you could improve communication in each case.

Case Study – social barriers to communication

A mother arrives at school with her four and a half-year-old daughter, Melissa. Both the mother and Melissa are well dressed. As Melissa comes in the door, she goes straight to the clay table and starts playing with the clay. She has obviously used it before and starts to make all sorts of little models with it. Her mother is horrified and says to you that she would really like her daughter to learn to read and write and not play with the clay. Her daughter is busy trying to get the other children to make models like she does and takes no notice of her mother.

- Make some notes about how you could communicate with the mother to discuss the situation, and how you could help Melissa to communicate with the other children in the group.
- Discuss your notes with your tutor or supervisor or with others in your student group.

Case Study – emotional barriers

A young mother arrives at the nursery with her two-year-old son. He is in tears and so is she. She wants him to stay at the nursery but she is as upset about him leaving her as about her leaving him. She feels that because he hasn't settled down straight away, she has failed to be a good mother. She is going to need some help to be able to leave him without getting upset and he is going to need help to settle down.

- Write some notes about how you could talk to them to help overcome some of their problems.

Rights and responsibilities of children and parents

All children have rights, which should be respected. In 1924 the United Nations stated that 'Mankind owes to the child the best it has to give'. In 1989 it produced a convention on the Rights of the Child. These rights included:

- The right to life, survival and development.
- The right to develop to the fullest and become a productive member of society.
- The right to protection from harmful influences, abuses and exploitation.
- The right to participate fully in family, cultural and social life without discrimination.
- The right to certain standards in health care, education, legal, civil and social services.
- The right to speak up and be heard and have views expressed and respected.

This is part of the United Nations' quest for a just, respectful and peaceful society. Respect for the rights of the child gives parents and early years practitioners the responsibility to empower children to exercise those rights.

Think It Over

Think about the responsibilities of parents in bringing up children. It is a responsibility that they have for the rest of their lives. Now think about the rights of the child and any rights the parents may have. Make a note of any ways you could support parents to understand their responsibilities so that children can exercise their rights.

Many of the strategies that can be used to support parents and carers involve good communication. It is very important to recognise that people have different ideas and values and that these may not be the same as yours. Although you may not agree with them, you must respect them and show that you will listen to them.

Parents will be different in their ability to look after their children. It will often depend on how they were brought up themselves and patterns of behaviour and child rearing are often handed down from one generation to another. You may hear a parent say that if something was good enough for them when they were children, it is good enough for their child now.

Working in partnership with parents is vital. Here are some of the ways it can be done.

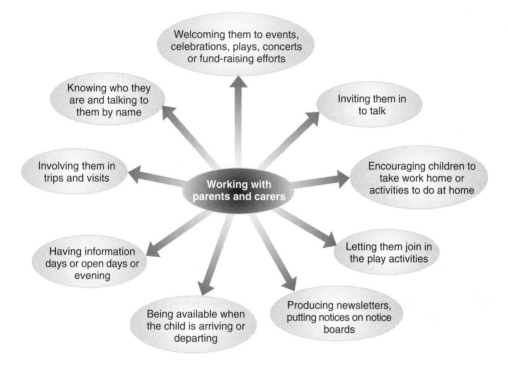

All of these should help parents and carers to work together with the staff of the setting, so that the best interests of the child can be served.

It is not your role at any time to become involved in arguments or disputes with parents. These do occasionally happen in settings and must be dealt with by a senior staff member.

Managing the effects of abuse

In Unit 5, Protecting children, you will have considered the difficult issue of child abuse very carefully. You will know that the disclosure of abuse can take place at any time, often when you are least expecting it. There are basic rules which must be followed when a child discloses that they have been the subject of abuse:

- Always believe the child.
- Never promise that you will keep it a secret, but reassure the child that you will only tell people who will help.
- Never keep it a secret – always report a disclosure of abuse.

- Do not ask the child any questions – apart from prompting questions such as 'and then what happened?'
- Reassure the child that nothing is their fault.
- Reassure the child that that they will be helped now that they have told you.
- Remember – children disclose abuse because they want it to stop

The process after disclosure will follow a set procedure. The key worker and the review group will make any plans for how an abused child is to be supported in the longer term and the setting will be involved in the planning process. This will be discussed among the team members in the setting, and activity and curriculum planning will take this into account.

Disclosure of abuse will have an enormous impact on the rest of the family. Other siblings and a parent who protects will need to be included in plans for supporting the family. There will be a range of professionals involved in supporting the family as they come to terms with the abuse. The support is likely to come from social workers, health visitors, possibly probation officers, specialist therapists and the relevant early years settings or schools if other siblings are involved.

The plans should be co-ordinated so that all agencies are working to the same goals, which will be to deal with the emotional trauma which follows abuse within a family.

You will have learned about the physical and emotional effects of abuse in Unit 5. The effect on other members of the family can be:

- guilt – that they allowed the abuse to happen
- anger – at the perpetrator of the abuse
- anger – at the survivor of the abuse because they 'disrupted the family' other family members may 'blame the victim'
- fear and anxiety – of what may happen to them
- feelings of insecurity – nothing will ever be the same again.

Family centres

Children who have been abused and their families can often be supported in a family centre. Such centres provide services for the entire family with a wide range of provision. A multi-disciplinary team of professionals will be able to provide support from a family centre with education and day care provision for pre-school children, after school care for older children, support and therapy groups for adults and children and specialist intervention such as play therapists and psychologists if necessary.

There may be other help available from the family centre, allowing each member of the family to find the agencies that can help them best. A variety of services can be offered in what is a 'one-stop-shop' for both the children and the adults in the family, ranging from play facilities to health, relationship or even housing and benefits advice.

Home visiting

Occasionally, you may have the opportunity to visit children at home. Some, but not most, early years settings will make a practice of visiting children at home before they start at the setting. This is obviously helpful for the child as it provides a link for them if they have seen you in the familiar surroundings of home, and they see you again when they start in the setting. It will also help you to be able to refer to familiar objects at home that the child can identify with.

Support for children and their families

When there are problems at home, both the children and the family need support. The Children Act 1989 requires that children and families are not automatically separated when things go wrong. The accepted view of the social work profession, that children should be kept within their family if at all possible, is now supported by legislation. Different forms of help may be needed by different members of the family but this should not require the splitting up of the family unless it is being done to protect the children from harm. Where children need to be separated from their parents, or they have been abandoned, then every effort will be made to accommodate the children with members of their extended family or friends. A placement in residential or foster care is a last resort if there are no less disruptive alternatives available.

Foster care

Foster parents provide care to children in their own homes. Children live as a member of the foster carers family. Some foster parents offer short-term temporary care, often in a crisis situation. This could be if a new baby was abandoned, or if young children were found left alone in a house, or even if a child with a long-term problem had to be taken into care quickly. The child may then go on to more permanent foster care, where they will stay with the family for some time, often many years. Sometimes the birth parents do not want to release the child for adoption or the child itself does not wish to be adopted, so they stay in a foster family instead.

Foster parents are registered with the local authority, after careful checks have been made, such as with the police or health authorities. They often have training in childcare and may have had specialist training to take particular groups of children. These could be children who have been in trouble with the law, children who have been subject to abuse or older children. They get paid for the work that they do to offset the cost of caring for the child. Very often, couples work together as foster carers, although single people can foster children.

Adoption

Adoption, unlike fostering, is permanent and because of this, very careful checks are made over a period of time before the legal processes are completed. The Family Court is always involved in adoptions and, having read all the reports presented to them, they make the final decision.

Adopted children are able to inherit from their adoptive parents and their new family, not the birth family, will take all the decisions about the child. The birth parent or parents will have given permission for the adoption to take place and there may be little contact after that, unless it has been specially negotiated and agreed. Couples may adopt a child, as can single people, but after the adoption has taken place, no payments are made, the child is the financial responsibility of the adoptive family.

Residential child care

Residential child care is only used for older children where they are unable to stay with their families. The local Social Services department may run small group homes, where specially trained professionals look after the children placed in their care in an atmosphere that is as like a home as they can make it. Older children sometimes prefer this kind of care to foster care, or it may be that they have had a number of foster placements which have not worked very well, so their time in residential care can bring a period of stability. Sometimes children stay in family group homes for a short time; sometimes for many years. They go to the local school and join in local organizations in the same way every other child does. Sometimes they are placed there by agreement with their natural parents and sometimes they are they on the order of a court, especially if something has gone wrong at home.

Assessment activity 6.8

Earlier in this unit, you considered the other professionals you might be working with. Using that list and your knowledge, write notes on how your work links with the work of others, describing their roles and yours clearly. Your notes should show that you understand what their particular specialist knowledge is and how your professional skills and understanding can contribute with theirs to work for the best interests of the child, so that everyone's roles and responsibilities are clear.

- Now consider what information should be shared and with whom.
- Find out how the first contact with other professionals could be made.
- What sort of information could be shared with other professionals?
- What sort of information could be shared with parents or carers and what sort of information would it be best not to share with them?
- What sort of information should remain confidential and not be shared with anyone?
- Who makes decisions about confidentiality: is it you as the early years worker, or somebody else?
- Discuss the notes you have made with your tutor or supervisor.

How to approach the assessment of this unit

Using the Practice Log

This Professional Practice Log has been designed to be completed over the whole period of your studies. For the majority of people this will be over two years.

Remember that you will need to use this log to show your skill at working as a professional with children. The log is not about recording what you know – it is about showing what you can do.

Demonstrating your competence

This Professional Practice Log is a record of your competence and skills in an early years context. How effective the Log is at demonstrating your competence is down to you. To meet the requirements of this Unit you must:

- complete each section of the Professional Practice Log
- present sufficient observation reports to meet the requirements of the qualification
- present sufficient witness reports to demonstrate your competence in a vocational context.

You should take care with the completion of each section and make sure that your records of observation are detailed.

Ways of demonstrating your competence

You should present evidence from many different areas of your practice. Evidence can be:

- witness statements of activities undertaken, practice demonstrated, involvement in meetings, discussions etc.
- reflective logs of placement
- child observations
- child assessment records – remember that the child should not be identifiable
- copies of children's work, photographic evidence with supportive evaluation as to their place in the evidence file – you must get parental permission to use photographs
- planning and evaluation sheets
- reflective accounts of incidents
- placement reports.

There are several ways of demonstrating your skills in an early years context. The most commonly used ways are:

- Asking your placement supervisor to observe you carrying out a task or activity. They then complete and sign a report detailing what they have seen and heard.
- Asking your placement supervisor for a signed witness statement relating to a piece of work that you have carried out in their workplace. They may not have seen you do the task but have seen the end result
- Asking your course tutor to observe you completing an activity or task and then obtaining a signed report detailing the results.
- Completing a 'reflective report' your self. This involves analysing what you have done. The report should include what worked well and what required change. A reflective report should always be supported by additional evidence that demonstrates how you carried out the task or activity

There are other types of evidence available, for example, a video of you working in placement. However, you would have to think about confidentiality and issues such as parental permission to film the children.

The most important part of your Professional Practice Log is that you and a credible witness compile it together. For example, it will be of no or very little value if you ask your 'best friend' to sign a witness statement or observation for you. The person providing observations and witness statements must be experienced/qualified in the particular vocational context that you are working in

Recording vocational hours

An essential part of your vocational practice is the completion of 800 hours of work placement/experience over two years.

Again, providing evidence of this vocational work is not easy. However, the Professional Practice Log does offer the opportunity for you to record the hours of experience that you gain over the period of your course.

As recording your practice is central to the Professional Practice Log you must ensure that all your hours are recorded to meet the requirements set for a 'pass' in this Unit of study.

Working through the Professional Practice Log

As you work through your Professional Practice Log you will find that each Outcome is listed in more detail along with suggestions for its achievement and evidence requirements.

In some cases an observation report from a placement supervisor or your tutor will be required, in other cases written work from another unit of study may be the evidence that you are submitting.

Outcome 1

Observe and identify the individual needs of the child appropriate to the requirements of the setting.

Introduction to the Outcome

Observing the children in your care is an important part of your job role. Through observation and correct evaluation of those observations, you can help in the identification of the needs of a particular child or group of children. As you will be working with many children in a variety of settings and age ranges you will carry out many different observations.

You will also need to show your understand and use of the different codes of practice relating to observation in the range of placements.

You must demonstrate your observation skills with children aged:

> 0–1 years
> 1–4 years
> 4–8 years

in at least four of the following possible settings:

the child's home, childminders, voluntary pre-school, private nursery provision, nursery schools/classes, primary schools, schools for children with special needs, paediatric hospital units.

Assessment criteria

To achieve this outcome you must demonstrate the ability to:

1. observe and identify the individual needs of children in four different settings and three age ranges

2. observe and identify the individual needs of children with specific needs

3. identify the codes of practice of each setting and explain the differences and similarities.

Sample Outcome No. 1: Observe and identify the individual needs of the child appropriate to the requirements of the setting

Briefly describe how you have met the learning outcome.

Type of setting _____ Date _____	Location
	Signed by
Type of setting _____ Date _____	Location
	Signed by
Type of setting _____ Date _____	Location
	Signed by
Type of setting _____ Date _____	Location
	Signed by

Continue your evidence on supplementary sheets if appropriate.

Learning in the early years

Introduction

Children's learning is a major focus within most early years settings and one that is rewarding and exciting for early years practitioners. Understanding how children learn and how to support learning requires extensive and in-depth knowledge from those people who care for and educate young children. The term 'early years' is usually applied to children under eight years of age and is applied to all the settings where children under eight receive care and education.

Unit 7 provides you with the knowledge and understanding to promote children's learning in the early years. It includes an examination of how children learn and the historical perspectives that have influenced early years practice. The content and form of the early years curriculum are covered. You will use this knowledge to plan, carry out and evaluate routines and activities in the early years setting. This unit lays out the foundations of how children learn and acts as a starting point for you to develop your skills, and begin to see and understand the issues underpinning effective provision.

What you need to learn

- Theories of how children learn
- The work of early educators and their influence on current principles and practice
- The role of play in the development of early learning
- The identification and promotion of learning opportunities for young children
- Children with special educational needs and disabled children

Theories of how children learn

How children develop and learn has been a point of debate between philosophers, psychologists, scientists and educators over many years. Many of these debates are still taking place. Although they seem very theoretical, these debates have a direct influence on the type of education and care given to young children. They are therefore very important areas for early years practitioners to understand and from which to draw conclusions regarding their own practice and that of the setting in which they work.

This section will help you to understand the nature of these debates and the theories and views behind them, how they affect our views of children as learners and how they have affected provision for young children.

Nature/nurture debate

This is a very important debate that influences how we view children's learning and how we provide for it. The debate is about how much either nature (genetic inheritance

– inborn abilities) or nurture (the environment – the people, places and influences on a child) contribute to children's development, learning and potential achievement.

If theorists consider that nurture is a strong influence, this means that there is a greater emphasis on the environment. This is because it is believed that a child's early experiences will be the most important factor affecting their ability to achieve. If theorists consider that nature is a strong influence, this means less emphasis on the environment, as the potential to achieve is thought to be inborn. Theorists supporting 'nature' believe children cannot perform at a higher level than their genetic inheritance may allow.

For example, if a child had learning difficulties the 'nature' approach could offer love and care but might not expect the child to achieve very much. It might not offer a very stimulating environment, as this would not make much difference in the end. The 'nurture' approach would say that the child should have an enriched learning environment to make sure they achieved their full potential and who knows what that might be!

Learning and development debate

Development is how a child grows, matures and functions. It is often divided into different strands, for example:

- physical
- intellectual/cognitive
- language
- emotional
- social
- cultural
- spiritual/moral.

These strands come together to form a complete view of the child. Child development is a relatively new discipline based on psychology, sociology, anthropology, genetics, physiology, and health disciplines such as paediatrics. Children's development generally follows the same stage and sequence but at different rates. For example, the sequence is that children normally sit unaided before they walk unaided, but some will walk at twelve months and others at eighteen months. When they can walk unaided they are at the 'walking stage'.

Learning is what takes place as a response to something the child experiences. This may be through solving problems, through trial and error, in everyday interactions or through being taught. The mechanisms of how learning actually takes place are still not fully understood and the theories considered below all have different viewpoints.

Development occurs rapidly in the early years and it is the child's stage of development and readiness to learn that should control the learning they are offered. This means each child is considered as an individual. It would be bad practice to treat a group of young children as if they were exactly the same and could all learn the same things at the same time. By carefully observing children, most early years practitioners will assess the individual child's stage of development and will make sure the time is right for each child to move on in their learning. They will do this by creating an environment where children can grow and develop freely with adult support offered sensitively in a way that will not dominate the child's learning.

Think It Over

Some people believe that a group of children aged four can sit together in a classroom, pick up their pencils at the same time and learn to write simple words. They are surprised when an early years practitioner says that some of the children are not ready to hold and control a pencil, others need a good deal of practice, whilst others can already write their names clearly.

- Discuss the difference between these points of view. How does this link to ideas about development and learning?

Factor affecting learning and development

Meeting basic needs first

Other issues affect the stages and sequence of development and of learning. Maslow's hierarchy of needs suggests that basic needs at the bottom of the hierarchy must be met before effective learning takes place.

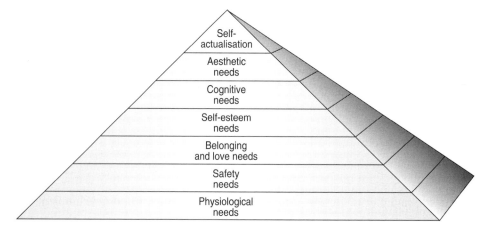

Maslow's hierarchy of needs

Opportunity

Children need opportunity, for example toddlers kept in cots (like those found in some orphanages in Eastern Europe) had not learned to walk as their muscles, co-ordination and balance had not been allowed to develop to create the opportunity for the child to learn how to walk. Sick or disabled children may also share some of those problems and require extra support in their learning.

Motivation

Children also need motivation and positive encouragement, for example if toddlers who are usually intrepid explorers are constantly told 'no' they become discouraged and frustrated. Most children when trying new skills need encouragement and support to move on. Children with low self-esteem such as those who have been abused or neglected also need special encouragement to take risks and do new things.

Timing

Learning and development take place when the time is right and the opportunities are there. For example, it is pointless trying to force children to write their names before they are developmentally ready. To write their name, children have to be able to hold a pencil securely, confidently and with control. This ability comes when children's nerves and muscles are able to cope with handling small objects with control, when they understand something about making marks on paper and when opportunities to practise and develop these skills are available.

Environment

Children need an environment which encourages them to learn and develop. They need to explore freely and safely from an early age and need encouragement and praise for their efforts as well as their achievements. This is discussed further below.

Gifted children

Children who are gifted in particular areas of learning also need to have their overall needs met. They should not be pressurised or pushed too hard before they are ready. Some children are gifted in, for example, mathematics, social relationships or music and this talent needs to be fostered; however, this does not mean they are gifted in all other areas. Children who are gifted will need encouragement to progress in all areas of their learning and development and should first and foremost be allowed to be children.

Assessment activity 7.1

Make a chart on the factors that affect children's learning. Prepare notes on each aspect you have identified and use these to contribute to a group discussion. Make sure you have covered each of the areas identified above and that you clearly explain why meeting children's basic needs is necessary if they are to learn effectively.

Theories and theorists

Early years settings base their provision on what they believe about children and learning. The setting's beliefs will be linked to the theories they accept as valid and important for children's learning in their early years. This section looks at three key theoretical models of children's learning, each of which has influenced current early years provision in the UK. The models themselves have their origins in the work of philosophers and thinkers and have more recently been developed by psychologists. You will see evidence of theories and theorists in your work placements although you may not always recognise them. This section considers the theories as follows:

- Their advantages and disadvantages.
- The effects on the role of the adult and the interaction with the child.
- The organisation of the learning environment.
- The nature/nurture debate.
- Links to current research.

Transmission model

The transmission model of learning builds on the thinking of the philosopher, John Locke (1632–1704), who thought of the child as an empty clay tablet (*tabula rasa*) or an 'empty vessel' capable of being moulded and shaped by adults. People working in this tradition are often called behaviourists. This theory sees human beings as basically passive, learning through their experiences and reacting predictably to outside stimulation. It also recognises that human behaviour can be modified by reinforcement; for example, if you put your hand in the fire, it will get burned and you are not likely to repeat the act.

Transmission theories are not greatly concerned with what goes on inside the mind being more concerned with the external inputs and influences on learning such as learning programmes, activities and experiences. Transmission models are concerned with the person's environment and experiences, not their genetic inheritance, i.e. nurture not nature.

There are two main components of transmission theory: **learning theory** and **social learning theory**.

Learning theory (learning from experience)
Classical conditioning

Pavlov's work on the behaviour of dogs is a well-known example of how learning theory developed during the twentieth century. Pavlov fed his dog when the church bells rang or a light was flashed before feeding; at the sight of the food the dog salivated. After some time the dog would salivate at the sound of the bell or when the light was flashed, even when no food was in sight as it associated the bell ringing or light flashing with the arrival of food. Salivation at the sound of the bell or flash of light indicated a conditioned response.

Food arrives when the bell has rung

After some time the dog associates food with the bell ringing and salivates ready to eat – this is a conditioned response

Operant conditioning

Operant conditioning was a further development of Pavlov's work by the psychologist B.F. Skinner. It is concerned mainly with shaping and modifying behaviour. Skinner also worked with animals but only rewarded them with food if they did as he required. The food reward acted as a positive reinforcement. When animals did not do as Skinner required he subjected them to unpleasant stimuli such as electric shocks; the unpleasant stimuli acted as negative reinforcers and these gradually extinguished the behaviour.

Learning theory has greatly influenced how adults shape or modify children's behaviour. By selectively reinforcing behaviour that is wanted, adults can change the way children behave. This is called **behaviour modification**.

Social learning theories (learning through example)
Social learning theory accepts the basics of learning theory but also emphasises that children learn behaviours by observing and imitating adults especially those adults who are important to them. Albert Bandura (b. 1925) is a well-known social learning theorist and he found that a wide range of behaviours was learned by observation including aggression, sharing, sex roles, and altruism (willingness to do things which benefit other people, even if it results in disadvantage for yourself). Social learning theory emphasises

the need to model socially acceptable behaviour to children. For example, if staff within the nursery regularly become angry and shout, children will learn that this is an acceptable way to behave and will copy the behaviour.

Key issues

In the new Day Care Standards for England (DfES, 2001) childminders are allowed to smoke in front of children if they have the parent's written permission. How could this affect children's attitudes to smoking even when other messages all around teach about its dangers?

Laissez-faire model (learning just happens)

This model is based on the work of the French philosopher Rousseau (1712–78). Rousseau thought that children learned naturally like the opening of a flower bud, and were programmed to learn certain things at certain times. Rousseau's thinking was that children's development would proceed anyway whether or not there was a significant influence from adults or the environment. Developmental scales were first developed as a result of the laissez-faire approach.

Expanding Rousseau's thinking, some psychologists (e.g. Fodor, 1983) believe that the development of mental concepts such as number, space, music and time, are 'wired in' to in-born internal structures and that the role of the adult in the child's development is limited. Noam Chomsky's (1968) work on language development is similar. Chomsky believed that children learned the complex grammatical structures of language just by hearing it spoken. He taught that children have innate structures within their brain that allow them to develop language and that children develop new sentences and apply rules of grammar to their speech rather than just copy sentences they have heard. This is often borne out by children making errors by applying speech rules to new situations, e.g. 'sheeps' instead of 'sheep' applies a common rule, i.e. adding an 's' to make it plural.

Freud

Freudian theory is based on the work of Sigmund Freud (1856–1939) who was the father of psychoanalysis. Psychoanalysis is based on the theory of personality development, introduced by Freud, that focuses on the unconscious mind. Freud's theory sees the child as passing through a series of pre-determined psychological stages in the development of personality based on the child's level of physical maturation. Freud's stages are called psycho-sexual stages as they are all part of the human being's drive to feed, grow and reproduce. Freud's view was that people were born with unconscious biological instincts much like animals and that we have to learn to control these instincts to live in society. Passing through these stages helps to ensure that children learn control and become mature. these are the stages:

Oral stage: This is where the baby has a drive to feed and engage in activities involving the mouth and lips, e.g. sucking, biting, exploring with the mouth. How children are weaned from the breast or bottle was thought by Freud to affect their future personality.

Anal stage: This is about young children learning to control their muscles especially anal muscles, e.g. during toilet training. How children are toilet trained was thought to affect their future personality. For example, over-strict toilet training was thought to lead to a more obsessive personality.

Phallic stage: This stage relates to children having sexual feelings towards their parents. Freud believed that boys had sexual feelings towards their mothers and wished their fathers did not exist and called this the Oedipus complex. Freud also believed that girls had sexual feelings towards their fathers and called this the Electra complex. By about the age of five or six years, children had to learn to give up these feelings and to identify with the parent of the same sex. How children managed this transition was thought by Freud to have an important impact on future relationships especially with the opposite sex.

Latency stage: This period covers middle childhood from about age six years until puberty. It is a latent period as children are not yet ready to express their sexuality.

Genital stage: This refers to the onset of puberty when adolescents become ready for full sexual activity.

Freud's view is that the environment is important as the child is involved in ongoing conflict situations with its parents and is not strictly a laissez-faire model; however, it has many similarities.

Psychoanalysis and psycho-analytic therapy looks at how these experiences are stored in the unconscious mind and how they affect people's personality, feelings and behaviour.

Social constructivist model

This model is based on the work of Piaget (1896–1980), Bruner (b. 1915) and Vygotsky (1896–1934) and is influential in current early years provision. The social constructivist model originated in the work of Kant (1724–1804) and views children as partly 'empty vessels' (transmission model) and partly as pre-programmed (laissez-faire model) with an interaction between the two. The social constructivist model emphasises environmental, biological and cultural factors and sees the child as an active participant in their own learning and development.

Piaget

Piaget was a constructivist whose work has been a major influence both on developmental psychology and on learning and education. Piaget's influence cannot be underestimated as he changed the way in which young children's learning was viewed and opened the door to further research and development.

Piaget's view was that, from birth, a child actively selects and interprets information from its environment and has the ability to adapt and learn. He believed that children constructed higher levels of knowledge by drawing on their own innate capacities to interpret the information coming through the environment. Piaget stated that children passed through a series of stages of cognitive or mental development always in the same order but at different rates. He emphasised that the child was an active participant in their own learning and development. Although recognising the social world of the child as having a role in development and learning, Piaget did not emphasise this and his work focuses on the role of the individual child in their own development.

Piaget's stages

Sensori-motor (birth to about two years). The child moves from basic reflexes and learns through its senses, gradually moving toward organising more complex physical action schemes such as hitting and grasping.

Pre-operational (two to about seven years). The child begins to think and represents actions with symbols. Early language is the best example of representation as words begin to represent objects and people in the child's thinking. At this stage, thought is very different from the ways adults think and has different logic.

Concrete–operational (seven to about twelve years). Children become capable of more systematic logical thought and begin to grasp abstract notions. They still need to relate their thinking to concrete objects and activities.

Formal-operational (twelve years onwards). Children become capable of abstract thought and are able to make hypotheses and test them. Abstract concepts such as truth or justice are able to be grasped. Critics state that not all adults fully reach this stage.

Piaget believed that children learn through processes of adaptation known as:

- assimilation – taking in new information from the environment through the child's existing patterns of action (sometimes called schemas)
- accommodation – modifying existing patterns of actions to accommodate new information and knowledge
- equilibration – balancing what they already know with new experience to make sense of the world.

Assimilation – toddler established concept of cats as black

Accommodation – toddler has 'accommodated' new information that cats can be different colours

Toddler needs to have this reinforced by further experiences – equilibration – before accommodating this into his understanding

Key definitions from the work of Piaget

Schemas   These are early ideas or concepts based on linked patterns of behaviour and are part of the child's powerful drive to understand its experiences. Adults take for granted that they know how objects relate together or about shapes and where things are positioned. Children have to learn about this. Schemas include the idea or concept in the mind of the child and the actions the child takes as a result of the idea. Often schemas occur in clusters. For example, children can be fascinated by positioning objects in certain ways such as on top of something, around the edge or behind. They spend a lot of time positioning objects or people in this manner and will show this in their paintings as well. They are learning about position.

Children will develop their schemas for hours on end and in many ways. There are many types of schema identified by early years practitioners, teachers and psychologists. Examples of common types of schema clusters are as follows:

- Transporting – moving objects or collections from one place to another. Look out for children doing this using bags, trucks or containers.
- Orientation – looking at things from different angles. Children turn things upside down or hang upside down themselves.
- Horizontal and vertical schemas – often shown in actions taken by the child such as climbing or stepping up and down or lying flat. They will also construct in this way using blocks, or show the schema in drawings and collage. When both horizontal and vertical schema have been explored separately children merge them by exploring grids and crosses.

Conservation of mass Young children judge situations on what they can see. The classic Piagetian test for conservation of mass is when a child who is pre-operational is shown two equal sized pieces of clay. The child agrees they are the same size but when one is rolled into a sausage shape they will say that it is larger. This means the child cannot 'conserve' mass, i.e. understand the concept of *reversibility* of materials.

Conservation is not just about mass as children have to learn to 'conserve' in other areas such as volume, number or weight (which is a more difficult concept and comes about a year later than the conservation of mass).

Egocentricity Piaget described young children as egocentric because they could not make a distinction between objects in the world and their own actions towards the objects, i.e. they cannot see from another's point of view.

Discovery learning Piaget felt that young children learned best by discovery, i.e. working out for themselves how to think and solve problems, in other words, the child as a solitary learner. The role of the adult was not emphasised.

Bruner and Vygotsky

Bruner and Vygotsky build on Piaget's work but stress the role of play, talking with adults and interacting with the social world. Piaget's view of the child as a solitary learner is replaced by that of the child as a social being. The child then uses the tools of learning and their knowledge of their own culture received from adults to develop ideas and learning that they could not do alone.

Like Piaget, Vygotsky saw children as active organisers of their own lives but unlike Piaget he believed that social relationships and interaction with another person was needed for human beings to develop intellectually. Vygotsky emphasised the role of adults in helping children learn. He identified the 'zone of proximal development'; that is when children begin to show signs that they are ready to move on in their development and learning. Adults need to intervene and help children to move into the zone of actual development and the cycle goes on.

Bruner believed that children learn through 'doing', imagining what they have been doing and then turning what they know into symbols such as speech, drawing, and writing. Bruner views the adult as important in supporting children's learning especially when informal, everyday interactions are utilised to help children make sense of the world.

Social constructivism is widely acknowledged to underpin and influence much early years provision. It emphasises that children have distinct and different ways of thinking, behaving and feeling at different stages of development and that children's thinking is different from adults. The following table outlines theories of how children learn.

	Transmission model	Laissez-faire model	Social constructivist model
Advantages	Behaviour modification Learning through experience Insights into learning through observing and imitating	Stages identified when children are sensitive to particular learning Child encouraged to take lead in learning Developmental scales are useful	Rewarding for children and adults involved. Many centres of excellence today use this model. Includes communities and families and recognises cultural diversity
Disadvantages	Does not explain complexity of children's learning and behaviour Children do not direct their learning and are less likely to explore or try new things Model does not consider the child's developmental stage affects how learning occurs	Child pre-programmed to develop regardless of adult or environment May be labelled backward if they do not conform with developmental scales Cultural differences in 'milestones' not recognised	Costly to operate demanding high staffing ratios and resourcing levels
Role of adult and interaction with child	Child seen as passive with adults making good what is lacking (as in compensatory education movement of 1960s)	'Leave it to nature' model with limited role for adult Adults may not intervene at appropriate time or offer sufficient stimulation Child seen as mostly passive	Child seen as active agent in their own learning Requires highly skilled multi-disciplinary teams to work together Adults observe and assess children, work closely with child, support their learning, extend play opportunities Parents are involved as partners
Organisation of the learning environment	Adults control environment Formal programmed approach to learning using small steps each building on the other Children sit quietly getting on with activities with little exploration or movement or need for much equipment	Well resourced with plenty of equipment and activities, and allowing children to explore freely Low adult intervention may miss learning opportunities	Carefully structured and well resourced encouraging exploration and discovery Emphasis on the crucial role of play in learning Balance of adult structured activities and play and learning opportunities freely chosen by child Outdoors important
Nature/ nurture debate	Supports 'nurture' as little notice taken of genetic or innate abilities	Supports 'nature' as environment does not really affect development	Both nature and nurture are important, development and learning are interdependent
Links to current research	Dowling (1995) argues behaviour modification is not long term There is little support for this model in current practice in the UK	Current research, especially concerning brain development, supports view that child has sensitive periods	Approach supported by current research, e.g. Athey (1990) and Pascal (1993)

Assessment activity 7.2

Working in a group, develop an article for the local press for three new nurseries opening in your area. Each nursery is based on one of the major theories of children's learning. In your article describe the advantages and disadvantages of using the individual nurseries, how the nursery views children's learning, how the adults work with the children and whether the approach of the nursery is up to date. Finally decide which nursery you would recommend and why.

The work of early educators and their influence on current principles and practice

As well as basing early years provision on key theories of how children learn, current early years practice has also grown out of the work of the early educators. This section explores the work of Froebel, Steiner, Montessori, McMillan and Isaacs and notes where their ideas are incorporated into mainstream practice today. The section also identifies curriculum models outside mainstream provision and explores current principles of good practice in early years settings.

The range of provision where early learning takes place

Early years care and education takes place wherever there are young children and usually starts in the home. By its very nature caring for a young child is also educating the child and encouraging its learning and development. Services for families and young children increasingly offer an integrated service, as both care and education need to be included to look after the needs of the whole child. Children will learn well in whatever settings they are in given the correct conditions.

Theory into practice

A baby is being bathed. During bath time the carer:

- talks and sings to the baby
- helps play with the water and the bubbles
- plays with toys pushing them under the water and letting them pop up again
- encourages the baby to listen to the noise made by the water
- lets the water trickle through their hands and pours from a plastic cup on to the baby's tummy
- laughs and enjoys the experience with the baby.

The learning here is endless: language development, sensory development, social and emotional development through a shared and pleasurable activity, early scientific learning about the properties of water, floating and sinking.

Bathing a baby can be valuable educationally as well as a basic care activity. Choose another everyday care activity and identify the learning that takes place.

From birth there are a range of different settings outside the home where babies and children receive care and education. These services are provided by different parts of the early years sector.

- **Statutory.** Usually government or local government provision and often set up under legislative requirements: includes schools and nursery schools, family centres, social service provision. Provision is usually free.
- **Voluntary.** Usually offered by a voluntary organisation using volunteers and some paid staff, e.g. pre-schools, playgroups, larger organisations such as Barnardos. Parents/carers usually pay a small fee and can be involved in the running of the setting.
- **Private/independent.** Usually businesses set up to make a profit or for reward, e.g. private day nurseries, childminders. Parents/carers will normally pay the costs.

Types of setting

The statutory, voluntary, private and independent sectors will offer different services for children under eight depending on their type and purpose. In England there are different requirements for registration by OFSTED. Under the Children Act 1989 these requirements have recently been revised and are detailed in the *National Standards for Under Eights Day Care and Childminding* (DfES, 2001). In the other countries of the UK the arrangements are different.

Key issues

Research the requirements of the Day Care Standards (DfES, 2001). Identify and discuss the differences in the requirements for different settings for Standard 3 'Care, Learning and Play'. Explore the standards for evidence of care and education. If you are studying in the other countries of the UK find out what their requirements are for approving early years settings and see if these cover both care and education.

Sessional care

Sessional care is for children in the absence of their parents/carers and is usually offered by pre-schools or playgroups that operate for less than four hours per day. Sessional care and education is also offered by nursery schools and classes. Sessional care usually concentrates on giving the child enriched play and learning opportunities. Sometimes family centres will offer sessional care and education to give the parents/carers a break or to work separately with them. Sessional care is offered either free via the nursery education grant or parents pay a small sum to a local voluntary organisation.

Full day care

Full day care is often for working parents who pay for the service. This is provided by private nurseries who are registered to provide for children under eight in the absence of their parents/carers for a continuous period of more than four hours per day. Children's centres and family centres may sometimes offer full day care and these are usually part of local authority provision.

Out of school care

This term is used to cover out of school provision for children between three and eight that takes place in the absence of their parents/carers providing it is over two hours in any day and for more than five days per year. Out of school care takes place before and after school or during the school holidays and will include breakfast clubs, holiday play schemes, summer camps, after school clubs and so on. Out-of-school clubs are often offered by the private or voluntary sector and require the payment of a fee that may or may not be subsidised by the local authority.

Crèches
These are facilities that provide occasional care for children under eight in the absence of their parents. They need to be registered if they run for more than two hours per day on more than five days per year. The children may not stay the full two hours. Crèches operate in many different places such as shopping malls, sports centres, exhibition or conference centres.

Childminders
Childminders are registered to look after one or more children under the age of eight to whom they are not related in their home for more than two hours per day. They are a very useful resource as they can often offer a highly flexible service including all day and after school care. Childminders are part of the independent sector and parents usually pay for their services. Some childminders work for social services supporting families and children.

Think It Over

Investigate the provision in your area for full day care and sessional care. If you can, get hold of materials from non-mainstream groups such as Steiner.

Collect examples of marketing leaflets, information for parents, inspection reports, or planning documents – anything that will tell you about the provision.

Develop a checklist to see which theoretical model/s are used in the settings you investigate. You could use headings such as learning environment, parents as partners, role of play, organisation – you may find it is not so easy as it seems!

Theories and influence of early educators
Friedrich Froebel (1782–1852)
Key beliefs and emphasis
Froebel emphasised the importance of physical activity and exploration involving real experiences, especially creative play, finger plays, songs and rhymes. His work stressed the importance of making one thing stand for another, i.e. symbolism. He stated how symbolic behaviour is best developed through play, especially imaginative and pretend play. Froebel developed play activities and materials to promote symbolic play. He called the play materials, e.g. wooden blocks, 'the gifts'. Activities such as songs, movements and dancing were called 'the occupations'. Froebel also felt that children were helped to think through being introduced to opposites, e.g. hard and soft, and this was a theme followed through in the play materials he used.

Froebel believed that everything in the world was linked and that children perceived the world best through integrated activities. He stressed the importance of encouraging art, literature, natural sciences, mathematical understanding and the appreciation of beauty. Froebel recognised that parents are the child's first educator and stated that teachers should be like 'mothers' to young children. He welcomed parents into schools and into the 'communities' where the children were cared for.

Influence on current practice and curriculum models

Most mainstream early years provision in the UK is based on Froebelian principles and most of his ideas are now taken for granted although in his lifetime they were ground breaking.

Current mainstream settings encourage learning through first-hand experiences and play remains central to provision for children's learning, including language development through rhymes and finger plays. Most early years settings encourage imagination to flow freely in play, and symbolic play is seen as very important for children's development.

Early years settings integrate care and education and today this is emphasised more than ever. Children's development is still encouraged through provision of a wide range of materials and activities tailored to the needs of the individual child. Current best practice still emphasises creativity, science and the humanities and learning opportunities are integrated across curriculum areas.

Current mainstream provision places emphasis on positive relationships and social development and values parent/educator partnerships.

Susan Isaacs (1885–1948)

Key beliefs and emphasis

Susan Isaacs worked in the Froebelian tradition but was influenced by Melanie Klein, a psychoanalyst, who believed in encouraging children to express their feelings. Isaacs valued play as giving children opportunity to think and learn and to express feelings.

Isaacs saw parents as the main educators of young children and felt that nurseries were an extension of home. She felt that children should remain in nursery until the age of seven before starting formal school and kept careful records of children's time at nursery. Through these records she demonstrated how children regressed after starting formal school.

Influence on current practice and curriculum models

Mainstream early years settings today give opportunities for children to 'let off steam' in a controlled way through vigorous physical play and encourage controlled expression of feelings through language and imaginative play. Play is still seen as central to learning and parents/carers are seen as partners. Careful observation of children and accurate record keeping is emphasised in early years settings.

Many countries throughout the world do not start children at school until age six or seven years and many early years educators in the UK argue that this should be the case here.

Margaret McMillan (1860–1931)

Key beliefs and emphasis

Margaret McMillan worked in the Froebel tradition. She believed in active learning through first-hand experiences and emphasised feelings and relationships as well as physical aspects of movement and learning. McMillan believed that play helped a child to become a 'whole person' and was an integrating force in learning and development.

McMillan was a pioneer in nursery education. She believed in the introduction of nursery schools as an extension of home and as communities in themselves. She emphasised the value of the open air and introduced gardens for families to play and explore. She believed in partnership with parents who developed with their children in the nursery environment. McMillan was the first to introduce school meals and medical services and stressed the importance of trained adults to work with children

Influence on current practice and curriculum models
McMillan has had a powerful influence on the provision of nursery education in the UK and many of her principles are widespread. Today children are given access wherever possible to outdoor areas and encouraged to make gardens and use natural materials. Early years settings give opportunities for children's physical, social, imaginative and creative play, and encourage expression of feelings. Active learning is encouraged through provision of a wide range of materials and equipment together with a skilled and qualified workforce.

McMillan's views on the nursery school as a community are followed through today as parents are invited into schools and seen as partners in the care and education of their children. As well as being a community in itself, early years settings extend provision into the community and become part of the community.

School meals and medical services are now an accepted part of provision.

Maria Montessori (1870–1952)
Key beliefs and emphasis
Maria Montessori was a doctor who practised in a poor part of Italy and who spent a good deal of time observing children especially those with special needs. There are Montessori schools in the UK within the private sector. Children are seen as active learners who go through sensitive periods in their development when they are more open to learning particular skills and concepts.

The Montessori method involves a series of graded activities through which every child progresses working through specially designed Montessori materials, e.g. solid geometric forms, knobbed puzzle maps, coloured beads, and various specialised rods and blocks. Each material isolates one quality for the child to discover, e.g. size, colour or shape. The materials are self-correcting – when a piece does not fit or is left over, the child can easily see what went wrong.

Montessori did not emphasise play or the free flow of ideas and did not allow children to draw or undertake creative activities until they had worked through all the graded learning activities. The child is thought to solve problems independently, building self-confidence, analytical thinking, and the satisfaction that comes from accomplishment.

Montessori did not think there was a need for adult 'correction'. The role of the adult was limited to facilitating the child's own activity; the teacher is known as 'directress'. Children are not seen as part of a community but work largely on their own in a quiet and peaceful environment of total concentration. Little parental involvement is encouraged.

Influence on current practice and curriculum models
Mainstream provision also sees the child as an active learner and some Montessori ideas and materials are used such as graded sizes of particular shapes, e.g. small, medium and large blocks.

Many of the other aspects of Montessori provision are different from mainstream early years practice. For example, mainstream settings emphasise the role of adults in intervening and supporting the child's learning. Current mainstream practice would not usually leave children to work through activities alone but encourages group work and sensitive intervention by adults to support learning. Sometimes quiet concentration is encouraged but according to individual children's needs rather than a basic approach to all learning activities. Current practice would involve parents/carers as partners with a high degree of involvement.

Rudolph Steiner (1861–1925)

Key beliefs and emphasis

Steiner believed in childhood as a special phase of life and that the young child needs a protected environment where all-round development can take place. He believed that a child's temperament was important in overall development and learning as well as academic progress. Steiner also emphasised the spiritual, moral, social, artistic and creative and the need to care for each other. He did not emphasise what is taught but how and when.

Steiner believed that young children need to be protected from formal learning and learn through imaginative and creative play using simple tasks and activities with natural materials. In Steiner schools the learning opportunities are often repeated as many times as necessary so that all children are confident including those with special needs.

Influence on current practice and curriculum models

Mainstream settings believe in early childhood as a unique phase of life that is more than just preparation for adulthood and that the individual child's needs and personality are important. As in Steiner schools, establishing relationships is valued and reaching out and serving the community is considered part of the nursery's role.

Mainstream settings consider the how and when (the process of learning) but also the content. Mainstream settings do not emphasise the spiritual dimension as much as Steiner.

Curriculum models outside mainstream provision

High/Scope

Aside from the curriculum models described above (Montessori and Steiner) there are other models currently practised in the UK, e.g. High/Scope. High/Scope is a structured programme developed in the 1960s in the USA, and now extended for use with pre-school children and babies. Some mainstream settings in the UK use the High/Scope approach. The method was well resourced in the USA and involved parents and children in more deprived areas. It was designed to meet the gaps in the child's learning and everyday experience. The results seem to promise good long-term benefits for children In the UK evidence for the success of High/Scope is less clear but new work is taking place in different parts of the country involving parents who themselves have basic skills needs and this seems to be opening new possibilities for High/Scope.

High/Scope is based on well-accepted educational principles:

- *Active learning*: the child is encouraged to become an active learner involved directly in their own learning.
- *Personal initiative*: the child is encouraged to use personal initiative to plan/do/review their own learning. For example, children are encouraged to plan their own learning at the start of the session, to undertake the learning experiences and to review how it went at the end of the session.
- *Consistency*: High/Scope believes that children need consistent, stable daily routines and organisation of the learning environment to help them become confident and independent learners.

- *Genuine relationships*: High/Scope practitioners aim to bring genuine warmth and trust to their relationships with children and respect and value cultural diversity.
- *Appropriate curriculum*: High/Scope has been developed through extensive observations of children and is designed to provide key learning experiences. The settings have a range of resources similar to most mainstream early years settings.

Hothousing young children

Other settings may offer highly structured programmes that 'hothouse' children into accelerated learning. Settings that attempt to push young children into learning in a formal way before they are ready may have serious long-term effects. The danger is that they deny children the opportunity to meet other children, relax and play without pressure. Children need time to grow and develop and to play freely to encourage their all-round development.

Current principles of good practice in early years provision

The principles of good practice in early years provision have integrated many of the key features of the work of the early educators. Over many years there have been debates about what good provision is and how it is organised and developed. Today there is general agreement about what constitutes 'good practice' and these ideas have been drawn together in the Curriculum Guidance for the Foundation Stage in England. The key areas for good practice are summarised in the table below. How the principles of good practice are implemented is detailed below.

Adults and children	Children are active learners, not passive recipients of learning. They engage with adults, materials, events and ideas in ways that are immediate, direct and meaningful to them	Adults are skilled and trained and understand how children learn and develop Children are viewed as a whole and their individual needs are met	Sensitive intervention by adults to support learning is the norm	Adults observe and assess children's progress and are able to respond appropriately	Imagination and symbolic play are seen as very important
Curriculum	Recognition that well planned and purposeful play is the most important vehicle for learning for young children	A balance exists between adult initiated activities and those children choose themselves	Equality of opportunity and access to learning for all children regardless of race, gender, culture, religion, disability, special educational needs, ability or home language	A broad, balanced, well planned relevant and appropriate learning curriculum is provided	A wide range of activities and equipment is available both indoors and outside to encourage all areas of children's development
Environment	A safe and stimulating environment	A secure and reassuring environment	Positive relationships with parents	A well planned and organised environment	Accurate records are kept

Assessment activity 7.3

Draw a diagram or table that highlights the key concepts of each of the early educators. Use the headings below and include other headings if you have extra information.

- Early educator's name.
- Key beliefs about children and how they learn.
- Views on play.
- Views on the role of parents and other adults involved in learning.
- Influence on current practice and curriculum models.
- Equipment they may have used to help children learn.

The role of play in the development of early learning

Wherever you see young children you are likely to see play taking place. Play is a term used to describe both adult and children's activity, for example an adult playing golf or cards or a child playing with their friend or with blocks in the garden. Although human beings play throughout their lives, adult play tends to be seen as something extra to do when work is over whereas for young children the term play is used to describe much of how they spend their time and energies. This section considers theories of play, the requirement for 'quality' play and the importance of play in the young child's learning.

Think It Over

What can you remember about your early play experiences? Discuss in a group and see if you remember similar things. Take it a step further and remember what it was like when an adult stopped your play even for good reasons – how did you feel?

Valuing play

Different cultures place different value on play. For some it is a fundamental right of the child (see UN Convention on Rights of the Child), for other cultures childhood is seen as a preparation for adulthood rather than a time unique and important in itself. Here the role of play is given less prominence and children are expected to engage in adult work from a very early age. In some cultures play is highly valued and encouraged throughout early childhood when formal schooling is postponed until the age of six or seven years.

Key issues

Get a copy of the Department of Health booklet 'The Rights of the Child – A Guide to the UN Convention (CAG9)' or read Article 31 of the Convention. What does this say about the child's right to play?

Children's play contributes both to their all-round development and has generally agreed characteristics and benefits such as:

- freely chosen and initiated by the child – no one can make a child play
- spontaneous
- content and intent of the play owned and directed by the child
- child is actively involved
- involves first-hand experiences
- usually pleasurable even where children are concentrating deeply
- usually a process not a product
- pretending is an important feature.

Through play children can:

- take risks and make mistakes in safe environment
- practise and build up ideas, concepts and skills
- explore, develop and represent their learning experiences
- learn how to control impulses and behaviour
- explore the identities and feelings of others
- express fears or feelings in a controlled way
- be creative and imaginative
- communicate and be sociable.

Common terms used to describe play

You will often notice that practitioners and researchers use a variety of terms to describe categories of play. These categories relate to the way the child is playing and are not to do with what or whom the child is playing with. All these categories could refer to different types of play such as playing with dolls, running and jumping outside or using sand and water.

Play terms	Description
Free play	Children playing where adult intervention is absent or minimal
Structured play	Adult led tasks, e.g. a modelling activity using clay. Adult demonstrates techniques and how to work with clay, encourages child to participate and learn how to manipulate the tools and materials. Once mastered the child knows how to play with clay and this can lead into deeper free flow play

Play terms	Description
Free flow play	When children learn through play at the deepest level using their experience of ideas, feelings and relationships and applying these with control, competence and mastery. In free flow play child uses: symbolic, manipulative, play with props, rough and tumble play. The term free flow play was first used by Tina Bruce who is a well-known researcher in early years education and play
Exploration, discovery and investigation of materials	Some early years practitioners and teachers do not categorise these activities as play but others do

Children who cannot play freely for whatever reason need adult support to play, e.g. an adult to hold their hand if they lack confidence or if they are disabled, special play equipment or environments to assist their play. Children need time to play and if they lead a busy life undertaking activities their parents choose for them, the opportunities for play are fewer. In addition unhappy children, sick children or those who are dislocated, perhaps as asylum seekers or refugees, need particular help to play. Sometimes practitioners need to show children how to play and then to stand back and let them. If they are emotionally damaged, children may need play therapy to help them to play. Finally children need space to play as cramped and restricted environments do not allow the full scope of play activity.

Is this play?

As well as the basic necessities of life, children must be allowed to play as a vital part of their healthy growth and development.

Theory in practice

Find out the local policy for inclusion of children with special educational needs. Are any special provisions made for play activities? How would you improve provision in your local area to ensure every child had the same chance to play? Why is it important that all children are able to participate in play activities?

The role of the early years practitioner in quality play

Many practitioners who work with young children recognise that there are two levels of play, one where children are just kept occupied and another that contributes to their educational development. Much early years research supports the view that children can spend time in low level play that has little real benefit for learning and development.

Many practitioners feel that play cannot be left to develop naturally and needs adults to plan, assist and support the play to ensure it aids learning. To ensure children's play brings them the maximum benefits and involvement will require sensitive and knowledgeable adult intervention to ensure that play is of high quality. This means practitioners must not interfere unnecessarily and control play but must observe children carefully and unobtrusively, extend and support play by introducing new ideas or materials building on the child's interest. They may also need to model playful behaviour to help the child learn to play more effectively.

Case Study

Irena is three years and four months old. Most days she plays with an empty doll's pram and wheels it round and round the outdoor area. She keeps stopping and looking at the children on the climbing frame and other equipment but does not attempt to talk or interact with the other children. Staff have observed Irena for a while and are concerned that she is not making the most of the play opportunities open to her. They have decided to spend time with Irena as she wheels the pram and talk to her as they walk around, suggesting other wheeled toys. They also wheel Irena around the garden laughing and having fun, and other children want to join in. After a week or so Irena seems to have made a friend and they take turns wheeling each other and using the dolls and teddies. They are beginning to use the dressing up clothes.

• Why were staff concerned about Irena? How did they check out their concerns? Why do you think the staff acted in the way they did? Were they successful?

There are other viewpoints regarding play and the basis for some of these can be found earlier in the philosophies of the early educators. Other disciplines such as playwork may have very different views of the role of the adult in play and believe that settings should allow for uninterrupted play with minimal adult intervention.

Play and learning

Children will learn well in whatever settings they are in, given the correct conditions. Children's play is one of the most important aspects of their lives. How they play will be the greatest influence on their development and learning but it is not the only influence on learning. Bruce (1996) describes play as co-ordinating a network of developmental and learning strategies. These include the following:

• Learning through first-hand experiences: children cannot learn by proxy. Second-hand experiences such as watching television or playing computer games are not likely to bring about quality learning experiences. However, if these build on the child's real experiences, it is more likely to deepen the learning. Listening to stories is not active play but has other benefits for the child.
• Taking part in games with rules: this allows the child to learn the rules of the game and of their own culture. They learn how rules are negotiated, who has authority, how to belong and be part of a community, e.g. the rule is to take turns or to count to 100 during hide and seek.

- Representation: children represent their experiences through language, dance and movement, drama and creative expression. They need to represent their own experiences, e.g. drawing from close observation of real things.

Moyles (1989) suggests that the learning process is like a spiral. It begins with free play, continues with structured or directed play and then returns to enriched free play as knowledge and abilities are acquired and consolidated. The first session of free play allows exploration whereas the second brings a degree of mastery and this is followed up by the adult who provides more structured play opportunities leading to a new cycle of play and exploration. This spiral goes on and on as children go through these cycles many times.

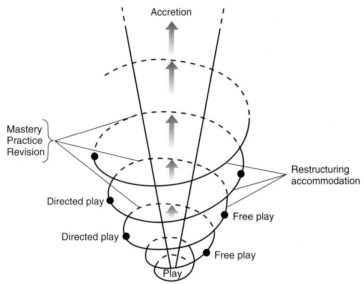

Moyles' learning spiral

Example of Moyles' learning spiral

- **Free play: exploration.** Mina is sitting at the modelling table for the first time. She has been watching other children playing with dough and clay for a couple of days but has never sat down to try it herself. Today she explores the dough by pushing and squeezing it and making holes with her finger.
- **Mastery.** Mina plays freely several times over the next few days and becomes more and more skilful in the way she handles the dough.
- **Adult provides structured play: baking dough shapes.** When the early years practitioner sets up a dough baking activity to make fruit shapes for the shop, Mina joins in. Over the next few weeks Mina develops real skills in modelling dough.
- **Free play.** Mina starts to investigate clay in exactly the same way.
- **Mastery.** As she is experienced in modelling dough her skill with clay grows more quickly.
- **Adult provides a structured play activity: making biscuits.** Mina joins in and makes biscuits, she rolls out the paste and cuts out the biscuits with control.
- **Free play.** Mina plays with the cooking utensils in the home corner.
- **Mastery.** She develops her play by entering into a rich sequence of imaginative domestic play centred on cooking.
- **Adult provides structured play activity: cooking bread.** Mina is enthusiastically entering into the cooking activity.

...and so the learning goes on.

Theories of play

Within early years practice there are two main theoretical views of play on which practitioners can base their work with children, outlined below. However, playworkers and others working with older children or within different disciplines have different theoretical perspectives that are not covered here.

Psycho-dynamic theories (feelings)

Psycho-dynamic theories were pioneered by Sigmund Freud and built on by workers such as Winnicott (1971) who thought play was the way in which children came to terms with their anxieties and fears. As children develop symbolic play (where one thing stands for another) they begin to act out their deepest feelings and concerns through language and role play. This approach to play is usually used in therapeutic situations. Play therapists often use techniques based on psycho-dynamic theory, for example using drawing and representation and encouraging children to express their feelings on paper. They sometimes use dolls and puppets so that children can express their feelings by pretending it's the doll or the puppet that has those feelings. This is a good way for some children to start to express what are often deep feelings of distress or anger that they simply cannot express openly.

Most early years provision will provide opportunities for children to express their deep feelings sometimes of frustration and anger or fear and despair. Vigorous physical activity can often help children to let off steam as can using a hammer and peg or pummelling clay. Many children will use puppets, masks or pretend play to act out their fears and concerns and this is normal behaviour. Adults have to provide adequate opportunities for children to express feelings and to observe children carefully to ensure that they notice if a child needs more specialised help.

Social constructivist theory (thinking)

Piaget saw play as the means by which the child's learning comes together and helps the child to make sense of the world. Vygotsky emphasised the importance of other people being involved in play. In particular he felt that children used play to act out and practise things before they managed them in real life circumstances and that play moved children from the zone of proximal development to the zone of actual development.

Most early years settings base their provision on social constructivist theory and will provide a wide range of activities and equipment for children to use in their learning. Careful observation of children's play and activity will show to observant adults when the child is ready to move on. For example, if a child is drawing circles and dots and recognisable letters, then says 'That's my name', it may be time for the adult to give opportunities for practice and encouragement to write purposefully.

Piaget's stages of play development

Piaget identified the following stages in play development:

- Sensori-motor play (using senses and movement) from 0 to eighteen months, for example exploring toys or their own hands, looking intently, sucking, banging the object on the ground, throwing objects.
- Symbolic play (where one thing stands for another) from eighteen months to five years, for example using language – words stand for something, blocks become cars, dolls become babies, they themselves become someone else such as a mummy or daddy when playing in a domestic play area.

- Co-operative play (using games with rules) five to eight years, for example playing chase or hide and seek and making up their own rules or playing a board game and learning to obey the rules or take turns.

Theory into practice

- Investigate how children in your placement can let off steam and express their feelings safely. What activities and equipment are provided to assist in this process? How does this relate to psycho-dynamic theory?
- Look at Piaget's stages of play development. For each stage think of activities and equipment that could be used with children to promote play development.

Co-operation in play

Early years practitioners work with children during their time at nursery to encourage co-operation but recognise that children go through different stages before they co-operate in play. Babies and toddlers usually play alone although they can be said to be aware of others. As they get older, children tend to watch others playing, then play alongside before joining in and co-operating. Co-operative play with rules usually means children make their own rules and play within those rules.

Assessment activity 7.4

Scenario 1: Mark is three years of age and has started at a local nursery school. He has settled well and enjoys the activities. Mark's parents are concerned that he spends a lot of time 'just playing'. They have written a note to the head expressing their concerns. Write a note to Mark's parents explaining why the nursery encourages children to join in play activities.

Scenario 2: Shenaz spends a good deal of her time in the construction area playing with large blocks. She is becoming very skilled in building various tall structures but staff have noticed she is becoming frustrated and knocks them down very quickly. Prepare a report outlining what the adult could do to support and extend Shenaz's play. Use ideas from Moyles' play spiral on which to base your report.

Scenario 3: Children in the pre-school are encouraged to enjoy vigorous outdoor activity, rough and tumble and activities that help children express strong feelings in a safe way, e.g. pounding clay, using a hammer. They are also encouraged to develop 'symbolic' pretend play sequences in a variety of nursery activities such as domestic play, imaginative play, building and making things.

- Explain to a new student how the psycho-dynamic and the social constructivist theories of play could be used to explain these activities.

The identification and promotion of learning opportunities for young children

This section looks at the curriculum and learning opportunities offered to young children. It considers the curriculum prior to formal schooling, the Foundation Stage and Early Learning Goals (ELGs) and the National Curriculum Key Stage 1.

What is the early years curriculum?

'The early years curriculum' is sometimes defined as all the learning opportunities and experiences offered to young children under eight years of age. However, in England, children normally start their formal education at five years of age when they commence the National Curriculum Key Stage 1, therefore this section uses the term 'early years curriculum' to refer to children at the Foundation Stage and earlier.

In a sense the early years curriculum starts at birth as babies are exposed to learning and development activities right from the start. Simply keeping children occupied with worksheets, colouring in, tracing and following templates or making up cards that adults have designed and prepared, does not constitute a learning opportunity. The early years curriculum should be broad, balanced and differentiated. It should cover all the six areas of learning in a balanced way. Differentiation means the curriculum is flexible and can be different for different children in order to meet individual needs. Differentiation must still ensure the curriculum remains broad and balanced.

Think It Over

You are in work placement where in your room a good deal of the children's time is taken up with watching TV or videos, colouring in cards to take home or working on displays that are basically the adults' work. You know this is not promoting children's learning except in a very limited way but the parents seem happy enough.

Imagine you were a new member of staff – how would you change things and how would you explain your reasons to the parents?

Basic principles for learning opportunities in the early years

What children are expected to learn is determined largely by the culture of the nation in which they live. In the UK there are some differences between the four countries but much of the learning and experiences are common. In England, the main areas of content known as the 'six areas of learning' are shown below:

- Personal, social and emotional development
- Communication, language and literacy

- Mathematical development

- Knowledge and understanding of the world

- Physical development

- Creative development

Babies learn through everyday routines

Babies are also highly motivated and curious learners and respond to a rich and stimulating learning environment. You may find in your placements that babies under one year and toddlers under three are in separate rooms in the nursery as they have distinct needs. As well as a stimulating environment babies and toddlers need to have quiet periods to rest and sleep. Some people believe that babies and toddlers should not be kept separate.

Babies learn primarily through their senses, i.e. sight, touch, taste, smell, hearing and through linking their own movements to the sensory information they receive from their environment. For example, the baby waves its hand around at random and hits a pram toy that makes an interesting sound. This happens a few times and the baby soon learns that they can control the pram toy and make the interesting sound. Babies need experiences that enable them to explore using all their senses from the earliest age. Babies need to be in a safe and secure environment where they trust the adults around them as this provides the basis for effective learning and development.

Provision for babies and very young children can draw on the six areas of learning but the

methods of delivery will be adapted to meet their needs As well as age-appropriate toys and equipment, babies are sometimes provided with a 'treasure basket' to explore. This is usually a basket containing everyday objects, usually not including manufactured items or toys, that is set on the floor with a small group of babies under one who play best if they are sitting up. A treasure basket will include items which can be explored with all the senses (remembering items go in babies' mouths) and changed regularly to ensure that babies' interest is kept going, e.g. wooden objects, fir cones, lemons, apples, shells, textiles or fur. Adults need to sit with the babies and supervise their play and exploration.

During the second year of life as children become more mobile some settings will provide children with a whole range of everyday items to explore. Children of this stage are often putting things inside one another or filling and emptying, and they can practice this with pots and pans, large hair curlers, ping pong balls, pompoms and many other safe items.

It is important when working with children, especially babies and younger children, that best use is made of every learning opportunity that occurs naturally throughout the day. This includes the routines of mealtimes, bathing and dressing, outings and play. During these everyday opportunities, the adults can use appropriate language and use the experiences to help learning as well as having fun with the baby. The environment should be suitable for the young child with plenty of opportunity to move around and explore in safety and to mix with other children and adults.

Case Study

Jamie is eighteen months old. He is 'helping' his mother with the housework and really wants to clean his bedroom. His mother provides him with a clean duster and they go up the stairs together counting them as they go. Jamie looks at the drawers where his clothes are kept and begins to polish. 'That's right Jamie, keep on polishing round and round and into edges until all the polish has disappeared and the marks are gone.' Jamie sings the 'wheels of the bus go round and round' and they change the words to 'the polish on the cloth goes round and round'. Jamie squeals with delight.

- Look at the six areas of learning and describe what Jamie has learned and into which area it fits. Observe children in their everyday routines and identify learning opportunities.

The learning content

The six areas of learning are evident in the experiences of young children right from birth but are made explicit in the Foundation Stage curriculum offered in England. The Foundation Stage applies to children in England aged three to five years who are being cared for and educated in settings that receive the nursery education grant. These children will be working towards the early learning goals (ELGs) (DfEE, 2000). The ELGs are expectations for most children to reach by the end of the Foundation Stage but are not a curriculum in themselves. The government recognises that some children will exceed the goals whereas others may still be working towards them, especially if they have not had high quality learning experiences, or have special educational needs or are learning English as an additional language.

Other countries of the UK have their own curriculum requirements or guidance as indicated below and you should obtain copies of the relevant documents as necessary:

- Wales: *Desirable Learning Outcomes for Children's Learning before Compulsory School Age Guidance for Local Early Years and Childcare Partnerships in Wales.*
- Northern Ireland: *CCEA Curricular Guidance for Pre-School Education.*
- Scotland: *Curriculum Framework for Children 3 to 5.*

The six areas of learning in more detail

The six areas of learning are common across most early years provision in the UK. The content may be expressed in different ways but is broadly similar, as shown in the table below.

Area of learning	Practitioners' role and experiences and activities that relate to the areas of learning (to be adapted according to stage of development)
Personal, social and emotional development	This area of learning is best developed through all other activities. Practitioners should make sure they encourage, praise and value all children, celebrate diversity, show sensitivity and make explicit equality of opportunity and anti-discriminatory practice
Learning to feel safe, secure and able to trust practitioners who work with them	Practitioners should create an environment and opportunities to develop children's:
Developing emotional well being, good self-esteem	• interest and motivation to learn • confidence and free expression of ideas • attention and concentration
Learning to respect themselves and others	• appropriate responses to significant experiences • awareness of child's own needs, views and feelings and sensitivity to others
Respecting children's culture so they develop a positive self-image	• understanding that differences should be respected • respect for their own culture and that of others
Learning about relationships	• ability to make relationships with adults and peers, work as part of a group, take turns and share fairly
Learning about the importance of friendships	• understanding of need for shared codes of behaviour and values and for groups to work together harmoniously
Developing a positive disposition to learn	• understanding of right from wrong and why • independence in activities and personal social skills, e.g. dressing
Having opportunities for problem solving	• awareness of similarities and differences between their experiences and others
Learning to be independent	• encouraging children to dress, undress and manage hygiene routines

Area of learning	Practitioners' role and experiences and activities that relate to the areas of learning (to be adapted according to stage of development)
Communication, language and literacy	
Interacting and communicating appropriately with others	Immerse children in language. Surround with print and other language opportunities. Model appropriate and rich use of language
Enjoying speaking, listening and written language	Explore, develop, experiment and use language with stories, nonsense rhymes, songs, rhymes, finger plays, role play, imaginative play, puppets
Extending and exploring new vocabulary	Use language to encourage to reflect on what they are doing
Speaking clearly and audibly, being confident and aware of the listener	Use sounds and experiment with how words are made up
Using language in imaginative and pretend play	
Exploring words and sounds	
Using language to talk, organise, sequence and clarify thinking, ideas, events	Use language to explore time and to anticipate events and predict outcomes, e.g. what might happen if we crack the eggs before we pour them into a bowl?
Linking sounds to letters, hearing and saying initial and final sounds of words, name and sound letters of alphabet	Tell and read stories using books, big books, poems
Recognising that print has meaning and in English goes left to right, front to back	
Enjoying stories and understanding their characteristics, e.g. main characters, sequence of events, how stories unfold	Use books to find information
Recognising that non-fiction books can answer questions of where, how and why	
Writing simple words using phonic knowledge and attempt more complex words	Practise writing in context, e.g. 'shopping lists', menus, instructions, stories. Make individual and class books
Developing pencil control	Pencil control activities
Mathematical development	
Saying and using numbers in everyday contexts	Practitioner to model maths language and create opportunities for children, e.g. how many, what if, how big, smaller than, larger than, more or less. Ball shape, box shape, heavy, light, full empty, inside, outside, between, above, below
Counting and recognising numerals	
Using mathematical language and ideas in everyday life and to solve simple problems	
Using counting rhymes	Using maths, rhymes and games, e.g. ten green bottles. Using opportunities in everyday routines and activities to
Asking maths questions	

Area of learning	Practitioners' role and experiences and activities that relate to the areas of learning (to be adapted according to stage of development)
	demonstrate that maths is all around in the environment
Posing maths problems	Adding and take away activities
Exploring shape, position, measures, space, sorting, matching, estimating, volume, capacity, pattern	Labelling shapes, looking at attributes, e.g. shape, colour, size of objects. sorting and matching
Knowledge and understanding of the world	
Investigating using all the senses: objects and materials such as animals and other living things, water, sand, earth, cycles of growing, planting, caring and harvesting	Practitioner to use appropriate language about the world. Children encouraged to answer 'what if', 'tell me more about' and similar questions about their world Cooking Use role play Growing, planting, preparing the soil How to care for animals
Observing and exploring their own environment	Use the local environment, talking to people and using maps and photos
Learning about similarities and differences	Note similarities and differences between objects and people. Explore cultures and beliefs through festivals and other activities
Learning about designing and making things, building and constructing	Designing, and making things using a wide variety of materials such as wood, plastic, string, dough; use real tools
Using computers and ICT	Use computers and programmable toys, different software
Looking back at things that happened in the past	Encourage children to talk to their families about their past, to ask questions about events in each others lives, compare artefacts from different times
Learning about their own culture	
Physical development	
Developing movement activities in everyday life, e.g. running, jumping and in dance and drama	Practitioner models appropriate language and give opportunities for physical development
Developing confidence and control in movement	Use small and large equipment, balance and climbing equipment, e.g. balls, bean bags, climbing frames, pushing and pulling toys
Developing balance and co-ordination	
Developing spatial awareness	Spatial awareness using own bodies and other objects
Becoming aware of safety issues	Healthy living projects and themes Use tools and materials safely

Area of learning	Practitioners' role and experiences and activities that relate to the areas of learning (to be adapted according to stage of development)
Creative development Using senses to explore key concepts Learning about different types of representation Learning about colour, texture, space, form, two and three dimensions Developing imagination Learning about music and musical instruments	Use creative activities including drawing, painting, collage, printing, modelling, sewing, natural material Explore sound patterns, patterns using objects Use movement and music, sounds, art, design, role play and stories Use musical instruments, songs and rhymes to explore ideas and feelings

Theory into practice

The children are playing in the sand, talking together and with an adult. They are pouring water into one corner and making a 'sea' and using moulds to make shapes. In the other corner they are using the dry sand to make patterns. In this one play activity the children are:

- learning scientific principles about the properties of materials, e.g. dry sand runs through their fingers, wet sand becomes solid and heavy and darkens in colour, water disappears and puddles (knowledge and understanding of the world)
- talking and developing their language e.g. 'The sand is brown and sticky and I can make holes in it' (communication and language)
- using maths concepts such as bigger than, smaller than, exploring volume and shape through filling and emptying the moulds (maths development)
- enjoying the feel of the sand and appreciating the shapes and patterns (creative development)

Observe one child or a small group of children in one particular play activity, e.g. water play area. Note briefly what you see them doing over a period of about 15 minutes. These need only be rough notes just to help you when you come to analyse what learning or development has been promoted. Note carefully:

- what equipment children use and how they use it
- if they are 'pretending' – describe what or who
- what language they are using (communication)
- how they relate to others around – both other children and adults (personal and social)
- if they are making or creating something (creative development)
- if they are exploring or investigating (knowledge and understanding of the world)
- what physical development being promoted, e.g. fine movements, large movements, co-ordination (physical)
- any maths concepts or language you notice (maths development)
- anything else of interest.

Write up your findings to summarise what learning and development could have been taking place under the six areas of learning. If there was no learning in a particular area say why you think that was and, if appropriate, how it might be possible to introduce this area of learning.

Promoting effective early learning

The main strategies for learning in young children are through playing and talking. In early years settings the six areas of learning will usually be presented to children through integrated activities, experiences, themes and projects. Children will approach the learning in different ways according to their age, level of experience, interest and confidence.

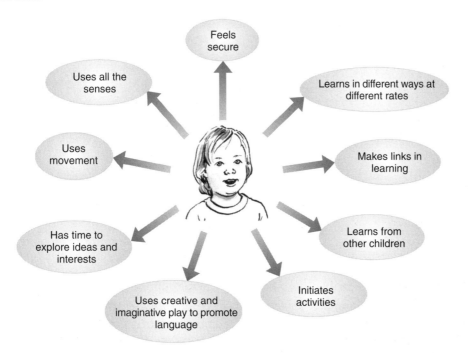

Strategies for effective learning

Theory into practice

Ben is just three years old and new to the nursery. He comes from a large family where he is a middle child. Ben has had little adult attention and does not know how to approach either the adults or the activities in the nursery.

Ben is greeted at nursery and then allowed a period of free play where he goes from activity to activity watching the other children, occasionally playing on the outside of the group. Staff notice Ben is reluctant to get his hands dirty or to touch the clay, dough, sand or water but during every session he watches other children play with dough.

What are your priorities for Ben's progress? Using the six areas of learning plan an individual programme for Ben that will fit into the nursery day.

Effective teaching

The QCA Guidance (QCA, 2000) defines early years teaching as 'systematically helping children to learn so that they are helped to make connections in their learning and are actively led forward, as well as helped to reflect on what they have already learnt'. Teaching has many aspects, including planning and creating a learning environment, organising time and material resources, interacting, questioning and responding to questions, working with and observing children, assessing and recording children's progress and sharing knowledge gained with other practitioners. The strategies shown in the following diagram draw on that definition.

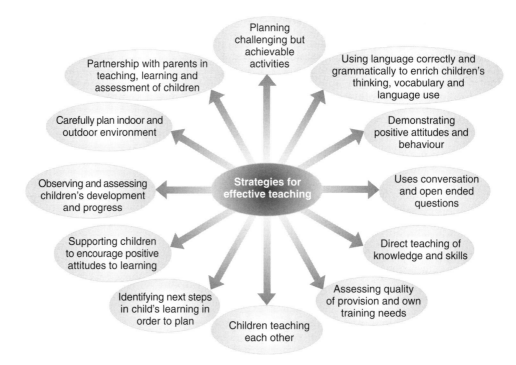

English as an additional language

Practitioners should value diversity and provide opportunities for children to play and develop in their home language as well as in English. This will mean providing print in the home language in everyday contexts such as books, labels or posters. Children will also need bi-lingual support to extend language and opportunities to hear their home language spoken, e.g. tapes, videos. Some children are bilingual from birth whereas others are acquiring English as an additional language. As with their home language children need to experience language in context. Children will need to listen to English spoken for some time before they can speak English.

Children with special educational needs and disabled children

Children with special learning requirements need the full range of appropriate support. Settings will have close links with parents and other agencies to clearly understand the children's needs. Depending on the circumstances, children may need help with:

- communication needs, e.g. use signs and symbols, large print, ICT, use all the senses to interpret the world and communicate
- adapting activities or providing alternatives
- using specialist aids and equipment
- encouraging self control and self help.

Assessing learning

There are many suggestions for assessment of learning detailed in 'Curriculum Guidance to the Foundation Stage' (QCA, 2000) and you should refer to this document or similar up-to-date guidance in your work with children.

Assessing learning requires close observation of children as they play and engage in curriculum activities. As well as observing, conversation and questions can ascertain the child's level of understanding. Assessment is based on:

- what children do
- what children say or communicate
- how children interact with others.

Case Study

Alice is busy examining an old telephone and taking it apart. She is playing with the dial making it move back and forth and enjoying the sound. Alice has found the telephone in an area of the nursery that has lots of discarded real objects such as old radios, clocks, watches, bells, metal coils to explore and is examining the object to find out more about it.

How does the adult assess her learning?

- Adult: 'That's a really old telephone'.
- Alice: 'My granddad's phone is a bit like this'.
- Adult: 'Tell me about your granddad's phone'.
- Alice: 'It's black and has a round bit – my new phone at home doesn't have a curly wire'.
- Adult: 'What sound does your granddads phone make?'.
- Alice: 'It goes ring ring ring ring'.

And so on…

During this conversation the adult is assessing how much Alice knows and understands about the purposes of telephones, the age of different objects and what makes them different, the sounds made by phones, the shapes and materials involved.

- Add to the conversation with Alice. What questions could you use to assess her learning and to extend her understanding? What structured activities could help her extend her knowledge?

The learning context

Learning can take place wherever the child is, e.g. at home or nursery, with friends, shopping or walking down the street. Formal places of learning such as classrooms are not needed for children to learn but well equipped and resourced settings staffed by knowledgeable adults can extend the range of possibilities. For example, if the children meet in a village hall with limited outdoor space and have to pack up after every session, their curriculum will to some extent be restricted as opposed to what is possible in a spacious purpose built nursery with its own garden. It is important to remember, however, that many groups in village halls provide excellent pre-school education and staff are creative and innovative.

Organisation and deployment of staff is important. There are minimum ratios for staff to children (DfEE, 2001). Children under three will normally only meet in small groups and will have key workers with special responsibility for them. A good deal of their time will be one to one with adults. Children between three and five spend most of their time in groups of less than eight children but will spend some time in bigger groups, e.g. story time. Once at school, children in reception or years 1 and 2 will be in larger groups of up to 25 children and sometimes more.

There are a range of different adults who are involved in children's learning:

* Parents who are the primary carers and educators of their children and with whom early years practitioners work in partnership.
* The early years staff team that is likely to include a range of staff with different qualifications and experiences. This group of staff should function as a team with mutual respect for each other and for the children and families. The team will include nursery nurses, early years practitioners, teachers, classroom assistants.
* Professionals whose work brings them into the nursery for different reasons such as health visitors, social workers, doctors, speech therapists, educational psychologists.

Values and beliefs

Values and beliefs also play a part in determining the kind of learning opportunities offered to young children. Adults have different views about how children learn and this will be reflected in the setting. Some settings will be much more formal than others and expect young children to work formally to a subject-based curriculum and not allow children to learn through play. In the UK today this is not considered to be good practice but this may not be the case in other cultures. Early years practitioners must be aware of the different beliefs and expectations that parents may have and work accordingly.

Think It Over

Children in the Yellow Room are all aged four years. They are all at slightly different stages of development. Some of the older children are well advanced in their literacy, can already read some words and follow the story from the book whereas others are only now learning how to hold a book and that print has some meaning. Every day the whole group hears a story and are then given worksheets to complete.

Think about how some children might be feeling and who is benefiting from the worksheet approach. Are any of the children likely to be engaged in real learning? Discuss alternative ways of working with children to follow up a story.

Planning the learning environment

The early years environment should be physically safe, e.g. safe equipment and supervision, include clean and hygienic washrooms and kitchens, safe care routines, home time routines and clear emergency procedures. The environment also needs to be predictable for the children, e.g. they know where things are, where to put things back and what the normal routine of the day is likely to bring. This does not mean it should be tightly scheduled as flexibility is needed, e.g. to spend time when a child comes in with something to show such as a pet or when someone has found an interesting insect in the garden. The needs of the child are the guiding principle.

Rooms will be laid out in many different ways but the following indicates the principles that should be observed:

- Rooms divided into smaller areas by screen or shelves to give privacy and encourage concentration and talking.
- Self-service principle where children help themselves to equipment and return it afterwards.
- Workshop style provision of activities according to curriculum plan – children joins in as they choose, activities often facilitated (anchored) by adults, e.g. making things, drawing from close observation.
- Other areas set up with equipment according to plans and some tables or floor space left empty.
- Large enough area for children to have circle or story time.
- Areas for sand and water (indoors and outdoors).
- Areas of learning grouped logically, e.g. science next to technology, books next to graphics, creative next to sinks.
- Layout avoids disruptive through traffic.
- Easy and constantly available access to outdoors (boots and waterproofs available).
- Displays at child height, furniture child sized.
- Child has own space to keep things, e.g. in a drawer.
- Comfortable areas for being quiet or using books.

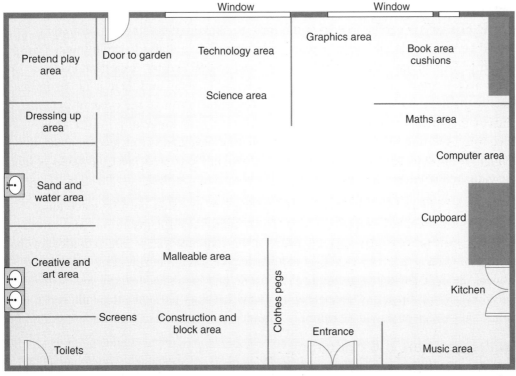

Example of a room layout

Routine of the day

This will vary between settings but for a two to three hour session most have a combination of:

- a greeting and settling down period
- open play and supported workshops activities
- free use of indoor and outdoor spaces
- circle time for games and singing
- opportunity for drinks throughout the session or perhaps with snack at a set time

- clearing away time
- story time
- going home.

Staff will be deployed according to an agreed plan; one may greet the children, comfort those who are distressed and help everyone to settle. Others may facilitate the workshops and be 'anchored' to that area during most of the session, giving opportunity for long conversations and support to the children.

Children should be given time to engage in periods of uninterrupted play when they are totally involved. During the session an adult will need to be free to cope with visits to the washrooms, comforting, clearing up accidents, pointing children towards the activities, and to ensure safe supervision both indoors and outside. Adults will need to carefully observe and assess the children during the session and record their progress. For example, where a child does not join in the workshops for a couple of weeks or if all the children are making items to decorate the nursery or to take home, extra encouragement may be needed.

Planning, implementing and evaluating the early years curriculum
Planning

Careful planning is needed to deliver the early years curriculum and the staff team should be involved at all levels; parents and children should also have an input. Plans should be written and available for all to see and to use, and for inspection evidence. Plans may be short/medium/long term each varying in detail and there is no set format. Usually planning builds on previous experiences gained through the cycle of planning, implementation and evaluation. Plans are based on a wide range of priorities and beliefs, e.g. meeting the ELGs, schema or promoting development in specific areas, but should ideally start from the interests of the children. Plans must meet the needs of both individual children and groups.

Planning for groups will follow an agreed format but provision must be made for individual children. For example, if a particular child has difficulty in fine movements, the early years practitioners must be aware of this and provide specific activities for that individual child at a level where they can participate. Therefore if a group of children is sewing, the child should be encouraged to join in and here the adult can help with threading and manipulating the needle in a way that does not make the child feel a failure. Achievement should be carefully recorded and built on in future sessions.

Implementation and evaluation

The implementation phase must be flexible according to children's needs especially the short-term plans. Evaluation should feed into the next cycle of planning. The staff team, parents and children will feed back on the implementation of the plan. The team will consider how well the plans went, how they could be improved next time, whether the children's needs were met and what learning took place.

Factors affecting planning

Plan duration	Factors to consider and include
Long-term plans/strategies (up to a year in advance)	• The ELGs/NC/Literacy and Numeracy strategies • Numbers and ages of children • Patterns of attendance • Available equipment and resources • Significant annual events • Family and community interests and concerns • Organisational factors such as staffing and room availability • Inspection recommendations • Meeting needs of individuals and groups
Medium-term plans (covering period of weeks)	• Planned topics and themes • Needs and interests of the children • Balance of programme • Knowledge and concepts to be gained • Skills to practise • Activities that will be used • Visits • The level of differentiation according to stage of development • Inclusion of anti-discriminatory practice • Health and safety • Existing routines • Arrangements for including children with special needs and English as an additional language
Short-term plans (usually detailed day to day, week to week or single activity)	• Staff deployment • Preparation and resources • Using visitors or parents who wish to be involved • Timing • Balance across week or day
Individual plans (for individual child's learning and development)	• Plans based on child's identified need, e.g. to encourage eye/hand co-ordination or confidence and self-esteem • Individual plans need to fit carefully with the medium/short-term plans

Examples of curriculum planning

Fairview Day Nursery

Fairview has decided to use the theme of 'Festival of Food' with two groups of three-to-four-year-olds. These children either attend the nursery on a sessional basis (each morning) or are part of the full-time groups that attend the nursery when their parents are at work. The nursery prepares its own lunchtime meals and snacks. The nursery has decided on this theme as it serves a diverse community who could all contribute and wishes to stress some healthy eating messages in a non-threatening way. Importantly the children themselves love cooking activities and have enjoyed visits to local markets. Two of the staff have allotments as have some grandparents, and children already enjoy visits to the allotment centre.

REMEMBER – there is no right and wrong way of planning and you will find excellent examples in your work placement. The figure below makes some suggestions.

Knowledge and understanding of the world

- Visit supermarkets, street markets, local allotments
- Help with cooking
- Discuss hot and cold cooking
- Identify healthy lunch boxes
- Understand simple food types and values including junk foods
- Use 'time' words
- Understand rationing and wartime menus
- Develop awareness of world foods and shortages
- Plant quick growing seeds
- Understand hygiene routines

Personal and social

- Learn about each festival – identify by name
- Provide food for festivals of Hanukkah, Diwali, Christmas
- Become familiar with different customs
- Welcome parents to help prepare and share food associated with different cultures
- Take turns to cook
- Share meals with families
- Dress up in chef's hats and aprons – pretend kitchen and café

Physical

- Develop fine manipulation using cutlery and cooking utensils in context and associate language (peeling, chopping, whipping, mashing)
- Develop large muscle – digging in allotment and preparing ground for planting

Festival of food

Creative

- Making models of food
- Draw and paint food themes for wall displays
- Design and print menus using IT and vegetable prints
- Identify colours and smells

Maths

- Buy ingredients
- Understand measuring and weighing vegetables and fruit in market
- Make price comparisons
- Practise selling and buying in pretend shop
- Lay table in café areas counting cutlery 1:1 correspondence
- Use computer and survey children's favourite foods
- Create database of information and then graphs to show findings
- Count using calculators and till

Communication

- Develop co-operative play in pretend shop
- Imaginative play and language in café area
- Make posters for menu of the day
- Write lists and notices
- Recognise print in environment
- Order on-line/phone
- Keep food diaries using cut out pictures, drawings and papier maché
- Understand social aspect of mealtimes
- Say and make up poems, rhymes and stories about food
- Act and model the Very Hungry Caterpillar
- Use food language (portion, helping, tasty, sour, sweet, salty)

Weekly plan based on 'Festival of Food' – learning objectives

- Visiting allotment (Monday and Tuesday) and developing understanding of growing things, where some foods come from, how they change when cooked.
- Talking about war time – developing understanding of time and continuity.
- Continuing work on personal hygiene.

The learning objectives are implemented in the ways shown in the following table.

Personal and social
- Sharing and taking turns with tools
- Encouraging talk about food likes and dislikes
- Cooking in group
- Sharing experience of allotment visit
- Eating together

Knowledge and understanding of the world
- Groups to visit Mrs Ash's allotment with 3 parents
- Bringing back potatoes, cooking, mashing with milk and butter and eating
- Noting change of appearance of potatoes, texture and taste
- Mrs Ash coming to talk about wartime recipes, showing real and dried eggs with pictures of Joel's great granddad digging large field
- Washing hands and need for hygiene both after gardening and before eating

Mathematical development
- How many potatoes for each person when they are mashed
- Sorting vegetables by colour and size
- Setting table ensuring correct numbers of plates and cutlery
- Selling vegetables in shop – using calculators and tills
- Serving food in café
- Maths language

Creative development
- Printing with potatoes
- Vegetable printing
- Comparing shapes and patterns
- Using prints on menus

Language and literacy
- 'Wash, wash, wash your hands' song to tune of row your boat
- Make posters and menus for café
- Develop gardening and food vocabulary
- Discuss what it was like in the war
- *The Very Hungry Caterpillar*

Physical development
- Digging potatoes
- Using potato masher
- Movement activity 'digging', 'raking' and 'stamping' the soil

Activity plan: making mashed potatoes
- Ask parents to help. Four children involved at a time.
- Prepare kitchen area. Peelers, chopping boards, masher, knives for chopping, wooden spoons, saucepans, salt, butter, milk, potatoes (from allotment), scales, nail brushes, bowls, towels.
- Select children in turn so that all can be involved over the week.
- Aprons.

Areas of learning

Knowledge and understanding of the world – life cycle of potato, change of state when cooked, mashing adding butter and milk – butter melting. Watching change of state. Tasting and adding salt and pepper to improve flavour, observing colour, understanding of how root vegetables look when taken out of the ground (children have dug up the potatoes). How to clean and prepare vegetables using brush and bowl of water (fine manipulative skills and hygiene rules for hand washing), cooking.

Physical development (control in fine movements and manipulative skills) – peeling user a potato peeler and noting change of appearance under the skin. Chopping using knife.

Communication – use of descriptive and mathematical language. Vocabulary – mashed, mashing, peeling, boiling, flavour, dirty, clean, earth, heavier than/bigger than, round, oval, knobbly, smooth, rough.

Maths development – language as above, weighing the potatoes.

Creative – pattern making on mashed potato.

Personal and social – working together, taking turns.

Review of 'mashed potatoes' activity

All the children participated and enjoyed the activity. Most of the time they were closely involved and talking to adults and each other.

Potatoes were really difficult to peel as the initial wash was not very successful.

Using peelers was difficult for Anita as she is left handed (must order left-handed equipment). Children enjoyed chopping but found it hard work as the knives are blunt.

Children picked up the language well and were fascinated by end product as we set the bowl next to a bowl of potatoes from the ground. Jane and Alex could not believe the mashed potatoes were the same thing as the dirty potatoes.

Katie and Anita asked if they could make chips next time.

Most enjoyed eating the mashed potatoes although some needed tomato ketchup and enjoyed making mash pink.

Learning

Discussions with the children as the activity took place showed they all understood how root vegetables look when taken out of ground but only Katie could transfer this knowledge to supermarket situation and that vegetables came from ground – to lorry – to supermarket. Concepts need reinforcement.

Weighing the potatoes – children seemed to understand weighing principles.

All understood need and reason to wash.

Use of descriptive and mathematical language – dirty/clean/earth/heavier than/bigger than/shapes/round/oval/knobbly/smooth. Alex could not use appropriate language to cover heavier/lighter, but everyone used terms fluently and accurately.

Children really interested in the life cycle of a potato and asked if they could eat when raw.

Mashing adding butter and milk – butter melting. Watching and describing change of state. Alex, Jane and Anita could describe mashed potato – white, soft, yellow runny butter, but could not grasp change of state, i.e. that this came out of original potatoes from allotments.

Follow-up activities

General

- Use potatoes for printing.
- Make chips.
- Plant in garden to see growth cycle – growing and harvesting.
- Broad beans in jam jar.
- Continue theme on food.
- More opportunities for observing change of state, pictures and books on life cycles.

Individual

Make sure Katie has enough practice with left-handed tools and fine movements are better controlled.

The feedback from activities is recorded against each child's individual record and future plans are based on identified needs.

Assessment activity 7.5

1   Plan a week's programme to extend creative play development for a small group of children, including one child who is in a wheelchair. Develop at least three activity plans showing how you will ensure that the child in the wheelchair can join in.

2   In discussion with your placement supervisor plan two activities that you could undertake with individuals or small groups of children. Implement and evaluate your plan.

Assessment of children starting school

Children entering schools in England have been subject to a baseline assessment scheme designed to record their abilities on starting school. There were 90 or so different variations of the assessment used in different local education authorities. These tests are to be replaced with a profile to be completed at the end of the reception year. The National Foundation Stage profile scheme will be based on ongoing assessment and observation of each child and will sum up each child's progress and learning needs in relation to the ELGs at the end of the Foundation Stage.

The profile scheme will be completed during the second half of the summer term and will be based on observations during planned classroom activity. The profile will not be a test that children pass or fail, but will represent a valuable tool to help build up knowledge of each child's capabilities throughout the year. It will be key in developing an accurate picture of what children, including those who have special educational needs, are able to do at the start of their primary schooling.

Assessment activity 7.6

You are opening your own nursery and need to draw up guidelines for use with your staff in training them to understand and support children's learning. Draw up guidelines that:

- explain your approach to children's learning and the theoretical basis
- include your beliefs about children's play
- describe the kind of learning environment you wish to create
- give examples of planning in the six areas of learning
- highlight the kind of staff you want to employ
- describe clearly how you would ensure equality of opportunity and anti-discriminatory practice
- discusse how you would involve parents
- describe how you would evaluate your work and ensure continuous improvement.

The National Curriculum

Early years practitioners will work with children from 0 to eight years and will need to have some understanding of the National Curriculum Key Stage 1 both if they work with children aged five to seven years in schools and if they work with younger children to prepare them for moving into Key Stage 1.

The National Curriculum follows on from the ELGs and should form a seamless progression for children moving into Key Stage 1 as it covers some of the same broad areas. Children entering Key Stage 1 who have achieved the ELGs will be well prepared to enter formal schooling.

What is the National Curriculum?

The National Curriculum was established by the Education Reform Act 1988. It defines the minimum educational entitlement for pupils of compulsory school age, and builds on the ELGs. The National Curriculum applies to all pupils aged 5–16 in maintained (state) schools. It does not apply in independent schools although those schools may choose to follow it.

There are differences in the curriculum within the four countries of the UK, e.g. Curriculum Cymreig applies to schools in Wales and stresses the need to provide a curriculum which includes the teaching of Welsh as a first or second language and the culture and heritage of Wales.

The Education Reform Act 1988 and the Education Act 1997 require all state schools to provide pupils with a curriculum that:

- is balanced and broadly based
- promotes their spiritual, moral, cultural, mental and physical development
- prepares them for the opportunities, responsibilities and experiences of adult life
- includes, in addition to the National Curriculum, religious education, and for secondary pupils, sex education.

The National Curriculum does not constitute the whole curriculum for schools. Schools have discretion to develop the curriculum to reflect their particular needs and circumstances.

The content of each National Curriculum subject is defined in a **Statutory Order**. Statutory Orders are legal requirements stating what has to be taught to children. Each Order consists of:

- **common requirements** which relate to access to the curriculum for all pupils, pupils' use of language, pupils' access to information technology and the Curriculum Cymreig (in Wales)
- the **programme of study** which sets out the minimum knowledge, understanding and skills for each subject at each key stage
- **attainment targets** which define the expected standards of pupil performance in terms of level descriptions or end of Key Stage descriptions.

National Curriculum content at Key Stage 1 (normally children aged 5–7 years)

English	Speaking and listening
	Reading
	Writing
Mathematics	Using and applying mathematics
	Number
	Shape, space and measures
Science	Experimental and investigative science
	Life processes and living things
	Materials and their properties
	Physical processes
Design and technology	Designing
	Making
Information technology	Using, exploring and discussing experiences of IT
	Communicating and handling information
	Controlling and modelling
History	Chronology
	Range and depth of historical knowledge and understanding
	Interpretations of history
	Historical enquiry
	Organisation and communication
Geography	Geographical skills
	Places
	Thematic study
Art	Investigating and making
	Knowledge and understanding
Music	Performing and composing
	Listening and appraising
Physical education	Games
	Gymnastic activities
	Dance
	(plus the option of swimming)
Additional statutory area	
Religious education	Content determined by LEAs (most schools) or faith foundation. Advised to cover:
	• Learning about religions
	• Learning from religions

National Curriculum Assessment

Attainment targets describe what pupils should be able to achieve at the end of each key stage in each subject area. During the primary school years the number of attainment targets varies between subjects, for example there are four for maths and one for history. Each attainment target is subdivided into levels.

Pupils are assessed, using national tests, at the end of the three key stages. They will normally be seven, eleven and fourteen when national testing occurs, although a minority maybe slightly younger or older.

	Range of most pupils	Expected attainment	
Key Stage 1	(5–7 years)	Levels 1–3	2
Key Stage 2	(7–11 years)	Levels 2–5	4

A typical seven-year-old will normally be working at Level 2 and a typical eleven-year-old will normally be working at Level 4. Some pupils will do well and achieve a higher level and others will achieve at a lower level. Pupils will often achieve at different levels in different subjects.

QCA develops the National Curriculum statutory tests and tasks for end of Key Stages 1, 2 and 3. In addition to national testing at the end of the three key stages, teacher assessment of a child's progress is required.

National Literacy and Numeracy strategies

Some years ago National Curriculum testing and other feedback showed that many children were not achieving well in literacy and numeracy. As a result the government established the National Literacy and National Numeracy strategies to ensure that these areas of the curriculum were given prominence and time by teachers. In many areas classroom assistants and early years practitioners have taken on extra responsibilities to help implement these strategies and have a direct role in teaching children to become more literate and numerate.

National Literacy Strategy

This initiative has been designed to improve levels of literacy in England. Literacy unites the important skills of reading and writing and also involves speaking and listening. The heart of the strategy is the introduction of a literacy hour and every school has to ensure that pupils are taught in accordance with the strategy. Special guidance has been issued by the DfES on using classroom assistants in a teaching role to deliver the Literacy Strategy.

Key issues

Research the role of classroom assistants who support the Literacy or Numeracy Strategy. How does their role support the class teacher?

National Numeracy Strategy

The Numeracy Strategy complements the Literacy Strategy and schools now provide a structured daily mathematics lesson of 45 minutes to one hour for all pupils of primary age. Teachers teach the whole class together for a high proportion of the time, and oral and mental work features strongly in each lesson. Classroom assistants are involved in planning and supporting teachers. The strategy contains a set of yearly teaching programmes illustrating how mathematics can be planned and taught from reception to year 6. It includes guidance on the daily mathematics lesson in which this teaching will take place and on the assessment of pupils' progress. The strategy recognises that well targeted positive support is needed to help those who have difficulties with mathematics to help them to keep up with their peers.

The National Curriculum and the early years practitioner

The early years practitioner has to understand the National Curriculum Key Stage 1, the National Literacy and the National Numeracy Strategies in order to:

- support children through the Foundation Stage
- work with children at National Curriculum Key Stage One.

It is important that you familiarise yourself with these aspects of children's learning to be able to understand learning from 0 to eight years of age, i.e. the early years. Early years practitioners are unique in that they consider the whole child from 0 to eight years of age and are able to see children's learning progress from babyhood until they are well established at formal school.

End-of-unit test

1. Which major theorist has most influenced current practice and why?
2. Social learning theory says that children learn through copying behaviour they see adults demonstrating. State whether this is true or false and give brief reasons for your answer.
3. Transmission theory encourages children to try new things. State whether this is true or false, and give brief reasons for your answer.
4. Social constructivists believe parents are partners in the education of their children. State whether this is true or false, and give brief reasons for your answer.
5. Why is the adult role less important within laissez-faire theory?
6. Explain the meaning and importance of symbolic play.
7. What equipment in your work placement most resembles that used by Maria Montessori? Describe the equipment and explain how it is used.
8. Describe three key aspects of Froebel's work that influences early years provision today?
9. Explain two theories of play commonly accepted in early years settings.
10. 'Adults should leave children to play and not interfere.' Does this statement represent the views of most early years settings? Give reasons for your answer.
11. A parent was overheard to say 'Young children should not just play all day; it's time they got down to the 3 Rs'. How would you explain to the parent why the nursery encourages the children to play?
12. Children can't learn much at home, they need to wait till they go to school. State whether this is true or false, and give brief reasons for your answer.
13. What are the six areas of learning?
14. From your own experience describe two practical activities you have undertaken with children and state how you identified the key areas of learning.

15 Comment on this statement pinned on the staff notice board in a nursery.

Planning the curriculum is an activity for senior staff only. Once published there should be no variation from the plan as otherwise no one knows what they are doing. After you have completed your planned activities you must clear away immediately and move to the next activity. All children MUST complete each activity. Staff must attend the monthly meeting and if they wish to make any suggestions or improvements these should be given in writing in advance of the meeting to the officer in charge. Anonymous suggestions will not be considered.

16 Describe the planning cycle and explain each stage.

References and further reading

Athey, C. (1990), *Extending Thought in Young Children*, London: Chapman Publishing

Bandura, A. (1993), *Aggression: A social learning analysis*, Prentice Hall: NJ Englewood Cliffs

Bruner, J. (1990), *Acts of Meaning*, Cambridge: MA, Harvard University Press

Bruce, T. (1991), *Time to Play in Early Childhood Education*, Sevenoaks: Hodder and Stoughton

Bruce, T. (1997), *Early Childhood Education*, London: Hodder and Stoughton

Bruner, J. (1977), *The Process of Education*, Cambridge, MA: Harvard University Press

Chomsky, N. (1968), *Language and Mind*, New York: Harcourt, Brace and World

Donaldson, (1986), *Children's Minds*, London: Fortuna

Dowling, M. (1995), *Starting School at Four: A joint endeavour*, London: Chapman Publishing

Drake, J. (2001), *Planning Children's Play and Learning in the Foundation Stage*, London: David Fulton

Fodor, J. (1983), *The Modularity of Mind,* Cambridge, MA: MIT Press

Hutt, J. F. *et al.,* (1988), *Play, Exploration and Learning: A Natural History of the Pre-school*, London: Routledge

Moyles, J. (1989), *Just Playing? The Role and Status of Play in Early Childhood Education*, Milton Keynes: Open University Press

National Standards for Under Eights Day Care, (2001), DfEE

Parry, M. and Archer, H. (1974), *Pre-school Education*, London: Schools Council/ Macmillan Education

Pascal, C. and Bertram, T. (eds) (1993), *Effective Early Learning*, London: Hodder and Stoughton

Piaget, J. (1962), *Play, Dreams and Imitation in Childhood*, London: Routledge & Kegan Paul

Siraj-Blatchford, I. (eds) (1998), *A Curriculum Development Handbook for Early Childhood Educators*, Stoke on Trent: Trentham Books

Siraj-Blatchford, I. *The Early Years Laying the Foundations for Racial Equality*, Stoke on Trent: Trentham Books

Vygotsky, L. (1978), *Mind in Society*, Cambridge, MA: Harvard University Press

Childcare practice

Introduction

The basic needs of babies and children remain the same throughout childhood, although the way practitioners provide for them slightly changes. It is now recognised that the healthy growth and development of children are linked closely to having these needs met. This unit looks at how early years practitioners can meet the basic needs of babies and young children.

What you need to learn
- Healthy development of babies
- Healthy development of children
- Children's behaviour
- Safe, secure and stimulating environment for children
- Key approaches to child rearing

Healthy development of babies

Working with babies is demanding work because babies rely entirely on their primary carers to meet not only their basic survival needs but also to promote their development.

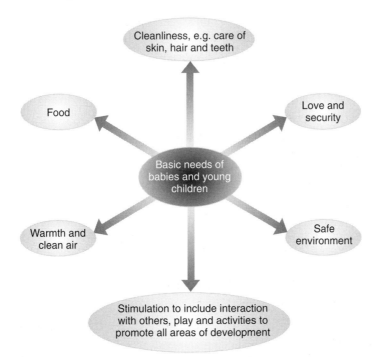

Views and advice about how to care for babies and toddlers have changed over time and so it is important that adults working with this age range keep themselves up to date on current information. For information about different childrearing approaches, see pages 317–20.

Care of the environment

Warmth

Babies are unable to regulate their internal temperature as the homeostatic systems within their bodies are still developing. They are, for example, unable to shiver to gain heat and so can be at risk of hypothermia, but equally of becoming overheated which is now thought to be a contributory factor in cot deaths (see page 286). It is therefore important to check on a baby's temperature regularly and be ready to add or remove a layer if necessary. Feeling the back of a baby's neck is a reliable guide as hands and feet are often cooler because of poor circulation. Note that young babies that are hypothermic will be pink in colour whilst older babies will look greyer.

Key issues

- Room temperatures should ideally be kept between 18–21°C.
- Blankets rather than duvets should be used in cots.
- Babies should not be swaddled tightly or be left in baby nests.
- Outdoor clothing should be removed when baby is brought indoors.
- Layers of clothing should be used as they can be removed or added to.
- Bonnets should be put on babies to help retain heat lost from their heads if temperatures are low.
- Socks and mittens may be needed to keep hands and feet warm.

Clean air and ventilation

Babies are vulnerable to infection and so providing an environment that is well ventilated is essential. Warm, stale air encourages the multiplication of viruses, fungi and bacteria. Stale air also contains a lower level of oxygen.

Smoking near babies, especially in places where babies will later sleep, has been proved to be a factor in cot death whilst also increasing the risk of a baby developing coughs, ear infections and asthma. The Health Education Authority also advises against handling a baby within 30–60 minutes of having smoked as smoke will be present in the exhaled air.

Safety

Babies have no sense of danger and once mobile are keen to explore their environment. The speed of babies' development requires adults to be one step ahead in ensuring that the environment remains safe, e.g. safety gates need to be fitted before a child begins to crawl. In home settings items such as plants, table cloths and electrical equipment may need to be moved. Baby walkers are now considered to be dangerous as they have been linked to many incidents involving scalds and falls. Current advice from organisations campaigning for safety is to avoid using them.

The table below shows common safety equipment used in most settings.

Equipment	Reason
Safety gates	To prevent falls in stairways and to prevent access to rooms such as kitchens and bathrooms
Socket covers	To prevent electric shocks from live sockets
Window, cupboard and drawer catches	To prevent falls and also access to potentially dangerous items such as cleaning fluids or tools

Equipment	Reason
Cooker guard	To prevent babies and toddlers from overturning saucepans
Safety corners	To prevent cuts and head injuries caused by children walking into corners of tables, etc.
Reins and harnesses	To prevent falls from highchairs, pushchairs and also to prevent toddlers from straying into the road

Key issues – safety

- Safety equipment should be installed and used according to manufacturer's instructions.
- Accidents happen very quickly. Always use safety equipment.
- Babies need constant and close supervision at all times unless they are soundly asleep in their cots.

Hygiene

Babies' immune systems are not fully developed which means that they are vulnerable to infection. In group-care settings a high level of hygiene must be maintained as there is a higher risk of cross-infection. Adults who are working with babies need high levels of personal hygiene to avoid bacteria from transferring from their hands and clothing onto babies. The table below shows the preventative hygiene measures that should be taken.

Measure	Reason
Sterilisation of feeding equipment and some toys	To prevent the ingestion (swallowing) of germs
Washing hands before handling babies, changing nappies, preparing foods	To prevent cross-infection
Use of disposable gloves and aprons	To prevent cross-infection
Disinfection of changing mats and other surfaces including kitchen	To prevent cross-infection
Use of separate towels, face cloths, comforters, beakers and other equipment for each baby	To prevent cross-infection
Ventilation of rooms	To prevent viruses and bacteria from being inhaled
Frequent washing of babies' clothes, bed linen and toys	To prevent cross-infection

Feeding and nutritional needs

In order to grow and develop, the nutritional needs of babies must be met. In the first four to six months of life, babies rely solely on milk. There are two types of milk: breast milk and formula milk.

Breastfeeding

Human breast milk is considered to be the best type of milk for babies to receive as it changes to meet babies' nutritional needs. In the first two to three days, it is thick and yellowish in colour. This is called colostrum and contains antibodies to protect the baby from infection and high levels of protein to promote growth. Over the following days milk comes in and the quantity of colostrum reduces.

Most babies who have breast milk take the milk directly from their mother's breasts although milk can be expressed and used in bottles. Expressed milk is often given to premature babies who are not strong enough to suckle as well as by mothers to allow someone else to feed their baby.

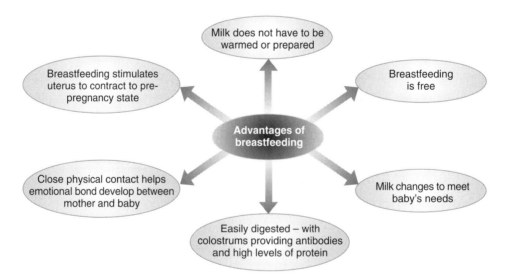

Supporting breastfeeding

Breastfeeding is more likely to succeed when mothers have had information about breastfeeding during the pregnancy and have been given help in the first few hours and days after the baby is born. Some mothers need help in getting their baby to 'latch on' to the nipple as this is a skill for both the mother and baby to learn. Once breastfeeding has been established, most mothers find it pain free and very rewarding. Approaches about how often mothers should offer the breast have changed but current advice is that mothers should breast feed 'on demand' (see page 326).

Key ways in which breastfeeding mothers can be supported
- Help mother to rest and relax, e.g. changing nappies, helping with household tasks.
- Prepare nutritious meals – breastfeeding mothers need to eat well. Dieting when breastfeeding is not recommended.
- Offer drinks before and during feeds – breastfeeding mothers need sufficient fluid to manufacture milk.

Formula milk – bottle feeding

There are two types of formula milk: cow's milk and soya milk. Soya milk is used for babies who are allergic to cow's milk or whose parents have objections to using animal products. Formula milk is designed to reproduce the composition of breast milk as closely as possible, although it is not as easily digested. Formula feeds are available in powdered form to which water is added or in ready-mixed packs which although costly can be useful when travelling.

Whilst breastfeeding is strongly recommended, some mothers may bottle feed. Common reasons include the wish to share the feeding with a partner, difficulties in establishing breastfeeding in the first few days or problems in coping with the night feeds. Mothers may also be advised to bottle feed in cases where they have a medical condition which requires that they take medications or in cases where the baby has difficulty feeding or is not putting on sufficient weight.

Sterilisation
An important aspect of feeding babies is the sterilisation of feeding equipment. Sterilisation prevents babies from ingesting bacteria and is required until babies are at least six months old, although in group-care settings, this may continue until twelve months to prevent possible cross-infection.

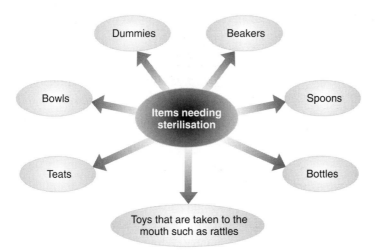

Methods of sterilisation

There are several ways of sterilising equipment. Many group-care settings use commercial sterilising units as although expensive they are fast and efficient. Whatever method is used, items have to be thoroughly cleaned first.

Name	Method	Comments
Chemical or 'cold water' sterilising	Sterilising fluid or tablets are added to cold water Items have to be completely immersed in solution (check for air bubbles in bottles) Items remain in solution until required Items must be rinsed thoroughly in cool, boiled water	Cheap Teats and rubber items need replacing frequently Solution has to be made accurately Solution needs changing every 24 hours
Boiling	All washed items are put in a saucepan with a lid Items have to be completely immersed Lid is placed on pan and water is boiled for at least ten minutes, although teats can be removed after three minutes Items are left in pan until required	Cheapest method Teats and rubber items need replacing often Saucepan should be kept just for sterilising Keep the pan out of reach of children Do not let pan boil dry
Steam steriliser units	Steam circulates in the unit and items reach high temperatures	Expensive, but fast and efficient Manufacturers' instructions must be carefully followed Units must be opened carefully as steam can scald
Microwave steam units	Steam circulates in the unit and items reach high temperatures	Commercial units must be used for this method Follow instructions carefully Allow items to cool Do not use metal items

Preparation of a formula feed

Powdered formula feeds are significantly cheaper than the ready-mixed types. Bottles are usually made up in advance and stored in a fridge to save time and prevent babies from becoming distressed when they are hungry. When making up feeds, it is important to find out from parents the type of powdered milk that should be used and also the weight of their baby as this, not the age, determines the amount of feed required. Follow the stages in the following list.

- Check that bottles have already been sterilised.
- Boil kettle – allow to cool to avoid being scalded.

- Read manufacturer's instructions to find out about amounts of water and powder to be used.

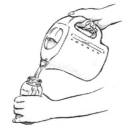

- Wash hands.

- Put required amount of water in sterilised bottles.

- Measure the exact amount of milk powder using scoop provided.
  Level off with a knife.
  The powder should not be pushed down as this will increase the amount.

- Put powder into bottle.
- Screw on top and shake.

- Allow to cool if bottle is to be given straight away, otherwise store in fridge.

Key issues – hygiene and safety

- Check that tin is still in date.
- Do not make up feeds for more than a day at a time.
- Throw away all unused feeds after 24 hours.
- Store feeds in a fridge.
- Read manufacturer's instructions carefully.
- Shake bottle carefully before use
- Make sure that bottle has cooled before giving to baby.

Bottle feeding a baby
As well as feeding providing babies with nutrients, bottle feeding also provides babies with emotional security. This means that whenever possible, babies should be fed by the same people. Follow the stages in the following list.

- Wash hands.
- Warm bottle by standing in a jug of boiling water.
- Check the flow and temperature of the milk by turning the bottle upside down and allowing it to drip onto your wrist.
- Find a comfortable chair to sit in and have tissues or a towel to hand.
- Gently touch the baby's lip with the teat.
- When mouth opens, gently place teat inside.
- Tilt the bottle to make sure that milk is covering the teat end of the bottle
- Allow the baby to take the milk at their own pace. This may include a baby not sucking strongly or wanting to have a rest. Some babies can be slow feeders whilst others are quick.
- Wind the baby after the feed by either sitting them upright on your lap and gently rubbing their back or by holding the baby upright slightly over your shoulder. It is advisable to put a towel over your shoulder as when babies burp, they may also bring up a little milk.
- Offer bottle again after winding in case baby is still hungry.
- Throw away remaining milk.
- Change the baby's nappy.

Key issues – safety points

- Never leave a baby alone with a bottle.
- Do not heat bottles in microwaves as they can heat the milk unevenly.
- Check the temperature of the bottle first.
- Throw away any unwanted feed.
- Follow manufacturer's instructions when making up feeds and using equipment.

Weaning babies

Weaning is the process by which babies learn to take foods other than milk. It is an important process because after six months babies' natural reserves of iron are running low and milk alone will not be sufficient to meet these or provide enough calories for the growing baby.

Weaning usually takes place between the ages of four and six months. It is currently recommended that babies should not be weaned earlier than four months because babies' digestive systems are not mature enough to cope with solid food (see also Key approaches to child rearing, pages 317–20).

Signs that a baby may need to be weaned
- Wakes in the night for feed after previously sleeping through.
- Seems hungry after a feed.
- Lacks energy and sleeps for longer periods.

Stages of weaning
There are three stages of weaning with new foods, as shown in the table below. The baby has to learn to take food from a spoon and swallow it. New foods are introduced gradually. This means that possible food allergies can be detected. By twelve months most babies eat a wide range of foods and can feed themselves using their hands. Milk remains an important food in babies' diets during the weaning process, although the

number of milk feeds decreases as the baby takes more food. Babies need to be offered drinks of cool boiled water or diluted fruit juice, as more water will be needed to aid digestion.

Stage	Food	Weaning process
Stage 1: 4-6 months	Puréd foods	Foods are introduced one by one, with rice, vegetables and fruit being given first. Wheat-based foods should be avoided at first as they can cause allergies. Foods are mixed with breast milk or formula milk so that they are a runny consistency and easy to swallow
Stage 2: 6-9 months	Mashed or minced foods	Foods are mashed down or minced up so that baby has to chew slightly before swallowing. Meat, fish and well-cooked eggs can be introduced. Foods can be mixed together. Cow's milk can be used for cooking, but formula or breast milk should be given for feeds up until 12 months
Stage 3: 9-12 months	Finger foods	Foods such as slices of bread, fish fingers and pieces of banana are given to babies to encourage them to feed themselves. Babies can be given the same food as the family, providing it is slightly mashed down and does not contain salt or sugar

Foods that should not be given to babies
Advice regarding the safety of foods can vary – always check the current advice. Some foods cannot be given to babies as they pose a health or safety risk.

Salt – salt should not be added to babies' food because the kidneys cannot process it.

Sugar – sugar is not given to babies as it can cause tooth decay.

Eggs – uncooked or partly uncooked eggs such as boiled eggs must not be served as they can contain salmonella, which causes food poisoning.

Nuts – nuts can pose a choking hazard and also in some children provoke a serious allergic reaction.

Liver – liver is no longer recommended for children as it can contain high levels of toxins.

Assessment activity 8.1

Marcia cares for a five-month-old baby. She started weaning him just before he was three months old. She usually gives him any food that she has to hand and tends not to worry about whether it is salty or sugary as he seems to eat everything she gives him. She has noticed that he does gag occasionally on larger pieces of food. She is also pleased that he can now hold his own bottle because this means that she can leave one in his cot so that if he wakes up early he can help himself to it.

- Examine the potential care and nutritional consequences of Marcia's actions.
- Provide recommendations to meet the nutritional needs of this baby.
- Critically evaluate two sources of advice about feeding babies that have been designed for parents.

Beginning the weaning process

Baby rice mixed with breast or formula milk is usually the first food that is offered to babies when beginning the weaning process as it is bland and is unlikely to provoke an allergic reaction. Some babies find it hard to take from a spoon and choke or spit out food and will need to be introduced to weaning slowly.

- Choose a time when the baby is not tired or very hungry. Most people give the first spoon part way through a feed.
- Place a bib on the baby and sit them on your knee.
- Place a very small amount of food onto a sterilised teaspoon.
- Gently rub the spoon against the baby's lips allowing them to suck it in
- Talk to the baby soothingly.
- Follow the baby's lead – if the food is spat out, try again at the next feed, but if taken, encourage them to have another go.

Key issues

- Do not force the spoon into the mouth.
- Be ready to take action if the baby chokes (see Unit 4 Safe environments, page 114).
- Teaspoon and bowl should be sterilised.
- Throw away any unused food.

Routines and continuity of care

Care of skin, hair and teeth

Skin is the largest organ of the human body and has several key functions which include forming a protective barrier to prevent germs from penetrating into our bodies. As babies are vulnerable to infections, it is vital that babies' skin is kept clean. Their skin is also sensitive and fragile which means that care must be taken in the selection of skin care products. Advice also changes over time with products such as barrier cream no longer being used systematically after a nappy change.

Respecting parents' wishes

As with any aspect of a baby's care, practitioners have to be sensitive to the wishes of the child's parents as there are cultural and religious variations in the way babies' physical care is provided. Afro-Caribbean children, for example, are often massaged after a bath. Parents will also know which skin care products suit their child and may have certain preferences about the types of product that are used.

Topping and tailing

Topping and tailing refers to the process of cleaning the vital parts of a baby, e.g. their face and hands and also their nappy area. Topping and tailing is often alternated with bathing as a young baby will not necessarily need a complete bath each day.

Items required

- Bowl of warm water
- A small cup of water that has been boiled and allowed to cool
- Cotton wool
- Towel
- Items for nappy change (see page 284)
- Clean clothes if necessary

Key issues – safety points

- Young babies lose heat easily and quickly. Ensure that room temperature is warm, at least 20°C, and prepare everything before beginning.
- Do not leave baby unattended on raised surfaces.
- Check temperature of water.
- Make sure that hands are washed before and after process.
- Talcum powder is not recommended for babies as it dries out the skin.
- Make sure each area of the baby's skin is thoroughly dry to prevent soreness.

How to top and tail a baby

- Hold baby on knee and undress leaving vest and nappy.
- Wrap baby in towel to prevent heat loss.

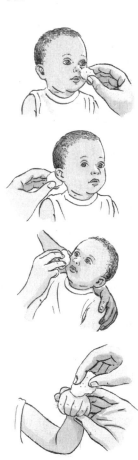

- Dip cotton wool in cool boiled water and use to wipe gently around eyes from the inner corner out. Use a separate piece of cotton wool for each eye.

- Using a fresh piece of cotton wool gently wipe around the rest of face and behind ears.

- Clean neck area by lifting chin slightly and cleaning in folds of skin.

- Dry all areas thoroughly by softly patting with towel.

- Using cotton wool, gently uncurl fingers and clean hands. Dry carefully.

- Change nappy and dress.

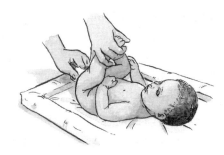

Bathing babies

The frequency of bathing depends very much on parental wishes and the child itself. Some young babies become very distressed when their clothes are removed whilst others quickly enjoy the experience. As babies become older they will need bathing each day. This is often incorporated into a bedtime routine.

Items required

- Baby bath with warm water, 38°C
- Non-slip mat (optional)
- Clean nappy and other items for nappy change
- Towel
- Bath thermometer (optional)
- Changing mat

Key issues – safety

- Do not leave babies in the bath or even near water without close adult supervision.
- Check carefully the temperature of the water.
- Make sure that room temperature is 20°C or slightly above.
- Remove any jewellery especially watches which can scratch the baby's skin.
- Be careful to bend from the knees to avoid back strain.

Bathing a young baby

It is important to be shown how to follow these procedures and to be supervised in doing so.

- Prepare equipment and fill bath. Check the temperature by using a thermometer or dipping in your elbow. It should feel lukewarm.
- Remove clothes from baby leaving on the nappy. Wrap in towel immediately.
- Wash face in the same way as for topping and tailing.
- Add bath product if requested to water.
- Keeping the towel around the baby, tuck baby under arm supporting head, neck and shoulders. Baby must be securely held. Practise this position first with a doll if unsure.
- Hold the baby's head over the bath and using the other hand, wet head to wash hair and scalp.
- Dry baby's head.
- Remove nappy and clean nappy area.
- Hold the baby's arm that is furthest away from you and support the head with your wrist. Lower the baby into the bath.
- Use your spare hand to wash the baby. Allow the baby time to kick and splash.
- Lift the baby back onto towel. Do not allow the baby to become chilled.
- Dry thoroughly checking that folds of skin around the neck and groin are dry. Rub in moisturiser or massage oil if requested by parents.
- Put on clean vest and then nappy. Check that baby is warm.

Bathing older babies

As babies become older, they can be bathed in an ordinary bath, although care has to be taken that they do not hurt themselves against taps or that they can turn on a hot tap. Water should always be kept shallow. Most older babies enjoy bath time and should be given time to play with the water.

Hair care

The way in which babies' hair should be cared for depends largely on the type and quantity of hair and also on the family's cultural and religious wishes. Some babies have their hair shampooed and brushed whilst others will need their hair oiling and plaiting.

Nail care

Babies' nails should be left in the first few weeks, but as they get older should be trimmed after a bath using a pair of blunt-ended nail scissors. The shape of the finger should be followed and care should be taken not to damage the skin. A soft nailbrush can be used to clean older babies' nails if necessary.

Tooth care

Most babies get their first teeth at around six months, although this can vary considerably with some babies being born with teeth and others being over a year in age. The first teeth to appear are usually the bottom incisors. Preventing tooth decay is essential even in very young babies as teeth can decay before they appear.

- Avoid sugary drinks – cool boiled water is the safest drink. Dilute fruit juice and serve only at meal times.
- Bottles should be kept only for milk or water – frequent coating of sugar on gums and teeth creates the ideal conditions for decay.
- Once teeth appear, clean twice a day with a baby toothbrush and a small amount of baby toothpaste.

Nappies

In Western cultures, babies are put into nappies that require regular changing. There are two categories of nappies: disposables and terry towelling (fabric) nappies. The choice of nappies depends on parental choice with the majority of parents currently choosing disposable nappies, although some parents prefer to use towelling nappies as they are re-usable and considered more environmentally friendly.

Key issues

Parents may have differing views on how best to care for their child's skin, hair and teeth.

Using a range of sources which may include questionnaires and interviews with a range of parents, produce a fact sheet which considers the cultural issues associated with caring for babies' skin, hair and teeth.

Changing nappies

Nappies should be changed after each feed and immediately after the passing of stools to avoid nappy rash (see page 284). Adults working with babies should check that stools and urine are normal for the age of the child. At first all babies produce meconium which is sticky and greenish-black in colour. After a few days, the stools change according to whether the baby is being breast or bottle fed. Breastfed babies have stools which are mustard in colour and fairly liquid. They should not smell unpleasant whilst the stools of bottle fed babies are browner, have some smell and are thicker in texture.

Once babies are weaned their stools become firmer and have a stronger odour. The frequency with which babies pass stools can vary, although medical advice should be sought if no stools have been passed after a week or if the stools are watery, very pale or contain any signs of blood. Medical advice should also be sought if urine is not being frequently passed as this may indicate dehydration.

The key to a successful nappy change is good organisation and plenty of practice!

Items required for nappy changing
- Disposable gloves (usually provided in settings)
- Clean nappy
- Cotton wool or baby wipes
- Spare change of clothes if necessary
- Changing mat or towel
- Nappy sack or access to bin

Key issues

- Babies should never be left unattended on high surfaces (some parents prefer to change their babies on the floor).
- Disposable gloves should always be worn in group settings to avoid possible infections.
- Nappies and soiled materials should be disposed carefully.
- Hands must be washed after nappy change.
- Care must be taken to wipe girls from the vagina back towards the rectum to prevent the spread of infection.

Method for nappy changing
- Wash hands and put on disposable gloves.
- Remove clothes from lower part of the body.
- Using a wet cloth or cotton wool remove stools from bottom taking care to wipe from front to back. Use a new piece of cotton wool for each wipe.
- Clean the nappy area thoroughly, avoiding pulling back the foreskin on a boy.
- Dry nappy area thoroughly.
- Check that clothing is not soiled or damp.
- If possible allow time for baby to kick without nappy especially if there is any indication of nappy rash.
- Put on a barrier cream if requested by parents.
- Place clean nappy on baby and dress.
- Place baby in safe place and clean mat and dispose of soiled nappies.
- Wash hands before handling baby.

Nappy rash
Nappy rash affects many babies under 18 months and has a variety of causes. The rash can cause severe discomfort to babies and therefore preventative steps are essential.

Some babies seem more susceptible to nappy rash than others and persistent bouts of nappy rash should be referred for medical attention. In some cases doctors will diagnose eczema or dermatitis caused by allergic reactions to creams and washing powders as the underlying cause of the rash.

Ammonia dermatitis

The most common type of nappy rash, ammonia dermatitis, is caused by the production of ammonia as bacteria from the baby's stools breaks down the urine. Ammonia is an irritant that burns the skin and thus causes nappy rash. The resulting rash is red and can spread quickly forming a spotty burning rash.

The table below describes the most common types of nappy rash.

Appearance	Cause	Treatment
Red rash forming around the genitals. Strong smell	Ammonia dermatitis	Increase frequency of nappy changes Wash and gently dry affected area thoroughly Allow time after changes without a nappy to allow air flow Seek medical advice if no improvement
Spotty ulcerated rash covering the genitals and bottom	Ammonia dermatitis	Use steps above, but seek medical advice promptly
Pink and pimply rash forming around the anus and spreading to bottom and genitals	Thrush dermatitis	Seek medical advice – an anti-fungal cream is likely to be prescribed
Small blisters or pimples around nappy area	Heat rash	Avoid using plastic pants if using terry towelling Leave off nappy for as long as possible Seek medical advice if condition does not improve
Brownish-red scaly rash around genitals and anywhere where skin is greasy	Seborrhoeic dermatitis (similar to cradle cap)	Seek medical advice as an ointment may be prescribed

Preventing nappy rash

The following steps can help prevent nappy rash and should be used at the first sign of any redness.

- Make sure that the nappy area is cleaned thoroughly.
- Leave the nappy off after each change to allow air flow to the skin.
- Change nappies more frequently.
- Check whether parents wish to use a barrier cream.

Rest and sleep

To grow and develop, babies need to sleep and take frequent naps, with newborns spending between sixteen and eighteen hours every day asleep. Older babies often require between twelve and fourteen hours sleep a day, although when and how this is taken will vary from baby to baby. Ongoing studies about the purpose of sleep suggest that one of its functions is to allow the processing of information as well as the release of hormones required for growth.

For the first few weeks of their lives, babies are unable to sleep for long periods as their stomachs cannot take the quantity of food necessary to sustain them and so will wake up frequently night and day, often at three- or four-hourly intervals. In theory, babies should be able to sleep through the night by four or five months if they are feeding well and have learnt how to get themselves off to sleep. Problems often arise when babies are unable to fall asleep without the assistance of a comforter or adult as during the sleep cycle, babies awaken slightly and need to be able to get back to sleep.

Key issues – putting babies to sleep

Cot death or Sudden Infant Death Syndrome is thought to be responsible for 8 deaths of infants a week in the UK. However, the number of deaths has recently been cut dramatically by encouraging parents and primary carers to follow these steps with young babies:

- Young babies should be placed on their backs and at the foot of their cots.
- Care should be taken to ensure that babies will not overheat and room temperatures should be between 16°C and 21°C.
- Cot bumpers, pillows and duvets should not be used in cots.
- Young babies should not be exposed to smoky environments or placed in rooms where adults have previously smoked.

Planning routines

Routines are important for babies and their carers. A good routine will not only meet a baby's care and nutritional needs, but will also stimulate their development. The term 'educare' is now often used in this context as child rearing approaches in the past tended to focus more on meeting babies' physical and care needs whilst potentially overlooking the role of the adult in stimulating babies and toddlers (see Key approaches to child rearing, pages 317–20).

Parents should always be involved in the planning of a routine as they may have particular preferences and knowledge that should be incorporated into a routine.

It is also important to remember that routines inevitably change as the baby grows and requires less sleep and has different needs. Understanding a baby's stage of development is therefore crucial when planning a routine to ensure that their play and exercise needs can be met. It is also important to allow sufficient time for dressing, changing nappies and feeding. These activities can be time consuming and babies do not react well if they sense tension or any impatience.

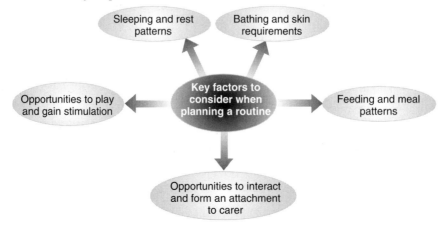

Implementing a routine

Spending a whole session with a baby and attending to their needs requires good planning, patience and good organisation. Most practitioners find that these skills develop with practice especially as most babies do not necessarily go along with any planned routine! Babies are also very aware of changes and react if they sense that their carers are not calm or are hurried.

Key issues – implementing a routine

- Make sure that enough time has been allowed for various tasks such as nappy changing, bathing and feeding.
- Use any time when the baby is asleep purposefully, e.g. making up feeds.
- Observe the baby carefully for signs of tiredness or hunger.
- Follow the baby's pace during the day as much as possible.

Evaluating a routine

Routines are best evaluated by considering how the needs of the baby have been met. The evaluation process could consider the following questions:

- Has the baby had periods of distress during the day?
- Has the baby appeared over-tired?
- How easily has the baby settled to sleep?
- How much food/milk has the baby consumed?
- How much interaction has the baby received in the course of the day?
- What type of activities and stimulation has the baby had?

Communication with babies

As well as providing for babies' care and nutritional needs, babies also need to interact with their carers. This helps them to 'bond' or form an attachment with their carer. Research on attachments (see Unit 12, pages 448–53) has shown that a child who has formed an attachment with their primary carers will be emotionally secure. Interaction with babies also stimulates their language and aids their overall development.

Touch and massage

Whilst hearing and vision are still developing in a young baby, they are able to process information by touching and being touched. Babies respond to being stroked, rubbed and held as this makes them feel secure. The use of massage in the everyday care of babies is increasing, although traditional in many cultures.

Crying

Babies are born with a range of reflexes (see Unit 9, page 330) including the crying reflex. Young babies rely on crying to signal their needs although the amount of crying decreases as babies' communication skills develop. Primary carers are usually able to identify the needs of their baby through the type of crying with breastfeeding mothers finding that some cries will stimulate the 'let down' milk reflex in their breasts.

Talking to babies and language development

Whilst research shows that babies have some innate ability to acquire language (see Unit 9, pages 348–52) they also rely on their carers to talk and interact with them. In the first few months, babies learn how to respond to others by smiling, making eye contact and trying to vocalise by babbling. Towards the end of the first year they 'tune' into the sounds of the language that they are hearing and gradually understand specific words and expressions. This cannot be achieved without carers taking the time to talk and communicate with them. Babies also respond well to nursery rhymes and singing as this promotes their auditory discrimination.

Stimulation

Babies learn about their world by taking information in from their senses. This stimulates brain activity and creates pathways in the brain. Babies who have not been stimulated are likely to show signs of developmental delay. There are many ways of stimulating babies including using toys and items such as baby gyms, but vital to the process is adult interaction and physical contact.

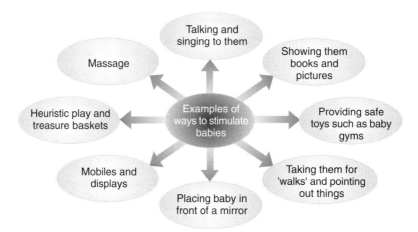

Heuristic play

Heuristic play is based upon the principle of stimulating babies through the provision of natural and everyday objects. Babies are given a range of objects to explore using their senses especially those of touch, taste and smell. The role of the adult is to encourage the baby, but to be passive allowing the baby to take the initiative. Objects can be chosen to help promote a concept, e.g. hard and soft, and can be presented in a soft bag or box.

Praise and encouragement

Babies notice and respond to adults' tone of voice, gesture and facial expression as part of the process of learning language. Praising and encouraging babies as they play, feed and concentrate helps them to

What concept might these objects promote?

feel secure and whilst they do not understand the exact meaning of words such as 'good', they are able to understand the message. Praising and encouraging babies therefore helps them to feel emotionally secure and gives them confidence to carry on exploring or playing.

Assessment activity 8.2

Daisy is eight months old and is cared for in her home. She has started to crawl and is eating a range of mashed foods. She wakes at 6.30am and has a two-hour nap during the late morning. She goes to bed at around 6.30pm.

- Produce a suggested routine which will meet her overall needs for care, nutrition and stimulation.
- Evaluate how the routine will meet her needs.
- Discuss factors that may influence babies' routines.

Management of a distressed baby

Babies cry as a signal that their needs are not being met. These signals should never be ignored as they may mean that the baby is in pain or needs feeding. Babies who cry persistently must be referred for medical advice promptly especially if they are normally easy to settle.

Colic: 0-three months

Some babies suffer from acute pain in the lower abdomen causing them to draw up their knees and scream. It is common in babies under three months and many parents report that it is worse towards early evening. Experts are divided as to the cause of colic, but it is generally linked with an immature digestive system and also with cow's milk intolerance. Dealing with a baby who has colic is not easy.

- Check that there is no other cause for the crying – seek medical advice if necessary.
- Remain calm and offer physical comfort by rubbing the baby's back and rocking.

Hunger

Young babies who are hungry will cry, but may also show signs such as trying to suck their hands or anything they are against. Being often hungry can indicate that a baby over four months needs to be weaned.

Key issues

- Prepare feeds and meals in advance so that the baby does not have to wait long.
- Offer a sip of cool boiled water if feed is not immediately ready to take the edge of hunger.

Tiredness

Many babies will fight to remain awake especially as they get older and more alert. Signs that a baby is tired include an intermittent cry and rubbing of head.

Loneliness

Young babies can feel lonely and cry because they want to be picked up and played with. They are unable to reach out and pick up things to entertain themselves and so rely heavily on adults to stimulate them (see Stimulation, page 288).

Pain

Babies cry when they are in pain, which is why a baby should never be left to cry without being checked.

Teething is a common cause of crying in babies as they approach five or six months. Signs include hot, red cheeks, dribbling and restlessness. Babies often gain temporary relief by biting on teething rings.

Ear infections are not uncommon in babies especially after a cold. Signs include raised temperature, distressed cries and rubbing of ears. Medical attention needs to be promptly sought.

Nappy rash and **eczema** can also cause babies distress and break their sleep patterns (see pages 284–6).

Separation anxiety

Most babies show separation anxiety from around eight to nine months, although it can occur earlier. Babies cry as they have formed a secure attachment to their primary carer and react if that person leaves (see Formation of early relationships, pages 448–53). Separation anxiety can be lessened if the baby has already formed an attachment with the person who they are left with. Babies who are showing separation anxiety will need plenty of physical contact and reassurance. Distraction with puppets or toys can also be helpful.

Healthy development of children

At the start of this unit, we looked at the basic needs of babies. The basic needs of children do not vary, although the way in which we provide them might.

Principles of diet and nutrition – planning meals

To be able to plan a meal effectively, it is important to have some understanding of how the body uses food. To grow and develop, the body needs a diet that contains food with sufficient nutrients to meet its needs. There are five nutrient groups with each nutrient having a specific function for growth and the maintenance of health – see table below. Many foods contain more than one nutrient and foods that are rich in nutrients are often referred to as **nutritious** or **nutrient-rich**. In addition to food, the body also needs water. Water does not contain any nutrients but has several essential functions in the body including regulating temperature.

Nutrient group	Function	Sources	Consequences of deficiency
Fats	Concentrated source of energy	Oils, butter, margarine, cheese, meat, fish, milk	Rarely deficient in the UK, although very low fat diets can prevent uptake of fat soluble vitamins such as vitamin E

Nutrient group	Function	Sources	Consequences of deficiency
Proteins	Growth and repair of cells – excess protein is converted into energy	Animal sources: milk and other dairy products, meat, fish, eggs Vegetables sources – thesemust be combined: soya, pulses, cereals, nuts,seeds, lentils	Lethargy, failure to thrive and susceptibility to infection
Carbohydrates	Energy Cellulose (commonly known as fibre) assists digestion	Bread, cereals, potatoes, rice, pasta, yams, bananas, fruit juice	Lack of energy will mean overall tiredness and difficulty in resisting infection
Vitamins Vitamin A – Retinol	Essential for vision in dim light, general health of eyes and skin	Yellow and dark green vegetables, e.g. carrots and spinach Also found in liver, butter and added to margarine	Poor vision, blindness (unusual in UK)
Vitamin B1 – Thiamin	Responsible for the steady release of energy from carbohydrate	Wholemeal flour and grains, milk, fortified cereal products, potatoes, eggs, vegetables and fruit	Beri-beri where carbohydrate intake is high and vitamin B1 level is low
Vitamin B2 – Riboflavin	Utilisation of energy from food	Milk, animal products, marmite	Sores in corners of mouth (rare in the UK)
Vitamin B6 – Pyridoxine	Metabolism of amino acids Needed for the formation of haemoglobin	Meat, fish, eggs, whole cereals, baked beans, banana	Deficiency is rare, although excess of this vitamin can cause damage to nerve function
Vitamin B12 – a compound Combines with folic acid	Needed by rapidly dividing cells such as bone marrow Folic acid taken before and during the first weeks of pregnancy is known to reduce the risk of spina bifida	Animal products, yeast, eggs, cheese, milk and fortified cereals Folic acid found in leafy green vegetables, yeast extract, breakfast cereals	Anaemia and degeneration of nerve cells – vegans can be at risk if no supplements are taken Deficiency of folic acid can result in anaemia

Nutrient group	Function	Sources	Consequences of deficiency
Vitamin C – Ascorbic acid	Needed for maintenance of connective tissue	Citrus fruits, blackcurrants, guavas, green pepper as well as other fresh fruit and vegetables. Vitamin C is fragile and damaged by heat	Bleeding from small blood vessels and from gums, wounds heal more slowly. Disease known as scurvy (rare in UK)
Vitamin D	Helps bone formation by ensuring a good supply of calcium in the blood	Sunlight, margarine, milk, yoghurt, other dairy products, breakfast cereals	Rickets and deformed bones
Vitamin E	Works as an antioxidant – full role still being researched	Most foods contain vitamin E especially vegetable oil, nuts, seeds and some cereal	Very rare, but occasionally anaemia in premature babies
Minerals – many minerals are required by the body. Key minerals include iron and calcium			
Iron	Helps the body take up oxygen	Meat, breakfast cereals, bread and vegetables. Iron is more easily absorbed into the body when vitamin C is present	Anaemia
Calcium	Strengthens bones, teeth, helps contraction of muscles including heart muscle, clotting of blood	Milk, cheese, bread, vegetables, yoghurt and other dairy products. Vitamin D needs to be present in order for calcium to be absorbed	Rickets, bone deformation

Achieving a balanced diet

It is virtually impossible to see foods just in terms of nutrients so many dieticians divide foods into groups and suggest that our daily intake of food is composed from each of these groups. It is also important that diets are varied as relying on only a limited number of foods reduces the likelihood of giving the body the range of minerals and vitamins required.

Key issues - effects of poor diets

Overweight and **obesity** occur when the body is taking in more energy or calories than it needs. Excess energy is converted by the body into layers of fat. Obesity has many damaging effects as it puts pressure on the cardiovascular system and the skeleton. It may also cause a great deal of unhappiness as a person may develop a poor self-image.

Malnutrition occurs when a diet lacks one or more nutrients and may cause specific diseases such as rickets – lack of vitamin D, and anaemia – lack of iron. It is therefore possible for someone to be overweight, but still be malnourished!

Under-nutrition occurs when the overall nutrient intake is insufficient even if the diet is balanced. This causes weight loss as well as increasing the risk of disease.

Assessment activity 8.3

Linda is fifteen years old and is overweight. She wants to lose weight in time for her sister's wedding as she is dreading everyone looking at her. She is trying a diet that promises rapid weight loss by eating only grapefruit and spinach for three weeks.

- What are the nutritional and health implications of such a diet?
- What recommendations would you make that would help Linda to lose weight effectively, based on current medical advice?

Planning meals for children

The principles of nutrition apply equally to feeding children as they need a range of foods that will provide sufficient nutrients. It is also important to consider the age of the child as nutrient requirements change, with younger children particularly requiring nutrient-rich foods such as milk to ensure that their small stomachs are taking in sufficient nutrients. Current advice is that a low fat, high fibre diet is unsuitable for young children especially under two years.

Snacks as part of the overall diet
Children also need to develop a healthy approach towards food and so do not use food as a reward or as a threat! Snacks and drinks should be thought of as part of the daily nutritional intake rather than something additional. This means that they should be nutritious. Good snacks include carrot sticks, tomatoes, apples, bread and rice sticks whilst the best drinks to serve are water, milk and occasionally fruit juices.

Breakfast
Porridge made with milk, orange juice, toast

Mid-morning snack
Milk and banana

Lunch
Cheese and potato pie, baked beans, and salad, blackcurrant mousse, water

Afternoon snack
Cheese and biscuits and an orange

Tea
Chicken, rice and spinach, fresh fruit salad and ice-cream, milk

A sample menu for a three-year-old

Think It Over

- Consider the sample menu above.
- Analyse its effectiveness in providing sufficient nutrients and calories for a three-year-old.
- Evaluate the nutritional consequences for this child if milk is not included.
- Explain why snacks are required for young children.

Meeting children's special dietary needs

Some children will have special food requirements because of cultural or religious restrictions or because of a medical condition. When planning meals and snacks for children with special dietary needs, advice and guidance should be sought from parents as the strictness with which families adhere to some religious and cultural restrictions can vary.

The following table is a guide.

	Requirements	Restrictions
Hindus	Mostly vegetarian	No beef No alcohol
Sikhs	Meat must be killed by one blow to the head	No beef No alcohol
Muslims	Meat must be 'halal' otherwise considered unclean	No pork No shellfish No alcohol
Jews	Meat must be 'kosher' otherwise considered unclean Fish has to have scales and fins Dairy and meat products cannot be consumed together. Dairy products must be prepared using separate utensils	No pork No shellfish No rabbit
Rastafarians	Mainly vegetarian although take milk products. Foods must be 'I-tal' or alive – no canned or processed foods. Foods should be organic	No salt No coffee No alcohol
Vegans	Vegans do not eat anything that originates from animals. Many vegans will only eat organically produced plants	No animal products
Vegetarians	Dairy products and eggs can be eaten, providing that the animals are humanely farmed	No foods that involve the killing of the animal
Diabetes	Diabetes is a disorder that reduces the ability of the body to control the amount of glucose in the blood. Fluctuation in glucose level can cause hypoglycaemia or hyperglycaemia Regular meals and snacks are required to avoid fluctuation in glucose levels	No foods containing sugar Follow parents' advice and any diet sheet carefully
Coeliac's disease	An intolerance to gluten means that it is not digested by the body. The disease can be fatal causing weight loss and anaemia. People with coeliac's disease must avoid products with gluten in them such as wheat, rye, barley and oats	No wheat, rye, barley and oats Look carefully at processed foods as gluten is often present, e.g. in soups, sauces

Case Study

Jaswinda is four years old and is a diabetic. She needs regular snacks and meals as well as insulin injections. It is home time and a nursery nurse gives all the children a small chocolate egg as a treat. She tells Jaswinda that she is sorry but she forgot that she was a diabetic and she can't give her one. Later, the mother comes into the nursery to explain that Jaswinda is allowed the occasional treat as explained on the diet sheet that is in Jaswinda's file. She is also concerned that Jaswinda is often made to feel 'different' in the setting.

- Use this case study to explain why it is important for staff to be aware of the dietary needs of children.
- Analyse the advantages and disadvantages of having separate menus for children who have dietary needs.

Theory into practice

Choose one of the following groups to find out more about their dietary needs: Coeliac's disease, diabetes, Sikhs, Muslims, Jews.

You may be able to find information on the Internet to assist you in your research

- Using your research as a basis, produce a day's menu for a five-year-old child with a dietary need
- Analyse the effectiveness of your menu in meeting this child's dietary requirements
- Consider the effects of ignoring the dietary need of the child
- Explain the role of nutrients in providing for children's overall health.

Preparing food and drink

Good food hygiene is essential when preparing food and drinks to avoid outbreaks of food poisoning. Food poisoning is a potential killer and young children are particularly vulnerable. If you are likely to be handling food in group settings, it is advisable to take a food hygiene course.

Hygiene routines

Outbreaks of food poisoning are often caused by poor hygiene routines in the kitchen, resulting in the contamination of foods.

- Wear aprons, tie hair back and take off jewellery.
- Wash hands thoroughly before handling foods and each time after visiting the toilet.
- Ensure that kitchen surfaces are disinfected regularly and towels are clean.
- Keep foods covered to prevent flies and bacteria reaching them.
- Keep raw and cooked foods separate. Raw foods contain bacteria especially poultry and meat.
- Wash hands after handling raw products, e.g. meat, poultry, etc.
- Use separate knives and chopping boards for raw products.
- Cover cuts or breaks in skin with plasters.
- Empty bins regularly and keep covered.

Storage of foods

Food has to be correctly stored to prevent contamination and to restrict the growth of any bacteria present. Bacteria flourish at room temperature and so foods such as meat, poultry and dairy products as well as cooked foods should be stored in the fridge.

- Check the temperature of fridges (0-5°C) and freezers (-18°C).
- Store raw and cooked foods in separate areas of a fridge.
- Read food manufacturers' instructions carefully.
- Throw away foods that are out of date.

Cooking and re-heating foods
Bacteria can be killed at high temperatures. Foods that are just 'warmed' will not kill bacteria, but are likely to encourage them to multiply.

- Cooked foods should not be re-heated more than once.
- Foods much reach at least 70°C for several minutes to kill off bacteria.
- Meat, eggs and poultry must be cooked completely through to avoid any 'cold spots'.

Daily routines

Toddlers and older children need to have good physical care in order to grow and develop. The principles of caring for skin, hair and teeth remain the same as with babies, but as children's physical skills develop, the adult should encourage them to take on increased responsibility for their own personal hygiene. This increased independence helps children to gain confidence and self-reliance. As with caring for babies, the views and advice of parents need to be sought.

Toilet training

The term 'toilet training' is in some ways misleading. It suggests that a child can be taught by an adult to use the toilet and this is no longer the approach taken today. It is now generally accepted that 'toilet training' needs to be a process which is child-led as it relies heavily on the child being physically and emotionally ready. This means that there is a wide variation in ages with some children moving out of nappies at fifteen months whilst others are ready at around three years.

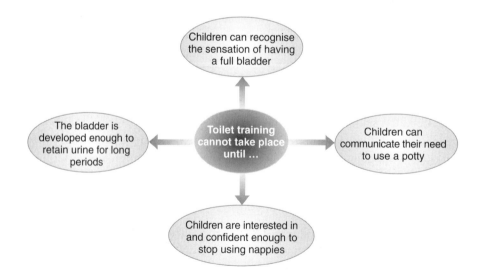

Role of the adult

The key to successful toilet training is to make sure that children are relaxed and happy and that it only takes place when children are showing that they are developmentally ready. Forcing children to sit on a potty often results in a child tensing up and so preventing the bladder from emptying. This in turn can lead to the child becoming distressed and associating the potty with the cause of their distress!

Once a child shows signs of being ready to use a potty or toilet adults should:

- make sure that clothes are easy to take off
- make sure that a potty is nearby the child
- avoid asking children if they need the potty as this creates potential pressure
- respond quickly when a child says that they need the potty
- react calmly to any accidents
- avoid putting undue stress on a child by bribing or rewarding a child for successfully 'performing' because if a child has an accident it can make them feel that they have failed.

Care of skin and hair

The table below shows the principles of caring for children's skin and hair at different ages. Note how children need to be given more privacy and independence as they become older.

Age	Physical care
1–3 years	High levels of supervision are required at this age to prevent possible accidents. **Children should never be left alone in a bathroom or toilet.** Cleaning products must be removed from their reach. During these years, children will learn to use a potty or toilet. Adults will need to make sure that they learn to wash their hands as part of this process. Adults may need to make hand-washing and general skincare fun by turning it into a game as many toddlers intensely dislike having their faces, hands and hair washed **Bathing** Children are likely to need a daily bath or shower. Adults should encourage children to play with the water so that bath time is seen as a positive experience. Water must be checked before children enter and bath mats are advised to prevent children from slipping. Children's skin needs to be dried carefully to prevent soreness **Hair care** Hair will need to be combed or brushed regularly. Check with parents about preferred hair products and styles. Many toddlers dislike having their hair washed. Encourage toddlers to wet their hair themselves as they are playing in the shower or bath. Use mild hair products and make sure that a towel is handy to wipe away any water or soap from eyes **Teeth** Milk teeth should be appearing. It is important that they are brushed twice a day by an adult as children of this age are likely to just suck the brush. To prevent tooth decay, sugary drinks and foods should be avoided and children should be seen by a dentist
3–6 years	Adults need to ensure that over this period, children are taking more responsibility for their personal hygiene. By 6 years, children should be able to

Age	Physical care
	use the toilet, dress and wash their hands independently. Personal hygiene can be used as a basis for learning topics, e.g. 'Looking after our teeth' **Bathing** Most parents will want their children to have a daily shower or bath. Children still need to be supervised at these times and the adult should take responsibility for running and checking the temperature of the water. They should encourage children to wash themselves, but do the 'final check' to ensure that all areas of the body are clean if necessary **Hair care** Adults should encourage children to brush or comb their hair, but may need to give some assistance. Hair needs to be checked for head lice. Children should be encouraged to wash their own hair, but may need to be given assistance when rinsing **Tooth care** Children can brush their own teeth, but adults should check and give a final brush. Avoid giving sugary foods and drinks to children. Six monthly check-ups at a dentist are advised
6 years+	Children should be given increased privacy and the adult should be aiming just to remind and praise children about looking after their hair, skin and teeth. Some children become less enthusiastic and thorough about keeping themselves clean as they get older. Interesting bath products and toys can help if this is the case

Head lice
Head lice are parasites that live on the human scalp. They have become a common problem in many group-care settings including schools as children have more head to head contact. Children's hair should be checked each week for the following signs of an infestation:

- itchy scalp
- red bite marks
- lice – tiny wingless translucent insects in the hair roots especially at the nape of neck
- eggs, known as nits – white or brown specks attached to hair.

Advice as to treatment changes, although thoroughly combing with a nit comb is the traditional method. Other methods include the use of lotions containing pesticides and electric combs.

Sun and skin care

Children's skin needs to be protected from the sun's rays to prevent heat stroke and the occurrence of skin cancer in later life. Current medical opinion suggests that even on a cloudy or cool summer's day, the sun's rays can still be harmful to skin. Research into the effects of the sun on the skin is ongoing and adults caring for children will need to check for the latest available advice. Current advice includes the following:

- Avoid taking babies and children out in the direct sunlight in the summer between 11am and 3pm when the sun is likely to be at its most powerful.
- Keep babies and children covered up in T-shirts or light fitting garments to prevent exposure to the sun's rays.
- Use wide brimmed hats and sunglasses to protect face and head.
- Apply a high factor sun cream to screen out UVB rays and apply regularly.
- Check that sun cream is not out of date as this can reduce effectiveness.
- Avoid taking babies under twelve months into the sun.

Stimulation and play

As with babies, children continue to need to be stimulated as part of their healthy development. Playing with toys, going on outings and walks are all ways of stimulating children's brain activity. One of the major roles of early years practitioners is to stimulate children's development through play and activities. For detailed information about this see Unit 7.

Sleep and rest

As part of a daily routine, children need opportunities to sleep and rest. The exact purpose of sleep is still being researched, but it is already known that the body requires sleep in order to maintain cells and also to process information. Lack of sleep can result in a lack of concentration and difficult behaviour. Many children under three years old will sleep for around ten to twelve hours a night and still require one or even two short naps in the day. Adults can help children to rest and sleep by creating a routine that helps children to relax and feel secure. In most home settings, bedtime is preceded by a bath and a story to help the child to wind down.

It is also important that during the day, children have opportunities to rest. Look out for activities that allow children to be more passive and where they can sit or lie down.

Key issues
- Make sure that children are not hungry or need a nappy change.
- Allow children to have a cuddly toy or other comforter.
- Check that the room is not too warm or cold.
- Check that the room is safe, e.g. no unsuitable toys or cleaning products left out.
- Allow enough time for children to settle and relax.

Theory into practice

Children's routines vary according to their age.

- Using questionnaires or structured interviews with parents or carers, research the routines of three children of different ages. Analyse how each routine meets the needs of the child.
- Explain the factors that can influence the routine of a child.
- Evaluate the importance of routines on a child's development.

Clothing and footwear

Suitable clothing and footwear is primarily needed for warmth and the protection of skin. It has, however, also become important in our society as a way of projecting a self-image. It is surprising how quickly children become aware of this secondary purpose and it is not unusual for quite young children to have clothing preferences.

Although parents are largely responsible for buying and choosing their children's clothes, adults working in home settings may also have an input. Clothes and footwear should be suitable for the time of year and also for the type of play and activity that children are undertaking. Carefully choosing clothes for the activity prevents situations when children are told to 'try and keep clean' which effectively restricts their play.

Key issues

- Clothes for toddlers and young children need to be easy to put on and take off.
- Garments should be easy to launder.
- Make sure that nightwear conforms with safety standards.
- Footwear including socks and tights should be checked for tightness.
- Garments should not restrict children's movements.

Choosing clothes for babies

Babies wet and soil their clothes easily and so several changes of clothes are needed. One of the key principles in dressing babies is to ensure that clothes are easy to put on and also easy to remove. Care should always be taken that a baby is not overheating. This means that items of outdoor clothing should always be removed when indoors.

There are strict regulations governing the manufacture of babies' clothing. This is to avoid possible accidents.

- Make sure that buttons on garments are sewn on securely.
- Avoid garments with ribbons as the baby may choke or be strangled.
- Dress babies in layers of clothes and check that they are not overheating.
- Do not put a baby down to sleep in a hat.
- Check homemade clothes carefully – babies tend to suck and also handle their clothes.
- Make sure that garments are easy to put over a baby's head.
- Avoid garments that are difficult to wash.
- Make sure that any socks or garments with feet allow the baby to move their toes freely.

Children's behaviour

One key aspect of working with children is to be able to manage their behaviour. There has been a shift in recent years towards understanding children's behaviour and looking for ways in which to promote wanted behaviour rather than just dealing with unwanted behaviour.

Defining behaviour

Acceptable behaviour

As children grow, they need to learn how to behave in a manner that is acceptable within the society or community in which they are growing up. This enables them as adults to 'fit in' and be tolerated by others. Socially acceptable behaviour can vary from society to society, e.g. spitting in the street is tolerated in some countries but frowned upon in others. Defining what is and is not acceptable behaviour is therefore not easy, but at the core of most societies is the underlying principle of respecting and considering others. For children, this means that practitioners try and encourage them to share, play co-operatively and be helpful.

As well as learning about behaviour that is essential to respect others, children also have to learn some codes of behaviour that are in place for more practical reasons. A setting may have a rule to stop children from running inside as a way of preventing accidents.

The language of behaviour

When writing or talking about behaviour, it is important not to use terms such as 'bad' behaviour as people's views about what constitutes 'good' or 'bad' behaviour can vary. Defining behaviour in such terms is therefore restrictive. When adults talk about 'good' behaviour, they are actually referring to behaviour that they want to encourage. It is therefore useful to use terms such as 'wanted' or 'acceptable'.

Variations in family values and practices

As part of showing respect for others, most families expect children to learn table manners and social courtesies but it is worth bearing in mind in our multi-cultural society that these are not universal. There are remarkable differences between manners in different cultures and even between families with similar backgrounds. Whilst some children are learning that putting their elbows on the table is rude, others will be learning that it is perfectly acceptable! Some children will also be encouraged to show behaviour that is linked to their families' religious beliefs. As a practitioner you will need an awareness of the social, cultural and religious manners that are promoted in the homes of the children you work with so that misunderstandings can be avoided.

Learning about behaviour

At first, the baby and young child learn about behaviour in the context of their family and main carers. They may learn to take their shoes off before going inside their home or to wait for others to be served before eating. Some aspects of wanted behaviour are linked to cultural or religious expectations whereas others are related to practical or safety issues. As children become older, they learn about the behaviour that is acceptable in a range of group and social situations and to adapt their behaviour to fit the context in which they find themselves, e.g. asking to go to the toilet in school, but not needing to do so at home.

Developmental effects on behaviour – links between children's behaviour and development

Children's ability to show socially acceptable or 'wanted' behaviour is partly linked to their development. Children need to have certain skills in place before they can show some types of behaviour that are considered to be desirable. Most children, for example, are unlikely to be able to share and play in a co-operative way until the age of three years, as sharing requires developed awareness of the needs of others. The following diagram shows some of the skills that children need in order to play co-operatively.

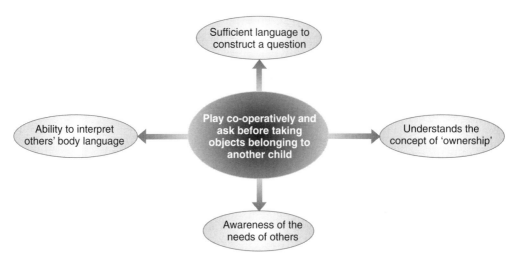

The need for children to acquire certain skills in areas of their development means that learning how to show acceptable behaviour is a gradual process. Children who have a developmental delay in one or more areas will therefore show behaviour that is not usual for their age range. This is particularly true with children who have communication or language difficulties as language allows children to express their needs and feelings.

The table below outlines children's development and the goals for children's behaviour. Note that goals represent the type of behaviour that adults should be encouraging children to show as this will be the child's next step.

Age	Developmental milestones	Goals for behaviour
1-2 years	Restless and keen to explore No sense of danger No understanding of sharing or playing with others of the same age Repeats actions that gain attention May cry or show anger if needs are not immediately met	Carry out simple instructions to develop independence Play alongside other children, but not sharing
2-3 years	Restless and keen to explore Wants to imitate adults and be independent, e.g. wants to try drinking tea, putting on own coat Cannot wait for things and finds sharing difficult Points and uses some language to express needs	Wait to have needs met, e.g. at meal times Play alongside other children Share toys with other children with significant adult support
3-4 years	Enjoys playing with other children Is able to be understood by other children, although may not have language to express feelings	Take turns and share equipment with some adult support Help tidy up Follow simple instructions Use language as a way of expressing feelings

Age	Developmental milestones	Goals for behaviour
4-5 years	Plays with other children, although occasionally squabbles Interested in helping others Learning how to play as part of a larger group Understands the need to wait	Ask permission to use other's possessions Play co-operatively with minimal adult help Take care of the environment and others Use language to negotiate and express feelings
5-8 years	Has strong friendships Able to use language to argue and reason Copies other children's actions, e.g. may repeat swearing Beginning to understand right from wrong for simple actions Has good self-help skills	Apologise and think of others' feelings and needs Listen, follow instructions and use initiative Be helpful and thoughtful Learn how to negotiate with others

Key issues

You should always consider a child's developmental stage rather than simply their age when working with them. Adjust your expectations of behaviour according to their stage of development.

Psychological perspectives on how children learn behaviour

In order to understand how to promote 'wanted' behaviour, it is important to have some understanding of how children learn behaviour. There are several psychological models that are usually drawn upon to help practitioners influence children's behaviour. Each of these models is discussed in detail in Unit 7 (pages 227–33) and Unit 12 (pages 433–38) but are summarised here.

Operant conditioning

At its simplest, the idea behind this theory is that children (and adults too) repeat actions and behaviours that have previously given us some reward or pleasure. We also avoid situations or actions that have been negative or unpleasant. According to this theory a child who has been praised for waiting for their turn is likely to repeat this behaviour again because it has been reinforced. B.F. Skinner, who led the research on operant conditioning, repeatedly found that positive reinforcing or rewarding people a more effective strategy than using punishers.

Types of positive reinforcers

There is a range of positive reinforcers that children respond well to. They include stickers, food rewards, toys, but the simplest positive reinforcer is adult attention. A word of praise, eye contact and a smile are strong reinforcers. It is worth noting here that some children will also show unwanted behaviour in order to gain adults' attention, even if the attention is quite negative.

As well as positive reinforcers that are given externally by someone else, children can also gain positive reinforcement from the actions themselves. A child may continually bounce on a chair, despite being praised when they are sitting properly in it, because the sensation of bouncing acts as a positive reinforcer.

Primary and secondary positive reinforcers
Positive reinforcers can also be divided into two groups: primary and secondary. A primary reinforcer gives you instant pleasure or reward such as a chocolate bar. Secondary reinforcers do not give instant pleasure but can lead to it, e.g. money is a secondary reinforcer because it is used to buy primary reinforcement such as sweets. It takes a while for children to associate secondary reinforcers with pleasure and this is one reason why a young child would choose a sweet over a £5 note!

Positive reinforcement for unwanted behaviour
Some unwanted behaviour is sometimes persistent because the child has received positive reinforcement for it in the past. A child may whine in the shop and be given some sweets to encourage them to be quiet. In this example the child has learnt that whining leads to something desirable and so is more likely to replicate this behaviour in future. In the same way, a child who needs adult attention may learn to gain attention by being aggressive to other children so that adults come and intervene.

Timing of reinforcements
The timing of reinforcements can increase their effectiveness. Skinner found that the closer the interval between the behaviour and the positive reinforcement, the more likely behaviour would be repeated. This means that praising a child at the time of their 'wanted' behaviour will be more powerful than mentioning it later on in the day.

Criticisms of using this theory to influence children's behaviour
There have been some criticisms of using this model to influence the way children behave. It can be thought of as manipulative as children should be encouraged to show 'wanted' behaviour for the 'right' reasons rather than simply to gain praise or reward from others. Clearly there is a danger that if practitioners use this as their only strategy, children risk losing some of their own creativity and resourcefulness in their attempt to 'please' adults. Effective practitioners, however, tend to use a range of strategies to help children manage their own behaviour.

It is also worth adding that a psychologist who subscribes to the theory of 'universal egoism' would suggest that, even when we help someone else, it is not necessarily a completely altruistic gesture because we are being positively reinforced when we enjoy feeling helpful or being thanked!

Key issues – reinforcers

- Primary reinforcers are more effective with young children. Star charts are secondary reinforcers because the child has to wait for a reward and so are better used with older children.
- When looking at a child's unwanted behaviour consider whether the child is being reinforced by the action itself.
- Give children immediate positive reinforcement for 'wanted' behaviour that you wish to encourage.
- Help children to understand why they are being praised or rewarded so that they understand which behaviour to repeat, e.g. 'Well done, you managed that puzzle by yourself'.

- Avoid phrases which make children believe that they have to do things to please an adult or simply to gain a reward. Explain the reason for the wanted behaviour, e.g. 'If you share that with Natalie, she will feel happy' rather than 'If you share that you can have a sticker'.

Social learning theory (see also Units 7 and 12)

The social learning theory (also known as observation learning) suggests that children learn 'wanted' and 'unwanted' behaviour by observing and imitating others. Research suggests that young children are heavily influenced by adults especially those who are important in their lives. They model their behaviour on them, hence the term 'role models'. Children who therefore see and hear adults demonstrating 'wanted' behaviour are more likely to reproduce it. The converse is also true with children who witness parents being aggressive, equally demonstrating this behaviour. As children become older, they also model behaviour of their peers or 'heroes' such as football players and film stars as the focus shifts away from their parents and immediate carers.

The social learning theory complements operant conditioning rather than competes with it. Children who copy an adult and then are praised for their actions will be more likely to repeat the wanted behaviour.

Key issues
- Social learning theory means that your actions and gestures are being observed and may later be modelled by children.
- Make sure that you demonstrate the 'wanted' behaviour that your setting is promoting.

Self-esteem and self-reliance

When managing children's behaviour, it is also useful to understand an effect known as the 'self-fulfilling prophecy'. The idea is that children will mirror the behaviour that adults expect of them. Adults who believe that they are working with children who are difficult are more likely to see unwanted behaviour whereas adults who have positive expectations of children are likely to see more positive behaviour.

One explanation for this is that children are building up a picture of themselves – their self concept. They look for reactions and messages from others around them to help them gain a vision of themselves. An adult who provides the child with a positive image of themselves will help the child feel good about themselves and thus allow the child to show 'wanted' behaviour. Children who are told that they are 'naughty' or hear people saying that they are 'difficult' are likely to decide that they are inherently so and therefore will behave accordingly.

To help children gain a positive view of themselves, it is important that practitioners praise children and also encourage them to do things for themselves. Being independent gives children inner confidence and thus aids self-esteem.

Preparing children for change – planned and unplanned

Changes in children's lives can affect their behaviour. It is a myth to suggest that children are adaptable, because although children may not have the language or the power to protest, they often mirror their worries through their behaviour. It is also harder for young children to adapt to changes in expectations of their behaviour as they tend to need consistency and routine. The way changes are handled by adults can affect the impact they have on children. The figure below shows the type of changes that may be expected to affect children's behaviour.

Reactions to change

The way in which children react to change can vary enormously. Some children react very quickly whilst other children may seem to cope at the time but later show a reaction. Common reactions to more prolonged changes include:

- tearfulness and clinginess – may not want to leave primary carer
- night waking and nightmares
- regression, e.g. wetting the bed, wanting to wear nappies, needing a previously discarded dummy
- sullenness and withdrawal
- aggression towards others
- attention seeking.

Helping children with planned changes

Wherever possible, it is important to talk to children about planned changes even if they seem relatively minor such as having a photographer in or going on an outing. Young children often rely on a sense of routine for their security and so disruptions to their normal routine can be hard for them.

The timescale when children should be prepared for change depends very much on the child's age. A young child may find it difficult to think about a change until just before it is due to happen because their concept of time is limited. Tomorrow or next week seems a very long time when you are two or three years old.

Older children, on the other hand, often respond well to knowing ahead because it gives them time to think and ask questions. It is not unusual for older children to want to go through various scenarios in order to gain reassurance. Books and resources can be a good way of helping children cope with more prolonged changes in their lives. It is also important to remember that children will need continued support even when they seem 'settled'.

Helping children with unplanned changes

Occasionally, a change of routine or circumstance will happen without any forewarning, e.g. evacuation of premises, sudden change of carer, hospitalisation. Children can find these types of changes very unnerving and will often look to the adults around them to understand how they should react. A calm, relaxed adult will give them reassurance, but a worried or harassed adult will cause them further distress.

Key issues – preparing children for changes

- Give plenty of reassurance.
- Make sure that you appear calm and remain approachable.
- Answer any questions as truthfully as possible.
- Observe the child carefully to look for signs of distress.
- Make sure that young children have access to comforters.
- Try and make some changes feel more like a game.
- Use books and resources to help children with planned changes.
- Where appropriate liaise with parents so that everyone knows what has happened or has been said.

Assessment activity 8.4

Design a leaflet for parents which explains the factors that might influence a child's behaviour. Your leaflet should include the following:

- the links between a child's stage of development and behaviour
- how changes in children's lives can affect behaviour
- strategies for helping children to cope with change.

Strategies for managing children's behaviour

There are times when children will show unwanted behaviour, although if practitioners are working to promote positive behaviour, these should be relatively rare and minor occurrences.

When managing unwanted behaviour it is essential for adults to remain calm and to consider their approach as it is important not just to manage the behaviour, but also to try and prevent it from recurring. In some cases where behaviour is recurrent, it will be important to gain more information from parents and also from observations (see page 310) in order to work out the underlying causes.

- Are there any immediate underlying causes of the behaviour that can be resolved? (e.g. children are hot, hungry or tired)
- How does the behaviour link to stage of development? (e.g. tantrums are not unusual with two-year-olds, toddlers tend to snatch other's toys)
- Is this behaviour linked to any ongoing changes or difficulties in a child's life?
- Is this repeated behaviour and, if so, is the child showing it to gain attention?
- Has the child learnt this behaviour from copying another child or adult?
- Is the unwanted behaviour a result of boredom or curiosity?
- Was the child aware of the goals and boundaries relating to the activity? (e.g. that they are not allowed to throw sand)

Common strategies to deal with unwanted behaviour

There are several strategies that can be used with children, although it is always essential to try and determine why children needed to show the unwanted behaviour. Some of the best strategies are non-confrontational because negatively dealing with children's behaviour by, for example, 'telling them off' can damage their self-esteem and create further problems. The following table includes a range of strategies.

Strategy	Rationale
Eye contact	Eye contact is a powerful way of reminding children about boundaries without saying anything. It is essential that a smile or praise is given once the child shows more suitable behaviour
Removal of eye contact or adult attention	If you suspect that a child is showing unwanted behaviour in order to gain adult attention, it is sometimes worth removing eye contact and pretending to ignore the behaviour unless the behaviour is likely to cause the child or another injury. Praise the child once more suitable behaviour is shown
Distraction	A young child can be distracted from unwanted behaviour by being shown a different toy or activity. This technique should always be tried with the under 3s as developmentally they find it difficult to share and think of others
Explanation	Explaining to children the consequences of their actions can be very effective with children from around $3^{1}/_{2}$ years when they have enough language and reasoning skills. It is also useful to ask older children how they can resolve any problems themselves, e.g. what do you think would be a better way of sorting this game out?
Adult participation	Actually joining in games or playing alongside children can help children in situations where they have been bored or are squabbling. It is also a good preventative measure to take when children are obviously needing more adult attention
Removal of items	In some situations, children are unable to cope with 'temptation', e.g. may find it hard not to throw sand or not to touch an item. Removing items can therefore be effective especially with young children

Dealing with specific types of behaviour

There are some types of behaviour that are common, although need careful handling as they can become recurrent – see the table below.

Behaviour	Explanation	Strategy
Comfort behaviour Masturbation Thumbsucking Rocking Head banging	This type of behaviour is not uncommon in children under 5 years old when they are tired or under stress	Distract the child by providing a stimulating activity Consider whether the child is tired or unwell Persistent comfort behaviour especially in older children can be a sign of emotional disturbance and should be referred to professionals
Biting	This type of behaviour is common in children aged 18 months – 3 years. It is	Give attention and comfort to the victim – do not focus your attention on the perpetrator

Behaviour	Explanation	Strategy
	generally linked to frustration, but the sensory satisfaction of a bite can mean that a child begins to enjoy biting	Supervise the perpetrator as carefully another bite can quickly follow the first Praise the perpetrator when they are playing well
Attention seeking behaviour Interrupting activities Answering back Challenging instructions	This type of behaviour is often linked to children's insecurity. Children will sometimes look at an adult before showing unwanted behaviour to check that they have an audience!	Avoid giving attention, even if negative, as this will reinforce the behaviour Consider withdrawing eye contact Praise the child when they are showing more suitable behaviour Look for opportunities to increase time spent with the child
Tantrums	Tantrums are common in children between the ages of 18 months and 3 years. They are generally a result of frustration and can be triggered by hunger and tiredness. Some children quickly learn that tantrums can be an effective way of gaining adults' attention. Occasional tantrums by older children often signal underlying unhappiness and require a different approach than with toddlers	Most practitioners can sense a looming tantrum – try first to use distraction Remain calm and do not fuel the situation with your own anger Avoid giving attention or reacting to tantrums in young children When the tantrum has subsided, be ready to offer comfort and praise Look for ways to avoid the same trigger in the future Make sure that a consistent strategy is being used with all who care for the young child Look for ways of promoting children's independence

Setting goals and boundaries for children's behaviour

Codes of behaviour change from environment to environment. Your behaviour at home is likely to be different from the behaviour that is expected from you in a place or worship or library. Children have to learn the codes of behaviour for the setting or environment that they are in. Unlike adults who can pick up cues or who have previous experience of situations, children need some guidance. Experienced practitioners give children clear messages about what is expected of them and also what they can and cannot do. This is what is meant by the terms 'setting goals' and 'boundaries'. Goals are targets for behaviour, e.g. a practitioner may say 'It would be nice if you could share this together', whilst boundaries are limits on behaviour, e.g. 'If you throw the sand again, I will put the lid on it'.

It is important to set goals and boundaries that are appropriate to children's stage of development otherwise children may not be able to meet them. Children who feel that they cannot live up to the expectations of a setting or an adult are more likely to have a low self-image and esteem. This in turn makes them think that they are 'no good at being good'.

Observing children's behaviour

A good starting point for managing children's behaviour is to observe the child carefully. This helps by giving everyone concerned a true picture of the child's overall development, any potential triggers and the incidents themselves. Observing children also reduces the possibility of children being unfairly labelled which can create its own set of problems (see Self-esteem and self-reliance, page 305). For observations to have any value, it is important that the observer is as objective as possible and that several observations of the child take place. The various methods of observation and their advantages/disadvantages are shown in the table below.

Method	Advantages and disadvantages
Event sample Every time the 'unwanted' behaviour is observed, a recording is made. It should include details about who the child was with, what happened and how the incident was handled. The event sample shows the frequency of incidents and also the timings	+ Gives clear indication of frequency of behaviour + Helps practitioners to see if a pattern of behaviour is emerging, e.g. after lunch + Can be used to monitor effectiveness of strategies, e.g. if number of incidents are decreasing. - Focuses only on poor behaviour, rather than on the whole child - May not show whether there is an underlying developmental cause for behaviour
Time sample The child is observed over a session at frequent intervals, e.g. every 10 minutes	+ Allows practitioner to build up a picture of what the child does during a session + May uncover underlying reason for behaviour, e.g. lack of friends, adult attention - May not catch the actual 'incident' of behaviour - Requires one member of staff to sit and observe
Video Some settings may be able to video part of a session, focusing on one or more children	+ Allows all staff members to look together at child's responses and play + Catches the whole scene and can be replayed + Can be replayed for other professionals - If children know they are being filmed, they will not show natural behaviour

Assessment activity 8.5

May-Lin is four years old. She has just had a tantrum because she has not been able to sit on her favourite chair at nursery. She often has tantrums and generally finds it hard to share with other children. Her parents say that she refuses to go to bed unless one of them stays in the room with her and this often means that she goes to bed very late at night. Staff in the nursery have also noticed that just before she shows 'unwanted' actions she often appears to check that one of them is near her and is looking. She has just started at this nursery because her previous childminder has left the area.

* Analyse the behaviour that May-Lin is demonstrating
* Evaluate a range of strategies that staff in the nursery might use to manage this behaviour.

Safe, secure and stimulating environment for children

Children need stimulation as part of their daily routine. This usually takes place in the form of play, activities and outings. This section looks at ways of making sure that the environment in which play and activities takes place is safe and secure.

Outdoor play environment

As part of a daily routine, it is important that children spend some time out of doors. There are many educational as well as health benefits when children play outdoors, as shown in the diagram below.

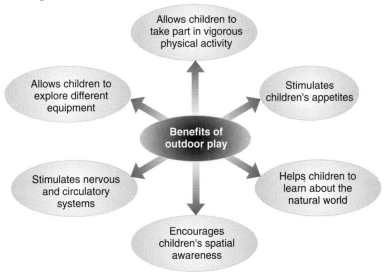

Designing and planning an outdoor play environment

A well-designed outdoor play area should maximise children's opportunities to explore and play freely whilst being safe. Traditionally, many settings only used their outdoor areas as places for children to 'let off steam'. This has now changed with many settings trying to provide opportunities for a variety of activities to promote learning. The amount of outdoor space can vary enormously between settings, with some settings having only a small tarmac surface which means that staff have to plan carefully how best to use the space. The table below shows how one nursery with a very limited amount of space managed to provide a range of outdoor activities for their children.

Type of learning opportunity	Learning benefits	Provision
Gardening and growing	To learn about how things grow To help children care for the environment	Children planted pots and tubs
Observing wildlife	To learn about natural environment	A bird feeder was placed near the window Children looked at mini-beasts in the park
Vigorous physical play	To control bodies, improve balance and co-ordination	Tricycles, slides, hoops were used as part of an obstacle course
Water and mud play	Learning through senses	Buckets and trays filled with peat, mud and water were put outside for children to play with
Constructing and digging	To enjoy constructing and modelling with new materials	Large tubs provided with diggers, scoops, pieces of wood
Imaginative play	To develop social skills and language	Pushchairs, dolls and teddies with shopping bags, trolleys and handbags were put out so that children could pretend 'shopping' Dens and houses are built by putting sheets and tables out for children to build with

Other factors affecting design of outdoor play environment

Safety and ease of supervision

Outdoor areas have to be safe and must be easy for adults to supervise. Layouts should be checked to ensure that they do not create potential 'blackspots' where children are likely to run into each other. Areas should also be secure to prevent children from wandering off or possible incidents from strangers. It is usual for settings to check the safeness of outdoor areas on a daily or sessional basis to look for possible hazards (see also Unit 4, pages 130–6).

Accessibility

Outdoor areas need to be easily accessible to all children especially those with mobility needs. This may mean installing ramps, raising flower beds and choosing equipment that can be adapted for children with mobility or other needs.

Low maintenance and durability

Outdoor areas need to be easily maintained and durable. Plants need to be chosen for hardiness in the face of possible onslaught by children's fingers, feet and sometimes ball games! Some settings use volunteers to help them maintain areas of garden or to give advice on ponds and creating natural habitats for wildlife.

Storage of equipment
Equipment needs to be properly stored. Many settings use an outdoor shed in which to store large pieces of equipment that are specifically used outdoors such as large slides and tricycles. This protects items from the weather and can allow settings to vary the type of equipment that they put out. In settings where space and storage is limited, equipment may be used both indoors and outdoors. They may, for example, take a sand tray outdoors or buy foam balls that can be used inside and outside.

Aesthetic appeal
The look of an outdoor area can affect its use. Settings that create aesthetically pleasing areas are also creating a pleasant atmosphere. This in turn can reflect on children's behaviour and care of their environment. Settings in residential areas may also have to consider their neighbours' feelings.

Play surfaces
There are a range of play surfaces that can be used in outdoor areas, including grass, bark chippings, gravel and cushioned tarmac. The surface chosen depends on the type of activity that will take place with the emphasis being on preventing serious injuries from falls. This has led to many settings using specially designed tarmac instead of concrete in areas where children may climb or fall off swings.

Case Study

The Millside pre-school is trying to improve its outdoor play area which is quite small, 10m x 6.5m, although it is flat and has already been fenced in. It is currently grassed, although the council has said that it will provide some concrete or tarmac surface if required. At present the pre-school only uses it for the children to ride tricycles. The pre-school raised £2000 and has a team of volunteers ready to help staff 'transform' the play area.

Constraints

- Millside does not want to spend the money on large items such as slides and swings as there is some vandalism on the estate.
- There is limited storage inside the building. Staff are concerned about the amount of lifting and packing away that they do.

Produce a report that includes:

- detailed recommendations as to how this outdoor play environment could be used
- the learning benefits of any equipment, activities or toys proposed.

Indoor play environments
Most children spend a large proportion of their time indoors and settings need to find ways of making sure that a range of play activities is available to them. Most settings do this by dividing the room into play and activity areas. The following types of play areas are commonly found in most settings.

Creative play area
This area is usually used for activities that are likely to be messy or require water, including paint, sand and water tray as well as junk modelling. This area is usually housed near to a sink or hand-washing facilities, and the floor surface is easy to clean.

Quiet area

This is often a carpeted, cosy area which allows children to rest, read or play with toys on the floor.

Role play area

In some settings this area is called the 'home corner' although they may turn it into a hospital, shop or other themed area. This area needs to be designed to allow children some feeling of privacy whilst still allowing adults to be able to supervise the children.

Activity tables

Many settings will also have some tables or areas in the room where a wide range of other activities can take place. There may be tables for jigsaw puzzles, emergent writing, maths and games.

Flexibility and adapting layouts

Many settings change their layouts during the session or during the week to allow them more space for physical activities. This is particularly true of settings that do not have a hall or a suitable outdoor play area. Tables and chairs may be moved back to allow children space to play on tricycles or to join in group activities such as parachute games. Changing layouts from time to time can also spark off new interest in children as they 'discover' an activity in a new place.

Creating an attractive and stimulating environment

The way in which activities are presented and the overall look of a play environment can affect the way in which children play and even behave. Most settings try to create a stimulating and aesthetically pleasing environment by displaying children's work, interesting artefacts and posters. Most settings also try to change their displays to provide a continually stimulating environment. Displays of children's work also help foster a sense of pride and achievement in children and so are considered essential.

Safety and other factors when planning a layout

Planning a layout also has to be considered in the context of health and safety. In addition, some settings have to put away their equipment after each session as the room is needed for other purposes. Unit 4 contains more information on safety factors to consider when planning a layout.

Risk assessment (see also Unit 4, pages 130–6)

It is virtually impossible to provide a totally risk-free environment, but settings have a duty under the 1974 Health and Safety Act to manage the risks in their environment. This process of identifying and then managing risks is known as risk assessment. Most settings have one person who is responsible for healthy and safety and who as part of their role produces a risk assessment.

Care of equipment and toys

The care of equipment and toys is extremely important especially in group-care settings where there is a potential risk of cross-infection. Toys and equipment are also under greater physical strain in group-care settings where the usage is greater than in homes. This increased usage can cause equipment made of plastic or metal to develop cracks or signs of metal fatigue. Most settings therefore purchase new toys rather than second-hand ones and also choose more sturdier and often costlier equipment.

Key issues

- Equipment, especially ones which are weight bearing such as tricycles and climbing frames, should be regularly checked for signs of corrosion, metal fatigue and cracks.
- Equipment and toys that are damaged should be removed and discarded if necessary.
- Toys that are frequently handled such as Duplo bricks should be wiped down regularly with a mild solution of disinfectant to destroy bacteria.
- Cuddly toys, dressing up clothes and other fabric items can also harbour bacteria and should be regularly machine washed.
- All toys and equipment should be age/stage appropriate for children.
- Manufacturers' instructions should be carefully followed when cleaning or using toys and equipment.

Babies and toddlers

Babies and toddlers are likely to be putting their hands in their mouths and then onto toys and equipment. High levels of hygiene are therefore essential to prevent cross-infection:

- Cuddly toys should be machine washed at least once a week.
- Toys should be either sterilised or wiped over with a mild solution of disinfectant.
- Toys should be checked to ensure that they are safe and age appropriate.

Supervision and adult intervention

Adults play a major part in ensuring children's safety and also providing stimulation. Whilst preventative measures such as using safety equipment are useful, close supervision by an adult remains the key way in which children can be kept safe.

Key issues

- Babies and toddlers need very close supervision – you should be physically near them at all times.
- Listen carefully to the way children are playing – loud angry voices or complete silence should always be investigated.
- Provide children with new play opportunities or suggestions if children are misusing equipment or appear bored.
- Make sure you position yourself to get a good all-round view of children.

Promotion of the environment and personal hygiene in children

Being able to take care of yourself and your environment are life skills. Adults can help children learn these skills by being a good role model and also through everyday routines and activities.

Promotion of care of the environment

Very young children can be taught to respect and care for their environment. The key to helping children is by presenting the activity in a fun way and also remembering to praise children when they pick up things or show interest in their environment. Toddlers will often help to tidy up if they see it as a game, whilst older children will enjoy tidying as a team game.

Promotion of care of personal hygiene

As children get older they should take on increased responsibility for their personal hygiene. At first, children are quite keen to do so, but as children get older, it helps if they understand the importance of why personal hygiene is important.

- Encourage toddlers and pre-school children to wash themselves by praising them and making it fun.
- Plan activities with older children to help them realise the importance of personal hygiene, e.g. place a tooth in a glass of cola and watch how it decays.
- Invite speakers, e.g. dentists, doctors and nurses.
- Encourage children to produce posters.
- Ensure that toilets and washbasins are attractive and clean.
- Gently remind older children to wash their hands and praise them.

Theory into practice – hand washing experiment

Ask two children to brush their hands with paint.

- Give one child some hot water, soap and a towel to wash their hands with.
- Give the other child some cold water and a towel to wash their hands with.

Which method of washing hands is the most effective?

- Decide the age range that this experiment would be suitable for.
- Consider the learning benefits for children.
- Link this activity into the Foundation Stage or other early years curriculum.

Safety in home settings (see also Unit 4, pages 130–6)

According to the Child Accident Prevention Trust, the majority of accidents involving young children occurs in the home. This means that close supervision of children is essential in home settings along with an awareness of the inherent risks in a home environment. Safety equipment should be used at all times to manage some of the risk, but it cannot be a substitute for close supervision. Safety is also an issue in gardens as ponds, plants and tools can all cause accidents.

Assessment activity 8.6

Write a report about the importance of outdoor play for children's learning and health. Your report should:

- examine the benefits of outdoor play on children's health and overall development
- consider a range of activities that would be suitable for the following ages of children: 0–1 years, 1–3 years, 3–5 years and 5–8 years
- discuss the safety issues involved in providing for outdoor play
- evaluate the role of the adult in providing for outdoor play.

Safety in the car

Many children are transported in cars and so adults must understand how to keep children safe. The key to safety is to ensure that children are strapped properly into fitting car seats or other restraints as well as ensuring that the driver is being careful.

By law the driver is responsible for ensuring that all passengers are wearing seatbelts or car seats if they are fitted and can be prosecuted if they are not.

- Children should be transported in appropriate childseats or restraints until they are tall enough for an adult seatbelt (1.5m).
- By law, children under three years are not allowed to be in the front seat of a car unless they are restrained by a car seat or appropriate restraint.
- Rear facing baby and child seats should not be used in the front seats where a car is fitted with an airbag.
- To avoid possible choking, it is not recommended for toddlers alone in the rear to be given drinks or foods on which they might choke. Toys also have to be carefully chosen.

Planning outings

Outings are important for children as a way of stimulating them. Outings can include trips to the park, a walk to post a letter as well as large-scale group outings such as going to a wildlife centre or the seaside. Changing environments inevitably means a new set of risks that need to be managed. Schools now follow national guidelines that were produced following a series of fatal accidents on trips, whilst pre-school settings have to increase staffing levels to comply with regulations.

Key issues – checklist for planning outings

For all outings
- Choose the venue carefully, looking for potential hazards such as traffic, weather, the type of activities.
- Make sure that you have parental consent.
- Make sure that children are adequately dressed.
- Take spare clothes, drinks, food and nappies, sun protection.
- Consider how to manage 'stranger danger' or children wandering off.
- Consider first aid/emergency arrangements.

For group-care outings
- Allow sufficient time to plan the outing.
- Find out whether you need insurance.
- Check what staffing ratios you need.
- Cost the trip carefully, allowing for hidden extras, e.g. driver's tip, parents who may not be able to contribute.
- Look at transport arrangements carefully, e.g. Do coaches have seatbelts? Do volunteer drivers have the necessary experience and insurance?
- Make sure that you have children's emergency contact details.
- Make sure that all staff and volunteers understand their role in the trip.
- Prepare and use registers to check that all children are present.

Key approaches to child rearing

Advice to parents on how to rear their children has changed considerably over the past hundred years. Mothers today are urged to breastfeed on demand, whilst this was considered bad for the baby in the 1930s. When to wean and even when to potty train a child has also changed over the years. This section looks at approaches to child rearing which have been widely influential.

Dr Truby King (1858–1938)

Although medically trained, Truby King became interested in the rearing of dairy calves and developed strategies for improving the mortality rates of calves. He then applied his scientific approach to the rearing of babies!

The Truby King 'system' was pioneered in New Zealand at the turn of the 1900s and claimed to have reduced rates of infant mortality. Many of King's ideas were adopted by health professionals in this country and the four-hourly approach to feeding babies stayed with the medical profession until the 1960s. King's wife, Mary, wrote the widely used book *Mothercraft* in which mothers were told how to bring up their children.

The Truby King 'system' of child rearing

Feeding
- Breastfeeding until nine months was the cornerstone of this approach
- Babies to be breastfed every four hours unless they were underweight or 'delicate', then every 3 hours
- No night time feeds
- Duration of feeds limited to 20 minutes

Weaning
- Weaning was not to begin until nine months
- Foods to be introduced one by one. Sugary foods considered unnecessary
- Lunch to be the main meal of the day
- 'Do not let him start the bad habit of refusing food because he does not like it'

Sleep
- Sleep was considered a vital component to keep children healthy and well behaved
- All children up to the age of six years to have a day time nap
- Children up to the age of five years to be in bed by 6pm

Potty training
- Referred to as 'holding out'.
- Potty training is suggested from day three of a baby's life. 'The bowels should be trained to move just after the 10am feed.' Babies were put onto a potty after the feed. The idea being that the association with cold rim of the potty would produce a reflexive action.
- Babies were also to be 'held out' over the pot just after they had woken as well as before and after meals. *Mothercraft* suggested that babies could be clean and dry at around 10 months

Thumbsucking
- Considered to be a bad habit and to be prevented early on by tucking hands away

Fresh air and sunshine
- Fresh air was considered as essential. Babies were to be wrapped up and put outside even when cold. Truby King also advocated babies being put in separate rooms from their parents to ensure that the child was not re-breathing the air its parents had 'used up and poisoned'
- Sun baths were considered to be healthy for children and so regular exposure to sunlight was advised

It is easy to be critical of King's methods, but viewed in the social context of the time, they are not too extreme.

Infant mortality was high, partly due to poor hygiene, but also because children were not vaccinated and antibiotics had not been invented. Science was rapidly changing people's lives and so a scientific approach to rearing children would seem appealing. King was effectively promising mothers a way of keeping their babies alive!

King has been much criticised for his insistence that babies should be fed at regular intervals – preferably four-hourly and not at night. Again, this needs to be seen in context. At that time women often died as a result of infections, had several children to care for and often had heavy domestic work. By allowing mothers to feed less often, King felt that they would be able to rest and sleep

Think It Over
- Why would early potty training seem a good idea in this period?
- What were the benefits of keeping babies out in the fresh air and sunlight and how would this contribute to preventing illness in babies?
- Why would late weaning of babies prevent possible infection?

Dr Benjamin Spock (1903–1998)

Dr Spock's first book was published in America in 1946. Entitled *The Commonsense Book of Baby and Childcare* it revolutionised attitudes towards children in America, although was not generally available in Britain until the 1960s. Spock was a medical practitioner, but also studied psychiatry and was heavily influenced by the psycho-analytical theories of development. His book became a best seller for many years and his books are still being sold.

The Spock 'system' of child rearing

Feeding
- Some limiting of time on breast, although Spock advocated a more relaxed approach
- Early weaning at around three months was suggested in the 1960s

Sleep
- Prefers baby to be put down on back
- Suggests that baby should be in own room by six months
- Does not advocate that baby should be brought into parents' bed

Potty training
- Not forcing the child to use the potty until the child shows interest

Thumbsucking/comforters
- Felt that thumbsucking was a result of young babies not being allowed enough time to suckle on the breast or at a bottle
- Suggests that parents should not restrain babies from sucking their thumbs or take away any comforters by force

Fresh air/sunbaths
- Advocates window being left wide open for babies sleeping indoors
- Suggests regular sunbaths

Spock's first book was produced after the World War II, when people were beginning to embrace the idea of a 'better world' and move away from strict social regimes. Unlike Truby King and other such approaches to child rearing, Spock concentrated on more than just the physical care side of raising children. He urged parents to treat their children with respect, rather than to view them as mere objects. This approach earned him the title 'father of permissiveness' and his early work was considered to be the cause of immorality amongst young people. Spock himself always rejected this view, claiming that he had just strived for a 'better understanding of children', although in later editions of his books, he revised his section on discipline.

Think It Over
- How do Spock's approaches to potty training and thumbsucking link with Freud's theory of personality development?

Child led approaches to child rearing

Following on from Spock, there have been several best selling books for parents which are child led in tone. These include Miriam Stoppard's *The Baby Book*. The child-led advice books tend to reflect recent work on child attachment by Ainsworth and Bowlby, as well as drawing on psycho-analytical approaches to child development.

The child-led approach

Feeding
- Breastfeeding, where possible, on demand and following the baby's pace

Sleeping
- Following the baby and child's pace. The 1983 edition of Stoppard's *Baby Care* book even suggested that if necessary the baby could be brought into the parent's bed

Crying
- Advice to parents to go to baby quickly rather than to leave them to cry as this may be damaging and could prevent the baby from forming a secure attachment

Theory into practice
- Write a commentary about the child-led approach that is favoured by many modern childcare writers.
- How does this approach contrast with Truby King's?
- Consider whether this approach would be feasible in the context in which Truby King was working, e.g. large families, poor health care, high infant mortality rate.

Behaviourist approaches to child rearing – Dr Christopher Green

It would be inaccurate to suggest that all parenting books are currently adopting a child-led approach. Since the mid 1980s, books such as *Toddler Taming* by Dr Christopher Green have been very popular. This takes a more behaviourist approach to child rearing, placing the parent very much in control. In America this type of parenting is sometimes referred to as 'Tough love' with the idea that parents may need to be firm.

Theory into practice

Using two books that have been written for parents about child rearing, look at the following topics:

- night time waking
- tantrums.

Consider if advice given to parents is consistent.

Evaluate each author's approach in terms of psychological perspectives, e.g. behaviourist, psycho-analytical or interactionist (child-led).

End-of-unit test

1   List the basic needs of babies.

2   What are the key advantages of breastfeeding?

3   Why is it important to clean and sterilise feeding equipment?

4   Explain the function of the five main nutrients.

5   What is the difference between malnutrition and under nutrition?

6   Give three reasons why it is important to talk to parents about the nutritional needs of their children.

7   Explain how the spread of head lice can be prevented.

8   Why is it important to work with parents when managing children's behaviour?

9   Briefly explain operant conditioning and how this theory may be used to manage children's behaviour.

10 Outline a situation where 'distraction' might be an effective strategy to manage a child's behaviour.

11 Explain why it is sometimes important to observe a child's behaviour.

12 Why is outdoor play considered to be beneficial for children?

13 What factors might be important when planning an outdoor environment?

14 Why is it important to sometimes change layouts of equipment?

15 Write down five factors that would need to be considered when planning an outing for children.

Human growth and development

Introduction

During life we both grow and develop. As a child increases in size so it grows. Growth is measured in terms of height and weight. Even before birth, the growth of the baby is monitored. After birth the baby is always weighed, its length recorded as well as the circumference of the head. The development of babies is also carefully monitored. Development is the increase in the complexity of body actions, the thinking processes, as well as a person's feelings, and social interactions. It is partly influenced by the genetically determined programme of maturation and partly by the interaction with the prevailing environment.

Growth and development normally follow an expected inter-related progressive pattern. However, when growth and development do not follow this linked expected pattern, unpredictable results occur. This unit examines developmental changes across the lifespan in order to gain an understanding of children's physical, intellectual, language, social and emotional development. This knowledge base will help you to structure children's educational and care environment, as well as equipping you with the skills to monitor and assess children's developmental progress and behaviour.

What you need to learn

- What determines our growth and development
- Physical, social and emotional development
- Children's cognitive and language development
- Observational techniques

What determines our growth and development

There are several aspects to a child's development. Development involves both the structure and the function of parts of the body. For instance, during its first few months, a young baby makes open vowel sounds, often called 'cooing'. The muscles of the mouth and tongue, which are important in producing clear speech, are still very slack. Later, when muscle tone and control improves consonants can be formed.

As the child grows, body actions become increasingly controlled and complex as **physical development** takes place. Children's thought processes become more organised and their understanding broadens as **intellectual development** progresses (this is sometimes called **cognitive development**). Babies are born with some skills to enable them to interact with others, mainly with their parents or carers. However, babies' social skills and abilities need greater refinement before they are competent in and adaptive to the social world around them. This process is called **social development**. Feelings or emotions, both negative (e.g fear and anger) and positive (e.g. happiness and pride),

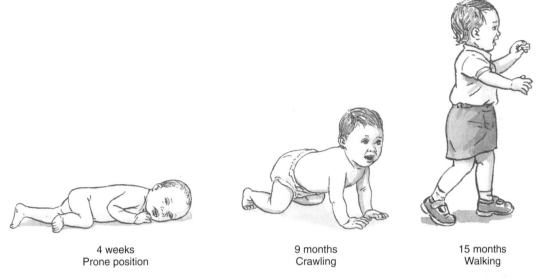

4 weeks
Prone position

9 months
Crawling

15 months
Walking

Figure 9.1: Stages of physical development

have to be understood by children and controlled. This process is called **emotional development**. All aspects of development are continually changing as people progress through life.

Factors that influence development

Cephalo–caudal development

Development does not take place evenly across the body but it does always follow the same sequence. The upper part of the body, especially the brain and the head, develops rapidly while the lower part of the body follows more slowly. This is called **cephalo-caudal development**. Legs and arms develop after the brain, heart and other organs within the centre of the body. Development progresses outwards from the mid-line to the outer edges of the body, called the 'extremities'.

Think It Over

Observe a group of babies and young children.

- When do they gain control over: (a) holding up their head, (b) sitting up on their own, (c) crawling, and (d) walking?
- Does this pattern follow cephalo-caudal development?
- From your observations, give an example of mid-line to extremities development.

Genetic information

When a baby is born, friends and relatives are usually very interested in who the baby looks like. We inherit genetic information from both parents. The millions of cells in our bodies arise from the division and subdivision of the single cell formed by the fusion of the ovum from the mother and the sperm from the father. Before a cell divides, its DNA is organised into paired formations called chromosomes. Human DNA forms 23 pairs of chromosomes. Each part of the pair is very similar but not identical. Units of DNA form a gene. Chromosomes are made up of hundreds of genes. Differences in details of our make-up are determined by our genes. At a certain point on a chromosome, there may be a gene determining the colour of the eyes. The mother may have a gene for brown eyes while the father has a gene for blue eyes. The 'brown' gene is more *dominant* than the blue gene, which is *recessive* and, therefore, not so influential. Consequently, the child will have the mother's brown eyes. If both parents have blue eyes, the child would have blue eyes.

Genetic information may affect other features of physical development such as height and build. It determines the limits of each child's potential to develop and grow. Currently, much exciting scientific research is unravelling the mystery of our genes and it is hoped that soon scientists will understand much more about how we are formed and function.

Theory into practice

Write down a description of your own physical features under the headings of (a) build/body shape, (b) height, (c) eye colour, (d) natural hair colour, (e) shape of hands, (f) skin colour, (g) facial features, and (h) size of feet.

- Draw a family tree.
- Identify which of the physical features identified above appear to be handed down from which members of your family.

Genetic disorders

Many human disorders are due to defective genes called *mutants*. Perhaps the most common disease is cystic fibrosis where the gene is recessive. The gene may have been passed down through many generations without any difficulties. However, the medical condition may occur when both the mother and the father are carriers of this recessive gene. Other disorders that are the result of inherited genes are sickle cell anaemia and haemophilia (the latter is transmitted by a sex-linked gene and is only exhibited in males). Some diseases, such as Down's syndrome, arise due to a faulty allocation of whole chromosomes. Early pregnancy tests involving amniocentesis and ultrasound scanning can reveal some of these genetic disorders prior to birth.

Other factors that influence development

It is clear that the potential for growth and development is affected by inherited factors. This is called the interaction of 'nature'. In addition, factors within our environment have a very influential effect on development. This is called the interaction of 'nurture'. There is much debate about how much and in what way either nature and/or nurture affects the process of development. It is generally considered that they interact within the developmental process which continues throughout life.

The factors outlined in the following figure can have different degrees of influence on individuals and at different stages of life. Individuals have a wide variety of lifestyles, so what is an important influence on one person may be of little consequence to another.

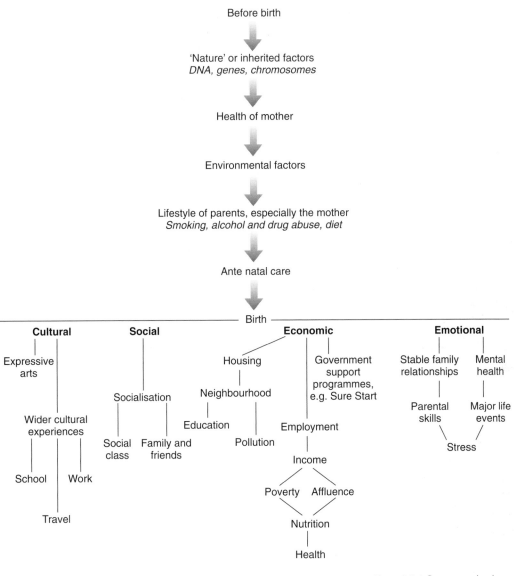

Figure 9.2: Influences on development

Think It Over
- Discuss with people of different ages or from different generations which factors in the chart they feel had an important influence on their development and why. Record your findings.
- Compare them with factors which you think are influential on your own ongoing development.

Environmental factors

Environmental factors are very important in a child's and adult's development. For instance, health visitors report that since the cot death scare, most mothers place their babies on their backs to sleep. Hence, many babies are not used to lying on their fronts in a prone position and are not content when placed so. These babies are tending to crawl slightly later.

Economic factors

Economic factors greatly affect children's development. People living in poverty have a poorer quality of life which can cause poor physical and mental health leading to lower life expectancies. Lack of money results in poor housing which is more likely to be in communities with fewer resources and higher rates of pollution and crime. Members of these households have a greater risk of being unemployed and having lower educational attainment and aspirations. With less money to spend, nutritional intake is often unbalanced and inadequate. The stress of these circumstances can lead to the breakdown of relationships which affect both emotional and social development.

Lifespan development

Lifespan is usually categorised into infants (0–3 years), young children (4–9), adolescents (10–18), adults (19–65), and elderly people (65+). The table on page 327 looks at developmental changes throughout the lifespan.

Major events occurring across the lifespan

During the course of life, events happen that change people's lives. Some are predictable and others are unpredictable. Predictable physical changes occur to everyone. We learn to walk and see the world from a different perspective than when crawling on the floor. Physical and emotional changes of puberty often alter young people's approach to life as do unexpected physical changes which occur due to injury or major illness.

Everyone experiences relationship changes, such as:

• leaving the warm security of a loving home
• adapting to school and work relationships
• involvement in intense emotional relationships with others, often resulting in long-term partnerships or marriage
• separation and divorce
• the birth of a child
• the predictable or unpredictable death of a loved one.

When these events occur, people have to find ways of adapting to new circumstances. Different people will react differently to the same event. This will influence their subsequent physical, emotional, social and intellectual development.

Social lives

Over the span of their lives, people live within social networks. Society is always changing. Social networks one hundred years ago were very different to those of today. For instance, people are judged on their ability far more today than previously when social class was considered to be more important. As society changes so culture changes. The multi-cultural society of today influences our lives in many ways as we adapt to understanding, recognising and valuing the diversity of lifestyles and interests.

Promoting good health across the lifespan

The UK government is very aware of the importance of early influences on development. As a consequence, it set up the Social Exclusion Unit in 1997. The government's aim is to end child poverty by 2020. One important initiative is the Sure Start Programme. This initiative is designed to support disadvantaged children under the age of four years and their families. In 1997–8, about 3.2 million children in Britain were living in households with incomes of less than 60 per cent of average income. The Sure Start programmes have been set up to enable children to be ready to thrive when they start school.

Developmental changes throughout our lives

	Infants	Young children	Adolescents	Adults	Elderly persons
Physical	Reflex action at birth ➡ gradually developing gross and fine motor control – sits ➡ walks ➡ runs, palmar ➡ pincher grip	Jumps, kicks, throws ball, good balance, start to learn to swim, good pencil control, writes, draws, uses preferred hand, rides two wheel bike	Highly developed gross and fine motor skills, very agile, muscle strength and co-ordination, e.g. learns to drive	Physically confident, complex gross and fine motor skills, often used in sports, e.g. ski-ing, golf	May suffer from stiffening joints, fine motor skills may deteriorate as fingers become less supple. Less physical strength. Risk of disability as life progresses, impairments such as vision and hearing loss
Intellectual	Uses senses and motor actions to explore. Achieves object permanence. Cries ➡ vocalises in turn with adult ➡ babbles ➡ single words ➡ speaks short sentences, shows intense curiosity	Uses grammar with growing accuracy, speaks confidently imaginative role-play. Develops self concept, increasingly understands abstract ideas	Seeks new challenges, develops new skills and knowledge especially linked to world of work	Period of learning, adapting to and consolidating new knowledge and skills	Many variations. Many use this period to enjoy new learning. Some slow to adapt to new ideas. Risk of mental impairment, memory loss, dementia
Emotional	Shows affection. Develop self-awareness and self-recognition. Shows attachment to main carer, becomes assertive, later strong emotions lead to temper tantrums	Shows caring attitude to others. Co-operates with routine, behaviour and emotions reasonably controlled	Conflict may develop between norms of friends and home, eager for emotional independence. Develops own gender role. Develops intense relationships with others. Has to adjust to strong emotions. May feel intensely for philanthropic or political causes – 'fire in the belly period'	*Early adult life (19–45)* Develops sexual relationships and partnerships/marriage, parenthood. Possible emotional trauma due to divorce. *Later adult life (46–65)* Support for both parents and children teenagers. "Empty Nest Syndrome" – loss of purpose as parent	May initially give close emotional support to family, especially grandchildren, later may need much support, especially after death of partner/if frail. Physical impairment may cause frustration. Some become fearful/anxious/self-centred and emotionally demanding
Social	Smiles ➡ laughs. Establishes a sense of self. Enjoys taking part in social interactions, notices other children ➡ enjoys playing alongside/co-operatively with others, becomes aware of own gender, aware of skills needed to be part of social group	Very sociable, wants friends' company, develops stable friendships, especially own gender. Complex co-operative play. Accepts rules. Develops social courtesies, shows affection, enjoys family social activities. Makes gender associations	More independent. Friendship groups very important and their norms are highly valued. Takes an affectionate and sexual interest in opposite or own gender	*Early adult life* Develops network of friends, work colleagues. Pressures from family and work may affect social activity. *Later adult life* Social pressure of maintaining work roles, family relationships, role in community	Wide variation. More free time in retirement. Many are very socially active. Opportunities to renew and develop friendships. Physical impairment and death of partner, reduced income may restrict social activities

The table shows current health education priorities and government initiatives.

Initiative	Objective
Saving Lives: Our Healthier Nation (1999)	This is the government's action plan to tackle poor health. It targets the main killers: cancer, coronary heart disease and stroke, accidents, mental illness. Targets, if achieved, will prevent up to 300,000 unnecessary deaths by 2010
Health Action Zones	Established in areas of deprivation and poor health to tackle health inequalities and to modernise services
Health Improvement Programmes	Each Health Authority produces a Health Improvement Programme setting out the strategic framework for improving health, reducing inequalities and delivering faster and more responsive services
Healthy Living Centres	Set up in 1999 by the New Opportunities Fund (funded by the National Lottery). They promote health in its broadest sense and target disadvantaged areas and groups and those who experience health worse than average
Social Exclusion Unit	A government co-ordinated committee to identify and consider ways of addressing inequalities within society and which result in individuals being prevented from reaching their potential
Sure Start	The government's major initiative to tackle child poverty and social exclusion. It aims to improve the health and well being of families and children before and from birth, so they are ready to thrive when they go to school
National Healthy School Standard	Devised to give practical support to schools to promote personal, social and health education. It covers an additional seven areas of citizenship, drug education, emotional health, healthy eating, physical activity, safety, sex and relationships. It sets a national quality standard for schools to achieve
National Childcare Strategy	This aims to provide good quality, affordable and accessible child care for up to 1.6 million children by 2004. Provides the funding, and inspection, of high quality pre-schooling for all 4-year-olds and eventually all 3-year-olds

Physical, social and emotional development

The development of children and adults is often studied as separate topics. However, each area of development influences the others.

- Physical development
- Social development
- Emotional development
- Cognitive development

A child is developing physical skills when trying to control the shaped pieces of a jigsaw. When successfully completing the jigsaw the child may express great emotional pleasure by enthusiastically telling the nearby adults about the success. In order for the physical skills of fine motor control and co-ordination to be used successfully, the child has to develop cognitive skills to identify and match the pattern.

If unsuccessful, the child may show frustration. The resulting social behaviour, of throwing the pieces of jigsaw around the room, arises due to the child's stage of physical, emotional and cognitive development. Hence, development should be seen as a whole or as **holistic development**.

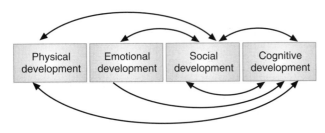

Figure 9.3: Holistic development

What is meant by physical development?

This is the gradual process by which children develop the use and control of muscles, thus gaining a wider range of movements. Physical development includes:

- *Changes in motor behaviour* – newborn babies display involuntary 'walking' movements arising from reflex actions. A fifteen-month-old child can increasingly voluntarily control their walking actions.
- *Fine motor development involving the movements of hands and fingers* – the early primitive squeeze grasp shown by some babies as young as four weeks develops into a very neat and co-ordinated grasp using the forefinger by five years.
- *Changes in some of the sensory organs, such as eyes* – the development of eye muscles enables most babies to see more clearly and over a larger area than at birth.

Why is physical development so important?

As a baby's physical development progresses, new skills are learnt. These enable the baby to become involved in more activities and to explore their immediate world. Further complex skills are learnt giving increasing control of activities. With success comes **emotional development**. The baby/child gains self-confidence through the control of their actions, thus promoting their self-esteem. With more mobility, children are able to play with others, thereby promoting their **social development**. The development of both gross and fine motor skills is important. Children become more personally independent, and, for instance, start dressing themselves. Children can then proceed to acquiring more advanced skills which they need as they grow older for school, work and leisure.

Children progress at different *rates* following the same sequence of physical development. The age at which children develop physical skills, such as walking, depends on the maturation of their nervous system, strength of muscles especially in their legs and back and achieving balance. For most children physical development is a continuous process until maturity.

Think It Over

Imagine you are confined to bed to lie on your back for three weeks and the muscles in your hands are weak and poorly co-ordinated.

* How would this affect your range of activities?
* How would this affect your awareness of the world around you?

Reflexes

Newborn babies are born with certain reflexes. These are involuntary, automatic, physical responses, triggered by a stimulus and determined by impulses in nerves. Everybody has some reflexes, e.g. knees jerk when tapped, which you do not learn to do; they are inborn. The reflexes described below are only present in the baby for a short time after birth.

Reflex	Stimulus	Response
Rooting	Stroking baby's check	Turns towards the side stroked as if seeking a nipple with the mouth
Sucking	An object put into the mouth, e.g. nipple	Sucks rhythmically
Hand grasp (palmar grasp)	An object, e.g. finger, put into the palm of the hand	Grasps tightly
Startle (Moro) reflex	Baby is startled by bright light/loud noise	Arms and legs splay open, back arches and then arms and legs close as if to hang onto carer to avoid falling
Stepping/walking reflex	Baby held upright with soles of feet on a flat surface or edge of table	Makes stepping/walking movements

These reflexes enable babies to survive, e.g. seek for food and suck. Gradually the reflexes disappear and the baby develops voluntary actions, i.e. they learn and can choose to do the actions. For instance, the walking reflex disappears after the first few weeks and babies learn to walk at around twelve months.

Development of gross motor control in first year

These are large movements including:

- gross motor actions which involve the use of the whole limb such as when hopping
- locomotive skills which are movements needed to travel, e.g. crawling and walking.

They develop as shown in the table below.

1 month	3 months	6 months	9 months	12 months
Head droops if unsupported	Head held erect for a few seconds before falling forwards	Raises head to look at feet	Can lean forward to pick up toy	May stand upright alone for a few minutes
Pulled to sit, head lags	Pulled to sit, little head lag	Sits with support in pram	Can sit alone for 10-15 minutes	Sits confidently on floor for long periods
Lies with head to one side	Lies with head in midline	Lifts head from pillow to look at feet	Can turn body sideways to pick up toy	Can pull up to standing and sit down again
Large jerky movements of limbs	Movements smoother and continuous	Holds arms up to be lifted. Can roll over	Moves on floor by rolling. Tries to crawl. When held steps purposefully on alternate feet	Crawls. Walks around furniture and may walk alone
Arms active	Kicks vigorously. Finger play – brings hands together	In cot lifts legs to 90 degrees and grasps foot	Very active movements	Drops and throws toys purposefully

When these milestones of sitting, crawling and walking are achieved depends upon the development of neuro-muscular co-ordination. Other factors such as the weight of the child and fitness level can also affect progress. For instance, an overweight baby who has little exercise may take longer to be able to walk unaided. Children's pattern of walking changes as they become more confident. The rate of development is also influenced by the inherited growth pattern from the parents.

Think It Over

Discuss in a group your actions when first learning to ice-skate or roller-blade.

- How relaxed were you at the different stages of learning? How far apart did you position your feet? How fast were you at first? How far did you attempt to go before choosing to stop? How much practice did you need to improve?
- Did your progress in learning to skate/roller blade match the progress children make when developing their walking skills.

Further development of gross motor movements

The table shows the development of gross motor movements from one to eight years.

Age	Pattern of development
12–15 months	Moves hesitantly and irregularly Poor balance, very unsteady Falls easily, body rigid Legs wide apart, arms outstretched to aid balance Arms and legs used to achieve balance by moving opposite each other
19–24 months	Body less rigid Feet only slightly apart, smooth pattern of walking Arms at side of body and not used for balance Stops and starts safely Runs carefully but cannot go round corners Walks upstairs with support, two feet to a stair Creeps downstairs backwards No attempt to move to catch ball
2–3 years	Can throw ball overhand Kicks balls enthusiastically Tries to catch a large ball by extending arms Can ride a tricycle Walks alone upstairs using alternate feet
4–5 years	Steady stride, arms used in walking action Can walk along a narrow line Runs lightly on toes Skips on alternate feet, can hop a short distance Moves rhythmically to music Skilfully climbs, slides and swings
6–7 years	Can catch ball by holding hands in cup-shape Moves legs, outstretches hands to intercept ball Takes impact of catching by moving body Good balance, both when moving and when static A smooth rhythmical action Arms and legs move in opposition to each other Feet close together When running slightly leans forward, arms swung backwards and forwards Co-ordinated jumping – able to jump a distance

By 8 years	Gross motor movements are precise, e.g. can walk along a thin line with arms outstretched for balance Expert rider of two-wheeled bicycle May develop skills in sports, e.g. swimming, roller-blading

In order to develop motor control, children need to:

- practise to improve and master the skill
- concentrate on small parts of the overall skill, e.g. children learn to place two feet to a stair before developing the more complex skill of alternate feet action
- pay a lot of attention to the action; later they can do the action almost automatically
- have experience of a range of movement activities to develop their memory of motor actions enabling them to cope with more complex situations.

Theory into practice

Observe two children of different ages and stages of motor development. Note their gross motor actions. What locomotion differences between the two children do you notice? Using the information above, identify at what age the toys listed below would be appropriate:

- baby bouncer
- roller-blades
- a toy on a rug for baby to lie on
- tricycle
- a trampette
- two-wheeled bicycle
- push-along wheeled toy.

Development of fine motor skills

At the same time as a child's gross motor movements changes are occurring, so too are their fine motor skills – see the table below. These involve wrists, hands and finger movements. It is important that these skills are fostered so children can develop good manual skills in adult life involving the use of tools and implements.

Age	Pattern of development	Play activities and play resources
Birth	Reflexes give automatic tight hand grasp	Talk, sing and rock baby to stimulate baby
4 weeks	Hands tightly clenched and will only open when touched. Not yet able to control hands	Provide mobiles, especially with faces, to stimulate baby
3 months	Watches own hands. Begins to clasp and unclasp hands together in finger play, presses palms together	Colourful rattles. Place toys in front of baby when on rug. Place baby on rug under overhead activity centre

Age	Pattern of development	Play activities and play resources
5 months	Primitive squeeze grasp appears but movement of hands uncontrolled. Finds it difficult to let go of object. Enjoys practising dropping and throwing, e.g. toys, food	Encourage baby to reach and grab toys by playing with baby or providing activity centres. Bath-time water play. Teething rings
6 months	Uses whole hand to grasp objects which are held in palm of hand	Rattles. Baby bouncer
9 months	Learns hand-eye co-ordination to pick up small objects – stretches out one hand leading to grasp small objects when catching sight of them. Handles objects enthusiastically – passing from one hand to another, turning over, etc. Early pincher grip – picks up small objects with finger and thumb	Drums, bells. Activity play gym. Beakers. Strong plastic spoons
12 months	Picks up small objects, e.g. crumbs with confident pincer grip – thumb and tip of index finger. Uses both hands freely, but may show preference for one	Treasure basket of items of different textures, shape and colour. Bath toys, e.g. beakers. Cardboard box. Bricks. Beakers
15 months	Picks up small objects with precise pincer grasp using either hand. Releases objects from grip skilfully, manipulates cubes – builds tower of 2 cubes after being shown. Grasps crayon with whole hand in palmar grasp, imitates to and fro scribble after being shown (large, forceful movements)	Push-along wheeled toys. Dolls. Large crayons. Bricks. Shape sorters. Musical toys. Picture books – cardboard books. Crayons
18 months	Holds pencil in primitive tripod grasp. Spontaneous to and fro scribble. Builds tower of 3 cubes after being shown. Turns pages of books	Dolls, bricks. Wooden train sets. Picture books. Sorting beakers. Push-along wheeled toys. Crayons
2 years	Picks up very small items, e.g. threads, accurately and releases with skill. Builds tower of 6 cubes. Holds pencil in preferred hand, well down shaft using thumb and two fingers	Large balls, large threading kits. Ride and sit-on toys, dough. Bricks. Books, crayons, paint. Small world toys. Dressing up clothes. Prams, train sets, large construction kits
2$\frac{1}{2}$ years	Holds pencil in tripod position using thumb, middle and index finger. Can imitate circle and 'T' and 'V'	Books, large balls, dressing up clothes and role play resources, crayons, paint

Age	Pattern of development	Play activities and play resources
3 years	Builds tower of 9 bricks. Threads large wooden beads on shoe lace. Enjoys painting with large brush. Cuts with scissors	Scissors, blackboard and chalks, bricks, jigsaws, writing materials, dough, sand and water, role play resources, small world toys, construction kits, books, computer assisted toys with keyboard
4 years	Threads small beads. Builds towers of 10 bricks and makes bridges. Holds pencil with good control in adult fashion. Draws recognisable house	Beads and threading kits, bricks, books, writing materials, balls, paints, crayons, complex construction kits, jigsaws, creative materials, tape recorder and tapes. Computer assisted toys, simple robots, cogs and wheels kits
5 years	Threads large needle alone and sews real stitches. Good control in writing and drawing using pencils and paint brushes. Colours pictures neatly, staying within the lines	Board games, jigsaws, books, writing materials, creative materials, glue, scissors, variety of different media, computer
By 8 years	Can build tall straight towers using bricks. Drawings and pictures show increased recognisable detail. Handwriting is even and may start to be joined. Ties and unties laces	Story books, small balls and bats, model kits, small jigsaws, simple DIY tools, board games, complex construction kits, tape recorder, computer

Figure 9.4: A four-year-old's picture of the Titanic. Tim's picture shows that his fine motor skills are well advanced. He has good pencil control and his drawing is clear. He is starting to form recognisable letters and numbers

Adverse factors affecting physical development

- Delayed maturation through the failure of the nervous system to develop properly.
- Poor environmental factors such as an inadequate diet and poor living conditions resulting in poor health.
- Lack of encouragement and opportunities to practise skills by parents/carers.

Key issues

Since the concern about salmonella bacteria in eggs, health visitors have noticed that some babies who are drinking cow's milk before the age of twelve months have been lethargic and their gross and fine motor movements have been delayed. The weaning foods and cow's milk lack iron and some babies have been diagnosed as having anaemia. The health visitors have recommended that babies up to the age of one year should drink formula milk, which contains iron.

Assessment activity 9.1

Refer to the section on 'Major events occurring across the lifespan' on page 326. Choose three of these life events and suggest why they might have a particular effect on physical development.

Measuring growth

Ros and Jobi Amina

are pleased to announce the safe arrival
of their daughter

Hannah Emily

on 10th November 2001

Weight: 3.9kg

Figure 9.5: A birth announcement

Nearly all birth announcements include the baby's weight. The baby's continued growth is carefully and routinely monitored to check that normal healthy progress is maintained. It also highlights any faltering growth and ensures early identification and referral of children with developmental disorders and health problems. For example, one in 3000-5000 babies suffer from growth hormone insufficiency, often linked with other disorders.

The tests undertaken, and their timing, may vary from one health authority to another. The information gathered aims to be soundly evidence-based. For instance, in some areas the baby's head circumference is measured shortly after birth. Health professionals in other areas prefer to do it two weeks later. This is to allow any distortion occurring during the birth process to have settled. There is no consistent agreement about the ages when measurements are made or recorded and the stage at which referral for specialist advice is desirable. Consequently, one area may monitor at six weeks, eight months, two years and three years while another area may monitor at other intervals.

Why is the head circumference measured?

Head circumference is measured to help detect two groups of disorders:

- those characterised by a large head including hydrocephalus – this is due to accumulation of cerebro-spinal fluid which can cause brain damage
- those characterised by a small head including microcephaly which may arise from some abnormality of brain development in pregnancy, or may be a sign of impaired brain growth.

Weight monitoring

'Normal' weight is seen by parents as a reassurance that all is well. However, satisfactory weight gain does not rule out growth disorders. For instance, growth hormone deficiency may be linked with normal or even increased weight gain.

Babies may have temporary slow weight gain or even temporary weight loss which may be due to minor illness or family disturbances. Hence, records have to be interpreted carefully. Prolonged failure to gain weight or continuing weight loss gives a more reliable indication that there are serious probable concerns. Factors such as parental build and height have to be considered. Faltering growth can only be used when there is evidence that the slow weight gain is abnormal for that baby.

Length and height monitoring

The Third Report on Child Health Surveillance casts doubt on the value of routinely measuring the length of newborn babies but recommends doing so at six to eight weeks in order to detect very short babies, such as those with severe endocrine disorders.

Efficient growth monitoring depends upon:

- correct measurement techniques
- use of suitable growth charts
- accurate transfer of measurements to the charts.

Children's growth is usually plotted on centile charts – the nine-centile charts first published in 1993 describe current growth more precisely. They can predict the adult height potential. There is a separate chart for boys and girls. A child's height is plotted between two allocated lines, calculated by the health visitor. An example of a growth chart is shown on the next page.

Measuring development

Parents generally view their child as a unique individual but, nevertheless, are usually eager to compare their child to others. Health professionals use both approaches in assessing and trying to understand children's state of physical and mental health and stages of development.

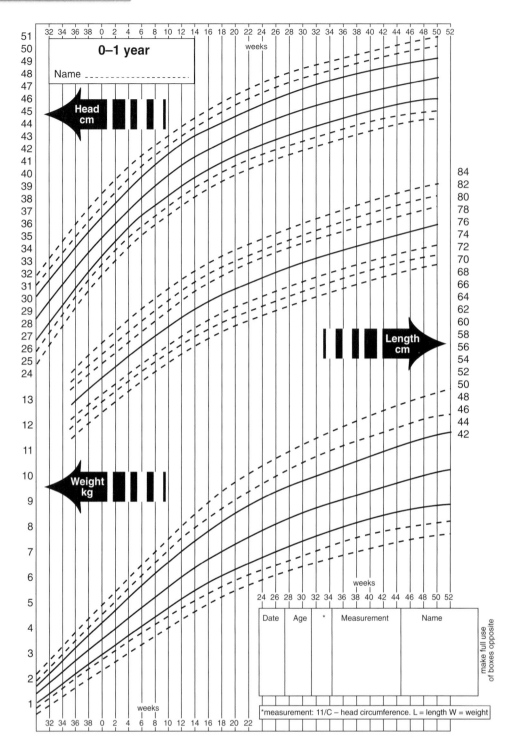

Figure 9.6: Boys growth chart 0–1 year. Boys Growth Charts (Birth – 18 Years) – designed and published by Child Growth Foundation 1994

Factors have been identified which enable children's progress to be compared. These factors are expected to be the normal level of development expected for a child according to their age and other factors, such as racial origin. For instance, children from Thailand are generally smaller than those from Western European countries. This is the **nomothetic approach** of assessment.

The **idiographic approach** to assessment involves the children's individual progress, with their uniqueness being observed and considered. This approach may be adopted by specialist health professionals, such as a child psychiatrist. Children with emotional problems may be referred to a child psychiatrist who will assess the individual child's problems, stage of development and needs. This may lead to the child having an individual therapy or support programme.

Child health screening

When a child is born, parents are given a Personal Child Health Record Book which contains charts on which the child's height, weight and head circumference are plotted and any advice offered by a health visitor (see also Unit 10, pages 370–1).

Information is gained through:

- growth monitoring
- discussions with parents
- physical examinations
- observations.

The information gained may indicate that further specialist monitoring of the child is needed. Many serious problems are found in the following ways:

- neonatal and six to eight week examinations
- follow-up of infants and children who have suffered various forms of trauma or illness affecting the nervous system
- detection by parents and carers
- detection by midwives, early years practitioners and teachers, health visitors and general practitioners in the course of their regular work
- some defects are first suspected when the baby/child is being examined for other reasons.

The child may be referred to a paediatrician for further tests or one of the specialists listed in the table below.

Health professional	Developmental concern
Speech therapist	Speech impairment or delay
Educational psychologist	Cognitive or behavioural development
Child psychiatrist	Emotional development

Social and emotional development

Children's social and emotional development are closely linked. Social interactions are also linked with language development which facilitates communication between people. Research suggests that newborn babies have an in-built need to make relationships. They watch their carer's face, start to smile and make noises to attract their carers.

Emotional development

John Bowlby thought both babies and mothers had a biological need to stay in close contact with one another. He suggested that an early, close emotional bond by the mother to the baby, which he called an *attachment*, was important for long-term development. See Unit 12 pages 449–50 for a discussion of Bowlby's attachment theory and the criticisms of his work.

Parental separation

Perhaps the most common form of parental separation today is divorce. During the breakdown of family relationships, parents suffer much stress and, as a consequence, their behaviour towards their children may change. This may affect their attachment to the children which may become insecure. Separation from the parent who leaves the family home may affect the attachment between that parent and the child. Research has shown that regular contact with this parent can reduce the effects of separation.

However, Mavis Hetherington's study (1978) found that where the family did not separate but there was much discord, children showed more disturbance than those whose parents separated, and subsequently divorced. She also found that where there is much social support, for instance from family and friends, the separated parents were more able to create a stable and happy home, thus reducing the stress on the children.

Key issues

When on a work placement in a nursery or early years setting, observe and record:

- how the children react to separation from parents
- the relationships the children have with the staff
- how the staff try to help children cope with this separation.

Compare your findings with the attachment theories highlighted above. Discuss with the staff the effect this separation is having on the children's development.

Developing self concept

One important aspect of emotional development is developing **self concept**. This is sometimes called self-identity or self-image (see also Unit 12 page 438).

Self concept is closely linked to self-esteem and revolves around the question 'How do I feel about myself?'. Self concept relates to the child's view of their own personality and what they can do. It also involves the child's perception of how others view them and their abilities.

The child has to recognise first that they are separate and unique individuals with their own characteristics and abilities. They develop this understanding through their interactions with others. Their first important interactions are with their family or carers, then friends and later with teachers and other school contacts. It is important that children have positive interactions so they learn to value themselves and their abilities.

Children with a positive self concept tend to live in families where there is much interaction between themselves and their parents or carers. The children are valued as interesting and important members of the household. Parents have high, but often realistic, expectations of them. The children are encouraged to express their views, parents/carers listen to them, respect their contributions and, at the appropriate age and in the appropriate way, these are discussed. Parents and carers offer discipline which is based on rewards which show approval or, if necessary, realistic sanctions and not on physical punishment.

Other factors such as stereotyping have negative effects on children's self concept. These include social, cultural, racial and gender stereotyping. Currently, the government is actively arguing that **social background** should not be considered an excuse for poor educational achievement. In the past, children from poorer environments were often expected to achieve less. It was common for them to follow in their parents' footsteps and go into the same type of work regardless of their innate ability.

Cultural and racial stereotyping can also have a negative effect. Often people from foreign countries are not fully valued for their abilities. There is a high percentage of young people from ethnic minorities in low status jobs. This may be for a variety of reasons including cultural and racial stereotyping.

How children view themselves and their own abilities is often influenced by others' expectations of them. Children are very sensitive to what others think of them and often behave in such ways as to meet these expectations. This is called a **self-fulfilling prophecy**. These expectations may be inappropriate or inaccurate but they influence the children's behaviour so that the expectations can become reality. The child who is expected to behave badly often does so in order not to disappoint adult expectations.

Theory into practice

- Write a short report entitled 'How do TV advertisements influence gender stereotyping?'.
- Undertake a simple survey of your group of how they think stereotyping has affected their self concept.

Personality

What is personality? Helen Bee defines personality as 'a broad range of individual characteristics, mostly having to do with the typical ways each of us interacts with the people and the world around us ... and which tend to be persisting aspects of the individual' (Bee 1989). Much interest is shown by parents in a child's developing personality. Babies of only a few weeks old display distinct personalities.

Personality is thought to be a result of a combination of nature and nurture. In other words, it is influenced not only by what is inherited from parents, but also by our environment. The child's initial temperament affects the child's developing personality. Environmental factors then come into play.

Our experiences are very important in forming our personality. Some babies are very placid and easily soothed whilst others seem to find it difficult to settle. The reaction of parents and carers to difficult children is thought to be crucial in reinforcing this type of temperament or helping not to emphasise it. Some studies, such as Olweus's (1982) suggest that early aggression in children is a good predictor of later aggressive behaviour. On the other hand, sociability seems to be well established by the age of two years and is a good indicator of it continuing into later stages of development. Environment is very influential in reinforcing and encouraging aggressive and sociable behaviours.

Social development

One important aspect of social development is the development of children's moral or pro-social behaviour. The family's role is vitally important in this development. Some psychologists believe that the rules of what is right and what is wrong are learnt through reward, punishment and imitation. This theory ignores the fact that some people develop part of their moral sense through thinking carefully and logically about their actions. For instance, young people often become vegetarian after much serious consideration of the issues involved and not as a result of any reward or punishment.

Freud believed that early childhood experiences had a profound effect on adult life including pro-social behaviour. He identified three different personality components – the 'id', 'ego' and 'superego' (see Unit 12, page 440). He suggested that moral behaviour is controlled by the 'superego' which develops around the age of three years during what he called the 'phallic stage'. At this stage, children feel a desire for the opposite-sex parent, and see the same-sex parent as a rival. This leads to feelings of guilt, unconscious hostility and a fear of punishment. The problem is resolved if the child identifies with the same-sex parent and in doing so takes on the attitudes and ideas of another which develops the 'conscience'. The 'conscience' punishes when the child does something wrong and this causes guilty feelings to arise. If the problem is not resolved this results in problems, such as homosexuality, amorality and rebelliousness. Freud's theory tries to explain how moral development involves both biological factors, such as inborn desires, and social factors, such as the influences of parents.

Psychologists of the humanist school view moral development as being promoted through family relationships which encourage emotional development. People who have difficult relationships with their parents are thought to be prevented from fully developing their personalities. They constantly seek social approval and have problems establishing their own identity.

Aggression

Freud believed that aggression comes from unconscious instinctive drives. He stressed the need to release this energy which would otherwise cause psychological disorders, such as depression. This act of release is called **catharsis** and may take the form of violent behaviour or more acceptable activities, such as sport.

Think It Over

Discuss in your group your own experiences of dealing with aggressive children. What causes them to become aggressive? How do you deal with their aggression?

There is some evidence to suggest that aggression may have a **biological explanation**. Connor's Danish study (1995) showed that if one of a pair of twins is a criminal, then the other twin is much more likely to have a criminal record than the average person. Brown *et al.* (1979) suggested that aggression is probably linked to high levels of certain hormones or chemicals. It is suggested that high levels of testosterone in males, women with pre-menstrual syndrome and increased levels of progesterone are linked to crime and negative behaviour.

Other theories stress that aggression may be reinforced and is, therefore, more likely to be repeated. For instance, parents may encourage boys to be tough and girls to be gentle. However, this is generally considered to be an oversimplified approach.

Patterson *et al.* (1991) studied families, some with aggressive children and some with children who were not a problem. Families were identified where the children were difficult to discipline. These seemed to have certain things in common, such as little affection shown, use of aggression to cope with tensions within family relationships, little use of approval and instead much use of physical punishment. The figure below shows the kind of home environment which may create aggressiveness.

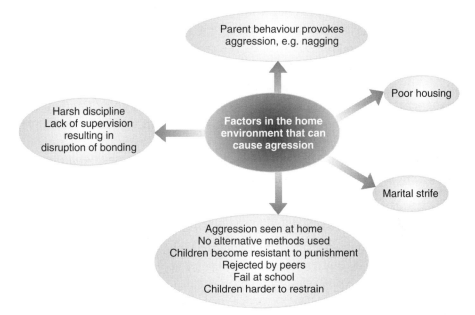

Ways of managing unwanted behaviour
- Positively reinforcing behaviour which is not aggressive, e.g. praising a child who helps another child. Aggressive behaviour should be calmly stopped and child given much warm attention when behaving well.
- Providing role models who are not aggressive. It is important that nursery staff always provide an excellent example of non-aggressive, calm, warm behaviour towards the children.
- Removing aggressive cues, e.g. playgroups have a policy that there are no toy guns for children to use.
- Use of humour and empathy to reduce aggressive behaviour.
- To encourage children to think about and discuss aggression.
- Encouraging the aggressor to experience the emotions of the victim, e.g. in role play.

Key issues
Review what you have learnt so far in this unit concerning managing unwanted behaviour. Imagine you have been asked to write a leaflet for a group of new parents called: 'How to Avoid Creating a Monster – how to live in peace with your children'. Write what you think are the most important ways of avoiding unwanted behaviour.

Role of play in promoting emotional and social development

Professor Kathy Sylva is clear in her view of the value of play: '... it is one of the activities most significant to the (child's) development.' Many other psychologists support Sylva's view:

- Erikson (1950) stressed the importance of children using play to help them deal with life experiences which the child tries to repeat, to master or to reduce their impact. The child tries to organise its personal world in relation to the real world. (Can you remember as a child playing schools and taking the role of the dominant teacher who tells the others what to do?)
- Hutt and Bhavnani's (1972) research found that children who were assessed as being low in exploratory play when they were pre-schoolers tended to be low in curiosity and to experience problems in social adjustment five years later. Children judged to be active explorers were more likely to score high on tests of creativity and show evidence of being independent and curious.
- Connolly and Doyle (1984) found that the amount and complexity of fantasy play were linked with social competence.

Researchers stress the importance of the emotional atmosphere around children during play. This appears to be more important than a vast array of toys. For instance, parents can play an important role in enhancing their children's play experiences. Cohen (1993) suggests that parents can encourage imaginative play by accepting and respecting their children when playing with them. They give children confidence to explore the world around them and to try out new roles.

Three stages of play are generally recognised, as shown in the diagram:

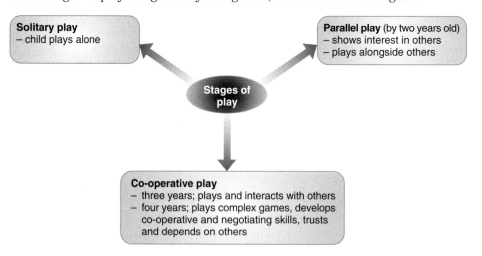

Solitary play
– child plays alone

Parallel play (by two years old)
– shows interest in others
– plays alongside others

Stages of play

Co-operative play
– three years; plays and interacts with others
– four years; plays complex games, develops co-operative and negotiating skills, trusts and depends on others

Children of all ages engage in solitary and parallel play at times but older children develop the skills to take part in co-operative play. Parallel play is the way a newcomer or younger member of the group is accepted as part of a group.

Research shows that play is vitally important in developing the child's ability to make good relationships. Children whose parents invite other children to come to play and have opportunities to play games involving co-operation are more popular among their peer group.

Read Unit 11 for more on the role of play in promoting physical, emotional and social development in children.

Assessment activity 9.2

- Describe the role of play in promoting social and emotional development.
- Why is attendance at a pre-school setting of importance in promoting all aspects of development?

Children's cognitive and language development

Learning theories

Throughout our lives we develop ideas or concepts and are influenced by what we perceive about the world around us (our **perception**). Gradually our knowledge develops together with an ability to reason, solve problems, comprehend abstract ideas and understand why people behave as they do. This is called **cognitive development**. Various theories explain how children learn and think and these are outlined in the table below.

Main theories	Theorist/research period	Key features
Behaviourism	Watson (early 20th century)	<ul><li>Concerned only with observable activities</li><li>Thoughts and feelings have little relevance to learning</li><li>Babies are born with biological reflexes which exist from birth (innate) and all other responses are learned (nurture)</li><li>Behaviour changes in response to rewards and punishments. Actions are encouraged by rewards and other actions discouraged by punishments</li><li>Theories developed through animal experiments and do not easily transfer to humans</li></ul>
Classical conditioning	Pavlov (late 19th century)	<ul><li>A new stimulus causes an existing response because of an association between two happenings</li><li>Baby's check touched gently (*Unconditioned stimulus*) ➞ baby turns head (*Unconditioned response – reflex*)</li><li>Baby's check touched + mother talks to baby (*Unconditioned stimulus*) ➞ (*Conditioned stimuli*) ➞ baby turns head (*Unconditioned response*)</li><li>Mother's voice (Conditioned stimuli) ➞ baby's head turns (*Conditioned response*)</li></ul>
Social learning (observational learning)	Bandura (1960s/1970s)	<ul><li>Children learn by observing another (a model) and then imitate, especially if the model is important and loving to them, such as a carer in a nursery</li></ul>
Constructivism	Piaget (1920–70)	<ul><li>Children's understanding of 'reality' is **constructed** through interacting with the world around them and **learning through discovery**</li></ul>

Main theories	Theorist/research period	Key features
(Constructivism cont'd.)		• Piaget believed children develop mental structures or **schemas** (knowledge about things, such as when shaken a rattle makes a noise). Children **assimilate** new information, they use their present simple schemas to **accommodate** or adapt to new experiences by developing more complex schemas and so achieve **equilibration** (a comfortable balance between the existing and the new experiences) • For instance, a baby develops a schema that a rattle when shaken makes a noise. Baby has to assimilate new schemas to accommodate that when the rattle is shaken fast by mother, a different rhythm is created compared to when the rattle is slowly shaken by the baby. Much experimenting by the baby enables the new information to be accommodated. This achieves equilibration This happens throughout the four distinct stages of cognitive development: 1. *Sensory-motor* (0-2 years) – a practical period of learning when children are **egocentric** 2. *Pre-operational* (2-6 years) – thinking is pre-logical and characterised by: symbolisation, e.g. language; egocentrism – an inability to imagine other people's perceptions; animism – attributing feelings and intentions to non-living things, e.g. a child's teddy bear becomes a trusty friend; moral realism – judging an action by its outcome rather by the intention of the person doing the act 3. *Concrete operational* (6-11 years) – thinking becomes more rationale 4. *Formal operational* (11 years on) – more abstract thinking

Assessment activity 9.3

- Name Piaget's four stages of cognitive development.
- Describe the Piagetian stage of development of children in a pre-school class, i.e. aged three to four years.
- Research further the key features of the learning theories listed above.

- Explain the key features of learning theories which may influence a nursery's policy:
  a) that staff act as excellent role models for the children
  b) to reward good behaviour by use of stickers
  c) to plan children's work carefully by allowing plenty of opportunities for them to assimilate new ideas and so consolidate their learning before being introduced to more complex knowledge.

Sensory development

Newborn babies take in, process and use a vast amount of information using their senses of sight, hearing, taste, smell and touch. The process by which each of us gains direct awareness through our senses of the world around us is called perception (Sylva and Lunt, 1998).

Hearing

From birth, babies seem to have an inborn preference for hearing the human voice. Condor and Sanders (1974) carried out some experiments on babies just a few hours old. Tapes of different sounds, including human speech were played. After two days the babies started to move their arms and bodies in time with the human speech and showed little interest in the other sounds.

Vision

Babies' visual sensory system is not fully mature at birth. Vision is more blurred than in an adult and their eyes focus best at about 25 centimetres. Fantz (1961) carried out research with young babies who were shown different stimuli the approximate size and shape of an adult's head. Babies looked at the face-pattern more than the others so Fantz concluded that babies have an innate preference for facedness. Other studies showed that babies have a preference for increasingly complex patterns and their capacity for differentiating patterns steadily develops.

Case Study

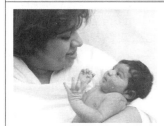

This is a picture of a mother talking to her fifteen-day-old baby.

- Comment on the distance between the mother's face and the baby. How can this influence the baby's perception?
- Comment on the baby's interest in the mother's face and her interaction with the baby. Is this interest to be expected by a baby of this age? Justify your answer with

Perception of depth and 3-D objects

Often babies roll and fall off chairs if unattended. They seem to have no sense of depth. Gibson and Walk (1960) tested babies' depth perception. They devised an experiment using a 'visual cliff' which consisted of a glass top covering a drop of several feet. Babies over six months refused to cross the 'cliff' which indicates that they are able to perceive depth.

Development of perceptual judgements

Vurpillot (1976) studied children from the age of three and a half years to seven and a half years to discover how they use their perceptual skills. She showed them a series of drawings, all of which were slightly different. She asked them to spot the differences.

Vurpillot found that:

- Three and a half-year-olds perceive anything missing in the picture and differences in form, e.g. round sun changes to crescent
- by seven and a half-years-old they perceive changes in sizes but not in detecting changes in location, e.g. the position of the house.

She concluded that younger children's perception is limited by their lack of capacity to gather, record and think about perceptual information, using only a few simple judgements. As children get older they are able to make more visual comparisons and are more skilled at selecting from a range of information presented to them.

Theories of language development

These are outlined in the table below.

Theorist/period of research	Type of theory	Main features of theory
Skinner (1930s)	Nurturist Language is taught through imitation	Parents and carers reinforce and therefore shape children's language
Chomsky (1960s)	Nativist Language is innate. Children are biologically programmed for language development	Children born with all the things we need to produce language called Language Acquisition Device and we are born with the potential to understand the structure of language (grammar)
Piaget (1920s-1970s)	Interactionist input theory	Language results from the children's cognitive development. As the cognitive processes develop so children's language develops, e.g. during the animism stage of the pre-operational period children often practise talking to their favourite toys. Language is influenced by their interaction with their environment. Children enrich the input and actively shape their perceptions through making it fit into pre-existing schemas or by generating new ones. They often use an expression which seems logical to them but does not follow the more complex formal rules of grammar, e.g. a child says 'one mouse' but when another is present a child may speak of 'two mouses'

Sequence of language development

The table below shows the sequence of development and the normal age at which children follow the sequence. However, there can be considerable variation in the age at which children pass through the stages, depending on the environment and their speed of development.

All children regardless of their ethnic origin follow the same sequence of language development.

Age	Pattern of development
1-2 months	Cooing – open vowel sounds like *oooh*, *aah* and uses *gestures* Shows skill of *turn taking* in 'conversations'
6-7 months	Babbling – adds consonants and makes strings of sounds e.g. *dah, dah, dah*
1-2 years	**12-18 months** First words linked to familiar things, e.g. 'Daddy', 'Car' First one or two-word sentences with gestures are called **holophrases**, e.g. child pointing to shoe with male figure, 'Daddy'- meaning Daddy's shoe First sentences – from 2 years **Telegraphic speech** (short sentences – 2 or 3 words but only essential words, e.g. 'I play ball')
2$\frac{1}{2}$ years	50 word **vocabulary** Uses plural, past tenses, prepositions Generalises speech, e.g. 'I goed' instead of 'I went', 3 mouses
5 years	2500 word vocabulary Uses complex sentences and questions Shows an interest in reading and writing. Can listen intently when interested
By 8 years	Able to pronounce most sounds but may have difficulty with some consonants, e.g. 'v', 's', 'l' Speaks confidently Uses most plural and past tenses correctly Can express abstract ideas, such as emotions, through language Writes short pieces of writing independently Can read simple text accurately

Assessment activity 9.4

Observe three-year-olds in a nursery including both (a) when they play together during role-play, and (b) when interacting with adults. Record the language used on both occasions.

- What stage of language development have the children reached? Give examples from your observations to explain your answer.
- How did the adult influence the child's language development?

Using your observations in the nursery, provide evidence to support Skinner's nurturist theory of language development. If possible, provide examples of children's use of language which does not support his theory. Provide an example of children's language which illustrates the interactionist input theory of language development which Piaget supported.

Language delay and language disabilities

Children mature at different rates. In order to talk, children need to hear spoken language and use their language. In extreme cases where children have little human contact, studies show that they do not learn to speak in isolation. In normal situations children with language delay in the early years can still progress well later.

Fluency – young children often hesitate to search for a word or how to say things. They lose track of what they are trying to say, may start again, taking time to complete what they want to say. If adults get impatient, then fluency can get worse. Most children gradually get more confident and become more skilful in expressing themselves fluently. For a few children fluency problems may lead to **stammering**, affecting a child's confidence and requiring specialist help.

Articulation – most children have difficulties saying some sounds, e.g. 'yellow'. Physical conditions, such as cleft palates, result in difficulties in forming sounds through control of mouth and tongue and need specialist help.

Children with mild or severe **learning difficulties** may have a delay in talking due to difficulty decoding the meaning of sounds.

Deaf children – if the emphasis is on developing oral language, then speech and reading problems may occur. Deaf children can be taught to communicate through lip reading, sign language and oral language at the same time. Most need special schooling.

Difficulty in reading and writing may be due to **dyslexia**. Children have problems organising themselves, with their memory as well as word recognition. Early identification and support are important.

Encouraging children's language development

Learning to listen, speak, read and write are all important interactive elements of language development. Children with a good knowledge of the sound and structure of language and the meaning of words usually make more progress in reading. They develop an ability to recognise individual letters (**phonemic awareness**) and that spoken and written words are made up of individual sounds.

From an early age, reading to children and sharing of books and stories are very important. Awareness of sounds, such as in rhymes, helps children's reading and writing. Children benefit from being in a 'text-rich' environment where they are made aware of the relevance of text and have good opportunities to make marks and write for their own simple purposes as in role play. Adult support helps them understand that letters are symbols for sounds they speak, read and write.

Theory into practice

- Observe or record children at different stages of language development. Identify the children's stage of language development.
- Find out the early learning goals for listening, speaking, reading and writing which children are expected to achieve by the end of the Foundation Stage.
- How can parents assist their children's language development?

Factors affecting intellectual, sensory and language development

Factors affecting intellectual, sensory and language development before birth:

Genes e.g. Down's syndrone, phenylketonuria	*Lifestyles of parents* Effect on foetus of drugs, alcohol, malnutrition, smoking
Age of mother If the mother is older there is more risk of Down's syndrome and genetic abnormalities	*Emotional stress*
	Social class
Health of parents Effects on foetus of mother's diseases during pregnancy, e.g. rubella Sexually transmitted diseases, e.g. Aids	*Poverty*
	Radiation and pollution

Assessment activity 9.5

- Take each factor listed in the box above and research the likely effects on a baby's intellectual, sensory or language development.
- Write a short paragraph explaining your findings.

Factors affecting intellectual, sensory and language development after birth.

Physical disabilities e.g. cleft palate	*Socialisation*
	Social class
Sensory disabilities e.g. deaf, blind	*Poverty*
	Emotional stress
Health of child e.g. meningitis	*Social and community support*
Family lifestyles e.g. effect of alcohol and drugs abuse, smoking, exercise, diet	*Family's cultural and religious traditions and personal preferences*
	Pre-school opportunities

Think It Over

Which of the factors listed in the above box could be described under the following headings:

- environmental
- social
- genetic
- cultural?

Assessment activity 9.6

A recent report highlighted that 'British families face the highest childcare bills in Europe. Many families cannot afford to use quality childcare. Millions of children are missing out on the benefits of early education.' ('The Price Parents Pay', Daycare Trust, 2001).

Sian and Cara are both only children and live in isolated communities. Sian's family can afford to send her to a nursery with a pre-school class. Cara's family is unable to afford to do so.

* Compare the range of opportunities the two children have for developing their language skills.

Role of play to promote language and cognitive development

Psychologists regard play as a vital tool in promoting language and cognitive development. Piaget believed that play was closely linked with cognitive development – see table below. The opportunity to master and practise skills at the different stages of development was vital in achieving equilibration. Children need different types of play for the different stages of development.

Piagetian stage	Type of play	Suitable activities	Examples
Sensory-motor	Mastery Exploration	Repetitive movements	Shaking a rattle
Pre-operational	Symbolic or make-believe play	Playing together Fantasy, make-believe, role play Learning to communicate symbolically through language	Dressing up Pretending a cardboard box is a car
Concrete operations	Play with rules	Use rules and reasoning, play games with rules Learn about rights and responsibilities	Card games, e.g. Snap, board games with fixed rules, e.g. Snakes and Ladders

Sylva (1980) studied children in a playgroup. She found that children learn from structured activities with clear goals, encouraging concentration and intellectual development. Children working in pairs improve the intellectual level of play and adults are invaluable in stimulating children's language and exploration during their play.

Case Study

Rasheda, an early years practitioner, took a group of children to the local airport and then, in the nursery, organised role play based on these experiences.

* Describe how role-play can extend the children's vocabulary.
* How could the children develop their interest in reading and writing?
* How is this project appropriate for the children's Piagetian stage of play?

Observational techniques

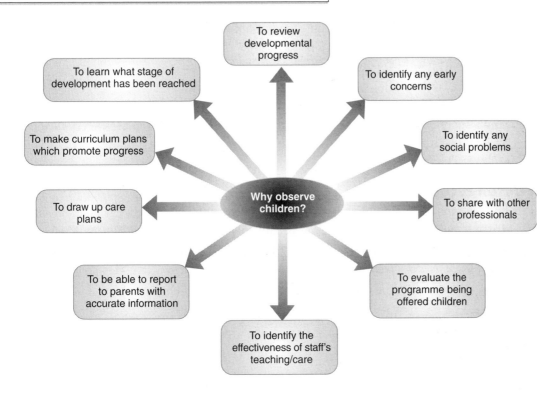

Observing children is a way of finding out how they are behaving in everyday life. Different methods can be used for observing children. Children might be observed during the normal activities of the early years setting, at home or at school. This is called **naturalistic observation**, since the child is observed in its natural setting.

When observing children it is usual for the observer to be concerned with a single child. This child is called the **target child**. The observer will concentrate on watching and recording the target child and only noting other children if they interact with the target child. However, on some occasions more than one child might be observed. For instance, the purpose of an observation might be to see how two children react to one another, so both children would be observed.

For many situations the observer has to sit quietly and try not to draw attention to themselves so they can concentrate fully on the observation. This is acting as a **non-participant observer**. Children are usually curious so this may be difficult. It is best to avoid eye contact with the child/ren. If successful as a non-participant observer the child is more likely to show more spontaneous behaviour and the observer is more likely to be able to be objective as they do not enter into a relationship with the child. However, by being slightly apart from the child it might be more difficult to have a good view of what is happening.

For some observations, the researcher has to become involved in order to direct the investigation, e.g. ask the child questions. This is acting as a **participant observer**. This allows the child to show behaviour which is to be observed. The child might be more responsive if the observer is a familiar adult. However, this may affect the resulting behaviour and it may restrict the opportunities to record the information gained.

Observations may take a variety of formats including:

- naturalistic
- checklists
- event sampling
- longitudinal.

- written record – narrative
- time sampling
- structured

Naturalistic observations

The child's spontaneous behaviour or learning is recorded. There is no pre-determined, specific activity to be observed.

Written record – narrative

This involves watching a child or group of children and noting down what you see. The record is written in the present tense and usually covers a short period of time. It is necessary to describe the scene but the main focus must be on the child being observed.

Observation

Date

Time commenced 9.30

Time completed 9.40

Name of child Anna

Age 4 years 1 month

Setting Home corner which is organised as a doctor's surgery

Anna barges in and demands the nurse's uniform to wear. She snatches it from a younger child who runs out crying. She tries to put the uniform on and has difficulty fastening the velcro tabs. She leaves the surgery to ask for help. Anna returns. The other children leave the home corner. Anna opens the doctor's case and drops all the contents except for the stethoscope. She walks over the other items without any concern. She has difficulty sorting out the stethoscope and first tries to put the wrong part in her ear. A doll is grabbed and the stethoscope is pushed into the doll's chest. After a few seconds she throws the doll to the ground and lies on the bed herself.

Checklists or tick charts

These can be used to record the activities of an individual child or a group of children. The checklist has to be prepared beforehand and what is to be observed has to be clearly identified. This method is regularly used in nurseries and schools to record children's progress and achievement, especially when they first start school, e.g. base line assessments.

Standard tick charts can be purchased or early years staff can make up their own – see example below. There are also several commercially produced tick charts. These record children's progress through the stepping stones leading to the early learning goals.

If recording major developmental progress the checklist is often supported by other evidence, e.g. a child's folder may include examples of written work to support the tick indicating the progress made in writing.

Activity	Shelagh	Darren	Graeme	Liam	Amin
Talks to friend	✓	✓	✓	✓	✓
Talks to adult on one-to-one	✓	✓	✓	✓	✓
Talks to two adults together	✓	✓	✓	✓	
Talks in small group of friends	✓	✓		✓	✓
Talks in small teaching group	✓				

Time sampling

This form of recording consists of a series of written records at equal intervals throughout a period of time. The reason for observing the child will determine the length of each observation and the length of time between each observation. For instance, you might want to record a child's level of concentration so you may record what the child is doing each minute, as shown below.

Time	Activity
10.00	Sat at playdough table, picked up dough and felt it in hands
10.01	Rolled dough into ball, broke it into pieces
10.02	Ran to book corner, choose book, opened it, dropped it
10.03	Opened another book, lay kicking bean bag, did not look at book
10.04	Now at construction kit rug, tries to put two pieces together, throws pieces when don't fit
10.05	Dressing up as a policeman, marches around room making noise of police car

Often coding is used in this method to provide a more detailed and valuable account, as shown on page 356.

You might observe the child again at a later stage of a session when other activities are available, thus recording concentration levels for a range of situations.

Target child: Ros Sex: F Age: 4 yrs 1 month Date: 13/12/2002				
Time	Activity	Code	Language	Social
10.00	TC sits at construction table	TC		SP
10.01	TC watches CL playing. Tries to make eye contact	TC-CL	NVC	PP
10.02	CL asks TC for a piece. TC snatches	TC-CL	Shouts 'No'	IP
10.03	CL hits TC	TC-CL	Cries and shouts	IP
10.04	A parts TC + CL Explains about please/thank you	A TC CL	CL asks + please TC nods (Yes)	IP
10.05	Both sulk	TC CL	None	PP

Code
TC = Targeted child   PP = Parallel play
CL = Liam (child involved with)   IP = Interactive play
A = Adult   NVC = Non-verbal communication
SP = Solitary play

Event sampling

This involves observing and recording certain events as they occur, e.g. temper tantrums, aggressive behaviour.

Structured observations

These involve observing children for a specific reason. For instance, Bandura structured his observations of children to discover their response to watching aggressive behaviour.

Longitudinal observations

These observations are undertaken over a period of time. One of the most famous longitudinal studies was the 'Seven-Up' TV series when children were observed every seven years from when they were seven years old until early middle age.

Structuring observations

All types of observations must be done in the child's best interest. There are clear ethical guidelines laid down by the British Psychological Society which *must* be followed. Neither the child nor the parents should be subjected to any distress. All information gained must be treated in strict confidence.

An observation should be well-organised so that they provide valuable documents of evidence. They may be used to provide evidence for other health professionals, perhaps as part of the Code of Practice for the Identification and Assessment of Special Educational Needs (1994). The observation can be used to help with curriculum planning. For instance, the evaluations and recommendations of observations can be used when planning activities for individual children or small groups of children to meet their individual needs. An observation may be undertaken in a care setting and may help to plan to meet a child's needs. For example, it could be undertaken in a foster home where a child has been placed after being abused. This may help a child psychiatrist assess the child's emotional needs and enable a social worker to provide an appropriate care plan.

Below is a typical observation format.

Observation

Observation No 1 – *(This allows progress to be reviewed across a series of observations)*

Date – *(This can help you time a repeat observation)*
Time commenced -
Time completed –

Number of adults – 2
Number of children – 4 *(Although there may be only one target child, it is useful to know how many other children were in the group as this may influence the targeted child's behaviour)*

Name of child – *(Only necessary to use the first name or a fictitious name so record remains confidential)*

Age – 3 years 6 months *(It is important to know the exact age in order to assess the progress or behaviour)*

Setting – The observation took place around a craft table in a playgroup *(Do not record the name of the venue but describe the general environment)*

Aim – Fine motor skills *(This should set out the broad area of development to be investigated)*

Objectives – *(These identify the specific abilities or area to be investigated, e.g. a child's ability to use scissors)*

Record of observation – *(This depends on the format of the observation, e.g whether it is a time sample/structured observation, etc.)*

Conclusion – *(Summarises what you observed)*

Evaluation – The developmental milestones for fine motor skills state that a child of 3 years should be able to cut using scissors. (Mary Sheridan: *From Birth to Five Years*) Hannah is 3 years and 6 months. She is not yet able to co-ordinate the use of her hands so she can hold the paper and cut using scissors at the same time *(This summarises the findings with what is expected for the age group. Use a recognised source of reference to make a comparison. The targeted child can also be compared with other children in the group)*

Recommendations – More activities which involve the use of scissors need to be provided. Staff support on a one-to-one basis should assist Hannah when engaged in these activities. Undertake a further observation of Hannah's cutting skills in 6 weeks' time *(How to help the child make progress)*

Using observations

- It is important to write up the observation as soon as possible after the event when it is still possible to visualise the happenings clearly and the 'rough' notes can be understood.

- A single observation may highlight a problem but important judgements should not be made on the basis of just one observation. This has to be followed up in order to make an informed evaluation.

- Care must be taken when carrying out an observation that it does not affect the way the child behaves. The child might be embarrassed and so behaviour could be inhibited. On the other hand, the child might take the opportunity to play-act for the observer and so the results are not valid.

- Judgements must be based on sound evidence. The observer must avoid any personal or cultural bias. For instance, if the target child has an older sibling with behavioural problems, avoid expecting that the target child will display the same problems. Base the evaluation on firm evidence. If a child comes from another culture the parenting styles may be very different and this must be taken into consideration. For instance, in some cultures children are breastfed beyond one year, hence, the child could have difficulty drinking out of a cup at twelve months.

Assessment activity 9.7

A student has an eight-week placement in a nursery. The staff have asked her to undertake two observations during this time. One observation is of a four-year-old child's concentration level and the other is of a three-year-old child's temper tantrums.

- Select different observational techniques for these two observations.
- Justify the selection of the techniques for recording the behaviour and development of the children.
- Evaluate the factors which can affect the accuracy and interpretation of the observational records.

End-of-unit test

1. a) State three different factors which can affect human growth and development.
   b) Describe how each factor affects either human growth or development.

2. a) Explain how fine motor skills develop in the first five years of a child's life.
   b) Give an example of an unpredictable life event which might affect an adult's fine motor skills.
   c) Describe what affect this life event might have on the adult's fine motor skills.

3. A health visitor is concerned about the development of a 3-year-old. For this age, what is the normal expected level of:

   i) physical development
   ii) social development
   iii) emotional development

   b) State two different methods the health visitor might consider using to measure the child's development.
   c) Evaluate the effectiveness of each method.

4 Describe one factor that might affect a child's (a) cognitive development, (b) speech, (c) writing skills.

5 Explain how a child's role play of being a shop assistant might promote:

a) physical skills
b) emotional development
c) language.

6 A three-year-old child is displaying severe anti-social behaviour during playgroup sessions.

a) Select two methods that could be used to observe the child's behaviour.
b) Choose one of the methods and explain:

i) why it could be used
ii) how the child's behaviour would be recorded using this method
iii) what factors might affect the accuracy and interpretation of this method.

7 Name and briefly describe the different stages of Piaget's theory of learning.

8 Describe, in detail, the stage of cognitive development, according to Piaget, that a child would be expected to reach by five years of age.

9 What sequence of language development would a baby normally follow in the first two years of life?

References

Bee, H. (1992) *The Developing Child*, London: Harper Collins College Publishers

Davenport, G. (1994) *An Introduction to Child Development*, London: Collins Educational

DfEE, (2000) *Curriculum Guidance for the Foundation Stage*, London: Qualifications and Curriculum Authority

Flanagan, C. (1999) *Applying Psychology to Early Child Development*, London: Hodder & Stoughton

Harding, J. and Meldon-Smith, L. (2000) *Helping Young Children To Develop*, 2nd edition, London: Hodder & Stoughton,

'Households Below Average Income 1994/5-1997/8', reported in *Social Inequalities 2000*, ONS, DSS, London: Stationery Office (2000)

Independent Inquiry into Inequalities in Health Report, (1998) Department of Health, London: Stationery Office

Lindon, J. (1998) *Understanding Child Development*, Basingstoke: Macmillan

Looking at Children's Learning, (1997) School Curriculum and Assessment Authority

ONS, (2000) *Social Inequalities 2000*, London: Stationery Office

Sharman, C., Cross, W. and Vennis, D. Cassell, (1995) *Observing Children: A Practical Guide*

Sheridan, M. *From Birth to Five Years*, Children's Developmental Progress, NFER Nelson

Sylva, K. and Lunt, I. (1998) *Child Development: A First Course*, Oxford: Blackwell

Tassoni, P., Beith, K., Eldridge, H. and Gough, A. (2000) *Diploma in Child Care and Education*, Oxford: Heinemann

Child health

Introduction

This unit covers aspects of child health with which all early years practitioners need to be familiar. It is therefore important that early years practitioners are able to recognise signs of illness and know how to deal with any situation that might arise. Health promotion and education is a growing area within the child education field and the UK government continues to initiate some changes in order that the health of the nation as a whole is improved.

What you need to learn
- Health promotion
- Causes of ill health
- The impact of ill health on children and families
- Treatment and care routines for children who are unwell

Health promotion

What is health?

To be healthy means very different things to different people, but it is generally associated with physical health rather than aspects of health such as mental or social health. The World Health Organisation (WHO) describes health as: 'a state of complete physical, mental and social well-being and not merely the absence of disease or infirmity'. Whilst some people think that being healthy relates to the ability to resist infection and to cope with life's stresses and strains, others might feel that good health is a person's ability to cope physically, emotionally and mentally with day-to-day life. To some people, however, good health might simply mean the absence of any illness and 'feeling well'.

Types of health

Although the World Health Organisation's definition only includes physical, mental and social health, health is generally considered to also include emotional, spiritual and environmental/community/societal health – i.e. a more holistic approach to health.

Health education and health promotion

Health education focuses on the prevention of illness in an individual, whereas health promotion, according to the World Health Organisation, is: 'The process of enabling people to increase their control over, and improve, their health'. It emphasises being healthy and improving health rather than focusing on illness. It also incorporates wider community issues, such as anti-smoking campaigns and employee health.

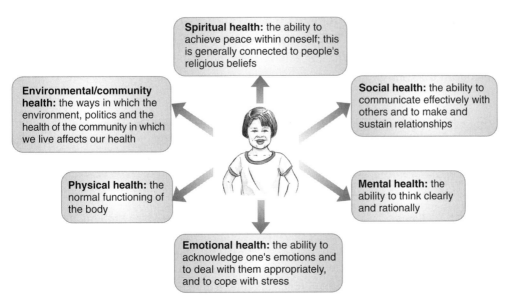

Figure 10.1: Types of health

Approaches to health education

There are many approaches to the health education issue which can be categorised in the following ways: primary, secondary and tertiary health education, and individual, community (or group), and organisational (including within education settings) health education.

Primary health education

This aims to improve the quality of health and therefore life by giving people information and advice on staying healthy. Most health education aimed at children falls within this category and includes care of the teeth, personal safety, road safety and healthy eating.

Secondary health education

This aims at early detection and treatment of conditions in order to prevent further complications or worsening of the condition. It can also involve educating people to change their behaviour in order to restore good health. This could include teaching diabetic children about their diet or ensuring that everybody knows some basic first aid.

Tertiary health education

This aims to reduce the impact of a chronic illness or disability by teaching children how to reach their maximum potential. This could involve the use of hearing aids in a profoundly deaf child or specially adapted wheelchairs.

Individual health education

Most health education will be aimed at individuals and their particular health need and can include leaflets and posters on smoking, healthy eating and safety in the home.

Community or group health education

This can involve local campaigns to improve health or the formation of self-help or pressure groups. Local groups for twins, or those with asthma or epilepsy are sometimes formed to give advice about how to cope with situations or conditions. These groups also come under the category of secondary health education.

Organisational health education

In early years settings, this can be about developing policies on promoting the health of staff and children. Settings might, for example, develop a policy on dealing with head lice, infectious diseases and asthma.

Approaches to health education and promotion by health educators

Health educators approach health education in different ways, as illustrated in the table below.

Approach	Aims	Examples
Medical	To prevent ill health by a series of public health measures. This is used most by doctors, health visitors and school nurses	The immunisation programme and health screening of children
Education	To provide information and/or the necessary skills to enable the child or parent to make an informed choice	Teaching of personal safety to children
Behavioural	To encourage people to change their behaviour or habits	Campaigns to stop smoking or to improve diets
Empowerment	To help people identify their own lifestyle changes and to facilitate them in developing the skills, confidence and self-esteem to change. This can be used on an individual basis or within the community	Parenting classes for young teenage mothers Building up children's self-esteem through personal safety role plays (e.g. the Kidscape programme)

Assessment activity 10.1

- Find three definitions of 'health' and ask at least six people how they would define health.
- Write a report on 'What is health?'.

Health educators and health promoters

Health education and promotion can be done both formally and informally to parents and their children:

- Formal health education targets a specific group at a specific time, e.g. antenatal and postnatal classes run by community midwives and health visitors; sex education in schools as part of the National Curriculum.
- Informal health education is done on a one-to-one basis or through television, the media, or magazines and provides information to those who are seeking it.

Everyone can be involved in promoting health, and early years practitioners and parents will be constantly doing this through activities and day-to-day routines, and by being a good role model.

The role of health educators and promoters

There are a number of organisations and professionals who promote health and provide health education.

The World Health Organisation (WHO)

The objectives of the WHO are 'the attainment by all peoples of the highest possible health'. Its main functions are to set worldwide standards for health, to give guidance and co-operate with governments in strenthening health programmes. Its role encompasses:

- promoting improved standards of teaching and training in the health professions
- researching ways of preventing infectious diseases
- co-ordinating health work internationally
- promoting improvements of nutrition, housing, sanitation, economic or working conditions.

Health Development Agency (formerly the Health Education Authority)

This is the UK's leading body in health promotion and exists to 'help people nationally and internationally to make sustainable improvements in health, and working to reduce health inequalities'. Its main functions are:

- to advise the government on health promotion strategy and to develop healthy public policies
- to work with and for health professionals involved in health education, providing training and resources
- to work with members of the public by providing leaflets, articles in the press and information for television programmes and advertisements on the television.

National voluntary organisations and pressure groups

Voluntary organisations strive to educate the public and promote health in particular health issues. They may also put pressure on the government to change policies (e.g. The Society for the Protection of Unborn Children). The National Childbirth Trust, for example, provides antenatal classes and promote breastfeeding, and part of the National Asthma Campaign's role is to educate the public and schools about asthma.

The media

The media have a very important role to play in informing the public about health issues and most organisations concerned with health will issue press releases in order to keep the press updated with accurate information.

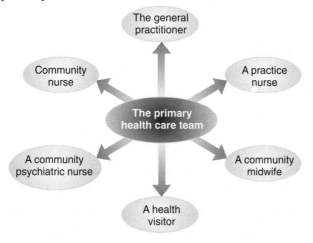

The primary health care team

The primary health care team's role within the community is to provide health education and to promote health, to detect and treat illnesses and conditions and to provide a caring service.

Health education is an increasing and essential part of the team's role. The health visitor, for example, works closely with parents giving advice and support on all parenting skills.

The school nurse

The school nurse's role is mainly concerned with screening, but their role is extending into other areas such as promoting health education within the classroom.

The dentist

Teaching on dental hygiene and the prevention of tooth decay is one of the dentist's roles. The school dentist service also visits children in schools.

The health promotion unit

This unit provides training, courses, exhibitions and advice and support on any health initiative. It also offers a free loan service of health education videos, displays, books, project packs, and CD-ROMs, and provides leaflets and posters.

Education services

Teaching on health issues is part of the PSE programme within schools and this area is being targeted in the National Healthy Schools Scheme (see page 365).

There are many others who have a role in health education including the police (teaching children to protect themselves, road safety and crime prevention) and the fire brigade (fire awareness).

The early years practitioner

Early years practitioners need to know and understand how to maintain their own personal health as well as that of the children in their care and to be a positive role model. It is also their role to help teach children about health issues as part of the curriculum.

Theory into practice

Devise a detailed plan for an activity about one of the following topics:

- Healthy eating
- Fire safety
- Caring for your teeth

Write down a list of resources you would need.

In what ways would the activity help the children to gain a better understanding of the topic?

Health promotion programmes

Health promotion programmes can vary in their extent. Some may target one particular class in a school and some will target a large population of the world. The WHO has managed to achieve the eradication of smallpox, whilst other diseases such as polio and leprosy are rapidly decreasing. In 1981, the World Health Authority adopted a worldwide strategy called the 'Health for All' movement, which aims to distribute health resources evenly and to ensure that everyone has access to essential health care.

Current health promotion campaigns in the UK

In February 1998, the government produced a document called 'Our Healthier Nation', which aimed to reduce deaths from cancer, heart disease, accidents and suicides by 2010. This paper identified that 'many of our attitudes to health and the influences on our lives are set in childhood ... education is one of the most important ways of giving children and young people a healthy start in life.' In October 1999, the Department of Health (DH) and the Department for Education and Employment (now the Department for Education and Skills) launched the 'National Healthy Schools Scheme' to support teachers in their role as health educators and to promote healthy schools.

The strands contained within the Healthy Schools Programme are shown in the table.

Programmes	Aims
Safer Routes to School	To encourage walking and safer travel
The National Healthy Schools Network	To provide information via a National Healthy Schools Network newsletter
Wired for Health	To inform teachers and children about health issues in schools through the website www.wiredforhealth.gov.uk
Cooking for Kids	To teach children about healthy eating, basic cookery skills and food hygiene
Healthy Teachers	To promote health in teachers

Assessment activity 10.2

Choose one health promotion programme aimed at children and examine three different health promotion leaflets, poster or activities. Evaluate the effectiveness of these resources and the roles that different health educators could have in promoting this topic to children.

Causes of ill health

Factors which affect children's health

In order that early years practitioners can understand how to help maintain and improve children's health, it is important to know what factors can influence a child's health.

Prenatal factors

There are many factors that can affect a child's health before it has even been born. The health and lifestyle of the parents, but particularly of the mother, has an important impact on the future health of the child as shown in the following table.

Prenatal factors	How they can affect the foetus
Smoking	Poor growth and development, reduced intellectual ability, and a higher risk of sudden infant death syndrome, respiratory diseases including asthma, and 'glue ear' (see pages 373–6)
Alcohol	Heavy drinking or occasional binge drinking can cause miscarriage, poor development or congenital abnormalities
Drugs	Women are advised not to take any medication whilst pregnant unless prescribed by the doctor Medications, e.g. aspirin, increase the risk of bleeding
Diet	Lack of folic acid in the diet can cause spina bifida and too much Vitamin A can cause foetal abnormalities
Infections (especially in the first 12 weeks of pregnancy)	
• Rubella	Deafness, blindness and congenital heart disease
• Toxoplasmosis	Blindness, brain damage, epilepsy and delayed intellectual development
• Listeria	Premature labour
• Cytomegalovir us (CMV)	Hepatitis, blindness, delayed motor skills and severe learning difficulties
• HIV	The baby can be born with the HIV virus (see page 393)
X-rays	Congenital abnormalities and childhood cancers
Maternal illness, e.g. pre-eclampsia (high blood pressure, protein in the urine and swelling in the tissues)	Poor foetal growth and a low birth weight or prematurity and death, in severe cases

Lifestyle

Factors within a family's lifestyle include the following:

- Diet – a healthy diet is necessary for normal growth and development. A malnourished child is likely to be unwell more often and to develop vitamin deficiencies. Children who are breastfed are less likely to have gastroenteritis, sudden infant death syndrome, respiratory and ear infections and allergies than bottle-fed babies.
- Exercise – regular exercise reduces the incidence of coronary heart disease in adults. It has been shown that children (particularly girls) take much less exercise than is recommended, and therefore it is important for the early years practitioner to encourage children to exercise every day. Emotionally, exercise can help cope with stress and is important socially.
- Smoking – children who grow up in a smoky atmosphere, and therefore passively smoke, have a higher incidence of respiratory and ear infections and asthma. These children are also more likely to smoke themselves. The long-term risks of smoking include a higher risk of heart disease, chronic respiratory infections and of developing cancers, especially of the lungs.

Socio-economic factors

- Poverty – there is an inverse proportion between wealth and health – the poorer the family, the greater the health risks. Children from socially deprived families are less likely to attend screening and developmental checks and for immunisations.
- The community – there are several factors which can effect health from our immediate environment: housing, income, social class, employment and the geographical location can all affect children's health.
- Housing – living in crowded damp conditions increases the risk of accidents and respiratory infections.
- Employment – some occupations are more at risk of accidents or from catching infectious diseases. Unemployment can cause mental health problems and stress-related diseases. Due to a poor income, families who are unemployed are more likely to have a poor diet and housing conditions.
- Health facilities – every area will have different priorities on how the money for the health service is spent, and how long their waiting lists are.

Genetic factors

We cannot change our genetic make-up, and everyone will inherit factors from both parents that will affect their health. Some conditions, such as sickle cell disease (see page 386) and cystic fibrosis (see page 376), are passed on from one or both parent to the child. Sometimes there can be an abnormality of one of the chromosomes (genetic factors), as in Down's syndrome. Other disorders are familial: this means that there is a tendency within the family to have certain conditions, such as asthma, eczema and hay fever.

Assessment activity 10.3

A child called Mariam has just started in the nursery. She is a refugee and has only been in this country for a few moths. She has apparently lived in great poverty although she speaks some English.

- Produce a report for the other staff on the socio-economic factors which could have affected her health, and the ways in which the negative affects can be alleviated.

Causes of illness

There are three main causes of illness: microbiological causes (when a micro-organism or germ enters the body), genetic causes and environmental causes.

Microbiological causes

Germs which enter the body and cause illness are called micro-organisms, and these are divided into four main groups: bacteria, viruses, fungi and parasites (which include protozoa). Some germs are non-pathogenic and aren't harmful to humans, e.g. the lactic acid bacillus which turns milk into yogurt, and the organisms that live in the bowel which manufacture Vitamin K which is essential in the blood clotting process.

Genetic causes

Some genetic conditions, such as sickle cell disease, can cause ill health. Sometimes ill health may be caused by a microbiological or genetic factor, but then made worse by the environment. For example, a child with sickle cell disease can be made worse by getting too cold.

Environmental causes

We generally have less control of these factors, because they are often organised at national level.

- Air – in 1998 the Committee on the Medical Effects of Air Pollutants published a report stating that air pollution is thought to shorten about 24,000 lives a year. This can be caused directly by pollutants in the air or by contributing to respiratory problems.
- Water supply – in the UK the water supply is well regulated and there are few problems with water-borne diseases such as cholera. However, there have been some well-publicised incidences where the water supply has become contaminated and caused ill health.
- Sewage and waste control – this is essential for community health.

Case Study

In July 1988, the public water supply to the town of Camelford in Cornwall was contaminated when aluminium sulphate solution, used in the purification of drinking water, was accidentally discharged into the treated water tank. Over 20,000 local people and 20,000 visitors plus the local farm animals were affected causing short- and long-term health problems.

How infection can be spread

Infection can be spread very quickly from one child to another through a variety of ways, as shown below.

Ways that infection can spread	Examples of infections
Droplet infection: speaking, sneezing, coughing and kissing	Colds, coughs and tuberculosis, rubella
Hands: contamination from air-borne droplets, urine and faeces	Gastroenteritis, colds, tapeworm
Body fluids	Hepatitis, sexually transmitted diseases and HIV
Contaminated water	Polio and typhoid
Contaminated food	Food poisoning, typhoid and cholera
Animals	Rabies (from dogs), toxoplasmosis (from cats)
Insects such as mosquitoes and flies	Malaria and food poisoning
Dust	Diptheria

Methods of preventing illness

Illness can be prevented in a variety of ways including:

- good personal hygiene of staff and children
- a healthy diet and plenty of exercise

- good living and care environment including housing
- proper disposal of waste
- easy access to high quality health care and medicines
- providing good health education and promotion
- child health screening
- immunisation.

(For information on providing a safe environment see Unit 4, pages 124–39 and for more detail on health diets and care routines, see Unit 8, pages 290–6.)

Immunisation

Immunisation is the use of vaccines to give immunity from a specific disease. They consist of a minute portion of the weakened bacteria, virus or of the toxins which they produce. These stimulate the immune system to produce antibodies against the disease. It is recommended that children have immunisations for the following reasons:

- They prevent a child from getting diseases and the associated side effects,
- They protect children who haven't been immunised (this is known as herd immunity: these children are less likely to be exposed to the disease itself),
- It is cheaper to immunise than to care for the children who suffer from side effects of the illness.

The table outlines the immunisation schedule.

Age	Vaccination	How given
Birth	BCG	Only given is there is a risk of contact with tuberculosis
2, 3 and 4 months	Diphtheria, whooping cough (pertussis), and tetanus. Hib (one type of meningitis)	One injection
	Polio	Taken by mouth
	Meningitis C	An injection against one type of meningitis
12-15 months	Measles, mumps and rubella (MMR)	This is given as one injection
3-5 years (before school starts)	Diphtheria and tetanus	One injection
	Polio	By mouth
	MMR	One injection
10-14 years	BCG (tuberculosis)	Skin test followed by one injection
13-18 years	Tetanus and diphtheria	One injection
	Polio	By mouth

Care of a child following immunisation

Serious side effects to immunisations are rare, but some babies may have a mild reaction, often within the first 48 hours. These include irritability, a mild fever or soreness, redness or a small lump around the injection site. It is often advised that infant paracetamol is given afterwards (with parental consent) if any of these symptoms appear. Serious symptoms such as a high fever or convulsions need to be seen immediately by a doctor.

The polio virus will be excreted in the baby's faeces for up to six weeks so handwashing is particularly important when changing nappies.

Child health screening

Every child is checked regularly to ensure normal growth and development and to detect any health problems or conditions. This is known as child health screening and is important because:

- conditions are treated as early as possible
- appropriate care can be provided for the child and the family
- the child can be referred to specialist help if required
- parents know how their child is developing
- genetic counselling can be offered to parents if applicable. This shows the likelihood of having a child with a particular genetic condition.

Developmental charts

Every health area will have their own chart on which development is recorded. The personal child health records contain graphs on which the weight, height and head circumference are plotted; these are called centile charts (see Unit 9, page 338).

Health screening and developmental checks

The main ways of checking on a child's development and health are by:

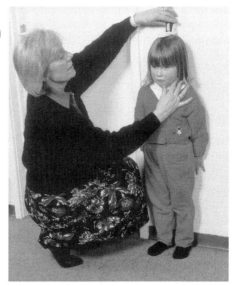

- measuring height, weight and head circumference (the latter in the first year only)
- a physical examination
- observing the child during structured or unstructured activities
- asking questions of, and listening to, the parents and/or carers about the child's development and health.

The midwife and paediatrician do neonatal checks, but the health visitor and occasionally the GP do all the subsequent checks. Each developmental area is checked to ensure that the child is developing at the expected rate, as well as examination of specific areas, such as hearing.

Child health screening programme

Each health authority will do checks at slightly different times, but most will follow a similar format to the one below. The way these checks are recorded will also differ from area to area.

The checks are normally done at the following times:

- A **neonatal check** is done at birth by the midwife and then by the paediatrician before the baby leaves the hospital.
- **Six to eight weeks** – this is usually done at the same time as the mother's postnatal check by the GP and the baby's first immunisation. This is a very important check, because it is a time when conditions are often detected.
- **Six to nine months** – this check is done at around eight months because the hearing distraction test, which ensures that babies can hear sounds of varying pitches, is best

done at this age. Health education will include: diet, play needs, accident prevention, sun safety and care of the teeth.

- **Eighteen to twenty-four months** – iron deficiency is fairly common at this age, which can cause anaemia. This can cause a child to be pale, tired and have headaches. Health education may include dental care, toilet training, diet, accident prevention, social contacts for the baby, dealing with temper tantrums and sun safety.
- **Three to three and a half years** – this is a pre-school check and may be done by the doctor and health visitor. Health education may include accident prevention, diet, dental care, toilet training, preparation for school, management of behaviour, socialising for the child.
- **Checks at school entry** – many health authorities are no longer doing routine physical checks in the term that the child is five years old, although the school nurse may do a developmental assessment, height and weight. Questionnaires are sometimes sent to the parents on health issues such as eating, sleeping, illnesses, allergies, medication, whether toilet trained at night, friendships, whether the child likes school or has any problems.

If any problems are picked up from checks, the child will be seen more regularly by the doctor or health visitor, or will be referred to a specialist if necessary.

The role of the early years practitioner in child health screening
Although health professionals do the health screening, the early years practitioner will be in daily contact with the children, so are in a very good position to identify any possible problems. Hearing problems, particularly glue ear, where there is intermittent hearing loss, is a common condition which can be detected by this means. If there are concerns about a child's health or development, the child's parents should be informed.

Assessment activity 10.4

The children in Noah's Ark Nursery are continually getting colds: two children have had scabies and two others have had gastroenteritis. Mariam, who is a refugee, appears to get one infection after another.

- Produce a fact sheet on the causes of illness in the setting and describe how the setting can prevent the spread of infection.

Common childhood illnesses
When working with children, it is important for early years practitioners to be able to recognise some of the common illnesses, and to know when it may be necessary to contact the child's parents or to call a doctor. Children sometimes do not have the experience to know that they are unwell, or the vocabulary to tell someone how they are feeling.

It is therefore important to observe children for changes to their behaviour or physical or emotional well being in order to detect signs of illness. It is also important to be able to record information about a child's health to the parent.

Signs that a child is unwell

Children's behaviour sometimes changes when they are becoming unwell before any specific signs and symptoms develop.

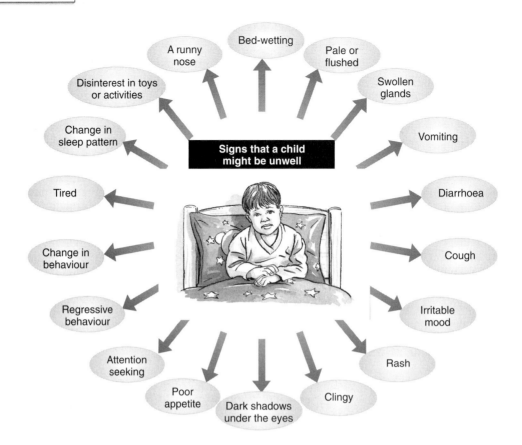

Signs that a child might be unwell

A runny nose · Bed-wetting · Pale or flushed · Disinterest in toys or activities · Swollen glands · Change in sleep pattern · Vomiting · Tired · Diarrhoea · Change in behaviour · Cough · Regressive behaviour · Irritable mood · Attention seeking · Rash · Poor appetite · Dark shadows under the eyes · Clingy

Illnesses of the upper respiratory tract and ears

Respiratory infections are the most common of the childhood illnesses. There are over 200 viruses that cause cold symptoms – which is why children seem to get one cold after another! Children are particularly prone to infections when they first start nursery or school because they are suddenly exposed to more germs.

Colds

Colds are caused by viruses and are spread by coughing, sneezing or by contact with secretions on toys and other surfaces. Cold-like symptoms are often the first sign of more infectious illnesses such as chicken pox. Colds often last for five to nine days, but children often have a runny nose for one to two weeks after this. Colds can spread to the lungs and to the middle ear and can also trigger an asthma attack. Signs and symptoms include a runny nose, a sore throat, sneezing, watery eyes, a slight temperature.

Sore throat and tonsillitis

The tonsils are fairly enlarged in a child because they are active in preventing infections. If there is a large invasion of germs, the tissues swell and become inflamed which usually causes pain. With tonsillitis, the throat initially becomes sore, the infection then spreads to the tonsils which become enlarged.

Coughs and chest infections

Coughing in children is usually associated with an upper respiratory infection and can sometimes follow a cold. It is one of the body's defence mechanisms to rid itself of irritants, chemicals or germs. Coughs can be caused by viruses or bacteria, dust, smoke, tuberculosis and asthma (a dry cough at night can sometimes be an early sign of asthma).

Asthma

Asthma is fairly common and affects more than three million people in the UK, including one in seven school children. It can occur at any age, and half of all children will grow out of it. There is often a family history of asthma, hay fever or eczema.

Causes of asthma

The airways in an asthmatic become oversensitive to certain conditions or triggers. These triggers cause the muscles around the airways to tighten, the lining of the airway to become inflamed and the airways themselves to fill with mucus. These cause the airways to narrow which causes the symptoms of asthma.

The 'triggers' which can cause the airways to become more sensitive are:

- an allergy to one or more irritants such as pollen, house mite dust, cats, dogs or horses (the allergen – substance which causes an allergy – is in the fur, saliva and urine)
- chemical irritants such as tobacco smoke, exhaust fumes, perfumes and household cleaners
- exercise
- cold air
- chest infections
- emotional stress such as anxiety or excitement
- food especially peanuts, seafood, eggs and some additives and food colourings
- mould (especially in damp living conditions)
- air pollution – although there is no evidence that this can cause asthma, it can be a trigger if the child has asthma.

There is also a higher incidence of asthma in children whose mother smoked in pregnancy and in those who were bottle fed.

Signs and symptoms

The symptoms vary in each child, and can range from mild to very severe or life threatening. Attacks may be very occasional or frequent and are a major cause of absence from school. The first signs might be:

- a persistent cough, especially in cold air, after exercise or at night
- colds which go 'straight to the chest'
- breathlessness and wheezing when the child exhales (breathes out)
- tightness in the chest

During an attack there may also be:

- difficulty in speaking
- a dry tickly cough
- grey-blue colour, especially around the lips

The child will also be frightened and anxious.

Management

This consists of medication and controlling the triggers. Medication consists of two types:

- The 'relievers' are used to treat the acute symptoms. They open up the air passages in the lungs and are given in syrup form, tablets or in an inhaler, which will always be blue.
- The 'preventers' reduce inflammation in the airways and prevent attacks or reduce

their severity. These are usually brown but sometimes in a maroon or orange inhaler, and they need to be taken regularly.

If a child is less than five years of age or has difficulty using an inhaler, they might use a spacer device such as a Volumatic or Nebuhaler, where the child inhales the drug as a mist. For under twos, there is a Babyhaler which has a soft mask.

Care and treatment of a child with an asthma attack

- Keep calm and reassure the child
- Help the child find a comfortable position
- Give the child the relief inhaler
- If the inhaler has no effect after five to ten minutes, call 999
- Check and record the child's breathing and pulse every ten minutes.

Avoiding triggers

Children should avoid contact with known triggers. Pets should be kept out of doors as much as possible (and especially out of the bedroom) and washed once a week, and hands should be washed after touching animals. The house dust mite is a particular problem and damp dusting should be done very regularly, but never when the child is present.

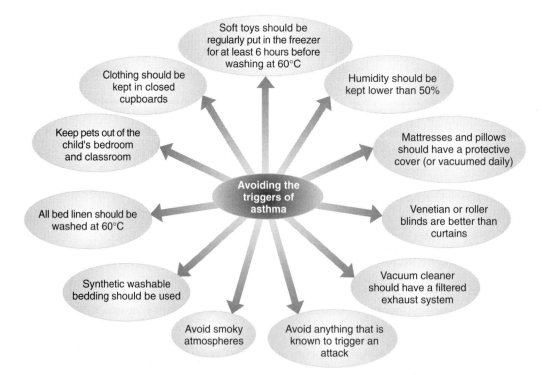

Key issues – supporting children with asthma

- Know the local education authority's and the setting's policy on asthma.
- Staff should know the signs, triggers, care and first aid for an asthma attack – the school nurse can give a talk if necessary.
- Be aware of children's triggers when planning activities and trips.
- Ensure that children have immediate access to their inhaler.
- Always take an asthmatic attack seriously.
- Keep the setting well ventilated.

Theory into practice

You have several children in your setting with asthma. Recently, one child had a severe asthma attack in the playground and the child needed to be admitted into hospital. The staff didn't feel confident about dealing with asthma. As a result of this, you have been asked to produce a booklet on asthma to inform staff about the condition.

- Describe the total care of a child, including treatments, medications and the early years practitioner's role in the care of children with asthma.
- How could the setting improve the care of children with asthma?

Earaches and middle ear infection (otitis media)

Middle ear infections are very common in children under eight years and often follow respiratory infections. They are caused by a virus or bacteria and some children have frequent attacks, especially children who are bottle fed, live in a smoky house and have frequent colds. Some of the signs and symptoms include painful ears, difficulty in hearing, vomiting and raised temperature. In severe cases the eardrum can perforate (a burst ear drum) which causes the ear to discharge pus and the pain to fade. To help relieve the feeling of tightness in the ear, get the child to yawn or swallow, and give them plenty to drink. Do *not* pack the ear with cotton wool if the ear discharges or allow the child to sleep with a hot water bottle.

Contact the doctor immediately if the child:
- has a stiff neck
- is unsteady on his feet
- had a head injury before the earache
- has a high fever and appears very unwell
- ears drain clear fluid.

Complications

If a middle ear infection is not properly treated, complications may occur, including inflammation of the outer ear, glue ear or brain abscesses (*very* rare).

Glue ear (chronic otitis media)

This is caused by a build up of thick mucus in the middle ear which is unable to drain. This prevents the movement of the ossicles (the bones in the ear) and the eardrum which prevents sound being conducted – this causes hearing loss. It is usually associated with recurrent ear infections and it occurs in both ears.

Glue ears affects young children; they will usually 'grow out of it' by the age of eight years. It is a very common cause of poor or intermittent school progress and unwanted behaviour. Some of the signs and symptoms are partial and intermittent deafness, changes in behaviour, lack of concentration and poor school performance, a tendency to talk loudly or shout, tiredness, and speech or reading difficulties.

Treatment and care
- The child will be monitored by a doctor.
- A hearing test will ascertain the degree of deafness.
- Decongestant nose drops may be used to unblock the Eustachian tube.
- Be understanding – it can be very confusing for a child to suffer intermittent hearing loss.
- Ensure that the child looks at you when you're speaking.
- Speak clearly and maintain the normal rhythm of speech.
- Check the child's understanding of instructions.
- Ensure there is as little background noise as possible.
- Provide as much one-to-one attention as possible in the setting.
- Occasionally grommets (small tubes) may be inserted into the eardrum. This allows the fluid, which is trapped in the ear, to escape, which relieves the symptoms.

Cystic fibrosis

Cystic fibrosis (CF) is an inherited condition which affects the respiratory and digestive systems. The mucus produced by the lungs is thick and sticky causing the airways to become infected or blocked and therefore causes difficulty in breathing. The ducts in the pancreas also become clogged with mucus which prevents the digestive enzymes produced here from digesting fats in the digestive tract. This results in poor weight gain.

CF is the most common life-threatening inherited disease and it affects more than 7000 people per year in the UK. Over the last 30 years life expectancy has risen from 5 to 31 years.

Effects of cystic fibrosis
- One in ten babies with CF are born with a blocked bowel
- Failure to grow normally and poor weight gain
- Repeated chest infections
- Salty sweat
- Stools are loose, oily and have a 'cheesy' smell

Care and treatment
- Children will have regular chest physiotherapy, breathing exercises and regular exercise to keep the lungs as free from mucus as possible
- A diet high in protein, energy and vitamins
- A replacement pancreatic enzyme enables the child to digest food properly

In many areas babies are screened routinely for CF as part of the neonatal screening programme. Due to better treatment of the symptoms, the outlook is now much better. Children should be watched carefully for signs of chest infections which can cause damage to the lungs.

Disorders and infections of the digestive system
Vomiting

Vomiting is a symptom that is very common in children and can be associated with an infection anywhere. Some children will be sick every time they have a slight fever, if they are excited or frightened. However, there are many causes and it is important to note the time of sickness, the colour, any pain or diarrhoea and whether the child appears unwell.

Causes of vomiting

- Travel sickness
- Meningitis (see pages 391–2)
- Food poisoning
- Gastroenteritis (see page 378)
- Hepatitis
- Appendicitis (see page 378)
- Pyloric stenosis (causing projectile vomiting in newborn babies)
- Food intolerance (see Unit 8 page 294)
- Possetting (babies less than 1 year old are slightly sick after feeds – this is normal)
- Urinary tract infection
- Whooping cough (see page 391)
- Respiratory infections and tonsillitis (see page 372)
- Ear infections (see page 375)
- Concussion (following a head injury)
- Excitement
- Stress
- Over eating (often associated with children's parties!)
- Sunstroke or heat exhaustion

Key issues – care of a child who is being sick

- Reassure and stay with the child.
- Ensure there is a bowl nearby and disinfect after use.
- Support the child's head when vomiting.
- Wash the child's hands and face after vomiting and encourage rinsing of the mouth with water.
- Allow the child to rest/lay their head on soft towels in case of accidents.
- Change clothes when necessary.
- Encourage sips of water to prevent dehydration (see page 379).
- Once the sickness has stopped, provide small portions of dry food, e.g. toast – this should be started gradually.

Diarrhoea

Diarrhoea (frequent runny stools) is fairly common in children and is often due to an infection. It can be distressing for a child and it may cause accidents in younger children, when unable to get to the toilet in time. Diarrhoea is not an illness in itself, but, like vomiting, is a symptom of many different conditions.

Causes of diarrhoea

- Toddler diarrhoea (see page 378)
- A side effect of some medicine (especially antibiotics)
- Food poisoning (see page 378)
- Gastroenteritis (see page 378)
- Food intolerance (see page 294)

- Excitement, nervousness or stress
- Chronic constipation which can cause an overflow of diarrhoea

Toddler diarrhoea

Toddler diarrhoea can affect healthy children of one to three years, and is characterised by watery diarrhoea containing undigested food. The child should be seen by the doctor to exclude other disorders, but there is no treatment other than chopping food up smaller. The child should grow out of it by the age of three years.

Key issues – care of a child with diarrhoea

- Reassure the child – it can be very distressing.
- Give regular drinks of clear fluid to prevent dehydration.
- Keep a potty nearby if possible for a younger child.
- Keep spare pants handy!
- Avoid going out (except if toddler diarrhoea).
- If gastroenteritis is suspected, isolate the child from others and send them home.
- Good hygiene is important – ensure that the child washes their hands after using the toilet.
- Soak soiled pants in Napisan solution before washing.

Appendicitis

Appendicitis is an infection of the appendix and is unusual in children less than two years of age, but is a common cause of abdominal pain in children under sixteen years of age. Some of the signs and symptoms are pain in the centre of the abdomen which moves to the right groin, nausea or vomiting, and possibly diarrhoea. If a child is suffering from appendicitis, take the child to hospital immediately, do not allow the child to eat or drink, and do not give paracetamol or other pain killers. A warmed hot water bottle might help the pain.

Gastroenteritis

Gastroenteritis is an irritation or inflammation of the stomach and intestines and is contagious. Because the infection is in the bowel, proper hand washing is essential. It is much more common in bottle-fed than in breastfed infants.

Causes

Gastroenteritis is caused by a virus, bacteria, parasites or food poisoning. Similar symptoms can also be produced by stress, medications or an over-indulgence in alcohol. These germs can be contracted by children from:

- contaminated food or feeding equipment
- contact with infected faeces (especially from poor hand washing)
- air-borne viruses or bacteria.

Symptoms

- Usually starts with vomiting and diarrhoea
- Loss of appetite
- A slight temperature
- Stomach pains
- Bloated abdomen
- Aching muscles

Viral gastroenteritis usually lasts 24–48 hours but the bacterial type lasts for longer, usually about a week.

Treatment

To avoid dehydration, the following will be necessary:

- Give clear fluids only for the first 24 hours – cooled previously boiled water or a rehydrating solution (such as Dioralyte), which can be recommended by the doctor or pharmacist and is available in different flavours; these contain glucose and some of the salts which are lost through diarrhoea and vomiting. Offer small amounts of fluids (30–60ml) very frequently (about every 30–60 minutes).
- If an infant is being breastfed, breastfeeding should continue, with extra fluid given too.
- Older children might like to suck ice cubes.
- After 24 hours, infants can recommence their bottle feeds, at half strength initially and little and often.
- Once the vomiting has stopped, children can be offered ice-lollies and clear soups, but avoid milk for 24 hours.
- When food is reintroduced, a soft, bland diet should be provided, e.g. pasta, cream crackers and rice. Avoid raw fruit, fatty food and highly seasoned food for several days.
- The child must be kept at home.
- Hygiene is extremely important and soiled linen and towels should be boil washed.
- Allow the child to rest and give plenty of reassurance.
- Remember, the vomit may be infected so cover the area where the child is resting with a towel and place a sick bucket nearby.
- The anal area may become sore and a barrier cream could be used.
- Watch out for signs of dehydration (see below).

Signs of dehydration

- Sunken eyes
- Pasty colour and dry skin
- Sunken fontanelle (in baby)
- Headache
- Dry skin, mouth/cracked lips
- Dark urine
- Increased pulse and breathing rates
- Passing no urine for six hours in the day
- Children don't always feel thirsty when dehydrated

Call a doctor if:

- a baby is under two months or has missed two feeds
- there are signs of dehydration
- the child cannot drink without vomiting
- there is no improvement after 24 hours
- there is blood in the vomit or stool
- there is a possibility of food poisoning
- there is persistent stomach pain or high temperature of over 38°C
- you are worried about the child.

If a child is very unwell or young, they might be admitted to hospital.

Complications

Possible complications, although rare, could include kidney failure, convulsions, anaemia and even death.

Prevention

This can be prevented by:

- ensuring bottles, dummies and feeding equipment are properly sterilised
- good personal hygiene, especially hand washing
- storing food at the correct temperature
- ensuring chicken and eggs are always cooked thoroughly
- keeping children with gastroenteritis away from others
- teaching children good personal hygiene
- ensuring that food preparation areas are clean.

Threadworms

Threadworms are parasitic worms which look like threads of white cotton, and are very common in children. They are caught by the eggs getting on children's hands from food, especially unwashed vegetables, soil, the sandpit, playdough, clothing and other equipment.

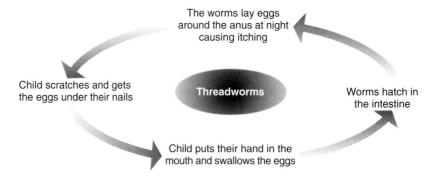

If hands haven't been washed properly, the child can pass on eggs to other children after touching food, playdough, sand or other equipment. The worms can survive for a while in dust at room temperature.

Symptoms

- Itching and soreness around the anus, especially at night
- Occasionally white worms can be seen in the faeces
- Bed-wetting
- Frequent waking at night

Treatment

The whole family will need to take medication from the doctor or the chemist

Prevention

- Good personal hygiene, especially hand washing and nail care
- Use of separate towels
- Keep child's nails short
- Ensure that all fruit and vegetables, and toys are washed carefully

Constipation

Constipation is a symptom rather than an illness itself, but it is very common in children and can cause great discomfort. Children can have their bowels open from four times a day to every four days, and as long as there is no pain or discomfort, and the stools are the normal soft consistency, there is usually nothing to worry about. A child who is constipated passes a hard dry stool infrequently. It is often a short-term problem, but can persist and becomes a chronic condition.

Causes
- Any illness causing dehydration
- Changes in diet
- Insufficient fibre in diet

Symptoms
- Dry hard stool
- Passing stool infrequently
- Abdominal pain
- Loss of appetite
- Blood in the stool
- Lethargy
- Soiling of the pants with a watery stool (which has trickled past the hard stool in the bowel)
- Distended abdomen

Treatment
- Give the child plenty of clear fluids
- Increase the fibre in the diet, e.g. fruit, vegetables and wholemeal bread
- Laxatives should not be given unless directed by a doctor

Refer to a doctor if:
- constipation lasts more than four days
- the child is in pain
- chronic constipation is suspected.

Skin conditions and infection
One of the main functions of the skin is as a protection against the environment – if the skin becomes broken, then infection can easily enter the body. Skin conditions and infections are fairly common in children and often cause great discomfort and itchiness. It is important that children are kept away from the early years setting if their condition is infectious, because these infections spread very quickly amongst children.

Some of the most common skin conditions and infections are shown in the following table.

Condition and cause	Spread	Recognition of condition	Treatment and care	Possible complications
Scabies *Insect*	Direct contact (the insect burrows under the skin and lays eggs), clothing and towels	Tiny grey swellings appear particularly between the fingers or on the wrist, armpits or sides of feet Intense itching especially at night Waking frequently at night	See a doctor All the family will need treatment with an insecticide lotion Isolate the child	Scratching can also cause impetigo
Cold sore *Herpes simplex virus*	Direct contact Triggers can be: cold weather, the wind, sunlight, or having a cold	Starts as tingling around the mouth Small blisters which form a crust after 1–2 days (these are smaller and more regular than impetigo) Itching	Often disappears on its own Anti-viral cream may be used early on After infection, the virus lays dormant until a 'trigger' restarts the infection Use lip salve in the winter and sun screen in summer	
Impetigo *Bacteria – usually Streptococcus or Staphylococcus*	Contact with other children Break in the skin caused by a cut, insect bite or eczema Chapped lips	Small blisters on the face (often around the mouth and nose) which crust and ooze The area spreads rapidly	Antibiotic cream which needs to be applied using gloves, or medicine Child should be isolated Discourage the child from touching the area Separate towels and flannels should be used Personal hygiene is very important	If untreated it spreads rapidly Can cause generalised infection and septicaemia (blood poisoning)
Wart or verruca *Virus*	Direct contact or from shower floors or swimming pools	Wart: raised lump on the surface of the skin, often on the knees, feet, face and hands Verruca: on the foot the lump is pushed in and can be painful especially during walking	Creams from the chemist Freezing with liquid nitrogen by the doctor Verruca: use rubber socks when swimming, and shoes for PE	It can spread

Condition and cause	Spread	Recognition of condition	Treatment and care	Possible complications
Ringworm *Fungus*	Direct contact from animals, shower trays or soil or from sharing hats or combs	Pink, ring-shaped scaly patch on the skin, usually the trunk, nails, feet, scalp or groin On the scalp it may cause bald patches Itching	An anti-fungal cream from the doctor	
Athletes foot Fungus	Bathroom floor, showers and swimming pools	Itchiness between the toes Sore, cracked skin between the toes	Cream, powder or foot spray from the doctor or chemist Wash and dry carefully between the toes Shoes made of natural fibres and cotton socks prevent the feet from overheating Avoid trainers Separate towels	
Urticaria (nettle rash or hives) *Allergy*	Contact with an allergen, e.g. contact with wool or nylon, biological washing powders or some foods: peanuts, egg, milk chocolate, strawberries, colours or food additives	Smooth raised pale lumps surrounded by a pink area Intense itching The rash may come and go May be widespread or infect a small area	None – calamine lotion may reduce itching Keep the skin cool	Scratching can lead to scarring
Psoriasis *Cause not known but there is a hereditary link*	Psoriasis is not infectious. It can be triggered by throat infections, stress, injury or some drugs	Raised red patches on the skin, covered with silvery scales Any part of the body can be affected, but the most common areas are the elbows, knees, scalp and nails	Moisturising creams and ointments Oils for the bath Sunshine can help	Scratching can lead to infections

Eczema

Eczema affects about one fifth of all school age children. It can start as early as two months and 60–70 per cent of children grow out of it by adulthood.

Characteristics

- A dry, itchy rash which becomes red and starts to weep. In very young children it can affect the face, scalp, trunk and the outside of the arms and legs. In older children it can affect the bends of the elbows and knees, the feet and the hands. The skin can become broken and be raw and bleed
- Itchiness, especially at night

Care of eczema

There is no cure for eczema but there are ways of dealing with the symptoms:

- The use of emollients. These can either be used in the bath (which makes the water oily) or instead of soap or as creams applied directly to the skin. These help prevent water loss from the skin ensuring that it is not so dry and less itchy. They should be applied with clean hands.
- The doctor may prescribe creams. Some of these contain steroids, and should only be used for the child for whom they are prescribed. The carer must ensure their hands are washed carefully after applying this.
- Avoid known irritants such as wool, biological washing powder, grass and jewellery containing nickel.
- Cotton clothes and bedding keep the skin cooler than man-made fabrics.
- Keep children's nails short.
- Cotton mittens can reduce scratching at night for babies.
- Elimination diets can sometimes exclude dietary causes, e.g. dairy products. This must be done with a dietician. Babies should be weaned very slowly and skin reactions observed.
- Ensure that the child doesn't become overheated, especially at night.

Caring for the child with eczema

Each child's eczema is very different and therefore it is important to discuss the child's treatment and care with the parents before coming to the setting. It is also important to keep updated on the child's condition. Some children are unable to touch paint, playdough, sand, clay or even water without causing the eczema to flare up, so it is important to find out from the parents what the child is unable to touch or use. This can potentially restrict the opportunities available for the child, and to ensure equality of opportunity, the early years practitioner needs to be aware of the child's needs and ways of coping with these in the classroom. Below are some suggested strategies.

Potential difficulty	Potential strategy
Contact with soap	Special emollients brought from home
Contact with paint, salt, dough, clay, sand or water	Cotton gloves can be worn or plenty of cream applied first
Swimming	Emollient cream can be applied beforehand. Remind the child to dry properly and then to reapply cream afterwards

Potential difficulty	Potential strategy
Pets	Some children will need to avoid the pet altogether
Becoming hot which will worsen the itching	Seating away from the radiator and windows. Plastic seats may be covered if necessary
Uniform	Children are better having cotton next to their skin
Scratching Lack of concentration due to itching	Distract the child as much as possible Try to avoid telling them not to scratch because it can make them worse or build up resentment Further applications of cream may help
Cooking: children should avoid contact with any food they are allergic to	Use different ingredients for all of the children It is important to know if any of the children has a severe reaction to a food such as anaphylactic shock
Worry over school work, friends or appearance can affect some children's eczema	Encourage the child to talk over any worries with the staff

Think It Over

How could you help to build confidence and self-esteem of a child with eczema within the setting?

Complications

Scratching can cause infections, including impetigo and herpes simplex (see page 382).

Hormonal disorders

Diabetes mellitus

There are two types of diabetes mellitus: childhood diabetes and age onset diabetes. Childhood diabetes is more serious because the body stops making insulin, a hormone which is necessary to enable the body to use and store sugar in the form of glucose properly. Without insulin, glucose cannot be used and passes out of the body in the urine. Before synthetic insulin was produced, many children died from diabetes. All children with diabetes have to have insulin injections for the rest of their lives and will have to watch their diet.

Signs and symptoms

- Excessive thirst
- Tiredness and lack of energy
- Poor appetite
- Weight loss
- Passing urine frequently

Management

The parent, carer and child (depending on the child's age) will be taught how to test the blood for glucose and how to give the injections.

The early years practitioner's role

The early years practitioner needs to have an understanding of the care of a diabetic child. The child's parents (and possibly the carer) will need to do the following with the child:

- Test for glucose in child's blood (a pin prick).
- Record the results.
- Give injections.
- Store and dispose of syringes.
- Manage the child's diet – the dietician will give the parents information on eating a regular and balanced diet.

If, for any reason, the child doesn't eat the correct amount, or has extra exercise or is sick, extra glucose or sugar may occasionally need to be given. It is essential that everyone who is involved in caring for the child knows that the child is diabetic, and what to do if the child has a hypoglycaemia attack, which occurs if the blood sugar level drops suddenly.

Sickle cell disease

Sickle cell disease is an inherited red blood cell disorder. Some children will be born with the disease which will be inherited from both parents, while others may be born with a 'sickle cell trait' which means that they are carriers of the disease. Sickle cell trait cannot turn into the disease and children will be perfectly healthy although some may struggle in high altitudes due to shortage of oxygen.

Sickle cell disease cannot be 'caught'; babies are born with it and will have it for life. In the UK, sickle cell disease is most common in people of African and Caribbean descent. Normal red blood cells are round like doughnuts but sickle red blood cells become hard, sticky and shaped like sickles, which can clog the flow of blood to an area of the body. This can cause pain, damage and anaemia.

Characteristics

Children with sickle cell disease will have episodes of anaemia (low blood counts), pain and increased susceptibility to infections. These are called crises. Some people have crises often whilst others have them only once every few years. In between the crises, the child is usually quite well, although they are more prone to infections. Crises are more likely to happen when there has been a reduction of oxygen in the blood, e.g. after exercise, during anaesthetics, in high altitudes, due to dehydration, during pregnancy and during times of illness with a fever.

Role of the early years practitioner

- Children with sickle cell disease may be absent more frequently because of crises or infections, which may require treatment in a hospital setting.
- Allow the child to drink plenty of water – they may need to keep a water bottle with them. This will necessitate frequent visits to the toilet as their kidneys cannot retain water as well.
- Try and prevent the child from becoming over heated or exposed to cold temperatures.
- Because of their anaemia, children with sickle cell may get tired before others and a rest period may be appropriate.

- Encourage gym and sports participation but allow the child to stop without undue attention.
- Some young children will be on permanent antibiotics to prevent infection.

Those with sickle cell should be treated as normally as possible with an awareness that they may have intermittent episodes of pain, infection or tiredness that can sometimes be prevented through adequate water intake, avoiding temperature extremes and over-doing it.

Medical attention is needed when the following occurs:

- fever
- joint pains
- abdominal pain or swelling
- shortness of breath
- unusual headache
- chest pain
- numbness or weakness
- sudden vision change.

Assessment activity 10.5

Jacob has sickle cell disease and has frequent absences from school due to crises. He is often admitted to hospital. Jacob's brother is in the reception class, and also has sickle cell disease but has very rarely had problems.

- How might the family and child be affected by Jacob's sickle cell disease?
- How may early years practitioners minimise the effects of ill health on the child and family?

Infectious diseases

The table on pages 388–92 offers a quick guide to common childhood diseases.

General care of a child with an infectious illness
- Isolate the child.
- Give paracetamol to reduce the temperature (with parental consent).
- Ensure child drinks plenty of fluids.
- Foods should be soft.
- Allow child to rest as much as they wish.

If the child has an itchy rash:
- keep the nails short – cotton mittens could be used for young children
- discourage the child from scratching, especially on the face – scratching can lead to permanent scarring.

Illness, incubation time, immunisation, method of spread	Signs and symptoms	Call doctor immediately if	Specific treatment/complications
Roseola infantum Viral infection which is very common between 6 months and 2 years and is uncomfortable but not usually serious *Incubation time:* 5–15 days *Method of spread:* droplet infection	• Irritable with an erratic temperature of 39–40°C • Mild diarrhoea • Cough • Enlarged glands in neck • Earache *After 4 days:* • Normal temperature • Rash of tiny distinct pink spots on the back, abdomen and head which lasts for 5 days	• Febrile convulsions • Drowsy or irritable • Rash appears with the fever	• Febrile convulsions Rarely: • Hepatitis • Pneumonia
Mumps Viral infection of salivary glands – not usually serious except in adolescent boys *Incubation time:* 14–24 days *Immunisation:* children can be immunised against mumps at 12–15 months as part of the MMR *Method of spread:* droplet infection	• Generally unwell initially • Fever *After 1–2 days:* • Swelling and pain on one or both sides of the face under the jaw line – lasts for 5 days • Dry mouth • Loss of appetite • Confirm diagnosis with doctor – it is a notifiable disease (see page 401)	• Severe headaches and signs of meningitis • Abdominal pain	• Orchitis (inflammation of the testes) in adolescent boys which very rarely can cause infertility Rarely: • Meningitis • Encephalitis (inflammation of the brain) • Deafness in one ear or both ears

Illness, incubation time, immunisation, method of spread	Signs and symptoms	Call doctor immediately if:	Specific treatment/complications
Chicken pox (varicella) (common in children under 10 years) Can be uncomfortable, and serious in very young babies, children who are HIV positive or taking medications for childhood cancer (and adults, especially pregnant women) *Incubation time:* 11–21 days *Method of spread:* droplet infection	• Rash starts on head and behind the ears • Pink spots turn to blisters which dry and form scabs • Spots often come in crops – new batches appear over a few days • Slight fever and headache • Child may *feel* well • Intense itching	• Coughing • Seizures • Abnormal drowsiness • Unsteady when walking	• Sodium bicarbonate in a cool bath and calamine lotion to relieve itchiness • Keep child cool as warmth makes the spots and itching worse • Dress in loose cotton clothing • Soft food if the mouth is affected • Scarring • Secondary infection from scratching especially impetigo • Pneumonia • Chest infection • Encephalitis
Measles Caused by a virus, is highly infectious and can be serious *Incubation time:* 10–14 days *Immunisation* is available for children at 12–15 months *Method of spread:* droplet infection	• Generally unwell initially • Koplick's spots (blueish white spots) appear on the inside of the cheeks • Temperature, runny nose, red eyes and cough • A flat, blotchy red rash starts behind the ears and on the face, and spreads to the rest of the body • Photophobia (dislike of bright light) – nurse in a slightly darkened room	• Severe headache • Earache • Vomiting • Rapid breathing • Drowsiness • Fits	• Conjunctivitus • Otitis media • Bronchitis • Pneumonia • Encephalitis

Illness, incubation time, immunisation, method of spread	Signs and symptoms	Call doctor immediately if:	Specific treatment/ complications
Erythema infectiosum (Fifth Disease or Slap Face) A viral infection which is very common in young children and is not usually serious *Incubation time:* 4–14 days *Method of spread:* droplet infection	• Bright red cheeks and a pale area around the mouth • Raised temperature *After 1–4 days:* • A blotchy lace-like rash may appear on arms and legs and occasionally on the trunk lasting 7–10 days • Rash may get worse when warm • Child may feel well		• Can be serious if child has sickle cell disease or thatassaemia (hereditary blood disorder)
Rubella (German Measles) A viral infection which causes a mild illness which is not serious (expect to pregnant women: it has serious effects on the unborn child) *Incubation time:* 14–21 days *Immunisation* is available for children at 12–15 months *Method of spread:* droplet infection	• Slight fever and generally slightly unwell • Swollen glands behind the ears and at the back of the neck • Rash of tiny flat pink spots which are not itchy and start on the face and spread to the body and limbs. These only last for a few days	• Joint pain • Any signs of meningitis	• Encephalitis • Can cause serious defects to the foetus if a woman contracts rubella in the first 12–16 weeks of pregnancy • Because the child can be infectious for 5–7 days before the rash develops, inform pregnant women who have had contact with the child

Illness, incubation time, immunisation, method of spread	Signs and symptoms	Call doctor immediately if:	Specific treatment/ complications
Pertussis (whooping cough) A bacterial infection which can be very serious, especially to babies *Incubation time:* 7–10 days *Immunisation* can be given to children at 8, 12 and 16 weeks *Method of spread:* droplet infection	- Slight temperature - Starts like a cold - Bouts of short dry coughing - Long attacks of coughing followed by a whoop (deep intake of breath) - Vomiting - A cough may last for 8–12 weeks	- Child has poor colour grey/blueish/pale - Difficulty in breathing - Baby not feeding - Convulsions	- Consult a doctor immediately - Antibiotics - Sit child up during attack and pat on back - It is a very frightening and exhausting experience so reassure the child and stay close by, especially at night
Meningitis Infection of the lining of the brain and spinal cord – always very serious *Incubation time:* 2–14 days *Method of spread:* There are 3 types: - viral - bacterial - meningococcal *Immunisation:* Hib vaccination can prevent one type of viral meningitis in children under 4 years (see page 369), and there is also a meningitis C vaccine available	Children can develop these signs and become seriously ill very quickly: - Signs of cold/flu initially - Drowsiness - Loss of appetite - Restlessness - Temperature - Nausea or vomiting - Severe headache - Photophobia (dislike of bright lights) - Stiff neck - Joint pains *In the late stages there may also be:* - a rash: flat purple or pink spots which DO NOT fade if pressed*	As soon as meningitis is suspected	- Antibiotics in bacterial meningitis - Will be nursed in hospital - Darkened room - Brain damage - Deafness - Epilepsy - Death

Illness, incubation time, immunisation, method of spread	Signs and symptoms	Call doctor immediately if:
Meningitis *(continued)*	*Babies may also:* • arch their backs • have a shrill cry • have a bulging fontanelle *The rash in meningitis is very distinctive, and can be recognised by doing the glass test: press a glass over the spots. If the rash is due to meningitis, the rash will not fade when pressed, whereas other rashes will.*	

AIDS/HIV infection and AIDS

AIDS (acquired immune deficiency syndrome) is caused by the human immunodeficiency virus (HIV). This virus attacks the immune system which means that the child is prone to infections, such as tonsillitis and ear infections, and lacks the ability to fight them. A child infected with the virus is said to be HIV positive and the advanced stage of the infection is called AIDS. HIV can be acquired by children in the following ways:

- Through the placenta in pregnancy from an untreated infected mother. If the mother has treatment and has a caesarean section, there is a 1 per cent risk of infection to the baby.
- During birth – this is the riskiest time, but delivery by caesarean section reduces the risks.
- During breastfeeding – there is about a 10 per cent risk of passing the virus to the baby.
- Through blood transfusion of infected blood – the risk is minimal now but this was a source of infection in the 1980s.

HIV can also be transmitted by:

- sexual contact with an infected partner through bodily fluids
- through infected blood from sharing contaminated needles or an accidental stab with a contaminated needle.

HIV is spread by infected bodily fluids (vaginal secretions, seminal fluid or breast milk) entering the blood stream via sexual contact, injection or through the mother to her baby. There is no evidence that it can be spread through sweat, urine, faeces or tears and cannot be caught from toilet seats, insect bites, casual contact such as sharing food utensils, touching, from bedding, towels or swimming pools.

Early signs and symptoms
- Swollen glands
- Frequent infections
- Failure to thrive and delay in development
- Lack of energy
- Recurrent diarrhoea

Symptoms might not show for years but children who are born with HIV may show symptoms around the age of two years. There are some children born with the HIV virus who have reached their teens without developing AIDS.

Diagnosis and treatment
A blood test for the virus cannot be done until one to three months after being infected. A number of anti-HIV drugs have been developed which slow the spread of HIV in the body, but cannot cure it.

Key issues – preventing HIV spread in the early years setting

Parents do not have to inform the school or early years setting if their child has HIV. All children should be treated equally and therefore a high standard of hygiene should prevail at all times. Each setting will include a policy for dealing with bodily fluids which includes the following:

- Always wear latex gloves when in contact with bodily fluids.
- Wear gloves when applying first aid to cuts and grazes.
- Cuts and grazes should be kept covered by a waterproof dressing.
- Hands should be washed after contact with spillages (even when gloves are worn).
- Nappies and used gloves should be disposed of in a sealed bag.
- Spillages of blood should be:
  – covered by 1 per cent hypochloride solution
  – wiped over using disposable gloves, and
  – the cloths should be placed in the appropriate bag (yellow) for incineration
  – the area should be washed with warm soapy water.

If someone has accidental contact with a bodily fluid on a cut or graze, wash the area thoroughly with soap and water and encourage the area to bleed.

The impact of ill health on children and families

Ill health can cause stress within the family, especially if it is chronic or life threatening. But even short-term illnesses can cause problems in the family. The effect of the illness on the child and family will depend on:

- whether the child is at school or early years setting
- the child's age and state of development
- the parent(s) work, and whether they would need to take time off to care for the child
- the illness itself, whether it is acute, chronic or life threatening
- the type of treatment
- previous experiences of illness
- how the family cope with the illness and the support they receive
- how often the child is away from school or the early years setting – this may affect their development
- whether the child needs hospitalisation.

The effect on the family of the child's illness

Even a short illness can cause disruption to family life and routine. If the parent works, alternative child care may need to be arranged. Chronic, long-term and life-threatening illnesses may cause the family to make adaptations to many aspects of their lives to meet the needs of the child and other family members. A child's illness may therefore affect the family in the following ways:

- **Physically:** it can be physically demanding to care for an unwell child, especially if any lifting is required. Lack of sleep can also lead to exhaustion.
- **Emotionally:** there is always a multitude of emotions, such as fear, uncertainty, anxiety, insecurity, guilt and depression, which arise when a child is ill, especially when there is a long-term illness, or if hospitalisation is required.
- **Financially:** if a parent has to give up work either temporarily or permanently, it can have huge financial implications on the family. If a child is in hospital, this can also cause more expense.
- **Isolation:** it is often not possible for the parent to have the same contact with friends or work colleagues when a child is ill, and this can cause the parent to feel isolated, especially if the care is very demanding.

An early years practitioner who is caring for an unwell child is also going to be affected in similar ways, and will need to be supported. Parents and carers will need to be given a break from the children and be able to have someone to listen while they talk.

The effect of a child's illness on siblings

When a child is unwell it can upset the routine of other children and can also cause a variety of different emotions to surface, especially if the child is seriously unwell. Siblings often have ambivalent feelings towards each other – they are the best of friends one minute and mortal enemies the next; illness can cause them to feel guilty if they think unkind thoughts about their sibling, and they might also feel that they have caused the illness in some way. Other children might feel jealous of the attention the ill child is getting or feel confused. Siblings may become attention seeking or develop behaviour problems and they therefore need time spent with them by themselves.

Older siblings may be expected to help more in the house and behave more responsibly; as one child explained: 'Just for once, I wish I wasn't the one that my parents say that they can always rely on'. If the child is seriously ill, siblings can worry that their brother or sister may die or that they may also catch the illness. Siblings therefore need time with parents and carers to be able to express these feelings and have the details about their sibling's illness explained in a simple way. They should be included in family discussions and know in advance whether their will be any change to their routine, e.g. who might pick them up from school. It is important that the early yeaars setting knows what is happening at home and any change to the routine, in order that the early years practitioner can support the child appropriately.

The impact of illness on the needs of a child

Children's needs can change when they become unwell. This can be a temporary change, as in an acute illness, or may be a profound change, as in a long-term or life-threatening illness.

Children's physical needs

The child's physical needs will change, often considerably during illness:

- The child's appetite will often decrease and therefore nutritional needs change.
- The child will often need more fluids to drink, especially in acute illnesses.
- The child's need for sleep and rest will usually increase.
- Clothing will need to be appropriate to the child's illness.
- The child may need more help with personal hygiene and have more washes instead of baths.
- The need for warmth and fresh air may change, especially if the child has a temperature.

These physical needs are discussed in further depth below.

Children's social and emotional needs

Children who are unwell need more support from their parents and carer than usual and will need to be cared for by someone they know and trust. Children in hospital cope far better if they have a parent or carer with them, and hospitals cater for this by providing beds and facilities for parents.

In the home environment, sick children need the security of their normal routine to continue as much as possible. Mealtimes and bedtimes should, where possible, continue as normal. It can be very worrying for a child to be ill and young children may not have the right vocabulary to express how they are feeling. Allow children to express their fears, and validate their feelings. There is nothing worse than feeling scared and confused and not being able to talk about it. Some children will become more clingy when unwell and behaviour changes might be noticed in others. They need to be reassured that they are going to get better and that they are still loved. It is often better to make up a bed on a sofa in the sitting room so that the child knows that the carer isn't far away.

If a child is seriously ill, it is usually better to be honest with the child about their condition and explain what is to happen in a clear and simple way. Part of growing up is learning how to deal with frustration, pain and loss. As carers, we can teach children effective ways of handling tough times with honesty and love.

Play is still very important for a child even when ill. When a child is first unwell, they often need to sleep more, but in between periods of sleep and rest the child can quickly become bored and frustrated In hospitals, play workers help children to work through their fears and worries using play. They can also explain what may be involved in their treatment through play.

Friendships can suffer is a child has frequent or prolonged absences from nursery or school. It is important that friends should be encouraged to visit the child, if possible, letter writing, emailing or sending pictures to each other can also help to sustain friendships.

Regression

If emotional needs are not being met, then the child may regress. Regression means that the child reverts back to the behaviour of a younger child. This can happen with any illness and is normal for a short period of time but over longer periods can affect development. It is important to recognise this and provide reassurance, routine, and extra attention.

Signs of regressive behaviour
* Behaviour typical of an earlier age group and refusal to do things that they previously did, e.g. talk, feed or dress themselves
* Plays with toys from an earlier age group
* Excessive crying
* Lack of concentration
* Inability to learn
* Clingy
* Aggressive
* Unusual behaviour such as head banging

Children's cognitive needs

Children who have to be absent from a learning environment for a period of time will lack the stimulation offered by the environment and will also be restricted from learning through observation and imitation of others.

Children often sleep for longer periods when unwell and they aren't interested in much, except perhaps being read to. During recovery, however, they may become bored and frustrated, and require activities which are short and simple, and which require little concentration. Children often play with toys and read books which are suitable for a younger age group when unwell, and the carer needs to play appropriate activities throughout the day.

Activities for children who are unwell

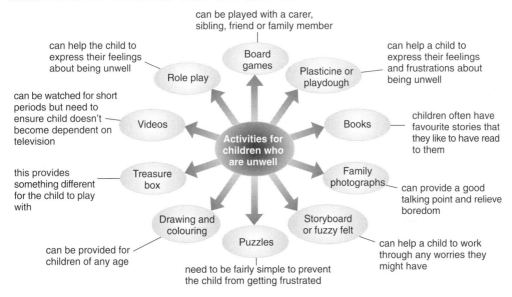

Children who are unwell for some time can miss out on work from school and their learning can then be affected. It is important that children be given the opportunity to have work from school, if appropriate, in order to minimise any disruption to the child's education. In hospital, the play worker may provide activities to help stimulate the child's mind.

Assessment activity 10.6

Jacob has sickle cell disease and has frequent absences from school due to crises. He is often admitted to hospital.

- How might disruption to Jacob's development in his school work be minimised?
- How can the early years practitioner provide for Jacob's social and emotional needs?
- How may Jacob's condition and his frequent absenses from school affect his development, appetite, behaviour, learning, social and emotional needs?

Treatment and care routines for children who are unwell

Different care settings for children who are unwell

The home

Most children who are unwell will be cared for at home because this is the place that can provide them with the security, comforts and attention that they require. At home, a bed can be made up in the sitting room if necessary, so that the child is not far away from the parent or carer. They can have their own toys and comfort objects and have their favourite foods cooked.

The hospital

Occasionally children need to be admitted to hospital but a parent or carer can always stay with the child throughout the stay – it is very frightening for a child to be admitted, especially in an emergency, when there is little time to prepare the child. Many children will have the experience of attending an accident and emergency department. It is useful if children have played 'hospitals' and have read books on hospitals in an early years setting.

If the child is having a planned admission to hospital, the early years practitioner may be able to help prepare the child. Generally, the child should start preparations two weeks before admission. They can visit the hospital and look at booklets or videos that the hospital may produce. The early years practitioner could play hospitals with the child and read books about hospitals. Children get very worried about being in hospital; these worries include being separated from their parents or carers and being left alone. Children have a poor concept of time and even a trip to the toilet will seem a long time. Some children believe that they are being punished and others become acutely anxious. Children who are well prepared for hospital are more likely to co-operate with hospital procedures and have a better recovery rate. The hospital will advise the child on what should be brought in, but the child's comforter and some favourite toys or books are also important.

Hospice

If a child is terminally ill, they may be admitted to a hospice, especially if they have a lot of pain that needs to be controlled.

Caring for the child who is unwell

Children who are unwell, in whatever setting, need extra care and attention; they will need reassurance and more attention than usual. If a child becomes unwell in the early years setting, it is important that they are removed from the other children and have a place to rest with an adult nearby. If they are  feeling sick they need a bucket and easy access to a toilet. The parent should be called straight away because it is unfair for the child to be kept at the setting and there is also a greater chance of other children catching an infectious illness.

Caring for the child's physical needs

Warmth

Children will need to be kept in a warm but well-ventilated room; if infectious, the child will need to be isolated from other children, but children will often prefer to be cared for in the sitting room on the sofa rather than in their own bedroom.

Food and drink

Children are often not very hungry when unwell but it is not generally a problem if they are drinking plenty of fluids. Food doesn't always taste the same as usual so it is important that the food is nutritious and presented in small appetising portions. However, it is far better to allow the child to have a favourite food than eating nothing at all! Food such as ice cream, fromage frais, toast and marmite, puréed fruit, eggs, ice lollies (made with fruit juice) will all provide the child with some energy and also with vital nutrients. It is often better to offer regular snacks when a child is unwell.

It is very important that the child drinks frequently whilst unwell to prevent dehydration (see page 379). It is better to offer a child their favourite drink, but drinks which are high in vitamin C, such a diluted orange juice or squashes, are ideal and will help the child fight infection. To encourage a child to drink, use a special cup with a straw, or make ice lollies or flavoured ice cubes from fruit juice and water; these should be offered at least every hour.

Personal hygiene
It is important that the child's normal hygiene routine continues although washes may be more acceptable than a bath; hair brushing and teeth brushing should continue as normal although this may also be done after a child has been sick. The child will need to wash their hands frequently especially if they have an infectious illness.

The carer must also ensure that they provide a good role model and take the following precautions:

- Wash hands after contact with the child's bedding, tissues, clothing and bodily fluids.
- Wear gloves if in contact with bodily fluids.
- If the child has an accident, use gloves and cover the area with a bleach solution (consult the setting's policies), wipe over the area with disposable towels which should be disposed of according to the setting's policy and then wash the area with soapy water.
- Use tissues instead of hankies and dispose of them into a bag.
- Ensure that the room is warm but well ventilated in order to disperse germs.
- Wash the child's bedding on a high heat to destroy germs.
- The child may need their own towel, especially if they have an infectious skin condition.
- Toys should be washed thoroughly.
- If a child has sickness or diarrhoea, cover their bed sheet/sofa with soft towels, because these are easy to wash on a high heat.
- Children are more likely to wet the bed when unwell, so you may need to use a mattress protector.

Rest and sleep
Most children require more sleep when they are unwell, giving the body time to recover. Children should therefore be encouraged to rest wherever they feel comfortable and be given quiet and simple activities to do.

Control of the child's temperature
When a child has an infection the body temperature is raised in order to fight the infection. The normal body temperature of a child is 36.5–37°C, and will vary throughout the day, often being higher in the evening, after exercise and bathing, and in hot weather. Babies, who have a very immature temperature regulating mechanism, can show large fluctuations in temperature and can develop high temperatures very quickly.

The termperature is usually taken under the armpit or by using a fever strip on the forehead in young children and babies. The temperature will be 0.5°C lower than if taken by mouth.

Thermometers
There are four different types of thermometer which can be used:

- A digital thermometer is unbreakable, easy to read, accurate and fairly quick to use.

- A mercury thermometer can be hazardous if made of glass because it contains mercury, which emits fumes if the glass is broken. It is accurate and cheap but is difficult to read and should never be placed in a child's mouth.
- A fever strip is not as accurate as other methods but is cheap and very easy to use by placing the strip onto the child's forehead. The strip changes colour and shows the temperature of the child.
- An infrared thermal scanning thermometer is very accurate and it only takes a few seconds when it is placed in the ear to take reading. It is expensive but very easy to use on children.

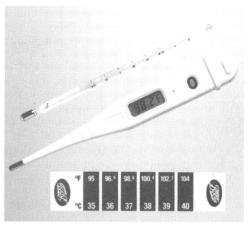

A clinical thermometer, a digital thermometer and a temperature strip

Key issues – taking a child's temperature

It is important that you note down the child's temperature so that you can inform the parent (or GP, if necessary).

- Ensure that the thermometer is cleaned and collect a book or toy to distract the child.
- Explain to the child what you are going to do. Try it on teddy first if the child is anxious.
- Shake a mercury thermometer until the mercury is at its lowest point.
- Sit the child down.
- Place the thermometer under the child's arm, ensuring that the bulb is directly in the armpit. Hold it in place.
- When the readings have stopped changing or the digital thermometer bleeps, record the temperature.
- Clean the thermometer and put it out of reach.
- Inform the parents if there has been a big change in the reading.

Care of a child with a temperature

A high temperature can cause febrile convulsions (see below); therefore the child should be cooled if the temperature exceeds 37.5°C:

- Maintain room temperature at 15°C (60°F) and remove clothing down to the underwear
- Offer sips of cool drink regularly.
- With parent's permission, paracetamol syrup (e.g. Calpol) can be given to children over three months (see Giving medicine, page 402).
- Fan the child.
- If the temperature is over 38.5°C, tepid sponging can be done – dip a sponge into lukewarm water, and sponge over the child's skin but do not dry. Repeat until the temperature falls below 38.5°C. The temperature should not fall too quickly because it can cause shock. *Never* use cold water.

Febrile convulsions

These can occur in children of six months to five years due to a rise in temperature. Children who have had a convulsion have an increased risk of further convulsions. It is frightening dealing with this and it is important to know whether the child has a history of convulsions (see Unit 4 page 115).

Who to contact when a child is unwell

Generally, it is not advisable to have children who are unwell at an early years setting. The following may be contacted when a child is unwell.

The parent/guardian

The parent should be informed if the child becomes unwell, has an accident or if their condition changes whilst in your care.

The general practitioner (GP)

Occasionally it may be necessary to contact the child's GP if the carer is unable to contact the parent and is concerned about the child's condition.

The emergency services

In an emergency call 999 (or 112) for an ambulance and be ready to answer some questions about the child and about the signs and symptoms. The parent would need to be informed and the child's key worker, first aider or head teacher may accompany the child from an early years setting.

It will depend on the setting as to who will contact the above.

- **Home setting**: if caring for a child at home, the early years practitioner will generally contact the parents initially when concerned about a child. It may occasionally be necessary to contact other services in an emergency situation.
- **Nursery setting**: the child's key worker will initially be informed if a child is unwell, but it will generally be the manager's responsibility to call parents and other services if necessary.
- **School setting**: the first aider will generally care for a child initially, but it will usually be the head teacher who will call parents in a primary school.

Records of a child's health

If you are caring for a child in their own home, it is good practice to ensure that you record any change in a child's health and any medication which you have been requested to give. In all other settings, it is important to keep accurate records of the following:

Key issues – recording children's medical history

- The name, age and address of child
- Parent(s) or guardian's contact numbers – at home and at work
- Two further contact names and their telephone numbers
- The GP's name, address and telephone number
- Long-term illnesses, allergies, conditions or operations
- Medication
- Special diet
- Difficulties with hearing, speech or vision and whether glasses are worn
- Immunisations

These records of a child's health are confidential, and should only be seen by those who really need to know. Parents might not want some information to be disclosed in case the child is treated differently. This does mean that you might not know if a child has an infectious condition, such as hepatitis or HIV. It is also very important that the carer does not discuss the contents of the record sheet with anyone else. Records should be kept in a locked cupboard and be updated regularly, usually manually.

When caring for a child at home, the carer needs to make records of the child's illness in order to show the parents, or doctor, if necessary. These need to contain:

- the child's temperature
- date and time of any medication given
- any changes in the child's condition, e.g. if the child develops an earache or a rash.

If the carer becomes concerned about a child's condition they should always contact the child's parents and/or seek medical assistance.

Record of medicines

Children often need medicine when unwell, but medicines are potentially dangerous and therefore great care should be taken in their giving and storage. Each early years setting will have a policy on this, and will require the parent to complete a form before any medicine can be given in the setting. If you are caring for a child at home, the parent should record all instructions for medicines. In most settings the first aider gives medicine. If you are caring for a child at home you must get permission from the parent before giving medicine.

Giving medicine

Children under the age of twelve years are usually supplied with medicines in syrup form which are flavoured and often sugar free. They are supplied with a 5ml spoon or a syringe (for babies and young children). Most children are happy to take their medicine, but some are not so eager! Try offering their favourite drink afterwards, making it into a game or if the taste is a problem, the child's parent could talk to the doctor about changing the flavour.

Key issues – giving medicines to children

- Before giving medicine ensure you know the reason for the medicine, the dosage, storage (some medication needs to be stored in the fridge), side effects and whether it should be given before or after food.
- Read the label on the medicine to ensure that it is the correct one.
- Check the dose and the time that the medicine should be given.
- If you are giving a medicine from the pharmacist such as paracetamol, check that the dose you have been asked to give matches the instructions provided.
- Check the expiry date.
- Wash hands.
- Shake the bottle if necessary.
- Always use the measure that is provided with the medicine (teaspoons are not equivalent to 5ml measure).
- Explain to the child about the medicine and sit the child down, preferably on the carer's knee.

- Pour medicines from the bottle with the label facing upwards, to prevent drips ruining the label.
- If using syringe, point this towards the inside of the cheek and give slowly to prevent choking.
- Ensure the child takes the full dose – medicine should never be added to drinks because the full dose might not be given.
- Give the child a drink after taking the medicine.
- Store the medicine correctly according to instructions.
- Record the date and time that you gave the medicine.
- For a baby, sterilise the syringe.
- If a child develops a side effect, such as a rash or diarrhoea, the GP needs to be informed before the next dose is given.
- It is important, when taking antibiotics, that the course is finished even if the child appears to get better, otherwise infection might reappear.

Storage of medicines

The Control of Substances Hazardous to Health Regulations 1994 (COSHH) require medicines to be in a locked cupboard out of the reach of children in an early years setting. Inhalers (which need to be easily accessible), and medicines which need to be in a locked fridge are the exception to this. It is important in a home setting that medicines are kept out of reach of children. Children can very quickly find an open medication, including those with a childproof lid – these only delay a child for a few seconds. Care must be taken never to keep any medicines in a handbag because children find these very quickly.

Assessment activity 10.7

You are caring for Michael and Sophie in the home setting. Sophie is an active and inquisitive two-year-old and Michael, who is four, is feeling very unwell with tonsillitis.
- Plan a routine for one day for both children, including your role in caring for Michael.
- Michael is to be admitted to hospital in two weeks to have his tonsils out. What might the early years practitioner's role be over the next two weeks and on admission to hospital?

End-of-unit test

1 What different types of health are there?
2 What is the early years practitioner's role in promoting health to children?
3 What environmental factors can affect health?
4 Name three different types of micro-organism and give three characteristics of each.
5 Name five different ways in which infections can be spread.
6 Which immunisations are given at two, three and four months and when is MMR given?
7 Why is it important to screen children's health and development? Give two ways this can be done.
8 What six signs indicate that a child is unwell?

9   What are the signs and symptoms of meningitis?

10   What could trigger an asthma attack and how should you deal with this?

11   What preventative measures can be taken in the setting to prevent gastroenteritis?

12   What signs indicate dehydration in a baby and how would you deal with this?

13   What is the normal temperature of a child and how would you reduce the temperature if it were high?

14   What would you do if a child had a febrile convulsion?

15   What information needs to be included in a child's health records?

16   Where should medicines be stored?

Play and learning activities

Introduction

Play is essential to all children's development and acts as a natural learning medium. Through play children develop skills, language and learn about their immediate environment and those in it. This unit will help you to develop an understanding of benefits of play and your role in maximising those potential benefits.

What you need to learn

- Play activities and learning experiences
- Individual learning plans
- Areas of early childhood development
- Evaluation

Play activities and learning experiences

Stages of play

The way in which children engage in play changes as they develop new skills and learn how to relate to others. Play begins early on in life. A young baby enjoys being played with and quickly learns how to smile and gain the attention of adults. By eight months, most babies are starting to enjoy peek-a-boo and will even initiate this type of play by pulling something over their faces. The way in which children are gradually able to play together with children of their own age suggests that there are social stages to play. These were recorded by Mildred Parten in 1932 and are still referred to today. Note that the age guide in the table below has to be considered as very approximate and that although most older children are capable of social activity, there will be times when they wish to play alone.

Age	Activity	Description
0-2 years	Solitary activity (or play)	Babies and toddlers spend time playing 'in their own world'. Babies for example may spend time touching, feeling and talking to their toes
2-4 years	Parallel activity (or play)	Children are beginning to notice other children and may play alongside each other. They may also imitate each other's play. Gradually children then become more and more involved in each other's play
4-7 years	Social activity (also known as co-operative play)	Children are able to play co-operatively together. They can decide how they want to play and make up rules for their play. They can also play complex games that require turn taking

The links between stages of development and play

The speed at which children's play becomes more social and sophisticated depends on their overall development and so adults need to be able to observe children playing in order to assess their play needs.

The table below shows the stages of play and development that most children show, although it should only be used as a broad guide.

Age	Stage of development	Social stages of play	Features of play	Examples of resources/ equipment
0-6 months	During this period, babies gain some control over their limbs. They learn about communication by cooing and babbling	**Solitary play** Babies enjoy playing with adults and older children, but also play and 'talk' by themselves	Senses are used to gain pleasure and explore Repetitive actions are used	Baby gyms Rattles
6-12 months	Most babies become mobile in this time. Babies are learning to gain adult attention by smiling, babbling and towards 12 months pointing	**Solitary play** although babies often show things to adults and initiate movements which will gain adult responses, e.g. dropping a toy on the floor	Senses are still being used. Play is repetitive and exploratory	Activity quilts balls, books, pop-up toys
1-2 years	Toddlers are mobile and gaining gross and fine manipulative skills. They can feed themselves and can stack bricks and manage very simple puzzles Language is just developing with first words emerging at 12-14 months. By 2 years many children are beginning to put two words together Children are very reliant on adults and want to be close to adults	**Solitary play** Most activity is still likely to be solitary	Trial and error learning Repetitive movements and play Toddlers 'talk'to toys Imaginative play is developing	Push and pull toys, dolls, trolleys
2-3 years	Children's overall co-ordination is becoming developed, although strength is often lacking. Many new words are learnt. Sentences are short, e.g. three words and not always understood by others Children often need adult	**Parallel play** Children begin to notice other children playing and will happily play alongside other children	Children enjoy imaginative play and imitate adult gestures, words and movements. Children may take each other's toys and equipment Sensory play is	Dressing up clothes Props used in the home, e.g. tea sets, telephones Water, sand, paint and dough

Age	Stage of development	Social stages of play	Features of play	Examples of resources/ equipment
	to support their play and to help organise games		also enjoyed, e.g. water, sand Play can be repetitive with children gaining mastery of their movements	
3–4 years	Children are usually confident at this age. Most children are well co-ordinated and are able to snip/cut with scissors, run and partly dress themselves They feel grown up as they are usually out of nappies Language is usually understood by others and by 4 years, speech has become fairly fluent Children require significant adult support	Parallel/co-operative play The way in which children play is usually determined by their level of confidence and language skills	Play is often imaginative play with children enjoying alongside or with others. Children also enjoy physical activities such as riding tricycles and climbing. Some play is beginning to be more planned, e.g. a child may tell an adult that they are making a house out of bricks	Small world play, e.g. farm animals, train sets Dressing up clothes and home props Water, sand, paint and dough
4–6 years	Friendships are beginning to be formed Single sex groups are not unusual Language is usually fluent with only minor errors Physically children are well co-ordinated Children often require adult support and help	Co-operative play Children are able to play together, share equipment and respond to each others' play	Imaginative play remains important for some children, although other children are more interested in games involving physical skills such as football, riding bicycles or making things, e.g. construction toys	Climbing frames, bicycles Drawing and painting Construction toys Creative materials
6 years+	Friendships are important to children Children are starting to see others' points of view and can negotiate Children are becoming increasingly independent	Co-operative play	Children begin to have strong play preferences, e.g. some children enjoy making things whilst others may enjoy physical games	Very dependent on children's preferences – creative materials, board games, complex construction toys, footballs, climbing frames, hoops, dressing up clothes

Assessment activity 11.1

Carry out the following structured observation using free description (see page 418). Observe two children of different ages playing with the same piece of equipment, i.e. give a football to a child of twelve months and then later to a child of four years.

- Analyse the differences in the way in which the children have played.
- Evaluate the extent to which their play links to their stages of development.
- Consider ways in which their play links to theories of child development.

Types of play

Play can be grouped into types, although remember that for children play is simply play! Categorising play into types helps practitioners to plan effectively as each play type has particular developmental benefits. Categories of play can vary from setting to setting, but in this unit play has been grouped into the following types:

- imaginative play
- creative and sensory play
- vigorous physical play.

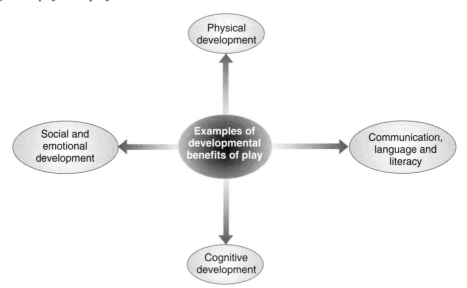

Imaginative play

This type of play is also referred to as 'pretend play' or 'role play'. It particularly stimulates children's language as at first they talk to themselves and later talk to each other. The language used often reflects the language that they have heard with children sometimes using imaginative play to make sense of situations that they have encountered.

Physical development
- Development of fine manipulative movements and hand-eye co-ordination, e.g. pretending to pour drinks
- Development of gross motor skills during play, e.g. pretending to go shopping by getting on a tricycle

Communication, language and literacy
- Development and awareness of social language, e.g. children 'practice' intonation, vocabulary that they have heard and expressions
- Development and awareness of non-verbal communication, e.g. children use facial expressions and hand gestures
- Interest in 'writing' as some children begin to write as part of their play, e.g. writing out a shopping list, calling the register

Cognitive development
- Imaginative play is often used by children as a way of interpreting the 'adult world', e.g. children often practise using 'numbers' in their play
- Development of problem-solving skills, e.g. a child may turn a table into a bed to suit their play needs or look for ways of making a blanket from a coat.

Social and emotional development
- Development and rehearsal of social conventions, e.g. children practise 'how to behave' and often act out the consequences of not behaving
- Understanding of gender and social roles. Children as part of trying to make sense of their world and their role in it, try to explore gender and adult roles through their role play
- Development and exploration of friendships
- Enjoyment and freedom, e.g. by creating their own world, children can feel 'released' from the world of adult expectations

Changes in the way children play
As children's language, cognitive and social skills develop, the way in which they engage in imaginative play also changes. At first, play is quite repetitive and simple. A child may offer an adult a 'pretend' cup of tea or wrap up a teddy and put it to bed. The same actions may be repeated with little dialogue.

As children get older, however, imaginative play becomes more complex and involved. Children begin to create worlds, characters and actual roles. In small world play, e.g. play people, farm animals, Fisher Price people, children will name and talk about each character and will take a 'directing role'. This type of imaginative play is slightly different in nature to 'role play' when children take on the roles themselves. By four years old, many children are together 'planning' their imaginative play, assigning each other 'scripts' and even devising endings. They increasingly show problem-solving skills as they 'convert' a climbing frame into a house or look around for materials as props. Later, many school-age children develop their play further by acting out 'set plays'.

Resources for imaginative play
Imaginative play is seen as important for children's development. Many settings provide a range of materials to support this type of play – see table below. In home settings, children often use 'real' props rather than ones specifically made. A feature of this type of play is the way in which children are adept at making one object stand for another, e.g. a box becomes a car or a piece of dough becomes a cake. They also adapt environments to suit their play purposes, e.g. a bench outdoors becomes the garage whilst the tricycle becomes a car.

Role play	Small world play
Materials for home corner, e.g. tea set, cooking utensils, bed, cooker, pushchairs, dolls and teddies, etc. Dressing up clothes Materials for a shop or office, e.g. cash till, shopping bags, type writer, note pad	Duplo people, animals Fisher Price people Playmobil people Farm animals

Creative play

Creative play is a broad heading to encompass materials and play that encourage children to express themselves. It is important to differentiate between creative play and activities which are adult led and result in children making things to a set formula. Creative play should allow children to be expressive and to bring to their play an interpretation of their own ideas, e.g. they may choose to paint but will not necessarily use the 'proper' colours. Another key feature of creative play is that it does not have to have a definite purpose or end product – only the purpose that the child ascribes it. For example, a three-year-old may enjoy the texture of ribbons and laces and may choose to stick different pieces onto a piece of paper.

Opportunities for creative play

Many settings provide varied opportunities for creative play. To maximise learning opportunities for creative play, it is important that wherever possible, children are provided with a varied range of resources, as shown in the following table and are encouraged to explore the materials freely.

Type of creative play	Features	Resources
Collage	Children from as young as 2 years enjoy selecting and feeling different textures and finally sticking them	Glue, selection of paper, fabrics, laces, ribbons, buttons, feathers, newspaper, magazines
Painting	Most children enjoy painting and printing with brushes, rollers, sponges and also with their hands	Selection of paints, large brushes, rollers, fine brushes
Musical instruments	Children love to use musical instruments and can quickly learn to identify a beat or rhythm. Exploring the sounds of instruments helps children's auditory discrimination	Homemade shakers and rattles, a selection of untuned percussion instruments such as tambours, drums and rattles. Tuned percussion instruments such as xylophone, chime bars
Junk modelling	From a selection of paper, boxes and other materials, children enjoy creating 3D models	Wide selection of interesting textures and materials which might include boxes, bubble wrap, corks, plastic lids, matchsticks, straws, tubing
Drawing and mark making	Early drawing and mark making forms part of the process of learning to write and communicate through symbols	Selection of paper, type writer, crayons, charcoals, pastels, felt tips, board markers, rubbers, etc.

Sensory play

Sensory play is sometimes referred to as 'play with natural materials'. It includes traditional nursery activities such as sand, water and malleable materials like dough. Sensory play has the capacity to hold some children's attention for long periods of time as the sensory nature of the materials seems to help them to focus. It is not unusual for quite sociable children to prefer to play in parallel with sensory activities, e.g. two four-year-olds may stand side to side at a sand tray and whilst looking occasionally across at each other may not actually play together.

Opportunities for sensory play

Most early years settings aim to provide for at least one type of sensory play. The equipment that is put out often shapes how children will use the materials, e.g. dough with scissors as opposed to dough with moulds and rollers. Some examples are given in the table.

Type of sensory play	Features	Examples of resources – these are usually rotated to encourage children to play in a variety of ways
Sand	Sand can be provided in walk-in large pits, free standing trays or also in small trays on tables. Children tend to spend time scooping, digging and shaping sand, although the dampness of sand will affect the way that they will play	Equipment for scooping and pouring, e.g. spoons, spades, bottles, egg cups Toys with wheels, e.g. trucks Animals, e.g. dinosaurs, farm animals Objects for hiding, e.g. shells, beads, 'treasure' Equipment for printing and making sand castles
Water	Water is usually provided in large trays. Children tend to enjoy changes in the water tray, e.g. inclusion of ice cubes, bubbles or coloured water	Items for floating, e.g. boats, corks, ducks Toys for 'washing' dolls clothes, dolls, plastic animals Equipment for pouring and scooping, e.g. beakers, bottles, tubes, funnels
Dough, plasticine and clay	Dough is used for children to model with as well as to pound and cut. Dough is versatile as there are many recipes which provide different textures	Tools, e.g. cutters, rollers, scissors Moulds Plates, cake tins to encourage children to make items for their role play
Gloop	Gloop is cornflour combined with water. It forms a runny paste	Trays and spoons although many children simply use their hands

Vigorous physical play

Most children enjoy running, climbing and balancing. This type of play is called vigorous physical play because it encourages children to use their whole bodies and take exercise in a natural way. Many settings will provide for this type of play outdoors, although it is possible to create opportunities indoors.

Opportunities for vigorous physical play
Where possible, children should be able to engage in this type of play freely, but more often 'set' times are used. This can create problems such as children all wishing to use the same pieces of equipment or children reacting to sudden 'freedom'. For some settings this is unavoidable, but it is good practice to look for ways of integrating physical play rather than seeing it as separate.

Combining play types

As children do not see play in terms of 'types', they tend to combine play materials to support their ongoing play. The climbing frame may become the house, dough may be used to make cakes for the home corner or farm animals may need to go for a swim in the water tray! Insisting that play materials can only be used in a certain way or have to remain in certain places generally inhibits children's learning experiences and creativity. It is good practice therefore for settings to be as flexible as possible and, unless materials or equipment are likely to be damaged, to try and allow children to combine materials.

Planning and preparation

Providing for children's play requires good organisation to ensure that there is sufficient materials, equipment and support to meet the needs of all children. This means that nearly all settings have some form of formal planning system in place, although the extent and type of plans can vary enormously.

Planning for the early years curricula

In the UK, at the time of writing, there are three early years frameworks in place: Foundation Stage curriculum in England, Desirable Outcomes in Wales and Play Framework in Scotland. Settings in receipt of government funding need to show that they are implementing the curriculum in their country.

School settings working with children aged six years and above in the UK have to plan using the country's National Curriculum.

Thematic and non-thematic frameworks

Many settings choose to deliver part or all of the curriculum using themes. The idea behind themes is that play and learning activities are interlinked and that children benefit from a cohesiveness. There are hundreds of popular themes including 'myself', 'growing' and 'colours'. It is generally accepted that 'themes' are not really appropriate with babies and very young children, although many settings working with children over 3 years tend to have some type of theme. There are criticisms as well as advantages of using themes in planning. These are outlined below in the table.

Advantages	Potential disadvantages
Provides cohesiveness in play and learning Enthuses children to learn about particular topics Helps staff remain focused and motivated Can provide a way of involving parents and even the community	Can be difficult to tie in all areas of the curriculum into the theme – this can result in 'false' or contrived links The play needs and interests of all children may not be met The theme may act as a restriction and staff may not put out certain activities because 'they do not link to the theme' May lead to an adult-led rather than a child-led curriculum

Types of planning

There are several types of planning and as this changes from setting to setting, it will be important to find out the type of planning that your setting uses. Good plans are based on correct assessment of children's stages of development and interests.

Long-term planning

The length of long-term plans varies incredibly. Some settings view a long-term plan as anything over 6 weeks, whilst in school settings it usually refers to a full academic year's work.

Common features of long-term plans
- Outline how curriculum is to be delivered
- Consider the themes that are to be used over the period

Medium-term plans

Medium-term plans are in some settings called curriculum plans. The length of a medium-term plan depends on the long-term plan. In some schools a medium-term plan shows coverage for half a term, whilst in some pre-school settings it shows coverage for a fortnight or a month.

Common features of medium-term plans
- Detail types of activities to be offered
- Show how the activities link to the early years or National Curriculum
- Indicate the order in which the activities are to be carried out
- Show learning outcomes

Short-term plans

Settings that plan for a month may also have short-term plans which show what is to happen each week or each session. Settings may refer to these type of plans as 'session planners' or 'weekly planners'.

Common features of short-term plans
- Details of staffing and resources
- Order of activities to be carried out
- Details of how individual activities may be adapted or extended to suit particular children
- Show learning outcomes for activities
- May show which activities are to be assessed
- Detail the role of the adult in supporting specific children

Activity plans

These can be referred to as detailed activity plans or even in schools lesson plans. Short-term plans are not used in every setting, but tend to be used by students to help them show that they can plan a single activity effectively.

Common features of an activity plan
- Shows resources
- Shows staffing
- Has specific learning outcomes
- Demonstrates how needs of individual children will be met
- Details the role of the adult

Curriculum planning

A curriculum can be thought of as a programme of activities or learning outcomes. Some settings plan an overall curriculum, which may be based on areas of development or on areas of learning from the curriculum they are following. Other settings may produce a separate curriculum plan for each area of learning or subject, i.e. some schools have a curriculum plan for literacy, another one for mathematics, etc.

Structured play and free play

Structured play is sometimes the term used when adult involvement is an essential part of an activity, e.g. planting bulbs. In recent early years curricula documents, the terms 'adult-directed activity' or 'adult-initiated activity' are often used instead of 'structured play'. These terms reflect the growing view that if play is highly structured, it is unlikely to be in essence 'play' as play by its nature should emanate from the child.

There are many advantages of structured play or adult-directed activities. If sensitively led, they can support specific areas of a child's development or enable coverage of a particular area of the curriculum. An adult, for example, may put ice cubes in the water tray and ask a group of children to observe and play with the cubes to see if they float or sink. This activity would help children to notice the properties of ice and through the activity they may learn specific vocabulary.

In contrast, free play is play that is completely chosen by the child and relies on children's interests, hence the growing trend to call this type of play 'child initiated' or 'child led'. There are many advantages to this type of play as children are able to spend time following their own interests and set their own challenges.

Most settings aim to provide a mix of play opportunities, some of which would be considered as structured play whilst others as free play. The table below shows the advantages of structured and free play.

Free play or child initiated activities		Structured play or adult directed activities	
Advantages	Disadvantages	Advantages	Disadvantages
+ Children can set their own goals + Children concentrate for longer periods when play is self chosen + Children are more likely to be creative + Child-initiated activities are less pressurised as the child is responsible + Children learn how to choose + Children can gain in confidence by being self-reliant + Children can repeat activities until they feel they have mastered them	– Children may not gain specific language or may choose not to engage in co-operative play – Sometimes child-initiated play can be repetitive and not challenge the child – Child-initiated play can be stereotypical – Some children find it hard to cope with choice – Children may not get a range of skills – Children with learning difficulties may not receive sufficient adult input	+ Coverage of the curriculum is insured + Children can gain specific vocabulary and skills + Areas of the curriculum such as mathematics need to be delivered sequentially in schools	– Children's attention span is shorter during adult-directed activities – Children may feel that they have failed if the adult's expectations are too high – Activities may not be sufficiently challenging or creative

Combining free and structured play

As both child-initiated play and activities involving adults have advantages, there is a growing trend towards combining both ways of working with children. The Foundation Stage curriculum advocates play as a vehicle for learning, but gives practitioners a vital role. To achieve this way of working, many settings now look for a combined approach as illustrated by the case study below.

Case Study

Anna, an early years practitioner, wants to encourage several children who are four years old to practise their sorting skills as part of delivering the mathematical development area of learning within the Foundation Stage. She puts out a large tray of buttons on a table. Two children come and start playing and touching the buttons. Anna asks them to show her their favourite buttons. She gives each child a small box to put their favourite buttons in. As the children show her their favourite buttons, she comments on them, 'This one is shiny. This one has four holes'. She then asks the children if they could find her some black buttons with four holes. After three or four minutes, Anna leaves them to carry on playing. The children make up their own sorting game using the small boxes that Anna has left.

Evaluate the effectiveness of this approach to learning by considering the following questions:

- How has the early years curriculum been implemented?
- How are the children learning through play?
- How is the practitioner able to meet individual children's needs and interests?
- How did the practitioner's intervention extend the children's skills and language development?

Differentiating the curriculum to meet children's needs

Within the planning process, play and learning experiences need to match children's needs. Experienced practitioners choose activities and resources that will allow the curriculum to be differentiated, e.g. one child may simply observe and play with ice cubes in the water, whilst another may be asked if they could find a way of keeping the ice cube from floating.

Encompassing diversity

In the planning process, thought has to be given to what has been dubbed the 'hidden curriculum' or underlying messages that children will be learning besides the ones intended. Are the activities in any way discriminatory? Will the activities help children to take a positive view of the differences in others and around them? Are the activities reinforcing undesirable stereotypes? These key questions should be at the forefront of practitioners' minds when planning and evaluating programmes.

Note that the Foundation Stage curriculum reflects the growing sentiment that before children can learn about the cultures and beliefs of others, they should feel secure about their own background and values and that by 'doing' major festivals that are not part of a child's life actually devalues and trivialises them as a young children cannot conceive of things beyond their own world. This represents a major change in thinking as early years settings have previously been encouraged to celebrate a variety of religious festivals outside of their immediate experience.

Factors for consideration

There are a range of factors that will influence the effectiveness of play and learning activities – see diagram below. By planning ahead, settings avoid confusion, duplication of activities and are able to check that sufficient resources are available.

Assessment activity 11.2

In order to carry out this assessment activity fully, you should gain the advice and permission of your placement supervisor.

- Produce an overall curriculum plan for at least six weeks showing a range of play activities that would be suitable for your placement setting.
- Choose five activities from the curriculum plan and produce activity plans for each of them.
- Implement the activity plans, keeping notes for later evaluation (see Assessment activity 11.4).

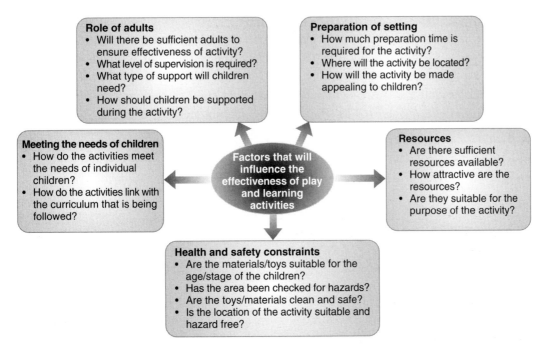

Role of adults
- Will there be sufficient adults to ensure effectiveness of activity?
- What level of supervision is required?
- What type of support will children need?
- How should children be supported during the activity?

Preparation of setting
- How much preparation time is required for the activity?
- Where will the activity be located?
- How will the activity be made appealing to children?

Meeting the needs of children
- How do the activities meet the needs of individual children?
- How do the activities link with the curriculum that is being followed?

Resources
- Are there sufficient resources available?
- How attractive are the resources?
- Are they suitable for the purpose of the activity?

Factors that will influence the effectiveness of play and learning activities

Health and safety constraints
- Are the materials/toys suitable for the age/stage of the children?
- Has the area been checked for hazards?
- Are the toys/materials clean and safe?
- Is the location of the activity suitable and hazard free?

Your curriculum plan should contain:
- a detailed rationale for the play activities chosen which considers the potential learning benefits from the plan
- detailed links between the early years or National Curriculum and the curriculum plan.

Each activity plan should contain:
- an explanation of how the activity is to be implemented
- an examination of the role of the adult in extending children's learning during the activity
- an exploration of the factors that might affect the success of the activity
- detailed links between the activities chosen and the stages of development of the children
- analysis of the potential developmental benefits of each activity
- detailed links between the play activities chosen and either the early years curriculum or the National Curriculum.

Individual learning plans

During the planning process, practitioners need to consider the individual needs of children and ensure that play opportunities will encourage their overall development. Many settings, particularly those working with babies and toddlers, produce outline plans that identify the needs of children and give strategies for meeting the needs. These types of plans can be known as individual learning plans or play plans.

Development of assessment and plans

The starting point for individual learning plans is the child. This means that practitioners begin the process of drawing up an individual learning plan or play plan by assessing the child's development, interests and needs.

Ways of assessing children

There are several methods that can be used to assess children's development. Ideally, a range of methods should be used to gain a full picture of the child although this in practice rarely happens as most settings find it hard to release one member of staff to carry out observations. It is also important to look at children in a range of situations, i.e. in group situations as well as when they are playing alone or with one other child.

Some settings also use commercially devised programmes or since the advent of the Foundation Stage in England use a scheme devised by the early years team in their area.

The table below briefly describes various observation methods but see pages 353–8 for a fuller description.

Method	Key features	Comments
Free description – also known as Specimen record Narrative record	The observer records whatever they see Simple, flexible method	This method allows the observer to be spontaneous as no special equipment or planning is required This method is particularly prone to observer bias as the observer has to choose while they are working what they wish to focus on
Time sample	Observer notes down what child is doing at regular intervals More than one child can be observed at a time	This method allows the observer to record a child over a period of time and build up a picture of what the child does
Event sample	Observer looks out for and records particular behaviours or responses, e.g. every time a child interacts with an adult	This method 'catches' specific features of a child's development or behaviour
Checklist/Tick chart	Observer has a series of statements or questions relating to specific skills or behaviours	This is a common method used in settings as checklists and tick charts are quick and simple to use These methods often do not allow the observer to note how easily or confidently the child manages tasks
Target child	Observer 'tracks' one child for a period of time using codes and symbols to save time	This type of observation can be very informative if the observer is able to provide a full and detailed picture of the child's movements

Factors affecting viability and reliability of assessments

It is very hard for practitioners who are closely involved with children to be completely objective when observing and assessing them. This is known as observer bias. The danger of observer bias is that the observer tends to home in on behaviours or skills that confirm their current view of the child. One way of limiting observer bias is by setting clear aims for observations, e.g. noting down every time a child interacts with an adult to gain a picture of a child's interactions with adults.

It is also important when completing checklists or tick charts which require adults to ask children to do certain tasks to remember that children may not always 'perform' well if they think that they are being watched or tested. Many skilled practitioners therefore try to incorporate these type of assessments into planned play opportunities, e.g. putting out some buttons for children to play with and then asking them if they would like to count how many there are.

Use of assessment

Once a practitioner has completed some observations, it is important to develop an overall picture of the child's development. What strengths and interests has the child shown? Are there any areas where the child has specific developmental needs? It is also good practice for early years settings to involve parents in the process. Parents see their children in a different context and will be able to provide additional information. It is also important to find out what parents feel are the priorities for their child, e.g. a parent of a toddler may want to concentrate on feeding skills.

The actual layout and content of an individualised learning plan can vary with some settings choosing to keep them quite brief. Most plans contain a resumé of the child's developmental progress and some aims for the future. It is important that these aims are achievable otherwise the child may be put under pressure.

Implementation

Once an individual learning plan has been drawn up, it is important for it to be reviewed regularly. Most settings review their children's progress each term or every three or four months. In settings where the child has a key worker, the key worker may be responsible for implementing the plan. They may plan particular activities for the child or make sure that activities designed for a whole group are adapted to meet the child's needs.

Think It Over

Matthew is three years old. His individual learning plan aims to promote his interaction with other children as although he plays alongside other children, he rarely talks to them. A small group of children, which includes Matthew, is to play sound lotto. Matthew's key worker puts Matthew with a slightly older child to play the game together as this will encourage Matthew to work with another child. She encourages them both and Matthew begins to make eye contact with the other child.

- Suggest two other activities that might encourage Matthew to interact with other children.

Assessment activity 11.3

In order to carry out this assessment activity, you will need to gain the advice and consent of your placement supervisor. Choose one child in your placement setting.

- Assess the overall development of the chosen child by carrying out five observations. You should use at least three different methods of observation and observe the child in a range of situations.
- Using your observations as a basis, produce an individual learning programme for the child.
- Produce and implement three activity plans based on the individual learning programme you have devised (keep notes during the activities for later evaluation; see Assessment activity 11.4).

The individual learning programme must contain:
- analysis of the observations linked to the child's stage of development and child development theory
- an evaluation of the child's overall development and subsequent needs
- a rationale of the aims and learning outcomes you have suggested for the child
- an explanation of how the proposed learning outcomes are to be evaluated and measured.

Each activity plan should contain:
- an explanation of how the activity is to be implemented
- an examination of the role of the adult in extending the child's learning during the activity
- an exploration of the factors that might affect the success of the activity
- detailed links between the activities chosen and the stages of development of the child
- analysis of the potential developmental benefits of each activity
- detailed links between the play activities chosen and the individual learning programme.

Areas of early childhood development

Planned and spontaneous play

In order to implement the early years curriculum, children will need a variety of play experiences, both planned and spontaneous. Spontaneous play experiences are often those that the children find the most rewarding because they are often child initiated and thus of interest to them. Sometimes spontaneous play and, in turn, learning arises out of planned activities, e.g. a practitioner may decide to encourage children to sort buttons, but a child may discover how to play tiddly winks with the buttons. This spontaneous play can then be used by the practitioner to further other learning by asking the child about the buttons which are the easiest to use.

Extending children's learning

Practitioners need to look at ways of extending children's learning whilst they are playing. This can take many forms and requires a flexible and thoughtful approach.

- **Providing further equipment**: a practitioner may feel that a child may benefit from a more challenging jigsaw puzzle or could be given further choice of materials in order to make the play more enjoyable.
- **Asking questions**: sometimes practitioners may ask questions to stimulate children's thinking and thus learning about a situation, e.g. 'What would happen if you mixed the colours?'. It is important that questioning is not carried out in the form of an interrogation and that the question is worth asking!
- **Playing alongside or with children**: practitioners can play alongside children as this may help children to gain ideas, e.g. a practitioner may start to make their own model and children may take some of the ideas and incorporate it into their own.

Language and communication activities

The development of language and communication is the key to later mastery of reading and writing. There is also a strong link between children's cognitive development and language, as language appears to be linked to thought processes. Most settings therefore provide a range of activities to develop this important area.

Games to develop language and communication

Children are more likely to remember and gain new vocabulary if it is introduced to them in an enjoyable way. Many settings working with young children play games such as picture lotto or guess what is in the feely bag.

Role of adult: these types of games often need an adult to direct and support the children. Adults need to be careful not to 'take over' so that they are speaking more than the children! It is also important to allow young children enough time to reflect and find 'the words' that they need. It is important to remember that most children are not able to internalise speech and thought until they are six or seven years old. This means that young children are likely to call out the answers or speak even when in theory it is not their turn. To avoid disruption, games tend to work better when played in very small groups.

Drama and role play

Imaginative play encourages children's speech and language development. To develop children's overall language, many early years settings 'theme' the role play area so that children begin to use new expressions and vocabulary (see the diagram below). Themes tend to work well when children have had some actual experience so that they draw from it into their play.

Role of the adult: children learn new vocabulary and expressions by hearing. This means that when introducing a new theme into the role play area, adults will need to introduce the target language. This can be done by having a visitor into the setting such as a vet to talk about how animals are cared for, if the role play area is an animal hospital. Language can also be introduced by reading a book or story to children and also by the adult at first taking a role in the area.

Music and rhymes

Songs, nursery rhymes and counting rhymes all stimulate children's language. Research carried out in the 1980s suggested a correlation between children's achievement in

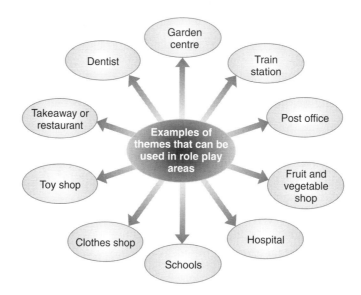

reading and their knowledge of traditional nursery rhymes. This is likely to exist because children learn to focus on patterns, rhymes and phonetic sounds in words as they speak or sing them. There are many songs that have actions or dances and these are particularly enjoyed by children.

Note: the use of traditional nursery rhymes is controversial in some settings as many nursery rhymes promote stereotypes and violence! There is also a school of thought which suggests that they should be learnt by children in order to keep a strong historical tradition alive. Many settings choose a compromise and combine traditional rhymes with modern songs and where necessary alter words.

Role of adult: adults need to be familiar with a range of songs and games and also, where necessary, to learn new ones. Traditional nursery rhymes often have several verses and these should be used so that children gain the pattern and sounds. It is also important for songs to be carefully planned and not just rely on children choosing them as otherwise their 'repertoire' will not develop. It is also a good idea to use props especially with counting rhymes as they help give meaning to the 'numbers' that the children are hearing. Nursery rhymes and songs have a huge advantage in that they can be done at any time and so it is good practice to 'burst' into song at odd times especially if children are waiting or are bored, e.g. at home time as they are waiting for their parents.

Poetry and literature

From as early as four months old, children can be introduced to books. In early years settings, a range of stories and poems will help children develop an interest in reading. Children who enjoy handling books and listening to stories and poems are more likely to be motivated to learn to read. Children's vocabulary and expressions are extended by hearing stories and poems and they also learn to associate print with reading. Poems and books can be used as starting points for a themed play during a session as the example below shows.

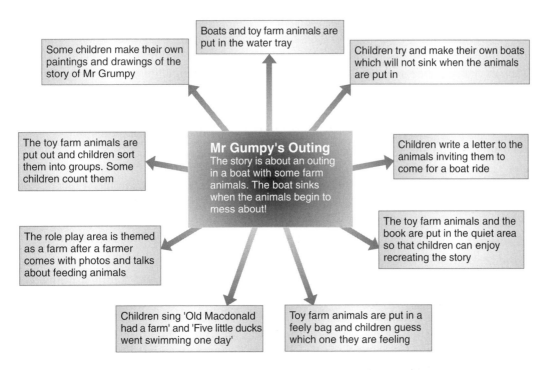

Some children make their own paintings and drawings of the story of Mr Grumpy

Boats and toy farm animals are put in the water tray

Children try and make their own boats which will not sink when the animals are put in

The toy farm animals are put out and children sort them into groups. Some children count them

Mr Gumpy's Outing
The story is about an outing in a boat with some farm animals. The boat sinks when the animals begin to mess about!

Children write a letter to the animals inviting them to come for a boat ride

The role play area is themed as a farm after a farmer comes with photos and talks about feeding animals

The toy farm animals and the book are put in the quiet area so that children can enjoy recreating the story

Children sing 'Old Macdonald had a farm' and 'Five little ducks went swimming one day'

Toy farm animals are put in a feely bag and children guess which one they are feeling

Mr Gumpy's Outing: examples of the different activities that this story might lead to

Theory into practice

Using the early years curriculum:

- discuss how the above activities would link to the curriculum
- explain the developmental benefits of these activities
- produce a short-term plan with identified aims and objectives for one of these activities.

Role of adult: it is essential that the experience of listening to stories and rhymes is a pleasurable one for children, otherwise they will not become motivated to learn to read for themselves. To achieve this, stories and rhymes are best shared with a very small group or even individual children. This allows for children to make comments about the story or ask questions and 'dwell' on pages that they find particularly interesting. Young children also rely heavily on pictures and will need to spend time looking and enjoying the pictures. To help children learn to identify print with the words being spoken, it is good practice for adults to run their fingers under the words as they are reading. This also helps children to learn that in English, print runs from left to right.

Note: whole group story time is very difficult to manage with young children as they are unable to 'hold' in their thoughts and tend to call out. The Foundation Stage curriculum in England, for example, does not give this as a model for working with three and four year olds, suggesting instead individual and small group sharing of books. In settings where whole group story time is being used, it is essential to use props and look for ways of making the story time interactive. This might mean choosing books with a repeated refrain which mean that children can join in.

Communication of information and reconstruction of events

Children need to be able to use language in a variety of ways including being able to describe events, give information and ask questions. Young children need plenty of support and practice at gaining these skills. Activities to help children gain these skills need to be carried out in small groups or with individual children. Children often benefit from the use of puppets, props, photos and objects which help them to visualise and sequence their thoughts. Adults often have to model language with young children as the case study below shows.

Case Study

Mike, an early years practitioner, has brought in a teddy bear. He tells a small group of children that teddy wants to see what happens in a nursery class. The children take turns at 'showing' teddy around and during the session he 'joins' in. Towards the end of the session, Mike asks pairs of children to use a telephone to tell 'teddy's mum' what he has been doing. To model the language to some of the younger children, Mike often talks to 'teddy's mum' first. The children listen to Mike and then often repeat the same type of expressions and phrases when it is their turn. Mike planned this activity to encourage children to use description and also to recount events.

Role of adults adults need to model new language to children. They may need to help children by asking them questions which help to sequence events, e.g. 'Do you remember what happened after story time?'. Large group situations should be avoided as they can create unnecessary stress as younger children may not be able to 'get out' what they want to say quickly and before older children call out. This can in turn cause some children to stammer or stutter.

Expression of emotion

Language development is linked to behaviour. Children who are articulate are often more able to control their behaviour and also to express their needs without being aggressive or attention seeking. Learning to express one's feelings requires specific language. Activities that can help children to do this include using puppets who 'say' what they are feeling, choosing stories where central characters express their emotions and also looking for ways of helping children talk about things that make them happy, sad, angry or jealous.

Role of adult: adults need to model language that children will need. They also need to look for opportunities to talk about emotions especially when children are experiencing potentially stressful events in their lives, e.g. arrival of a sibling, moving house, changes in family structure, visit to hospital. There are many resources including books and puppets that can be used to trigger discussions.

Case Study

Jaswinder, an early years practitioner, uses a teddy and some other cuddly toys to talk about feelings. Teddy tells Jaswinder that he is feeling sad. None of his friends want to play with him. Jaswinder asks another cuddly toy why. The cuddly toy says that teddy never wants to share any of his toys and that last time they played, teddy hurt him. He says that teddy makes him feel unhappy. Jaswinder asks a child or a small group of children what they think is the problem. Jaswinder asks the children if they can tell teddy what he should do. This activity can be used to introduce specific vocabulary and also to help children think about sharing and friendships.

Speaking and listening activities

A good starting point when considering speaking and listening activities is to re-visit children's stages of language development including their ability to internalise thought and process information (see Unit 9). Child development theories suggest that children will find it hard to process information gained by the spoken word alone (i.e. listening) as they rely heavily on images to process information. In the same way, they find it hard to wait for their turn to speak because they cannot internalise their thoughts which results in them needing to talk in order to think! It is therefore good practice for speaking and listening activities to be interactive and carried out with small groups of children. Some examples are given in the table below.

Speaking activities	Listening activities
Feely bags – children have to describe what they are feeling to the others	Simon says...
	Sound lotto
Guess what is in the box – children have to ask questions	Guess the sound (one child hides behind a screen and the other children guess or point to the instrument that is being played)
I went to the shops and I bought... (for young children put out real objects)	Stop and go type games – children run around and make certain movements according to the instructions

Role of adult: adults have to remember that children's ability to absorb the spoken word in the absence of pictures or gestures is limited. This is why many young children appear to find it hard to sit and listen. Listening activities need therefore to be kept focused and interactive, e.g. put your hand up when you hear a bell. It is also very hard for young children to listen to each other – as young children do not have 'entertainment' skills. This means that activities relying on large groups are unlikely to meet the needs of all the children.

Self-expression

Activities that encourage self-expression help children gain confidence, build imagination as well as develop language and fine manipulative skills.

Role play, dance and drama

Although the role play area can be used to stimulate children's language, it should also be a place where children can go, dress up and take on any role that they wish. As children get older, they may wish to plan their play with others and this then becomes 'drama'.

Children can also show self-expression when moving to music. Children enjoy having space and music to move to. Props such as ribbons and scarves can be put out as some children enjoy moving and creating shapes with them.

Note: whilst concerts and plays organised by adults may be enjoyed by children, it is important to understand that generally they are not good vehicles for self-expression as they originate with the adult rather than with the child.

Creative art

Drawing, painting and making models are all ways of encouraging self-expression in children. The key to helping children show their creativity is to provide them with a good choice of materials rather than to show them what to make. Most settings provide a drawing and writing table as well as malleable materials and paint.

Role of the adult: in order for children to be able to express themselves, adults have to give them choices and a feeling of 'freedom'. Children will need to feel that there is no 'right way' or 'wrong way' and that whatever they do will be free of judgement. Adults have therefore to learn to take a 'step back' and support rather than direct children. It is also important that adults praise children for what they are doing, rather than for what they are producing, e.g. 'You look like you are enjoying painting' rather than 'Well done, that's a lovely painting'.

Physical development

There is increasing research to suggest that children's physical development is important in order to help children's literacy. Physical skills also give children confidence and independence as, for example, they can put on their coats or complete a jigsaw. Physical skills can be divided into gross and locomotive motor skills and fine motor skills, although some activities encompass both types of skill (see table below).

Activity	Skills promoted	Comments
Obstacle courses – indoor and outdoors	Promotes gross and locomotive skills and develops general co-ordination and balance	Obstacle courses are enjoyed by children and can be varied according to children's stage of development. Hoops, play tunnels as well as beams can be used to encourage children to use a range of movements
Parachute games	Promotes listening skills, co-ordination as well as gross motor and locomotive skills	Parachute games can be used indoors as well as outdoors. Tablecloths or sheets can be used to improvise as parachutes
Tricycles, scooters, roller skates and bicycles	Promotes hand-eye co-ordination, gross locomotive skills and also helps children to learn about speed and distance	Children need to gain in confidence to use these pieces of equipment. Protective headgear should be offered where possible in case of falls. Children enjoy the feeling of speed and independence
Climbing frames, seesaws, swings	Balance, co-ordination and gross motor skills, spatial awareness	This type of equipment helps children to gain in confidence as they enjoy the sensations of climbing and swinging

Activity	Skills promoted	Comments
Throwing and catching	Gross motor skills, hand-eye and foot-eye co-ordination	Young children will need significant input before they can throw and catch.
Kicking	co-ordination, perceptual skills	There are a range of balls, bean bags and coils available. Children will also enjoy simply throwing and then collecting objects Children enjoy kicking from an early age although children find it hard to play co-operatively with a football until they are older
Running games	Gross motor and locomotive skills, co-ordination, spatial awareness	There are a range of 'running games' that can be enjoyed by children, e.g. chase or what's the time Mr Wolf? Young children also appreciate catching bubbles that have been blown into the wind or running with ribbons

Fine motor skills

Children need to develop the muscles in their hands to allow them later to use tools such as scissors with accuracy and also in order to be able to write.

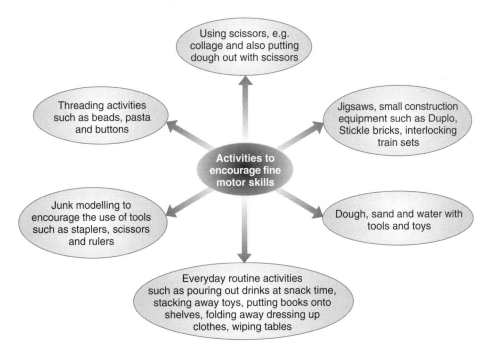

Role of adult: many physical skills involve practice and early failure can discourage children from continuing. This means that activities need to be planned to ensure that whilst presenting some level of challenge, the child is likely to succeed. Children also need to gain in confidence before attempting some activities such as climbing or attempting to ride a bicycle. Adults therefore need to adopt a sensitive approach to encouraging children to attempt such activities and avoid pressuring children.

Evaluation

It is important for practitioners to evaluate the effectiveness of their plans and ways of working with children. Ongoing evaluation helps us to consider whether we are meeting the needs of children and also helps us to consider what further activities they may need.

Setting and using criteria for evaluation

To assist the evaluation process, it will be important to set criteria for success during the planning process so that the success of strategies or activities can be measured. Criteria for evaluation is often seen on individual learning plans, school curriculum plans and individual education plans for use with children with special needs (see Unit 13). Setting some criteria for evaluation is essential in situations where a child needs to have mastered a concept or skill before being presented with a further task. Judging whether the child has met the criteria will therefore help the practitioner to decide whether further reinforcement and practice is needed or whether a child is ready to move on. An example of a curriculum area where this is particularly useful as an approach is maths. A child who cannot count accurately to five, will not be ready to carry out an activity which involves counting to ten.

Building in assessment tasks into activities

Most evaluation criteria involve checking whether children have gained the intended learning outcomes. This is difficult to measure unless some type of assessment is carried out either during or after the activity. A child appears to have understood a concept or may have happily played with materials, but not necessarily have learnt anything new! By building in some assessment into the activity itself, practitioners can see what the child has understood and learnt. It is important that the assessment is not seen in any way as a test as this would undermine the child's confidence. Good assessment happens as part of the activity.

Case Study

Jo has planned a series of activities to improve cutting skills for four year olds. She put out some scissors on the dough table and three children are happily snipping and cutting away. Jo sits with them and flattens a piece of dough. She draws a line on the dough and then cuts it along the line. One of the children looks at what she is doing. She then flattens another piece of dough and draws a line on it. She passes it to the child who smiles and then has a go. Jo notices how the child handles the scissors and how easily he is managing the scissor action. Jo also notes that the child is almost able to cut on the line.

- Discuss the advantages of this type of assessment.
- Consider ways in which this assessment will help further planning of activities.

Student evaluation

As a student, you will need to show that you can evaluate the effectiveness of your work as well as the activities. Student evaluations can also be used to provide evidence of:

- knowledge of child development
- ability to assess accurately a child's stage of development
- understanding of the early years curricula
- awareness of your strengths and weaknesses
- ability to review and plan effectively.

Producing a student evaluation

There is no set format for producing student evaluations, although most contain the following:

- an overall introduction to the nature of the plan and the intended learning outcomes
- a brief review of how the plans were implemented
- an analysis of how the children responded and an evaluation of the effectiveness of the activity or activities
- an analysis of the effectiveness of your role and your planning
- detailed recommendations of how to extend the child's learning
- detailed recommendations of how to improve and consolidate your practice.

Gaining information for evaluations

One of the key ways of gaining information for use in later evaluations is through careful observation of children during the activity. Most students find it helpful to keep a pad of paper near them to make notes.

- How engaged are children in the activity?
- Do children appear to be interested and enthusiastic?
- How easily are children distracted?
- Do children appear settled?
- How confident do the children seem?
- Are their bodies relaxed or tensed?
- How easily are children managing the activity?
- Are there any children who appear frustrated or bored?
- How much support is being given in order for children to manage the activity?
- Is support being given because the activity is too challenging?
- Are the children active or passive?
- Are the children using language during the activity?
- What has interested the children during the activity – can this be used as a starting point for further activities?

Self-evaluation

In order to analyse the effectiveness of your practice, it can be useful to ask yourself the following questions:

- How well have I prepared for this activity?
- Is this activity meeting the needs of all the children?
- Are the learning outcomes planned being gained by the children?
- What other learning is taking place?
- How much control have the children over their learning?
- Am I encouraging children to be spontaneous and to develop their own thinking?

Discussion with colleagues

Other practitioners, particularly those who are very experienced or who are familiar with the children you have been working with, can also be a useful source of information. They may be able to make practical suggestions as to how to improve certain aspects of your practice, provide you with written information about the curriculum and also make recommendations as to the future needs of children.

Many settings also try and spend time reviewing their plans and activities so that they can set targets for individual children and help them prepare future curriculum plans. The level of written evaluations varies with some settings keeping quite detailed records of activities and others preferring to focus more heavily on children's achievements.

Extension of play activities

During activities, sensitive practitioners will also be looking for scope to extend children's language, skills or thinking. This requires an amount of skill and knowledge of child development as the practitioner has to consider the child's stage of development, their interest in the activity and ways of developing the child further. Opportunities to extend children's learning are sometimes built into the activity or they can be spontaneous. Good practitioners also look for ways of building on from one play activity to another so that children consolidate and extend their learning.

Theory into practice

A practitioner is working alongside a group of children who are enjoying painting. One of the children dips their brush into the blue paint and a few spots of blue paint fall into the yellow palette. Another child moans, 'He's spilt blue paint'. The practitioner smiles as she recognises that there is an opportunity to discuss colours of paints. She asks the children what they think will happen if the yellow paint is then mixed.

- Explain why this is an example of a spontaneous learning opportunity?
- Consider ways in which the practitioner may be able to use this activity and learning as a starting point for further activities?

Assessment activity 11.4

- Produce an evaluation of your curriculum plan and associated activity plans (see Assessment activity 11.2).
- Produce an evaluation of your individual learning programme and associated activity plans.

In each evaluation you should:
- explain how the plans were implemented
- analyse the responses of the children in relation to child developmental theory
- consider the effectiveness of your planning based upon self-evaluation, responses from children and feedback from others
- evaluate your role in implementing the plans and extending children's learning and play
- examine your effectiveness in meeting children's play and developmental needs
- consider ways of improving your professional practice.

Computer programs for young children

The use of computers, whilst being widespread in adult life, remains controversial in early years settings. In some settings, children have frequent access to computer technology whilst in others, staff are sceptical about the benefits to children. The range of computer software is also variable and so before planning activities involving the computer an analysis of the potential learning benefits must be made. The Foundation Stage in England includes an aspect of learning (within the area Knowledge and Understanding of the world) on Information Communication Technology. This aspect is quite wide and includes the use of programmable toys and remote controlled vehicles such as cars. It is interesting to note that it suggests that younger children should be using information technology in a practical way.

The table below shows some of the commonly expressed views in favour and against the use of computers in early years settings.

For	Against
• Computers now form part of everyday life and children will naturally express an interest in using them • Using a keyboard and mouse can encourage fine motor skills and hand-eye co-ordination • Children enjoy using computers and can show periods of concentration • Good software can introduce and reinforce concepts such as number, shapes	• Computers make children passive rather than active learners • Children should learn using their whole body and senses • Computers in addition to television are limiting children's opportunities to take exercise • Computers do not encourage children's socialisation with others • Some software is very repetitive and similar in style to worksheets

Think It Over

• Does your placement setting use computers with children? If so, how are activities planned and organised? If not, find out from staff whether this is a policy or financial decision.

• Choose one computer software program designed for pre-school children. Critically evaluate its learning potential.

End-of-unit test

1   What is meant by the term 'parallel' activity?
2   List the developmental benefits of imaginative play.
3   Suggest three toys that might be given to a child aged three years.
4   Describe the advantages of free play.
5   What factors might an adult take into consideration when choosing activities and equipment for children?
6   List three activities that will promote children's spoken language skills.
7   Why is it important that young children work in small groups or individually with adults?
8   Why are observations important when working with children?
9   List four pieces of equipment that would promote children's physical development.
10 What are the main benefits of using computers with children?

Developmental psychology

Introduction

Most early years practitioners find it useful to have a basic knowledge of child psychology as it helps them to work more effectively with children. Using psychology can help them to manage children's behaviour, help children to settle in as well as consider how best to present activities.

What you need to learn
- Issues in developmental psychology
- Development of social behaviour
- Processing and using information
- Language development
- How early years practitioners influence children's development

Issues in developmental psychology

Why study children?
There are many different branches of psychology, but developmental psychology looks at the skills and thoughts that we have and considers how we might have acquired them. It studies how we grow and develop and includes areas such as how we learn, language and personality development. Having an understanding of how children learn will help us when planning activities, whilst knowing about the way children learn language will enable us to provide the best conditions for this.

A brief outline of the history of psychology
The study of psychology is relatively new. Psychology has grown out of the disciplines of philosophy and biology. Modern psychology has been influenced by both early philosophers and biologists.

John Locke and empiricism
John Locke and other philosophers in the seventeenth and eighteenth centuries argued that the way to truly learn about the world is by using our senses, i.e. observing, listening. Empiricists reject the idea of innate knowledge and instincts, i.e. being born with understanding. Locke suggested that we are born with no knowledge and that our minds are clean slates! If correct, this suggests that early years practitioners should aim to put plenty of knowledge into children.

Charles Darwin
Charles Darwin is famous for his publication *The Origin of Species* (1859). He suggested that the reason why there are so many species of plants and animals is because they had

had to adapt to different climatic and environmental changes. Characteristics which would ensure survival were passed onto successive generations. Darwin's work has influenced some psychologists who believe that some of our behaviour is innate (inborn). This approach is often referred to as the ethological perspective.

The key figures in developmental psychology are shown in the following table.

Name	Area	Key theory	Comments
Freud, Sigmund	Personality and emotional development	Psychosexual stages of development	Freud made a distinction between our conscious and unconscious minds
Erikson, Erik	Personality and emotional development	Psychosocial stages of development	Erikson produced his theory based on Freud's work. Considered that our personalities carry on developing into adulthood
Bowlby, John	Attachment	Maternal deprivation	Bowlby showed in his work that for healthy development, babies and young children need to form a bond with their parents or key carers
Bandura, Albert	Behaviour/learning	Social learning theory	Bandura showed that children can learn through imitating others
Skinner, Burrhus Frank	Behaviour/learning	Operant conditioning	Skinner suggested that behaviour can be manipulated through the use of reinforcements
Pavlov, Ivan	Behaviour/learning	Classic conditioning	Pavlov through his works with dogs showed that humans can learn through association
Piaget, Jean	Learning/cognitive development	Stages of cognitive development	Piaget suggested that children's thinking passed through stages
Vygotsky, Lev	Language/cognitive development	Zone of proximal development	Vygotsky placed emphasis on the importance of adults to help children understand concepts

The nature v. nurture debate

At the heart of the nature v. nurture debate are two questions:

• Are our personalities, behaviour patterns, thoughts, etc., a result of our genes?
Or
• Are our personalities, behaviour patterns , thoughts, etc., a result of environmental influences such as the way we were parented or where we live?

Psychology as a separate subject has gradually evolved from biology. This means that many of the early theories were influenced by the idea that we inherited skills, abilities and behaviour. Work by behaviourists such as Skinner have since shown that our behaviour can also be shaped. The issue for many psychologists is to define how much of our skills, personalities, etc., are inherited and how much is influenced by our environment as most psychologists accept that both influences are probably at work.

A practitioner who fundamentally believes that children's abilities and personalities are with them when they are born may take a non-interventionist approach e.g. 'boys will be boys' or 'she's very shy'. A practitioner who believes that nurture has a bigger impact may take a different stance believing that the children's progress and behaviour will be a reflection on their own abilities as an educator.

Continuity v. discontinuity (is development continuous or does it occur in stages?)

Some theories discussed in this unit are 'stage' theories, e.g. Freud's psychosexual stages of personality and Piaget's stages of cognitive development. Such theories are based on the idea that development passes through defined and separate stages and that each stage will have recognisable features, e.g in language development children babble before they speak words so babbling is seen as a stage in itself. Others feel that development is more gradual or a continuous process.

Think It Over

Many early years practitioners may feel that children don't jump from stage to stage, but that development is often so gradual that it is hard to see, although over a few weeks they can see that children's development has progressed.

*   In your work setting, ask staff what they think. Do they think that children's progress fits into stages or that development is continual? Ask if there are any areas of development which seem particularly stage like.

Nomethetic v. idiographic

This debate looks at whether we are all unique (the idiographic approach) or share essential characteristics but that we have some differences (the nomothetic approach). This debate is particularly relevant when we consider our personalities.

Assessment activity 12.1

Prepare a presentation for other students based on one of the following debates within psychology:

*   Nature v. nurture.
*   Continuity v. discontinuity.
*   Nomothetic v. ideographic.

Prepare a handout giving information about both sides of the debates and explain how the different perspectives may affect practice. Use at least one of the following sources:

*   Results of questionnaires with parents and/or practitioners.
*   Results of face-to-face interviews with children.
*   Examples of children's work (permission must be sought).
*   Observations of children.

Acquiring behaviour

When the term behaviour is used in ordinary conversation, we may think of actions of some kind – good or bad. Psychologists use the term in a different and broader way, e.g.

the study of behaviour encompasses the way we learn, form attitudes and how we behave towards others.

Acquiring behaviour through learning

Behaviour and learning are linked. It is through behaviour that psychologists can see that learning has taken place. If we can understand how we learn, we could be more effective in our teaching and improve society. Psychologists in this area are interested in the process of how we learn rather than what we learn.

There are several theories that explain the learning process, broadly dividing into two strands: the behaviourist approach and social learning. There is also a third strand which centres around how children learn to think and develop thought processes (see pages 227–33).

The importance of learning theories in psychology

Learning theories are extremely important as they can be applied to many situations. This means that when studying other aspects of child development, such as language, behaviour management, etc., the same terms and theories will keep reappearing!

Behaviourist approach to learning – conditioning

This approach suggests that learning is influenced by rewards, punishments and environmental factors. The term **conditioning** is often used by behaviourists – it means that we learn to act in a certain way because past experiences have taught us to do or not do something. We may know this as 'learning by association', e.g. not touching a flame because we were once burnt. There are two types of conditioning which are well documented: classical conditioning and operant conditioning.

Classical conditioning

Ivan Pavlov was a physiologist who whilst studying dogs, noticed that they always started to salivate before food was put down for them. He concluded that the dogs were anticipating the food and were salivating because they had learnt to associate the arrival of food with other things such as footsteps, buckets etc. He devised an experiment where he fed dogs whilst a bell was sounded. Normally dogs do not salivate when hearing bells, but the dogs began to associate the bell with food and would salivate simply on hearing the bell.

Applying classical conditioning to humans

Pavlov's work was built on by Watson who showed that it was possible to use classical conditioning on humans. In a famous experiment he was able to make a baby of eleven months afraid of a white rat. The child had previously shown no fear of rats, but by pairing the rat with something that did frighten the child, the child was conditioned to be afraid of the rat.

Theory into practice

Classical conditioning can help us to understand how some children might develop seemingly irrational fears – for example suddenly being afraid of the dark, particular foods or animals. Look at the example below:

Mary was five years old and had gone to bed without being afraid of the dark. One night she was violently sick and her room was in darkness. Afterwards Mary cried if no light was left on at night.

Operant conditioning

The basis of operant conditioning is that our learning is based on the type of consequence or reinforcement that follows our initial behaviour. B.F. Skinner (1904–90) is a key figure in the development of the behaviourist approach to learning theory and the theory of operant conditioning. Whilst Skinner accepted the work of Pavlov and Watson, he suggested that most humans and animals learn through exploring the environment and then drawing conclusions based on the consequences of their behaviour. This means that we tend to be active in the learning process which is an important difference from classical conditioning.

Skinner divided the consequences of actions into three groups:

- positive reinforcers
- negative reinforcers
- punishments.

Positive reinforcers and negative reinforcers are described in Unit 8, pages 303–4. **Punishers** are likely to stop us from repeating behaviour, e.g. we may learn to stay away from an electric fence after receiving a shock.

Theory into practice

Operant conditioning is often used to encourage children to show wanted behaviour, although many parents and early years practitioners will think of it as offering a bribe! A child may be given a sticker if they have helped to tidy up. In this way, the child will be more likely to help in future as their behaviour has been positively reinforced.

Skinner further divided positive reinforcers into two groups: primary and secondary. These are described in Unit 8, page 304.

Social learning theory

This is another widely accepted learning theory. The key figure among social learning theorists is Albert Bandura (b. 1925). Social learning theorists accept the principles of conditioning, but suggest that learning by classical and operant conditioning alone would not explain other behaviours. Social learning theorists are particularly interested in looking at moral and social behaviour (see also Unit 7 and Unit 8).

Bandura's Bobo doll experiment

Bandura's famous experiment, often referred to as the Bobo doll experiment (1965), showed that children can learn behaviour by watching adults. Bandura showed a film to three groups of children. The film showed an adult in a room with a Bobo doll (a large inflatable doll similar to Mr Blobby!). The three groups saw different versions:

- Group A saw the adult acting aggressively to the doll.
- Group B saw the adult being aggressive to the doll, but at the end of the film, the adult was rewarded with sweets and lemonade by another adult.
- Group C saw the adult being aggressive to the doll, but at the end a second adult appeared and told the adult off.

After the film, each group of children was shown in turn into a playroom that had a variety of toys including the Bobo doll. The reactions of the children were recorded. Group C were the least aggressive to the doll, but there was little difference between groups A and B. This suggested that they were less influenced by the reward that had been offered to the adult.

A follow-up to the experiment asked the children if they could demonstrate how the doll had been attacked and were rewarded for doing so. There was little difference between the three groups showing that they could all imitate the behaviour they had seen.

Theory into practice

Early years practitioners may agree that children learn through observational learning. A toddler may try to cross their legs in adult fashion after seeing an adult. If children do learn through observational learning, this has powerful implications for early years practitioners. We must act as good role models for children and be responsible when children are with us.

The development of self

Who are we? What are we like? These are fundamental questions for children, almost like being able to place oneself on a map. The development of self concept is the process by which we gather information about ourselves. Self concept is important because it is closely linked with self-esteem. It is useful to understand the difference between the terms used when talking about self concept.

Self concept – this is our vision of our whole selves, which includes our self-esteem, our self-image and our ideal self.

Self-image or self-identity – this is the way in which we define ourselves – who we are, where we live, our gender: etc.

Ideal self – this is our view of what we would like to be.

Self-esteem – also referred to as self-confidence. Once we have developed a self-image and an ideal self, we then judge ourselves: how close are we to being the person we want to be? This judgment either gives us high or low self-esteem.

Developing self-image

Children gradually develop self-image. The first step for children is to be able to recognise themselves. A well-known test to see if children can recognise themselves is to put a touch of red lipstick on a baby's nose and then put the baby in front of the mirror. A child who is beginning to recognise themselves will touch their nose, rather than the nose in the reflection. Most babies are doing this by eighteen months old.

Theory into practice

Classical conditioning can help us to understand how some children might develop seemingly irrational fears – for example suddenly being afraid of the dark, particular foods or animals. Look at the example below:

Mary was five years old and had gone to bed without being afraid of the dark. One night she was violently sick and her room was in darkness. Afterwards Mary cried if no light was left on at night.

Robert Selman's levels of social role-taking

Role play or role-taking is also seen as important by Selman, who concludes that children develop in their abilities to understand themselves and others – see the table below.

Stage	Age	Description
Stage 0: Egocentric role-taking	3-6 years	Children assume that everyone will be the same and feel the same as they do
Stage 1 Social-informational role-taking	6-8 years	Children see that others do not act or appear to have the same feelings, but do not understand the reasons behind this
Stage 2: Self-reflective role-taking	8-10 years	Children accept that others have different points of views to theirs, but find it hard to bring together the different perspectives
Stage 3: Mutual role-taking	10-12 years	Children can understand two points of view at the same time, and realise that other people can do the same
Stage 4: Social and conventional system role-taking	12-15 years	Adolescents are beginning to have a more detached view on how other people may be feeling and are able to understand behaviour in the light of this

How self-esteem and self-image are linked

Once we have established what we think we are like (our perceptions of ourselves), we then consider whether we are happy with the result! Someone with a high self-esteem will be reasonably happy about their self-image, whereas someone with a low self-esteem feels that they are not 'measuring up'. This means that self-esteem and self-image are linked. The process of how we come to make our judgments has been researched. There seems to be three main factors that affect this process which carries on through our lives.

- reaction of others to us
- comparison to others
- ideal self-image.

Why does self-esteem matter?

Low self-esteem is linked to low achievement. Children who have low self-esteem will be less likely to put themselves in challenging and new situations. They have low expectations of what they can do and so do not meet their full potential. This means that early years practitioners must raise children's self-esteem through praise, showing genuine warmth and affection.

Coppersmith's study of self esteem

Coppersmith (1967) carried out a large study in which hundreds of boys aged between nine aand ten years underwent a series of tests to discover whether there was a link between achievement and self-esteem. Although the boys came from similar social backgrounds, he found that where the boys had high scores of self-esteem they were also achieving more highly. He found that boys with lower self-esteem consistently underestimated themselves.

Coppersmith then looked to see if there was a link between self-esteem and parenting. Using questionnaires and interviews, he found that children with high self-esteem had parents who had set firm boundaries but who had allowed them some freedom and security. Later, Coppersmith looked at the same children as adults. He found that men who had high self-esteem as children in the study had fared better in their education and careers.

Personality development

One of the greatest influences in psychology is Sigmund Freud. He is particularly famous for his psychosexual theory of development, often used to explain our unconscious thoughts and actions.

Freud's structure of personality

Freud suggested that there were three parts that made up our personality: the id, the ego and the superego. Not all of these parts are present at birth but develop with the child.

The id

This is the instinctive part of our personality, governed by the drives and needs of the body, e.g. hunger, pleasure. The id does not consider how meeting our desires and wants will affect others and so is often thought of as the selfish and passionate component.

Freud suggested that babies only had the id when they were born – hence a baby will cry and cry until it is fed, regardless of how tired the carer is or whether there are other children that also need feeding. Getting the desire or need met is known as gratification.

The ego

The ego has a planning role. It works out how to meet the id's needs and desires in the best way. The ego develops from the id in the first few months – as babies might learn that by smiling in some situations, they are more likely to get their needs met, whilst in others it is better to cry. In some situations the ego may sometimes make the id wait for its demands to be met, e.g. a child may learn that if they snatch a cake from a tray, they may have it taken away from them, but by waiting to be offered it, they will eventually get it. The term **deferred gratification** is used when this happens.

The superego

The superego develops later in childhood and is that part of our personality that gives us our 'conscience'. It tries to control the ego. It comprises of two elements: the conscience and the ego-ideal.

- The conscience will punish the ego if it misbehaves, i.e. does something that the superego considers wrong. This is the source of our guilt.

- The ego-ideal will reward the ego if it shows good behaviour, i.e. pride, high self-esteem. This is the source of our pride and confidence.

Freud's psychosexual stages

Freud believed that our personalities are based mainly on biological needs or drives – the id factor! He felt that the main drives were sexual and aggressive ones and he shocked Victorian and Edwardian society by suggesting that the sexual drive was present in babies and children. The energy behind these drives, Freud called **libido**. He suggested that there were five stages through which we pass in childhood and on which our libido concentrated. The stages linked to physical development of the body. Freud felt that if we did not pass through these stages satisfactorily, part of our energy or libido would be stuck – or fixated. This would affect our behaviour and personality.

Oedipus complex

One of the theories that made Freud famous is the Oedipus complex. In the Greek tragedy, a man, Oedipus, falls in love with his mother and kills his father. Freud suggests that in the phallic stage, children fall in love with the opposite sex parent – hence the title of the theory. They then see the other parent as a rival. This is also a stage where children have become aware of the physical differences between men and women. Freud argued that the absence of a penis is thought by children to be as a result of castration. This leads boys to fear being castrated 'castration anxiety'. Boys therefore have a decision to make, should they continue to love their mothers and risk being castrated by their fathers? Freud suggests that the conflict is resolved because boys decide to try and make a friend of their fathers by copying and admiring them.

For girls the situation is slightly different. Freud called this the female Oedipus (or Electra) complex. Girls will believe that they have already being castrated and develop 'penis envy'. Eventually realising that they cannot have a penis, they develop a desire for a baby and turn to their fathers. Freud is not so clear why girls then begin to develop closer ties with their mothers. He suggested that the ties are not as profound and that a girl tries to identify with the mother fearing that her mother will stop loving her.

Theory into practice

It is interesting that many children do have strong links with the opposite sex parent. We may hear the expression 'he's a mother's boy' for example or hear a girl saying that one day she is going to marry her father. The phallic stage does correspond with children often showing very sex-stereotypical play. Freud would argue that this play helps the child to identify and copy the actions of the parent they fear.

It is also interesting to note that boys do seem often to hold their penises at this age, particularly when they are anxious!

Erikson's theory of personality development

Erikson was influenced by Freud's work, but considered that the social environment, e.g. parenting and friendships, also affect personality. He accepted Freud's theory of the structure of personality being divided into three, but did not feel that Freud's work went far enough. He considered that our personalities were not fixed, and that we kept on changing during the course of our lives. His stages of personality development are life stages and are linked to social stages. He considered that at each stage, we face a dilemma or conflict and that, like Freud, the outcome of each stage would determine our personality.

Personality – a behaviourist approach

Do children learn some aspects of their personality from their parents through imitation and reinforcement? This would be the behaviourist and social learning approach to personality development. Many children share some characteristics of their parents. They can also develop similar attitudes to them. The difficulty with this approach is that it does not explain why children brought up in the same families can be so different.

Acquiring gender role

Gender concept and sex role concept is an important part of self concept and image. Our gender and the expectations of our gender become part of our self-image – of who we are. It is important not to confuse gender concept with sex role concept. Sex role concept is learnt alongside gender concept and means that children come to understand how as a boy or girl they are expected to act.

Gender identity

Children need to understand if they are a boy or a girl. By nine or ten months, babies are already starting to respond differently to male and female faces. By the age of two years, most children can correctly pick out a same sex picture (Thompson, 1975). Children seem to be using clues such as hair length and dress. Understanding gender identity is the first step in the gender concept process.

Gender constancy

Children also need to understand that regardless of the way people dress, act or cut their hair, they remain either male or female. This is called gender constancy. Understanding that some things remain the same, even if their appearances change links to Piaget's theory of conservation (see also page 232) which suggests that this understanding marks a significant stage in children's cognitive development.

Sex concept

This is always an interesting area in the light of equal opportunities practice and policies! How do children learn the sex roles that are associated with gender and how are these learnt? The table below outlines some of the stages of the development of gender concept and sex concept.

Age	Stage of development
9-12 months	Babies react differently to male and female faces
18-24 months	Toddlers start to show preferences for gender stereotyped toys
By 2 years	Children can point to a picture of a same sex child
$2^1/_2$–3 years	Children identify differences between genders by using clues such as hair length and style and dress
3-4 years	Children begin to associate tasks and objects with gender, i.e. some roles are determined through gender
5-6 years	Children have acquired the concept of gender stability. They know that gender is not dependent on type of clothes or hair cut

Sex role behaviour

Researchers have found that sex role behaviour is often shown earlier than we imagine. By 18-24 months children start to show some preference amongst playthings, with boys choosing building blocks and cars, and girls choosing dolls and 'caring' toys (O' Brien, 1992). Even so, many children of this age are still not showing understanding of their own gender. Children as young as three years start to show a preference for their own sex playmates.

Children also seem to be quickly aware of stereotypical roles, e.g. tasks and occupations that are seen as men's or women's work are identified by children as young as three years.

How do children learn these stereotypes and sex role behaviours?

There are three strands of thinking that relate to learning theories and theories of personality.

Social learning theory – Bandura

This theory suggests that children learn sex role behaviour by the way in which they are played with and with what they see. Children will imitate their parents' and carers' roles and actions. There is some research to support this approach as parents seem to respond in different ways to boy and girls (see page 228).

Cognitive development theories of gender

The idea behind one widely supported theory by Lawrence Kohlberg (1966) is that the child develops an understanding of what it is to be a boy or a girl – a schema – and behaves in such a way as to fit in with their understanding once they have understood that gender is permanent and they will always be a boy or girl. This would explain why some girls at around three years old refuse to wear trousers, because they know that they are a girl and believe that wearing trousers is what makes a boy a boy!

Gender schema theory

Another cognitive development theory put forward by Martin (1991) builds upon Kohlberg's theory. It suggests that children begin to develop an idea of what it is to be a boy or girl at around two or three years and show behaviour to match this. As they grow up they learn more about gender roles and sex roles and adapt and develop their ideas or schemas. It differs from Kohlberg's theory because the original schema is developed even though children have not shown an understanding that gender is permanent.

Aggression

In many early years settings guns are banned, but children may still go around waving a stick and pretend to be shooting each other. This begs the question whether aggression is instinctive or whether it is learnt – the nature versus nurture debate again!

The ethological perspective (Lorenz) – nature!

This considers whether aggression is an inborn instinct that has its roots in the survival of the species. This is an appealing theory – animals fight each other to protect their territory and females. One of the most famous ethologists is Konrad Lorenz who believed that the fighting instinct in animals has parallels with aggression in humans. He notes that fighting is often ritualised in animals – the triumphant male shows enough aggression just to make his point; shows of aggression without actual violence lead to the other party backing off and appeasing the aggressor. Through ritual aggression, animals avoid killing each other. According to Lorenz, humans have inherited the 'warrior' instinct, but no longer ritualise aggression because they have developed weapons. Weapons where the aggressor no longer needs to make face-to-face contact with the other party has meant appeasement rituals such as cowering, begging for mercy, etc., are no longer so effective. Lorenz also suggested that aggression in animals and humans is spontaneous as if the aggression has built up inside and needs to show itself.

Criticisms of Lorenz's theory of aggression
- **Where does the 'warrior' instinct come from?** Evidence about early man suggests he was a hunter-gatherer rather than a warrior fighting other tribes, so he would not have the basic instinct to attack.
- **Animals do frequently kill each other.** Lorenz talks about ritualised aggression where animals do not actually destroy each other. Although this can be seen, there are also many documented cases where groups of chimps have attacked and killed each other. It is also not uncommon to find animals eating their young offspring.
- **Aggression is inevitable.** Lorenz's idea that aggression builds up inside and needs an outlet has been criticised by other ethologists and biologists who suggest that aggression in animals is shown as a result of environmental factors, i.e. if food is plentiful, territorial fights might not be needed.
- **Aggression is learnt behaviour.** Lorenz did not consider that learning played a part in aggressive behaviour. Studies have, however, shown a correlation between learning and aggression (see Nurture below).

Think It Over

Many early years practitioners programme for time for physical play or activities that allow children to be 'legitimately aggressive', believing that children need to 'vent their aggression'.

- Is this the case in your setting?
- What happens if the children are not able to go outside for vigorous play activity?

Aggression is the result of frustration

A theory known as the frustration-aggression hypothesis combines the instinctive nature of aggression with learning theory. It was put forward by Dollard *et al.* in 1939 although was later revised. The basis is that although there is an inborn aggressive instinct, it tends to be triggered when people are feeling frustrated. This linking of frustration with aggression may explain why some children have dolls or objects onto which they heap their anger! The later theory proposed by Miller (1941) suggested that although aggression can be triggered through frustration, other factors may prevent the aggression from being shown, i.e. realising that any aggression might be punished afterwards.

Aggressive cue-theory - Nurture

This theory builds on the frustration aggression hypothesis, but looks carefully at why aggression is not automatically shown when people become frustrated. This theory suggests that although frustration causes anger, it might not necessarily cause aggression. Experiments carried out by Berkowitz (1966, 1967 and 1993) suggested that in order for aggression to be shown there needs to be some other triggers. Triggers used in experiments included weapons being available and participants seeing violent films. The aggressive cue theory would therefore explain why sometimes we can cope in some situations when we are angry, whereas in similar situations we might show some types of aggressive behaviour

Aggression and biological factors

There is some support for believing that aggressive behaviour might be linked to biological factors such as hormones, drugs or alcohol. Chemicals produced by the brain may lead us to be more highly aroused and therefore more prone to show aggressive behaviour. A study in 1979 by Brown *et al.* looked at levels of serotonin. Low levels of serotonin are likely to produce high levels of arousal and therefore possibly aggressive behaviour. There have also been cases where women suffering from pre-menstrual tension have committed acts of aggression. These acts have been linked to the higher levels of progesterone produced prior to menstruation.

Aggression is learnt behaviour

The social learning theory approach suggests that our behaviour is shaped by what we have seen. Bandura's Bobo doll experiment (see page 437) seems to support this view. Children who had seen violent behaviour seemed more likely to show aggressive behaviour, whereas children who had seen how adults and other children control their anger were more likely to cope when they were angry. Although this theory is valuable, Bandura warns that not all children will be aggressive if they have seen an aggressive act.

Development of social behaviour

Pro-social behaviour is the type that we tend to encourage in young children, e.g. comforting another child or sharing equipment. Psychologists have studied this behaviour to consider whether pro-social behaviour is instinctive or learnt.

Moral development

At what age are children able to judge right from wrong? In the UK the age of legal responsibility is one of the lowest in Europe. The boys involved in the murder of Jamie Bulger faced criminal prosecution as our legal system felt that although they were 10 years old, they were at an age to know right from wrong. The Early Learning Goals for England suggest that by the end of the reception year 'most children will understand what is right and wrong, and why'.

Piaget's theory of moral development – a cognitive approach

One of the most famous approaches to understanding moral development is a cognitive, i.e. stage, model. This cognitive approach was put forward by Jean Piaget. Piaget used a clinical interview approach, asking children to explain how they were playing games and telling them stories. He suggested that children's moral development was a three-stage process.

Pre-moral (0-4 years): children learn about right and wrong through their own actions and consider the results of adults around them.

Moral realism (four to seven years): children's moral development is greatly influenced by the adults in their lives. Their judgments very much depend on what they think the adult's expectations would be.

Moral relativism (eight to eleven years): children preoccupied with justice and following rules. This means that children have developed a concept of fairness.

Moral relativism (eleven years +): children understand the concept of equity, i.e. that treating people in exactly the same way may not result in fairness – a child who does not understand their homework may need more teacher's time than a child who does. The motives for people's actions are also considered by children.

Think It Over

If moral development follows a stage process, with children learning more as they develop, it would mean that an 'age' approach to children knowing right from wrong is not a helpful one. It also means that it is difficult to 'teach' children right from wrong.

* What do you think?

Kohlberg's theory of moral development – a cognitive approach

Lawrence Kohlberg's work on moral development is well known. He built on Piaget's description of moral development and suggested that, as with other cognitive areas, moral reasoning is linked to stages of development. He suggests that there are three levels of moral development that are subdivided into stages.

The chart below outlines the three levels and stages.

Age	Level	Stages
6–13	Pre-conventional	1. Punishment and obedience 2. Individualism, instrumental purpose and exchange
13–16	Conventional	3. 'good boy/nice girl' 4. Law and order
16–20+	Post conventional/ principled	5. Social contract 6. Universal ethical principles

Pre-conventional

This is divided into two stages. At this level, children are not being guided by their own moral reasoning, but following their parents or carers. They are doing this to either seek reward or to avoid punishment.

Stage 1: Punishment and obedience

The child finds out about what is wrong and right through seeing the consequences of their actions.

Stage 2: Individualism, instrumental purpose and exchange

The child is learning that some actions and behaviours are rewarded. The child is also learning to avoid behaviours that might mean punishment. By the end of this stage the child is also beginning to enjoy helping people and has learnt the 'if I help you, you might be able to help me' approach.

Conventional

The next level of moral development consists of an awareness of group behaviour and the idea that of what is and isn't acceptable in society.

Mutual interpersonal expectations, relationships and interpersonal conformity (often known as the 'good boy/nice girl' stage)

In this stage children come to believe that good behaviour pleases other people e.g. friends, teachers and parents. Children are also becoming aware of the motive factor i.e. 'he meant to help really'.

Social system and conscience (also referred to as law and order orientation)

This is a widening out stage – before children were wanting to show good and correct behaviour to please people they knew. In this stage, we become more aware of society's needs and interests and what is deemed by society to be right or wrong. People in this stage are keen to obey regulations and laws.

Post-conventional or principled morality

This level is very different to the others. At this level, people are not accepting the morality of the group or society unquestioningly. Demonstrators who break laws, e.g. animal right's campaigners who illegally set animals free, would be demonstrating this level of morality.

Social contract

At this stage rules and regulations are seen as useful tools to make sure that there is some protection and fairness in society. People working at this level are prepared to tolerate rules being broken, if they do not see that they are fair or just rules.

Universal ethical principles

This last stage was in some ways an unclear one for Kohlberg and difficult one to test. People working at this stage would be extremely principled people who are not swayed by society and have inner principles which they have developed. People in history who may have reached this level were often killed or persecuted as they were often seen as troublemakers as they would be unwilling to compromise their position.

Testing moral reasoning

Kohlberg used hypothetical stories to test his theory (see Think It Over activity below). His ideas have also been tested in many countries by John Snarey (1985) to see if his stage theory was relevant to other cultures. The result of his studies showed that the development of moral reasoning did fit the stage and level model, although in some societies, a norm of stage 2 reasoning was shown.

Think It Over

You might like to try out one of Kohlberg's stories to look at the reaction of children you work with. (The story has been simplified and adapted so that you can use it with children aged four plus.)

A man was trying to save his wife's life. He could not afford to pay for the special medicine she needed. He asked the only chemist who sold it, but the chemist would not give it to him. Later the man broke into the chemist's shop and stole the medicine.

Should he have stolen the medicine?

Theory into practice

If moral development follows a stage process, with children learning more as they develop, it would mean that an 'age' approach to children knowing right from wrong is not a helpful one. It also means that it is difficult to 'teach' children right from wrong. What do you think?

Psychoanalytical – Freud and moral development

Freud suggested that moral development was also part of personality development. He suggested that moral behaviour is controlled by the superego (see page 440). He also suggested that children would be influenced by their parents through the process of identification during the phallic stage. Freud believed that children identify, that is to say, try to be the same as their same-sex parents. This would mean that a boy who had an authoritarian father would be likely to show the same characteristics.

Assessment activity 12.2

Using at least three observations of one child in a setting, prepare a report about how the child is learning behaviour. The report should:

- analyse how the child's behaviour is being managed or reinforced in the setting
- evaluate ways in which the child is learning behaviours
- consider how the theories of how children learn behaviour link to practice.

Formation of early relationships

The study of children's early relationships and their importance in a child's overall development did not really start until the 1950s when John Bowlby published *Maternal Care and Mental Health*. The results of this and subsequent research has had noticeable and continuing effects on childcare practice. This means that adults working with babies and children need to have a good understanding of the stages in attachment, attachment theory and the effects of separation.

What is meant by the term attachment?

The term **attachment** is widely used by psychologists studying children's early relationships. An attachment can be thought of as a unique emotional tie between a child and another person, usually an adult. Research has repeatedly shown that the quality of these ties or attachments will shape a child's ability to form other relationships later in life. Attachment is often seen as a process.

Age	Stage	Features
6 weeks – 3 months		Babies begin to be attracted to human faces and voices. First smiles begin at around six weeks
3 months – 7/8 months	Indiscriminate attachments	Babies are learning to distinguish between faces showing obvious pleasure when they recognise familiar faces. They are happy to be handled by strangers preferring to be in human company rather than left alone – hence the term indiscriminate attachments

Age	Stage	Features
7/8 months	Specific attachments	At around 7 or 8 months, babies begin to miss key people in their lives and show signs of distress – for example, crying when they leave the room. Most babies also seem to have developed one particularly strong attachment – often to the mother. Babies also show a wariness of strangers even when in the presence of their 'key people'. This wariness may quickly develop into fear if the stranger makes some form of direct contact with the baby, for example, by touching them
From 8 months	Multiple attachments	After making specific attachments, babies then go on to form multiple attachments. This is an important part of their socialisation process

Bowlby's theory of attachment

The work of John Bowlby has greatly influenced social care policy, childcare practices and research into early relationships. Immediately after the World War II, he was asked to investigate the effects on children's development of being brought up in orphanages or other institutions. In 1951 his findings showed that meeting children's physical needs alone was not sufficient – children were being psychologically damaged because of the absence of their mothers. The term 'maternal deprivation' was used to describe this effect. He reached this conclusion by looking at the life histories of children who had been referred to his clinic. He noticed an overwhelming trend – most of these children had suffered early separations from their mothers and families.

Main features of Bowlby's theory

- **Monotropy** – Bowlby believed that babies need to form one main attachment and that this relationship would be special and of more importance to the child than any other. Bowlby suggested that in most cases this relationship would be formed with the mother, but that it could be formed with the father or another person.
- **Critical period** – Bowlby was greatly influenced by ethologists such as Lorenz and he believed that in the same way that humans too would have a '**critical period**'. He felt that babies needed to have developed their main attachment by the age of one year and that during a child's first four years, prolonged separation from this person would cause long-term psychological damage.
- **Children need 'parenting'** – Bowlby showed through his findings that simply meeting a child's physical and care needs is not enough for healthy growth and development. Children need to have a main attachment in their early lives that gives them consistent support. His early papers suggested that the mother should play this role, although his position changed in later years.
- **Children show distress when separated from main attachment** – Bowlby outlined a pattern of distress that babies and children show when separated from their carers. This is often referred to as **separation anxiety** (see page 452) He also made links to show that when adults had been separated from their mothers in infancy, they would not form deep and lasting relationships. He called this effect '**maternal deprivation**'.

Criticism of Bowlby's work

There are many criticisms of Bowlby's work and his work has been superseded by other pieces of research. When looking at the criticisms of his work, it is, however, important to remember the political, economic and social climate of the time.

The role of the mother was overemphasised

This has been a major criticism of Bowlby's early work. At the time of writing, women were the traditional care-givers and economically after the war the government was keen for women to return to their traditional roles within the home. Bowlby's later work did emphasise that babies could form an attachment with someone other than the mother.

Attachments to more than one person were not explored

Bowlby placed a lot of emphasis on the importance of one single attachment. Subsequent research (Schaffer and Emerson, 1964) has shown that as children get older, they can develop equally strong attachments to other figures such as their fathers and siblings (see table, page 449).

Quality of the substitute care was not taken into consideration

Bowlby did not take into consideration the effect of being in poor quality care. This means that it is hard to be absolutely sure that the psychological damage done to the children was only the result of 'maternal deprivation'. Later studies have suggested that good quality care can help children to adjust to separation as children are able to substitute the main attachment to another person (Hodges and Tizard, 1989).

Maternal deprivation as a concept was too general

Michael Rutter criticises Bowlby's 'maternal deprivation' as being too general. Factors such as discord in the family, the nature of separation and the quality of attachments made would all affect outcome. This explains why some children are more adversely affected by their earlier experiences than others (see also Key issues box about Koluchova, page 453).

Schaffer and Emerson's work on attachment

Until the 1950s, it was generally thought that babies and children automatically formed the strongest relationships with the people who fed them and met their physical needs. This is sometimes referred to as 'cupboard love'! Several pieces of research have shown that this is not necessarily true. One strong piece of research by Schaffer and Emerson (1964) showed that babies and children can form the equally strong attachments to their fathers even when the father is not the main giver. Over a period of eighteen months they visited babies at four-weekly intervals and found that most children by eighteen months protested equally when they were separated from either the mother or the father. This piece of research showed that care giving alone did not automatically mean that a child would form a main attachment.

Theory into practice

One of the major concerns most parents have when leaving babies with nannies or childminders is that the child will attach itself to the care-giver and not know who their parent is. Although in theory this is possible, it is unlikely providing the parents spend time responding to and interacting with the baby. This is the idea behind 'quality time' where the quality of the interaction and responsiveness of the parents is more important than the actual time spent with children.

The role of fathers

Recent research has highlighted the importance of a father's role in children's social and emotional development. Fathers seem to offer a different type of contribution, which is nonetheless valued by babies and children.

Research also shows the following:

- Most children aged 7-30 months chose their father to be playmates in preference to their mother (Clarke-Stewart, 1978).
- Fathers hold their children in order to play with them, whereas most holding by mothers is linked to care-giving or restricting (Lamb, 1977).
- Fathers play in different ways with their children, giving children more vigorous physical play (Parke, 1981).
- Strong attachments to both parents rather than just one also seems to help children in unfamiliar situations (Main and Weston, 1981).

Theory into practice

Interestingly these pieces of research also coincide with a greater public awareness of the importance of fathers, although ironically, due to an increase in divorce and separation, a large proportion of children grow up in families without fathers. The understanding that men relate in different ways to children is also a reason why many early years settings are trying to employ male members of staff.

Attachment behaviour

It is important for early years practitioners to be able to identify when babies and children have made attachments. This generally can be observed through looking at their behaviour. There are four broad indicators that babies and children might show:

- Actively seeking to be near the other person.
- Crying or showing visible distress when that person leaves or for babies is no longer visible.
- Showing joy or relief when that person appears.
- Acute awareness of that person's presence, e.g. looking up at them from time to time, responding to their voices, following their movements

Looking at the quality of attachments

There has been some research that has looked at the quality of babies' early attachments. It would seem that where babies and children are 'securely' attached they are able to explore and develop their independence. Babies and children whose attachment is less secure seem to show either indifference or clingy types of behaviour.

The 'strange situation'

The quality of attachments was looked at by Ainsworth who is considered alongside Bowlby to a be key figure in this area of pyschology. Ainsworth and her colleagues (1978) created a scenario by which babies' reactions to being left with a stranger and then reunited with their mothers (and or fathers) was measured. This scenario is now widely used to study attachment behaviour.

The scenario is known as the 'strange situation' and is divided into eight parts with each part lasting about three minutes. During the experiment, the baby (a one-year-old) has some time by itself as well as with a stranger.

1 Parent and baby enters room.
2 Parent remains inactive, baby is free to explore room.
3 Stranger joins parent and infant.
4 Parent leaves room.
5 Parent returns, settles baby and stranger leaves.
6 Baby is alone in the room.
7 Stranger returns and interacts with baby.
8 Parent returns again and stranger leaves.

Ainsworth and her colleagues were particularly interested in the reactions of the baby to the parent when they left or returned and the way in which the parent interacted with the baby. They categorised the behaviour into three types.

Type A – anxious-avoidant
Baby largely ignores parent and shows little signs of distress when parent leaves continuing to play. Baby ignores or avoids parent on their return. Baby dislikes being alone, but can be comforted by stranger.

Type B – securely attached
Baby plays while parent is present, but shows visible distress when parent leaves and play is reduced. Baby is easily comforted on return of parent and carries on playing. Cries when alone because parent is not there, but can be partly comforted by stranger. Reactions towards stranger and parents are markedly different.

Type C – anxious-resistant
Baby is wary and explores less than other types. Very distressed when parent leaves and actively resists stranger's attempts to comfort. Wants immediate contact with parent on return but is ambivalent, showing frustration and anger alongside clinginess, e.g. wanting to be held but then immediately struggling to get down.

Why are some children more securely attached than others?
Ainsworth came to the conclusion that the quality of attachment depended on the parenting that the baby received. Where parents were able to sense and predict their babies' needs and frustrations, the babies showed type B behaviour. This meant that they were able to explore and play, knowing that their parent was as a safe base.

What happens when babies and children are separated from their main attachments?
Most early years practitioners will notice that as children become older, they find it easier to separate from their parents. This is because they have formed other attachments to staff and as they get older to other children. They have also learnt that although their parent is absent, they will return. Babies and toddlers, however, find it difficult to cope with the absence of their main atttachments and will show distress.

Bowlby noted that there seemed to be a pattern to the way children reacted if they were separated from their main attachments. This pattern is often referred to as **separation anxiety**. Separation anxiety is clearly seen in babies from around seven months and seems to reach a peak at around twelve to fifteen months. Older children will show separation anxiety if they are separated for long periods, e.g. if a parent dies or goes away for a period of time.

There seems to be three distinct stages of separation anxiety, as shown in the table below.

Stage	Features
Protest	Children may cry, struggle to escape, kick and show anger
Despair	Children show calmer behaviour almost as though they have accepted the separation. They may be withdrawn and sad. Comfort behaviour such as thumbsucking or rocking may be shown
Detachment	Children may appear to be 'over' the separation and start to join in activities. The child is actually coping by trying to 'forget' the relationship – hence the title detachment. The effects of detachment may be longer lasting as the child may have learnt not to trust people they care for

What are the effects of parents leaving their children to go to work?

A number of studies in America have compared groups of children – those with working parents and those with a parent who has stayed at home. One of the largest studies (Kagan *et al.*, 1980) would suggest that children receiving high quality day care fare no differently from children whose parents stay at home. The importance of good standards of care and attention cannot however be emphasised enough!

Privation is the term used when babies and children have not formed a main attachment.

There is a difference between the terms 'deprivation' and 'privation'. Deprivation means that a child has made a main attachment and then has been separated from the person. Privation means that the baby or child has never formed a main attachment. Fortunately, an increased awareness of child abuse and child protection has meant that cases of extreme privation in the UK are rare. There are, however, some famous case studies that have helped psychologists look at privation in children. Below is the case study of the Czech twins reported by Koluchova in 1972.

Key issues – the Czech twins reported by Koluchova (1972)

In 1967, twin boys aged seven years were found to be in a neglected state in Czechoslovakia. They had been cruelly treated and beaten by their stepmother and had often been locked in a cupboard together. They had little speech when they were rescued and after spending two years in a children's home were fostered. Follow-up reports in 1976 suggested that they had made significant progress in their speech and cognitive development and by 1984 they had completed an apprenticeship. They also seem to be psychologically stable and had developed a good relationship with the foster family.

This case study seems to show that children can form main attachments to each other – almost as a survival mechanism. This and similar case studies also cast doubt on beliefs that poor early experiences will automatically create irreversible damage on children's social and cognitive development.

Assessment activity 12.3

Produce a report about attachment and settling in procedures.

Your report should:
- be based on information that you have collected about settling procedures at two different settings that care for children aged four years and under
- analyse the settling in procedures studied in relation to attachment theories
- examine the influence of attachment theories on early years practice
- evaluate factors that might affect the settling in process.

Processing and using information

From birth onwards, we are constantly being bombarded with information – light, sounds, tastes and language. The way we process this information, sometimes filtering it out, has been a study of research in recent years. This section looks at the following aspects of processing and using information:

- Piaget's approach to cognitive development.
- Vygotsky's and Bruner's theories of cognitive development.
- The information processing approach to learning.

Piaget's theory of cognitive development

Jean Piaget was a zoologist who became interested in children's cognitive development as a result of working on intelligence tests. He noticed that children consistently gave similar 'wrong' answers to some questions and began to consider why this was. Piaget used his own children to make detailed observations and gradually developed a theory of learning. This theory is sometimes referred to as a **constructivist approach** as he suggested that children constructed or built up their thoughts according to their experiences of the world around them. Piaget used the term **schema** to mean a child's conclusions or thoughts. Piaget felt that this was an ongoing process with children needing to adapt (hence Piaget's term **adaption**) their original ideas if a new piece of information seemed to contradict their conclusions.

Understanding why children think differently to adults

Piaget's belief that children develop schemas based on their direct experiences can help us to understand why sometimes young children's thinking is so different to ours. Piaget also suggested that as children develop so does their thinking. He grouped children's cognitive development into four broad stages. (See also Unit 7.)

Sensori-motor stage (0–2 years)
This is the first stage of children's lives. It begins at birth with babies using their reflexes to survive. Babies are also very reliant on using their senses in the first two years especially taste and touch. Babies' first schemas are physical ones with babies learning to repeat and then control their movements.

Pre-operational stage (2–7 years)
During this stage, children develop their skills at using symbols, i.e. language. Many early years practitioners will find that children in this stage are using a lot of imaginative play where children use objects to stand in a representational way, e.g. sticks become guns, cardboard boxes become cars. Piaget did divide this stage into two

further substages – pre-conceptual and intuitive – although there are four main features which run through both of these substages:

- Egocentrism – the child can only see things from their own perspective.
- Conservation – children find it difficult to understand that things can remain the same, even though their appearance might change.
- Centration – children are beginning to classify objects and make associations but are often only looking at one attribute at a time e.g. sorting objects according to size but not size and colour.
- Animism – the child believes that objects must have feelings, e.g. 'That wall is bad, it hurt me'. Children's drawings can also be animistic.

Concrete operations stage (7-11 years)
This stage marks a great leap in children's logical abilities. They begin to use rules and strategies to help their thinking. Piaget called this the concrete stage because children are helped in their thinking when they can do it in practical ways, e.g. using counters to find the answer to 15 – 9 = ?.

Theory into practice

Children in the concrete operations stage will need plenty of practical support to help them, e.g. they may use their fingers to help them count or need to see something actually laid out or acted out for them to understand it.

- Find out about the national Numeracy Strategy in schools. What is the balance between practical and mental mathematics?
- Ask one teacher in Key Stage 1 and another in Key Stage 2 how easily children find it to carry out mental calculations.

Formal operations stage (11-15 years)
The main difference between this stage and the concrete operations stage is that children are now able to manipulate thoughts and ideas to solve problems without needing practical props. This means that, in theory, tasks such as map reading can be done without having to turn the map around to work out whether a turning is on the right or left.

Criticism of Piaget's work
Piaget's work has been very influential and widely accepted, but there have been many criticisms of his work as further research has been carried out.

Piaget's research methods may have been biased
Piaget did use clinical interviews as the major research method with children. This method is open to bias, but Piaget did carry out hundreds of interviews and the type of data that was collected is qualitative, but very informative. Piaget also used experiments, but the tests he constructed have also been criticised (see below).

Does cognitive development really happen in stages?

This is one of the criticisms of Piaget's early work, although from the 1970s Piaget suggested a spiralling process and considered that at times children will show features of more than one stage at once. This he referred to as *d'ecalage*, but maintained that children would not be able to skip whole elements of the stages and progress to another stage.

Piaget underestimated children

One of the most widely accepted criticisms of Piaget's work is that the ages that he gave for children's thinking are inaccurate. He underestimated children's level of thinking. One of the reasons given for his inaccuracies is the type of tasks that he used with children.

Piaget underestimated how training and practice can help children

Piaget suggested that the cognitive development of children was heavily linked to maturation and therefore children could not be 'fast tracked' through the stages. There has, however, been some research which suggests that children can achieve tasks if they are given experiences to help them, e.g. Bruner felt that five- and six-year-olds can be taught to conserve, although training is only partially effective.

Think It Over

In your work setting, consider the following questions in relation to Piaget's theory of how children learn:

- Is there an assumption that children need to work at their own pace (i.e. are children grouped according to their stages of development or according to their ages)?
- What type of activities are chosen that encourage learning through discovery (e.g. children using beakers and water to find out about properties of water)?

Other constructivist approaches to cognitive development

Although Piaget's work is well known, there are two other approaches which are in some ways similar to Piaget's and have also influenced early years practice: Vygotsky's theory of cognitive development and Bruner's developmental theory.

Vygotsky's theory of cognitive development

Vygotksy's work was not published in English until the early 1960s, even though his work was known in Russia in the 1920s and 1930s. He believed that children's social environment and experiences are very important. He considered that children were born to be sociable and that by being with their parents and then with their friends they acquired skills and concepts. Vygotsky saw children as 'apprentices', learning and gaining understanding through being with others. The term 'scaffolding' is often used alongside Vygotsky's ideas as the idea of the child being helped by adults around them to learn concepts is a strong feature of his work.

Vygotsky also suggested that maturation was an important element in children's development and that we needed to extend children's learning so that they could use their emerging skills and concepts. He used the term **zone of proximal development** to define this idea, although we might think of this as potential.

Bruner's developmental theory

Jerome Bruner's work was influenced by Piaget but particularly by Vygotsky's work. Bruner's is not a stage theory as such but he suggests that children gradually acquire cognitive skills which Bruner refers to as modes of thinking – see the table below.

Mode	Age (approx.)	Description and use
Enactive	0–1 years	Learning and thought take place because of physical movements
Iconic	1–7 years	Thoughts are developed as mental images
Symbolic	7+ years	Symbols including language are used in thinking

Information processing theory of cognitive development

Information processing theories (IP) of cognitive development consider the actual processes used when information is presented to us. Information is constantly being gathered in the brain through our five senses – we may hear a sound in the street whilst also having the television on – some information we store and use whilst others we filter out and disregard. Information processing theories often use similar language to the terms used in computing as they suggest that the brain acts in similar ways! In much the same ways as computers, IP theorists suggest that tasks are broken down as part of the process involved in handling information. This breaking down into stages is often referred to as 'task analysis'.

Memory

Memory is an important component in our ability to process information. It was not until the 1950s that memory was really studied by psychologists and at present the most influential work carried out on memory has been by Atkinson and Shiffrin. They have proposed a 'multi-store' model which looks at the way information is coded and retrieved.

Theories about the way we store and retrieve information vary, but most psychologists agree that there is a process system to our memory – a simplified version of this process is shown below.

Primary and secondary memory (short- and long-term memory)

Most psychologists also agree and have worked on the concept which William James (1890) suggested that memory storage is divided into two – commonly called short- and long-term memory. Our short-term or (primary) memory is the one we use when we are holding a new telephone number for a few seconds before dialling it. An hour later we might not remember the order of the digits. By contrast the long-term memory can hold information for a few minutes or for a lifetime! The long-term memory is seen as having unlimited capacity – this may come as a surprise if you are someone who has difficulty remembering things, but storage capacity is completely different to the process of retrieving information.

Storing information

In order to be able to retrieve information from either our long- or short-term memories, we have to encode it. If information is not encoded properly, it will be lost to us. Researchers are still looking at the way we encode information, but it would seem that our long-term memory uses three main methods: visual, semantic (signs, written and spoken language) and acoustic. In addition, we may also learn some of the following strategies that help us hold onto information that we do not want to forget.

Rehearsal

Repeating to ourselves what we want to remember, e.g. repeating a telephone number or practising actions to a song.

Clustering or chunking

This involves grouping pieces of information – rather than remembering a telephone number as 0-0-3-3-5-6-0-6-7-9-9-7, you would remember it in clusters or chunks 00-33-56-06-79-97. Children as young as two years can begin to chunk information.

Elaboration

Elaboration means finding connections between things that need to be remembered. If you find a person's name difficult to remember, you might think about one feature about that person to help you. Mnemoics such as <u>N</u>ever <u>E</u>at <u>S</u>hredded <u>W</u>heat, to remember the points around a compass are forms of elaboration.

Assessment activity 12.4

Produce an information sheet for other students on the theories of cognitive development.

- Outline each of the following theories: Piaget, Bruner and Vygotsky.
- Analyse the differences and similarities between these theories.
- Evaluate each theory's contribution to current early years practice using examples based on your placement experience.

Language development

Language either spoken or written plays an important part in most people's lives. Some psychologists, theologians and philosophers would suggest that our ability to use language to communicate and think separates us from the animal kingdom.

Understanding the structure of language

It is important to have some understanding of the structure of language. All languages have rules which are understood and used by both the speaker and listener. The rules are often usually referred to as grammar. By following the rules or grammar, speakers and listeners can understand each other. Linguists who study the structure of language use the term grammar to describe the 'package' of a language. This package is formed of three key elements:

- phonology
- semantics
- Syntax.

Phonology

Languages have a sound system – phonology. When we hear someone speaking, we may recognise the language that they are using, even if we cannot speak it. This recognition may be based on listening to the sounds that are being used. The individual sounds that are used in a language are called phones – some languages use fewer phones than others, i.e. there are 40 phones used in English. Individual sounds that are combined together are called phonemes.

Semantics

Languages are composed of words or units of meaning. When we learn a language we also have to learn what these units are and how they can be changed, i.e. if we add 'less' onto the end of some words, it changes their meaning.

Syntax

Finally, we have to learn the rules for using the words and how their place in a sentence can change their meaning, e.g. 'The cat ate the mouse' has a different meaning to 'The mouse ate the cat' even though the same words have been used.

The sequence of language development

A good starting point when considering language development is to look at the pattern by which children learn to speak. It is interesting to note that babies and children in whichever country they are born all follow a similar pattern. The first year of a baby's life is spent trying to 'tune in' on the language that they are hearing and learning the skills of communication, i.e. making eye contact, responding to others' facial expressions and words. This first year is often known as the pre-linguistic phase and is now considered to be vital in children's overall language development.

The major stages in language development are shown in the table below.

Stage	Age	Features	Comments
Pre-linguistic			
Cooing	6 weeks	Cooing	Babies making cooing sounds. Cooing sounds made to show pleasure. These early sounds are different to sounds made later on mainly because the mouth is still developing
Babbling (phonemic expansion)	6–9 months	Babies blend vowels and consonants together to make tuneful sounds, e.g. ba, ma, da	Babbling has been described as learning the tune before the words. The baby seems to be practising its sounds. Babies increase the number of sounds or phonemes. This is sometimes called phonemic expansion. All babies, even deaf babies, produce a wide range of sounds during this period
Babbling (phonemic contraction) Echolalia	9–10 months	Babies babble but the range of sounds is limited	The range of sounds or phonemes that babies phonemes used in the language that they are hearing. At this stage, it would in theory be possible to distinguish between babies who are in different language environments. At 10 months babies are also understanding 17 or more words

Stage	Age	Features	Comments
Linguistic stage			
First words	Around 12 months	Babies repeatedly use one or more sounds which has meaning for them	The first words are often unclear and so gradually emerge. They are often one sound, but are used regularly in similar situations, e.g. 'ba' to mean drink and cuddle. Babbling still continues
Holophrases	12-18 months	Toddlers start to use one word in a variety of ways	Toddlers use holophrases to make their limited vocabulary more useful for them. One word is used in several situations, but the tone of voice and the context helps the adult understand what the toddler means. Most toddlers have 10-15 words by 18 months
Two-word utterances – telegraphic speech	18-24 months	Two words are put together to make a mini sentence	Toddlers begin to combine words to make sentences. They seem to have grasped which are the key words in a sentence – 'dada gone' or 'dada come'
Language explosion	24-36 months	A large increase in children's vocabulary combined with increasing use of sentences	This is a period in which children's language seems to evolve rapidly. Children learn words so rapidly that it becomes hard for parents to count them! At the same time the child uses more complicated structures in their speech. Plurals and negatives begin to be used, e.g. no dogs here!
	3-4 years	Sentences become longer and vocabulary continues to increase	Children are using language in a more complete way. Mistakes in grammar show that they are still absorbing the rules and sometimes misapplying them! Mistakes such as 'I wented' show that they have learnt that '-ed' makes a past tense. These type of mistakes are known as 'virtuous errors'
Fluency	4-5 years	Mastered the basic skills of the language	Children have mastered the basic rules of English grammar and are fluent, although will still be making some 'virtuous' errors

Theories of how children use language

The nature versus nurture debate appears once more when we look at the theories of how children learn language.

Skinner's operant conditioning theory – behaviourist perspective

This is a 'nurture' theory as Skinner suggests that we learn language mainly because when babies try and communicate their efforts are rewarded or reinforced in some way, e.g. a baby may get a smile from a parent if they gurgle. Skinner used this idea of reinforcement to explain why babies stop making some sounds – he reasoned that when babies made sounds that parents did not recognise, they would not receive any attention, whilst sounds which were recognisable were noticed and reinforced. He called this process selective reinforcement. This approach would explain why children speak in similar ways to their parents using the familiar phrases and intonation.

However, there have been criticisms of Skinner's theory. For example, the theory does not explain why all babies and children follow the same pattern of gaining language. If Skinner's theory was correct, you would expect to see that children's language would develop very differently depending on the amount and type of reinforcement that adults and others were giving. This is not the case, however, as most children seem to pass through the same stages. Also, the theory does not explain why children speak in different ways to adults around them, e.g. 'dada gone'. If children are learning by imitating what they are hearing and not having incorrect sounds or sentences reinforced, why do children say things such as 'wented' or 'swimmed'?

Noam Chomsky – nativist perspective

Chomsky's work on language is based on the idea that our ability to learn language is instinctive. This is a 'nature' or nativist theory. His theory has been widely accepted as it is comprehensive and unlike Skinner's ideas explains why all babies' language development follows a pattern. He is famous for suggesting that humans have a Language Acquisition Device (LAD). This is not an actual physical part of the brain, but a structure within our brains that allows babies to absorb and understand the rules of the language they are being exposed to. The brain is able to analyse the language and work out the system that the language uses. This is a complex process, but explains why children can quickly understand and then use their language creatively and correctly without ever being formally taught or 'knowing' the rules.

How language links to thought

There seems to be a strong link to language and thought, although there are different views of the relationship between them. Piaget differed in his views from Vygotsky and Bruner because he suggested that language was a tool that was used by us whereas Vygotsky and Bruner suggest that language organises and drives the thought process.

Vygotsky

Vygotsky suggested that thought and language begin as two different activities – when a baby babbles they are not using babbling as a way of thinking. At around the age of two years, they merge and at this point the child uses language to help them think. Vygotsky also differentiated between two types of speech – inner speech which helps us to think and external speech which we use to communicate with others. An example of inner speech would be when we say either aloud or inwardly 'Then, I am going to...' as a way of directing ourselves. Between the ages of two and seven years, Vygotsky felt that children were not able to use them in distinct ways and therefore their speech was often a blend of the two with young children often providing a running commentary of what they are doing. Vygtotsky referred to this early speech and thought as egocentric.

Bruner

Bruner suggested that language is also linked to thought and that it was why children were able to develop a symbolic mode of thought. Previously children were using visual imagery to hold and use information in their learning, but language allowed them to use abstract thoughts, e.g. symbolic.

Assessment activity 12.5

Prepare a presentation on language development for other students. You should also produce a handout to support your presentation. Your presentation should:

- evaluate the different theories of language development
- analyse the links between language and thought
- examine ways in which the early years practitioner can contribute to language development.

How early years practitioners influence children's development

To end this unit we look at how we might be able to influence the development of children we work with. We have already seen that many aspects of children's development rely on the adults around them, e.g. language development and learning through imitation. This might already make us believe that we can influence development, but one piece of research shows that we can clearly make the difference. The experiment is very famous because it had a lot of implications for those working with children – it is known as the 'Pygmalion' experiment.

Key issues – Pygmalion in the classroom (1968)

Two researchers, Rosenthal and Jacobson, carried out an experiment in which they told classroom teachers that some of the children they were due to teach were likely to make significant progress in the school year. They named these children (who had actually been chosen on a random basis) and then monitored their progress later. The researchers were then staggered to find that the named children had made the 'predicted' progress! They associated the children's progress with the teachers having high expectations of these children and the children in turn living up to these expectations. The link between expectations of others and actual behaviour is known as the self-fulfilling prophecy.

The importance of understanding the self-fulfilling prophecy

This experiment, although based in a school setting, shows clearly that the way adults think about children will influence children's behaviour and achievement, i.e. if we show children that we believe in them and have high expectations of them, they will demonstrate this behaviour to us.

Think It Over

In pairs, using the self-fulfilling prophecy can you explain why:

- labelling children as difficult or naughty can be unhelpful
- some children are 'good', i.e. show wanted behaviour for some adults, but not for others
- saying to a child 'Never mind, you have done your best' may actually send out the wrong signals to a child?

End-of-unit test

1 Briefly explain the theory of operant conditioning.

2 What is the difference between operant and classical conditioning?

3 Why has Lorenz's theory of aggression been criticised?

4 Explain how the social learning theory may be used to explain differences in personality.

5 Explain the role of the id, ego and superego according to Freud.

6 What were the key effects of Bowlby's work on the childcare practices?

7 What are the major criticisms of Bowlby's early work?

8 List Piaget's stages of cognitive development.

9 Why were Piaget's research methods criticised?

10 What are the differences between the nativist and the behaviourist perspectives of language development?

Further reading

Bee, Helen (1999) *The Developing Child*, London: Longman

Bukatko, Danuta & Daehler, Marvin (1997) *Child Development: A Thematic Approach* (3rd edition), London: Houghton and Mifflin

Gross, Richard (2001) *Psychology: The Science of Mind and Behaviour* (4th edition), London: Hodder and Stoughton

Gross, Richard, McIlveen, Rob, Coolican, Hugh, Russell, Julia & Clamp, Alan (2000) *Psychology: a New Introduction for A Level* (2nd edition), London: Hodder and Stoughton

Introduction

According to the 1994 Code of Practice on the Identification and Assessment of Special Educational Needs, around 22 per cent of all children will have some sort of special educational need during their childhood. The term 'special needs' is an extremely broad one and takes in children who may have short-term educational needs, alongside those who are gifted and those who have inherited a severe learning difficulty. The number of children who are considered to have a special need means that a good understanding and awareness of special needs is important for early years practitioners and adults working with children.

What you need to learn
- Terminology and definitions
- Legislation and assessment procedures
- Disability equality in practice
- Working in partnership
- Issues in communicating

Terminology and definitions

This section looks at the terminology and definitions that are used in relation to special needs. It also looks at some of the factors that may create disabilities as well as some types of disability.

Getting the terminology right

A good starting point is the language and terms that are used in relation to special needs. Language is a powerful tool; words and phrases can reveal our deep-seated attitudes and so getting the language right when talking about special needs is important. There has been quite a shift in thinking about disability in the past 20 years and this has been reflected in the language we use and it is quite possible that it will change again to reflect further changes in society's thinking. An example of this is the current debate within some organisations such as SCOPE as to whether the term 'disabled people' should be used.

The key to working successfully with anyone who has special needs is to think about the person, not about the condition. At the time of writing the following words are often used:

Impairment: the loss or abnormality of development of growth, e.g. a hearing impairment means that a person has a loss of hearing.

Disability: the restrictions that the impairment causes, e.g. a person with a hearing disability has a disability in hearing.

Handicap: the disadvantage that the person has in relation to others in certain situations. Note that the person is not themselves 'handicapped' – they are being handicapped by the situation, e.g. a person with a hearing impairment is being handicapped when announcements are being broadcast in an airport because they have a hearing disability. Their disability does not prevent them from reading the signs and getting onto the aircraft and so they are not being handicapped.

Definitions of special educational needs

There are several definitions of special needs. Definitions often reflect the attitudes of society and they gradually change over time. The following definitions are used in current legislation.

Education Act 1996

Children have special educational needs if they have a learning difficulty which calls for special educational provision to be made for them. Children have a learning difficulty if they:

- have a significantly greater difficulty in learning than the majority of children of the same age, *or*
- have a disability which prevents or hinders them from making use of educational facilities of a kind generally provided for children of the same age in schools within the area of the local education authority, *or*
- are under compulsory school age and fall within the two definitions above or would do so if special educational provision was not made for them.

Disability Discrimination Act 1995, Section 1 (1)

A person has a disability for the purposes of this Act if they have a physical or mental impairment which has substantial and long-term adverse effect on their ability to carry out normal day-to-day activities.

Children Act 1989, Section 17 (11)

A child is disabled if they are blind, deaf or dumb or suffers from a mental disorder of any kind or is substantially and permanently handicapped by illness, injury or congenital deformity or such other disability as they may be prescribed.

Classifications of special need

As well as legal definitions of children with special needs the following terms are also currently used to classify children into broad groups according to their overall needs rather than to focus on the 'medical cause' of the disability (see Warnock Report, 1978).

Mild learning difficulties

It has been suggested that about 18 per cent of all children will at some time in their school career have some form of mild learning difficulty. Most of these children will not need a statement but will be given extra attention and support within settings.

Case Study

Joshua has some difficulty with spelling and writing. His writing is neat but very slow and he works painstakingly hard to produce a few lines. He often rubs out his work, as he prefers to get his spelling correct. Recently the special needs assistant working with Joshua suspected that Joshua has adopted task avoidance strategies as he constantly asks for spellings and spends a lot of his time either looking for the rubber or rubbing out. He also spends time asking other children for help in finding the rubber and is generally the last child to sit down and actually start a task. At a review meeting, it is decided that Joshua will be given much shorter work tasks that involve less writing and that instead of praising the neatness of his work, he will be praised for finishing the task. It is also decided to make Joshua responsible for counting and giving out the milk straws each day. Within a few days, Joshua has become more enthusiastic about his work as he can see that he can easily complete it and he is enjoying helping the adults in the classroom.

Moderate learning difficulties

Before the 1981 Education Act, the majority of children who had moderate learning difficulties, such as children with Down's syndrome, would have been educated in special schools. Children with moderate learning difficulties often have limited ability to follow instructions and think independently.

Severe learning difficulties

Many children with severe learning difficulties need specialist help and care which means that they attend special schools or specialist units within mainstream schools. Many children will have genetic disorders or have had a medical injury, e.g. during birth or an accident during childhood. Children with severe learning difficulties need a high level of adult support and find it difficult to act independently.

Profound and multiple learning difficulties (PMLD)

Children with profound and multiple learning difficulties will mostly have a combination of severe physical disabilities and severe learning difficulties. Many children may also have difficulty with their vision and hearing. Most of these children will require adult support to carry out basic tasks such as feeding, dressing and toileting. The majority of children with PMLD will be cared for and supported in special schools where the key priority will be ensuring children's physical comfort. Many children are unable to communicate and so finding ways to break into their world is essential.

Specific learning difficulties

Children with specific learning difficulties may have learning difficulties which are specific rather than general, e.g. they find it difficult learning to read, but otherwise have no difficulty in communicating or coping with abstract concepts. They are often of average or even above average ability but have a difficulty in one or more specific areas. The most common type of specific learning difficulty is commonly referred to as dyslexia, although this is a general 'umbrella' term.

Emotional and behavioural difficulties (EBD)

The term covers a range of behaviours, but in general children with EBD will have some type of emotional or social difficulties. In many cases these difficulties often cause children to show disruptive and unwanted behaviour which in turn will interfere with their ability to learn effectively.

Physical disability

This term covers a range of conditions, many of which will not affect children's ability to learn (see the diagram below). This is an important point to consider as many people with physical disability feel very frustrated when they are treated as if they had some sort of learning difficulty.

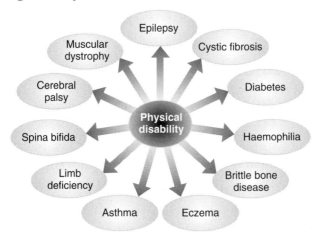

Sensory impairment

There are two main types of sensory impairment – hearing impairment and visual impairment – although the term can be used to describe any condition that affects the senses and prevents normal progress. Many children with either a hearing impairment or a visual impairment used to be educated separately despite their having no actual learning difficulties. Some children may also have a sensory impairment alongside other conditions, for example children with profound and multiple disabilities.

Language impairment

Language impairment is one of the most common impairments that early years practitioners are likely to meet. The term 'language impairment' can cover a wide range of difficulties, e.g. stammering, difficulty in pronunciation as well as poor vocabulary and reluctance to speak. In some cases, children's language impairment is part of another condition, but for many children the language impairment is temporary.

Communication impairment

For nearly all children the desire to communicate and break into the social world is instinctive, even though they may have learning difficulties or a language impairment. Most children learn quickly to smile or acknowledge others. There are, however, a range of conditions which include autism and Asperger's syndrome which prevent children from having the desire to communicate or understand social conventions.

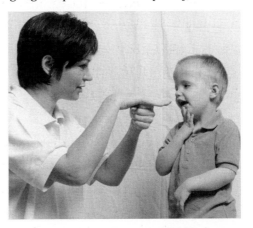

Using sign language

467

Social and medical models of disability

Attitudes towards disabled people have changed in recent times, although in terms of equal rights, there is still some way to go. Throughout history, the birth of a baby which was in any way different was seen as a tragedy or a curse. This attitude towards disability is sometimes known as the 'medical model'. Anyone with a disability was seen as being helpless and requiring a cure. Today, attitudes are changing with disabled people being increasingly viewed as being part of society rather than outcasts. This view of disability is known as the 'social model' (see also pages 483–4).

Labelling and stereotyping

One of the dangers of using any classification system is that people can be stereotyped. This means that instead of seeing the person, we hear the label – this is one of the things that disabled people find most frustrating. The danger of labelling and stereotyping is that people working with children with special needs can concentrate more on the condition and the disability than on what the child can actually do. This means that the children's potential is not fulfilled and is one of the reasons why integration into mainstream classes is considered a preferred option wherever possible.

Causative factors

Identification

There are several ways in which children with special needs are identified. Wherever possible, early identification is sought which has meant that many routine tests are carried out before babies are born. Early identification is not always possible because some impairments only become noticeable as a child develops. The table below outlines the main ways in which a child with special needs might be recognised.

When?	Test	Identification
Pre-natal tests	Ultrasound scan Blood tests Amniocentesis Chorionic villus sampling	Tests are carried out during pregnancy Where a family has a medical history that might indicate a possible difficulty, specific tests will be carried out Modern technology has meant some life-saving operations can be carried out in the womb. These include heart surgery as well as repairing the lesion in the spine of babies who have spina bifida
At birth	Apgar tests Blood tests Physical examination	At birth babies are carefully checked. In some cases immediate operations might be carried out
During health surveillance checks	Physical examinations including height, weight and head circumference Speech and language	The need for early identification means that parents are offered regular health surveillance checks for their babies and children (see pages 336–9). Health visitors and family doctors normally carry out these health checks

When?	Test	Identification
Recognition by parents or other family members		Parents might have a concern about their child (especially, if they have had more than one child). They may report their concern to their health visitor or to the family doctor
Recognition by early years practitioners		Early years practitioners may carry out observations or notice that a child has specific difficulties compared to a child of a similar age
Recognition in school settings	Diagnostic language and numeracy tests	Some children will have their needs identified in schools because teachers may carry out routine educational tests or they may notice discrepancies in areas of a child's performance, e.g. a child may be orally very fluent, but have difficulty in remembering and recognising letters
During an illness or following an accident		Sometimes identification will be made during a routine visit to the family doctor, e.g. a cough that is persisting or whilst other medical conditions are being investigated. In addition, there are some illnesses that can cause an impairment, e.g. measles can occasionally cause hearing impairments

Causes of special needs

Many parents of children with special needs find it very helpful to understand the cause of their child's condition. It can affect whether they go on to have another child, inform them of support organisations as well help them deal with their own feelings of guilt. Many parents, especially mothers, are afraid that they might have taken something or done something to cause the condition. Unfortunately, although scientific knowledge has developed enormously, not every condition has a clear cause.

Case Study

Wendy is Sophie's mum. She realised that Sophie was not making the same developmental progress as other children during Sophie's first year. She was keen for Sophie to be checked out and was at first disappointed when the doctors could not find out what exactly was wrong, although they could recognise that she had some learning difficulties. It was several years before the exact cause of Sophie's learning difficulties was recognised – a chromosomal disorder. Wendy was relieved as she had been worried that she might have unknowingly taken something during the pregnancy to cause the condition. It also meant that she could conceive another child knowing that it was unlikely for a subsequent child to have the same disorder. Once Sophie's disability had been recognised, it was also easier for Wendy to get support as there was a voluntary organisation for children with the same disorder.

Hereditary factors

Many conditions are thought to be caused by hereditary factors which means they were passed down to the child via one or both parents. In some cases, such as Down's syndrome, the condition can even be traced to the presence or absence of specific chromosomes, whereas in others the condition is caused by a damaged chromosome. Substantial medical research is now being done to identify the genes within our chromosomes and to define their effects on our bodies. Some conditions are only seen in particular races, e.g. sickle cell anaemia affects Afro-Caribbean children, whilst others affect only one gender, e.g. haemophilia in boys.

Prenatal factors

Some conditions are thought to be caused during pregnancy. The foetus is particularly vulnerable in the first few weeks of life and often before a woman knows that she is pregnant. This means that drugs taken for medical reasons as well as for recreational use, excess alcohol and smoking can sometimes have an effect on the developing baby. Recently, scientists are becoming more aware of the need for women planning on becoming pregnant to take extra supplements before conception. Conditions such as spina bifida seem to be linked to a lack of folic acid in the woman's body. Diet during pregnancy can also be a factor, for example it is known that eating unpasteurised foods can lead to women contracting listeria. Illnesses contracted during pregnancy can also cause damage to the embryo, e.g. rubella can cause sensory impairments.

During the process of birth

The process of birth itself can be the cause of some conditions. Damage to the brain can be caused by lack of oxygen during the first moments of life, similarly some babies suffer physical damage during the actual delivery. Some babies are also born too soon (prematurely) and this can lead to several difficulties as the lungs and other organs such as the eyes are often not mature. Conditions that are present at birth are known as congenital, whether they are inherited or not.

Postnatal factors

Postnatal factors covers illnesses, accidents and diseases that the child might be subject to during their childhood. For example, a child might fall off their bike and have a brain injury, or contract meningitis and develop a hearing impairment. It is now known that shaking a baby or toddler can cause severe brain injuries. The environment where the child lives can also have an effect on their general health and some conditions such a asthma can be triggered by pollution, damp and chemicals. Sometimes the way that children are receiving care in the home can contribute towards learning or behavioural difficulties. Children might be exposed to a tense and aggressive atmosphere or their carer might not be coping with the demands of parenthood. Children in these situations might develop emotional and behavioural difficulties. Finally, child abuse of any kind can also mean that children develop special needs.

Hereditary and congenital conditions
Down's syndrome

Children with Down's syndrome have one extra chromosome in their genetic make up. The diagnosis of Down's syndrome is often made at birth as the baby's facial features have certain characteristics, although women who have had an amniocentesis test will be aware that they are carrying a Down's syndrome baby.

Children with Down's syndrome develop and learn in the same way as other children, although their progress will be slower and their eventual ability to reason in the abstract is often limited. The extent of their learning difficulties varies enormously from individual to individual, although many children are able to remain with support in mainstream settings. Some children go on to be able to lead relatively independent lives in sheltered accommodation.

Cystic fibrosis

Cystic fibrosis is a disease that is present at birth and is caused by a recessive gene. A child with cystic fibrosis will have both parents who are carriers of the gene. Diagnosis is usually made early on in a baby's life as they may be failing to put on weight and also have recurrent lung infections.

Children with cystic fibrosis have difficulty in digesting food properly and are unable to take in all the nutrients required for a balanced diet. They are also prone to chronic lung infections, diabetes and pancreatic disorders. Children with cystic fibrosis often require daily physiotherapy to clear their lungs of mucus which builds up. Tablets are also required at meal and snack times to help children digest their food.

Whilst children with cystic fibrosis do not have learning difficulties as such, they may need extra support due to absences caused by the disease which is physically tiring and can shorten the lifespan of a child due to the damage caused to the lungs. Children with cystic fibrosis may not be able to join in physically demanding activities and may quickly feel tired. The nature of the disease can affect children's ability to concentrate.

Fragile X syndrome

This is an inherited genetic disorder which causes learning difficulties in children. There are wide differences in the type of learning difficulties that children may show, with some children needing significant adult support.

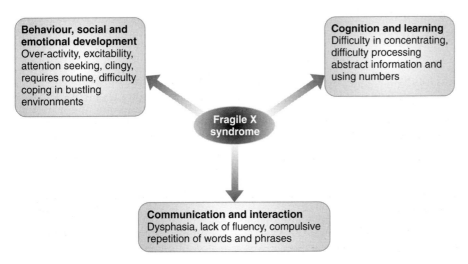

Behaviour, social and emotional development
Over-activity, excitability, attention seeking, clingy, requires routine, difficulty coping in bustling environments

Cognition and learning
Difficulty in concentrating, difficulty processing abstract information and using numbers

Fragile X syndrome

Communication and interaction
Dysphasia, lack of fluency, compulsive repetition of words and phrases

Cerebral palsy

This is a general term to describe disorders which prevent the brain from controlling muscles in the body. There are a multitude of causes of cerebral palsy which include birth injuries, maternal infection in the first few weeks of a pregnancy, head trauma and genetic disorders.

There are three main types of cerebal palsy with some people having a combination of two or more:

- Spastic cerebal palsy – one or more limbs are stiff and the muscles are contracted.
- Ataxic cerebal palsy – difficulty in balancing, controlling whole limb movements and focusing.
- Athetoid cerebal palsy – involuntary movements caused by muscles contracting and then stiffening.

The extent to which a child may be affected can vary enormously with some children having only slight indications of cerebal palsy. Whilst children with cerebal palsy may have difficulties with co-ordination and use of their limbs, they will not necessarily have learning difficulties.

Spina bifida and hydrocephalus

Spina bifida is a congenital disorder which occurs early in pregnancy. The vertebrae in the spine do not properly form leaving part of the spinal cord exposed. The spinal cord serves as the passage way for messages to be passed to and from the brain from the limbs. Any blockages can result in loss of sensation and use of the limbs. Hydrocephalus often accompanies spina bifida at birth. Hydrocephalus is sometimes referred to as water on the brain and is the result of a build up of spinal fluid in the brain. In order to prevent brain damage, the excess fluid is drained.

The extent of damage to the body depends on how exposed the spinal cord is, with the severest type of spina bifida (myelomeningocele) often resulting in partial or complete paralysis from the waist down. Children with severe spina bifida will often require a wheelchair for mobility and will remain incontinent. Many children with spina bifida do not have any learning difficulties although they may need extra support in terms of coping with their disability.

Physical disabilities

Epilepsy

Epilepsy is the term used when the brain shows abnormal electric activity. This can result in 'absences' where a child or person simply seems to have 'shut down' or makes involuntary twitches and movements or, at its most extreme, dramatic convulsions or seizures.

In the past, children with epilepsy were discriminated against as it was thought that they were 'mentally deranged' or even that the devil had taken control of their minds. It is now known that epilepsy in itself is not linked to a person's mental state and that children with epilepsy do not have learning difficulties.

There are three types of epilepsy:

- Partial – where a person may be conscious of feeling 'strange'.
- Generalised absence (previously called petit mal) – where a person 'switches off' and afterwards has no recollection of what they were doing or thinking about.
- Generalised tonic clonic (previously called grand mal) – where a person falls unconscious and has a seizure. Seizures are often dramatic with a person arching their back and then going on to make large involuntary movements before the body relaxes. A person may then regain consciousness and feel dazed or fall into a deep sleep.

Most children with epilepsy take medication which suppresses extraneous brain activity. Medication can cause drowsiness especially at first when the dosage is being fixed. If a child has a seizure, it is important to clear the area of anything that may cause them to injure themselves and stay on hand until the seizure has finished. The child should then be put in the recovery position until they feel better. Children may then need to rest.

HIV

HIV stands for human immunodeficiency virus. Once a person has the HIV virus, they may later develop AIDS (acquired immune deficiency syndrome) although some people with the HIV virus are at present showing no signs of developing AIDS. It is AIDS that people fear as the virus attacks the immune system preventing the body from fighting off bacteria, viruses and cancers which inevitably shortens the lifespan.

Children with HIV are likely to have gained this virus from their infected mothers either in the womb or through breast milk. In the past, a relatively few number of children may have contracted the virus through having received contaminated blood products, although careful screening now makes this unlikely.

Children with HIV pose no risk to other children or staff providing that the usual procedures of wearing gloves when dealing with bodily fluids, including blood, are followed. Children with HIV have often been discriminated against because of a widespread and unfounded fear of HIV. Children with HIV have no particular learning difficulties although they may show emotional and behavioural difficulties caused by the awareness of the disease and in some cases bereavement of their parents.

Asthma

Children with asthma have difficulty in breathing. Asthma affects one in ten children, and can occasionally be fatal, which is why when a child has an attack, the correct medication should be available.

Children with asthma do not have learning difficulties as a result of this condition, although they may get behind academically due to prolonged absences from school. If it is properly controlled by medications, there should be no restriction on active play for children with asthma.

Eczema

Eczema is a skin condition which is caused by an allergic reaction. Eczema can cause severe itchiness, dryness of skin and discomfort. Children with eczema do not have learning difficulties, but may find it hard to concentrate and in severe cases may not be able to touch certain play materials such as sand or dough.

Sickle cell anaemia

Sickle cell anaemia is an inherited blood disorder which causes the red cells to be 'sickle' shaped. This in turn prevents the normal flow of blood and causes anaemia. Sickle cell anaemia is prevalent among people of African or Caribbean descent. The symptoms of anaemia include tiredness and lethargy and poor blood flow can create pains in the arms, legs and back.

The disease also causes children to have difficulty in fighting off infections and adults caring for children need to be vigilant for signs that the child is having a crisis that will require immediate medical attention. Children with sickle cell anaemia do not have learning difficulties, but may fall behind with their work due to prolonged absences and constant fatigue which may affect concentration.

Diabetes

Diabetes is a disease where the pancreas is unable to produce sufficient insulin to maintain blood sugar levels in the body. Untreated, the disease can be fatal, although this is extremely rare. Children who have diabetes are likely to require daily injections of insulin and will have a diet to follow which will exclude sugar. They are also likely to need regular meals and snacks to prevent low blood sugar. Children with diabetes have no particular learning difficulties and generally go unnoticed by the other children.

Coeliac disease

Children with this disease have an intolerance to gluten. Gluten is found in wheat and many other cereals such as rye and oats. Children have no learning difficulties and as with diabetics, usually go unnoticed by others. Adults caring for children with this condition must be careful not to offer any products containing gluten and adhere to the dietary arrangements agreed with the parents.

Dyslexia

Dyslexia is a global term used to describe specific learning difficulties in reading and writing. It is sometimes referred to as 'word blindness'. It is usually recognised when children reach seven or eight years and have made limited progress in reading and writing, although they may be performing well in other areas of the curriculum.

The needs of children with dyslexia are often very different and the type of support required can vary among individuals. Most children, however, develop low self-esteem as literacy skills are often valued in schools by teachers and their peers. The causes of dyslexia are not completely understood, although there appears to be an inherited tendency and a difference in the way the brain processes information. Dyslexia appears to affect boys more than girls and a correlation between children who have not crawled as babies.

Gifted children

Whilst gifted children are not usually defined as special educational needs children, there is an increasing recognition that they do have particular needs. The Special Educational Needs Code of Practice 2001 does not cover gifted children, but at the time of writing the government is producing initiatives to identify and support gifted children.

Parents of gifted children often report that their children have behavioural or emotional and social difficulties. These can be the result of frustration, boredom or low self-esteem as children feel that they are 'different'. Traditionally many parents have found that the education system cannot cater for their child's needs and some parents have decided to educate their children at home

Communication difficulties

There are a range of disorders which cause children to have difficulty in responding and communicating with others. Autistic spectrum disorders are often the most common.

Autism and Asperger's syndrome

The causes of autistic spectrum disorders are currently unknown although there is some speculation that there may be some genetic factors at work. Children who have autistic spectrum disorders find it hard to understand and communicate with other people including their own families. Some people liken autism to being 'trapped in a bubble'; seeing others, but not being able to share their world. Characteristics of severely autistic children may include:

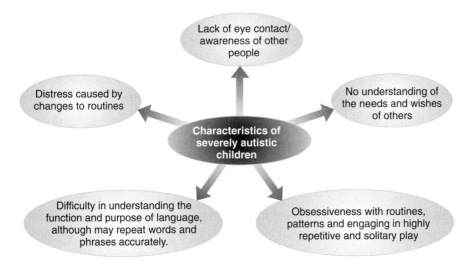

The extent of autism can vary enormously with children who have slight tendencies towards autistic behaviours usually being diagnosed with Asperger's syndrome. Children with Asperger's syndrome are usually able to use language effectively, but find it hard to guess what others want or are thinking and so find it hard to socialise effectively. Their play is often highly structured and individual.

Parents of children with autistic spectrum disorders can feel isolated as their child's behaviour is not conducive to shopping or social occasions especially as members of the public cannot see the 'disability' and assume that the behaviour is a result of poor parenting.

Attention deficit hyperactivity disorder (ADHD)

Children with ADHD have difficulty in maintaining concentration and are easily distracted and thus show restless behaviour. The diagnosis of ADHD is not straightforward as some of the signs are similar to those found in autistic spectrum disorders. Some children whose parents feel that their children are ADHD have been found in the past to respond well to behavioural modification programmes, which has led to some professionals feeling that the true number of children with ADHD may be quite small. Where ADHD is diagnosed, children may be treated with a stimulant called Ritalin which arouses the child and thus allows them to maintain concentration.

The impact on families of children with special needs

The families of children with special needs often have their own special needs. Couples can find that their own relationship is put under enormous stress at times. It is not uncommon for couples to split up soon or shortly after a child is found to have special needs, especially if they are complex or severe. Many parents of children with special needs find that so much of their time and energy is used in caring for the child, that it is hard to find the extra time for each other or for themselves especially where there are other children in the family. Money is another source of worry for most families as in many cases one parent has to give up work in order to care for the child. Places with childminders or in day nurseries for children with special needs are rare especially if the child has moderate or severe learning difficulties. This means that the family income is often hit and many families especially lone parents find themselves reliant on state benefits.

Some parents find that having a child with special needs, particularly learning difficulties or emotional and behavioural difficulties, is isolating. Public places can be nightmares to negotiate and finding friends who can cope with the behaviour of the child can be difficult. Most parents find that local support groups give them opportunities to make friends.

Finally, the future of their children is often a major concern for parents – most parents expect their offspring to lead independent lives at some point, but for some parents of children with special needs this will not be the case. Most parents cope with the future, simply by blocking it out and living one day at a time, especially where a child has a life-threatening condition.

Assessment activity 13.1

Produce an information sheet for other students about two different groups of children who have 'special needs'. This should be based on at least three different sources of information and should provide information about:

- the causative factors
- the impact on children and their families
- further sources of information for parents.

Legislation and assessment procedures

This section looks at current legislation and the way in which children's needs are assessed.

Children Act 1989

The Children Act has been generally well received. It brought together many pieces of legislation related to children and was based on the idea that children have rights. It sought to protect all children, but also looked at the needs and rights of vulnerable children. In respect of children with special needs the following points are important:

- Children's welfare must be given priority.
- Parents are important.
- Children need to be listened to.

- Local education authorities have legal duties towards all children, but especially vulnerably children.

Education (Handicapped Children) Act 1970

This piece of legislation made all children the responsibility of the local education authority (they had previously been the responsibility of the health service) and as a result full-time education had to be provided for them. This meant that many special schools were built in the 1970s to provide an education. Towards the end of the 1970s, the consensus changed towards trying to integrate children into society. This was a backdrop to the now famous Warnock Report.

Warnock Report 1978

In 1978 a report was published by a committee chaired by Mary Warnock. Its report was to prove one of the most influential pieces of legislation to affect disabled children in the twentieth century. In 1981, many of the recommendations suggested by the committee became law. The committee had undertaken a comprehensive study of the whole area of disabled children, their education and their needs. The committee took evidence from parents, the voluntary sector, educationalists and the medical profession.

Introduction of the term 'special educational need'

For years, people had talked about handicapped children or labelled children according to their disability. The report suggested a title of 'special education need' (SEN), which would include any child who needed some form of extra support. The report suggested three types of support:

- special means of access to the curriculum
- changes to the curriculum
- changes to the environment – including emotional or social support.

The term 'special educational need' was an all-encompassing one and included children who had slight difficulties with their reading and writing to children who had major care needs. It also included children who had short-term needs that were causing them difficulties in fulfilling their potential alongside children who had long-term needs. In this way it focused professionals on the idea of how to meet the needs that the children might have, rather than on the condition or cause of them. This was a major breakthrough and one that the Warnock Report will be noted for.

Education Act 1981

This Act was heavily based on the recommendations of the Warnock Report and gave local education authorities legal duties to fulfil. The Act placed a clear responsibility on local education authorities to provide support for children who have special educational needs. It also introduced the process now known as 'statementing'. This is the process by which children are assessed by a team of professionals alongside the parents and a statement is drawn up of how the child's needs are to be supported. The statement of special educational needs is a legally binding one and commits the local authority to providing for the child.

The Act is also important because it gave parents power for the first time. Parents were to be involved in the process of producing a statement and deciding on the best course of education for their children, but more importantly the parents were given the legal power to challenge local education authorities.

Statementing and funding

The idea behind producing a statement was to ensure that children with special educational needs were given support. By recording their needs and the action required to meet these needs, children were supposed to be more likely to have these needs met. See pages 482–3 for more on statementing.

Education Act 1993

The Act was built upon the Education Act 1981 legislation and is currently legislation in England and Wales. Its key points are summarised below and are important because they still form the basis of the Education Act of 2001.

Key issues

Code of Practice	The Act required that the Secretary of State for Education publish a code of practice which was to give local education authorities and others practical guidance in following the legislation. The Code of Practice was in effect between September 1994 and December 2001.
Parents	The 1993 Act made it clear that local education authorities needed to work alongside parents. It also established special educational needs tribunals that would hear cases where parents and local authorities were able to agree. Parents' rights of appeal were extended and information was published to help parents understand their rights.
Definition of special educational needs	The Act stated that where health services identified that a child under five years old might have special educational needs, they had a duty to both the local education authority and the parents. It also stated that they should pass on information about voluntary organisations that might be able to help parents. This meant that health services, the voluntary sector (including charities such as Scope, Mind) and the local education authority have to work together.
Assessment of children under two years	The Act gave parents the right to ask for the child under two years to be assessed and if appropriate be given a statement of special educational needs.

Special Education Needs and Disability Act 2001

This Act has been fairly well received by major disability charities and is divided into two sections. Part 1 of the Act reforms the framework of special educational needs to strengthen the rights of parents and children to access mainstream education. Part 2 extends the Disability Discrimination Act 1995 to education, extending the civil rights of disabled children and adults in schools, colleges and universities.

Key features of the Act include:

- the right of children with special educational needs to be educated in mainstream schools (where this is what parents want and where it is appropriate for the child)
- the requirement of local education authorities to arrange to provide parents of children with special educational needs with advice and information, and a means of resolving disputes with schools and local education authorities
- the requirement for local educational authorities to comply with orders of the special educational needs tribunal
- the requirement of education settings to tell parents where they are making special educational provision for their child and allow schools to request a statutory assessment of a pupil's special educational needs
- the introduction of disability discrimination rights in the provision of education in schools, further education, higher education, adult education and the youth service
- the requirement not to treat disabled students less favourably, without justification, than non-disabled students.

Carers and Disabled Children Act 2000

This legislation came into force in April 2001. It is designed to help the people who care for children to get their needs met alongside those of their children. The idea behind this law is to help carers manage more effectively. They may be given respite vouchers as well as being offered services directly from social services.

Code of Practice 2001

This Code of Practice was implemented in January 2002 and acts as the key guidance for local education authorities, schools, early years education settings and parents.

Fundamental principles

The Code of Practice outlines the following principles:

- A child with special educational needs should have their needs met.
- The special educational needs of children will be met in mainstream schools or settings.
- The views of the child should be sought and taken into account.
- Parents have a vital role to play in supporting their child's education.
- Children with special educational needs should be offered full access to a broad, balanced and relevant education, including an appropriate curriculum for the Foundation Stage and the National Curriculum.

The philosophy behind the Code of Practice

Behind the Code of Practice there are several themes which represent trends in society.

Inclusion

The Code of Practice forms part of the government's drive towards establishing an 'inclusive' society. This trend is generally welcomed by voluntary organisations representing groups who are traditionally discriminated against. Therefore the aim of the Code is to look for ways of keeping children who have special educational needs within mainstream school and early years settings by supporting them.

Involvement of children

The Code of Practice emphasises that children have rights and that they should be involved in making decisions and exercising choices. The importance of recognising the views of children was one of the main themes of the Children Act 1989 and also forms two of the articles of the United Nations Convention on the Rights of the Child. The Code of Practice clearly states that from an early age, children should be involved in making decisions where possible including the drawing up of individual education plans as well as during the statementing process and subsequent reviews.

Acknowledgement of the role of parents

The importance of parents in supporting their children and also in educating them is recognised within the Code of Practice. There is emphasis on making sure that parents are informed when settings have concerns about their children and also emphasis on gaining the expertise of parents when discussing arrangements to meet the needs of children. The Code of Practice also reminds local education authorities of their duty under the Education Act 1996 to provide parents of children with special educational needs with advice and information.

Assessment procedures

The identification and assessment procedures laid out in the Code of Practice 2001 are based on the idea that the majority of children with special educational needs should remain in mainstream education and will not require a statement of special educational needs (see pages 478 and 482–3). It also assumes that practitioners at all levels with appropriate training and support should be able to provide and meet the needs of children.

Identification, assessment and provision in early education settings

It is increasingly being recognised that early identification of special educational needs is essential in order to support the child and their family and also in some cases to minimise the impact of the special needs. The Code of Practice 2001 requires all early years settings that receive government funding to have a special educational needs policy and appoint a member of staff to be the special needs co-ordinator (SENCO) (see page 491 for the role of SENCOs).

Theory into practice

Find out about the special educational needs policy in your setting. How is the policy implemented?

Graduated response

The Code of Practice uses the term 'graduated response' within the context of identifying, assessing and providing for young children. (See diagram on page 486.)

Early Years Action level

At this level, the setting will be providing most or all of the support for the child, although advice and help from local education authorities and other external agencies may be sought. In some cases, children will be provided with extra adult support, but in other cases, the staff in the setting may differentiate the curriculum or concentrate on particular activities with the child.

A child's progress is noticed by parents, practitioners or the setting's SENCO as being of concern

The SENCO in consultation with parents and other practitioners assesses the child's strengths and weaknesses. These are recorded and a decision will be made as to the type of support that the child needs. The Code of Practice categorises two levels of support: Early Years Action and Early Years Action Plus

Individual education plans are drawn up which show short-term targets and the strategies that the child will need (see page 483)

Early Years Action Plus level

At this level, the setting has identified that it will need additional support in order to meet the child's needs. It may approach the local education authority or other external agencies with records of the child's progress and previous individual education plans.

Requests for statutory statements

Where additional support is required beyond the scope of Early Years Action Plus, education settings, external agencies or the parents may request a statutory statement from the local education authority (see Statutory assessments, page 482).

Identification, assessment and provision in the primary phase

In theory, many children with special educational needs may have already had their needs identified by the time that they begin their primary education. The Foundation Stage in England now spans the pre-school and primary sectors. Individual education plans from the child's pre-school settings are likely to be passed to the primary school. The assessment process suggested by the Code of Practice is similar to that of the early education settings with primary schools using a graduated response.

School Action level

At this level, the school will make plans to meet the child's needs and the SENCO will draw up individual education plans in association with class teachers, parents and other professionals. The implementation of the individual education plan is the responsibility of the class teacher, although advice can be gained from the SENCO.

School Action Plus level

At this level, schools will seek the assistance of external support and involvement. An educational psychologist may assist in drawing up individual education plans, although any involvement of external support will require the consent of parents.

Statutory assessment

Where a school is still concerned that the child is not making adequate progress, they may seek a statutory assessment from the local education authority.

Statementing

A statement is a legal document that outlines a child's special educational needs and the local authority's duties towards the child. The process by which a statement is drawn up is often referred to as 'statementing' (see the diagram below).

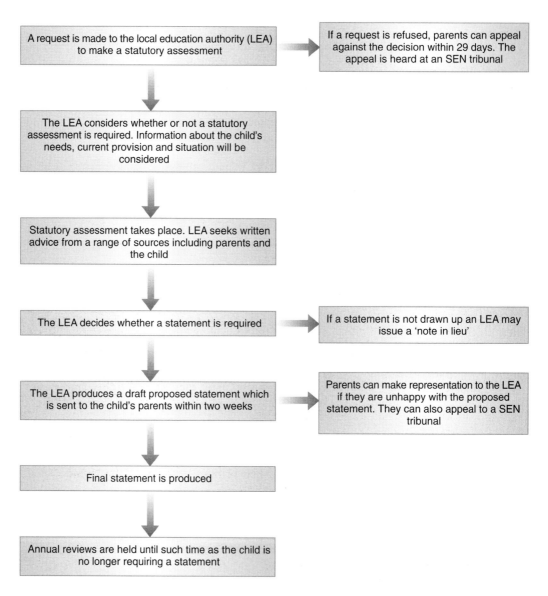

| A request is made to the local education authority (LEA) to make a statutory assessment | → | If a request is refused, parents can appeal against the decision within 29 days. The appeal is heard at an SEN tribunal |

↓

The LEA considers whether or not a statutory assessment is required. Information about the child's needs, current provision and situation will be considered

↓

Statutory assessment takes place. LEA seeks written advice from a range of sources including parents and the child

↓

| The LEA decides whether a statement is required | → | If a statement is not drawn up an LEA may issue a 'note in lieu' |

↓

| The LEA produces a draft proposed statement which is sent to the child's parents within two weeks | → | Parents can make representation to the LEA if they are unhappy with the proposed statement. They can also appeal to a SEN tribunal |

↓

Final statement is produced

↓

Annual reviews are held until such time as the child is no longer requiring a statement

The statementing process

The trend towards reducing the number of statements

Since statementing began, there have been concerns that too many children were gaining statements which were not required as they were already receiving sufficient support. It was often felt by local education authorities and others involved in the statementing process, that too much time and money was spent on preparing reports and reviewing previous statements when the money would be better allocated in actually making provisions.

One of the reasons given for parents and schools asking for a statement for a child was budgetary. By having a statement, schools could often ask for additional funds whilst parents could in theory take a local education authority to court if the support indicated in a statement was not given.

Changes in school funding to include a budget to support children with special educational needs has meant that fewer statements should be required.

Individual education plans – short-term plans

These are considered to be essential in helping a child to make progress. Individual education plans are normally drawn up by the SENCO together with staff members who work with the child and also the parents. They contain:

- short-term targets for the child (usually three or four at a time)
- details of the teaching strategies
- the provision to be put in place (this includes resources)
- when the plan is to be reviewed
- criteria for success, e.g. that a child may be able to put on their coat alone
- outcomes, e.g. a brief evaluation once the plan has been implemented.

Assessment activity 13.2

Sam is four years old. He attends a local pre-school three mornings a week. The staff have become concerned about his language development. He has made some progress over the past six months, but the staff feel that he will need further support.

- Produce a flow chart which shows how this child may have his needs met in relation to the latest legislation. The flow chart should also show the roles of a range of people in the assessment process.
- Consider the impact that a language impairment may have on a child's overall development.
- Explain which professionals may become involved with Sam if his language development is considered to be seriously delayed.
- Produce a sample individual education plan for Sam.

Disability equality in practice

Different models of disability

The way we think about disability has affected the care and education of people with disabilities. Two models of disability (or attitudes towards disability) are usually contrasted – the medical model and the social model.

Medical model of disability

The medical model of disability is in many ways the traditional way of thinking about disability. It reflects society's faith in doctors and perhaps has come about because of the advances in medical knowledge. The medical model views disability as something that must whenever possible be cured and, where that is not possible, a feeling of failure results unless the person can be made to 'look' or 'act' normally. The medical model of disability therefore treats people with impairments as victims and patients – words such as handicapped, incurable, suffering and wheelchair bound are associated with this attitude. The medical model of disability tends to put the emphasis more on the condition rather than on the person. The tendency to label people according to their impairments stems from this attitude, e.g. 'the one who's wheelchair bound' rather than 'James, who uses a wheelchair'.

Social model of disability

The social model of disability reflects a new attitude towards people with impairments. It considers that first and foremost they are people with rights and feelings. The social model of disability has been a very empowering one for many disabled people, as it emphasises their rights to make choices, question values and asks whether it is society with the real problem. The social model of disability has meant that terms such as 'mentally handicapped' and 'wheelchair bound' are now considered unhelpful. The case study below shows clearly how attitudes have changed and the social model of disability is now being increasingly accepted as the way forward.

Case Study

Emma was born with one arm foreshortened above the elbow. Her mother was determined that this should not affect Emma's life and she refused anyone to feel sorry for Emma or consider her a victim. Emma was given a prosthesis (false limb) which, although uncomfortable and restricting, made her look like other children. At home Emma never wore her prosthesis as her family completely accepted the way she looked without it. Emma learnt to ride a horse, manage everyday tasks and was to all intents and purposes a very happy and confident child. She left school and started to work in a restaurant. As she became older she gradually started to question society's attitude towards disability and began to feel unhappy that she was in effect disguising her disability. One day she decided that she would no longer wear her false arm. Her employer was unhappy about this decision. He said that seeing a person with only one arm would make customers feel uneasy and it could affect his business. Emma turned the argument around and said that if she had spent her life learning to cope without an arm, perhaps his customers could spend five minutes learning to see her without one, especially as they had already learnt to cope with seeing his bald head!

Think It Over

In pairs, consider the following questions:

- Is there pressure on people to look 'perfect'? If so, where do you think this pressure comes from?
- Would you ever consider plastic surgery to improve your appearance?
- Do you use any products to disguise 'imperfections', such as spots, or improve your appearance?
- Would you or do you wear contact lenses rather than glasses simply for the sake of appearances?

Self-esteem

Self-esteem and empowerment are linked. Children with special needs can often have low self-esteem, especially if they are in mainstream settings where they might compare themselves to other children. Self-esteem can also be lowered by people around them doing too much for them and thus taking control away from them.

In some cases, this means that children become very passive because adults around them reward them for 'being so good' – which actually means that they have kept still and allowed the adult to take control. This is sometimes referred to as 'learned helplessness'. In the long term it can mean that children's potential is not being developed, as the focus becomes their condition or disability.

Adults working with children with special needs have therefore got to encourage children to be active rather than passive and build in them self-reliance and self-confidence. This is achieved through praise, positive expectations and giving children unconditional love (see page 439 on self-esteem).

Empowerment

The word 'empowerment' is often used in connection with the idea of people taking responsibility for decisions that will affect them. Previously, disabled people tended to have things either done for them or done to them! They were often protected and treated as helpless victims to be nurtured. Currently this attitude is being revised and people working with children with special needs have to make sure that whenever possible thay are empowering children. This means giving children choices and looking for ways in which we can develop their independence.

In an everyday routine, this might mean asking children to choose what they wear, the colour of the pen they use or which activity they want to do first. Empowerment has become a key feature of many disability campaigning groups. This campaigning has resulted in changes to legislation, voluntary organisations and education policy.

Disability Discrimination Act 1995

The aim of the Act is to ensure that services and employment opportunities are not denied to disabled people on the grounds of their impairment. An example of this would be if a disabled person using a wheelchair wanted to go into a restaurant. The owners of the restaurant must now make sure that they provide the same level of service to the disabled person as for any other member of the public. They can no longer say that they cannot serve wheelchair users.

The Act was divided into seven parts, with parts of the Act being gradually phased in to allow time for businesses and employers to make necessary adjustments. It created a National Disability Council to advise and work with the government on matters relating to disability and ways to introduce all parts of the Act.

Criticisms of the Disability Discrimination Act

The Disability Discrimination Act disappointed campaigners because unlike other previous discrimination acts, no commission to actively uphold rights was created. They were also unhappy that the Act was to be phased in over a number of years. The Conservative and subsequent Labour governments have argued that enforcing all parts at once would be too expensive for many employers, although the Labour government has now set up a Disability Rights Commission. The Act has also been criticised because test cases have shown that some of the phrases are vague and can be hard to interpret, for example employers are asked to make 'reasonable adjustments' where necessary to prevent discrimination. The term 'reasonable' is open to wide interpretation.

Empowerment and voluntary organisations

Voluntary organisations have evolved in the last ten years. They increasingly look to involve the people who they represent. This has meant that wherever possible, positions are being filled by people with special needs. This is a significant shift from the days when many of these charities were set up and disabled people were seen as victims who needed helping. In some cases, the transition has not always been smooth and some disabled people have gone on to set up their own splinter organisations.

Many disabled people would like to see the fund raising aspect of these organisations disappear in favour of adequate statutory funding whilst continuing the advisory and campaigning role. They feel that they should have the right to be properly educated and cared for and that it should not be left to others to raise funds. They also see that raising funds creates an image of helplessness in the public's eye – the opposite of what they are hoping to achieve.

Assessment activity 13.3

Choose a national or local voluntary organisation of your choice.

Find out its history, its purpose and its work. Try and ask some of the following questions:

*   How are disabled people encouraged to be involved in its decisions?
*   How has its work changed over the past 20 years?
*   Do they see that statutory funding will ever improve to allow this aspect of their work to disappear?

Produce a report that critically evaluates the work of the organisation.

Advocacy

Today great care is taken to involve parents and children with special needs in the decision-making process. Generally parents act as advocates for their children or the children are able to speak for themselves if the issues are explained to them. Where for some reason, there is no one available to represent the child, an advocate will speak for the child. The advocate will be thinking about the needs and wishes of the child and putting these forward. Advocates are particularly used in cases where children are being 'looked after' by the local authority.

Developing an anti-bias curriculum for all children

All children need to learn to respect and value others. Early years practitioners, teachers and other adults have a vital role in doing this. Developing an anti-bias curriculum means raising children's awareness of others in a positive but not patronising way.

Raising money for the 'poor children who cannot see', for example, does not teach sighted children to respect and value visually impaired children. On the other hand showing children how Braille as a system works and getting children to have a go at writing messages in Braille is a more positive approach. Below are some simple ideas that might be used to help children to learn about others:

- Write and send letters in Braille.
- Learn songs and rhymes using Makaton signing.
- Encourage children to say and also use signing to say 'hello', 'thank you' and 'please'.
- When taking a register, ask the children to spell their names using the sign alphabet.
- Have dolls and other role play materials that reflect the 'real world', e.g. dolls with glasses.

(See Unit 1 on Equality, diversity and rights.)

Assessment activity 13.4

Produce a leaflet for other students about the issues surrounding the labelling of children with special needs and the importance of promoting anti-discriminatory practice. The leaflet should:

- examine the effects of labelling on children with special needs
- consider ways in which inclusiveness can be promoted in early years settings
- evaluate a range of strategies to promote anti-discriminatory practice.

Working in partnership

Statutory and voluntary support

The multi-disciplinary team

Most families and children with special needs will gain support from the many different agencies and professionals. Before 1994, many parents became very frustrated as there seemed to be little communication between many of the different professionals and agencies. This meant that time was wasted in giving the children the support that they needed. The Code of Practice 1994 improved this aspect of supporting families as it stressed the importance of inter-team collaboration. An outline of the roles of different professionals and agencies is given below.

Educational psychologists
Educational psychologists consider how children learn and so are used to help identify learning difficulties in children. They visit schools and settings regularly and work alongside parents and professionals in the setting. They draw up individual educational programmes and give guidance to staff as to how they can be implemented. Where a child needs a statement or has a statement, they will be involved in the assessments and drawing up of the statements.

Physiotherapists
A physiotherapist helps to identify a child's main physical problems working alongside other professionals and parents. They often devise a programme of exercises or treatments which either they administer themselves or they help parents and others to learn how to administer.

Case Study

Oliver is three years old. His mother and the portage worker have decided to work on Oliver's feeding skills. The aim for this week is to get Oliver to put his fingers around a spoon. Three times a day, his mother will enclose his fingers around a spoon at meal times. She will praise him during this process.

Speech and language therapists
Speech and language therapists work with children who have some difficulties with their language. They identify the causes of the problems as well as devise speech and language programmes. These may include exercises, advice for parents, early years teachers and other professionals. The range of children that they work with can be quite wide and includes children with cleft palate, lisps, as well as children who are autistic.

Health visitors
Health visitors are important members of the community health team. In some areas health visitors have a mixed client list and work with many ages and needs of people in the community. In other areas, some health visitors will be specifically assigned to work with families with children under five and families who have children with special needs. Health visitors are able to give support, advice and information in their own homes.

Paediatricians
Paediatricians are mainly based in hospitals and clinics. They have specialised training in children's medicine and children are referred to them via their family doctor for diagnosis. They make regular assessments of children's progress and medical needs. They are able to refer children to other health services such as the speech and language therapy and dieticians.

Family doctor (general practitioner)
The family doctor has general training in medicine. They form part of the community health team and act as a base for a child's ongoing medical treatment and notes. The family doctor will often have been the person who referred the child to the paediatrician when impairment was suspected.

Child psychologists and psychotherapists
These professionals are often used when children show emotional and behaviour difficulties. They work with other professionals to determine the root cause of the unwanted or disturbed behaviour. Play therapy or family counselling is often used as a way of helping children and their families. Child psychiatrists may sometimes be called upon to give guidance to other professionals in some cases.

Educational welfare officer/education social worker
The main function of these professionals is to liaise between home and families in cases where school attendance is infrequent. (It is an offence for children not to be in some sort of full-time educational provision.) Their role is particularly helpful in cases where children are refusing to attend school – 'school refusal'. They are often able to work alongside parents, the child and other professionals to make sure that children's needs are being met.

Special needs support teacher
These teachers travel between schools or visit children in their homes or in pre-school settings. They are able to help a wide range of children and are often seen as useful sources of support and guidance. Special needs support teachers tend to build up a good

relationship with the child and may even work with children when they are admitted to hospitals.

Special needs assistant/learning support assistant

There are many variations on the title used for special needs assistants. Their main purpose is to support an individual child or group of children within a classroom under the direction of the classroom teacher. They may also be responsible for carrying out the activities listed in the individual education plan as well as recording the child's progress. Most classroom teachers, SENCOs and special needs assistants work closely together and draw up the individual education plan.

Social worker

The majority of social workers are employed by the local authority, although some are employed by voluntary organisations. They are generally deployed in teams according to specialist areas, e.g. some social workers are involved in caring for older clients, others for adoption and fostering work. Children with special needs often have an assigned social worker as they are seen as potentially vulnerable. Social workers are often able to provide guidance, advice as well as practical support for families and as such are often welcome visitors.

Types of education provision

There is a variety of provision that is provided for by education authorities and also in the case of residential care, voluntary and private organisations.

Residential care and education

Despite the move towards inclusive and integrated education, there is still a need for some children to be cared for in residential centres, although a very small minority of children need this type of help. Many of these specialised centres are run by voluntary and private organisations but are funded by local authorities, although some of them are privately run. These centres tend to help children with severe learning disabilities where the family would have difficulty in caring for them at home, or where children need short-term respite care, although there are also private schools that specialise in educating children with specific learning disabilities such as dyslexia. School services are responsible for inspecting and checking that these centres are providing good care, education and protection for the children.

Provision within mainstream classes and settings

This is the favoured option wherever possible for children. The advantages of receiving education alongside other children means that expectations tend to be higher and that children with special needs are not 'ghettoised'. Support can vary according to the needs of the child. Some children have permanent one-to-one help, often a special needs assistant who only works alongside them and changes classes or group in early years settings with them at the end of the year. Other children might have a support teacher who works regularly with them whilst other children might be given extra attention by the classroom teacher.

Units within mainstream schools

In some areas where special schools have been closed, local education authorities have provided units within mainstream schools. The units allow children to have access to specialised equipment and low staff ratios. Children may visit the unit for certain periods during the day or they may spend most of the day there.

Special schools

There are still many special schools to help children whose needs cannot be met within mainstream provision. These include children with moderate and severe learning difficulties, profound and multiple learning difficulties and emotional and behavioural difficulties. The move towards integration means that children who have mild, physical or sensory impairments are generally being catered for in mainstream schools.

Special schools have many advantages for these children including:

- specialist equipment such as multi-sensory rooms, hydrotherapy pools
- specialist staff trained and experienced in working with children with special needs
- special schools often take children from two to nineteen years of age which means that children do not have to move site and readjust to new staff
- on-site speech and language therapists and occupational therapists
- active parent support groups
- small, homely atmosphere with 40 to 60 pupils.

The role of the voluntary sector

Charities were originally founded either because the state did not provide facilities or the standards of care were very poor for disabled people. Once the welfare reforms were introduced in the 1940s it was expected that charities would no longer be needed as social benefits and assistance became statutory provision. This was not the case as it quickly emerged that there was not enough provision or funds to provide the quality of care required, thus the voluntary sector has carried on its traditional role in raising funds for specific groups of people and children. In the past few years, the role of the voluntary sector has become not only broad but also very professional. Many positions in voluntary organisations are paid ones, recognising the transition from perhaps amateurish attempts at helping to being thought of as specialists in their field. The spidergram below shows the type of activities that many charities and voluntary organisations carry out:

The role of SENCOs

In all education settings that receive government funding a member of staff will be appointed to take on responsibility for co-ordinating the special educational needs policy and also the needs of children with special educational needs. SENCOs have a key role in developing and maintaining partnerships as they have frequent contact with parents, other professionals and the children. SENCOs do not necessarily work directly with individual children, although many settings will include this as part of their role. In some schools, SENCOs are part of the senior management team. SENCOs play a vital part in liaising with parents and social and health services to make sure that children are having their needs met. The Code of Practice 2001 sets out the role of SENCOs in early years settings as well as in primary settings.

The role of the SENCO in early education settings
- Liaises with parents and other professionals
- Advises and supports other members of the team
- Ensures that individual education plans are in place
- Collects, records and updates information about individual children with special educational needs

The role of the SENCO in primary schools
- Oversees the day-to-day operation of the school's special educational needs policy
- Co-ordinates provision for children with special educational needs
- Liaises with and advises fellow teachers
- Manages learning support assistants
- Oversees the records of all children with special educational needs
- Liaises with the parents of children with special educational needs
- Contributes to the in-service training of staff
- Liaises with external agencies including the local education authority's support and educational psychology services, health and social services, and voluntary bodies

Working partnerships

Parents and families are often forgotten when we think about children with special needs. Previously, parents had to fight to gain information from the medical profession about their child's needs and condition, and then fight local authorities to get the support they needed. Most parents of children with special needs became seasoned campaigners and often helped each other by forming support groups. The need for campaigning and fighting has not completely gone away as many parents believe that there are insufficient resources within the system.

The attitudes among many health and education professionals have, however, started to change, mainly because parents have been given more legal rights than ever before. The need for parents to be involved in decisions about their children was first recommended in the Warnock Report and was then enshrined in several Acts including the Children Act 1989. The move to working in partnership with parents can be seen in the following ways:

- Information is transferred from home to school using 'home books'.
- Parents are encouraged to take part in exercises and programmes at home, e.g. carrying out physiotherapy, administering drugs, following a portage programme.
- Parents can express choices about schooling arrangements for their children.

- Parents can challenge the local education authority's decisions at special educational needs tribunals.
- Parents are involved in decisions about children's medical treatment.

Respite care

The strains on families are alleviated by respite care and holidays. Respite care allows parents time to be by themselves, rest and have time with their other children. Siblings of special needs children often feel neglected and a common complaint is that they missed out on their childhood because they were forced to grow up and take on responsibilities.

Assessment activity 13.5

Produce a report that looks at the services and support that a family with a child with special needs receives. The report should be based on interviews with the family, but should not compromise the child or the family's right to privacy and confidentiality.

The report should include:

- details about the child's special needs and the impact on the child and family
- an evaluation of the support that parents receive from statutory and voluntary organisations
- an analysis of the effectiveness of the approach to parent partnership working.

Issues in communicating

Communication methods

Several methods of communicating are used with children with special needs.

Key issues – communicating

There is an ongoing debate between groups and individuals about whether hearing impaired children and other children with language difficulties should as a priority be taught to speak or whether they should learn to sign. In some ways this debate has echoes of the medical versus social model of disability. The arguments for each side are outlined below.

Pro signing

- Signing is easier and progress is quicker than teaching children to speak.
- Signing is a two-way process and means that children can really join in. Two children with severe hearing impairments playing side by side can communicate with each other.
- The effort and time spent in teaching children how to speak does not result in children always being able to be understood by non-signing people – hence it is a wasted effort.
- Hearing people should make more of an effort to learn sign language – it should be taught in schools as a second language.
- Wanting children to be able to speak, even if they cannot hear themselves, is simply another way of society trying to 'normalise' people.

Pro speech
- Signing can isolate children as most people in wider society do not know how to sign and this may limit job choices and lifestyle.
- Signing limits children because there are more spoken works than there are signs.

Portage

Portage is a system that was developed in the United States which has been adopted, although often modified, in the UK. It concentrates on helping children under five by working with parents in their home. It is based on the idea that early stimulation can help children with special needs. A portage worker will visit the home (in some areas this is a volunteer, whereas in others this is a trained teacher) and will carry out some assessments on the child. The parents and the portage worker together decide which skill or area of learning should be worked on. A step-by-step approach is decided upon with the parents being largely responsible for carrying out the programme. To support the programme, families are visited at least once a week by the portage worker where the child's progress is discussed. Portage workers take on the role of being a 'support' rather than a professional and parents are very much seen as equal partners.

Braille

Braille is a well-known and widely used system of written language for the visually impaired who are unable to read large print. It uses sequences of raised dots that can be felt and therefore read. A machine called a Perkins brailler can be used to transcribe text into Braille and vice versa.

Makaton

Makaton has become increasingly used to support speech and language development with children who have communication difficulties. It is based on signs that resemble actions or objects. Makaton is often chosen as the major sign language in many schools because it is easy to learn. (Remember that parents and other family members as well as staff need to be taught to sign.)

British sign language (BSL)

British sign language is a different language to Makaton. Users of BSL have a complete language and can make complex and abstract statements.

Soft play rooms

Soft play rooms are used to help develop children's gross motor skills safely. Rooms are filled with brightly coloured foam-filled shapes. Some areas also have ball pools where children can throw and also 'swim' in the balls. Soft play areas are particularly helpful for children who have conditions where a fall or a cut can result in a fracture or bleeding. Soft play areas have been so successful that they are now being seen in crèches and play areas for the use of all children.

Sensory rooms

Sensory rooms are sometimes called light rooms. These specially designed rooms are used with a range of children who have special needs. The aim is to stimulate as well as relax and reassure children who may have difficulties in communicating. The rooms are generally quite small and often have a wide range of equipment that can stimulate the senses, e.g. rotating coloured lights, reflective materials, textured surfaces, music and wind machines which can be gently blown into a child's face. Aromatherapy (the use of smells) has also been introduced into the sensory rooms. The rooms are particularly useful with children who have profound and multiple learning difficulties as they may also have language and sensory impairments.

End-of-unit test

1 How is disability represented in the medical model of disability?
2 Explain ways in which disability can affect a child?
3 List three features of the Special Education Needs and Disability Act 2001.
4 Explain the purpose of an Individual Education Plan.
5 Give two reasons why it is important to empower children who have a disability or special need.
6 Why is the Disability Discrimination Act 1995 seen as being important?
7 What are the main criticisms of the Act?
8 List three types of professional who may be involved in the care and education of a child who has multiple disabilities.
9 What are the arguments in favour of inclusive education?
10 Explain three features of the role of the SENCO in an early years setting.

Useful addresses – support groups

Coeliac UK, PO Box 220, High Wycombe, Bucks HP11 2HY

Cystic Fibrosis Trust, 11 London Road, Bromley, Kent BR1 1BY

Diabetes UK, 10 Parkway, London NW1 17AA

Down's Syndrome Association, 155 Mitcham Road, London SW17 9PG

Epilepsy Action, New Anstey House, Gateway Drive, Yeadon, Leeds LS19 7XY

HIV and AIDS, Terence Higgins Trust, 52-54 Gray's Inn Road, London WC1X 8JU

Hyperactive Children's Support Group, 71 Whyke Lane, Chichester, West Sussex PO19 7PD

National Association for Gifted Children, Suite 14, Challenge House, Sherwood Drive, Bletchley, Milton Keynes MK3 6DP

National Asthma Campaign, Providence House, Providence Place, London NW1 0NT

National Autistic Association, 393 City Road, London EC1V 1NG

SCOPE, 6 Market Road, London, N7 9PW

Sickle Cell Society, 54 Station Road, Harlesden, London NW10 4UA

Glossary

Abstract	A brief summary of a study and its results. It states what the study was about, how it was done and what the results showed.
Acute illness	A sudden illness that is usually short-lived; the symptoms might change from one day to the next. Some cases may be severe. Examples are tonsillitis or an ear infection.
Advocacy	When a person communicates on behalf of someone else.
Ageism	Discrimination on the grounds of age.
Animism	A child attributes feeling and intentions to non-living things, e.g. a toy.
Antibiotics	Medication which kills bacteria.
Anti-discrimination	Actively opposing discrimination.
Attachment	A close emotional bond between baby and carer.
Bacteria	A pathogenic organism that can cause infections.
Bias	Something that could alter, or interferes with, the results of a study.
Cartoid artery	The main artery carrying blood to the head.
Case conference	A number of professionals representing different agencies (health, police, education etc..) who meet to keep each other informed and make decisions about a particular case.
Chastisement	To punish by physical harm or beating
Checklist	To observe and record specific activities or aspects of development on a pre-set list
Child Protection Register	A list of names of children who are deemed to be 'at risk' held by Social Services departments
Chronic illness	A prolonged illness where the signs and symptoms change very little from day to day. Some chronic illnesses have acute episodes. Examples include asthma and glue ear.
Colostrum	Fluid rich in antibodies, produced from the breasts following the birth of a baby.
Communicable diseases	Diseases that can be communicated or transmitted.
Congenital	A condition that a baby is born with such as cystic fibrosis.
Correlation	A statistical term describing the presence of a relationship between variables. A 'positive' correlation or association is one where an increase in one variable results in an increase in the other variable being considered. A 'negative' association occurs when an increase in one variable results in a decrease in the other variable.
Cross-sectional study	A 'snapshot' of a group of people at one point in time.
COSHH	Control of Hazardous Substances Hazardous to Health Regulations (1994): legislation that requires medicines and chemicals to be stored correctly.
Culture	The total range of activities, beliefs, values, knowledge and ideas shared by a group of people from the same tradition or background.
Curriculum	An outline of knowledge, skills or concepts to be presented to children.
Curriculum plan	A programme of activities.
Deficiency	A lack of a particular substance e.g. vitamins.
Deprivation	Term used when babies and children have formed an attachment, but are subsequently separated.
Development	The increase in the complexity of body actions, the thinking processes as well as a person's feelings and social interactions. It is partly influenced by the genetically determined programme of maturation and partly by the interaction with the prevailing environment.

Disability	The consequence of an impairment, or other individual difference. The disability a person experiences is determined by the way in which other people respond to that difference.
Discrimination	Unfavourable treatment of individuals or groups of the population based on prejudice.
Distraction hearing test	A hearing test done at approximately 8 months.
Diversity	Having variety; being different; accepting that we are not all the same.
Droplet infection	An infection spread by coughing, sneezing or spitting.
Early years curriculum	Everything children do, see, hear or feel in the early years setting, whether planned or unplanned.
Egocentrism	The inability to imagine things from another's perspective.
Equality	Having the same rights as other people.
Ethnicity	Identification with a group (ethnic group) who share some or all of the following features: lifestyle, culture, religion, nationality, language, history, geographical area.
Ethnocentrism	Viewing the world from the perspective of one particular ethnic group.
Event sampling	Observing and recording certain events as they occur, e.g. aggressive behaviour.
Febrile convulsion	A fit caused by a raised temperature in children under 5 years.
Folic acid	A B-vitamin that can be found in some enriched foods and vitamin pills.
Free-flow play	When a child learns through play at the deepest level using their experience of ideas, feelings and relationships and applying these with control, competence and mastery. Adult intervention is absent or minimal
Frequency	The number of times an event occurs.
Frequency histogram	A chart of numerical values ranging from the lowest to the highest (class intervals), showing the number of times each value occurs (frequency).
Full day care	Facilities that provide day care for children under eight for a period of four hours or more which are not domestic premises.
Gender discrimination	Sometimes termed sexism, practices that discriminate on the grounds of gender difference.
Genetics	The study of inherited conditions.
Genetic counselling	Tests and screening done on a man and woman who have a history of an inherited condition. This will give the couple the potential risks of having a child with the condition.
Head circumference	A measurement of the baby's head to ensure correct growth.
Health education	This focuses on the prevention of illness in an individual.
Health promotion	Encouraging people to increase their control over, and improve, their own health.
Hepatitis	Inflammation of the liver caused by a virus.
HIV	Human immuno-deficiency virus; the virus that causes AIDS.
Holophrases	Word and gesture combinations.
Homophobia	Hatred or fear of homosexuals.
Hypoglycaemia attack	A sudden drop in the level of blood sugar in the body, often associated with diabetes.
Hypothesis	A statement that predicts the relationship between variables, i.e. the relationship between the independent and dependent variables. A hypothesis can be written as an experimental hypothesis that predicts the outcome of the study or as a null hypothesis that does not predict the outcome of the study.
Immunisation	The use of vaccinations to prevent specific illnesses.
Immunity	The body's ability to resist infection.
Incubation period	The time between infection with a micro-organism and the development of any symptoms.

Insulin	A hormone that is necessary in enabling the body to use and store sugar in the form of glucose.
Interpersonal interaction	Ways in which people communicate with each other.
Interpreter	Someone who translates speech from one language to another.
Longitudinal study	The study of an individual or group of people over a period of time.
Malnourished	Lacking in essential nutrients.
Marginalised groups	The socially excluded: groups of people on the fringe of mainstream society and who feel unimportant and uninvolved, e.g. travellers, asylum seekers, those in poverty, the elderly, those who lack basic skills such as the ability to read or write.
Maturation	A genetically determined programme of progressive changes leading to full development.
Micro-organism	An organism such as bacteria or a virus that cannot be seen.
Minority ethnic group	People who belong to ethnic groups who are not in the majority.
Moral realism	An action that is judged by the intention of the person doing the act and not by the outcome
Multiculturalism	Recognition and sharing of different cultures in our society.
Naturalistic observation	A study that observes behaviour as it occurs naturally.
Observation	The report of a study or examination on what is happening, without deliberately intervening in the course of events. Observation can be participant where the researcher is part of what is happening or non participant where the researcher observes from a distance.
OFSTED	Office for Standards in Education: responsible for inspecting all early years settings and schools.
Out of school care	Facilities that provide day care for children under eight which operate during one or more of the following periods: before school, after school, during school holidays.
Paediatric nurse	A nurse who specialises in sick children.
Paediatrition	A doctor who specialises in sick children.
Phonemic awareness	An understanding of the sounds that individual letters (phonemes) make.
Placebo	A fake treatment given to people in a control group so they don't know whether or not they are in an experimental or control group. A placebo should not have any effect, however, occasionally if someone in the control group believes they are getting a real or active treatment, they can experience effects, good or bad.
Population	A group of people or objects that have particular characteristics.
Portage	A system of structured teaching of skills to children in their homes by parents.
Pre-eclampsia	A condition that occurs in pregnancy with the symptoms of: high blood pressure, protein in the urine and swelling in the tissues.
Prejudice	Having preconceived opinions about a group or individual that results in negative effects.
Premature	A baby born before 37 weeks of completed pregnancy.
Privation	The term used when babies and children have not formed a main attachment.
Qualitative	Information gathered in narrative (non-numeric) form, e.g. a transcript of an interview.
Quantitative	Information gathered in the form of numbers.
Race	The categorisation of people based on attributes such as skin colour and general physical appearance
Racism	Practices that discriminate because of colour, culture, race or ethnicity.
Range	A measure of the variability of quantitative data. The difference between the

	highest and lowest values in a set of data.
Referral	Passing on information to a person or agency more suited to deal with the issue.
Regression	Reverting to behaviour of an earlier age.
Reflective practitioner	Someone who is able to review the way in which they work and identify and plan for necessary changes, developments and improvements.
Reinforcers	Consequences that might encourage or discourage repeated actions.
Reliability	Reliability is concerned with the consistency and dependability of a research method. It is an indication of the extent to which the method used gives the same answers at different times, with similar yet different groups of people and irrespective of who administers it.
Research question	A clear statement in the form of a question of what a researcher wishes to find out.
Sample	A subgroup of a population that is selected to represent the entire population. Ideally, all people or objects in the population have an equal chance of being chosen. This will give a random sample. Random samples can be selected using. Some samples may not be truly random and as such may be subject to bias.
Screening	A programme that examines all children to detect certain conditions, illnesses or disabilities.
SENCO	Special Education Needs Co-ordinator – a person with responsibility for providing support for children with Special Needs
Separation anxiety	An unhappy response by a child when attached carer leaves. The response is usually in three stages: (1) protest, e.g. crying, (2) despair, child becomes calmer but apathetic, and (3) detachment (if situation continues for weeks or longer) gives up hope and ignores attachment figure on return.
Sessional care	Facilities that provide day care for children under eight for a period of less than four continuous hours which are not domestic premises.
SIDS	Sudden infant death syndrome: sudden and unexplained death in an infant.
Social learning theory	A theory of learning that suggests that we learn by imitating others.
Standard deviation	A statistical measure of how far things vary from the average result (the mean).
Statistic	A characteristic of a sample.
Stranger fear	Distress shown by a child if a stranger appears and moves nearer. Babies tend to move away and cling to their attachment figure.
Structured play	Activities that are planned and usually led by adults.
Time sampling	Observing and recording what a child is doing every minute for a short period.
Trial study	Sometimes called a pilot study. An initial use of the research method, usually a questionnaire, to test its effectiveness.
Validity	The extent to which a particular research method produces results that likely to be 'true' and free of **bias**.
Variable	A factor or characteristic of a person or object that varies, i.e. can have different values. Variables include things like age, height, gender, how much someone smokes, number of children, etc. In experimental research the variable that is assumed to cause or influence the outcome of the experiment is called the **independent variable**. The independent variable is altered in some way to observe its effect on a factor or characteristic of the person or object. This factor is called the **dependent variable** and is the variable that can be measured. Other factors may affect the results of the experiment and these are called **confounding variables**.
Virus	A very small micro-organism which can cause disease. It cannot be treated with antibiotics.

Index